M E R R I L L
EARTH SCIENCE

GLENCOE

Macmillan/McGraw-Hill

New York, New York   Columbus, Ohio   Mission Hills, California   Peoria, Illinois

A GLENCOE PROGRAM

MERRILL EARTH SCIENCE

Student Edition
Teacher Wraparound Edition
Teacher Resource Package
Study Guide, Student Edition
Reinforcement, Student Edition
Enrichment, Student Edition
Transparency Package

Laboratory Manual
Laboratory Manual,
   Teacher Annotated Edition
Spanish Resources
Chapter Review Software
Computer Test Bank
Videodisc Correlation

REVIEWERS

Marilyn W. Miles
Nowlin Middle School
Independence, Missouri

Ellis Eugene Underkoffler
1989 Recipient, Presidential Award for Excellence in
Science and Math Teaching
Talley Junior High School
Wilmington, Delaware

Jeffery W. Tolhurst
1989 Recipient, Outstanding Earth-Science Teacher
Award
San Benito High School
Hollister, California

Larry G. Friedrichs
1989 Recipient, Presidential Award for Excellence in
Science and Math Teaching
Palmer High School
Colorado Springs, Colorado

David M. Barlow
1989 Recipient, Outstanding Earth-Science Teacher
Award
Mooresville High School
Mooresville, North Carolina

Susan Tarwick Roberts
Wirt County High School
Elizabeth, West Virginia

Edward Wayne Gordon, Jr.
President, Science Teachers Association of Texas
San Antonio, Texas

Priscilla Jane Lee
Venice High School
Los Angeles, California

John A. Fradiska, Jr.
Gov. Thomas Johnson Middle School
Frederick, Maryland

Tracy Day
Nevis School
Nevis, Minnesota

James Michael Henry
Kazen Middle School
San Antonio, Texas

Joyce Rowland Johnson
Miller Intermediate School
Pasadena, Texas

Michael Scott Goodrich
Lake Oswega High School
Lake Oswega, Oregon

Cover Photograph: Mount Dana at dawn over Mono Lake by Galen Rowell

Send all inquiries to:
GLENCOE DIVISION
Macmillan/McGraw-Hill
936 Eastwind Drive
Westerville, OH 43081

ISBN 0-675-16744-2

Printed in the United States of America.

5 6 7 8 9-RRD-W-99 98 97 96 95 94

AUTHORS

Ralph M. Feather, Jr. is a teacher of geology, astronomy, and earth science, and serves as Science Department Chair in the Derry Area School District in Derry, PA. He holds a B.S. in Geology and a M.Ed in Geoscience from the Indiana University of Pennsylvania, and is currently working on his Ph.D. at the University of Pittsburgh. Mr. Feather has more than 20 years of teaching experience in secondary science and has supervised student teachers for over 15 years. He is a past recipient of the Outstanding Earth Science Teacher Award from the National Association of Geology Teachers and the Keivin Burns Citation from the Spectroscopy Society of Pittsburgh. In 1989, Mr. Feather was nominated for Excellence in Science Teaching. He is also a member of the Geological Society of America, the National Science Teachers Association, the American Association for the Advancement of Science, and the Association for Supervision and Curriculum Development.

Susan Leach Snyder is a teacher of earth science at Jones Middle School, Upper Arlington School District, Columbus, Ohio. She serves on the Board of Trustees of North American Astrophysical Observatory and has served on the Boards of Directors for state and national science organizations. Ms. Snyder received a B.S. in Comprehensive Science from Miami University, Oxford, Ohio, and an M.S. in Entomology from the University of Hawaii. She has 18 years of teaching experience and is author of various educational materials. Ms. Snyder, in addition to receiving Exemplary Earth Science and Career Awareness in Science Teaching Team awards from NSTA, was the 1987 Ohio Teacher of the Year, and one of four finalists for the 1987 National Teacher of the Year.

Dale T. Hesser currently serves as the Assistant Superintendent of Schools in North Syracuse, New York. A past recipient of the Outstanding Earth Science Teacher award from the National Association of Geology Teachers, Mr. Hesser received his B.S. in earth science from Buffalo State College, New York, and holds an M.S. and Certificate of Advanced Studies in Science Education from Syracuse University. He has over 20 years of classroom teaching experience in the earth sciences ranging from junior/senior high school through college astronomy, and numerous pre-service and in-service teacher training institutes. Mr. Hesser currently serves as an adjunct instructor for Syracuse University in Earth Science Teaching.

CONSULTANTS

Dr. Gerald H. Newsom
Professor of Astronomy
The Ohio State University
Columbus, Ohio

Dr. Robert C. Howe
Professor of Geology
Indiana State University
Terre Haute, Indiana

Dr. James B. Phipps
Professor of Geology and
Oceanography
Grays Harbor College
Aberdeen, Washington

Dr. Allan A. Ekdale
Professor of Geology
University of Utah
Salt Lake City, Utah

Eric Danielson
Associate Professor of Meteorology
Hartford College for Women
Hartford, Connecticut

Dr. George Moore
Professor Emeritus, Geology
The Ohio State University
Columbus, Ohio
Reading:

Barbara Pettegrew, Ph.D.
Director of Reading/Study Center
Assistant Professor of Education
Otterbein College
Westerville, Ohio
Safety

Robert Tatz, Ph.D.
Instructional Lab Supervisor
Department of Chemistry
The Ohio State University
Columbus, Ohio

Special Features:
Stephen C. Blume
St. Tammany Pubic School System
Slidell, Louisiana

Gifted and Mainstreamed:
Barbara Murdock
Elementary Consultant For
Instruction
Gahanna - Jefferson Public Schools
Gahanna, Ohio

Judy Ratzenberger
Middle School Science Instructor
Gahanna Middle School West
Gahanna, Ohio

CONTENTS

UNIT 3   THE CHANGING SURFACE OF EARTH   118

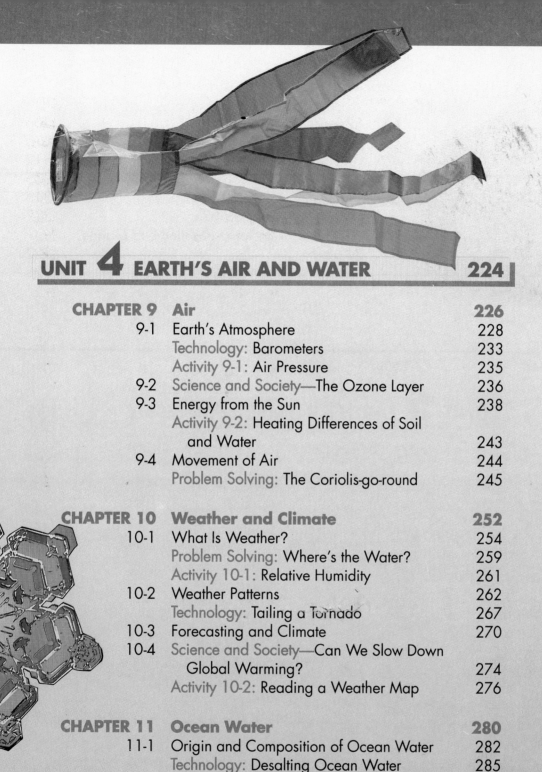

UNIT 4 EARTH'S AIR AND WATER 224

UNIT 5 EARTH'S INTERNAL PROCESSES 332

UNIT 6 CHANGE AND EARTH'S HISTORY 414

UNIT 8 ASTRONOMY 548

ACTIVITIES

MINI-Labs

PROBLEM SOLVING

TECHNOLOGY

SKILL BUILDERS

ORGANIZING INFORMATION

Classifying: 53, 67, 113, 291, 327, 409, 443, 521, 543, 573

Sequencing: 25, 98, 139, 165, 175, 219, 402, 467, 471, 499, 556, 573, 625, 640

Outlining: 33, 83, 139, 160, 193, 219, 303, 339, 357, 385, 443, 471, 514, 543, 570

THINKING CRITICALLY

Observing and Inferring: 53, 83, 251, 279, 327, 409, 443, 597, 651

Comparing and Contrasting: 17, 25, 113, 151, 187, 248, 273, 279, 296, 303, 314, 327, 357, 406, 409, 499, 597, 657

Recognizing Cause and Effect: 113, 127, 139, 269, 303, 353, 443, 453, 521, 543, 582, 616, 632, 651

EXPERIMENTATION SKILLS

Measuring in SI: 21, 25, 83, 113, 212, 219, 327, 357, 385, 409, 521, 573, 591, 625, 657

Hypothesizing: 53, 113, 169, 251, 279, 357, 471, 492, 543, 597, 625, 645

Using Variables, Constants, and Controls: 25, 139, 193, 251, 321, 385, 597

Interpreting Data: 83, 107, 193, 219, 303, 435, 471, 609

Designing an Experiment: 169

GRAPHICS

Concept Mapping: 9, 25, 38, 53, 77, 83, 88, 133, 139, 147, 169, 181, 201, 219, 242, 251, 260, 285, 310, 327, 346, 357, 364, 392, 409, 425, 484, 499, 529, 543, 565, 573, 597, 604, 625, 657

Making and Using Tables: 47, 53, 169, 193, 279, 379, 439, 461, 499, 505, 539, 573, 625, 657

Making and Using Graphs: 53, 72, 193, 234, 251, 303, 372, 443, 505, 521

Interpreting Scientific Illustrations: 94, 169, 205, 279, 385, 471, 499, 521, 539, 622, 645

GLOBAL CONNECTIONS

CAREERS

SCIENCE AND LITERATURE/ART

USING MERRILL EARTH SCIENCE

Earth Science is a subject you're familiar with because your every activity depends on the natural environment around you. The types of clothes you wear depend on the weather and every item you buy is produced from natural resources. Your link to Earth and its environment is an important one. How you view your world is determined by your understanding of how it works. **Merrill Earth Science** will help you understand the many natural processes occurring around you. And once you've learned about your own planet, you'll explore other worlds and objects in the universe. As you read this text, you'll discover much about your natural environment and how you can help preserve it for your future.

a quick tour of your textbook

What's happening here? Why have we built a model of planet Earth? Each unit begins with thought-provoking photographs that will make you wonder. The unit introduction then explains what is happening in the photographs and how the two relate to each other and to the content of the unit. Why is this model of Earth important to your future? Read the opener to Unit 7 to find out.

It's clearly organized to get you started and keep you going.

As you begin each new chapter, use the **Gearing Up** to preview what topics are covered and how they are organized. You will also preview the skills you will use in this chapter.

After you've performed the **FIND OUT** activity and previewed the chapter, you're ready to further explore the topics ahead. Read **What's Next** to see what's ahead.

Chapters are organized into three to five numbered sections. The **Objectives** at the beginning of the numbered section tell you what major topics you'll be covering and what you should expect to learn about them. The **New Science Words** are also listed in the order in which they appear in the section.

Experience science by observing,
experimenting, and asking questions.

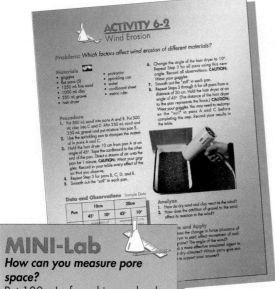

Science is more than words in a book. The two Activities and the MINI-Labs in each chapter give you the chance to further explore and investigate the science topics covered in your textbook.

In the **Activities,** you'll use household items and laboratory equipment as you follow the easy, step-by-step procedure. At the end of each Activity are questions that ask you to analyze what you've done.

MINI-Lab

How can you measure pore space?

Put 100 mL of sand in one beaker and 100 mL of gravel in another beaker. Fill a graduated cylinder with 100 mL of water. Pour the water slowly into the gravel and stop when the water just covers the top of the gravel. Record the volume of water used. Repeat the procedure with the sand. Which substance has more pore space—gravel or sand? Why?

Most **MINI-Labs** are designed so you can do them on your own or with friends outside of the science classroom using materials you find around the house. Doing a MINI-Lab is an easy and fun way to further your knowledge about the topics you're studying.

Each **Problem Solving** feature gives you a chance to solve a real world problem or understand a science principle.

Flex Your Brain is a unique activity you can use to sharpen your critical thinking skills. Starting from what you already know about a science topic, you will apply a simple ten-step procedure to extend your knowledge about the topic from a perspective that interests you.

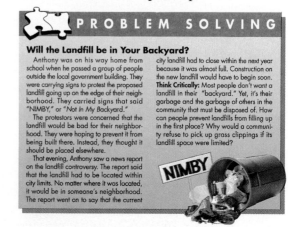

PROBLEM SOLVING

Will the Landfill be in Your Backyard?

Anthony was on his way home from school when he passed a group of people outside the local government building. They were carrying signs to protest the proposed landfill going up on the edge of their neighborhood. They carried signs that said "NIMBY," or "Not In My Backyard."

The protestors were concerned that the landfill would be bad for their neighborhood. They were hoping to prevent it from being built there. Instead, they thought it should be placed elsewhere.

That evening, Anthony saw a news report on the landfill controversy. The report said that the landfill had to be located within city limits. No matter where it was located, it would be in someone's neighborhood. The report went on to say that the current

city landfill had to close within the next year because it was almost full. Construction on the new landfill would have to begin soon. **Think Critically:** Most people don't want a landfill in their "backyard." Yet, it's their garbage and the garbage of others in the community that must be disposed of. How can people prevent landfills from filling up in the first place? Why would a community refuse to pick up grass clippings if its landfill space were limited?

Explore news-making issues, concerns about the environment, and how science shapes your world through technology.

The impact of science on society directly affects you. In the **Science and Society** section in each chapter, you'll learn about an issue that's affecting the world around you. The topics you'll read about are controversial, and you'll explore them from several sides. Then, you'll have a chance to express your opinion in the You Decide feature that follows.

In the **Technology** feature in each chapter, you'll read about recent discoveries, newly developed instruments, and applications of technology that have shaped our world and furthered our knowledge.

TECHNOLOGY

Recovering Fossils

When scientists locate an area thought to have fossils, large earth-moving equipment or explosives are used to remove overlying rocks and soil. Smaller and smaller tools are then used as the excavation draws nearer to the fossils. In the final phases of fossil recovery, tiny picks and brushes are used to remove soil from the fossils.

In order for the fossils to be removed or transported, they must be strengthened and protected. Large, brittle bones, such as dinosaur remains, are first covered with a layer of shellac. Then, strips of wet newspaper are molded onto the fossils. Finally, a plaster mixture is used to coat burlap straps, which are then applied to the fossils. This final step produces a kind of cast that protects and supports the fossils. The cast can be made even stronger with wooden sticks. The reinforced fossils are now ready to be transported to a museum, where they will undergo final preparations before being placed on exhibit.

Think Critically: Why are remains such as dinosaur bones so fragile?

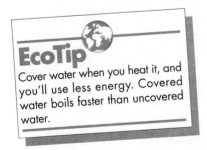

EcoTip

Cover water when you heat it, and you'll use less energy. Covered water boils faster than uncovered water.

Each **EcoTip** suggests a simple step you can take to help improve the environment. EcoTips explain how you can get involved in making Earth a better place to live.

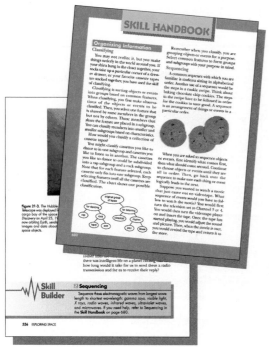

Discover that you can apply what you've learned as you answer questions and practice your science skills.

At the end of each section are several Section Review questions that help you test your knowledge. The last question challenges you to think critically and **Apply** what you've learned.

The **Skill Builder** feature lets you sharpen your science skills using only paper and pencil. If you need help with these skills, refer to the **Skill Handbook** at the back of the book. Here, you can find complete information about each type of skill covered in the Skill Builders

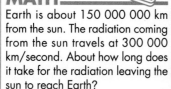

Science and MATH

Earth is about 150 000 000 km from the sun. The radiation coming from the sun travels at 300 000 km/second. About how long does it take for the radiation leaving the sun to reach Earth?

Science is related to every other subject you study. The **Science And** features challenge you to solve math problems, read literature excerpts, and to write about topics you're studying as you make the connections between science and other disciplines.

The **Chapter Review** starts with a summary so you can review the major concepts from each section. Then, you'll apply your knowledge and practice thinking skills as you answer the questions that follow.

Discover how earth science topics relate to people and places all over the world.

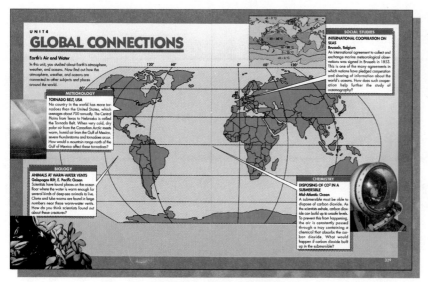

Global Connections help you to see how earth science is related to other sciences as well as social studies, history and health.

Also at the end of each unit you will find two **Careers** that relate to the material in the unit you just read. What jobs may be related to Earth's air and water? Read the careers at the end of Unit 4 to find out.

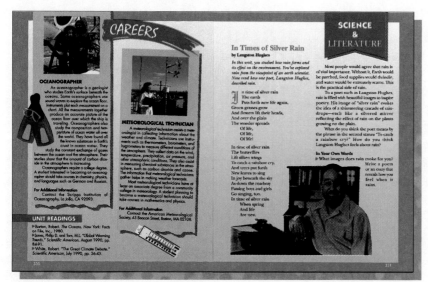

What do earth science and poetry have in common? A lot, as you'll discover when you read the unit close to Unit 4. Each unit is closed with a reading from literature or an example of art that makes a connection with earth science.

1 FOUNDATIONS OF EARTH SCIENCE

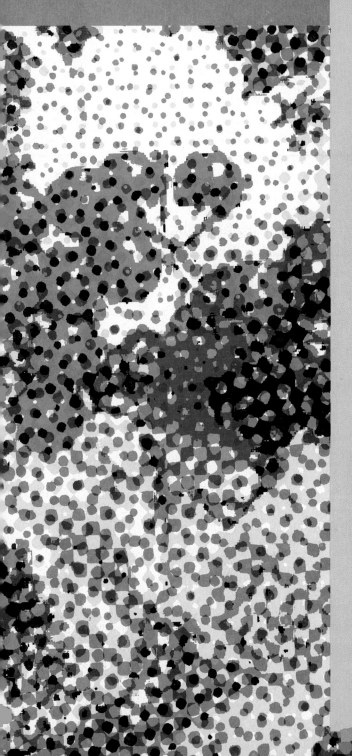

What's Happening Here?

The small photograph below has been enlarged to show the individual color dots that make up the large picture on these two pages. To see how scale affects observation, have another student hold the large photograph about three meters from you. The many colored dots in the photograph work together to produce an understandable image. As you study the chapters in this unit, you will see how the varied branches of science relate to earth science. You will also learn that the small-scale structure of objects in nature relates to a wider understanding of Earth itself.

UNIT CONTENTS

1 The Nature of Science

The parachutist in this photo is using the results of scientific experiments to enjoy skydiving. Previous experiments led to the modern design of the parachute.

FIND OUT!

Do this activity to find the best parachute design.

Fold a piece of notebook paper it in half, then in half again. You should have a piece of paper one-fourth as big as you started with. Have a friend hold the folded paper over his or her head. Using a watch with a second hand, record the time it takes for the paper to fall to the floor. Now unfold the paper so it is folded in half just once. Again, record the time it takes for this folded paper to fall to the floor. Now completely unfold the paper and flatten it out. Record the time it takes for the paper to fall to the floor. What is the best design for your parachute? How did you come to this conclusion?

Gearing Up
Previewing the Chapter
Use this outline to help you focus on important ideas in this chapter.

Section 1-1   What Is Science?
▶ Science
▶ Earth Science
Section 1-2   Science and Society
Science and Technology
▶ Technology and You
▶ The Effects of Technology
Section 1-3   Solving Problems
▶ Problem-Solving Strategies
▶ Critical Thinking
▶ Using Scientific Methods
▶ Theories and Laws
Section 1-4   Measurement and Safety
▶ Measurement
▶ Safety

Previewing Science Skills
▶ In the **Skill Builders,** you will make a concept map, compare and contrast, and measure in SI.
▶ In the **Activities,** you will think critically and calculate and experiment.
▶ In the **MINI-Labs,** you will investigate specific areas of study in earth science, and learn about SI conversions.

What's next?
Now that you've seen how science can be used in solving the problem of parachute design, you're ready to explore earth science. In this chapter, you'll learn about other sciences related to earth science. You'll also become aware of the relationship between science and technology, and you'll study measurement and safety.

1-1 What Is Science?

New Science Words

science
geology
meteorology
astronomy
oceanography

Objectives

▶ Differentiate among the following sciences: chemistry, physics, biology, and earth science.
▶ Identify the topics you'll be studying this year in earth science.

Science

Science is all around you. It is such a common part of your life that you probably take it for granted. Have you ever wondered why a refrigerator keeps food cold or what makes a hair dryer blow hot air? Most everything you see has some connection to science. Think about the radio or stereo you listen to. It operates on scientific principles of electricity. The speakers change an electrical signal into a sound wave that you hear as your favorite song. The radio is constructed out of metal and plastic compounds. Determining the best compounds to use involves the science of chemistry. By simply turning on the radio, you are using science in many ways.

Figure 1-1. Science is used in many common objects such as radios.

But where did all the scientific knowledge used in making radios and other appliances come from? This knowledge has accumulated since people first began observing the world around them.

At first, people had only their senses to rely on for their observations. Early astronomers studied the night sky with just their eyes because they didn't have telescopes yet. They acquired knowledge very slowly. Today, we have complex instruments such as microscopes that magnify small objects, satellites that take photographs of Earth and other planets, telescopes that probe the depths of space, and computers that store and analyze information. Today, we are learning more information, we are learning it faster, and there are more new inventions and discoveries than ever before.

Science means "having knowledge." It's a process of observing and studying things in our world. Many of these observations can't be explained easily and therefore present a problem. Science involves trying to solve these problems. Science is a process that enables you to understand your world. Every time you try to find out how and why things look and act the way they do, you are a scientist. For example, if you wonder and try to figure out why you keep getting a cold, you are doing science.

Science can be applied to just about anything, and hundreds of special subject areas fall within the broad scope of "science."

But basically, science can be divided into four general areas: chemistry, physics, biology, and earth science. These general topics do overlap. For example, in earth science, chemistry, physics, and biology are studied as they relate to Earth. In Table 1-1 you'll see what these different sciences are about and how they are connected to each other.

EcoTip

Find out how many trees are used for your junk mail in one year. Save your junk mail for one month. Then multiply the weight by 12 months. For every 907 kg of paper, 17 trees are used.

What are four general areas of science?

Table 1-1

THE MAJOR SCIENCES

Title	Topic of Study	Title	Topic of Study
Chemistry	Properties and composition of matter. *You'll learn basic concepts about matter when you study rocks and minerals.*	Physics	Forces, motion, energy, and their effects on matter. *You'll learn basic concepts of physics when you study the motions of Earth and the moon.*
Biology	Living organisms. *You'll learn basic concepts of biology when you study Earth history and the environment.*	Earth Science	Planet Earth. *You'll study planet Earth and its place in space.*

Figure 1-2. The study of volcanic lava is one area of earth science.

Earth Science

Just as science can be divided into the four general areas of earth science, chemistry, physics, and biology, earth science in this book is divided into four specific areas of study.

Geology is the study of Earth, its matter, and the processes that form and change Earth. Some of the things you'll look at are volcanoes, earthquakes, maps, fossils, mountains, and land use. Geologists search for oil, study volcanoes, identify rocks and minerals, study fossils and glaciers, and determine how mountains form.

Meteorology is the study of weather and the forces and processes that cause it. You'll learn about storm patterns, climates, and what factors cause our daily weather. A mete-

Science and READING

Look at the table of contents in this book and try to name ten careers in earth science. Check the career resources in the library or guidance office for help.

Figure 1-3. Astronomers study objects in space using telescopes.

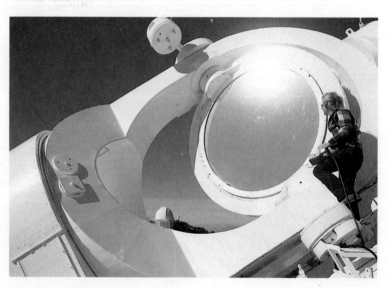

orologist is a scientist who studies weather patterns in order to predict daily weather.

Astronomy is the study of objects in space, including stars, planets, and comets. Before telescopes were invented, this branch of earth science mainly dealt with descriptions of the positions of the stars and planets. Today, scientists who study space objects seek evidence about the beginning of the universe. The study of astronomy helps scientists understand Earth's origin.

Oceanography is the study of Earth's oceans. Scientists who study the oceans conduct research on the physical and chemical properties of ocean water. Oceanographers also study the processes that occur within oceans and the effects humans have on these processes.

As you study these topics, imagine how all this information was collected over the years. People just like you had questions about the universe, and they used science to find the answers. In Section 1-3, you'll learn ways that you too can find answers to questions and solutions to problems.

MINI-Lab

How many earth sciences are there?

Although the four major areas of earth science are geology, meteorology, astronomy, and oceanography, each of these are composed of subtopic areas of its own. Listed below are some very specific areas of study. In which of the four major areas of earth science do they belong? What would a scientist working in each of these fields study?

hydrology	seismology
volcanology	petrology
mineralogy	geomorphology
paleontology	geochemistry
stratigraphy	crystallography

SECTION REVIEW

1. What topics are studied in each of the following sciences: chemistry, physics, biology, and earth science?
2. How can chemistry and physics relate to earth science?
3. **Apply:** The following paragraph summarizes one idea of how the dinosaurs may have died. Explain how this paragraph relates to geology, oceanography, astronomy, and meteorology.

   Scientists think that in the past, large objects from outer space crashed onto Earth's crust. So much dust was created from these collisions that the sun's light was blocked out. Earth became colder, killing some plants and animals.

☑ Concept Mapping

Make a Network Tree concept map that shows which of the following topics are studied in a particular topic of earth science. Use the following words: *earth science, geology, waves, currents, astronomy, oceanography, stars, volcanoes, planets, meteorology, fossils, weather, climate.* If you need help, refer to Concept Mapping in the **Skill Handbook** on pages 688 and 689.

Skill Builder

1-2 Science and Technology

New Science Words

technology

Objectives

▶ List ways technology helps you.
▶ Discuss ways that the use of technology can be harmful.

Figure 1-4. New technology has improved telephones over the years.

Technology and You

The study of science doesn't just add to our understanding of our natural surroundings, it allows us to make discoveries that help us. **Technology** is the use of scientific discoveries. Technology has produced such diverse and important things as televisions, artificial hearts, jets, computers, calculators, telephones, and satellites, to name just a few.

Everywhere you look, you can see ways that science and technology have shaped your world. You simply have to turn on a switch or a knob, and you light your room, microwave your food, control the temperature in your house, or watch a television program coming from another part of the world.

Because of technology we have robots and computers that help us in many ways. For example, robots work in assembly lines, explore other planets, and go to the bottom of oceans to perform work that would be dangerous

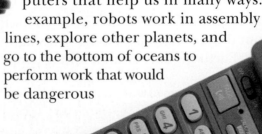

for people to do. Computers do everything from helping us predict weather to monitoring patients in hospitals. Advancements in robotics, computers, and medicine have enabled us to make artificial arms, legs, and other body parts to replace those that are diseased or injured. Technology has enabled us to live longer because we have improved medicines, health care, and foods.

We have the technology to clear forests, build cities, breed animals, and even create new types of organisms. Humans are unique because we're the only creatures on Earth that can change our surroundings to meet our needs.

The Effects of Technology

Not all of the changes created by technology are good. Advances in medical technology have extended the time people live. But sometimes the quality of life for these people is very low. For example, people can be kept alive by machines, even though they are permanently unconscious—in a coma.

Technology has also led to the development of modern machines, such as cars. Cars allow us to be mobile and travel freely, but they also create pollution and contribute to congestion in cities. Another machine, the air conditioner, provides cool comfort but uses electricity; and the freon chemical released during its use harms the environment.

Figure 1-5. Disposable items use resources and contribute to problems such as full landfills.

SECTION REVIEW

1. List ways technology helps you.
2. What problems can technology cause?

You Decide!

SCIENCE & SOCIETY

Many things, such as plastic razors and food wraps, are "disposable." Technology has made the cost of manufacturing these products so low that they can be thrown away. Even small appliances, such as blow dryers and curling irons, cost less to buy new than to repair. This use of technology has made us a "throwaway" society. Many people simply throw things away when they are broken and buy new ones. Is it better to have the convenience of disposable items, or does the excessive waste created by disposable items make them an unwise use of technology?

1-3 Solving Problems

New Science Words

scientific methods
hypothesis
variable
control
theory
law

Objectives

▶ Describe some problem-solving strategies.
▶ List steps commonly used as scientific methods.
▶ Distinguish between hypotheses, theories, and laws.

Problem-Solving Strategies

Soccer practice, dinner, homework, chores, watching your favorite television program...how will you squeeze them all in tonight? This might be a problem you are facing. There are many methods you can use to find solutions to problems. These are called strategies. Let's look at a strategy you can use to solve the problem of how to squeeze so many activities into one evening.

To solve any problem, you need to have a strategy. Identifying the problem is the first step of any strategy. Next, you need to collect information about the problem. You need to know the basic facts of when soccer practice begins and ends, how much homework you have, what chores need to be done, and when the TV program

Figure 1-6. Solving schedule problems is just one problem you can learn to solve.

is on. After you have determined these things, you might try writing out a time schedule. First, write in the activities that have fixed times. Then, fill in each of the other activities. You may have to try different arrangements before you find the solution that you think is the best.

In solving this problem, making a list helped you organize the parts of your problem. There are other ways to solve problems. You might try the strategy of eliminating possibilities. You could do this by trying options until you find the one that works. This method is also known as trial and error. Sometimes it is easier to solve a problem by finding out what does *not* work. Another strategy is to solve a simpler, related problem, or to make a model, drawing, or graph to help you visualize the problem. If your first strategy does not work, keep trying different strategies.

Name three problem-solving strategies.

TECHNOLOGY

Building a Better Bicycle

Would you be able to ride your bicycle if it didn't have any pedals? It would be difficult, but you probably could. In fact, that's how the first bicyclists rode their vehicles. People pushed their feet along the ground to propel a machine made of only two wheels and a seat.

In the early 1800s, bicycles were mostly wood, with two metal wheels that were the same size, a handlebar, and no pedals. Bicycle makers then worked on the problem of how to propel the bicycle. They used problem-solving strategies to add pedals and a gear. This allowed the bicycle to be propelled by the rider.

Today's bicycles are radically different from the first bicycles. Problem-solving strategies are used to make bikes lighter. Bicycle makers have experimented with aluminum,

carbon fiber, molybdenum, and other very lightweight metals and alloys. Bicycles have been advanced and improved through the use of problem-solving skills.

Think Critically: How could you use problem-solving techniques to choose the most lightweight substance for a bike frame?

Critical Thinking

Imagine yourself coming home from school on a cold, wintery Friday afternoon. It had begun to snow and the forecast for Saturday was one to three inches of snow. Saturday would be a great day for chili. You get out all of the ingredients and make the chili in a crock-pot so it will be ready for Saturday. After sledding on Saturday morning, you come home and get a bowl of chili.

What is critical thinking?

What went wrong with the chili? Even though you followed your usual recipe, it just seemed to taste bland. After thinking for a bit, you realized that you left out an essential ingredient—chili powder. How did you figure out that lack of chili powder was to blame? Without being aware of it, you probably used some aspect of critical thinking.

Critical thinking is a process that uses certain skills to solve problems. For example, you identified the problem by mentally comparing the bad batch of chili with other batches of chili you've eaten. You separated important information from unimportant information if you realized that the temperature of the chili had little to do with its flavor. You may have examined your assumption that you followed the recipe correctly. After looking at the recipe again, you concluded that chili powder had been left out.

You probably went one step further and analyzed your conclusion. Would leaving out the chili powder have made the chili taste bland? If your answer was "yes," then you may have solved the problem.

This book uses an activity called "Flex Your Brain" to help you think about and examine your thinking. "Flex Your Brain" is a way to keep your thinking on track when you are investigating a topic. It takes you through steps of exploration from what you already know and believe, to new conclusions and awareness. Then, it encourages you to review and talk about the steps you took.

"Flex Your Brain" and other features of this book will help you improve your critical thinking skills. You can get your first chance to "Flex Your Brain" on the next page. You'll become a better problem solver, and your next batch of chili will taste great.

FLEX Your Brain

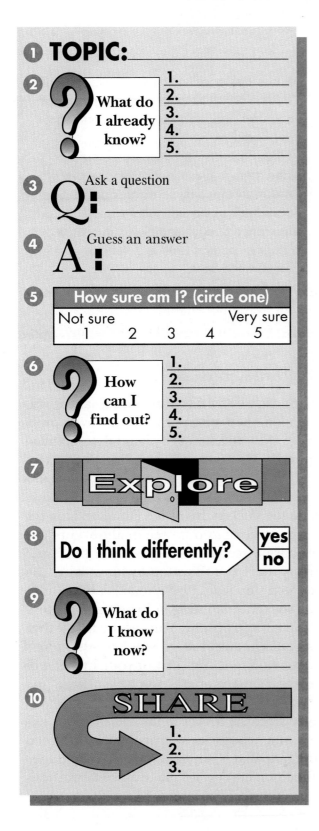

1 TOPIC: _____

2 **?** What do I already know?
1. _____
2. _____
3. _____
4. _____
5. _____

3 Ask a question
Q: _____

4 Guess an answer
A: _____

5 | How sure am I? (circle one) | |
|---|---|
| Not sure | Very sure |
| 1   2   3 | 4   5 |

6 **?** How can I find out?
1. _____
2. _____
3. _____
4. _____
5. _____

7 Explore

8 Do I think differently? | yes |
| no |

9 **?** What do I know now?
_____
_____
_____

10 SHARE
1. _____
2. _____
3. _____

1 Fill in the topic your teacher gives you.

2 Jot down what you already know about the topic.

3 Using what you already know (Step 2), form a question about the topic. Are you unsure about one of the items you listed? Do you want to know more? Do you want to know what, how, or why? Write down your question.

4 Guess an answer to your question. In the next few steps, you will be exploring the reasonableness of your answer. Write down your guess.

5 Circle the number in the box that matches how sure you are of your answer in Step 4. This is your chance to rate your confidence in what you've done so far and, later, to see how your level of sureness affects your thinking.

6 How can you find out more about your topic? You might want to read a book, ask an expert, or do an experiment. Write down ways you can find out more.

7 Make a plan to explore your answer. Use the resources you listed in Step 6. Then, carry out your plan.

8 Now that you've explored, go back to your answer in Step 4. Would you answer differently? Mark one of the boxes.

9 Considering what you learned in your exploration, answer your question again, adding new things you've learned. You may completely change your answer.

10 It's important to be able to talk about thinking. Choose three people to tell about how you arrived at your response in every step. For example, don't just read what you wrote down in Step 2. Try to share how you thought of those things.

PROBLEM SOLVING

New Uniforms for the Band

The students in the band had worked hard to raise money to purchase new uniforms. The students were concerned about how hot they would get during football games and parades. Chris determined which color of uniform was the coolest.

Chris designed a scientific experiment to determine which color absorbed the least amount of heat. He obtained fabric samples of each color.

He cut the samples the same size and folded them into pockets. Then, he placed a thermometer inside each pocket and placed them in the sun. After recording the temperature of each sample after a set period of time, he was able to determine which color was the best.

Think Critically: How did Chris use scientific methods in his experiment?

Using Scientific Methods

What are scientific methods?

Suppose that nearly every day, your locker jams. First, you can't get it open, then it won't close. You have a problem to solve. Scientists use a series of planned steps, called **scientific methods,** to solve problems. The basic scientific methods are listed in Table 1-2 on the next page. It's portant to note that scientists don't always follow these exact steps or do the steps in this order. However, most scientists follow some type of step-by-step method. How can scientific methods be used to solve the locker problem?

You've already done the first step by identifying the problem. The next step would be to make a hypothesis about why your locker is jamming. A **hypothesis** is a testable prediction of a problem. You might think that something is getting caught in your locker door. You hypothesize that taking things out of your locker will allow it to open and close properly. You have made a prediction. Now you're ready to test it.

EcoTip

Design an experiment to determine which things break down in the environment in one month's time. Use items such as an apple core, a foam cup, a plastic bag, and a carrot.

If you remove all of the locker items and the door still doesn't work, your hypothesis was probably incorrect. You would conclude that it isn't jamming because things are stuck in the door. You would make a new hypothesis and start the problem-solving process over again.

Every experiment includes variables and controls. A **variable** is a changeable factor in an experiment. The variables in you locker experiment would be the things in your locker, the hinges on the locker, the door, the latch, and the way you open and close your locker. Experiments should only test one variable at a time.

A **control** is a standard for comparison. In the experiment with your jammed locker, a neighbor's locker that doesn't jam could be your control. By looking at it, you could tell how a locker should work.

Theories and Laws

Many things we learn about in science, such as how animals evolve or how continents move, are called theories. Scientists are constantly testing hypotheses. When new data gathered over a long period of time support a hypothesis, scientists become convinced that the hypothesis is correct. They can use such hypotheses to form theories. An explanation backed by results obtained from repeated tests or experiments is a **theory.**

A scientific **law** is a "rule of nature" that describes the behavior of something in nature. Generally, laws predict or describe what will happen in a given situation, but don't explain why. An example of a law is Newton's first law of motion. It states that an object continues in motion, or at rest, until it's acted upon by an outside force.

In this section, you've learned a variety of problem-solving strategies. The "Flex Your Brain" activities will help you improve your critical thinking skills, and by understanding scientific methods, you'll better understand the activities in this book.

Table 1-2

COMMONLY USED SCIENTIFIC METHODS
1. Determine the problem
2. Make a hypothesis
3. Test your hypothesis
4. Analyze the results
5. Draw conclusions

What's the difference between a theory and a law?

SECTION REVIEW

1. What are some strategies you can use to solve problems?
2. **Apply:** Imagine that your bike chain came off after riding over a stick, and you think the stick must have been the cause. Is that a hypothesis or a theory?

☑ Comparing and Contrasting

Compare and contrast a scientific variable with a control. If you need help, refer to Comparing and Contrasting in the **Skill Handbook** on page 683.

Skill Builder

1-4 Measurement and Safety

New Science Words

International System of Units (SI)
mass
weight
gravitational force

Objectives

▶ List the SI units for the following measurements: length, mass, weight, area, volume, density, and temperature.
▶ Differentiate between the terms *mass* and *weight* and the terms *area* and *volume*.
▶ State three lab safety rules.

Figure 1-7. A guitar is about one meter long.

Measurement

How could you measure your classroom without a ruler or measuring tape? You might count your steps across the room. You could then say that the room is 25 steps by 30 steps. But this step measurement wouldn't mean the same thing to your friends because their steps would be different from yours. Because of this problem, there are standard units used for measurement.

Today, the measuring system used by most people around the world is the **International System of Units (SI).** SI is a modern version of the metric system, although some forms of the metric system are used in this book. SI is based on a decimal system which uses the number *10* as the base unit.

The standard unit in SI for length is the meter. It's about the length of a guitar. A decimeter is one-tenth of a meter. A centimeter is one one-hundredth of a meter. And a millimeter is one one-thousandth of a meter. Another common unit for longer distances is the kilometer. A kilometer is 1000 times greater than a meter. Refer to Appendixes A and B for further explanation of SI and English/SI conversions.

Mass

Mass is a measure of the amount of matter in an object. Mass depends on the number and kinds of atoms that make up an object. It is measured using a balance. On a balance, it's determined by adding known masses to balance out the mass being studied.

The standard unit of measure for mass is a gram. The mass of one bagel is about 57 grams. One gram equals 1000 milligrams, so what would be the mass of one bagel in milligrams? It would be 5700 milligrams.

Weight is a measure of gravitational force. **Gravitational force** is an attractive force that exists between all objects. A scale measures the force of Earth's gravitational pull on your mass. If you could weigh yourself on the moon, you would weigh one-sixth the amount you weigh on Earth. This is because the moon's gravitational force is one-sixth that of Earth's.

The standard unit for weight is a newton, named after Sir Isaac Newton, who was the first person to describe gravity. In SI, a can of soup weighs 0.4 newtons.

Area, Volume, and Density

Some measurements, such as area, volume, and density, require a combination of SI units. Area is the amount of surface included within a set of boundaries. Let's say you want to know the area of your desk top. First, you'd measure its length and width with a meterstick, and then you'd multiply these two measurements to find the area. In SI, area is expressed in units such as square centimeters (cm^2).

Density is a measure of the amount of matter that occupies a particular space. It's determined by dividing the mass of an object by its volume.

Liquid volume measurements are made using graduated cylinders and beakers. These volumes are usually expressed in milliliters (mL). Because one milliliter of a liquid will just fill a container with a 1 cm^3 volume, milliliters can be expressed as cubic centimeters. For example, a full can of soft drink is 355 mL or 355 cm^3.

Volume is a measure of how much space an object occupies, so if you wanted to know the volume of a solid object, like your book, you'd need to know its length, width, and height. Then you'd multiply these three measurements to find the volume. The cubic meter (m^3) is the basic unit of volume in SI, but liquid volumes are often measured in liters (L) and milliliters (mL).

$$\text{density} = \frac{\text{mass}}{\text{volume}} \qquad D = \frac{m}{v}$$

An SI unit that is often used to express density is grams per cubic centimeter (g/cm^3). How might you express the density of a liquid? We often use grams per milliliter (g/mL).

Figure 1-8. When you weigh yourself, you are measuring the force of gravity.

How is volume calculated?

Temperature

Temperature is a measure of how hot or cold something is. As you probably know, temperature is measured with a thermometer. What you probably didn't know is that the SI unit for temperature is a kelvin. On the Kelvin scale, absolute zero is 0, the coldest temperature. The symbol for kelvin is K. Instead of using kelvin thermometers, many scientists use Celsius thermometers. The symbol for a Celsius degree is °C. The Celsius temperature scale is based on the freezing and boiling points of water. The freezing point of pure water is 0°C, and the boiling point is 100°C. A comfortable room temperature is 21°C, and the average human body temperature is about 37°C. You can use these temperatures as reference points when you measure other Celsius temperatures. Now, suppose you wanted to change Celsius temperatures to SI. You'd simply add 273.16 to the degrees Celsius to find the number of kelvins.

$$\text{degrees Celsius} + 273.16 = \text{kelvin}$$

Making accurate measurements in SI is an important part of any experiment. If you don't make accurate measurements, your results and conclusions are invalid.

Safety

The laboratory activities you'll complete in this book will require you to handle potentially hazardous materials. When performing these activities, safe practices and methods must be used. Scientific equipment and chem-

Figure 1-9. Temperature is a measurement we use almost daily.

icals need to be handled safely and properly. The safety rules that follow will help you protect yourself and others from injury and will make you aware of possible hazards.

1. Before beginning any lab, understand the safety symbols shown in Appendix D, on page 665.
2. Wear goggles and a safety apron whenever an investigation involves heating, pouring, or using chemicals.
3. Always slant test tubes away from yourself and others when heating them. Keep all materials away from open flames. Tie back long hair and loose clothing.
4. Never eat or drink in the lab, and never use laboratory glassware as food or drink containers. Never inhale chemicals, and don't taste any substance or draw any material into a tube with your mouth.
5. Know what to do in case of fire. Also, know the location and proper use of the fire extinguisher, safety shower, fire blanket, first aid kit, and fire alarm.
6. Report any accident or injury to your teacher.
7. When cleaning up, dispose of chemicals and other materials as directed by your teacher, and always wash your hands thoroughly after working in the lab.

Figure 1-10. Several safety rules are being followed by this student.

SECTION REVIEW

1. List the SI units for the following measurements: length, mass, weight, area, volume, density, and temperature.
2. Explain the differences between mass and weight and between area and volume.
3. When should you use safety goggles? Refer to Appendix D on page 665.
4. **Apply:** Why do you suppose you should always slant test tubes away from yourself and others when heating them? Why should you tie back long hair and loose clothing?

☑ Measuring in SI

Use your knowledge of SI units to answer the following questions. If you need help, refer to Measuring in SI in the **Skill Handbook** on page 684.

1. Which SI unit would you use to measure the amount of orange juice in a glass?
2. How many meters are in a kilometer?
3. Which unit would you use to measure the amount of carpet needed to cover the floor of your bedroom?

Skill Builder

ACTIVITY 1-1
Determining Length, Area, and Volume

Problem: *How are length, area, and volume determined?*

Materials

- graph paper
- metric ruler
- string
- graduated cylinder (100 mL)
- small rock
- shoe box
- water

Procedure

1. Measure and record the length, width, and height of the shoe box using the metric ruler.
2. Calculate and record the area of the top, side, and end of the shoe box using the equation: area = length × width.
3. Calculate and record the volume of the shoe box using the equation: volume = length × width × height.
4. Trace the outline of the rock on a piece of graph paper. Determine the surface area of the rock. Explain your answer.
5. Fill the graduated cylinder half full of water and record the volume in mL.
6. Tie a piece of string around the rock and lower it into the cylinder. Record the volume reading. Remember to express each volume measurement in cm³ or mL.
7. Remove the rock. Check to make sure that the cylinder has the same volume of water in it as when you started.

8. Subtract the volume of the cylinder with water from the volume of the cylinder with the water and the rock. Record the volume of the rock.

Analyze

1. How did you determine the volume of the box?
2. Which was easier to measure, the area or the volume of the rock?
3. Why did you need to know the volume of water in the cylinder before you added the rock?

Conclude and Apply

4. How could you determine the volume of an oddly shaped object that floats in water?
5. What area does a house 10 m wide, 15 m long and 18 meters high cover?

Data and Observations

Object	Length	Width	Height	Area	Volume
Shoe box					
Coffee can					
Rock					
Graduated cylinder					

CHAPTER
REVIEW

1-1: What Is Science?

1. Chemistry is the study of properties and composition of matter. Physics is the study of forces, energy, motion, and their effects on matter. Biology is the study of living organisms. The study of Earth is earth science.

2. Some topics studied in earth science are volcanoes, earthquakes, fossils, weather, climate, mountains, land use, planets, stars, and oceans.

1-2: Science and Technology

1. Technology has made possible various appliances you use every day, such as calculators and TVs. Technology also has allowed people to explore space and make advances in medicine.

2. Technology allows some people to live longer, but sometimes with a poor quality of life. Technology also contributes to pollution.

1-3: Solving Problems

1. Problem-solving strategies include identifying the problem; collecting data about the problem; eliminating possibilities; using trial and error; solving a simpler, related problem; and making a model or drawing.

2. Commonly used scientific methods include determining the problem, making a hypothesis, testing, analyzing results, drawing conclusions.

3. A hypothesis is a testable prediction for a problem. Hypotheses may be used to form theories, which are explanations backed by results obtained from repeated tests or experiments. A law is a "rule of nature" that generally describes what will happen in a given situation, but not why it happens.

1-4: Measurement and Safety

1. In SI, the unit for length is the meter; mass, the gram; weight, the newton; area, square centimeters; volume, cubic meters; and density, grams per cubic centimeter.

2. Mass is the amount of matter in an object. Weight is a measure of the force of gravity. Area is the amount of surface in a set of boundaries.

3. Lab safety includes: understanding how to do the activity, using caution while working with flames, never eating or drinking in the lab, using care with all substances, and reporting any accident to your teacher.

KEY SCIENCE WORDS

a. **astronomy**
b. **control**
c. **geology**
d. **gravitational force**
e. **hypothesis**
f. **International System of Units (SI)**
g. **law**
h. **mass**
i. **meteorology**
j. **oceanography**
k. **science**
l. **scientific methods**
m. **technology**
n. **theory**
o. **variable**
p. **weight**

UNDERSTANDING VOCABULARY

Match each phrase with the correct term from the list of Key Science Words.

1. having knowledge by observing and studying things around you
2. the study of objects in space
3. the use of scientific discoveries
4. a testable prediction
5. a factor in an experiment that changes
6. a scientific "rule of nature"
7. a modern version of the metric system
8. the amount of matter in an object
9. a measure of gravitational force
10. the study of weather conditions

CHAPTER
REVIEW

CHECKING CONCEPTS

Choose the word or phrase that completes the sentence or answers the question.

1. The word *science* means to _____.
   a. have knowledge   c. observe things
   b. solve problems   d. all of these

2. _____ is the study of organisms.
   a. Chemistry   c. Geology
   b. Biology   d. Physics

3. Oceanographers study Earth's _____
   a. place in space   c. weather
   b. oceans   d. glaciers

4. _____ involves the study of stars.
   a. Chemistry   c. Astronomy
   b. Physics   d. None of these

5. Technology has resulted in _____.
   a. advances in medicine   c. computers
   b. air pollution   d. all of these

6. A _____ is a standard used for comparison in an experiment.
   a. variable   c. control
   b. theory   d. law

7. The length of your toe is best measured in _____.
   a. meters   c. cubic centimeters
   b. centimeters   d. degrees Celsius

8. A balance is used to measure _____.
   a. mass   c. volume
   b. weight   d. density

9. _____ is measured with a thermometer.
   a. Length   c. Temperature
   b. Area   d. Volume

10. Which of these is *not* a lab safety rule?
    a. Slant tests tubes away from people when heating them.
    b. Know where the fire extinguisher is.
    c. Wash your hands after working in the lab.
    d. Taste substances to find out what they are.

UNDERSTANDING CONCEPTS

Complete each sentence.

11. Finding out how sea lillies feed would be studied in _____.
12. Soils are studied in the field of _____.
13. _____ could be used to find out how light affects plants.
14. The SI unit of _____ is the newton.
15. _____ is a measure of how much space an object occupies.

THINK AND WRITE CRITICALLY

16. Why would a scientist studying a volcano like Mount Saint Helens also need some knowledge of physics and chemistry?
17. How have advances in technology been harmful to our planet?
18. How does a theory differ from a hypothesis?
19. Compare and contrast mass and weight.
20. How could you determine the volume of a cardboard box given that its area is 100 m²?

APPLY

21. Brent had decided to go to college to become a sports trainer. In addition to human biology courses, she was required to take a physics course. Explain
22. Describe how you use technology to do your homework.
23. Suppose you had two plants—a cactus and a palm. You planted them both in potting soil and watered them daily. After a week, the cactus was dead. What problem-solving strategies could you use to find out why the cactus died?
24. Are the steps of the scientific method always followed in the order given on page 17? Explain.

25. The moon's gravitational force is one-sixth hat of our planet. How would your mass differ on the moon?

If you need help, refer to the Skill Handbook.

MORE SKILL BUILDERS

1. **Concept Mapping:** Make a concept map using the following terms and phrases: *centimeters; kilometer; deciliter; liquid medicine for a baby; distance from Houston, TX, to Columbus, OH; and area of a postage stamp, the appropriate use.*

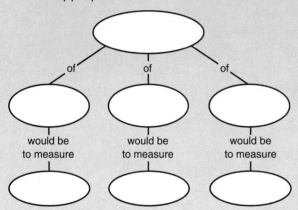

2. **Using Variables, Constants, and Controls:** Suppose you wanted to know whether cold water causes fish to breathe slower than they do in warm water. How would you set up a simple experiment to test this?

3. **Comparing and Contrasting:** Contrast science and technology.

4. **Sequencing:** Ann wants to see how much rain falls in her city during March. Sequence the following steps in the most logical order that she needs to follow to solve her problem.
   a. Collect rain.
   b. Make a rain gauge.
   c. Measure the amount of rainfall each day.
   d. Research how much rain usually falls during March in her city.
   e. Hypothesize how much rain will fall.
   f. Graph her results.

5. **Measuring in SI:** Describe how you would calculate the volume of a coffee can.

PROJECTS

1. Perform an activity to study what happens to air as it is heated. Partially fill a balloon with air. Tape two wooden sticks parallel to the sides of the balloon. Then tape the balloon to a ring stand with a heating lamp above it. Record the temperature near the balloon, the size of the balloon, and the time at set intervals. Use SI units. Record your data in a table.

2. Design an experiment to determine the effects of water on small plants. Use three identical plants and give each a different amount of water every other day. Record the amount of water used and plant growth using SI units.

2 Matter and Its Changes

You've probably combined ingredients to form a mixture called a pizza. You may have made ice tea to drink with your pizza. If you added sugar to your tea, you created another mixture called a solution. In fact, you make and use many mixtures each day. But do you know what mixtures are? Why is sweetened tea a special type of mixture called a solution?

FIND OUT!

Do this activity to find out how much sugar can be dissolved in tea.

Make yourself a cup of warm tea in a cup that allows you to see the bottom. Place a sugar cube in the tea and stir until all of the sugar dissolves. Continue adding sugar cubes, one at a time, until no more sugar can be dissolved. How many sugar cubes dissolved in the tea before sugar started collecting on the bottom of the cup? Try the activity again using cold tea. Does temperature affect the amount of sugar that can dissolve?

Gearing Up
Previewing the Chapter
Use this outline to help you focus on important ideas in this chapter.

Previewing Science Skills
▶ In the **Skill Builders**, you will outline, make concept maps, and make and use tables.
▶ In the **Activities**, you will observe, collect and organize data.
▶ In the **MINI-Labs**, you will classify, observe, and infer.

What's next?

Now that you've discovered how much sugar dissolves in a cup of tea, learn why this happens. In this chapter, you'll investigate the basic building blocks of matter — atoms and molecules. And you'll learn that the structure of atoms and molecules in a substance affects how it behaves in the presence of other substances.

2-1 Atoms

New Science Words

matter
atoms
elements
protons
neutrons
electrons
isotopes

Objectives

▶ Identify matter as anything that has mass and takes up space.
▶ Describe the internal structure of an atom.
▶ Relate that isotopes of the same element have the same atomic number but different mass numbers.

The Building Blocks of Matter

What do this book, the air you breathe, and the food you eat all have in common? The book, the air, and the food are all matter. **Matter** is anything that takes up space and has mass. You can't always see matter; for example, you can't see air. On the other hand, not everything you see is matter. You can see light reflecting off surfaces, but light doesn't take up space or have mass. Light, despite being visible, isn't matter.

Matter is all around you, yet various forms can be very different. Air is a colorless gas, water is a transparent liquid, and rocks are colorful solids. Why do the characteristics of one form of matter differ from the characteristics of another? This chapter will help you answer that question.

Figure 2-1. More than 99 percent of the matter in our solar system is contained in the sun.

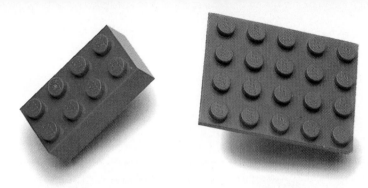

All matter is composed of "building blocks." The structure of these building blocks determines the structure of the matter you observe. Think about when you were younger and played with snap-together blocks. You could snap the blocks together in many ways to build cars, ships, or buildings. Matter is put together in a similar way. The building blocks of matter are **atoms.** The arrangement and types of atoms give matter its properties.

Atoms combine, like the blocks snapping together, to form many different types of matter. Your body has only a few of these atoms in it, but they have combined in many different ways to form the matter that composes your body. Other forms of matter contain only one type of atom. Such substances are **elements.** Let's take a look at the structure of an element.

Suppose you have a copper wire. What kind of atoms are in the wire? Because copper is an element, it's made up of only copper atoms. Look at Table 2-1. It shows copper and some other common elements and their uses. Appendix E of your book is a table of the known elements called the periodic table.

Figure 2-2. Like atoms, the same few blocks can combine in many different ways.

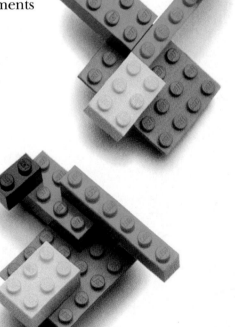

Table 2-1

COMMON ELEMENTS AND THEIR USES

| Copper ore | Aluminum ore | Silicon (quartz) | Fluorine |
| Electrical wire | Soft drink cans | Computer chip | Toothpaste |

The Structure of Atoms

You already know that atoms are very small. Atoms are far too small to be seen, even with a microscope. How can you study something this small? How can you determine the internal structure of an atom?

Why are models useful?

When substances are too large or too small to handle or directly observe, models are often used to take their place. Have you ever worked with model cars, trains, or houses? If so, your model was a small version of a large object. In the case of atoms, the opposite is true. A large model is made of a very small object. We construct drawings, sculptures, and mental pictures of the internal structure of atoms. These models are based on information we've gathered by observing the ways atoms of elements react when in contact with other atoms or with light.

Let's construct a mental model of the internal structure of an atom. Three basic particles make up an atom—protons, neutrons, and electrons. Protons and neutrons are located in the center of an atom and make up its nucleus. **Protons** are particles that have a positive electric charge. **Neutrons** are particles that have no electric charge. The nucleus, therefore, has a positive charge because of the positively charged protons in it. This positive electric charge of the nucleus is balanced by the electrons of the atom.

Electrons are negatively charged particles that circle the nucleus. There is one electron for each proton. Our model in Figure 2-4 shows electrons existing as a negatively charged electron cloud. This cloud completely surrounds the nucleus of the atom. Electrons can be anywhere within the cloud, but evidence suggests that they are located near the nucleus most of the time. A swarm of bees flying around its hive can be a model of an atom. The hive represents the nucleus of the atom. The bees flying around the hive in all directions are like the electrons circling the nucleus. You can't determine exactly where each bee is, but each is usually close to the hive.

Figure 2-3. Bees model electrons as they swarm around their hive —the nucleus.

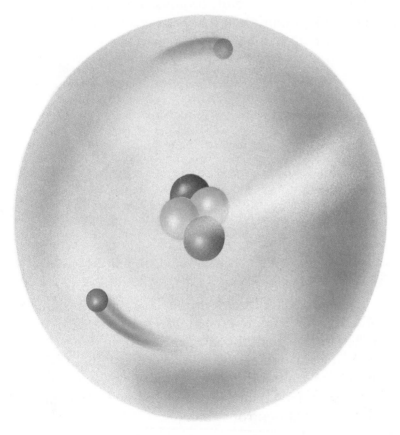

Figure 2-4. This model of a helium atom shows two protons and two neutrons in the nucleus and two electrons in the electron cloud.

Mass Numbers and Atomic Numbers

Just as an atom has a characteristic number of protons, neutrons, and electrons, it also has a characteristic mass. The mass number of an atom is equal to the number of protons and neutrons making up its nucleus. Just as you have more mass when you are carrying many books, an atom has more mass if it contains more particles. So oxygen, which contains eight protons and eight neutrons, has a mass number of 16. Carbon has a mass number of 12. How many protons and neutrons does carbon have?

You've probably noticed that electrons aren't counted when we compute an atom's mass number. This is because electrons aren't massive enough to add much to the atom's mass. They have much less mass than protons and neutrons.

Another property of an atom that's convenient to know is its atomic number. An atom's atomic number equals the number of protons in its nucleus. This number also equals the number of electrons contained in its electron cloud. All atoms of a specific element have the same atomic number. For example, all atoms of iron have an atomic number of 26. How many protons does an atom of iron contain? Whether it's in the metal of a car fender or in the nails in a bookcase, an iron atom has 26 protons.

If the number of protons in an atom is changed, a new element is formed.

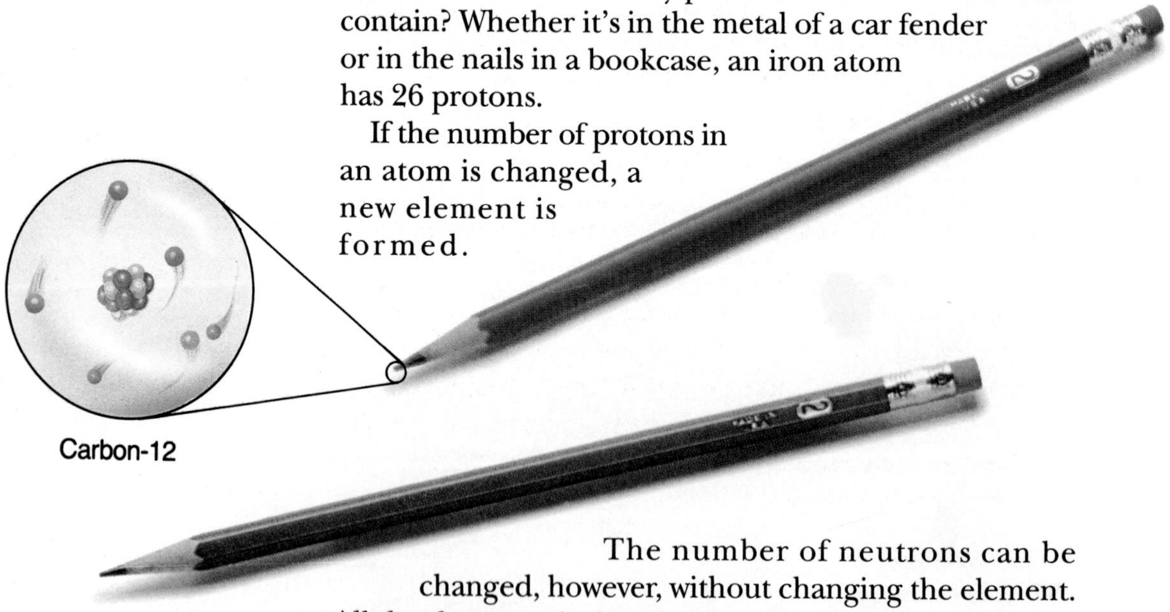

Carbon-12

Figure 2-5. The carbon in your pencil lead is mostly carbon-12. Its atomic mass is 12 and its atomic number is 6.

The number of neutrons can be changed, however, without changing the element. All that happens is that the atom's mass changes. Atoms of the same element that have different numbers of neutrons in their nuclei are called **isotopes.** Table 2-2 lists isotopes of some common elements. Note that the number of protons remains the same for each element, but the number of neutrons changes.

Table 2-2

ISOTOPES			
Isotope	Number of Protons	Number of Neutrons	Number of Electrons
Hydrogen-1	1	0	1
Hydrogen-2	1	1	1
Hydrogen-3	1	2	1
Carbon-12	6	6	6
Carbon-14	6	8	6
Uranium-234	92	142	92
Uranium-235	92	143	92
Uranium-238	92	146	92

Isotopes provide us with a way to determine the age of ancient objects. Geologists use isotopes to date fossils and layers of rock. Archeologists use them to determine the age of artifacts such as clothing, wood, bones, and structures. You will be learning more about isotopes and some of their uses in Chapter 16.

Our model of an atom allows us to predict how a particular element will react when it's in contact with another element. As you continue to investigate matter in this chapter, you will explore how atoms of different elements combine to form the matter around you.

Figure 2-6. Isotopes have helped geologists verify the dates of rock layers and fossils.

SECTION REVIEW

1. List two facts that are true of all matter.
2. What is the electric charge of each of the particles of an atom?
3. **Apply:** Oxygen-16 and oxygen-17 are two different isotopes of oxygen. The numbers 16 and 17 represent their mass numbers. How many protons and neutrons are in each isotope?

⊠ Outlining

Outline the material in Section 2-1. What is the main topic of this section? How do atoms and elements differ? If you need help, refer to Outlining in the **Skill Handbook** on page 681.

Skill Builder

2-2 Combinations of Atoms

New Science Words

molecule
compound
chemical properties
ions
mixture

Objectives

▶ Discuss several ways atoms combine to form compounds.
▶ Compare and contrast compounds and mixtures.

How Atoms Combine

Suppose you've just eaten a snack such as an apple or an orange. It's unlikely that you were concerned about the elements that were in the snack. Yet anything you have ever eaten and anything you've ever touched has had the same few elements in it. The sugar in the apple or orange contains the elements carbon, oxygen, and hydrogen. The air you're breathing contains nitrogen, oxygen, argon, and other elements.

Notice that both the apple and the air contain the element oxygen. Yet in one case oxygen is in a colorless gaseous form. In the other case it's part of a structure that's hard and colorful. How can the same element, made from the same type of atom, help make up two objects that are so different? The atoms of elements combine to form new substances called compounds. When they do, the properties of the individual elements change. Let's see how this happens.

One way that atoms combine is by sharing the electrons in the outermost portion of their electron clouds. The combined atoms form a **molecule**. For example, two atoms of hydrogen can share electrons with one atom of oxygen to form one molecule of water. Water is a compound. A **compound** is a type of matter that has properties different from the properties of each of the elements in it.

The properties of hydrogen and oxygen are changed when they combine to form water. Under normal conditions on Earth, you will find the elements oxygen and hydrogen only as gases. Yet water can be a liquid or a solid as well as a gas. When hydrogen and oxygen com-

Figure 2-7. Carbonated drinks are a mixture of carbon dioxide and other compounds.

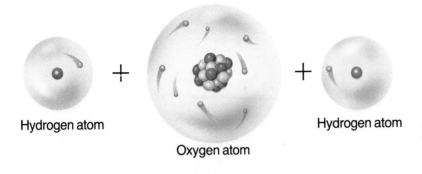

Hydrogen atom

Oxygen atom

Hydrogen atom

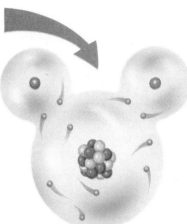

Water molecule

Figure 2-8. A molecule of water has chemical properties that are different than those of hydrogen and oxygen atoms.

bine, a chemical change occurs. A new substance forms with chemical properties that are different from those of the elements in it.

The properties of hydrogen that determine how it will react with oxygen are chemical properties. **Chemical properties** describe how one substance changes when it reacts with other substances. For example, the chemical properties of iron cause it to change to rust when it reacts with water and oxygen.

TECHNOLOGY

One at a Time!

Atoms are extremely small. Many are hundreds of billionths of centimeters in diameter. Yet, scientists have discovered how to move individual atoms in much the same way you may have used a magnet to move small game pieces around a plastic covered board. Using a scanning tunnel microscope (STM), physicists drag a fine-tipped needle over the material's surface. When the desired position is reached, the needle is raised and the atom "drops" into this new position.

This discovery may lead to the building of molecules one atom at a time. Even smaller electrical circuits could be made

for everything from watches to computers. New drugs that would cure or eliminate certain illnesses could be constructed using this method. The illustration shows xenon atoms arranged to spell out "IBM."

Think Critically: How could STMs be used to permanently store information?

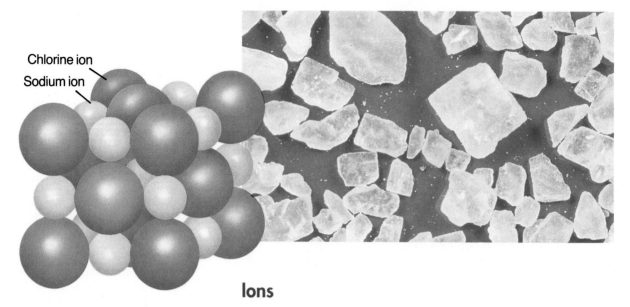

Chlorine ion

Sodium ion

Figure 2-9. The cubic arrangement of sodium and chlorine ions gives salt crystals their cubic shape.

Ions

You know that atoms combine by sharing electrons of the outer portion of their electron cloud. But atoms also combine because they've become positively or negatively charged.

As you discovered earlier, atoms are usually neutral—they have no overall electric charge. Under certain conditions, however, atoms can lose or gain electrons. When an atom loses electrons, it has more protons than electrons so the atom is positively charged. When an atom gains electrons, it has more electrons than protons so the atom is negatively charged. Electrically charged atoms are called **ions.**

Ions are attracted to each other when they have opposite charges. Oppositely charged ions join to form electrically neutral compounds. Table salt forms in this way. A sodium (Na) atom loses an electron and becomes a positively charged ion. Then it comes close to a negatively charged chlorine (Cl) ion. They are attracted to each other and form the compound NaCl. This is the compound that you use on your french fries or popcorn.

Mixtures

If you look into your book bag, you will see an example of a **mixture.** Many different objects are mixed together, but each retains its own properties. Your math book isn't any different whether it's beside your comb or beside your history book.

Another example of a mixture is a cup of tea with sugar dissolved in it. The sweetness of the sugar can be tasted whether it's in the tea or not. So, the properties of the sugar molecules aren't changed just because they're mixed in with the tea.

Sweetened tea is an example of a kind of mixture called a solution. When one substance of a mixture is dissolved in another substance, a solution is formed. In the case of our sweetened tea, the sugar molecules are separated from each other by other molecules within the tea. Therefore, the sugar has dissolved in the tea. Another property of a solution is that it is the same throughout. One part of a solution is the same as all other parts. To make the sweetened tea a solution, we had to stir it. If we've stirred the tea enough, the sugar molecules are spread evenly throughout. Our first drink of tea will taste as sweet as our last.

Define solution.

The components of a mixture can be separated by physical means. You can sit at your desk and pick out the separate items in your book bag. You can let the tea evaporate and the sugar will remain in the cup. But is it possible to separate the components of a compound in a similar way?

PROBLEM SOLVING

Filled to the Rim?

Janice went to her favorite delicatessen on a bitter cold day in January. After carefully studying the menu, she ordered a cheese sandwich on rye bread and a cup of hot tea. Her waiter brought the food to her table, but much to Janice's dismay, he filled her teacup to the rim. Janice wondered how she was going to put her usual two teaspoons of sugar into the tea. Rather than risk burning her fingers by trying to pour some of the tea onto the saucer, Janice put a heaping spoonful of sugar into the tea. It didn't overflow. Janice was surprised. She then added another spoonful of sugar. Intrigued, she added still another

spoonful of sugar. As she ate her sandwich, Janice thought about the seemingly full cup of tea.

Think Critically: Why didn't the tea spill from the cup when the sugar was added? If Janice had ordered ice tea, would she have been able to add as much sugar?

Figure 2-10. Water can be easily separated from the spaghetti mixture. However, it is more difficult to separate the compound water into its component parts.

Suppose you take the sugar in the cup and try to separate its carbon atoms from its hydrogen and oxygen atoms. How can you do it? It's much more difficult than separating the components of a mixture. The only way is to separate the carbon, hydrogen, and oxygen atoms of each sugar molecule. This is an example of a chemical change. A chemical change converts one substance into one or more new substances.

Sweetened tea, air, ocean water, and the contents of your book bag are all examples of mixtures. These mixtures are made from materials that have mixed together but still retain their individual properties. The materials themselves are made of compounds. The atoms of these compounds lost their individual chemical properties when they combined. As you continue to explore matter, use the mental models you've developed for atoms, elements, molecules, compounds, and mixtures.

EcoTip

When making homemade cleaners, never combine chlorine products with ammonia products. A dangerous gas is produced.

SECTION REVIEW

1. How do atoms or ions combine to form molecules?
2. Is the basic unit of water an atom, a molecule, or an element? Write water's molecular formula.
3. **Apply:** How can you determine if salt water is a solution or a compound?

Skill Builder

☑ Concept Mapping

Make an events chain map using the terms *mixtures, atoms, molecules, compounds, electrons, protons,* and *neutrons.* If you need help, refer to Concept Mapping in the **Skill Handbook** on pages 688 and 689.

ACTIVITY 2-1
Measuring Physical Properties

Problem: *How can you use laboratory equipment to make observations about physical properties of objects?*

Materials

- balance (beam)
- graduated cylinder (100 mL or larger)
- metersticks (2)
- thermometers (3)
- stick or dowel
- rock sample
- string
- globe
- water

Procedure

1. Begin at any station and determine the measurement requested. Record the data and list sources of error.

   a. Use a balance to determine the mass, to the nearest 0.1 g, of a rock sample.

   b. Use a graduated cylinder to determine the volume, to the nearest 0.5 mL, of the water.

   c. Use 3 thermometers to measure the average temperature, to the nearest 0.5°C, at a certain location in the room.

   d. Use a meterstick to measure the length, to the nearest 0.1 cm, of a stick or dowel.

   e. Use a meterstick and string to measure the circumference of a globe. Be accurate to the nearest 0.1 cm.

2. Proceed to the other four stations as directed by your teacher. Complete the procedure, as in Step 1, at each station.

Analyze

1. Compare your measurements with those who used the same objects. Review the values provided by your teacher. How do the values you obtained compare to those provided by your teacher and those of other students?

2. Determine your percentage of error in each case. Use this formula.

$$\frac{\text{your value} - \text{teacher's value}}{\text{teacher's value}} \times 100 = \text{\% of error}$$

Conclude and Apply

3. Decide what percentage error will be acceptable. Generally, being within 5% to 7% of the correct value is considered good. If your values exceed 10% error, try the measurement again to see where the error occurred. What was the most common source of error?

Data and Observations

Station	Sample #	Value of Measurement	Causes of Error
a	____	Mass = ____ g	
b	____	Volume = ____ mL	
c	____ (location)	Average temp. = ____ °C	
d	____	Length = ____ cm	
e	____ (globe)	Circumference = ____ cm	

2-3 Matter

New Science Words

physical properties
density

Objectives

▶ Distinguish between chemical and physical properties.
▶ Contrast the four states of matter.

Physical Properties of Matter

So far in this chapter, you've been investigating chemical properties of matter—the properties that describe how one substance changes into another substance. But you can observe other properties of matter. The properties that you can observe without changing a substance into a new substance are **physical properties.**

What are some physical properties of your clothing? If you say your jeans are blue, soft, and about 80 cm long, you've described some of their physical properties. You can observe these without changing the material in your jeans into new substances.

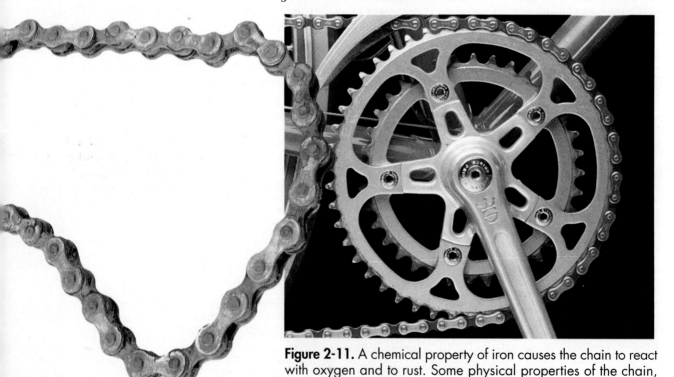

Figure 2-11. A chemical property of iron causes the chain to react with oxygen and to rust. Some physical properties of the chain, such as length and hardness, make it useful.

Density

One physical property that you will use to describe matter is density. **Density** is a measure of the mass of an object divided by its volume. Generally, this measurement is given in grams per cubic centimeter (g/cm^3). For example, the average density of liquid water is $1 \ g/cm^3$. So $1 \ cm^3$ of water has a mass of 1 g.

Suppose you have a small pebble and need to find its density. First measure its mass and volume. If its volume is $2 \ cm^3$ and its mass is 8 g, its density is:

$$\text{Density} = \frac{\text{mass}}{\text{volume}}$$

$$D = \frac{8 \ g}{2 \ cm^3}$$

$$D = \frac{4 \ g}{cm^3} \quad \text{or} \quad 4 \ g/cm^3$$

An object that's denser than water will sink, whereas one that's less dense will float. You've heard about the oil spills off the coast of the United States. Why does this oil float on the surface of the water and wash up on the beaches?

Science and MATH

Suppose you have a small object with a volume of $7 \ cm^3$ and a mass of 4.2 g. What is the density? Will the object float in water?

States of Matter

Think back to breakfast this morning. You may have had solid toast, liquid milk or juice, and of course you breathed air, which is a gas. If you happen to have a fluorescent light in your home, you also used matter in its plasma state. On Earth matter occurs in four physical states. These four states are solid, liquid, gas, and plasma. What causes the differences among these four states of matter?

Solids

The reason some matter is solid is that its atoms or molecules are in a fixed position relative to each other. The individual atoms may vibrate but they don't switch positions with each other. You can make a mental model of this.

Suppose you have a puzzle with its many pieces in place. The pieces are packed so tightly that no one piece can switch positions with another piece. But the pieces can move a little. For example, you can twist the whole puzzle a few millimeters without breaking it apart. If it's on a table, you can shake the table and the puzzle's individual pieces will vibrate. But the pieces of the puzzle are held together even though they do move some.

The puzzle pieces in our model represent atoms or molecules of a substance in a solid state. Such atoms or molecules are strongly attracted to each other and resist being separated.

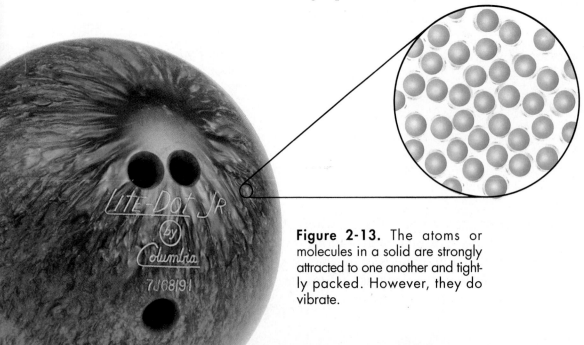

Figure 2-13. The atoms or molecules in a solid are strongly attracted to one another and tightly packed. However, they do vibrate.

Figure 2-14. The atoms or molecules in a liquid are not as strongly attracted to each other as those of a solid. They are free to move over and around each other.

Liquids

Atoms or molecules in a liquid are also strongly attracted to each other, but they aren't as strongly attracted as they are in a solid. Atoms or molecules remain close to one another in a liquid but are free to change positions with each other. This allows liquids to flow.

When you sit down to breakfast, you may have several liquids at the table. You may have milk in a glass and syrup on your pancakes. Both are substances in the liquid state, even though one flows more freely than the other.

A liquid flows as it takes the shape of the container it's placed in, but it resists changes in volume. You can pour orange juice into a short, wide glass and it will match the shape of the glass. You can then pour the same juice into a tall, skinny glass and it will flow until it matches the shape of its new container. It does so because its molecules move over and around each other.

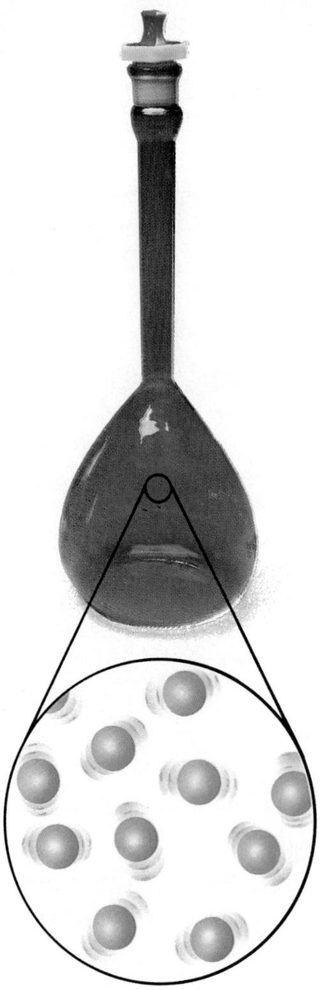

Gases

Gases behave the way they do because their atoms or molecules have very little attractive force on each other. This causes them to move freely and independently. Air fresheners work because of this property. If an air freshener is placed in a corner, it isn't long before molecules from the air freshener have spread throughout the room. Gases fill the entire container they are placed in no matter what size or shape it is. The atoms or molecules move apart until they're evenly spaced throughout the container.

Plasma

What's the most common state of matter? So far we've investigated matter in the solid, liquid, and gaseous states. But most of the matter in the universe is in the plasma state. Matter in this state is composed of ions and electrons. Many of the electrons normally in the electron cloud have escaped and are outside of the ion's electron cloud.

Stars are composed of matter in the plasma state. And plasma exists in the space between the stars. On Earth, plasma is found in fluorescent lights and lightning bolts.

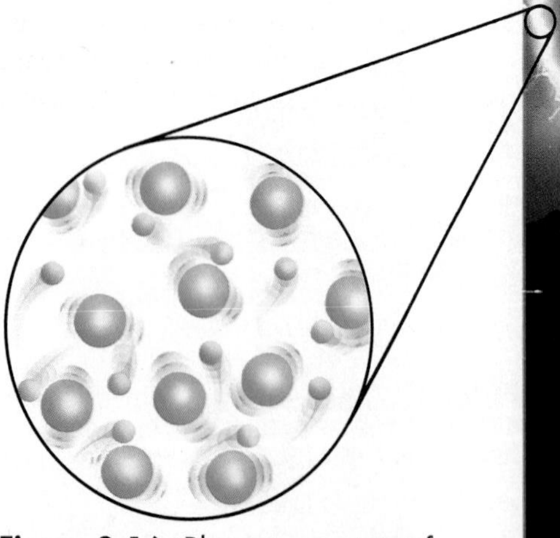

Figure 2-15. Molecules in a gas are not strongly attracted to each other.

Figure 2-16. Plasma consists of ions and electrons moving freely.

Changing the State of Matter

Matter is changed from a liquid to a solid at its freezing point and from a liquid to a gas at its boiling point. You're probably familiar with the freezing and boiling points of water. Water changes from a liquid to a solid at its freezing point of 0°C. It boils at 100°C. Water is the only substance that occurs naturally on Earth as a solid, liquid, and gas.

Most substances don't naturally exist in these three states on Earth. Their boiling and freezing points are above or below the temperatures we experience. Temperatures and conditions needed for matter to exist as plasma are even less common on Earth.

The attraction between atoms or molecules and their rate of movement are two factors that determine the state of matter. When you melt ice you increase the rate of movement of its molecules. They are then able to move apart. Adding thermal energy to the ice causes this change.

Changes in state can also occur because of increases or decreases in pressure. You can demonstrate this by applying pressure to an ice cube. It will change to liquid water even though its temperature stays the same.

Figure 2-17. A solid metal can be converted into liquid by adding thermal energy to its molecules.

EcoTip

Cover water when you heat it, and you'll use less energy. Covered water boils faster than uncovered water.

What are two factors that determine matter's state?

MINI-Lab

What happens when water freezes?

Pour water into a graduated cylinder or small beaker so that it is about half filled. Mark the level of the water with a small piece of masking tape. Then place the uncovered container of water into a freezer until all of the water turns to ice. How does the level of the ice in the container compare to the original level of the water? Describe some of the changes in the physical properties of water when it changes to ice.

Figure 2-18. If ice was more dense than water, lakes would freeze solid from the bottom up. What would happen to the life in a pond if this were true?

Changes in Physical Properties

Chemical properties of matter don't change when the matter changes state. But some of its physical properties change. For example, the density of water changes as it changes state. In which state is water the most dense? You may be tempted to say when it's a solid, but think critically about this. Ice will float in liquid water, therefore ice is less dense than liquid water. This is because water molecules move farther apart and the water expands as it freezes.

Some physical properties of substances don't change when they change state. For example, water is colorless and transparent in each of its states.

Chemical and physical properties allow us to identify and classify matter. One way to classify matter is by its state. Matter in one state can often be changed to another state by adding or removing heat. When matter changes state in this way, it retains its chemical properties while some of its physical properties change.

Figure 2-19. Water-carved valley on the Planet Mars

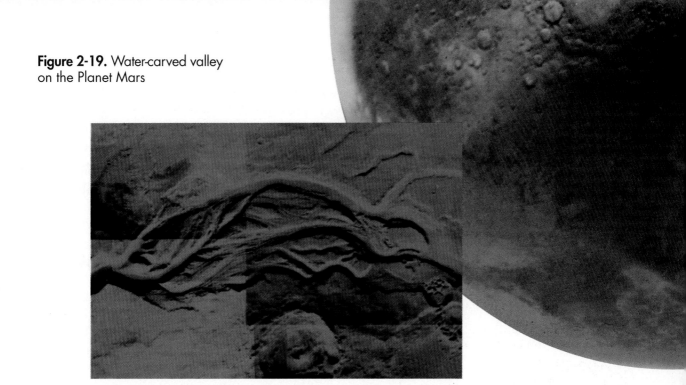

SECTION REVIEW

1. What property of a substance is calculated by dividing its mass by its volume? Is it a chemical or physical property?
2. In which state are the molecules of water prevented from moving over and around each other? In which state can water molecules spread the farthest apart?
3. Suppose you blow up a balloon and then place it in a freezer. Later, you find the balloon has shrunk and it contains liquid in it. Explain what has happened.
4. **Apply:** The planet Mars has what appears to be ancient stream beds, yet there's no liquid water on Mars. Explain what may have happened to Mars' liquid water.

☑ Making and Using Tables

Jonathon had a glass of milk, an orange, celery sticks, and a peanut butter and jelly sandwich for lunch. Make a table listing the state of matter of each item of his lunch. Also list at least one physical property of each item. If you need help, refer to Making and Using Tables in the **Skill Handbook** on page 690.

2-4 Superconductors

New Science Words

superconductors

Objectives

▶ Compare and contrast superconductors with other conductors.
▶ Discuss one possible use of superconducting materials.

How Can Superconductors Store Energy?

It's 8:00 PM and the electricity in your home suddenly goes out. You have no lights, no radio, no refrigeration, and no television. Your local power company didn't produce enough electricity to power all the homes and businesses in your neighborhood. How can this be? Isn't there a way to prevent this from happening?

When coal-burning and nuclear power plants produce electricity, they send it out over utility lines and it eventually reaches your house. But if the power company produces more energy than is needed, the electricity can't be stored; it goes to waste. If they don't produce enough, you and your neighbors lose power. If there were a way for power companies to store electricity, they could produce more than was needed at one time, store it, and tap into it when energy demands are high. Superconductors may make this possible.

Any material that allows electrons to pass through it is called a conductor. Electrons flowing through a conductor produce the electricity you use in your home.

As electrons pass through a wire they collide with atoms in the wire. This resistance to the flow of electricity causes the material to heat up. Part of the electric energy is wasted as it's converted to thermal energy. But in **superconductors,** no electricity is wasted because there's no resistance to the flow of electrons.

Materials such as titanium, zinc, lead, and mercury conduct electricity with no resistance when they are cooled to extremely low temperatures. Planes of atoms provide highways for electrons to flow without collisions with atoms.

Because there's no resistance in a superconductor, electric current continues once it's started. Electric currents

Figure 2-20. Wires made of conducting material carry electricity to your home.

can even be stored in a superconducting ring. The current continually flows around the ring and can be tapped when the electricity is needed in another circuit. Power plants could have a way to store excess electricity that would otherwise be wasted.

The biggest problem with superconductors is that extremely low temperatures are needed to make materials into superconductors. So far the highest temperature superconductor must be cooled to about –150°C. In fact, much of the energy saved by using superconductors must then be used to keep them cool.

Figure 2-21. Superconductors generate powerful magnetic fields as they conduct electricity. This magnet is suspended in a magnetic field over a superconductor.

SECTION REVIEW

1. Why is some of the energy flowing through conductors wasted? How are superconductors different?
2. Why can't superconductors be used to replace the wires in utility lines so that no electricity would be wasted as it passes through them?
3. How might power companies use superconductors?

You Decide!

It's unlikely that materials will ever be developed that can superconduct at room temperature. Is the possibility of reduced cost and reduced waste of electric energy worth the expense in an attempt to find higher temperature superconductors? Or would it be better to spend the money on educating people on how to conserve energy?

SCIENCE & SOCIETY

ACTIVITY 2-2
Determining Density

Problem: *How are the densities of substances determined?*

Materials

- pan balance
- beaker (100 mL)
- piece of quartz
- graduated cylinder (250 mL)
- water
- piece of clay
- small wood block
- small metal block

Procedure

1. Using the pan balance, measure the mass of the wood block, metal block, clay, and quartz. Record these values.
2. Use the graduated cylinder to determine the volume of each sample. Record these values.
3. Calculate the density of each sample by using this equation:

    density = mass/volume

4. After completing these calculations, split the piece of clay into two pieces. Predict what the density of each of the two smaller pieces of clay will be. Determine the density of each piece using the procedure outlined above.
5. Empty the graduated cylinder and determine its mass.
6. Put 100 mL of water in the graduated cylinder and determine the mass of the cylinder and water. Calculate the mass of the water using this equation:

$$\text{mass of water} = \text{mass of cylinder and water} - \text{mass of empty cylinder}$$

7. Calculate the density of water.

Analyze

1. How does the density of each of the smaller pieces of clay compare to the original larger piece?
2. If you broke the quartz into many small pieces, would one of these pieces be more dense, less dense, or equally dense as the one large original piece?

Conclude and Apply

3. What effect does the size or amount of a substance have on its density?
4. Isopropyl alcohol is less dense than liquid water and ice. How could you use isopropyl alcohol to determine the density of an ice cube?
5. How are the densities of various substances determined?

Data and Observations

Object	Mass	Volume	Density
Wood			
Metal			
Clay (lg. piece)			
Quartz			
Clay (sm. piece)			
Water			

CHAPTER
REVIEW

2-1: Atoms

1. Matter is everything that has mass and takes up space. Atoms are the building blocks of matter.
2. Protons and neutrons make up the nucleus of an atom. Protons have a positive charge whereas neutrons have no charge. Electrons circle the nucleus, forming an electron cloud. Electrons are negatively charged.
3. Isotopes are atoms of the same element. Isotopes have the same atomic number, but differ in the number of neutrons.

2-2: Combinations of Atoms

1. A compound is a substance made of two or more elements. The properties of a compound differ from the chemical and physical properties of the elements of which it is composed.
2. Atoms join to form molecules — the building blocks of compounds. A mixture is a substance in which each of the components retains its own properties.

2-3: Matter

1. Physical properties can be observed and measured without causing a chemical change in a substance. Chemical properties can only be observed when one substance reacts with another substance.
2. Atoms or molecules in a solid are in fixed positions relative to one another. In a liquid, the atoms or molecules are close together but are freer to change positions. Atoms or molecules in a gas have very little attractive force on one another. Plasma is composed of ions and electrons.

2-4: Science and Society: Superconductors

1. Electrons flow through superconductors with no resistance.
2. Superconducting rings may be used to store electricity.

KEY SCIENCE WORDS

a. **atoms**
b. **chemical properties**
c. **compound**
d. **density**
e. **electrons**
f. **elements**
g. **ions**
h. **isotopes**
i. **matter**
j. **mixture**
k. **molecule**
l. **neutrons**
m. **physical properties**
n. **protons**
o. **superconductors**

UNDERSTANDING VOCABULARY

Match each phrase with the correct term from the list of Key Science Words.

1. building blocks of matter
2. particles with no electric charge
3. allow electrons to flow with no resistance
4. anything that takes up space and has mass
5. a solution is one type
6. circle the nucleus of an atom
7. composed of only one type of atom
8. mass divided by volume
9. two or more atoms combine to form this building block of compounds
10. atoms of the same element but with different numbers of neutrons

REVIEW

CHECKING CONCEPTS

Choose the word or phrase that completes the sentence.

1. _____ contain only one type of atom.
   a. Plasmas   c. Elements
   b. Mixtures   d. Solids

2. A(n) _____ has a positive charge.
   a. electron   c. neutron
   b. proton   d. plasma

3. In an atom, the _____ form a cloud around the nucleus.
   a. electrons   c. neutrons
   b. protons   d. all of these

4. Carbon has a mass number of 12. Thus, it has _____ protons and _____ neutrons.
   a. 6, 6   c. 6, 12
   b. 12, 12   d. 12, 6

5. On Earth, oxygen is usually a _____.
   a. solid   c. liquid
   b. gas   d. plasma

6. An isotope of carbon is _____.
   a. boron-12   c. carbon-14
   b. nitrogen-12   d. hydrogen-2

7. Electrically charged atoms are _____.
   a. molecules   c. isotopes
   b. solutions   d. ions

8. The color of your clothes is a(n) _____.
   a. chemical property
   b. physical property
   c. isotope property
   d. all of these

9. A rock with a volume of 4.0 cm^3 and a density of 3.0 g/cm^3 has a mass of _____.
   a. 0.75 g   c. 12.0 g
   b. 3.0 g   d. 4.0 g

10. Water changes state at _____.
    a. 0°C and 100°C   c. 0°C and 32°C
    b. 32°C and 100°C d. none of these

UNDERSTANDING CONCEPTS

Complete each sentence.

11. Carbon-12 and carbon-14 have the same number of _____.

12. Sodium has 11 protons and 12 neutrons. Its mass number is _____.

13. The atomic number of sodium is _____.

14. A bowl of fruit salad can best be classified as a(n) _____.

15. Liquid water changes to ice at its _____.

THINK AND WRITE CRITICALLY

16. Compare and contrast protons, electrons, and neutrons.

17. Arrange the following terms in order of size, from smallest to largest: *atomic nucleus, proton, molecule, atom, compound, element.*

18. One isotope of argon is argon-39. What is the mass number of this element?

19. What is the density of 25 cm^3 of salad oil if its mass is 23 grams?

20. How do conductors and superconductors differ?

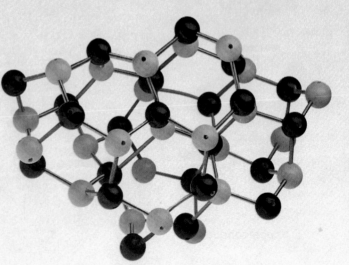

21. Would isotopes of the same element have the same number of electrons? Explain.
22. Two chlorine ions are both negatively charged. Will they combine to form a compound? Why or why not?
23. You pour salad oil into a glass of water. After several minutes, you observe that the water is at the bottom of the glass and all of the oil is floating on top of the water. Does your glass contain a mixture? Does it contain a solution?
24. When oxygen combines with iron, rust is formed. Is this a chemical or physical property of iron?
25. Would rubber or copper make a better superconductor? Explain.

Element	Atomic No.	Mass No.
Fluorine	9	19
Lithium	3	7
Carbon	6	12
Nitrogen	7	14
Beryllium	4	9
Boron	5	11
Oxygen	8	16
Neon	10	20

5. **Making and Using Graphs:** Use the data above to make a line graph of increasing mass number and atomic number of each element. What is the relationship between mass number and atomic number?

MORE SKILL BUILDERS

If you need help, refer to the Skill Handbook.

1. **Classifying:** Use Appendix E to classify the following substances as elements or compounds: *iron, aluminum, carbon dioxide, gold, water,* and *sugar.*
2. **Concept Mapping:** Make a network tree to illustrate the three main parts of an atom.
3. **Hypothesizing:** You put a bottle full of water in the freezer to cool it quickly. You forgot about it, though, and found a broken glass when you went to get it. What hypothesis can you make about water as it changes from a liquid to a solid?
4. **Observing and Inferring:** Your brother is drinking a dark-colored liquid from a clear glass. As you watch from across the room, you think to yourself that the cola is probably refreshing. Is thinking that the liquid is cola an observation or an inference?

PROJECTS

1. Use different-sized foam balls and wooden sticks to make scale models of the atomic structure of the first ten elements in the periodic table.
2. Classify all the items in your family's refrigerator according to physical state. Then list at least two chemical and two physical properties of each item.
3. Research how the model of an atom has evolved with time. Include sketches that compare and contrast the different models.

GLOBAL CONNECTIONS

Foundations of Earth Science

In this unit, you studied about scientific investigation and properties of matter. Now find out how these topics are connected to other subjects and places around the world.

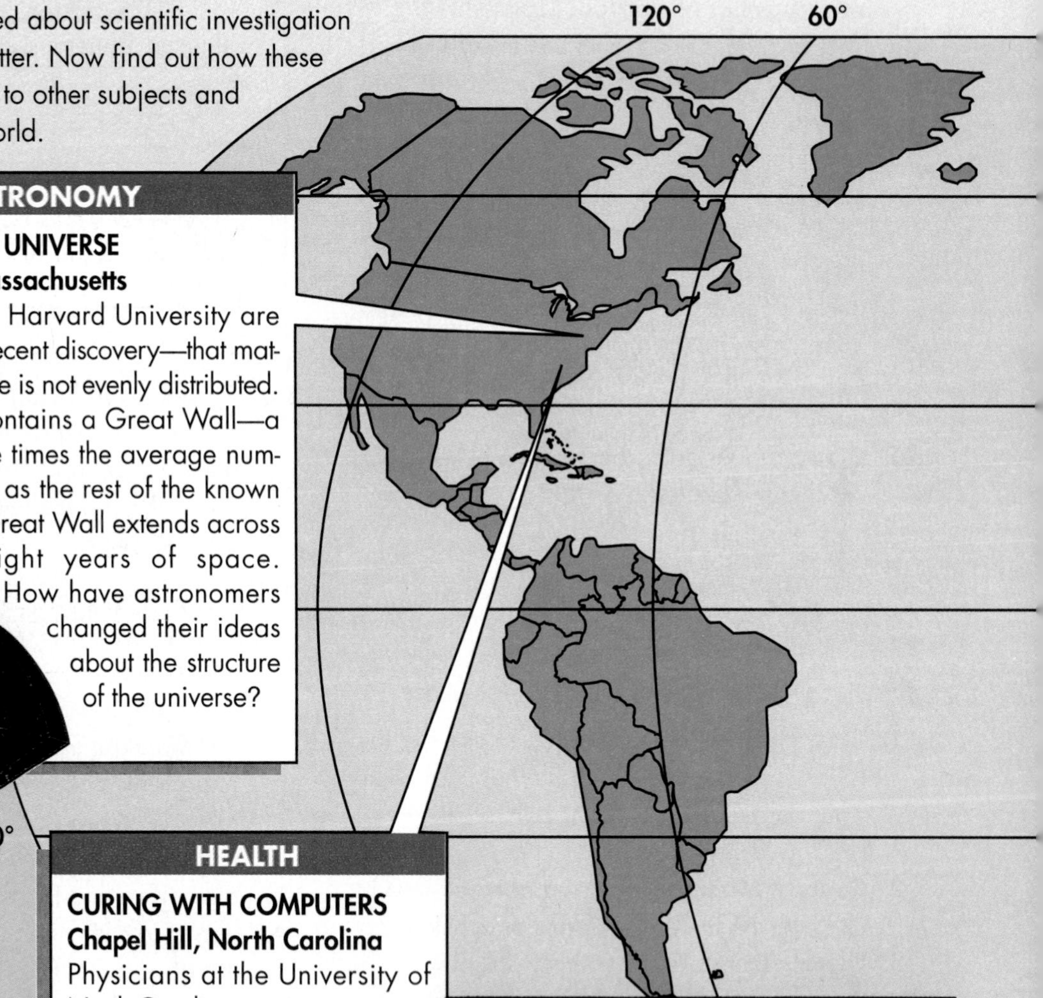

120°   60°

ASTRONOMY

MATTER IN THE UNIVERSE
Cambridge, Massachusetts

Astronomers at Harvard University are interested in a recent discovery—that matter in the universe is not evenly distributed. The universe contains a Great Wall—a region with five times the average number of galaxies as the rest of the known universe. The Great Wall extends across 500-million light years of space. How have astronomers changed their ideas about the structure of the universe?

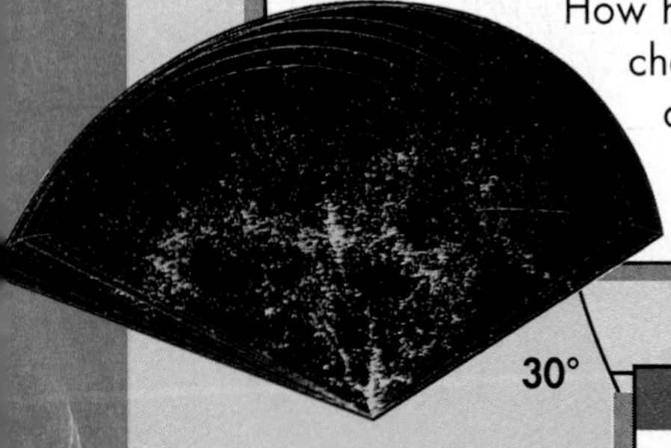

30°

HEALTH

CURING WITH COMPUTERS
Chapel Hill, North Carolina

Physicians at the University of North Carolina want an accurate way to beam radiation at a tumor so they can increase the amount of radiation and kill the cancer. A supercomputer, calculating the amount of radiation needed, could be connected to a special graphics computer to produce a three-dimensional model showing where the radiation must strike. How would linking computers help?

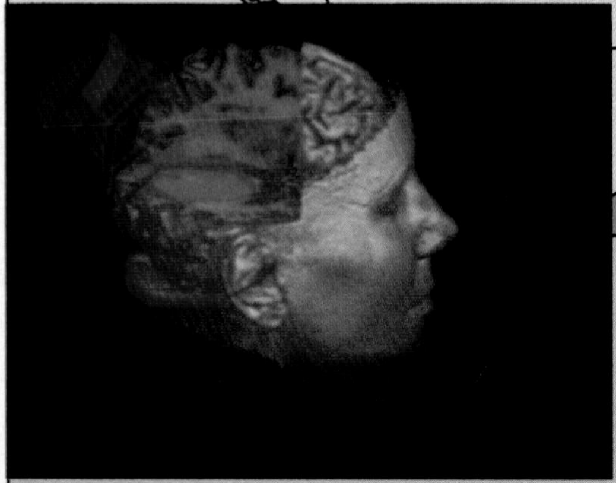

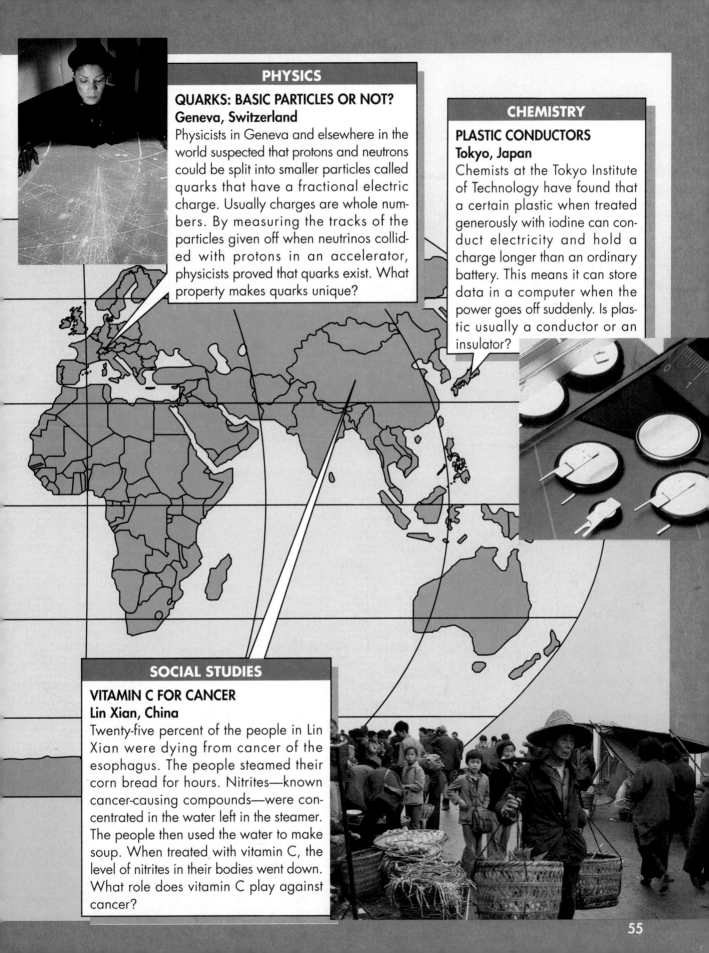

PHYSICS

QUARKS: BASIC PARTICLES OR NOT?
Geneva, Switzerland

Physicists in Geneva and elsewhere in the world suspected that protons and neutrons could be split into smaller particles called quarks that have a fractional electric charge. Usually charges are whole numbers. By measuring the tracks of the particles given off when neutrinos collided with protons in an accelerator, physicists proved that quarks exist. What property makes quarks unique?

CHEMISTRY

PLASTIC CONDUCTORS
Tokyo, Japan

Chemists at the Tokyo Institute of Technology have found that a certain plastic when treated generously with iodine can conduct electricity and hold a charge longer than an ordinary battery. This means it can store data in a computer when the power goes off suddenly. Is plastic usually a conductor or an insulator?

SOCIAL STUDIES

VITAMIN C FOR CANCER
Lin Xian, China

Twenty-five percent of the people in Lin Xian were dying from cancer of the esophagus. The people steamed their corn bread for hours. Nitrites—known cancer-causing compounds—were concentrated in the water left in the steamer. The people then used the water to make soup. When treated with vitamin C, the level of nitrites in their bodies went down. What role does vitamin C play against cancer?

55

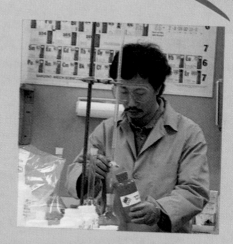

CAREERS

RESEARCH CHEMIST

A *research chemist* may do basic research to learn how chemical substances react. Some research chemists try to develop new products. One new product chemists are working on is polymers, or plastics, that can conduct electricity.

A research chemist needs a college degree in chemistry. Many earn doctorates. A student interested in becoming a research chemist should take courses in chemistry, physics, and mathematics.

For Additional Information

Contact the American Chemical Society, 1155 16th Street NW, Washington, DC 20036.

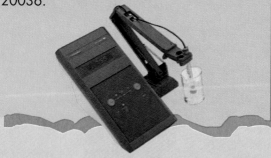

CHEMICAL TECHNICIAN

A *chemical technician* has an opportunity to work on projects in which new materials are developed by a chemical company. A technician's work consists of routine analyses of materials. They also help research chemists perform experiments and record accurate data. They may also test new products.

A chemical technician requires a degree in laboratory techniques from a two-year college. A student interested in becoming a chemical technician should study chemistry and mathematics in high school.

For Additional Information

Contact the American Chemical Society, 1155 16th Street NW, Washington, DC 20036.

UNIT READINGS

▶ Ballard, Robert. *Exploring Our Living Planet.* Washington, DC: National Geographic Society, 1983.
▶ Edelson, Edward. "The Strangest Plastics." *Popular Science,* June, 1990, pp. 90-93.
▶ Zewail, Ahmed. "The Birth of Molecules." *Scientific American,* December, 1990, pp. 76-82.

Computer Impressionist

How has science and technology led to a new generation of art? Read the following paragraphs to find out.

If you've watched television documentaries you've probably been amazed by the beauty of many of the computer-drawn scenes. Computer animations can even make it possible to travel back in time and envision what occurred before people inhabited Earth.

Many artists have begun to use computers, lasers, and holograms to express their creative talents. You may wonder if artists will someday turn in their paint brushes altogether and let computers do their work. But artists that work with computers must make the computer do what they want it to do. As long as the artists feel that they are creating something beautiful and others are pleased with the results, computer art will thrive.

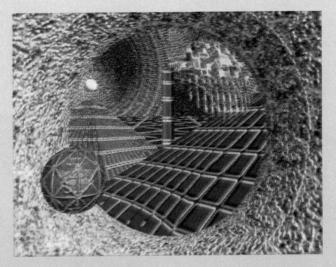

David Em, who produced the art on this page, is one of the new kind of artists. He uses high-tech computer programs produced by James Blinn at the Jet Propulsion Laboratory in Pasadena. Blinn didn't plan his programs in order to produce purely creative images. His purpose was to produce scientifically accurate images of the surfaces of planets. Em uses the textures and twists that are made possible by Blinn's programs to create graphically unique impressions.

Many artists wouldn't find inspiration in staring at a blank computer screen. David Em does. He uses a metal-tipped stylus to draw lightly across a pad. The pad transmits the corresponding lines to the screen. The artist claims that the computer expands his artistic abilities. He can choose from an almost infinite choice of colors and dimensions and can manipulate them in many ways.

In Your Own Words

▶ Do you think someone needs artistic ability to create computer art? Support your opinions in an essay.

UNIT
2 ROCKS AND MINERALS

What's Happening Here?

The gold bars and chains pictured here are considered treasures because of their rarity and beauty. However, gold has properties that make it useful for many purposes. NASA astronauts have gold foil in their face masks and on delicate equipment that's exposed to high radiation levels in space. Gold foil reflects 98 percent of the infrared radiation that strikes it. This makes it useful for controlling temperature inside an astronaut's helmet. As you study the chapters in this unit, you'll discover how properties of other minerals and rocks make them useful.

UNIT CONTENTS

3 Minerals

Minerals are used for many things. They are used in jewelry, pencil lead, powders, and in the metal used in bicycles. Table salt, for example, is the mineral halite. The huge cavern shown at the left is the interior of a salt mine. How does this mineral form?

FIND OUT!

Do this simple activity to see how halite forms.

Fill a cup about half full of warm tap water. Place two teaspoons of salt in the water. Stir the water until all of the salt has dissolved. Pour the water into a pan. Place the pan somewhere where it won't be disturbed. Check on the pan each day for two or three days. Has the water level gone down? What happened to the water? Is anything forming in the pan? Try to describe the cause of what you have observed. How does this relate to the formation of the mineral halite?

Gearing Up
Previewing the Chapter

Use this outline to help you focus on important ideas in this chapter.

Previewing Science Skills

► In the **Skill Builders**, you will classify, graph, and make a concept map.
► In the **Activities**, you will observe, collect, and organize data.
► In the **MINI-Labs**, you will experiment and compare.

What's next?

Now that you've seen how a mineral can form, read to find out more about what minerals are, their properties, and their uses. You'll also find out about a mineral that can be harmful.

3-1 Minerals

Objectives

▶ List five characteristics all minerals share.
▶ Describe the structure of minerals.
▶ Give examples of two ways that minerals form.

What Is a Mineral?

Have you ever used minerals? You may not realize it, but you use them all of the time. Rock salt, a diamond, and the graphite in a pencil are all minerals. A **mineral** is a naturally occurring, nonliving solid, with a definite structure and composition. Although more than 4000 different minerals are found on Earth, they all share five characteristics. Let's look at rock salt, diamonds, and graphite, and the characteristics they share.

First, all minerals are formed by natural processes. Rock salt, diamonds, and graphite are minerals because they formed naturally. You'll investigate more about these processes later in this lesson.

Second, minerals are nonliving. They aren't alive and never were alive. Diamonds and coal are both made from the element carbon, but they are not both minerals. Diamonds form from nonliving carbon inside Earth, whereas coal is made of carbon from living things. Which one would you classify as a mineral?

The third characteristic that minerals share is that they are all solids. Remember that all solids have a definite volume and shape. A gas such as air or a liquid such as water isn't a mineral because its shape changes. Neither a gas nor a liquid have definite shape.

Fourth, every mineral is an element or compound with a chemical composition unique to that mineral. Rock salt's composition gives it a distinctive flavor. Graphite's arrangement of atoms makes it feel soft and slippery.

Finally, the atoms in a mineral are arranged in a pattern, repeated over and over again. Read on to find out more about the structure of minerals.

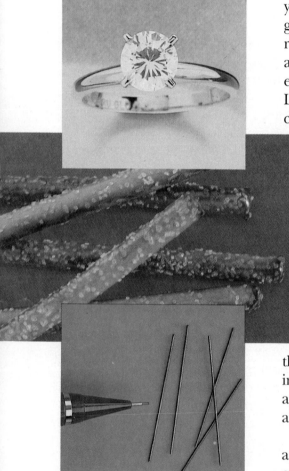

Figure 3-1. Shown here are just a few examples of how we use minerals.

a

b

Figure 3-2. Some mineral specimens have flat surfaces and sharp edges, showing crystal structure on the outside (a). Even if a mineral doesn't show its crystal structure on the outside, its atoms are still arranged in a crystal structure (b).

The Structure of Minerals

Did you know that each little grain of salt in a salt shaker is a cube? The atoms contained in each grain of salt are grouped in such a way that they form a cube. These cubes are crystals. A **crystal** is a solid in which the atoms are arranged in repeating patterns.

Even though all minerals are crystals, they don't all have smooth surfaces and sharp edges like the quartz crystal in Figure 3-2a. The quartz in Figure 3-2b has atoms arranged in repeating patterns, but you can't see the crystal structure on the outside of the mineral. This is because quartz 3-2b developed in a tight space. Quartz 3-2a, on the other hand, developed freely in an open space. Quartz has a hexagonal crystal shape.

Science and READING

The word *mineral* comes from the Latin word *minare,* which means "to mine." Go to the library and research the origin of the word *crystal.*

Table 3-1

CRYSTAL SYSTEMS

Examples

Halite	Wolfenite	Corundum	Topaz	Gypsum	Plagioclase

Systems

Cubic	Tetragonal	Hexagonal	Orthorhombic	Monoclinic	Triclinic

There are six major crystal systems, as shown in Table 3-1. These crystal systems refer to the set patterns that atoms form in a crystal. The simplest crystal system is cubic. Salt and pyrite are minerals whose crystals form cubes. Quartz belongs to the hexagonal crystal system.

How Minerals Form

There are two main ways that minerals can form. One way is from the cooling of hot melted rock, called **magma,** inside Earth. As magma cools, its atoms form a crystal structure and it becomes a mineral. The atoms will continue to line up in repeated patterns until there are no more atoms of the mineral available. The type of mineral that is formed depends on the type of elements present in the magma.

Crystals may also form from minerals dissolved in liquids. When the liquid evaporates, the atoms in the minerals stay behind and form crystals. Perfectly shaped crystals of a mineral can form when they have an open space to grow. Without space to grow, a mineral still has crystal form, but you can't see the crystal shape on the outside. When salt water evaporates, perfectly shaped crystals of halite—rock salt—are left behind.

Figure 3-3. Atoms of the mineral galena arrange themselves in a cubic crystal system.

ACTIVITY 3-1
Crystal Formation

Problem: *In what two ways can crystals form?*

Materials

- salt solution
- sugar solution
- large test tube
- toothpick
- cotton string
- hand lens
- shallow pan (2)
- thermal mitt
- test-tube rack
- cardboard
- table salt
- granulated sugar
- hot plate

Procedure

1. Pour the sugar solution into one of the shallow pans. Use the hot plate to gently heat the solution.
2. Place the test tube in the test-tube rack. Using a thermal mitt to protect your hand, pour some of the hot sugar solution into the test tube. **CAUTION:** *The liquid is hot. Do not touch the test tube without protecting your hands.*
3. Tie the thread to one end of the toothpick. Place the thread in the test tube. Be sure that it does not touch the sides or bottom of the tube.
4. Cover the test tube with a piece of cardboard and place the rack containing the test tube in a location where it will not be disturbed.
5. Pour a thin layer of the salt solution into the second shallow pan.
6. Place the pan in a warm area in the room.
7. Leave both the test tube and the shallow pan undisturbed for at least one week.
8. Examine sample grains of table salt and sugar with the hand lens. Note any similarities or differences.
9. At the end of one week, examine each solution and see if crystals have formed. Use a hand lens to observe the crystals.

Analyze

1. Describe the crystals that formed from the salt and sugar solutions. Include a sketch of each crystal.
2. What happened to the salt water in the shallow pan?
3. Did this same process occur in the test tube? Explain.

Conclude and Apply

4. What caused the formation of crystals in the test tube? What caused the formation of crystals in the shallow pan?
5. Are salt and sugar both minerals? Explain your answer.
6. In what two ways can crystals form?

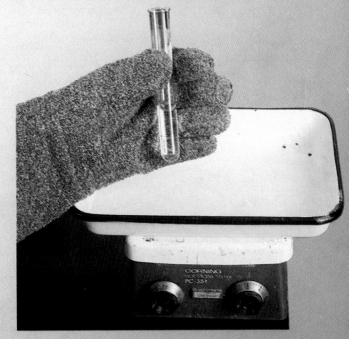

Mineral Compositions and Groups

With over 4000 known minerals, studying all of their compositions might seem very hard. This isn't the case, though, because most of the known minerals are made of only eight elements. In fact, these eight elements make up 98 percent of Earth's crust, as shown in Figure 3-4.

There are twelve common rock-forming minerals that are composed almost entirely of these eight elements. Most of the rock-forming minerals are silicates. Feldspar, quartz, and calcite are examples of rock-forming minerals. All minerals are classified according to their compositions.

The largest group of minerals is the silicates. **Silicates** are minerals that contain silicon and oxygen and one or more other elements. Silicon and oxygen are the two most abundant elements in Earth's crust. Because of this, silicates are the most common group of minerals.

Other major groups of minerals are carbonates, oxides, sulfides, sulfates, halides, and native elements. Table 3-2 lists these groups, what each is made of, and an example of each.

You now know a lot more about common rock salt than you did before reading this section. You know that its real name is halite and that it is a mineral. You also know that halite has a cubic crystal shape that is formed when salt water evaporates. And remember, halite is just one of over 4000 minerals on Earth.

How are minerals classified?

EcoTip

The glass in bottles is made from the mineral resource quartz. The aluminum in cans comes from mineral resources in Earth also. Help conserve energy and resources by recycling glass bottles and aluminum cans.

Figure 3-4. Most of Earth's crust is composed of these elements.

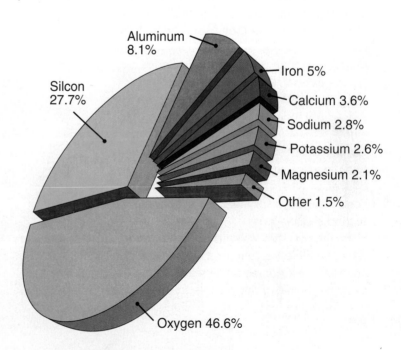

Aluminum 8.1%

Iron 5%

Calcium 3.6%

Sodium 2.8%

Potassium 2.6%

Magnesium 2.1%

Other 1.5%

Silcon 27.7%

Oxygen 46.6%

Table 3-2

NONSILICATE MINERAL GROUPS

Carbonates
Compounds of certain elements and a carbon atom with three oxygen atoms.

Example: Malachite

Sulfates
Compounds of certain elements and a sulfur atom with four oxygen atoms.

Example: Gypsum

Halides
Compounds of certain elements and chlorine, fluorine, iodine, or bromine.

Example: Fluorite

Oxides
Compounds of elements and oxygen.

Example: Hematite

Sulfides
Compounds of elements and sulfur.

Example: Chalcopyrite

Native Elements
Elements found uncombined with other elements.

Example: Native Copper

SECTION REVIEW

1. List briefly the five conditions a substance must meet to be a mineral.
2. To what crystal system does halite belong?
3. What are the silicate minerals made of?
4. What are two ways that minerals can form?
5. **Apply:** Is ice a mineral? Explain.

✉ **Classifying**

Skill Builder

Classify each of these minerals into the correct mineral group. Evaluate their chemical formulas using Appendix E on page 666 and Table 3-2. If you need help, refer to Classifying in the **Skill Handbook** on page 680.

siderite ($FeCO_3$)

barite ($BaSO_4$)

talc ($Mg_3Si_4O_{10}(OH)_2$)

enstatite ($MgSiO_3$)

cinnabar (HgS)

malachite($Cu_2CO_3(OH)_2$)

silver (Ag)

sylvite (KCl)

3-2 Mineral Identification

New Science Words

hardness
luster
streak
cleavage
fracture

Objectives

▶ List the physical characteristics used to identify minerals.
▶ Describe how physical characteristics such as hardness and streak are used to identify minerals.

Physical Properties

How can you tell the difference between one of your classmates and another? You can tell the difference between them without even thinking about it because you observe things about them that make them different. The color of a classmate's hair or the type of shoe he or she wears helps you tell him or her from the rest of your class. Hair color and shoe type are two properties unique to that individual.

Individual minerals also have unique properties. These properties help us tell the difference between minerals. Color and appearance are just two of the clues that are used to identify minerals.

But color and appearance alone aren't enough to tell most minerals apart. The minerals pyrite and gold are both gold in color and can appear to be the same. But we all know they are very different. Gold is worth a lot of money, whereas pyrite has little value. You need to look at other properties of minerals such as hardness to tell them apart.

Figure 3-5. Minerals have many different characteristics.

Hardness

A measure of how easily a mineral can be scratched is its **hardness.** The mineral talc is so soft, you can scratch it loose with your fingernail. You might be familiar with talcum powder made from this mineral. Diamonds, on the other hand, are the hardest mineral. Some diamonds are used as cutting tools. A diamond can be scratched only by another diamond.

In order to compare the hardnesses of minerals, a list of common minerals and their hardnesses was developed. The German scientist Friedrich Mohs developed Mohs' Scale of Hardness, as seen in Table 3-3. The scale lists the hardnesses of ten minerals, with 1 being the softest and 10 the hardest.

Here's how the scale works. Let's say you have a clear or whitish colored mineral that you know is either calcite or quartz. You scratch it on your fingernail and then on a copper penny. You find that the mineral scratches your fingernail but doesn't scratch the penny. Because the hardness of your fingernail is 2.5 and that of a copper penny is 3.5, you can determine the unknown mineral's hardness to be about 3. Now you know it's not quartz because quartz has a hardness of 7. Your mystery mineral must be calcite.

Figure 3-6. Talc can be scratched with your fingernail.

Table 3-3

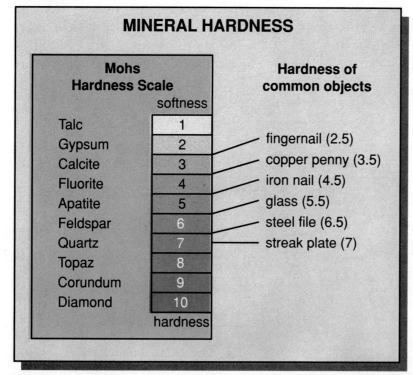

MINERAL HARDNESS

Mohs Hardness Scale		Hardness of common objects
	softness	
Talc	1	
Gypsum	2	fingernail (2.5)
Calcite	3	copper penny (3.5)
Fluorite	4	iron nail (4.5)
Apatite	5	glass (5.5)
Feldspar	6	steel file (6.5)
Quartz	7	streak plate (7)
Topaz	8	
Corundum	9	
Diamond	10	
	hardness	

a

b

Figure 3-7. A mineral may have a metallic (a) or a dull (b) luster.

Luster

Luster describes how light is reflected from a mineral's surface. Luster is defined as either metallic or nonmetallic. Minerals with a metallic luster always shine like metal. Metallic luster can be compared to the shine of a fancy metal belt buckle or the shiny chrome trim on some cars.

When a mineral does not shine like metal, its luster is nonmetallic. Examples of names for nonmetallic luster include dull, pearly, silky, glassy, and brilliant. Examples of minerals with metallic and nonmetallic lusters can be seen in Figure 3-7.

Color

The color of a mineral can also be a clue to its identity. An example of a mineral whose color helps in identification is sulfur. Sulfur has a very distinctive yellow color. Just remember that, as you learned with gold and pyrite, color alone usually isn't enough to identify a mineral.

Streak

Streak is the color of the mineral when it is broken up and powdered. When a mineral is rubbed across a piece of unglazed porcelain tile such as in Figure 3-8, a streak is left behind. This streak is the powdered mineral. Gold and pyrite can be identified with the streak test. Gold has a yellow streak and pyrite has a greenish-black streak.

The streak test works only for minerals that are softer than the streak plate. Very soft minerals will even leave a streak on paper. The last time you used a pencil to write on paper, you used the streak of the mineral graphite. Graphite is used in pencil lead because it is soft enough to leave a streak on paper.

Figure 3-8. A streak test reveals the color of a mineral's powder.

Is It Real?

Hazel has visited several areas of California. At one stop, a place called Sutter's Mill, where gold was discovered in 1849, Hazel saw some bright yellow metallic objects glistening in the clear water of a fast moving stream. Reaching into the stream, she found what appeared to be four or five nuggets of gold.

Excitedly, Hazel, who had been working in a jewelry store, tested the nuggets. She found that the gold nuggets left a greenish-black powder when rubbed across a piece of white porcelain. The nuggets scratched a copper penny she had with her.

Think Critically: Did Hazel hit pay dirt?

Cleavage and Fracture

The way a mineral breaks is also a clue to its identity. Minerals that break along smooth, flat surfaces have **cleavage.** Mica is a mineral that has perfect cleavage. You can see in Figure 3-9 how it breaks along smooth, flat surfaces. If you were to take a layer cake and separate its layers, you would show that the cake has cleavage. But not all minerals have cleavage. Minerals that break with rough or jagged edges have **fracture.** Quartz is a mineral with fracture. If you were to grab a chunk out of the side of that cake, it would be like breaking a mineral with fracture.

Why is mica said to have perfect cleavage?

Figure 3-9. Mica's perfect cleavage allows it to be broken along smooth, flat surfaces.

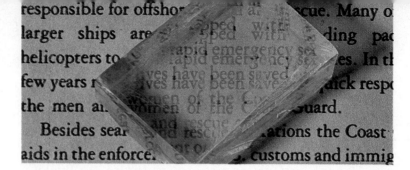

Figure 3-10. A clear specimen of calcite can be identified by its unique ability to bend light, causing a double image.

Other Properties

Here are some less common properties of minerals. Some mineral specimens are in the form of perfect crystals and are easy to recognize by their crystal system. The crystal form of quartz has six sides. Halite and pyrite have cubic crystals.

Other minerals have unique properties. Magnetite, as you can guess by its name, attracts metal objects like a magnet. Light bends when it passes through some calcite specimens, causing you to see a double image, as in Figure 3-10. Calcite can also be identified because it fizzes when hydrochloric acid is put on it.

You can see that you sometimes need more information than just color and appearance to identify most minerals. You might also need to test its streak, its hardness, its luster, and its cleavage or fracture. You can be just as good at identifying minerals as you are recognizing your friends in class.

SECTION REVIEW

1. What's the difference between a mineral that has cleavage and one that has fracture?
2. Which property of a mineral refers to how light reflects from its surface?
3. How can an unglazed porcelain tile be used to identify a mineral?
4. What happens to calcite when hydrochloric acid is placed on it?
5. **Apply:** What hardness does a mineral have if it is scratched by glass but scratches an iron nail?

Skill Builder

☒ Making and Using Graphs

Make a bar graph of the hardnesses of the common objects used for comparison to the minerals in Mohs' Scale of Hardness. If you need help, refer to Making and Using Graphs in the **Skill Handbook** on page 691.

ACTIVITY 3-2
Mineral Identification

Problem: How are minerals identified?

Materials

- mineral samples
- hand lens
- pan balance
- graduated cylinder
- water
- copper penny
- glass slide
- steel file
- streak plate
- 5% hydrochloric acid with dropper
- goggles
- Mohs' Scale of Hardness
- Appendices L and M

Procedure

1. Use the hand lens to examine the mineral samples. Determine and record the luster, hardness, streak, cleavage or fracture, and color of each sample.
2. Test the samples for special properties such as reaction to hydrochloric acid. **CAUTION:** *HCl may cause burns. If spillage occurs, rinse with water. Wear your goggles.*
3. Record all observable characteristics in a table like the one shown.

Analyze

1. What property was most useful to you in mineral identification?
2. Which test was most difficult to perform?

Conclude and Apply

3. What property was least helpful in identifying minerals? Why?
4. How are minerals identified?

Data and Observations

Mineral	Luster	Hardness	Streak	Cleavage/ fracture	Color	Other properties
quartz	non-metallic, glassy	7	none	fracture	white/clear	none

Uses of Minerals

New Science Words

gems
ore

Objectives

▶ Discuss characteristics gems have that make them different from and more valuable than other minerals.
▶ List the conditions necessary for a mineral to be classified as an ore.

Gems

What makes one mineral more useful or valuable to us than another? Why are diamonds and rubies so valuable? The next time you go shopping, look in the window of a jewelry store. Chances are you will see rings, bracelets, and maybe even a watch with diamonds or other gems on them. What properties do gems possess that make them valuable?

Gems or gemstones are highly prized minerals because they are rare and beautiful. Many gems are cut and polished and used for jewelry. They are more bright and colorful than common samples of the same mineral.

The difference between a gem and the common form of the same mineral can be very slight. Amethyst, a gem form of quartz, contains just traces of iron in its structure. This iron gives amethyst a desirable purple color. And sometimes a gem has a crystal structure that allows it to be cut and polished to a higher quality than a non-gem mineral.

What makes a gem different from other minerals?

Figure 3-11. It is easy to see why gems are prized—for their beauty and rarity.

Figure 3-12. Ores must be processed and refined into more useful materials.

Ores

If you look around your room at home, you will find many things made from mineral resources. See how many you can name. Is there anything in your room with iron in it? If so, the iron may have come from the mineral hematite. The aluminum in soft drink cans comes from the mineral bauxite.

Bauxite and hematite are minerals that can also be called ores. A mineral is an **ore** if it contains a useful substance that can be mined at a profit. Aluminum can be taken from bauxite and made into useful and valuable products. These products are worth more money than the cost of the mining, so bauxite is an ore.

Science and READING

Find some jewelry advertisements in your local paper. Read them to find out some of the gems that are commonly used in jewelry. Also, find out what kinds of minerals the gems are set in.

Figure 3-13. Bauxite ore (a) is used to make aluminum products (b).

a

b

Did You Know?

The state of Colorado is famous for its mineral resources. In 1894, the largest silver nugget ever found in North America was discovered there. The nugget had a mass of 835 kg. That's about 15 times the mass of the average person in your class.

Most ore contains unwanted material along with the valuable material. The waste rock or material must be removed before a mineral can be used. Removing the waste rock can be very expensive. If the cost of removing the waste rock gets higher than the value of the desired material, the mineral will no longer be classified as an ore.

Think back to the last soft drink you had in an aluminum can. What do you think would happen if people stopped using aluminum cans? This would cause the demand for aluminum to go down. Some bauxite mines would close down because they would no longer be able to make money. The bauxite mined at these locations would no longer be an ore. The value of a mineral can change if the supply of or the demand for that mineral changes.

TECHNOLOGY

Diamonds Are Forever?

You probably knew that diamonds were used in jewelry, but did you know that diamonds are used on drill bits and other instruments? Diamond-tipped drill bits can cut through very hard substances such as steel and rock. Diamonds are used on the bits because they are the hardest mineral.

Recently, scientists developed a way to put a thin coating of diamonds on objects, as shown in this photo. They use a gas called methane and microwaves to make the diamonds. A methane molecule consists of a carbon atom surrounded by four hydrogen atoms. Microwaves are used to strip the hydrogen atoms away from the molecule. Then the carbon atoms link together on the surface of the object being coated, forming tiny rows of diamonds. This process can be used to make diamond-edged surgical scalpels, razor blades, diamond surfaces that can't be scratched, and diamond coated computer parts.

Think Critically: These diamonds aren't true minerals. Why not?

Figure 3-14. Many ores are obtained from large open pit mines.

You'd be surprised to find out all of the things that come from ores. Magnetite is used to make iron used in everything from buildings to ships. Sulfur is used to make fertilizers, and clay is used in bricks and pottery. Garnet and corundum are used to make abrasives such as sandpaper. There's probably even an ore in the walls where you live. Gypsum is used to make plaster. Gems and ores are important mineral resources.

REVIEW

1. List some physical properties that are used to classify a mineral as a gem.
2. When is a mineral deposit classified as an ore?
3. **Apply:** Why couldn't a company stay in business if the mineral it was mining was no longer an ore?

☑ Concept Mapping

Make an events chain showing why bauxite can be an ore. Use the following terms: *gives aluminum, ore, mined at profit, bauxite.* If you need help, refer to Concept Mapping in the **Skill Handbook** on page 688.

Skill Builder

3-4 Asbestos Removal

New Science Words

asbestos

Objectives

▶ List the properties of asbestos that make it useful as a flame retardant and an insulator.
▶ State why people are so concerned about the asbestos used in buildings.
▶ Compare the pros and cons of asbestos removal.

a

Figure 3-15. The mineral asbestos is made of threadlike fibers (a). Asbestos is being removed from many buildings (b).

Should All Asbestos Be Removed?

Do you know of a building where asbestos has been removed? Perhaps your school has had asbestos removed. The Environmental Protection Agency (EPA) requires school officials to inspect buildings every six months. If flaking asbestos is found, it must be removed or contained. Some people want all asbestos removed from schools and other public buildings. Why is the public so concerned about asbestos?

Asbestos is a mineral with threadlike, flexible fibers. Different forms of the mineral are used as insulation and as fire protection. Asbestos fibers have been shown to cause cancer.

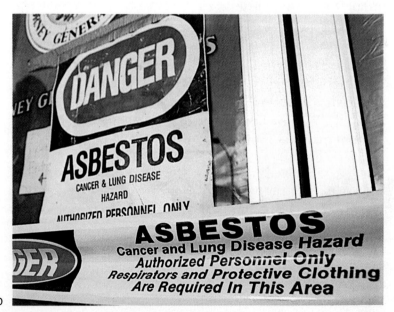

b

The threadlike structure and flexibility of asbestos allow it to be woven into cloth or pressed into sheets. Asbestos materials don't burn easily and don't conduct heat or electricity very well. When you pick up something hot from the stove, you use a hot pad to insulate your hand against the heat. Asbestos is used in the same way. Asbestos is also used to make flame retardant material because it resists burning. Asbestos is often found in the insulation around hot water pipes and electrical wires and motors.

The properties that make asbestos useful, also make it dangerous. If fibers break loose, they can float around in the air. Breathing in some types of asbestos fibers can cause several diseases, including lung cancer. The fibers get into the lungs where they can cause healthy cells to change into cancer cells. This is the reason that asbestos is removed.

How can asbestos be harmful?

Some people think that removing all asbestos from buildings is an overreaction. It has been shown that the amount of asbestos fibers contained in the air of buildings with asbestos is not much more than the amount in air outside the building. The only time asbestos in a building sheds fibers into the air is when it is damaged. In fact, the removal process releases fibers into the air that are a hazard to the people removing the asbestos.

Figure 3-17. Removing asbestos is hazardous.

As stated earlier, there are different forms of asbestos used in buildings. The type that is used most often has been shown to be much less dangerous than some less common types of asbestos. The curly nature of the fibers in this common asbestos keeps it from being imbedded in the outer portion of the lungs. It also disappears from tissue over time. Removing this type of asbestos may be unnecessary.

Another type of asbestos has been shown to cause other diseases. This form of asbestos has long, thin, straight fibers. The fibers penetrate into the lungs, causing cancer. This asbestos has not been used very often.

SECTION REVIEW

1. Why is asbestos used in buildings?
2. Why is asbestos being removed from buildings?

SCIENCE
&
SOCIETY

You Decide!

Some people feel all asbestos shouldn't be removed because removal is very expensive and not all asbestos is harmful. They feel that removing all asbestos even if it isn't shedding fibers is a waste of money. On the other hand, some asbestos has been linked to cancer. What do you think? Should all asbestos be removed?

REVIEW

SUMMARY

3-1: Minerals

1. All minerals are formed by natural processes, are nonliving solids, with unique compositions and distinct internal structures.
2. Minerals have crystal structures in one of six major crystal systems.
3. Minerals can form when magma cools or when liquids containing dissolved minerals evaporate.

3-2: Mineral Identification

1. Hardness is a measure of how easily a mineral can be scratched. Luster describes how light is reflected from a mineral's surface. Color is sometimes a property that can be used to identify a mineral.
2. Streak is the color left by a mineral on an unglazed porcelain tile. Minerals that break along smooth, flat surfaces have cleavage.

Minerals that break with rough or jagged surfaces have fracture.

3-3: Uses of Minerals

1. Gems are minerals that are more rare and beautiful than common minerals.
2. An ore is a mineral or group of minerals that can be mined at a profit.

3-4: Science and Society: Asbestos Removal

1. Asbestos is used as a flame retardant and an insulator because it is a poor conductor of heat and electricity.
2. Some kinds of asbestos used in building construction have been shown to cause cancer.
3. Removing asbestos can reduce the threat of cancer caused by asbestos. On the other hand, not all asbestos causes cancer.

KEY SCIENCE WORDS

a. asbestos
b. cleavage
c. crystal
d. fracture
e. gems
f. hardness
g. luster
h. magma
i. mineral
j. ore
k. silicates
l. streak

UNDERSTANDING VOCABULARY

Match each phrase with the correct term from the list of Key Science Words.

1. naturally occurring solid
2. hot, melted rock
3. minerals containing silicon, oxygen, and one or more other elements
4. how light is reflected from a mineral
5. fiber mineral used as insulation
6. valuable, rare minerals
7. a mineral mined at a profit
8. breakage along smooth, flat planes
9. solid with a repeating arrangement of atoms
10. the color of a mineral's powder

CHAPTER
REVIEW

CHECKING CONCEPTS

Choose the word or phrase that completes the sentence.

1. Minerals _____ .
   - **a.** are solids
   - **b.** have crystal structure
   - **c.** are not alive
   - **d.** all of these

2. All silicates contain _____ .
   - **a.** magnesium
   - **b.** silicon and aluminum
   - **c.** silicon and oxygen
   - **d.** oxygen and carbon

3. _____ is hot, melted material.
   - **a.** Magma
   - **b.** Quartz
   - **c.** Salt water
   - **d.** None of these

4. Graphite is a(n) _____ .
   - **a.** oxide
   - **b.** carbonate
   - **c.** silicate
   - **d.** none of these

5. _____ is a measure of how easily a mineral can be scratched.
   - **a.** Luster
   - **b.** Hardness
   - **c.** Cleavage
   - **d.** Fracture

6. The color of a powdered mineral on an unglazed porcelain tile is its _____ .
   - **a.** luster
   - **b.** density
   - **c.** hardness
   - **d.** streak

7. Quartz breaks with _____ .
   - **a.** cleavage
   - **b.** fracture
   - **c.** luster
   - **d.** all of these

8. _____ can cause cancer.
   - **a.** Aluminum
   - **b.** Hematite
   - **c.** Asbestos
   - **d.** Quartz

9. The largest group of rock-forming minerals is the _____ .
   - **a.** oxides
   - **b.** halides
   - **c.** silicates
   - **d.** sulfides

10. Halite is _____ .
    - **a.** cubic
    - **b.** rock salt
    - **c.** formed by evaporation
    - **d.** all of these

UNDERSTANDING CONCEPTS

Complete each sentence.

11. Halite forms _____ crystals.

12. _____ contain the two most abundant elements in Earth's crust.

13. The mineral _____ is harder than apatite and softer than quartz.

14. Diamonds and coal are both made of _____ .

15. _____ have a definite volume and shape.

THINK AND WRITE CRITICALLY

16. What's the difference between an ore and a gem?

17. Describe the dangers of asbestos fibers.

18. Explain why air is not a mineral.

19. Compare and contrast the properties of cleavage and fracture. List an example of a mineral that cleaves and one that fractures.

20. Why is asbestos removal a controversy?

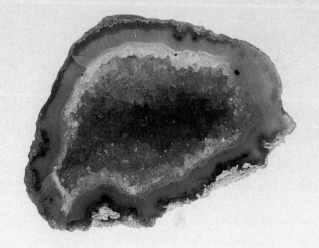

APPLY

21. Water is a nonliving substance formed by natural processes on Earth. It has a unique composition. Sometimes water is a mineral and other times it is not. Explain.

22. How many sides are there to a perfect salt crystal?

23. Suppose you let a sugar solution evaporate, leaving sugar crystals behind. Are these crystals minerals? Explain.

24. Will diamond leave a streak on a streak plate? Explain.

25. Explain how you would use Table 3-3 to determine the hardness of any mineral.

MORE SKILL BUILDERS

If you need help, refer to the Skill Handbook.

1. **Observing and Inferring:** Suppose you found a white, nonmetallic mineral that was harder than calcite. You identify the sample as quartz. What are your observations? What is your inference?

2. **Interpreting Data:** Suppose you were given these properties of a mineral: pink color; nonmetallic; softer than topaz and quartz; scratches apatite; harder than fluorite; has cleavage; and is scratched by a steel file. What is it?

3. **Outlining:** Make an outline of how at least seven physical properties can be used to identify unknown materials.

4. **Measuring in SI:** The volume of water in a graduated cylinder is 107.5 mL. A specimen of quartz, tied to a piece of string, is immersed into the water. The new water level reads 186 mL. What is the volume of the piece of quartz?

5. **Concept Mapping:** Make a network tree concept map showing the six nonsilicate mineral groups and examples from that group. Use the following words and phrases: *nonsilicate groups, carbonates, oxides, sulfides, sulfates, halides, native elements, corundum, galena, halite, azurite, gypsum, gold, hematite, pyrite, fluorite, malachite, barite, copper.*

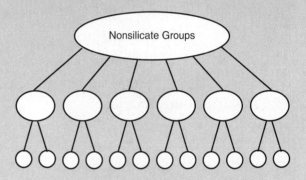

PROJECTS

1. Do research to find out about the six major crystal systems. Use cardboard to make models of each major crystal shape for each system.

2. Go to the library or bookstore to find books that explain how to grow crystals. Follow the instructions given to grow your own crystals.

3. Collect samples of objects that you think are minerals. Then use a mineral identification book to find out which specimens actually are minerals. Identify each mineral and list some of its uses.

CHAPTER
4 Rocks

The Great Wall of China was constructed more than 2000 years ago. The wall is a collection of rocks, 6400 kilometers long. Today, we use rocks to construct our buildings, roads, and monuments. Minerals from rocks are even in the foods you eat. Rocks are all around you. Can you describe what rocks are made of?

FIND OUT!

Do this simple activity to find out what rocks are made of.

Collect three or four rocks from around your home. Look at each rock carefully. Use a magnifying glass so you can see each rock more clearly. What do you notice? Try drawing a picture of the details in each rock. Can you see different types of material within the same rock? Think of the terms used in Chapter 2. Would you classify rocks as mixtures? If so, what are they mixtures of?

Gearing Up
Previewing the Chapter
Use this outline to help you focus on important ideas in this chapter.

Previewing Science Skills

▶ In the **Skill Builders,** you will make concept maps, interpret scientific illustrations, sequence events, and interpret data.
▶ In the **Activities,** you will classify, analyze, and draw conclusions.
▶ In the **MINI-Labs,** you will classify, observe, and infer.

What's next?

Now you can investigate what kinds of materials make up rocks. As you read this chapter, you will explore how rocks are formed and how they change from one form to another.

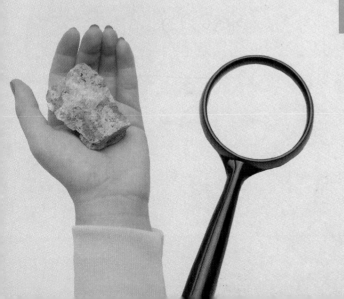

4-1 The Rock Cycle

New Science Words

rock
rock cycle

Objectives

▶ Differentiate between a rock and a mineral.
▶ Describe the rock cycle and the changes that a rock may undergo.

What Is a Rock?

Imagine that you're on your way home from a friend's house when you notice an unusual rock in a driveway. You pick it up, wondering why it looks different from most of the other rocks in the driveway. Most of the other rocks are flat and dull, but this one is rounded and has shiny crystals in it. You decide to stick the interesting rock in your pocket and ask your earth science teacher about it tomorrow.

What exactly should you ask your teacher? You might begin by asking, "What is a rock?" and "Why are rocks so different from one another?"

Figure 4-1. Granite is a mixture of mica (a), quartz (b), feldspar (c), hornblende (d), and other minerals.

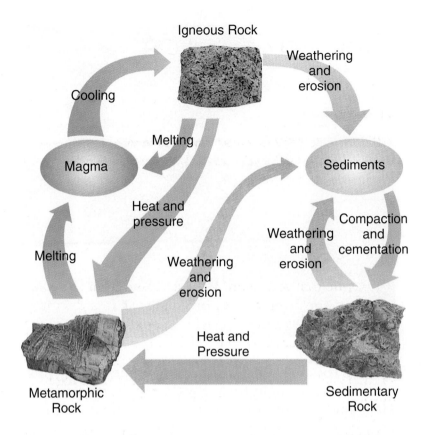

Igneous Rock

Cooling

Weathering and erosion

Melting

Magma

Sediments

Heat and pressure

Melting

Weathering and erosion

Compaction and cementation

Weathering and erosion

Heat and Pressure

Metamorphic Rock

Sedimentary Rock

Figure 4-2. This model of the rock cycle shows how rocks are constantly changed from one form to another.

What is a rock?

A **rock** is a mixture of minerals. You learned about the mineral quartz in the last chapter. You know that it's a common mineral found in rocks. Other common minerals include feldspar, hornblende, and mica. Look at Figure 4-1. It shows that all of these minerals mix together to form the rock granite.

But how do these minerals mix together? And once they've formed a rock, do they stay in that same rock forever? You can answer these questions by studying the rock cycle.

The Rock Cycle

Figure 4-2 is a model of the **rock cycle.** It shows how one rock changes into another. Notice that rocks are classified as igneous, metamorphic, or sedimentary. You will learn more about each of these groups of rocks in this chapter.

Rocks are changed by processes such as weathering, erosion, compaction, cementation, melting, and cooling. For example, the minerals of a sedimentary rock can melt and later cool to form an igneous rock. The

Figure 4-3. By studying rocks and the changes they undergo, geologists have helped explain how our world formed and how it is changing.

What are the three major classifications of rocks?

igneous rock may then weather and erode and the fragments from it might form another sedimentary rock. Heat and pressure can change both sedimentary and igneous rocks into metamorphic rocks.

In Chapters 5 and 6, you will explore weathering, erosion, deposition, and other processes involved in the rock cycle. And you already know something about minerals. The rock cycle shows how all of these things interact to form and change the rocks around you. Let's now investigate how igneous, metamorphic, and sedimentary rocks fit into the rock cycle.

SECTION REVIEW

1. What materials mix together to form a rock?
2. What is the rock cycle?
3. **Apply:** Look at the model of the rock cycle. How would you define *magma* based on Figure 4-2? How would you define *sediments* and *sedimentary rock*?

Skill Builder

☑ Concept Mapping

Make a concept map that explains how igneous rocks can become sedimentary, then metamorphic, and finally other igneous rocks. If you need help, refer to Concept Mapping in the **Skill Handbook** on pages 688 and 689.

ACTIVITY 4-1
Igneous Rocks

Problem: *How are igneous rocks classified?*

Materials

- igneous rock specimens, A-F
- hand lens
- Table 4-1

Procedure

1. Examine each rock specimen with a hand lens. Determine the texture of each rock sample. If the grains or crystals are large and easily seen, the texture is coarse. If the grains are so small that they are not easily distinguished, the texture is described as fine. Separate the rocks into groups based on the texture.
2. Answer Analyze 1 and 2.
3. Determine the color of each rock. Is the rock light-colored, dark-colored, or intermediate? Regroup your samples based on color.
4. Answer Analyze 3 and 4.
5. Examine the coarse-grained rocks to determine the minerals present.
6. Refer to Table 4-1 and give each sample a name according to its composition and grain size.

Analyze

1. What's the difference between the size of the grains in intrusive and extrusive igneous rocks?
2. If grain sizes within one sample are noticeably different, what type of rock is it?
3. What minerals must be responsible for the color of sample B?
4. Name at least two other igneous rocks that owe their colors to the presence of these minerals.

Conclude and Apply

5. Why do igneous rocks of the same composition sometimes have different sizes of grains?
6. What two characteristics determine the identity of an igneous rock?
7. How does obsidian differ from most other igneous rocks?

Data and Observations

Rock Sample	Texture	Color	Minerals present	Rock name
A				
B				
C				
D				
E				
F				

4-2 Igneous Rocks

New Science Words

igneous rocks
lava
intrusive
extrusive
basaltic
granitic

Objectives

▶ Recognize magma and lava as the materials that cool to form igneous rocks.
▶ Contrast the formation of intrusive and extrusive igneous rocks.
▶ Contrast granitic and basaltic igneous rocks.

Origin of Igneous Rocks

In December of 1989, Mount Redoubt in Alaska began to erupt. Perhaps you've heard of other recent volcanic eruptions. When most volcanoes erupt, they eject a thick, gooey flow of molten material. This material is similar to fudge candy before it has cooled. You know that if you allow the fudge to cool, it becomes hard and you have to cut it with a knife. When molten material from a volcano or from deep inside Earth cools, it forms **igneous rocks.** But why do volcanoes erupt and where does the molten material come from?

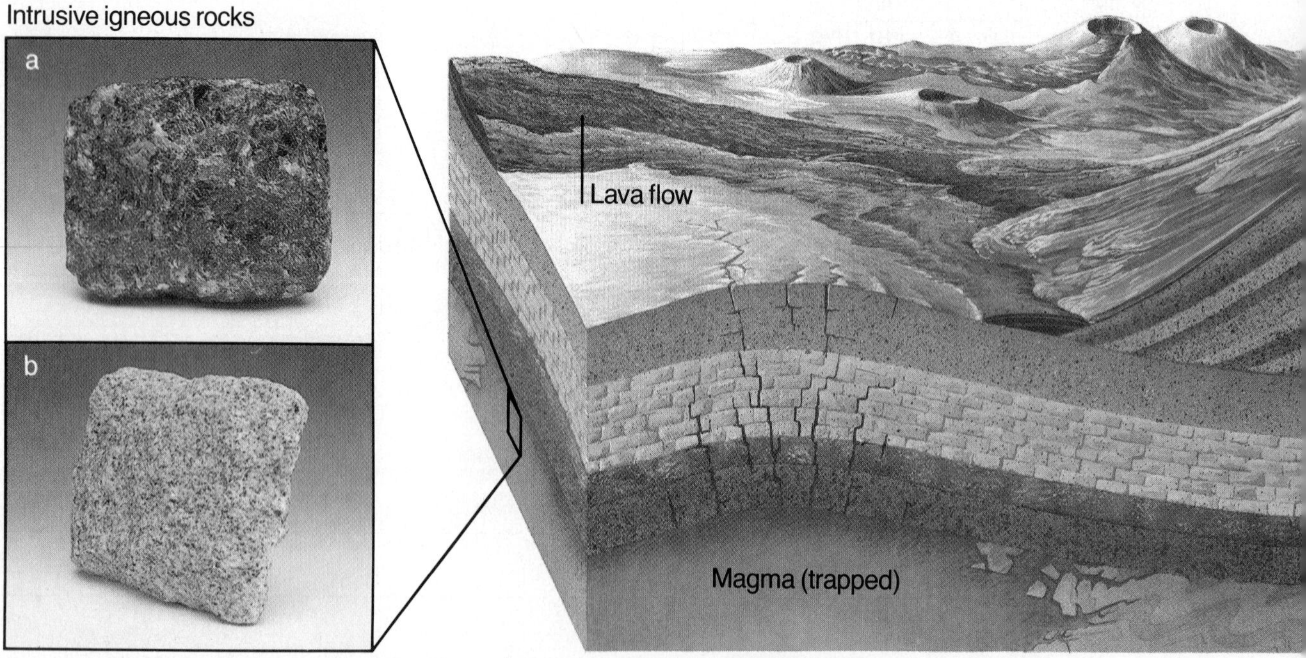

Figure 4-4. Intrusive rocks such as gabbro (a) and diorite (b) form when magma cools slowly.

Intrusive igneous rocks

Lava flow

Magma (trapped)

Temperatures reach about 1400°C at depths ranging from 60 to 200 km below Earth's surface. The rocks at this depth are under great pressure from overlying rocks. Radioactive elements in the rocks generate thermal energy, heating the rocks. In certain locations on Earth, the temperature and pressure are just right to melt the minerals and form magma.

The magma is less dense than the surrounding solid rock, so it tends to rise toward Earth's surface. Magma that eventually reaches Earth's surface flows from volcanoes as **lava.**

Magma that's trapped below Earth's surface is insulated by the rocks surrounding it. This holds in the heat and causes the magma to cool very slowly. Remember, magma is made up of atoms of melted minerals. When it cools, these atoms rearrange themselves into new mineral crystals. If the magma cools slowly, the atoms have time to arrange into large crystals. These crystals are called mineral grains.

Compare and contrast lava and magma.

Extrusive igneous rocks

Magma

Figure 4-5. Extrusive rocks such as rhyolite (a) and andesite (b) form from fast-cooling lava.

a　　　　　b　　　　　c

Figure 4-6. Pumice (a), Obsidian (b), and Scoria (c)

Figure 4-7. Processes bring magma to Earth's surface where it cools to form extrusive igneous rocks.

Rock forms as these mineral grains grow together. Rocks that form below Earth's surface are **intrusive** igneous rocks. Generally, intrusive igneous rocks have large mineral grains. Look at Figure 4-4. It shows coarse-grained, intrusive igneous rocks. Intrusive rocks are found at Earth's surface when the kilometers of rock and soil that once covered them have been removed, or when forces in Earth have pushed them up. You will be investigating these forces in later chapters.

Extrusive igneous rocks are formed when lava cools on Earth's surface. When lava flows on Earth's surface, it is exposed to air and moisture. Lava cools quickly under these conditions. The quick rate of cooling keeps large mineral grains from growing. The atoms don't have time to arrange into large crystals. Extrusive igneous rocks have a fine-grained texture. Often, the individual grains are too small to be seen without a magnifying glass. Figure 4-5 shows some extrusive igneous rocks.

Table 4-1

COMMON IGNEOUS ROCKS		
Type of Magma or Lava	Intrusive	Extrusive
Basaltic	Gabbro	Basalt
		Scoria
Andesitic	Diorite	Andesite
Granitic	Granite	Rhyolite
		Pumice
		Obsidian

Figure 4-6 shows pumice, obsidian, and scoria. These objects cooled so quickly that no mineral grains formed at all. The atoms in these objects are not arranged into neat crystal patterns. Obsidian, scoria, and pumice are actually glass, and not a mixture of minerals. However, they are classified as extrusive igneous rocks.

In the case of pumice and scoria, air and other gases are trapped in the gooey molten material as it cools. Many of these gases eventually escape, but holes are left behind where the rock formed around the pockets of gas.

Classification of Igneous Rocks

You've learned to classify igneous rocks as either intrusive or extrusive depending on where they formed. A way to further classify these rocks is by the types of minerals in them. An igneous rock can be either basaltic, granitic, or andesitic.

Basaltic igneous rocks are dense, heavy, dark-colored rocks that form from basaltic magma or lava. Basaltic magma and lava are rich in iron and magnesium. These elements make the molten materials dense and dark colored. Basaltic lava flows from the volcanoes in Hawaii.

Granitic igneous rocks are light-colored rocks of a lower density than basaltic rocks. Granitic magma and lava are thick and stiff and contain a lot of silicon and oxygen. Granitic magma can build up a great deal of pressure, which is released during violent volcanic eruptions.

Andesitic rocks have mineral compositions between those of granitic and basaltic rocks. Many volcanoes in the Pacific Ocean are andesitic.

Science and READING

The word *igneous* comes from the Latin word *ignis* which means "fire." Find out where the words *intrusive* and *extrusive* come from. Look them up in a dictionary that shows the roots of these words.

Figure 4-8. Basalt is the most common extrusive rock. Sediments from weathered and eroded basalt form the black-sand beaches of the Hawaiian Islands.

The classification of an igneous rock tells you quite a bit about its formation and composition. Granite, for example, is an intrusive, granitic igneous rock. This means that it formed deep in Earth, where cooling was very slow and large mineral grains had a chance to grow. The rock has a high concentration of silicon and oxygen because it formed from granitic magma.

Igneous rocks are the most abundant type of rock on Earth. They've been classified to make them easier to study. By studying all rocks, geologists and other scientists have been able to hypothesize how Earth formed.

SECTION REVIEW

1. How do igneous rocks form?
2. Which type of magma and lava form igneous rocks that are dark-colored and dense?
3. How do intrusive and extrusive igneous rocks differ?
4. **Apply:** How are granite and rhyolite similar? How are they different?

Skill Builder

☑ Interpreting Scientific Illustrations

Suppose you are given a photograph of two igneous rocks. You are told one is an intrusive rock and one is extrusive. By looking only at the photographs, how could you know which is which? If you need help, refer to Interpreting Scientific Illustrations in the **Skill Handbook** on page 693.

Metamorphic Rocks

Objectives

▶ Describe conditions that cause metamorphic rocks to form.
▶ Classify metamorphic rocks as foliated or nonfoliated.

New Science Words

metamorphic rocks
foliated
nonfoliated

Origin of Metamorphic Rocks

You wake up, go into the kitchen, and pack a lunch for school. You place a sandwich and a cream-filled cake in the bag. As you leave for school, you decide to throw in an apple. At lunch-time, you open your lunch bag and notice things have changed. Your cream-filled cake doesn't look too good anymore. The apple was resting on your cake all morning. The heat in your locker and the pressure from the apple have changed the form of your lunch. Rocks can also be affected by temperature changes and pressure.

Rocks that have changed due to temperature and pressure increases are **metamorphic rocks.** Metamorphic rocks can be formed from changes in igneous, sedimentary, or other metamorphic rocks. What occurs in Earth to change these rocks?

Figure 4-9. The mineral grains in granite (a) are flattened and aligned when pressure is applied to them. Gneiss (b) is formed.

Pressure

a

b

TECHNOLOGY

Solid As a Rock?

Rocks are used as building materials because of their durability and appearance. Large slabs of rock, however, are expensive and difficult to work with.

A company in Iowa has made a material that looks like granite, wears like granite, and in fact, is about 90 percent granite. Granitech is a humanmade material made of crushed granite that's glued together. This material weighs less than natural granite and ranges in thickness from less than 0.5 cm to almost 1 cm. Granitech can be used on countertops, as floors, to make furniture, and to cover walls.

Think Critically: Granite is made of interlocking mineral crystals that have grown together. How does Granitech differ from this?

Rocks beneath Earth's surface are under great pressure from overlying rock layers. They also experience heat generated by the radioactive elements in them. If the heat and pressure are great enough, the rocks melt and magma forms. But what happens if the heat and pressure are not great enough to melt the rocks?

In areas where melting doesn't occur, mineral grains in the rock change in size or shape. Some are flattened like the cake in your lunch bag. Sometimes minerals exchange atoms with surrounding minerals and new or bigger minerals form.

Look at the model of the rock cycle in Section 4-1. You see that a rock that is classified as igneous can be transformed into a rock classified as metamorphic. For example, the igneous rock granite can be changed into the metamorphic rock gneiss (NISE).

One type of metamorphic rock can form from different types of existing rock. For example, the metamorphic rock schist (SHIHST) can form from igneous rock, basalt; from sedimentary rock, shale; or it can form from metamorphic rock, slate.

What type of rocks does schist form from?

Classification of Metamorphic Rocks

When mineral grains flatten and line up in parallel bands, the metamorphic rock has a **foliated** texture. Foliated rocks form when minerals in the original rock flatten under pressure.

Two examples of foliated rocks are slate and gneiss. Slate forms from the sedimentary rock shale. The minerals in shale are arranged into layers when they're exposed to heat and pressure. Slate is easily separated along these foliation layers. The minerals in slate are so tightly compacted that water can't pass between them.

Gneiss, another foliated rock, forms when granite and other rocks are changed. Quartz, feldspar, mica, and other minerals in granite aren't changed much, but they are rearranged into alternating bands.

In some metamorphic rocks, no banding occurs. The mineral grains change, grow, and rearrange but they don't form bands. This process produces a **nonfoliated** texture. Such rocks don't separate into layers. Instead they fracture into pieces of random size and shape.

Sandstone is a sedimentary rock that's often composed mostly of quartz minerals. When its mineral grains are changed by heat and pressure, the nonfoliated rock quartzite is formed. The only change that occurs is in the size of the mineral grains.

MINI-Lab
What do metamorphic rocks form from?

Your teacher will provide you with samples of four metamorphic rocks and four nonmetamorphic rocks. Each of the metamorphic rocks formed from one of the nonmetamorphic rocks. For each metamorphic rock, determine which nonmetamorphic rock was its "parent."

Figure 4-10. The varying abundances of minerals in shale result in the many different colors of slate. The properties of slate make it useful as patio and stepping stones and roofing shingles.

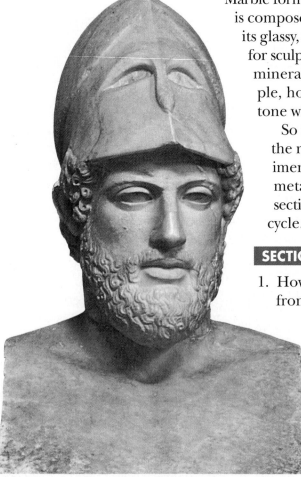

Another nonfoliated metamorphic rock is marble. Marble forms from the sedimentary rock limestone which is composed of calcite. The calcite crystals give marble its glassy, shiny luster that makes it a popular material for sculpturing. Usually, marble contains several other minerals besides calcite which color it. For example, hornblende and serpentine give it a greenish tone whereas hematite makes it red.

So far, we've traveled through only a portion of the rock cycle. We still haven't observed how sedimentary rocks are formed and how igneous and metamorphic rocks evolve from them. The next section will complete our investigation of the rock cycle.

SECTION REVIEW

1. How is the formation of igneous rock different from that of metamorphic rock?
2. How are metamorphic rocks classified? What are the characteristics of rocks in each of these classifications?
3. Marble rarely contains fossils even though limestone does. Explain.
4. **Apply:** Slate is sometimes used as roofing tiles for houses. What properties of slate make it useful for this purpose?

Figure 4-11. Sculptors often work with marble because it's soft and easy to shape. Its calcite crystals also give it a glassy, shiny luster.

Skill Builder

☑ Sequencing

Put the following events in a sequence that could explain how a metamorphic rock might form from an igneous rock. (HINT: Start with *igneous rock forms*.) Use each event just once. If you need help, refer to Sequencing in the **Skill Handbook** on page 680.

Events: *sedimentary rock forms, weathering occurs, heat and pressure are applied, igneous rock forms, metamorphic rock forms, erosion occurs, sediments are formed, deposition occurs*

ACTIVITY 4-2
Sedimentary Rocks

Problem: *How can you classify sedimentary rocks?*

Materials

- unknown sedimentary rock samples
- marking pen
- 5% hydrochloric acid (HCl)
- dropper
- hand lens
- paper towels
- water

Procedure

1. On your paper, make a Data and Observations chart similar to the one shown below.
2. Determine the types of sediments in each sample. What size are the sediments in the clastic rocks? Classify them as pebbles, sand, silt, or clay.
3. Put a few drops of HCl on each rock sample. **CAUTION:** *HCl is an acid and can cause burns. Wear goggles. Rinse spills with water.* "Bubbling" on a rock indicates the presence of carbonate minerals.
4. Look for fossils and describe them if any are present.
5. Classify your samples as clastic, chemical, or organic. Identify each rock sample.

Analyze

1. Why did you test the rocks with hydrochloric acid?
2. What mineral reacts with hydrochloric acid?
3. What is needed in order for sedimentary rocks to form from fragments?

Conclude and Apply

4. How do clastic sedimentary rocks differ from nonclastics?
5. How can you classify sedimentary rocks?

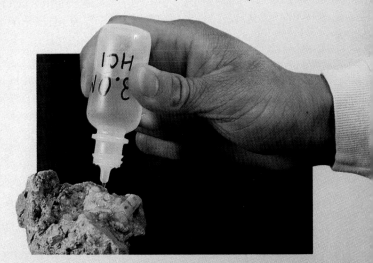

Data and Observations

Sample	Observations	Minerals or fossils present	Sediment size	Clastic, Chemical, or Organic	Rock name
A					
B					
C					
D					
E					

4-4 Sedimentary Rocks

New Science Words

sedimentary rocks
sediments
compaction
cementation

Objectives

▶ Explain how sedimentary rocks form from sediments.
▶ Classify sedimentary rocks as clastic, chemical, or organic in origin.

Origin of Sedimentary Rocks

Most of the rocks below Earth's surface are igneous rocks. Igneous rocks are the most common rocks on Earth. But chances are, you've seen more sedimentary rocks than igneous rocks. Seventy-five percent of the rocks at Earth's surface are sedimentary rocks.

Sedimentary rocks form when sediments become pressed or cemented together or when sediments fall out of solution. **Sediments** are loose materials such as rock fragments, mineral grains, and bits of plant and animal remains that have been transported. Minerals that are

Define sediments.

Table 4-2

SEDIMENT SIZES			
Sediment	Clay	Silt	Sand	Pebbles
Size range	< 0.004 mm	0.004 - 0.06 mm	0.06 - 2 mm	2 - 64 mm
Examples of rock formed from	 Mudstone	 Siltstone	 Sandstone	 Conglomerate

Figure 4-12. Two processes that form sedimentary rocks are compaction (a) and cementation (b).

dissolved in water are also sediments. But where do sediments come from? If you look at the model of the rock cycle, you will see that they come from already-existing rocks that are weathered and eroded.

Weathering is the process that breaks rocks into smaller pieces. Table 4-2 shows how these pieces are classified by size. These sediments are usually moved by water, wind, ice, or gravity. The movement of sediments is called erosion. You will learn more about these processes in Chapters 5 and 6.

Erosion moves sediments to a new location, where they are then deposited. Here, layer upon layer of sediment builds up. Pressure from the upper layers pushes down on the lower layers. If the sediments are very small, they can stick together and form solid rock. This process is called **compaction.**

You've compacted sediments if you've ever made "mud pies." Mud is made of small, clay-sized sediments. They easily stick together under the pressure applied by your hands. However, if you tried the same thing with large particles, such as driveway gravel, you couldn't make them compact into one mass.

If sediments are large, like sand and pebbles, pressure alone can't make them stick together. Large sediments have to be cemented together. **Cementation** (see men TAY shun) occurs in the following way. Water soaks through soil and rock. As it moves, it dissolves minerals in the rock such as quartz and calcite. These minerals

MINI-Lab

What are rocks made of?
Spread some sediments on a sheet of paper. Using tweezers or a dissecting probe, separate the sediments into three piles based on size—large, medium, or small. Now separate each of these piles into two piles based on shape: rounded or angular. You should now have six piles. Describe each of the six types of sediments you have.

are natural cements. The solution of water and dissolved minerals moves through open spaces between sediments. The natural cements are deposited around the pieces of sediment and they stick together. A group of sediments cemented together in this way forms a sedimentary rock.

Sedimentary rocks often form as layers. The older layers are on the bottom because they were deposited first. Then, more sediments pile up and they, too, become compacted and cemented together to form another layer of rock.

How do sedimentary rock layers form?

Sedimentary rock layers are a lot like the papers in your locker. The oldest papers are on bottom and the ones you get back today will be deposited on top of them. If, however, you disturb the papers, searching through them for a pencil at the bottom of the pile, the older ones may come to the top. Sometimes layers of rock are disturbed by forces within Earth. The layers are overturned, and the oldest are no longer on the bottom. The forces that cause such disturbances will be discussed in Chapter 13.

Classification of Sedimentary Rocks

Sedimentary rocks can be composed of just about anything. Sediments come from weathered and eroded igneous, metamorphic, and sedimentary rocks. Sediments also come from plants, insects, and animals. The composition of a sedimentary rock depends on the composition of the rocks and living things its sediments came from.

Like igneous and metamorphic rocks, sedimentary rocks are classified by their composition and by the way they formed. Sedimentary rocks are usually classified as clastic, chemical, or organic.

Clastic Sedimentary Rocks

The word *clastic* comes from the Greek word *klastos,* which means "broken." Clastic sedimentary rocks are made of the broken fragment of plants, animals, and other rocks. These sediments are compacted and cemented together.

The shape and size of the sediments are used to name a clastic rock. For example, conglomerate and breccia both form from large sediments. If the sediments have been well rounded, the rock is called conglomerate. If the sediments are not rounded and have sharp angles, the rock is called breccia.

The pebble-sized sediments in both conglomerate and breccia may consist of any type of rock or mineral. Often, they are chunks of the minerals quartz or feldspar. They can also be pieces of rocks such as gneiss, granite, or limestone. The cement holding them all together is usually quartz or calcite.

Have you ever looked at the concrete in sidewalks and driveways. It's made of pebbles and sand grains that have been cemented together. Since concrete is made by people, it's not a rock, but it does have a structure similar to that of naturally occurring conglomerate.

Figure 4-14. The concrete making up the sidewalk is similar to naturally occurring conglomerate (above).

Figure 4-15. Rock salt is a chemical sedimentary rock.

Sandstone is formed from smaller particles than conglomerates and breccias. Its sand-sized sediments are usually grains of the minerals quartz and feldspar, but can be just about any mineral. These sand grains can be compacted together if clay particles are also present, or they can be cemented.

Layers of sandstone beneath Earth's surface transport large volumes of groundwater. Groundwater is rain or surface water that has soaked into the ground. It reaches the sandstone deposits and moves through them. People drill wells into sandstone deposits and pump the groundwater to the surface to use as drinking water.

Shale is a clastic sedimentary rock that requires no cementation to hold its particles together. Its sediments are clay-sized particles. Clay-sized sediments are compacted together by pressure from overlying layers.

Chemical Sedimentary Rocks

Chemical sedimentary rocks form from minerals dissolved in solution. In rock formation these minerals separate from the water. Think back to our discussion of solutions in Chapter 2. We found that sugar is deposited in the bottom of a glass when tea evaporates. In a similar way, minerals collect when seas or lakes evaporate. The deposits of minerals that fall out of solution form rocks.

The mineral calcite is carried in solution in ocean water. When calcite comes out of solution and its many crystals grow together, limestone is formed. Limestone may also contain other minerals and sediments, but it's at least 50

Figure 4-16. Why does this sandstone look so much like desert sand dunes? This rock formed from sand deposited in layers by desert winds.

PROBLEM SOLVING

A Geology Trip in the City

While on a class field trip in the city, Peter and his classmates observed rocks used as building materials. In the city square Peter noticed flowers arranged in a rock terrace. The rocks were light-colored and contained many small fossils.

Soon, the class left the square and entered a historical district with an assortment of buildings. The first building Peter noticed was light pink with small crystals of quartz that felt gritty to the touch. Continuing down the street, he observed another building with columns. This building was constructed of a light-colored rock containing large mineral grains. Next, he saw a wooden building with a roof made of dark tiles. Some of the tiles had been broken off in layers.

On the bus trip back to school, students were asked to describe and name the rocks they observed on the field trip.

Think Critically: Using what you have learned about minerals and rocks, name the rocks that Peter observed. What rocklike materials do people make and use for buildings and other structures?

percent calcite. Limestone is usually deposited on ocean floors. Large areas of the United States are underlain by limestone because oceans once covered much of the United States for millions of years.

When lakes and seas evaporate, they often deposit the mineral halite. Halite, mixed with a few other minerals, forms rock salt. Rock salt deposits range in thickness from a few meters to over 400 meters. People mine these deposits because rock salt is an important resource. It's used in the manufacturing of glass, paper, soap, and dairy products. The halite in rock salt is even used as table salt.

How does rock salt form?

Organic Sedimentary Rocks

When rocks form from the remains of once-living things, they are organic sedimentary rocks. One of the most common organic sedimentary rocks is fossil-rich limestone. Like chemical limestone, fossil-rich limestone is made of the mineral calcite. But fossil-rich limestone

Figure 4-17. The White Cliffs of Dover, England, are composed mostly of chalk.

also contains remains of once-living ocean animals instead of just calcite that has separated from ocean water.

Animals such as mussels, coral, and snails make their shells from the mineral calcite. When they die, their shells accumulate on the ocean floor. These calcite shells are compacted and cemented together and fossil-rich limestone is formed. If the shell fragments are relatively large, the rock is called coquina (koh KEE nuh). If the shells are microscopic, the rock is called chalk. When your teachers use naturally occurring chalk to write with, they're actually crushing and smearing the calcite shells of once-living ocean animals.

Another very useful sedimentary rock is coal. Coal forms when pieces of dead plants are buried under other sediments. These plant materials are chemically changed by microorganisms. The resulting sediments are compacted over millions of years to form coal. In Chapter 18, you will learn how we use coal as a source of energy.

Another Look at the Rock Cycle

You have seen that the rock cycle has no beginning and no end. Rocks are continually changing from one form to another. Sediments come from rocks and other objects that have been broken apart. Even the magma and lava that form igneous rocks come from the melting of rocks that already exist.

All of the rocks that you've learned about in this chapter evolved because of the processes of the rock cycle. And all of the rocks around you, including those used to build houses and monuments, are part of the rock cycle. They are all changing.

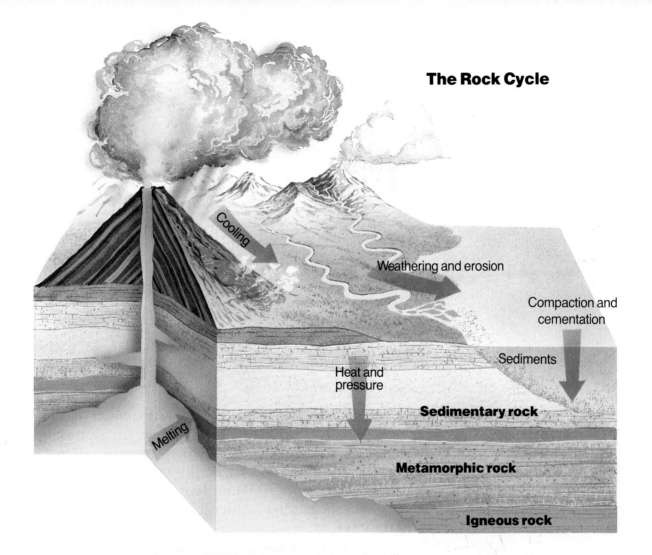

The Rock Cycle

Cooling

Weathering and erosion

Compaction and cementation

Sediments

Heat and pressure

Sedimentary rock

Melting

Metamorphic rock

Igneous rock

SECTION REVIEW

1. Where do sediments come from?
2. Explain why limestone can be classified as a chemical or organic sedimentary rock.
3. **Apply:** Use the rock cycle to explain how pieces of granite and slate could be found in the same piece of conglomerate.

☒ Interpreting Data

You are told that a clastic sedimentary rock is composed of sediments of the following sizes: pebbles, sand, and silt. The larger sediments are surrounded by the smaller sediments which are cemented together by quartz. What is the name of this rock? If you need help, refer to Interpreting Data in the **Skill Handbook** on page 687.

Skill Builder

4-5 Environmental Effects of Coal Mines

New Science Words

strip mine

Objectives

▶ Contrast characteristics of strip mines and underground coal mines.

▶ List several environmental effects associated with coal mining.

How Are Coal Mines Harmful to the Environment?

Every day of your life, you use electric power in some way. The coal used to generate the electricity must be taken from Earth. Two basic methods are used to remove the coal. If the coal is near Earth's surface, strip mining is used to remove it. When layers of coal are deeper beneath the surface, underground mines are used to take it out.

In a **strip mine,** layers of soil and rock above the coal are removed. These materials are piled up to one side. The exposed coal is then removed and loaded into trucks or trains to be moved elsewhere. A large open pit exists where the coal, soil, and rock were removed.

Mining companies are required to return the soil and rock to the open pit and cover it with topsoil. Usually, they plant trees and grass as well. This process is called land reclamation.

In underground mining, tunnels are dug to reach the coal. Large amounts of coal can be removed, but some must be left behind as walls or pillars to support the rocks and soil above. Otherwise, the mine would cave in.

Removal of coal by either method causes problems with the environment. Strip mining requires the removal of all vegetation. It temporarily scars the land with open pits. Wildlife lose their habitats.

Abandoned underground coal mines can collapse, causing large pits on Earth's surface. If people built homes above a mine, their homes would end up at the bottom of a pit when the mine collapsed.

Both mining methods pollute streams and kill fish and other wildlife. Since the vegetation has been removed, the soil is exposed. Heavy rains wash exposed soil into streams. The water can become so polluted with sediments that fish can no longer survive.

An even bigger problem occurs when water flows through mines and then into streams or lakes. The water dissolves sulfur from the coal and carries it in solution. Such water is acidic. The acidic water kills wildlife and severely pollutes drinking water.

From 1930 to 1970, only 40 percent of the mines in the United States were reclaimed. Since then, states have passed laws that require mining companies to reclaim the land. Today, almost all the land affected by mining is reclaimed. Mining companies put great effort and money into making the land as it was before they mined it. But the land can't always be restored to its original form. Forests take hundreds of years to develop, and wildlife that left the area when the mines came in may never return.

Differentiate between strip mines and underground mines.

Figure 4-18. Tunnels used in underground mining can collapse or fill with water which may then contaminate drinking water supplies.

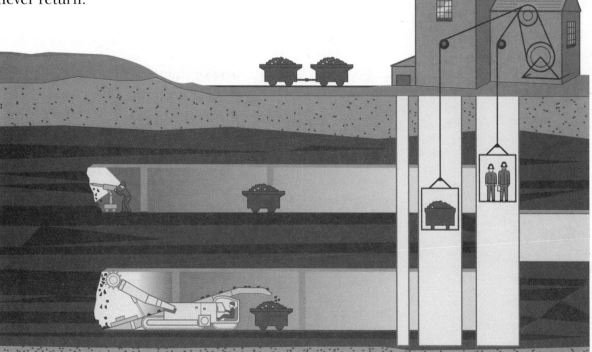

Figure 4-19. A strip mined area before and after reclamation.

Mines exist because we all want the energy that comes from coal. Would you be willing to give up electricity so that our environment didn't suffer? Probably not. Whole communities rely on mining operations for their survival. Men and women work in mines to make money to support themselves and their families. Mines are an important economic and energy resource for all of us.

SECTION REVIEW

1. What type of mine removes coal by removing overlying vegetation, soil, and rock?
2. List two environmental problems caused by underground mining.

You Decide!

Should you be required to use less electricity so that less damage is done to our environment? Should you have to wash dishes only by hand and reduce the use of your TV and stereo? Should people be required to give up energy-using luxuries such as hot tubs and air conditioners? What would you be willing to give up in order to conserve energy and protect our environment?

REVIEW

SUMMARY

4-1: The Rock Cycle

1. A rock is a mixture of one or more minerals.
2. The rock cycle includes all processes by which rocks form. A model of the rock cycle shows how rocks change into other rocks.

4-2: Igneous Rocks

1. Magma and lava are molten materials that harden to form igneous rocks.
2. Intrusive igneous rocks form when magma cools below Earth's surface. Extrusive igneous rocks form when lava cools at Earth's surface.
3. Basaltic rocks are dense, heavy, dark-colored rocks. Granitic rocks are light-colored and less dense than basalts. Andesitic rocks are intermediate between basaltics and granitics.

4-3: Metamorphic Rocks

1. Increases in heat and pressure can cause metamorphic rocks to form.
2. Slate and gneiss are classified as foliated, or banded, metamorphic rocks. When banding is not visible, as in quartzite, metamorphic rocks are classified as nonfoliated.

4-4: Sedimentary Rocks

1. Sedimentary rocks form when fragments of rocks, minerals, and/or organic materials are compacted and cemented together.
2. Clastic sedimentary rocks form when sediments are compacted and/or cemented together. Chemical sedimentary rocks form from minerals dissolved in solution. Organic sedimentary rocks are made mostly of once-living organisms.

4-5: Science and Society: Environmental Effects of Coal Mines

1. Strip mines are mines in which vegetation, rocks, and soil are removed from an area. Tunnels are dug to reach resources in underground mines.
2. Both strip and underground mining pollute the environment and kill wildlife.

KEY SCIENCE WORDS

a. basaltic
b. cementation
c. compaction
d. extrusive
e. foliated
f. granitic
g. igneous rocks
h. intrusive
i. lava
j. metamorphic rocks
k. nonfoliated
l. rock
m. rock cycle
n. sedimentary rocks
o. sediments
p. strip mine

UNDERSTANDING VOCABULARY

Match each phrase with the correct term from the list of Key Science Words.

1. mixture of one or more minerals
2. processes that form and change rocks
3. molten material at Earth's surface
4. igneous rocks that form when lava cools
5. rocks formed by heat and pressure
6. quartzite has this kind of texture
7. fragments of rocks, minerals, plants, and animals
8. process by which sediments are pressed together
9. process by which sediments become glued together
10. a mine at Earth's surface

CHAPTER
REVIEW

CHECKING CONCEPTS

Choose the word or phrase that completes the sentence or answers the question.

1. Which process is a part of the rock cycle?
   - **a.** weathering
   - **b.** deposition
   - **c.** melting
   - **d.** all of these

2. Igneous rocks form from _____ rocks.
   - **a.** sedimentary
   - **b.** metamorphic
   - **c.** other igneous
   - **d.** all of these

3. _____ rocks have large mineral grains.
   - **a.** Intrusive
   - **b.** Extrusive
   - **c.** Obsidian
   - **d.** All of these

4. During metamorphism, minerals can _____.
   - **a.** partly melt
   - **b.** become new minerals
   - **c.** grow larger
   - **d.** all of these

5. Gneiss is a(n) _____ rock.
   - **a.** foliated
   - **b.** nonfoliated
   - **c.** intrusive
   - **d.** extrusive

6. _____ is a rock made of large, angular pieces of sediments.
   - **a.** Conglomerate
   - **b.** Breccia
   - **c.** Limestone
   - **d.** Chalk

7. Which of these is not an organic rock?
   - **a.** shale
   - **b.** coal
   - **c.** chalk
   - **d.** coquina

8. A(n) _____ mine removes overlying rocks and soil to get to the material being mined.
   - **a.** underground
   - **b.** tunnel
   - **c.** strip
   - **d.** none of these

9. _____ mines scar Earth's surface because they require the removal of all vegetation.
   - **a.** Underground
   - **b.** Tunnel
   - **c.** Strip
   - **d.** Reclaimed

10. _____ forms when water carries sulfur from coal in solution.
    - **a.** An open pit
    - **b.** Soil
    - **c.** Strip
    - **d.** Acidic water

UNDERSTANDING CONCEPTS

Complete each sentence.

11. _____ and _____ can cause metamorphic rocks to form from sedimentary rocks.

12. Magma reaches Earth's surface because it is _____ than the surrounding rocks.

13. Rocks with fine-grained textures are the result of _____ cooling.

14. Conglomerates form in much the same way as shales, sandstones, and _____.

15. Erosion of soil is often _____ due to strip mining.

THINK AND WRITE CRITICALLY

16. Explain why the rock cycle has no beginning and no end.
17. Compare magma and lava.
18. Compare and contrast clastic rocks with organic and chemical rocks.
19. How do strip mines harm wildlife?
20. List the steps from first to last that a mining company would have to take to reclaim an area that was strip mined.

APPLY

21. Granite, pumice, and scoria are igneous rocks. Why doesn't granite have air holes like the other two?
22. Contrast the process that forms igneous rocks with the process that forms metamorphic rocks.
23. Why are only a few fossils found in marble?
24. Recall that a mineral is an inorganic solid with a definite structure. Rocks are mixtures of one or more minerals. Why do some scientists not consider coal a rock?
25. Explain why coquina could also be classified as a clastic rock.

MORE SKILL BUILDERS

If you need help, refer to the Skill Handbook.

1. **Concept Mapping:** Copy and complete the concept map shown. Add ovals and connecting lines so you can include examples of each classification of rock.

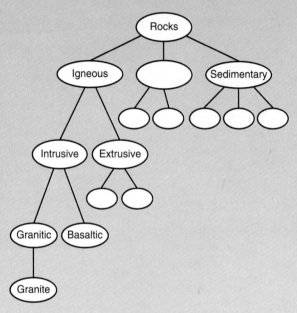

2. **Comparing and Contrasting:** Compare and contrast basaltic and granitic magmas.

3. **Hypothesizing:** A geologist found a sequence of rocks in which 200 million year-old shales were lying on top of 100 million year-old sandstones. Hypothesize how this could happen.
4. **Measuring in SI:** The rock shown below is a limestone that contains fossils. Find the average length of the fossils.
5. **Recognizing Cause and Effect:** Explain the cause and effects of pressure and temperature on shale.

PROJECTS

1. Use sand, gravel, mud, clay, and a salt solution to make at least three igneous, three metamorphic, and three sedimentary "rocks." Label your "rocks" and explain how each forms in nature.
2. Do some research to find out where coal is mined in the United States. Include the type of mining that is done for each deposit. Also include a discussion of how successful the reclamation efforts of the area have been.

GLOBAL CONNECTIONS

Rocks and Minerals

In this unit, you studied rocks and minerals. Now find out how rocks and minerals are connected to other subjects and places around the world.

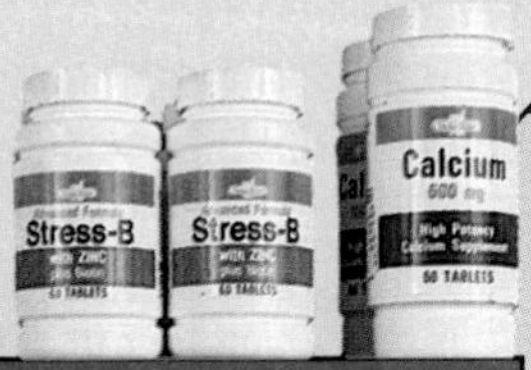

120° 60°

HEALTH

MINERALS FOR NUTRITION
Los Angeles, California
People of California obtain important minerals from the local soils. Calcium, magnesium, and phosphorus are minerals essential to bones and teeth. Iron is an important part of hemoglobin, which carries oxygen in the blood. How does the body obtain these essential minerals?

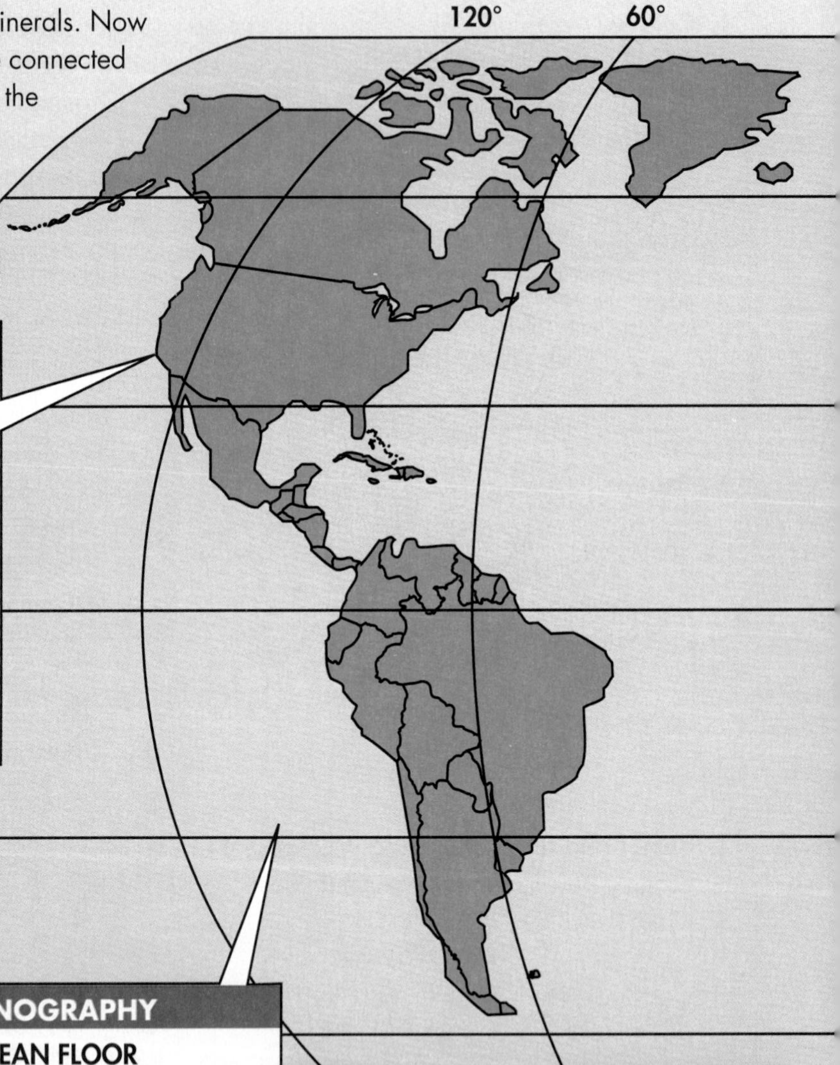

30°

OCEANOGRAPHY

MINING THE OCEAN FLOOR
South Pacific Ocean
Manganese nodules look like dark stones on the ocean floor. They contain valuable metals such as manganese, nickel, cobalt, and copper. The nodules are formed from minerals in seawater. Which do you think are more difficult to mine, materials from the ocean or from the land?

BIOLOGY

BACTERIA PUT MINERALS IN THE SOIL
Seville, Spain

All living things need nitrogen to make protein molecules. There is abundant nitrogen in the air, but only bacteria can convert the nitrogen to useful minerals. The bacteria live in the roots of plants such as peas, beans, and alfalfa, which are called legumes. The animals that eat these plants take in the minerals. What do you think happens to these minerals when the legumes die?

PHYSICS

PERFECT TIMING
Zurich, Switzerland

For decades, Zurich has been famous for its watchmakers. Today, they make sophisticated quartz watches. A quartz watch is more accurate than a spring-driven watch. If an electric current is applied to a quartz crystal, the crystal expands and compresses with almost perfect regularity. This makes quartz ideal for keeping time. Why are some quartz watches better than others at keeping time?

HISTORY

THE IRON AGE
Cairo, Egypt

The period of history that began between 1500 and 1000 B.C. was called the Iron Age. During that time, people in Egypt and elsewhere in the world began to mine iron ore. They also smelted iron ore to extract iron for making tools and weapons. Why is iron still used today to make good tools and weapons?

METALLURGICAL ENGINEER

Metallurgical engineers develop new types of metals with properties required for special tasks. For example, they may produce a material that is heat resistant for use in machinery that operates at very high temperatures. Metallurgical engineers also search for new ways to extract metals from their ores. Some of them determine ways to convert metals into useful products.

Metallurgical engineers usually have a degree in engineering with a specialty in metallurgy. A student interested in becoming a metallurgical engineer should take courses in mathematics, chemistry, and physics.

For Additional Information

Contact the Minerals, Metals, and Materials Society, 420 Commonwealth Drive, Warrendale, PA 15086.

GEMOLOGIST

A *gemologist* examines gems to grade them for purity and to estimate their value. Jewelers depend on the expertise of gemologists to appraise gems at a fair price. One benefit of being a gemologist is that you can look at and enjoy the beauty of precious stones.

Most gemologists receive training at a trade school after high school. Students learn to use a refractometer to measure how light passing through the gems is refracted, or bent. They also use a stone's specific gravity for identification purposes.

For Additional Information

Contact the Jewelers of America, Time-Life Building, Suite 650, 1271 Avenue of the Americas, New York, NY 10020.

UNIT READINGS

▶Amato, Ivan. "Diamond Fever." *Science News*, August 4, 1990, p. 72.
▶Pough, Frederick H. *Rocks and Minerals*. Boston: Houghton Mifflin, 1983.
▶"Trapping Wastes in Glass." *Popular Science*, November 1990.

Native American Pottery

In Chapters 3 and 4, you read about the properties of rocks and minerals. As you read the following paragraphs about Maria Martinez and her pottery, you'll discover that rocks and minerals can be used to fashion works of art.

The Pueblo people of the Southwest had one of the most highly developed civilizations to ever inhabit North America. Like other Native Americans, the Pueblos have always had a good understanding of how to make use of the natural resources of their environment. They employed minerals and rocks to produce useful and artistic products. Of particular interest are the beautiful hand-painted pieces of pottery fashioned by Pueblo craftspeople.

In the twentieth century, modern utensils have replaced pottery for kitchen use. So now Native Americans are producing pottery that is treasured mostly for its artistic value. One Pueblo artist whose works are in many museums of the world was Maria Martinez. Most of her long life of ninety-nine years was dedicated to producing the exquisite black-on-black pottery such as the pieces shown on this page.

Black pottery had not been produced by Native Americans for over 700 years until an archaeologist discovered some black pottery shards in an excavation of an ancient Native American village near San Ildefonso. He brought them to Maria who had already become well known for her multicolored pottery. Maria began working with a clay, rich in several minerals, found near her home, hoping to find the secret of how to make black pottery. Then one day she and her husband smothered the flames while the clay pots were being fired. When they removed the pots, they found that the clay had blackened! They had finally discovered how to duplicate the ancient black pottery.

Maria later devised a way to make the black pots shine by polishing the surface with a smooth stone before firing. After awhile, she combined polished designs with a flat finish called matte.

When demands for her black-on-black pottery exceeded her ability to produce them, Maria taught others in her village the secret. Soon Maria Martinez's black-on-black pottery replaced the earlier styles in several villages. Other Native Americans, influenced by Maria, have received recognition for their artistic pottery: Grace Medicine Flower, Cristina Naranjo, Joy "Frogwoman" Navasie, Blue Corn, and Nampeyo (a Hopi artist).

In Your Own Words

▶ Maria Martinez's rediscovery of an ancient skill came after many trials and errors. Write an essay to compare and contrast the techniques of artists and scientists. Explain how both must experiment, observe, and analyze results to achieve their goals.

What's Happening Here?

Earth's surface is constantly changing. Some processes of change occur so slowly that they are difficult to observe. Movement of a glacier, for example, can slowly carry large rocks from one place to another. A glacier can reshape mountains and fill in river valleys as its ice creeps along. Some processes of change are fast enough that they can be directly observed. Ocean waves moving grains of sand swiftly along the shore are easy to see. As you study this unit, you'll learn about the many processes that change the shape of our world.

UNIT CONTENTS

119

These stone carvings stand guard on tiny Easter Island in the South Pacific Ocean. They show the results of being exposed to weathering for hundreds of years. What happens to rock that is weathered?

FIND OUT!

Do this simple activity to find out what happens to different types of rocks when they are exposed to weather.

Obtain small samples of several different types of rocks. You could use sandstone, shale, granite, and basalt. Hold any two of the rocks above a piece of white paper and rub them together.

Observe the small particles of rock that fell to the white paper. Which rock broke apart more easily when rubbed? Repeat this process with the other rocks. Which rocks do you think would last the longest if exposed to wind and rain?

Gearing Up
Previewing the Chapter
Use this outline to help you focus on important ideas in this chapter.

Section 5-1 Weathering
▶ About Weathering
▶ Mechanical Weathering
▶ Chemical Weathering
▶ Effects of Climate on Weathering

Section 5-2 Soil
▶ Formation of Soil
▶ Soil Profiles
▶ Types of Soil

Section 5-3 Science and Society
Soil Loss
▶ Human Activities and Soil Loss

Previewing Science Skills
▶ In the **Skill Builders**, you will recognize cause and effect and make a concept map.
▶ In the **Activities**, you will observe, infer, interpret data, and measure.
▶ In the **MINI-Labs**, you will observe, and compare and contrast.

What's next?

Now that you've seen how rocks can break down, you'll learn about the processes that cause rocks to break down. You will have a better understanding of the rock cycle by studying these processes.

5-1 Weathering

Objectives

▶ Contrast mechanical weathering and chemical weathering.
▶ Explain the effects of climate on weathering.

About Weathering

Have you ever noticed, while you've been walking down a sidewalk, that there is sand and grit along the sidewalk and the curb? Also, there always seems to be a layer of gritty dirt on the sidewalk at the bottom of stone or concrete buildings. Where do you suppose this dirt comes from? Actually, it is made up of small particles that break loose from the concrete in the curbs and the stones or concrete in the buildings.

Conditions and processes in the environment cause stone and concrete to break apart. In Chapter 4, the rock cycle showed you how sedimentary rocks form from pieces of other rocks. But you haven't investigated the conditions and processes that create these sediments. Let's see how it all happens.

Figure 5-1. Weathering changes sharp, jagged mountains into smooth, rolling mountains and hills over long periods of time.

Weathering is the term used to describe the breaking of rocks into smaller fragments. Weathering changes things around us gradually over long periods of time. It wears mountains down to hills over thousands of years. Weathering affects both naturally formed rocks and human-made structures such as buildings and streets. There are two main types of weathering processes— mechanical and chemical.

What is weathering?

Mechanical Weathering

Mechanical weathering is weathering that breaks apart rocks without changing their chemical composition. This can happen in many different ways. Suppose you are sitting beside a swiftly moving river. As you watch the swift water move by, you can only imagine what's happening below the surface. There, water is lifting rocks from the bottom and forcing them to collide with other rocks. When they hit, tiny pieces break off of the rocks. In this example, the force of the water creates the energy necessary to cause mechanical weathering.

You've probably seen the results of another type of mechanical weathering if you've ever ridden a skateboard on an old sidewalk. Some old sidewalks near trees are so cracked that you can't ride on them. Can you guess what causes this to happen? As trees grow, their roots spread through the soil. As roots grow under the sidewalks, they expand and force the concrete to break. Roots can break up naturally formed rocks the same way. This is how plant roots cause mechanical weathering.

How can plants cause weathering?

Figure 5-2. Tree roots break up naturally formed rocks the same way that they break up sidewalks.

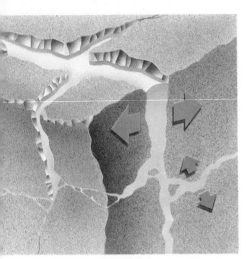

A third example of mechanical weathering occurs when water gets into the cracks in rocks and freezes. **Ice wedging** occurs when water freezes in cracks, expands, and forces the rocks apart. This process repeats itself when the ice thaws and the water freezes again. Mountain peaks are weathered rapidly by this process because they are often exposed to warm temperatures during the day and freezing temperatures at night. This cycle of freezing and thawing also breaks up roads and highways. When water gets into cracks in road pavement and freezes, it forces the pavement apart. This can lead to the formation of "potholes" in roads.

Figure 5-3. When water gets into cracks in rock and freezes, it expands, forcing the rock apart.

Chemical Weathering

The second main type of weathering occurs when water, air, and other substances react with the minerals in rocks. This type of weathering is called **chemical weathering** because the mineral composition of the rock is changed. Let's see how chemical weathering can happen.

PROBLEM SOLVING

Jamie's Frozen Failure

Jamie had promised her dad she would cut the lawn before he got home from work. She had heard on the weather report that

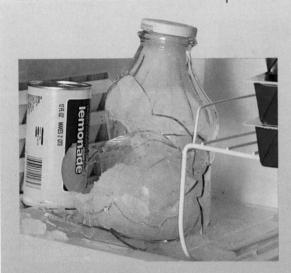

the temperature might reach a record high on that day. Jamie found that the weather report was right. It was a very hot afternoon and she knew she would be very thirsty by the time she finished such a big job. She decided to make herself a jar of lemonade. She poured the lemonade into a glass jar, put a lid on it, and put it in the freezer to make it really cold.

At the end of two hours she finally returned for a glass of lemonade. She opened the freezer to find the glass jar broken. It didn't take Jamie long to guess what had caused the glass to break.

Think Critically: What do you think caused the glass to break? How does the same process weather rocks?

ACTIVITY 5-1
Weathering Rocks

Problem: How can physical weathering break down rocks?

Materials

- 100 g limestone or shale samples
- plastic bottle with cap
- wire strainer
- pan balance
- water

Procedure

1. Determine the mass of the presoaked limestone or shale using the pan balance.
2. Place the chips into the plastic bottle and add enough water so that the bottle is about half filled. Seal the bottle with the cap.
3. Before continuing, make a list of the factors that you think will affect the weathering rate of the rocks.
4. Shake the bottle vigorously for two minutes. Uncap the bottle and pour the water and rock through the strainer. Rinse the rocks off, and again determine the mass of the rock material. Record this measurement.
5. Repeat Steps 2 and 4 until 20 minutes of shaking time have been completed, broken into shaking intervals of two minutes each. Record the original mass and the final mass of the rock material at each shaking time. Extend your data table to include 10-, 12-, 14-, 16-, and 18-minute shaking times.

Analyze

1. What happened to the mass of the rock material after each period of shaking?
2. What was the total change in mass of the rock from the beginning to the end of the 20-minute shaking time?
3. What were some of the factors in this activity that affected the rate that the rock was physically weathered?

Conclude and Apply

4. Where on Earth would you find rocks undergoing weathering similar to this activity?
5. What are some factors that would affect the physical weathering rate of rocks in a natural weathering situation outside of your classroom?

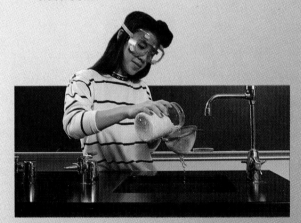

Data and Observations

Shaking Time	2 min.	4 min.	6 min.	8 min.	10 min.	12 min.	14 min.	16 min.	18 min.	20 min.
Original mass										
Final mass										
Change in mass										

MINI-Lab

How does rust form?

Put a piece of steel wool in a shallow pan containing about 1 cm of water. Observe it for several days. What changes are occurring? How can you explain these changes?

Water is the main cause of chemical weathering. What happens to a sugar cube when you put it in a cup of tea? The water dissolves the cube. Water does the same thing to some minerals in rock. It dissolves them and carries them away. The rock that is left behind now has a different composition.

Sometimes compounds in the air combine with water. When this water comes in contact with some minerals in rocks, new minerals are formed. For example, when water mixes with the mineral feldspar, clay minerals such as kaolinite are formed.

Oxygen also helps cause chemical weathering. Have you ever seen a rusty car? **Oxidation** occurs when a metal such as iron is exposed to oxygen and water. Paint usually protects metal and keeps it from rusting, but if the metal under the paint gets exposed to oxygen and water, rust forms. Rocks that contain iron also "rust."

Another type of chemical weathering occurs when naturally formed acids come in contact with rocks. When water mixes with carbon dioxide from the air, a very weak acid called carbonic acid forms. This acid dissolves minerals such as calcite, the main mineral in the rock limestone. Over thousands of years, the acid can dissolve enough limestone to form caves as shown in Figure 5-5.

Acids are also given off by some plant roots and decaying plants. These acids dissolve some of the minerals in the rocks. When these minerals are gone, the rock is weaker and will eventually break into smaller pieces. The next time you find a moss-covered rock, peel back the moss and you'll find small pits in the rock. These pits are caused by the plant root acids.

Figure 5-4. Oxidation causes rocks that contain iron to "rust," giving them a reddish color.

Effects of Climate on Weathering

Mechanical and chemical weathering occur all around the world. However, the climate of a particular region determines how fast weathering happens. Climate is the pattern of weather an area has over many years. Climate also has an effect on what types of weathering are occurring. For example, in regions where freezing and thawing occur frequently, rocks weather rapidly because of the expansion of freezing water. You may have seen the effects of this type of weathering on the streets in your neighborhood. The pavement cracks and buckles during the winter, and potholes seem to be everywhere.

Figure 5-5. Chemical weathering dissolves limestone, forming caves.

Chemical weathering is most rapid in regions with lots of moisture and warm temperatures. Thus, chemical weathering is very rapid in tropical areas such as the Amazon River region of South America. In desert areas and polar regions, the lack of moisture and low temperatures keep chemical weathering at a minimum.

Now that you know what weathering is, you can see its results in many places. You also know that weathering does more than just break up rocks. Weathering contributes to the rock cycle by making sediment. When you see a broken sidewalk near a tree, you know that roots caused mechanical weathering. Roots break up rocks, forming sediments that form sedimentary rocks.

Why is chemical weathering rapid in the Amazon region?

Science and WRITING

The rate of chemical weathering in the Amazon River region is very different from that in Antarctica. Find information on these two places in an encyclopedia and write a short paper describing reasons for their different climates and their different rates of chemical weathering.

SECTION REVIEW

1. What is the difference between mechanical and chemical weathering?
2. How is mechanical weathering affected by climate?
3. How do some plant roots cause chemical weathering?
4. **Apply:** How can water cause both mechanical and chemical weathering?

☑ Recognizing Cause and Effect

Identify the cause and effect in each of these examples of weathering. If you need help, refer to Recognizing Cause and Effect in the **Skill Handbook** on page 683.

1. Acid rain has turned a bronze statue green in a major city.

2. Tree roots are exposed in cracks in your sidewalk.

3. A piece of limestone has a honeycomb appearance.

Skill Builder

5-2 Soil

Objectives

▶ Explain how soil evolves from rock.
▶ Describe soil by comparing the A, B, and C soil horizons.
▶ Discuss how environmental conditions affect the evolution of soils.

Formation of Soil

How often have you been told, "Take off those dirty shoes before you come into this house"? Ever since you were a young child, you've had many experiences with dirt. Usually, this dirt is actually soil. You can find soil in lots of places. An empty lot may have exposed soil in it. A garden or a flower bed has soil.

But what is soil and where does it come from? As you learned in Section 5-1, weathering gradually breaks rocks into smaller and smaller fragments. When plants and animals live in these fragments, organic matter, such as leaves, twigs, and dead worms and insects, is added. When organic matter is gradually added to the weathered rock, soil evolves. **Soil** is a mixture of weathered rock and organic matter. Most soil is made up of about 50 percent rock and mineral fragments and 50 percent air, water, and

Figure 5-6. Soil evolves from weathered rock.

Figure 5-7. Soil is a mixture of weathered rock and organic matter.

organic matter. Soil can take hundreds of years to form and can range in thickness from 60 meters in some areas to just a few centimeters in others.

As rock weathers into smaller and smaller fragments, plants begin to grow in the weathered rock. Then worms, insects, bacteria, and fungi begin living among the plant roots. These organisms don't just live in the weathered rock, they help it evolve into soil by adding organic matter. When the plants and animals that live in the soil eventually die, they break down in a process called decay. The dark-colored organic matter made of pieces of decaying plants and animals is called **humus.** As worms and insects burrow throughout the soil, they mix the humus with the fragments of rock. As you can see, weathered rock is constantly evolving into soil.

Soil Profiles

You may have seen layers of soil if you've ever been near a steep slope such as a road cut where the soil and rock are exposed. You might have noticed that plants grow in the top layer of soil, which is a darker color than the other soil layers below it. These different layers of soil make up what is called a **soil profile.** Each layer in the soil profile is called a **horizon.** There are generally three horizons, and they are labeled A, B, and C.

MINI-Lab

What is soil made of?
Collect a sample of soil. Observe it closely with a magnifying glass or microscope. Try to identify the different particles by describing them. Do any of the materials appear to be remains of once-living organisms? Compare your samples to those of other students in your class. In what ways are those samples different or similar to yours?

ACTIVITY 5-2
Soil Characteristics

Problem: *What are the characteristics of soil?*

Materials

- soil sample
- sand
- clay
- gravel
- hand lens
- water
- paper
- watch
- scissors
- plastic coffee can lids (3)
- cheesecloth squares
- rubber bands
- pencil
- 250-mL beakers (3)
- thumbtack
- large polystyrene cups (3)
- graduated cylinder

Procedure

1. Describe the color of the soil sample.
2. Spread some of the sample on a sheet of paper and examine it with a hand lens. Name or describe some of the different particles you see.
3. Place a small amount of soil in your hand and rub it between your fingers. Describe the texture (how it feels).
4. Punch the same number of holes in the bottom and around the lower part of each of three polystyrene cups with a thumbtack.
5. Cover the holes in each cup with a square of cheesecloth. Secure the cloth with a rubber band.
6. Cut a hole in each plastic lid so that a cup will fit just inside the hole.
7. Place each cup in a lid and place each lid over a beaker.
8. Label the cups A, B, and C.
9. Fill cup A half full of dry sand, cup B half full of clay. Half fill cup C with an equal mixture of sand, gravel, and clay.
10. Use the graduated cylinder to pour 100 mL of water into each cup. Record the time when the water is first poured into each cup and when the water first drips from each cup.

11. Allow the water to drip for 25 minutes, then measure and record the amount of water in each beaker.

Analyze

1. Based on your examination of the soil sample in Steps 1-3, describe your soil sample in as much detail as possible.
2. Permeability refers to the ability of water to move through a substance. Which substance that you tested in Steps 4-11 is most permeable? least permeable?

Conclude and Apply

3. How does the addition of gravel affect the permeability of clay?
4. What are three characteristics of soil?

The A horizon is the top layer of soil. It's also known as topsoil. If you could dig up a scoop of topsoil from the top of that steep slope and look at it very closely, what would you see? The soil would be dark in color and would contain sediments, decayed leaves, the roots of plants, and even insects and worms. The A horizon is the most fully evolved soil layer in a soil profile. This means that the A horizon has changed the most since it was just weathered rock. It generally has more humus and smaller sediments in it than the other, less evolved layers in a soil profile.

The next layer below the A horizon is the B horizon. This layer is less evolved and lighter in color than the A horizon because it has little or no humus. Some plant roots reach into this layer. This horizon usually contains minerals that were washed down from the A horizon. The process in which minerals are dissolved in water and carried down in a soil profile is called **leaching.** The process of leaching is similar to how coffee is made in an automatic drip coffee maker. Like water seeping into the A horizon, hot water drips into coffee grounds in a filter. There, like water dissolving minerals in the B horizon, the water absorbs flavor and color from the coffee grounds. Then, like water carrying the dissolved minerals to the C horizon, water in a coffee maker flows through the filter and into the pot.

EcoTip

Roses and azaleas love an acid soil. Coffee grounds acidify soil. Recycle coffee grounds by placing them around these acid-loving plants.

Why does the B horizon contain minerals from the A horizon?

Figure 5-9. This scientist is analyzing soil.

Below the B horizon you will find the C horizon. This is the bottom layer in a soil profile. Some of the materials in this layer were leached from the B horizon. The C horizon also contains partly weathered rock, but no humus. This rock is just beginning the long, slow process of evolving into soil. What do you suppose you will find if you dig all the way to the bottom of the C horizon? As you might have guessed, there will be solid rock.

Types of Soil

Are all soil profiles the same no matter where you dig? No, soil profiles vary greatly from one location to the next. The thickness of the horizons and the soil composition depend on many conditions. These include the climate of the area and the type of rock the soil has evolved from. Other factors include the slope of the land, the amount of humus in the soil, and the length of time the soil has been evolving.

T E C H N O L O G Y

Knock on Wood!

Soil is estimated to be lost from about 56 000 square kilometers of land per year around the world. Some of this soil loss is caused by the cutting of trees.

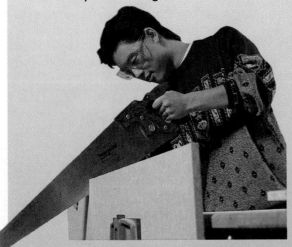

Engineers and scientists have developed a way to reduce the number of trees that must be cut to provide lumber. "Reconstituted lumber" is wood that is made from logs that aren't long enough or in good enough shape to be cut for lumber. These logs are ground up into small chips; and then the chips are glued together. Because it is dried in special kilns, reconstituted lumber is less prone to shrinkage, warping, and bowing. The manufacturers of this engineered lumber also say that their products can be up to 2.5 times stronger than natural wood.

Think Critically: How does using reconstituted lumber help conserve soil? What are the benefits of reconstituted lumber?

a

b

For example, if you consider just the climate of an area, you can see how one factor affects the soil. Soil in an area where there is little rainfall is very different from soil in an area with a lot of rainfall. Chemical weathering is slower in the area where there is little rainfall, so the soil horizons there are thinner than horizons from a rainy climate. Soil from a rainy climate with a lot of plant life is thick with humus. So as you can see, soil profiles are quite different depending on many factors.

Figure 5-10. Soils in cold, dry climates have thin horizons (a). Soils in warm, humid climates have well-developed horizons because of chemical weathering (b).

SECTION REVIEW

1. How do organisms help soils to evolve?
2. What is the difference between the A horizon and the C horizon?
3. Why does horizon B contain minerals from horizon A?
4. **Apply:** Why aren't all soil profiles the same?

☑ Concept Mapping

Skill Builder

Make an events chain map that explains how soil evolves. Use the following terms and phrases: soil is formed, humus develops, rock is weathered, plants grow, worms and insects added, humus mixes with weathered rock. If you need help, refer to Concept Mapping in the **Skill Handbook** on pages 688 and 689.

5-3 Soil Loss

New Science Words

desertification

Objectives

▶ Explain the importance of soil.
▶ Identify and describe activities that lead to soil loss.

Human Activities and Soil Loss

You probably don't realize how important soil is. Have you ever thought about where bread comes from? How about the paper in this book or the cotton fabric in your clothes? Bread, paper, and cotton fabric all have a direct connection to soil. Bread comes from grains that grow in soil. Paper is made from trees that need soil to grow in. Cotton comes from another plant that grows in soil. Without soil, we simply couldn't grow food and other resources. You can see how important soil is.

We've seen the results of soil loss in the past. In the 1930s, poor farming practices and a drought in the Great Plains area of the United States led to what is known as the "dust bowl." It was called the dust bowl because topsoil was carried away by the wind, creating dust storms. Thousands of metric tons of soil were carried away by wind during the dust bowl.

One of the poor farming practices that contributed to the dust bowl was overgrazing. Overgrazing occurs when livestock such as cattle or sheep eat every bit of grass off of the land. Without grass on the land, wind and water

Why is soil important to us?

Figure 5-11. Many products we use and depend on come from resources grown in soil.

Figure 5-12. Poor farming practices and drought turned the Great Plains into a "dust bowl" in the 1930s.

carry away the valuable topsoil. Also, without plants, soil evolution stops and no new soil develops. In some places around the world, when one area is overgrazed, livestock are simply moved to a new location to overgraze again.

Another poor farming practice is growing crops every year in the same area until all of the soil nutrients are used up. When this soil is no longer good for growing crops, the crops are moved to a new area and all of the soil nutrients there are used up. These ruined soils can take many years to recover. It takes 10 to 30 years for 1 mm of soil to evolve! Rotating crops so that an area doesn't have the same crop every year allows soil to recover nutrients after a crop uses them.

When soils are damaged by overgrazing in areas that receive little rain, a desert can form. Desert formation, also called **desertification,** is currently happening in some areas of Africa, China, and the United States. Desertification is so rapid that each year it claims an area of land that is nearly the size of the state of Maine.

Another human activity that is destroying soil is the clearing of forests for farming. Each year, thousands of square kilometers of tropical rain forest are cleared for farming and grazing. That soil depends on the rich nutrients provided by the lush rain forest. When the rain forest is removed, the soil is useful to farmers for only a few years before the nutrients are gone. Then the productivity of the soil is lost, and farmers clear more rain forest, repeating the process.

How does rotating crops help soil?

Did You Know?

Each year about 146 000 square kilometers of tropical rain forest is destroyed. This area is roughly the same size as the state of Illinois.

Figure 5-13. Clear cutting of forests leads to soil loss.

Developers in many locations clear forests to make way for buildings and roads. This type of development stops the evolution of soil also.

Overgrazing is one of the largest causes of soil loss in the United States. There are almost 2.5 million square kilometers acres of public land in the U.S. This is land that the federal government controls but lets people use for different purposes. Some of this land is used by ranchers for grazing cattle and other livestock. Grazing livestock on this public land costs ranchers about half as much as it would if they had to rent private land.

SECTION REVIEW

1. Why are soils important?
2. What are some human activities that destroy soils and prevent the evolution of new soils?

SCIENCE & SOCIETY

You Decide!

Public land is overgrazed. In Colorado, 84 percent of the public land is overgrazed, making soil loss very likely. On the other hand, the low grazing fees make it cheaper for ranchers to raise livestock. People benefit by paying lower prices for products made from cattle such as meat and leather products. What do you think? Should public land be better protected against soil erosion?

REVIEW

SUMMARY

5-1: Weathering

1. Mechanical weathering breaks apart rocks without changing their chemical composition. Chemical weathering changes the composition of the rock. Ice and plant roots are two things that can cause mechanical weathering. Chemical weathering can be caused by water, oxygen, and acids.

2. Climate affects the rate and type of weathering in an area.

5-2: Soil

1. When rock is weathered and organic matter is added, soil evolves.

2. In a soil profile, the A horizon, or topsoil, is dark in color, and contains weathered rock and organic matter such as leaves, roots, insects,

and worms. The B horizon has little or no humus and usually contains minerals leached from the A horizon. The C horizon contains partly weathered rock and some minerals leached from the B horizon.

3. Soil characteristics depend on the climate of the area, the type of rock the soil formed from, the slope of the land, the amount of humus in the soil, and the length of time the soil has been evolving.

5-3: Science and Society: Soil Loss

1. Soil is important because we use things such as grain and wood that grow in soil.

2. Soil loss is due to poor farming practices, overgrazing, the clearing of forests, and construction.

KEY SCIENCE WORDS

a. chemical weathering
b. desertification
c. horizon
d. humus
e. ice wedging
f. leaching
g. mechanical weathering
h. oxidation
i. soil
j. soil profile
k. weathering

UNDERSTANDING VOCABULARY

Match each phrase with the correct term from the list of Key Science Words.

1. breaking down rocks without changing their chemical composition
2. weathering in which the composition of the rock is changed
3. mixture of weathered rock and organic matter
4. decayed organic matter
5. all layers that make up a soil
6. each layer in a soil profile
7. a process that carries dissolved minerals downward in soil
8. desert formation
9. rock is forced apart by ice
10. chemical weathering due to exposure to water and oxygen

CHAPTER
REVIEW

CHECKING CONCEPTS

Choose the word or phrase that completes the sentence.

1. _____ break(s) rocks into sediments.
   a. Water   c. Roots
   b. Other rocks   d. All of these

2. Freezing and thawing weathers rocks because water _____ as it freezes.
   a. contracts   c. expands
   b. gets less dense   d. none of these

3. Air, water, and other substances react with rocks to produce _____ weathering.
   a. mechanical   c. physical
   b. chemical   d. all of these

4. _____ causes rust to form.
   a. Oxygen   c. Feldspar
   b. Carbon dioxide   d. Paint

5. _____ determines how fast weathering takes place.
   a. Acid   c. Water
   b. Slope of the land d. Climate

6. Chemical weathering is most rapid in _____ regions.
   a. cold, dry   c. warm, moist
   b. cold, moist d. warm, dry

7. _____ is a mixture of weathered rock and organic matter.
   a. Soil   c. Carbon dioxide
   b. Limestone d. All of these

8. Decayed organic matter is called _____ .
   a. leaching   c. soil
   b. humus   d. sediment

9. The _____ has little or no humus.
   a. A horizon   c. C horizon
   b. B horizon   d. D horizon

10. _____ is destroying the world's soils.
    a. Overgrazing   c. Clearing of trees
    b. Construction   d. All of these

UNDERSTANDING CONCEPTS

Complete each sentence.

11. _____ are formed as the result of mechanical weathering.

12. Minerals are washed to lower soil horizons in a process called _____.

13. Poor farming practices in areas that receive little rain results in _____.

14. _____ occurs when livestock eat all of the grass off the land.

15. The _____ in a soil profile is the least weathered layer.

THINK AND WRITE CRITICALLY

16. Compare and contrast mechanical weathering and chemical weathering.
17. Explain how soil evolves from rock.
18. How can a worm help soil to evolve?
19. Hypothesize why the B horizon is less weathered than the A horizon.
20. Explain how the clearing of tropical rain forests contributes to soil loss.

21. Which type of weathering, mechanical or chemical, would you expect to be more effective in a desert region? Explain.
22. How does ice wedging damage roads and streets in areas that have cold temperatures?
23. Why does some metal rust?
24. Why are some areas around the world changing to deserts?
25. Explain how chemical weathering can form a cavern.

MORE SKILL BUILDERS

If you need help, refer to the Skill Handbook.

1. **Outlining:** Make an outline of Section 5-2, Soil.
2. **Concept Mapping:** Make an events chain concept map that shows two ways in which acids can cause chemical weathering.

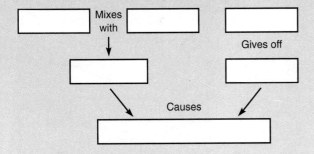

3. **Using Variables, Constants, and Controls:** Juan Carlos did an activity to test the ability of water to wash away soil. He put the same amount and kind of soil in three identical pans. He was careful to pour the same amount of water at the same rate over two pans: one that contained only soil and another that contained soil and grass. What is Juan Carlos' control? Which factors in his activity are con-

stants? What is the independent variable? the dependent variable?

4. **Recognizing Cause and Effect:** In Juan Carlos' activity, he found that in the pan containing soil and grass, the least amount of soil washed away. What are the cause and the effect in his observation?
5. **Sequencing:** Sequence the following types of soil in proper soil profile order from top to bottom: light colored soil with little humus, weathered rock, topsoil. Label the soils A, B, and C horizon.

PROJECTS

1. Obtain several different soil samples from around your community. Compare and contrast the samples, looking at color, texture, composition, number of organisms present, and the permeability. Construct a table on posterboard of your findings. Include an actual sample of each soil in the table.
2. Use reference books and current magazines to find out what is being done to prevent desertification. Prepare a written report that summarizes your findings.

CHAPTER 6

Erosion and Deposition

The water in the waterfall you see here looks clear and clean. But it's actually carrying tonnes of sediments.

There are little bits and pieces of rocks, soil, plants, insects, and animals all around you. These sediments don't just stay in one place—they are continually moving from one location to another. Your world is constantly changing because these bits and pieces are part of a cycle that keeps them moving and changing.

FIND OUT!

Do this simple activity to find out how sediments are moved from one location to another.

Place a small pile of sand and gravel on your desk. Now move the pile across your desk without touching any of the grains with your hands. How many ways can you think of to move the particles? Compare each of your methods with a force in nature that might cause sediments to move.

Gearing Up
Previewing the Chapter

Use this outline to help you focus on important ideas in this chapter.

Section 6-1   Gravity
▶ Erosion and Deposition
▶ Erosion and Deposition by Gravity

Section 6-2   Running Water
▶ Water Erosion
▶ Deposition by Water

Section 6-3   Science and Society
Developing Land Prone to Erosion
▶ Should We Develop Land Prone to Erosion?

Section 6-4   Glaciers
▶ Continental and Valley Glaciers
▶ Glacial Erosion
▶ Deposition by Glaciers

Section 6-5   Wind
▶ Wind Erosion
▶ Deposition by Wind

Previewing Science Skills

▶ In the **Skill Builders**, you will make concept maps, compare and contrast, recognize cause and effect, outline, and sequence.
▶ In the **Activities**, you will observe, infer, and analyze.
▶ In the **MINI-Labs**, you will design experiments, observe, and infer.

What's next?

Now that you've experimented with moving sediments, learn how the forces in nature transport sediments. You will explore how sediments are moved and dropped off at new locations by the agents of erosion.

6-1 Gravity

New Science Words

erosion
deposition
slump
creep

Objectives

▶ Define erosion and deposition.
▶ Compare and contrast slumps, creep, rockslides, and mud-flows.

Erosion and Deposition

Have you ever ridden your bike by a river just after a heavy rain? The water was so muddy that it looked like chocolate milk. Where do you suppose all of the mud came from? As you might guess, some of it came from dirt along the river's bank, but the rest of it was carried to the river from much more distant sources.

Mud is a product of erosion. **Erosion** (ih ROH zhun) is the process that moves weathered sediments from one location to another. As you investigate the processes of

Figure 6-1. Streams are part of the cycle that erodes and then deposits sediments.

Figure 6-2 . You are an agent of erosion when you transport coins and then deposit them in your bank.

erosion, you will see that eroded sediments are eventually deposited. But what moves the sediments in the first place? The four major agents of erosion are gravity, running water, glaciers, and wind.

As you investigate these four agents of erosion, you will notice that they have several things in common. For one thing, they all carry sediments only when they have enough energy of motion. For example, air doesn't have the ability to erode sediments as long as it's standing still. But once air begins moving and develops into wind, it can carry dust, soil, and even large rocks along with it.

Another thing that the agents of erosion have in common is that they all drop their load of sediments when their energy of motion decreases. This dropping of sediments is called **deposition** (dep uh ZIHSH un). Now let's take a look at how gravity, running water, glaciers, and wind erode and deposit sediments.

Erosion and Deposition by Gravity

Gravity causes loose materials to move down a slope. When gravity alone causes materials to move downslope, it's called mass movement. Some mass movements are very slow; you hardly notice that they're happening. Other types, however, happen very quickly. Let's examine some different types of mass movements.

What is mass movement?

Scar

Slump mass

Weakened material

Figure 6-3. Slumps occur when material slips downslope as one large mass.

Figure 6-4. When the ground freezes, soil particles are lifted at a right angle to the slope. Upon thawing, they fall downslope resulting in soil creep.

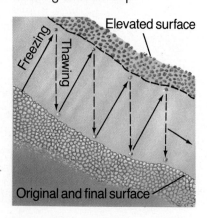

Freezing

Thawing

Elevated surface

Original and final surface

Slump

A **slump** is a type of mass movement that takes place on steep slopes. It occurs when loose materials or rock layers slip downward as one large mass. The material doesn't travel very fast or very far, but when it happens, a curved scar is left where the slumped material originally rested. Slumps occur because the material underlying the slumped material weakened. It could no longer support the overlying material, so it slipped downslope.

Creep

The next time you travel by car or bus, look along the roadway for slopes where trees, utility poles, and fenceposts lean downhill. These indicate that another type of mass movement is happening. It's called creep. **Creep** gets its name from the way sediments slowly creep down a hill. It is especially common in areas where freezing and thawing occur. As the ground freezes, small sediments are pushed up by the expanding water in the soil. Then, when the soil thaws, the sediments fall downslope, often less than a millimeter at a time. Several years of soil creeping downslope can cause objects such as utility poles and fenceposts to lean.

Rockslides

You may have seen signs along the road warning you to "Beware of Falling Rocks." Falling rocks are a type of mass movement called a rockslide. A rockslide happens when large blocks of rock break loose from steep slopes and tumble quickly to the bottom. As they fall, these rocks crash into other rocks, and they too break loose. Rockslides commonly occur in mountainous areas. They happen most often after heavy rains or during earthquakes, but they can happen on any rocky slope at any time without warning. Piles of broken rock at the bottom of a cliff tell you that rockslides have occurred there in the past and are likely to occur there again.

Weathering breaks rocks apart

Gravity erodes sediments

Sediments are deposited in piles called *talus slopes.*

Why do mudflows eventually deposit sediments?

Figure 6-5. How does the deposit from a mudflow differ from deposits from slumps, creeps, and rockslides?

Mudflows

Can you imagine being in a car traveling along a mountain road during a storm, when suddenly a wall of chocolate pudding slides down a slope and covers your car? This is similar to what might happen if you were caught in a mudflow. Instead of chocolate pudding, a thick mixture of sediments and water would flow down the slope in a type of mass movement called a mudflow.

Mudflows usually occur in relatively dry areas where weathering forms thick layers of dry sediments. When heavy rains fall in these areas, the water mixes with the sediments and forms a thick, pasty substance. Gravity causes this mass to slide downhill. A mudflow has enough energy to move almost anything in its path, including houses, cars, and large rocks. When a mudflow finally reaches the bottom of a slope, it loses its energy of motion and deposits all the sediments and debris it has been carrying. These deposits are usually a cone-shaped mass.

Now that you've thought about mudflows, rockslides, creep, and slump, think about how all these mass movements are similar. They're all more likely to happen where there are steep slopes. They all depend on gravity to make them happen. And, regardless of the type of mass movement, it will occur more often after a heavy rain because the water adds mass and makes the sediments slippery.

MINI-Lab

What causes mass movements?
Using a large pan and moist sand, construct model landforms that will show how the mass movements of sediments or loose materials can be demonstrated. Try to set up situations where each of the four types of mass movements is created. If a camera is available, take before and after pictures that will show the effects of these movements. What factors must be present for mass movements to occur? In what ways are each of these forms of mass movements similar?

Now, can you think of one more way they are all alike? All mass movements are the erosion of sediments from the top of a slope to a place farther downslope. The result is that mass movements constantly change the shape of a slope so that it becomes less steep.

SECTION REVIEW

1. Define erosion and deposition.
2. What is the difference between slump and creep?
3. What characteristics do all types of mass movements have in common?
4. **Apply:** People pile up dirt or cut into the sides of hills when they build houses and roads. Why does this speed up erosion by mass movement?

☑ Concept Mapping

Make a concept map about mass movements using these terms: gravity, slump, creep, rockslides, mudflows, curved scar, leaning trees and poles, rock piles, and cone-shaped mass. If you need help, refer to Concept Mapping in the **Skill Handbook** on pages 688 and 689.

Skill Builder

6-2 Running Water

New Science Words

rill erosion
gully erosion
sheet erosion
alluvial fan
delta

Objectives

▶ Compare rill, gully, and sheet erosion.
▶ Describe how alluvial fans and deltas form.

Water Erosion

Water erodes more sediments than any other agent of erosion. It's easy to see why—running water has great energy of motion. Usually, water moves downslope because of gravity's pull. As long as it has its energy of motion, water carries its load of sediments. But when it loses some of its energy, water must deposit the sediments that it's eroding.

As the water in a stream moves along, it constantly picks up sediments from the bottom and sides of its channel. Water picks up and carries some of the lightweight sediments, while large, heavy sediments just roll along the bottom of the stream channel. All of these different-sized materials scrape against the bottom and sides of the channel, where they knock loose even more sediments. Because of this, a stream continually cuts a deeper and wider channel.

Figure 6-6. Cross Section of a Stream Channel

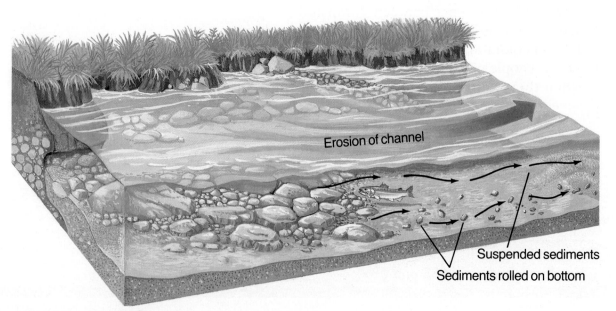

Erosion of channel

Suspended sediments

Sediments rolled on bottom

Figure 6-7. As the Colorado River flows, it erodes a huge load of sediments. Over the past several million years, the Colorado River has carved out the Grand Canyon by carrying away the rock and soil that were once there.

Rill and Gully Erosion

Suppose you and several friends walk the same way to school each day. Perhaps you cross the same field or empty lot, always walking in the same footsteps as you did the day before. By now, you've worn a path through the lot. Water also wears a path as it travels down a slope.

You may have seen a scar or small channel on the side of a slope that was left behind by running water. If you have, then you've seen evidence of rill erosion. **Rill erosion** begins when a small stream forms during a heavy rain. As this stream flows along, it has enough energy to carry away plants and soil. There's a scar left on the slope where the water eroded the plants and soil. If a stream frequently flows in the same path, rill erosion may evolve into gully erosion.

In **gully erosion,** a stream channel becomes broader and deeper, and large amounts of soil are removed from an area. Deep canyons, such as the Grand Canyon in Arizona, evolve from this type of erosion.

How do rill and gully erosion differ?

Science and READING

Research recent news articles to find which planets in the solar system have evidence of erosion by running water.

Sheet Erosion

Water often erodes without being in a stream channel. For example, when it rains over a fairly flat area, the rainwater accumulates until it eventually begins moving down a gentle slope. **Sheet erosion** happens when this rainwater flows into lower elevations, carrying sediments with it. In these lower elevations, the water loses some of its energy of motion and it drains into the soil or slowly evaporates. The sediments left behind cover the soil like a sheet.

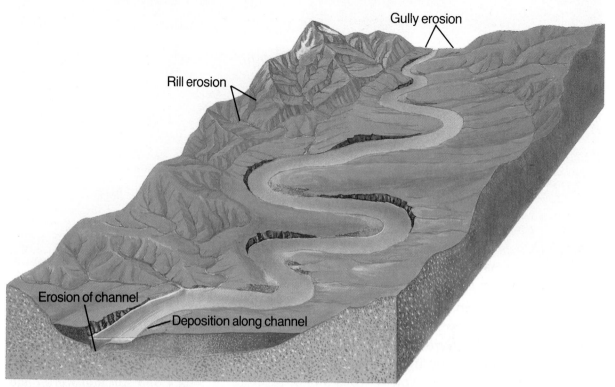

Rill erosion

Gully erosion

Erosion of channel

Deposition along channel

Figure 6-8. Streams are eroding and depositing material at the same time.

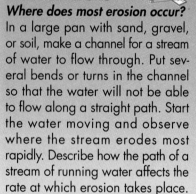

Deposition by Water

Where do you suppose the sediments from sheet, rill, and gully erosion end up? Why doesn't the stream just carry the sediments forever?

Some stream sediments aren't carried very far before being deposited. In fact, many sediments are deposited within the stream channel itself. Whenever the water in a stream isn't moving fast enough to carry sediments, they settle to the bottom.

Some stream sediments travel great distances before they are deposited. Sediments picked up when rill and gully erosion occur are examples. Water usually has a lot of energy of motion as it moves down a steep slope. When the water begins flowing on a level surface, it slows down, loses energy of motion, and drops its sediments.

One type of deposit that results, an **alluvial fan,** is shaped like a triangle. If the sediments are not deposited until the water empties into an ocean, gulf, or lake, the alluvial fan is known as a **delta.**

Let's use the Mississippi River as an example to tie all of this together. Thousands of small streams flow into the Mississippi. These streams are causing rill or gully erosion as they pick up sediments and dump them into the

Mississippi River. The Mississippi is quite large and has a lot of energy. It can erode many sediments. As it flows, it cuts into its banks and picks up more sediments. In other places, where the land is flat, the river deposits some of its sediments in its own channel.

Eventually, the Mississippi River reaches the Gulf of Mexico. There, it flows into the gulf, loses most of its energy of motion, and dumps its sediments in a large triangular deposit on the Louisiana coast. This deposit, shown in Figure 6-9, is the Mississippi Delta.

Describe how the Mississippi Delta grows.

SECTION REVIEW

1. What causes rill erosion?
2. How do alluvial fans and deltas form?
3. **Apply:** How can rill erosion evolve into gully erosion?

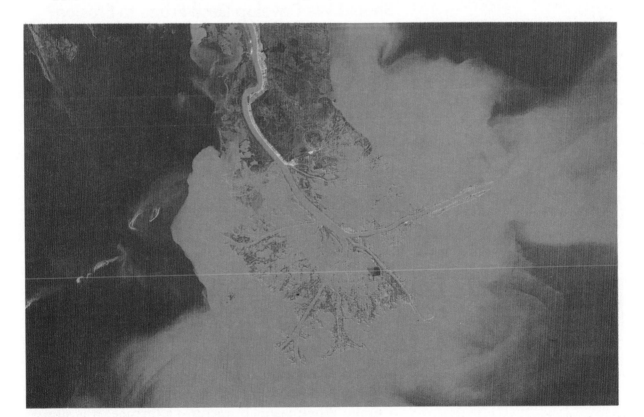

Figure 6-9. This satellite image of the Mississippi Delta shows how sediments accumulate when the Mississippi River empties into the Gulf of Mexico.

☒ Comparing and Contrasting

Compare and contrast sheet, rill, and gully erosion. If you need help, refer to Comparing and Contrasting in the **Skill Handbook** on page 683.

Skill Builder

SCIENCE & SOCIETY

6-3 Developing Land Prone to Erosion

New Science Words

terraces

Objectives

▶ Explain why problems develop when people live in places where land is prone to excessive erosion.
▶ Describe ways that erosion can be reduced in some high risk areas.

Should We Develop Land Prone to Erosion?

Have you noticed that many people live in houses and apartments beside rivers and lakes and on the sides of hills and mountains? If you ask real-estate agents, they'll tell you that people like to live where there's a good view. People like to look down on a valley or watch boats sail along a river. However, when you think of the effects of gravity and water, do you think steep slopes and river banks are good places for people to live? Perhaps not.

When people settle in these locations, they must constantly battle erosion problems. They have to deal not only with erosion that occurs naturally, but sometimes with additional problems they create themselves. When people make a slope steeper or remove vegetation, they are speeding up the erosion process.

There are a variety of things that people can do to reduce erosion. Planting vegetation is one of the best ways because not only do roots hold soil, but plants absorb a lot of water. A person living on a steep slope might also build terraces or retaining walls.

Terraces are broad, steplike cuts made into the side of a slope. When water flows onto a terrace, it is slowed down and its energy of motion is reduced, so it can't erode as much. Retaining walls are often made of concrete, stones, wood, or railroad ties. Their purpose is to keep soil and rocks from sliding downhill. These walls can also be built along stream channels, lakes, or ocean beaches to reduce erosion caused by flooding, running water, or waves.

EcoTip

In nature areas, stay on marked trails. You will protect fragile plant life and prevent excessive erosion.

Why do terraces reduce erosion?

People who live in areas with erosion problems spend a lot of time and money trying to preserve their land. Sometimes they're successful in slowing down erosion, but they can never eliminate it. Eventually, cliffs cave in and streams overflow their banks. Sediments constantly move from place to place, changing the shape of the land forever.

Figure 6-10. Building on steep slopes can have severe consequences.

SECTION REVIEW

1. How do people increase erosion when they develop an area?
2. How can erosion be reduced in areas where there are steep slopes?

You Decide!

Suppose you live beside a river. You love it there. It's beautiful, and there's so much to do. The only problem is that the river frequently floods. Several times your family has been evacuated to higher ground. One day, the mayor informs your family that you must move. She tells you that living along the river is not only dangerous, but it costs the city too much money each time you're evacuated. Do you think this is fair? Should communities be able to control where people live?

6-4 Glaciers

New Science Words

glacier
plucking
till
outwash

Objectives

▶ Describe how plucking occurs.
▶ Explain how striations are created.
▶ Compare and contrast till and outwash.

Continental and Valley Glaciers

Does it snow where you live? Does it snow only a few months out of the year? In some areas of the world, temperatures are low enough that it snows year-round. If the snow doesn't melt, it begins piling up. When it accumulates, the weight of the snow is great enough to compress the bottom layers into ice. When the snow piles up to 50 to 60 meters high, the ice on bottom partially melts and becomes putty-like. The whole mass begins to slide on this putty-like layer and it moves downhill. This moving mass of ice and snow is a **glacier.**

Figure 6-11. This map shows the extent of continental glaciation in North America.

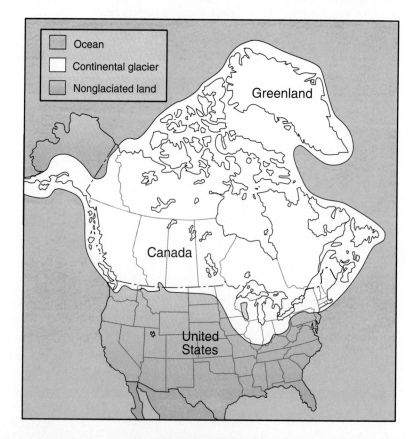

a

b

Figure 6-12. A continental glacier in Antarctica (a) and a valley glacier (b).

Glaciers, along with gravity, running water, and wind, are agents of erosion. There are two types of glaciers: continental glaciers and valley glaciers. Continental glaciers are huge masses of ice and snow found near Earth's polar regions. Today, they are found only in Greenland and Antarctica. But during past ice ages, continental glaciers covered large portions of the world. An ice age is a period of time when ice and snow cover much of Earth's surface. The most recent ice age began 2 million years ago and ended about 12 000 years ago. During that time, the average temperature on Earth was about 4°C lower than it is today.

Valley glaciers are fairly common even in today's warmer climate. They are located in mountainous areas where the average temperature is low enough that snow doesn't melt over the summer season. The glaciers of Glacier National Park in Montana are valley glaciers.

How is it possible that something as fragile as snow or ice can erode something as hard as rock? It may not seem likely, but much of Earth's landscape has been shaped by glacial ice. Let's explore how this is possible.

When did the last ice age occur?

Figure 6-13. The material plucked from the sides and bases of valleys can flow within glaciers as streams of rock and soil.

Glacial Erosion

As they move over land, glaciers act like bulldozers, pushing any loose materials out of their path. These eroded sediments are added to the mass of the glacier or piled up along its sides.

But glaciers do more than just move loose sediments. They also weather and erode rock and soil that isn't loose. Glacial snow and ice melt and the water flows down into cracks in rocks. Later, the water refreezes in these cracks, expands, and breaks the rock into pieces. The rock fragments are moved along with the glacial ice. This process, called **plucking,** results in boulders, gravel, and sand being added to the bottom and sides of a glacier.

These materials at the base of a glacier act like the blades of a plow. They scrape the soil and bedrock that the glacier moves over. They cause the glacier to erode even more than the ice and snow alone could.

Why do striations form?

When bedrock is gouged by rock fragments being dragged across it, marks are left behind. These striations (stri AY shunz) are usually long, parallel scars in rocks. Very large striations are called glacial grooves. Figure 6-14 shows a set of glacial grooves.

Did You Know?

The Great Lakes were gouged out of rock by glacial ice that covered the area from about 250 000 to 11 000 years ago.

Figure 6-14. This set of grooves at Kelleys Island, Ohio, are 10 m wide and 5 m deep.

If you live in the mountains and want to know if there were ever valley glaciers in your area, how could you find out? You might begin by looking for striations. But what other evidence of glacial erosion could you find? Glacial plucking often occurs near the top of a mountain, where a glacier is in contact with a wall of rock. A bowl-shaped basin, called a cirque (SURK), is created in the side of the mountain. If two or more glaciers erode a mountain summit from several directions, a ridge or sharpened peak forms.

Figure 6-15. Plucking by valley glaciers produces characteristic landforms.

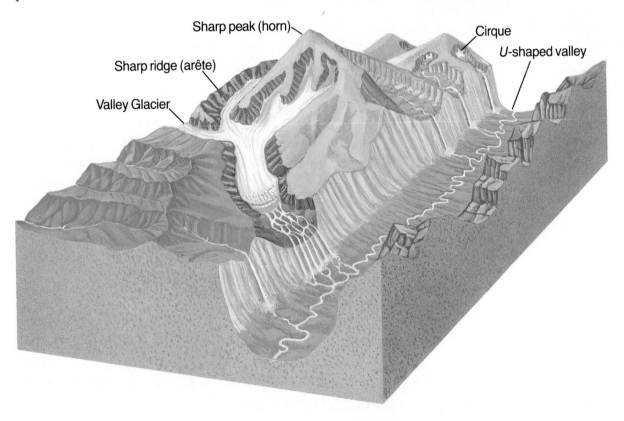

Sharp peak (horn)

Sharp ridge (arête)

Valley Glacier

Cirque

U-shaped valley

Bergy Bits?

Icebergs are large chunks of ice that break loose from continental glaciers. In the North Atlantic each year, about 16 000 icebergs break loose from Greenland's glaciers. As these vast chunks of ice move southward, the warmer waters and heat from the sun cause pieces to break off from the icebergs. Pieces the size of an average house are called bergy bits. Smaller pieces of ice are called growlers due to the noises they make as they float in the water.

Because more than 75 percent of Earth's fresh water is locked up in glacial ice, scientists have been studying ways to tow icebergs to areas that need fresh water. It has been estimated that an iceberg about 270 square kilometers in area would provide over 7080 million cubic meters of fresh water! A supertanker tug could tow an iceberg of this size at a rate of about 32 kilometers per day. This may be the only way to bring drinking water to some areas of the world.

Think Critically: What area of the world would benefit most from using icebergs as a source of fresh water?

Valley glaciers flow down mountain slopes and valleys, eroding as they go. Valleys that have been eroded by glaciers are a different shape from those that have been eroded by streams. Stream-eroded valleys are normally V-shaped; glacially eroded valleys are usually U-shaped. This is because glaciers pluck and scrape soil and rock along their sides as well as on their bottoms. Streams tend to erode downward into underlying rock more than glaciers do. Figure 6-17 shows a U-shaped valley.

Deposition by Glaciers

As you might guess, when glaciers begin to melt, they no longer have enough energy of motion to continue carrying many sediments. Therefore, these materials are deposited. Glacial deposits are classified into two major types. One is a jumble of different-sized sediments that is deposited from the glacial ice and snow. This mixture of boulders, sand, clay, and silt is called **till.** When a glacier stops moving, till begins dropping from its base. These sediments cover huge areas of land. In fact, during the last ice age, continental glaciers moving across the northern United States dropped so much till that it completely filled valleys and covered hills. Today, these areas appear quite flat.

Till is also deposited in front of a glacier when it stops moving forward. Unlike the till that is dropped from a glacier's base, this type of deposit doesn't cover a very wide area. Because it's made of the rocks and soil that the glacier has been pushing along, it looks like a big ridge of material left behind by a bulldozer. Similar ridges are deposited along the sides of glaciers. These mounds of material are called moraines.

The other major type of glacial deposit is outwash. **Outwash** is deposited from the glacier's melted ice. This meltwater carries sediments and deposits them much like a river does. For example, one type of outwash deposit

Science and WRITING

An erratic is a rock fragment deposited by a glacier. The word *erratic* comes form the Latin word *errare,* which means "to wander." Research how erratics are eroded and deposited by glaciers. Then, write a poem about the "life" of an erratic.

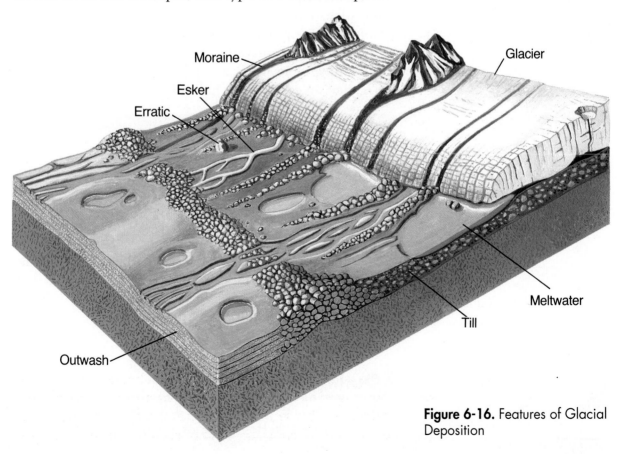

Figure 6-16. Features of Glacial Deposition

Figure 6-17. A *U*-shaped valley formed by a glacier looks much different than a valley cut by a river.

is an alluvial fan made of sediments eroded by the glacier. It forms when a stream of meltwater drops sand and gravel in front of the glacier.

Another type of outwash deposit looks like a long winding ridge. This deposit forms beneath a melting glacier. Meltwater forms rivers within the ice. These rivers carry sand and gravel and deposit them within their channels. When the glacier melts, a winding ridge of sand and gravel, called an esker, is left behind.

SECTION REVIEW

1. How does the expansion of water when it freezes result in plucking?
2. How do striations form?
3. Explain how till and outwash are different. Which one is deposited directly from ice? Which is deposited from meltwater?
4. **Apply:** Suppose you find a large boulder in the middle of a field in Indiana. Later, you find out that it's a type of rock normally found in Canada but not in Indiana. Give one explanation of how it got there.

Skill Builder

☑ Outlining

Make an outline of Section 6-4. If you need help, refer to Outlining in the **Skill Handbook** on page 681.

ACTIVITY 6-1
Glacial Erosion

Problem: *How do valley glaciers affect the surface?*

Materials

- stream table with sand
- pail
- ice block containing sand, clay, and gravel
- wood block
- metric ruler
- overhead light source with reflector

Procedure

1. Set up the stream table as shown.
2. Make a river channel. Measure and record its width and depth. Draw a sketch that includes these measurements.
3. Position the light source so that the light shines on the stream bed as shown.

4. Place the ice block in the river channel at the upper end of the stream table.
5. Gently push the "glacier" along the river channel until it's halfway between the top and bottom of the stream table and is positioned directly under the light.
6. Turn on the light and allow the ice to melt. Observe and record what happens.
7. Measure and record the width and depth of the glacial channel. Draw a sketch of the channel and include these measurements.

Analyze

1. Explain how you can determine the direction from which a glacier traveled by considering the shape of the channel and location of deposits.

Conclude and Apply

2. Can you determine the direction of glacial movement from sediments deposited by meltwater? Explain.
3. How do valley glaciers affect the surface over which they move?

Data and Observations

	Width	Depth	Observations
River			
Glacier			

6-5 Wind

New Science Words

deflation
abrasion
loess

Objectives

▶ Explain how wind causes deflation and abrasion.
▶ Discuss how loess and dunes form.

Wind Erosion

Wind erodes sediments in two ways—by deflation and by abrasion. Both types occur over all of Earth's land surface. However, they are most common in deserts, beaches, and plowed fields. In these places, the sediments are exposed to the wind because there aren't many plants to protect them.

Wind easily picks up and moves small sediments such as clay, silt, and sand. Pebbles and boulders too heavy to move are left behind. This type of erosion is **deflation.**

a

Figure 6-18. Deflation produces airborne sediments (a) and leaves behind what is called *desert pavement* (b).

b

162 EROSION AND DEPOSITION

The second type of wind erosion is abrasion. It's similar to the action of a crew of restoration workers sandblasting a building. These workers use machines that spray a mixture of sand and water against a building. The blast of sand removes dirt from stone, concrete, or brick walls. It also polishes the building walls by breaking away small pieces and leaving an even, smooth finish. Wind is like a sandblasting machine at work.

Wind makes sand grains roll and skip along the ground. As the grains move along, they bump into other grains. The sand grains and the rocks they strike become pitted and polished when small fragments are broken off. This sandblasting is a type of erosion called **abrasion.**

Deposition by Wind

What do you think happens to the sediments that are blown away when deflation and abrasion occur? Eventually, they are deposited. These windblown deposits form several types of landforms.

Figure 6-19. Egypt's desert winds, carrying sand-sized sediments, have abraded this sculpture of a sphinx.

Define deflation and abrasion.

Science and WRITING

Pretend you are a radio news reporter during the great dust storms in the Dust Bowl of the 1930's. Research the cause of the Dust Bowl and the effects on the land and people. Then, give a report to your class as if you were broadcasting on the radio.

One of the largest deposits of windblown sediments in the world is near the Mississippi River. The small sediments in this deposit were carried by strong winds that blew from the continental glaciers that once covered the northern United States and Canada. When the sediments finally settled, they fell onto hilltops and into valleys. Once there, the particles were packed together, creating a thick deposit known as **loess** (LES).

Loess is as fine as talcum powder. Many of the farmlands of the midwestern United States are on the fertile soils that have evolved from loess deposits. Loess is also found in China, where the sand and silt blow in from the Gobi and Ordos deserts.

What happens when wind blows sediments against an obstacle such as a rock or a clump of vegetation? The sediments settle behind the obstacle. More and more

PROBLEM SOLVING

A Trip across the Desert

Emmanuel and Jason had been best friends for years. But two years ago Emmanuel moved to southern California with his family. One day Emmanuel's father announced he was taking a business trip

to their old hometown, where Jason still lived. When his father said he could come with him, Emmanuel was excited at the prospect of seeing Jason again.

Soon, Emmanuel and his father were on their way. As they crossed the desert of the southwestern United States, Emmanuel noticed large rocks had been piled up at the bases of utility poles. Rocks had also been stacked up along the bases of some houses. His father said the rocks had been put there by people. Emmanuel also noticed that sand dunes were forming on parts of the highway. However, where fences had been built along the highways, no sand dunes formed.

Think Critically: Why had people piled rocks at the bases of poles and houses? How did fences help control the natural deposition of sand on the desert highways?

sediments build up and eventually a dune is formed. Dunes are the most common wind deposits and are usually composed of sand. These sand dunes form in deserts and beaches where sand is abundant. They are constantly changing and moving as wind erodes them.

When dunes and loess form, the landscape is changed. Wind, like gravity, running water, and glaciers, shapes the land as it erodes sediments. But the new landforms created by these agents of erosion are themselves being eroded. Erosion and deposition are part of a cycle of change that constantly shapes and reshapes the land around us.

Figure 6-20. Sand dunes typically have a gentle slope on one side and a steep slope on the other side.

EcoTip

Don't disturb grass or other plants on beach sand dunes. These plants prevent excessive beach erosion by slowing running water and by holding the sediments together with their roots.

SECTION REVIEW

1. How does deflation happen? What is abrasion?
2. How do loess deposits form?
3. **Apply:** You notice that snow is piling up behind a fence outside your apartment building. The wind is blowing strong but it's depositing snow when it comes to the fence. Why?

☑ Sequencing

Skill Builder

Sequence the following events that describe how a sand dune forms. If you need help, refer to Sequencing in the **Skill Handbook** on page 680.
- a. Grains collect to form a mound.
- b. Wind blows sand grains until they hit an obstacle.
- c. Wind blows over an area and causes deflation.
- d. Vegetation grows on the dune.

ACTIVITY 6-2
Wind Erosion

Problem: Which factors affect wind erosion of different materials?

Materials

- goggles
- flat pans (5)
- 1250 mL fine sand
- 1000 mL clay
- 250 mL gravel
- hair dryer
- protractor
- sprinkling can
- water
- cardboard sheet
- metric ruler

Procedure

1. Put 500 mL sand into pans A and B. Put 500 mL clay into C and D. Mix 250 mL sand and 250 mL gravel and put mixture into pan E.
2. Use the sprinkling can to dampen the material in pans A and C.
3. Hold the hair dryer 10 cm from pan A at an angle of 45°. Tape the cardboard to the other end of the pan. Direct a stream of air onto the pan for 1 minute. **CAUTION:** *Wear your goggles.* Record in your table every effect of the air that you observe.
4. Repeat Step 3 for pans B, C, D, and E.
5. Smooth out the "soil" in each pan.

6. Change the angle of the hair dryer to 10°. Repeat Step 3 for all pans using this new angle. Record all observations. **CAUTION:** *Wear your goggles.*
7. Smooth out the "soil" in each pan.
8. Repeat Steps 3 through 6 for all pans from a distance of 20 cm. Hold the hair dryer at an angle of 45°. (The distance of the hair dryer to the pan represents the force.) **CAUTION:** *Wear your goggles.* You may need to redampen the "soil" in pans A and C before completing this step. Record your results in the table.

Data and Observations

Pan	10cm		20cm	
	45°	**10°**	**45°**	**10°**
A				
B				
C				
D				
E				

Analyze

1. How do dry sand and clay react to the wind?
2. How does the addition of gravel to the sand affect its reaction to the wind?

Conclude and Apply

3. How does the change in force (distance of hair dryer to pan) affect movement of sediment grains? The angle of the wind?
4. Is wind a more effective erosional agent in wet or dry climates? Which pans give evidence to support your answer?

CHAPTER
REVIEW

6-1: Gravity

1. Erosion is the process that moves weathered sediments. Deposition occurs when an agent of erosion can no longer transport its load.
2. Slump, creep, rockslides, and mudflows are all mass movements.

6-2: Running Water

1. Rill and gully erosion create stream channels on slopes. Large canyons can eventually evolve from gully erosion. Sheet erosion occurs outside of a stream channel.
2. Alluvial fans and deltas are triangular-shaped deposits that form when water loses energy of motion.

6-3: Science and Society: Developing Land Prone to Erosion

1. Increasing slopes and removing vegetation increase erosion.
2. Vegetation, terraces, and retaining walls can reduce erosion on slopes.

6-4: Glaciers

1. Plucking adds rock and soil to a glacier's sides and bottom as water freezes and thaws in surrounding rocks.
2. Striations are formed when bedrock is gouged by rock fragments being transported by a glacier.
3. Till is a jumble of sediments deposited directly from glacial ice and snow. Outwash is glacial debris deposited by melted ice.

6-5: Wind

1. Deflation occurs when wind erodes only small-sized sediments and pebbles and boulders are left behind. The pitting and polishing of rocks and sediments by windblown sediments is called abrasion.
2. Deposits of fine-grained particles that are tightly packed are called loess. Dunes begin to form when windblown sediments pile up behind an obstacle.

KEY SCIENCE WORDS

a. abrasion
b. alluvial fan
c. creep
d. deflation
e. delta
f. deposition
g. erosion
h. glacier
i. gully erosion
j. loess
k. outwash
l. plucking
m. rill erosion
n. sheet erosion
o. slump
p. terraces
q. till

UNDERSTANDING VOCABULARY

Match each phrase with the correct term from the list of Key Science Words.

1. process of moving weathered sediments
2. slow movement of sediments downhill because of freezing and thawing
3. steplike cuts in the side of a slope
4. mass movement in which materials move as one large mass
5. erosion caused by freezing and thawing of glacial ice
6. wind erosion that leaves large sediments
7. mixture of rocks and sediments deposited by glacial snow and ice
8. sediments deposited by glacial meltwater
9. erosion caused by natural sandblasting
10. thick, densely packed deposits of dust

CHAPTER
REVIEW

CHECKING CONCEPTS

Choose the word or phrase that completes the sentence or answers the question.

1. Which of the following is not a type of mass movement?
   - **a.** abrasion
   - **b.** creep
   - **c.** slump
   - **d.** mudflow

2. _____ is not an agent of erosion.
   - **a.** Gravity
   - **b.** A rockslide
   - **c.** A glacier
   - **d.** Wind

3. Which of these is not a type of erosion by water?
   - **a.** rill erosion
   - **b.** abrasion
   - **c.** sheet erosion
   - **d.** plucking

4. _____ reduces erosion.
   - **a.** Planting vegetation
   - **b.** Building a wall
   - **c.** Making terraces
   - **d.** All of these

5. A mass of snow and ice in motion is a(n) _____.
   - **a.** loess deposit
   - **b.** glacier
   - **c.** outwash
   - **d.** abrasion

6. _____ glaciers are found in Greenland.
   - **a.** U-shaped
   - **b.** Till
   - **c.** Outwash
   - **d.** None of these

7. Glacial valleys are _____.
   - **a.** V-shaped
   - **b.** L-shaped
   - **c.** U-shaped
   - **d.** None of these

8. Glaciers have changed Earth by _____.
   - **a.** erosion
   - **b.** plucking
   - **c.** deposition
   - **d.** all of these

9. Wind erosion in which pebbles and boulders are left behind is called _____.
   - **a.** deflation
   - **b.** loess
   - **c.** abrasion
   - **d.** sandblasting

10. A(n)_____ is a bowl-shaped erosional feature formed by glacial plucking.
    - **a.** striation
    - **b.** esker
    - **c.** cirque
    - **d.** moraine

UNDERSTANDING CONCEPTS

Complete each sentence.

11. _____ is the slowest type of mass movement.
12. Water _____ the chances of mass movement on a slope.
13. Deltas differ from alluvial fans because deltas are deposited in _____.
14. Building by people often _____ erosion.
15. A(n) _____ is a long, winding ridge formed by deposits from outwash.

THINK AND WRITE CRITICALLY

16. Discuss the causes and effects of slumping.
17. Explain how a river carries its load of sediments.
18. Compare and contrast continental and valley glaciers.
19. How does the deposition of till differ from the deposition of outwash?
20. Arrange these sediments according to size from smallest to largest: boulders, clay, sand, pebbles, and silt. (HINT: Refer to Table 4-2 in Chapter 4.)

21. How can striations give information about the direction of movement of a glacier?
22. How effective would a retaining wall made of fine wire mesh be against erosion?
23. Sand dunes often migrate. What can be done to prevent the migration of beach dunes?
24. Scientists have found evidence of movement of ice within a glacier. Explain how this may occur. (HINT: Recall how putty-like ice forms at the base of a glacier.)
25. Often the front end of a valley glacier is at a lower elevation than the tail end. How does this explain melting at its front end while snow is still accumulating at its tail end?

MORE SKILL BUILDERS

If you need help, refer to the Skill Handbook.

1. **Making and Using Tables:** Make a table that contrasts rockslides and mudflows.
2. **Designing an Experiment:** Explain how you could test the effect of glacial thickness on a glacier's ability to erode.
3. **Concept Mapping:** Copy and complete the cycle map to show how sediments form from and result in sedimentary rocks.

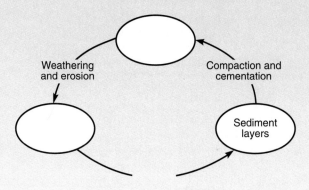

4. **Hypothesizing:** Hypothesize why most of the silt in the Mississippi Delta is found farther out to sea than the sand-sized particles.
5. **Interpreting Scientific Illustrations:** Look at the map of Ohio below. In which part of Ohio would you find erosion and deposition caused by glaciers of the last ice age? How would you expect the terrains to differ throughout the state?

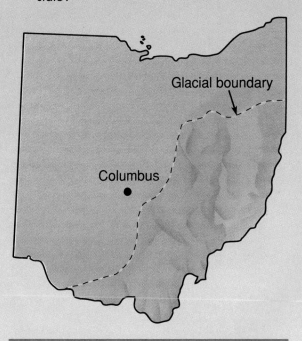

PROJECTS

1. Design an experiment to study the effects of a thin layer of oil on the ability of wind to erode sand.
2. Obtain a map of your area and find the local streams that drain into a major river in the area. Compute the area in square kilometers that is eroded by the main river and the smaller streams.

You've probably seen pictures of a river like this one. What determines the direction a river takes? Does the surface of the land have any effect on the water?

FIND OUT!

Do this activity to find out about water systems.

Place a piece of waxed paper on top of a piece of cardboard. Then, using eye droppers, place water droplets onto the waxed paper as close as you can without having them touch. Next, gently tip the cardboard and observe what happens. Repeat the procedure, using cardboard covered with a paper towel instead of waxed paper. What happens to the water droplets on the waxed paper when the cardboard is tilted? What differences are there between the two types of surfaces? How could the surface of Earth affect how water flows?

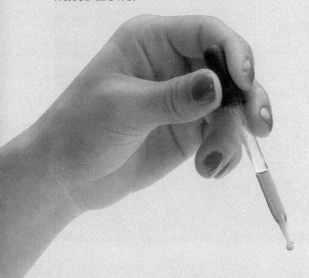

Gearing Up
Previewing the Chapter

Use this outline to help you focus on important ideas in this chapter.

Section 7-1   Water on Earth
► The Water Planet
► The Water Cycle
► Runoff

Section 7-2   Development of River Systems
► River System Development
► Stages of Stream Development

Section 7-3   The Action of Groundwater
► Groundwater Systems
► Wells and Springs
► Hot Springs and Geysers
► Caves and Sinkholes

Section 7-4   Science and Society
Water Wars
► Water As a Resource
► Water Diversion

Previewing Science Skills
► In the **Skill Builders,** you will sequence, compare and contrast, and make a concept map.
► In the **Activities,** you will observe and record data.
► In the **MINI-Labs,** you will make a model, observe and infer, and record observations.

What's next?

In Chapter 6, you learned that water is the primary agent of erosion. You just saw in the Find Out activity some things that can happen to water on Earth's surface. In this chapter, you'll learn more about how water interacts with Earth.

Water on Earth

New Science Words

hydrosphere
water cycle
runoff

Objectives

▶ Describe the water cycle.
▶ Explain what happens to water that doesn't soak into the ground or evaporate.
▶ List three factors that affect runoff.

The Water Planet

Earth is very different from the other planets in the solar system. Unlike the other planets, Earth's surface is about 70 percent covered with water. Most of this water is in the oceans. But water can also be found in lakes, streams, rivers, underground, and frozen in glaciers. All the water on Earth's surface is called the **hydrosphere**. Even though there's a lot of water on Earth, 97 percent of it is salt water. Of the remaining three percent, two-thirds of it is frozen in ice caps at the north and south poles. Therefore, only

Figure 7-1. Most of the water in the hydrosphere is salt water (a). Earth's surface is about 70 percent water (b).

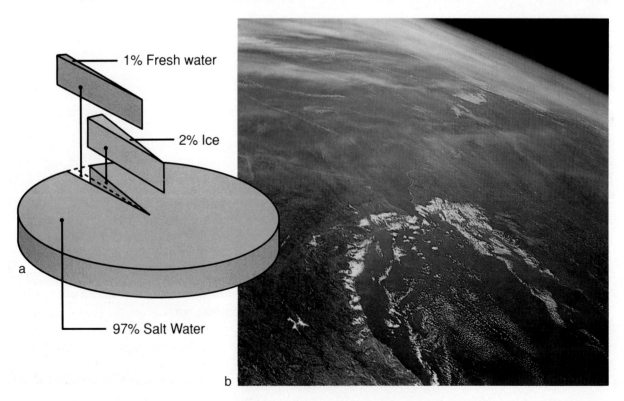

1% Fresh water

2% Ice

a

97% Salt Water

b

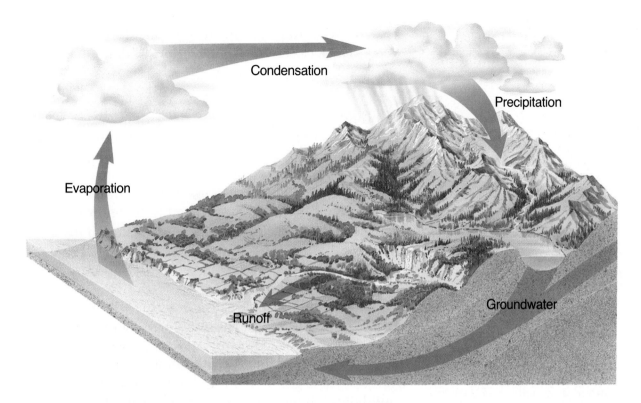

Condensation

Precipitation

Evaporation

Runoff

Groundwater

Figure 7-2. Water moves from Earth to the atmosphere and back to Earth again in the water cycle.

about one percent of the water in the hydrosphere is water we can drink and use to grow food.

The Water Cycle

Think back to the last time you experienced a hard rain. You could see it forming puddles on the grass and in the streets. Where did the water go after it rained? How did the water get in the atmosphere in the first place?

Water constantly moves between the atmosphere and Earth in the **water cycle,** as seen in Figure 7-2. The sun provides the energy for the water cycle. Heat from the sun causes water to change to a gas called water vapor. This process is called evaporation. Water evaporates from lakes, streams, and oceans and rises into Earth's atmosphere.

In the next step of the water cycle, water vapor changes back into a liquid in the atmosphere. This process is called condensation and forms clouds. Clouds are made of tiny droplets of water that have condensed.

The third step in the water cycle is precipitation. When the clouds can no longer hold the condensed water vapor, it falls back to Earth as precipitation such as rain. Rain can do three things when it falls to Earth. It either soaks into the ground, runs along the ground to someplace

MINI-Lab

How does the water cycle work?
Pour 2 cm of water into a large beaker. Place a small beaker in the center of the large beaker. Cover the large beaker loosely with plastic wrap and seal it with a rubber band. Put a marble in the middle of the plastic wrap. Place the beaker in direct sunlight for several hours. How does this simulate the water cycle?

else, or evaporates to repeat the cycle. In this chapter, you will look closely at what water does while it is on Earth.

Runoff

Water that doesn't soak into the ground or evaporate flows across Earth's surface and is called **runoff.** If you've ever spilled milk while pouring it, you've experienced something similar to runoff. You can picture it in your mind. You start pouring yourself a glass of milk, and it overflows and spills all over the table. Then, before you can grab a towel to clean up the mess, it runs off the table onto the floor. This is similar to rainwater that doesn't soak into the ground or evaporate. It runs along the ground and eventually enters streams.

But what factors determine whether rain soaks into the ground or runs off? The amount of rain and the time span over which it falls are two factors that affect the amount of runoff. Light rain falling over several hours will probably have time to soak into the ground. Heavy rain falling in just an hour or so will run off because it doesn't have time to soak in.

Another factor that affects the amount of runoff is the slope of the land. Gentle slopes and flat areas hold water

What happens to water that doesn't soak into the ground or evaporate?

Figure 7-3. Runoff is less likely to occur where there is vegetation (a). Runoff is more likely to occur where there is little or no vegetation (b).

a

b

Figure 7-4. Runoff can cause erosion.

EcoTip

Adopt a stream or pond. Keep it clean by picking up trash along the banks. Recycle the trash you collect.

in place until it has a chance to evaporate or sink into the ground. On steep slopes, however, water runs off before these things can happen.

The amount of vegetation, such as grass, also affects the amount of runoff. Just like milk running off the table, water will tend to run off smooth surfaces with little or no vegetation. Plants and their roots act like sponges to soak up and hold water. By slowing down runoff, plants and roots help prevent the erosion of soil.

How do plants slow down runoff?

Runoff is just one part of the water cycle. This water will pass through many stages on its trip through the cycle. In the next stage, runoff enters streams and rivers and becomes a part of a water system, which you will learn about in Section 7-2.

SECTION REVIEW

1. What does the sun do in the water cycle?
2. What are three things water can do on Earth's surface?
3. What are three factors that affect runoff?
4. **Apply:** How does the water cycle keep river systems full of water?

☑ **Sequencing**

Sequence the events in the water cycle beginning with rain falling to Earth. If you need help, refer to Sequencing in the **Skill Handbook** on page 680.

Skill Builder

Development of River Systems

New Science Words

drainage basin
meander
floodplain

Objectives

▶ Describe how a river system is like a tree.
▶ Explain what a drainage basin is.
▶ Discuss the three different stages of river development.

River System Development

Do you know of a stream in your neighborhood or town? Maybe you've been fishing or swimming in that stream. Each day, thousands of liters of water flow through your neighborhood or town in that stream. But just where does that water come from?

The stream in your neighborhood is really a part of a river system. The water in the stream came from smaller channels located upstream. Just as a tree is a system

Figure 7-5. The system of twigs, branches, and a trunk that make up a tree (a) is similar to a river system (b).

a

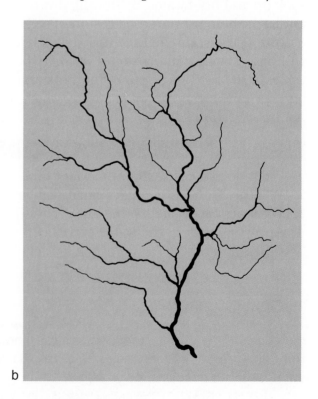

b

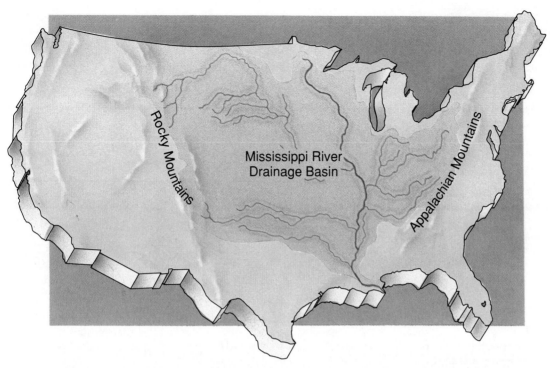

Rocky Mountains

Mississippi River
Drainage Basin

Appalachian Mountains

containing stems, twigs, branches, and a trunk, a river system also has many parts. Water runs off of the ground and enters small streams. Where small streams join, a larger stream forms. Finally, where streams merge, a larger body of water called a river forms.

The land area from which a stream gets its water is called a **drainage basin.** A drainage basin can be compared to a bathtub. Water that collects in a bathtub flows toward the drain. Likewise, all of the water in a river system eventually flows to one location—the main river. The largest drainage basin in the United States is the Mississippi River drainage basin. Most of the rain that falls between the Rocky Mountains and the Appalachian Mountains drains into the Missouri and Ohio rivers. These rivers and others flow into the Mississippi River, as seen in Figure 7-6.

Figure 7-6. Water from a large portion of the United States drains into the Mississippi River.

Where does rain that falls between the Rocky Mountains and the Appalachian Mountains go?

Stages of Stream Development

There are many different types of streams. Some are narrow and swift-moving, and others are very wide and slow-moving. Streams differ because they are in different stages of development. These stages depend on the slope of the ground over which the stream flows. Streams are classified as young, mature, or old.

Figure 7-7. The characteristics of a young stream can be seen in the diagram and in the photo.

No floodplain

Rapids

A stream that flows swiftly through a steep valley and has steep sides is a young stream. These streams are found in mountainous or hilly regions. The water is flowing rapidly down a steep slope. A young stream may have white water rapids and waterfalls. Because the water is flowing rapidly downhill, it has a high level of energy and erodes the stream bottom more than its sides.

PROBLEM SOLVING

Washed Out

David stared at the cloudy sky. He knew from weather reports that northern areas of the state had received heavy rain.

However, his hometown had not received a drop. He hoped the rain would come and go by the weekend so the baseball game would not be rained out. His team was in the playoffs, and the day of the big game was almost here.

It never did rain that week. Saturday morning arrived and David had hardly slept. He arrived at the field early and could not believe his eyes. The playing field next to the river was underwater.

Think Critically: How could the field be flooded if it didn't rain?

The next stage in the development of a stream is the mature stage. A curving stream that flows down a gradual slope and erodes its sides is a mature stream. A mature stream flows less swiftly through its valley. Most of the rocks in the stream bed that cause waterfalls and rapids have been eroded away.

The erosional energy of a mature stream is no longer concentrated on its bottom. Now, the stream starts to erode its sides, developing curves. These curves form because the speed of the water varies throughout the width of a channel. Water in shallow areas of a stream is slowed down by the friction created by the bottom of the river. In deep areas, less of the water comes in contact with the bottom. This means that deep water has less friction with the bottom of the stream and therefore flows faster.

This faster moving water erodes the side of the stream where the current is strongest, forming curves. A curve that forms in this way is called a **meander.** Figure 7-8 shows what a meandering stream looks like from the air.

When a stream enters its mature stage and starts to meander, it erodes the valley walls and widens the valley floor. This broad, flat valley floor carved by a meandering stream is called a **floodplain.** When a stream floods, it often covers a part of or the whole floodplain.

Why does water flow faster in an area of deeper water?

Figure 7-8. The characteristics of a mature stream can be seen in the diagram and in the photo.

Meandering stream

Floodplain

ACTIVITY 7-1
Stream Velocity

Problem: *How does the slope of a stream affect its velocity and load?*

Materials

- stream table
- plastic pails (2)
- rubber tubing
- meterstick
- wooden blocks (2)
- stopwatch
- small cork
- sand to fill stream table
- books (2)
- plastic sheet
- water

Procedure

1. Arrange the stream table as shown.
2. Make a stream channel down the center of the sand so that it ends at the short length of rubber tubing.
3. Measure and record the length of the stream channel.
4. Fill the pail at the top of the table with water. Set up a siphon using a long piece of rubber tubing.

5. Put one block of wood under the upper end of the stream table.
6. Put the cork at the upper end of the stream bed. Start the water into the stream bed.
7. Record the time the cork takes to travel the length of the stream channel.
8. Observe and record whether or not the water carries material other than the cork downstream. Stop the flow of water. Allow excess water to drain from the stream table.
9. Repeat the procedure in Steps 6-8 two more times. Record the average flow time in a table.
10. Stack another block on top of the first at the upper end of the stream table.
11. Repeat Steps 6, 7, 8, and 9 and record all observations in a table.

Data and Observations

Slope	Stream length	Flow time	Observations
one block			
two blocks			

Analyze

1. Calculate the velocity of the stream for a slope of one block and for a slope of two blocks.

$$\text{velocity} = \frac{\text{distance}}{\text{time}}$$

2. Did your stream meander?

Conclude and Apply

3. How does the increase in slope affect the amount of sediment the stream carries?
4. What was the purpose of the cork?
5. How does the velocity of the stream change when you increase the slope?

Well developed meanders

Very wide floodplain

Figure 7-9. The characteristics of an old stream can be seen in the diagram and in the photo.

The last stage in the development of a stream is the old stage. An old stream flows very slowly through a very broad, flat floodplain that it has carved. A river in this stage erodes its sides mostly causing changes in its meanders. The lower Mississippi River is a river in the old stage of development.

River systems usually contain streams in all stages of development. At the outer edges of a river system, you find white water streams moving swiftly down mountains and hills. At the bottom of mountains and hills, you find streams that are starting to meander and are in the mature stage of development. These streams meet at the lowest point in the drainage basin to form a major river, which is usually in the old stage of development.

What kind of stream is found at the bottoms of hills and mountains?

SECTION REVIEW

1. Why can a river be described as a system?
2. What is a drainage basin?
3. In which stage of development is a stream that erodes its sides?
4. **Apply:** How is a stream's rate of flow related to the amount of erosion it causes?

☑ Concept Mapping

Make an events chain concept map showing the stages of stream development. Use the following words or phrases: *old stream, mature stream, young stream, slow-moving, meanders, waterfalls.* If you need help, refer to Concept Mapping in the **Skill Handbook** on page 688.

Skill Builder

The Action of Groundwater

New Science Words

groundwater
permeable
impermeable
aquifer
zone of saturation
water table
artesian well
spring
hot spring
geyser
cave

Objectives

▶ Explain what happens to water when it soaks into the ground.
▶ Describe the relationship between the water table and springs.
▶ Explain the cause of geysers and how caves form.

Groundwater Systems

What would have happened if the spilled milk from Section 7-1 had run off the table onto a carpeted floor? It would have quickly soaked into the carpet. Water that falls on Earth can also soak into the ground.

But what happens to water then? Water that soaks into the ground becomes a part of a system, just as water that stays above ground becomes a part of a river system. You already know that soil is made up of many small rock fragments and that there is weathered rock beneath the soil. Between these fragments and pieces of weathered rock are spaces called pores. Water that soaks into the ground collects in these pores and becomes part of what is called **groundwater.**

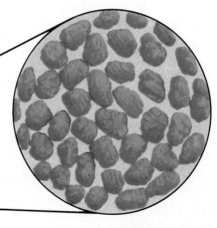

Figure 7-10. Water disappears into soil because it has pore spaces.

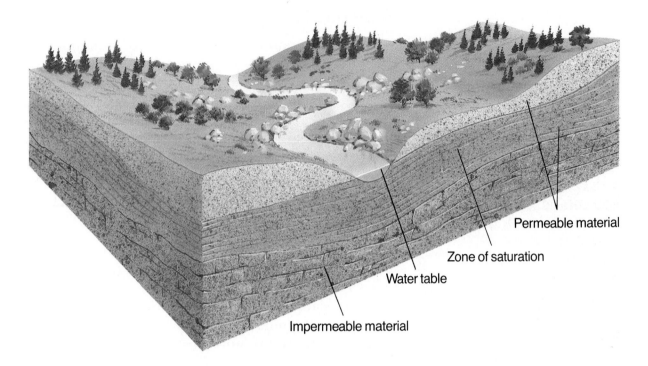

Permeable material

Zone of saturation

Water table

Impermeable material

The groundwater system is similar to a river system. However, instead of having channels that connect different parts of the drainage basin, the groundwater system has connecting pores. Some soils and rock have connecting pores, as shown in Figure 7-10, that water can move through. Soils and rock are **permeable** if water can pass through them this way. Sandstone is a common permeable rock.

Soil or rock that has many large connected pores is very permeable. Water can pass through it easily. Soil or rock that has few or small pores is less permeable because water can't easily pass through. Some material, such as clay, has very small pores or no pores at all. Water can't pass through this **impermeable** material.

How deep into Earth's crust do you suppose groundwater can go? That depends on the permeability of the soil and rock. Groundwater will keep going to lower elevations until it reaches a layer of impermeable rock. When this happens, the impermeable rock acts like a dam and the water can't move down any deeper. So, it begins filling up the pores in the rocks above the impermeable layer. A layer of permeable rock that transmits water freely is an **aquifer.** The area where all of the pores in the rock are completely filled with water is the **zone of saturation.** The upper surface of this zone is the **water table.**

Figure 7-11. A stream's surface is the level of the water table in that area.

Science and MATH

In an experiment, you find that 100 mL of gravel (Total Volume) can hold 31 mL (Volume of Pore Spaces, VPS) of water. Calculate the percentage of pore space (porosity) using the following formula.

$$\frac{VPS}{Total\ Volume} \times 100 = \%\ Porosity$$

Wells and Springs

What's so important about the zone of saturation and the water table? Many people get drinking water from groundwater in the zone of saturation. Water wells are drilled down into the zone of saturation. Water flows into the well, and a pump brings it to the surface. A well must go down at least past the water table to reach water. Sometimes during dry seasons, a well goes dry because the water table drops. Having too many wells in one area can also cause the water table to drop. This happens because more water is taken out of the ground than can be replaced by rain.

There is another type of well that doesn't need a pump to bring water to the surface. An **artesian** (ar TEE zhun) **well** is a well in which water under pressure rises to the surface. Artesian wells are less common than other wells because of the unique conditions they require.

An artesian well requires a sloping aquifer located between two impermeable layers. Water must be able to enter the aquifer at the high part of the sloping aquifer. Water in the higher part of the aquifer puts pressure on the water in the lower part. If a well is drilled into the lower part of the aquifer, the pressurized water will come to the surface. Sometimes there is enough pressure to force the water into the air, forming a fountain.

In some places, the water table meets Earth's surface. When this happens, water flows out and forms a **spring.** Springs can be found on hillsides or any other place where the water table is exposed at the surface. Springs can be used as a source of fresh water.

Figure 7-12. Water is forced out of the artesian well (b) because of pressure applied by the water in the aquifer at (a) above the well.

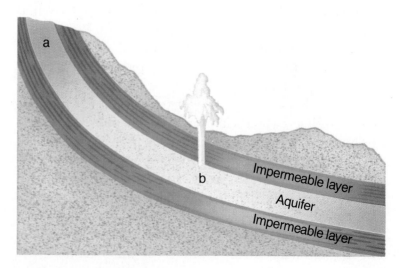

ACTIVITY 7-2
Artesian Wells

Problem: How does an artesian well work?

Materials

- 30-cm plastic or rubber tube
- funnel
- protractor
- water
- scissors
- sink
- beaker
- tape

Procedure

1. Use the scissors to cut a hole 2 mm in diameter in the tube 2 cm from the end.
2. Put tape over the end nearest the hole you just made.
3. Copy the Data and Observations table.
4. Place the tube in the sink at a 45° angle as shown below. Put the end with the 2-mm hole down first.
5. Place a funnel into the top end and use a beaker to pour water in the tube in a steady stream.

6. Be careful not to pour water down the outsides of the tube.
7. Observe what happens at the 2-mm hole. Record your observations in the table.
8. Reduce the angle that you hold the tube to 20°. Record what happens at the hole.
9. Repeat Steps 3-6 for angles of 30° and 40°. Record your observations.
10. Increase the angle that you hold the tube to 60°. Record what happens at the hole.

Analyze

1. Which angle allowed the greatest flow of water out of the hole? Which allowed the least?

Conclude and Apply

2. Compare the inside of the tube to an aquifer. How are they similar?
3. Compare the rubber sides of the tube to impermeable rock. How are they similar?
4. What does the 2-mm hole represent?

Data and Observations

Angle	Observations
45°	
20°	
30°	
40°	
60°	

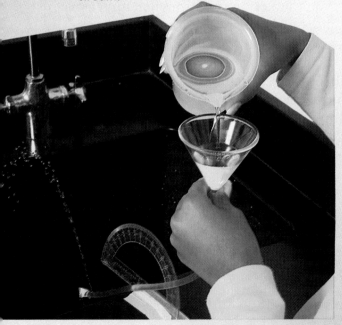

Science and READING

Read an article about geothermal energy and draw a diagram explaining how it works. Also, list the limitations of this energy source.

Hot Springs and Geysers

The water from most springs is cold. But in some places, groundwater is heated and comes to the surface as a **hot spring.** The groundwater is heated by rocks that come in contact with molten material under Earth's surface.

One of these places where groundwater is heated is Yellowstone National Park in Wyoming. In Yellowstone, there are hot springs and geysers. A **geyser** is a hot spring that erupts periodically, shooting water and steam into the air. Water is heated to very high temperatures, causing it to expand underground. This expanding water forces some of it out of the ground, taking the pressure off of the remaining water. The remaining water boils quickly, with much of it turning to steam. The steam shoots out of the opening like steam out of a tea kettle, forcing the remaining water out with it. Yellowstone's famous geyser, Old Faithful, shoots about 45 000 liters of water and steam into the air once each hour.

Caves and Sinkholes

Just as water is the most powerful agent of erosion on Earth's surface, it can also have a great effect underground. As mentioned in Chapter 5, when water mixes with carbon dioxide in the air, it forms a weak acid. This carbonic acid eventually becomes groundwater. One type of rock that is easily dissolved by this acid is limestone. As this acidic groundwater moves through natural cracks in limestone, it dissolves the rock. Gradually, the cracks in the limestone are enlarged until an underground opening called a **cave** is formed.

You've probably seen a picture of the inside of a cave, or perhaps you've visited one. Groundwater not only dissolves limestone to make caves, but it also can make spectacular deposits on the insides of caves. The long, pointed objects hanging from the roof of the cave in Figure 7-14 are stalactites.

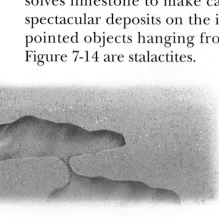

Figure 7-13. After a geyser erupts, water runs back into the underground openings where it is heated and erupts again.

Water often drips slowly from cracks in the cave walls and ceilings. This water contains calcite dissolved from the limestone. If this water evaporates while hanging from the roof of a cave, a deposit of calcite is left behind. Stalactites form when this process happens over and over. Where drops of water fall to the floor of the cave, a stalagmite forms. Sometimes a stalactite and a stalagmite grow together to form a column.

If underground rock is dissolved near the surface, a sinkhole may form. A sinkhole is a depression that forms when the roof of a cave collapses. You probably never thought that all these things could happen to water. You can see that this portion of the water cycle is very complex. When rain falls and becomes groundwater, it might dissolve a cave, erupt from a geyser, or be pumped from a well to be used at your house.

Figure 7-14. This large sinkhole in Florida caused major damage (a). Water containing dissolved calcite forms interesting features in caves. (b).

How do sinkholes form?

SECTION REVIEW

1. How does water enter the groundwater system?
2. What causes a geyser to erupt?
3. What is the difference between a stalagmite and a stalactite?
4. **Apply:** Explain how a well can go dry.

☑ **Comparing and Contrasting**

Compare and contrast wells, geysers, and hot springs. If you need help, refer to Comparing and Contrasting in the **Skill Handbook** on page 683.

Skill Builder

Water Wars

New Science Words

water diversion

Objectives

▶ Give examples of ways people use water.
▶ Explain why some communities must rely on water diversion methods for their water supply.
▶ Identify a problem caused by water diversion.

Why is it easy to underestimate the amount of water you use every day?

Water As a Resource

How much water do you use each day? An average person in the United States uses about 227 liters each day. That's equal to the amount of liquid in 678 soft drink cans. How could you possibly use that much water? Think about it. You use it whenever you shower, bathe, and flush the toilet. Also, you use a lot of water indirectly. Water is used in making paper, plastic, and metal products that you use, and to irrigate crops that become your food. You can see that you use a lot of water each day.

Just imagine how much water a whole community of people uses each day. Do you know where your town gets its water? Some towns use nearby rivers and lakes, or they have wells. But, many communities don't have enough water to supply all their needs. Where do they get their water?

Figure 7-15. Water is a resource that many people take for granted.

Figure 7-16. Reservoirs are constructed to hold water for when it is needed.

Water Diversion

Many towns are forced to get water from other locations. Dams and pipelines are used to divert water to other locations. When the natural flow of water is changed by people, it is called **water diversion.** Dams and pipelines have been used successfully in many places around the world. However, taking water from one location for another town leaves less water for the people at the original location.

T E C H N O L O G Y

Water Shortage in Florida?

The southern tip of Florida receives between 102 and 165 centimeters of rain per year. However, after evaporation and runoff, only one-fifth, or about 26 cm, of the rain seeps into the ground and shallow lakes. In addition to the loss of fresh water by natural processes, daily usage of water in some areas of southern Florida is about 6000 liters per person! This is a little over 14 times the national average.

In order to preserve and protect the much needed fresh water, a new technique has been implemented. Some farmers are now using purified sewage water to irrigate their crops. This water-cycling method is an alternative to irrigating crops with fresh water from wells.

Think Critically: What environmental factors contribute to a water shortage in Florida? What human factors contribute to the water shortage?

b

a

Figure 7-17. The ancient Romans constructed aqueducts (a) to carry water over long distances. Today, pipelines carry water over long distances in some places (b).

Water diversion is becoming a big issue. In some areas of the United States, individuals, communities, and even states have gone to court over water rights. As Earth's population continues to increase, more and more demands are placed on Earth's freshwater supply. With more people, water needed for industrial, agricultural, and recreational uses increases.

SECTION REVIEW

1. What are four ways that you use water each day?
2. Why must some communities rely on water diversion methods for their water supply?

SCIENCE & SOCIETY

You Decide!

Each year, more and more people move to the southern United States. As a result, a large and growing quantity of water is needed in an already dry climate. To solve this problem, some people would like to build a giant canal to divert water from the Great Lakes. However, if the lakes are slowly drained, their states will suffer economically. Industries, recreation, and agriculture will be affected. Do you think a canal should be built?

CHAPTER
REVIEW

7-1: Water on Earth

1. The water cycle is the movement of water between Earth and its atmosphere.

2. When water from the atmosphere doesn't soak into the ground or evaporate, it flows across Earth's surface as runoff.

3. The amount of runoff in an area depends on the amount of rain that falls and the time period over which it falls. Runoff is also affected by slope of the land and the amount of vegetation.

7-2: Development of River Systems

1. A river system can be compared to a tree whose "branches" include small streams. The main river can be compared to the tree trunk.

2. A drainage basin is the land area from which a river system gets its water.

3. Young streams flow swiftly through steep-sided valleys and erode the bottoms of their channels more than the sides. Mature streams erode the sides of their channels and form meanders. A stream in the old stage has less energy than a young stream because it moves very slowly. Broad, carved floodplains are common along old streams.

7-3: The Action of Groundwater

1. Water that soaks into the ground becomes part of an underground system called groundwater.

2. When the water table reaches Earth's surface, a spring forms.

3. Geysers are eruptions of steam and water caused by the heating of water underground. Caves form when water dissolves limestone.

7-4: Science and Society: Water Wars

1. People use water by drinking it, bathing, showering, and flushing the toilet.

2. Because many communities don't have enough water to meet their needs, they must divert water from other places.

3. Water diversion takes water away from other places that may need it.

KEY SCIENCE WORDS

a. **aquifer**
b. **artesian well**
c. **cave**
d. **drainage basin**
e. **floodplain**
f. **geyser**
g. **groundwater**
h. **hot spring**
i. **hydrosphere**
j. **impermeable**
k. **meander**
l. **permeable**
m. **runoff**
n. **spring**
o. **water cycle**
p. **water diversion**
q. **water table**
r. **zone of saturation**

UNDERSTANDING VOCABULARY

Match each phrase with the correct term from the list of Key Science Words.

1. water that flows over Earth's surface
2. land area drained by a river system
3. a curve in a stream channel
4. water that soaks into the ground
5. rocks through which fluids are unable to pass
6. the upper surface of the zone of saturation
7. hot springs that erupt
8. a large underground opening formed when limestone dissolves
9. the low flat part of a river valley
10. the changing of natural water flow by people

CHECKING CONCEPTS

Choose the word or phrase that completes the sentence or answers the question.

1. The movement of water between Earth and the air is the _____.
   - **a.** groundwater
   - **c.** water cycle
   - **b.** floodplain
   - **d.** drainage basin

2. _____ affects the runoff in an area.
   - **a.** Amount of rain
   - **c.** Slope of the land
   - **b.** Vegetation
   - **d.** All of these

3. A layer of rock that water flows through is a(n) _____.
   - **a.** aquifer
   - **c.** well
   - **b.** pore
   - **d.** artesian well

4. The network formed by a river and all the smaller streams that contribute to it is a _____.
   - **a.** water cycle
   - **c.** drainage basin
   - **b.** water table
   - **d.** zone of saturation

5. Soils through which fluids can easily flow are _____.
   - **a.** impermeable
   - **c.** saturated
   - **b.** geysers
   - **d.** permeable

6. Underground rocks completely filled with water belong to the _____.
   - **a.** zone of saturation
   - **c.** lower water table
   - **b.** limestone caves
   - **d.** water diversion

7. A(n) _____ forms when the water table is exposed at the surface.
   - **a.** meander
   - **c.** aquifer
   - **b.** spring
   - **d.** all of these

8. Heated groundwater that reaches Earth's surface is a(n) _____.
   - **a.** water table
   - **c.** aquifer
   - **b.** cave
   - **d.** hot spring

9. At the outer edge of a drainage basin, streams are in the _____ stage.
   - **a.** young
   - **c.** old
   - **b.** mature
   - **d.** none of these

10. Water rises in an artesian well because of _____.
    - **a.** a pump
    - **c.** gravity
    - **b.** none of these
    - **d.** pressure

UNDERSTANDING CONCEPTS

Complete each sentence.

11. When water containing dissolved calcite drips in a cave, a(n) _____ can form on the cave floor.

12. A V-shaped valley is typical of a river in the _____ stage of development.

13. When water mixes with carbon dioxide, _____ acid is formed.

14. Water in a shallow part of a stream is slowed by _____.

15. Water on Earth's surface makes up the _____.

THINK AND WRITE CRITICALLY

16. Would you expect more runoff from a parking lot or a backyard with the same slope? Explain.

17. Compare and contrast the valleys of young, mature, and old rivers.

18. Compare a river system to a groundwater system.

19. Explain the relationship among the zone of saturation, the water table, and an aquifer.

20. Sequence the major events in the water cycle.

21. Explain why the Mississippi River has meanders.

22. What determines whether a stream erodes its bottom or its sides?

23. Why would you be concerned if developers of a new housing project started drilling wells near your well?

24. If you had an artesian well, would the water come from a higher or lower elevation? Explain.

25. How is a tea kettle like a geyser?

MORE SKILL BUILDERS

If you need help, refer to the Skill Handbook.

1. Making and Using Tables: Use the table below to answer these questions. Which river has the highest flow? Which has the lowest flow rate? Which two rivers have nearly the same flow rate?

River	Waterflow (m³/sec)
Mississippi	17 500
Brahmaputra	19 800
La Plata	79 300
Ganges	18 700
Congo	39 600
Yangtze	21 800
Amazon	113 330

2. Interpreting Data: Compare the rates of flow of the Brahmaputra and the La Plata Rivers.

3. Making and Using Graphs: Make a bar graph showing the flow of the five slowest rivers listed in the table at left.

4. Outlining: Make an outline that explains the three stages of stream development.

5. Using Variables, Constants, and Controls: Explain how you could test the effect of slope on the amount of runoff produced.

PROJECTS

1. Use the map of North America in Appendix G to locate the source and mouth of the Mississippi River. Then, carefully outline the boundaries of the Mississippi drainage basin and compute its approximate area.

2. Research the topic of water diversion. Discover as many pros and cons of this technique of supplying water to places as you can. Choose a stance and then debate the topic with a classmate.

This astronaut is using a jet powered maneuvering unit outside the space shuttle during a space walk. It's hard to imagine what it would be like to view Earth from space. Astronauts can see the outlines of some land masses from space. How can you become familiar with views of Earth?

FIND OUT!

Do this simple activity to find out more about views of Earth.

Using a globe or a world map, first look for natural features such as rivers and lakes that you may have heard of before. Can you find the Amazon, the Ganges, or the Mississippi River? Next, look at the bodies of water on Earth. Where is the Indian Ocean, the Sea of Japan, and the Baltic Sea? Then try to identify the continents. Where is Australia, South America, and North America? Locate your country. Where is your home on this view of Earth?

Gearing Up

Previewing the Chapter

Use this outline to help you focus on important ideas in this chapter.

Section 8-1   Landforms
▶ Plains
▶ Plateaus
▶ Mountains

Section 8-2   Viewpoints
▶ Latitude and Longitude
▶ Earth Time

Section 8-3   Maps
▶ Map Projections
▶ Topographic Maps
▶ Map Scale and Legends

Section 8-4   Science and Society
Secret Maps
▶ Intentional Distortion of Maps
▶ Sea Beam

Previewing Science Skills

▶ In the **Skill Builders**, you will make a concept map, interpret a scientific illustration, and measure in SI.
▶ In the **Activities**, you will observe, measure, use numbers, and interpret data.
▶ In the **MINI-Labs**, you will interpret a scientific illustration and make a scientific illustration.

What's next?

Now that you've seen one view of Earth, you should be ready to explore some others. You'll first learn about some landscapes found on Earth's surface. Then you'll see how exact locations on Earth are found using longitude and latitude. Section 8-3 shows you how Earth's irregular surface can be captured on a topographic map.

Landforms

New Science Words

plains
plateaus
folded mountains
upwarped mountains
fault-block mountains
volcanic mountains

What is a landform?

Objectives

▶ Differentiate between plains and plateaus.
▶ Compare and contrast folded, upwarped, fault-block, and volcanic mountains.

Plains

There are a lot of interesting landforms around the world. A landform is a feature that makes up the shape of the land at Earth's surface. Three basic types of landforms are plains, plateaus, and mountains.

What do you think of when you hear the word *plains*? You might think of endless flat fields of wheat or grass. That's true, many plains are used to grow crops. **Plains** are large, relatively flat areas that cover much of the United States. About one-half of all the land in the United States is plains.

Coastal Plains

Coastal plains are broad areas along coastlines that are called lowlands because of their low elevations. Elevation refers to distance above or below sea level. Sea level has zero elevation. The Atlantic Coastal Plain stretches along the East Coast of the United States. This area is characterized by low rolling hills, swamps, and marshes. A marsh is grassy wetland, usually flooded with water.

Figure 8-1. The Florida Everglades is a marsh area on a coastal plain.

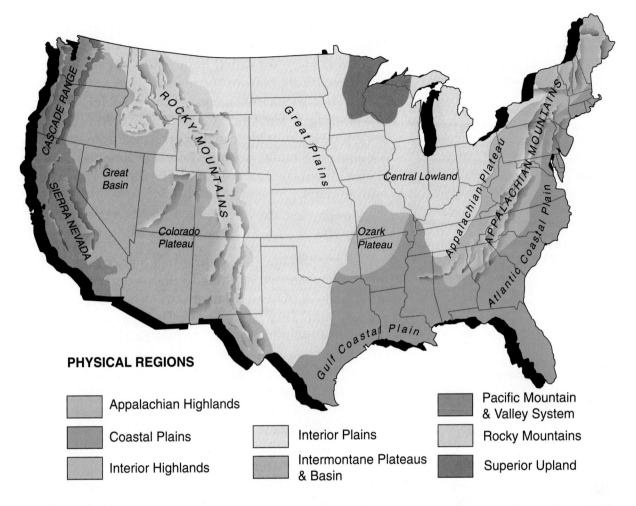

PHYSICAL REGIONS

Appalachian Highlands

Coastal Plains

Interior Highlands

Interior Plains

Intermontane Plateaus & Basin

Pacific Mountain & Valley System

Rocky Mountains

Superior Upland

Figure 8-2. The United States is made up of eight major types of landforms called physical regions.

If you hiked along this plain, you would realize it isn't perfectly flat. Many low hills and valleys have been carved by rivers. What do you suppose caused the Atlantic Coastal Plain to form? It formed as land emerged from the Atlantic Ocean during the last few million years.

Another coastal plain is the Gulf Coastal Plain. It includes the lowland in the southern United States that surrounds the Gulf of Mexico.

Interior Plains

A large portion of the center of the United States is called the interior plains. They extend from the Appalachian Mountains in the east, to the Rocky Mountains in the west, to the Gulf Coastal Plain in the south. The interior plains include the rolling hills of the Great Lakes area and the central lowland around the Missouri and Mississippi rivers.

What are the boundaries of the interior plains?

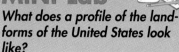
How are plateaus different from plains?

Figure 8-3. Rivers cut deep into the Colorado Plateau.

To the west of the Mississippi lowlands lie the Great Plains. The Great Plains are flat, grassy, dry plains with few trees. They are called high plains because of their elevation. It ranges from 350 meters above sea level at its eastern border to 1500 meters above sea level at its western boundary. The Great Plains are covered with nearly horizontal layers of loose materials eroded from the Rocky Mountains. Streams deposited these sediments that were eroded from the Rocky Mountains during the last few million years.

Plateaus

If you would like to explore some higher regions, you might be interested in going to the second basic type of landform—a plateau. **Plateaus** are relatively flat raised areas of land. They're areas of nearly horizontal rocks that have been uplifted by forces within Earth. They are different from plains in that they rise steeply from the land around them. A good example of a plateau in the United States is the Colorado Plateau that lies just west of the Rocky Mountains. Here, the Colorado River has cut deep into the rock layers of the plateau, forming the Grand Canyon. Because the Colorado Plateau is located in a very dry region, only a few river systems have developed on its surface. If you hiked around on this plateau, you'd see a desert landscape.

Mountains

Are plateaus still not high enough? How about hiking on a mountain ridge, or climbing steep rock faces? To do these activities, you must go to the third basic type of landform—mountains. Mountains rise high above the surrounding land, providing a spectacular view from the top. The world's highest peak is Mt. Everest in the Himalayan Mountains. It's more than 8800 meters above sea level. Mountain peaks in the United States reach just a little more than 4000 meters high. Mountains vary greatly in size and in how they are formed.

Folded Mountains

The first mountains we'll investigate are folded mountains. If you ever travel through a road cut in the Appalachian Mountains, you'll see rock layers that are folded. Folded rock layers look like a rug that has been pushed up against a wall. What do you think caused this to happen? Tremendous forces inside Earth force rock layers together. When rock layers are squeezed from opposite sides, rock layers buckle and fold into **folded mountains.** You'll learn more about the forces that create mountains in Chapters 13, 14, and 15.

The Appalachian Mountains are folded mountains that were formed in this way between 450 and 200 million years ago. They are the oldest mountains in North America and also one of the longest ranges, stretching from Quebec, Canada, south to Alabama. The Appalachians were higher than the Rocky Mountains at one time, but weathering and erosion have worn them down to less than 2000 meters above sea level.

How do folded mountains form?

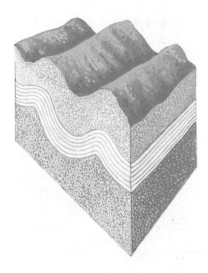

Figure 8-4. The Appalachian Mountains are folded mountains.

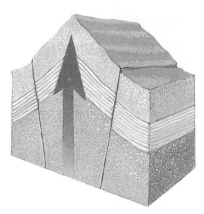

Figure 8-5. Some parts of the Rocky Mountains are upwarped mountains.

How do upwarped mountains become sharp peaks?

Upwarped Mountains

The southern Rocky Mountains in Colorado and New Mexico, the Black Hills in South Dakota, and the Adirondak Mountains in New York are **upwarped mountains.** These mountains were formed when crust was pushed up by forces inside Earth. Over time, the sedimentary rock on top of the crust was eroded, leaving behind the igneous and metamorphic rock underneath. These igneous and metamorphic rocks were then eroded to form sharp peaks and ridges as found in the southern Rockies.

Fault-Block Mountains

The Grand Teton Mountains of Wyoming and the Sierra Nevada Mountains in California formed in yet another way. **Fault-block mountains** are made of huge tilted blocks of rocks that are separated from surrounding rock by faults. A fault is a large crack in rocks along which there is movement. When the Grand Tetons were formed, one block was tilted and pushed up. The other block was pushed down. If you decide to go to the Tetons or the Sierra Nevadas, you'll see the sharp, jagged peaks that are characteristic of these mountains.

Figure 8-6. The Grand Tetons of Wyoming are fault-block mountains.

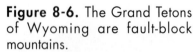

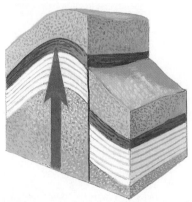

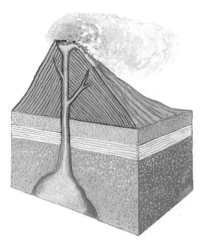

Figure 8-7. Mountains in the Cascade range of Washington and Oregon are volcanic mountains.

Volcanic Mountains

The last type of mountain that you could choose to explore is a volcano. Mount St. Helens in Washington state and Mauna Loa in Hawaii are two of the many volcanic mountains in the United States. **Volcanic mountains** begin when molten material reaches the surface through a weak area of the crust. The materials pile up, one layer on top of another, until a cone-shaped structure forms. The Hawaiian Islands are volcanic mountains formed on the floor of the Pacific Ocean. The islands are just the peaks of huge volcanoes that stick out above the water.

Plains, plateaus, and mountains offer a wide variety of landforms to explore. They range from low coastal plains, high desert plateaus, to mountain ranges thousands of meters high. Have you made up your mind yet? Where would you like to go?

EcoTip

When camping in the woods, always make sure your campfire is out before leaving the campsite. Douse the fire with water and then cover it with dirt.

SECTION REVIEW

1. How do folded mountains form?
2. What's the difference between a plain and a plateau?
3. **Apply:** If you climbed the volcano Mauna Loa in Hawaii, why would it be inaccurate to say that you climbed from the bottom to the top of the mountain?

☑ Concept Mapping

Make a concept map that explains how upwarped mountains form. If you need help, refer to Concept Mapping in the **Skill Handbook** on pages 688 and 689.

Skill Builder

8-2 Viewpoints

New Science Words

equator
latitude
prime meridian
longitude
International Date Line

Objectives

▶ Differentiate between latitude and longitude.
▶ Describe how latitude and longitude are used to identify locations.
▶ Calculate the time and date in different time zones.

Latitude and Longitude

If you're going to explore landforms, you might want to learn how to find locations on Earth. If you wanted to go to the Hawaiian Islands, how would you describe their location? You might say that they're located in the Pacific Ocean. That's correct, but there's a more precise way to locate places on Earth. You could use lines of latitude and longitude. These lines form an imaginary grid system that enables points on Earth to be located exactly.

First, look at Figure 8-8. The **equator** is an imaginary line that circles Earth exactly halfway between the North and South Poles. The equator separates Earth into two

Figure 8-8. The degree value used for latitude is the measurement of the imaginary angle created between the equator, the center of Earth, and that location (a). Likewise, longitude is the measurement of the angle created between the prime meridian, the center of Earth, and that location.

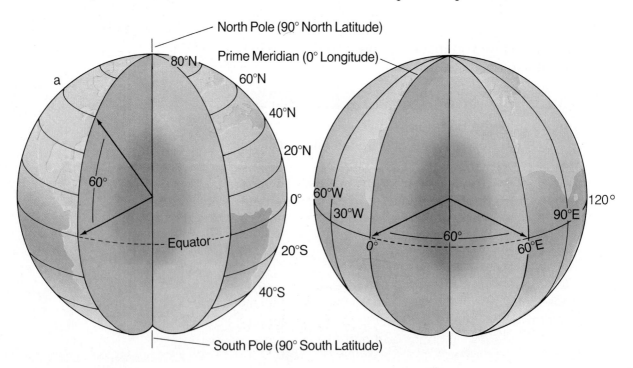

equal halves, called the Northern Hemisphere and the Southern Hemisphere. The lines running parallel to the equator are called lines of latitude. Because these lines are parallel to each other, they are also called parallels. **Latitude** refers to distance in degrees either north or south of the equator. This system uses numbers with degree symbols, such as 59° north latitude.

The equator is numbered 0° latitude. The poles are each numbered 90°. Therefore, latitude is measured from 0° at the equator to 90° at the poles. Locations north of the equator are referred to by degrees north latitude. Locations south of the equator are referrred to by degrees south latitude. For example, Minneapolis, Minnesota, is located at 45° north latitude.

Latitude lines are used for locations north and south of the equator, but what about locations in east and west directions? These vertical lines seen in Figure 8-8 have two names—meridians and lines of longitude. Just as the equator is used as a reference point for north/south grid lines, there's a reference point for east/west grid lines. This reference point is the **prime meridian.** This imaginary line runs through Greenwich (GREN itch), England, and represents 0° longitude. In 1884, astronomers decided the prime meridian should go through the Greenwich Observatory near London. The observatory has since been moved, but the prime meridian remains in its original location in Greenwich. **Longitude** refers to distances in degrees east or west of the prime meridian. Points west of the prime meridian have west longitude measured from 0° to 180°, while points east of the prime meridian have east longitude, also measured from 0° to 180°.

The prime meridian does not circle Earth like the equator does. It runs from the North Pole through Greenwich, England, to the South Pole. The line of longitude on the opposite side of Earth from the prime meridian where east lines of longitude meet west lines of longitude is the 180° meridian. This line is also known as the International Date Line, which you will learn about on page 205.

Using latitude and longitude, you can locate Hawaii more accurately as seen in Figure 8-9. Hawaii is located at 20° north latitude and about 155° west longitude. Read on to see how longitude lines are used to tell time on Earth.

MINI-Lab

How Do You Use Latitude and Longitude?

On a world map that shows latitude and longitude, identify the cities that have the following coordinates:

1. 56°N; 38°E 4. 13°N; 101°E
2. 34°S; 18°E 5. 38°N; 9°W
3. 23°N; 82°W

Now determine the latitude and longitude coordinates of the following cities:

6. London, England
7. Melbourne, Australia
8. Buenos Aires, Argentina
9. Paris, France
10. Anchorage, Alaska

List your answers on a sheet of paper and compare them with your classmates'.

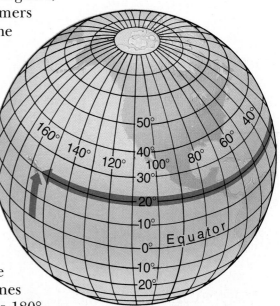

Figure 8-9. Hawaii is located at about 20°N, 155°W.

Earth Time

What time is it right now? That depends on where you are on Earth. We keep track of time by measuring Earth's movement in relation to the sun. Earth rotates one full turn every 24 hours. When one half of Earth is facing the sun, the other half is facing away from it. For the half facing the sunlight, it's daytime. For the half in darkness, it's nighttime. Half of Earth is experiencing sunlight, while the other half is in darkness. And because Earth is constantly spinning, time is always changing.

How can you know what time it is at any particular location on Earth? Earth is divided into time zones. Because Earth takes 24 hours to rotate once, it is divided into 24 time zones, each one hour different. Each time zone is 15 degrees wide. There are six different time zones in the United States. Because Earth is rotating, the sun rises earlier in Atlanta, Georgia, than it does in Los Angeles, California. When the sun is rising in Atlanta at 7:00 AM, it's still dark in Los Angeles, and the time is earlier—4:00 AM. If you lived in Los Angeles, and were in your first or second period class, a student in Atlanta would be at lunch.

Did You Know?

If you left London on the Concord jet airplane, at 8 AM, London time, you would arrive in New York at 6 AM, New York time. The Concord can make the trip through five time zones in just three hours, which means you would gain two hours.

Figure 8-10. Time zones are roughly determined by lines of longitude.

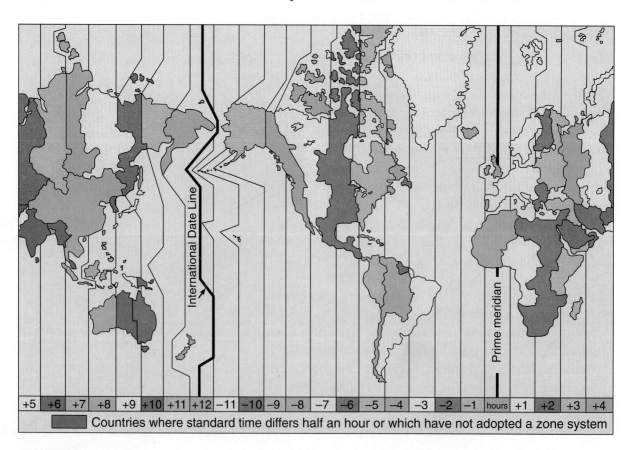

| +5 | +6 | +7 | +8 | +9 | +10 | +11 | +12 | −11 | −10 | −9 | −8 | −7 | −6 | −5 | −4 | −3 | −2 | −1 | hours | +1 | +2 | +3 | +4 |

Countries where standard time differs half an hour or which have not adopted a zone system

As you can see in Figure 8-10, the time zones do not strictly follow lines of longitude. Time zone boundaries have been adjusted in local areas. For example, if a city were split by a time zone boundary, great confusion would result. In such a situation, the time zone boundary is moved to outside of the city.

We all know that a day ends and the next day begins at 12 midnight. If it is 11:59 PM Tuesday, two minutes later it is 12:01 AM Wednesday. Over the period of a day, every time zone experiences this transition from one day to the next. The calendar advances to the next day in each time zone at midnight.

But if you were traveling around the world, you'd have a harder time keeping track of the days. You gain or lose time at each time zone you travel through until at some point you gain or lose a whole day. The **International Date Line** is the 180 degree meridian that is the transition line for calendar days. The International Date Line is one-half of one day, or 12 time zones, from the prime meridian. If you were traveling west across the International Date Line, you would lose one day. If you were traveling east across the International Date Line, you would gain one day.

Exploring different locations on Earth could be tricky. If you moved from Los Angeles to Atlanta without changing your watch, you would be three hours late to school the first day.

What meridian is directly opposite the prime meridian?

SECTION REVIEW

1. What is the difference between latitude and longitude?
2. What is the longitude and latitude of New Orleans, Louisiana?
3. If it's 9:00 AM in Maine, what time is it in California?
4. **Apply:** How could you go fishing on Monday, fish for an hour on Sunday, and return on Monday.

☑ Interpreting Scientific Illustrations

Skill Builder

Use Appendix F on page 668 to find the approximate longitude and latitude of the following locations: the Hawaiian Islands; Sri Lanka; Tokyo, Japan; London, England; and the Falkland Islands. If you need help, refer to Interpreting Scientific Illustrations in the **Skill Handbook** on page 693.

8-3 Maps

New Science Words

Mercator projection
Robinson projection
conic projection
topographic map
contour line
contour interval
map scale

Objectives

▶ Differentiate between Mercator, Robinson, and conic projections.
▶ Describe how contour lines and contour intervals are used to illustrate elevation on a topographic map.
▶ Explain why topographic maps have scales.

Map Projections

One of the things that you would take with you if you went hiking is a map. It would sure be hard to get to a certain mountain without a map showing where it is. There are road maps, political maps showing the boundaries between states and countries, and maps that show physical features such as mountains and valleys. They all have one thing in common. They are models of Earth's surface. But because Earth's surface is curved, it's not easy to represent on a flat piece of paper.

Maps are made using projections. A map projection is made when points and lines on a globe's surface are transferred onto paper. There are several different ways to

Figure 8-11. A Mercator projection exaggerates the areas near the poles.

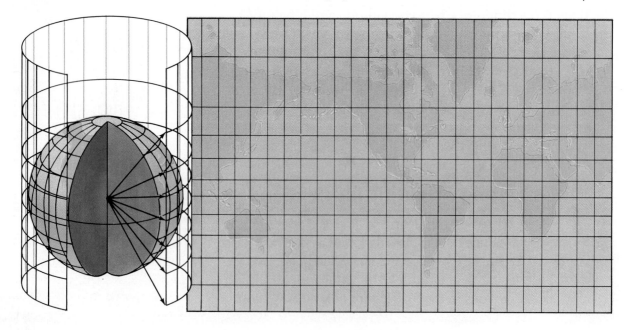

Figure 8-12. A Robinson projection is less distorted near the poles.

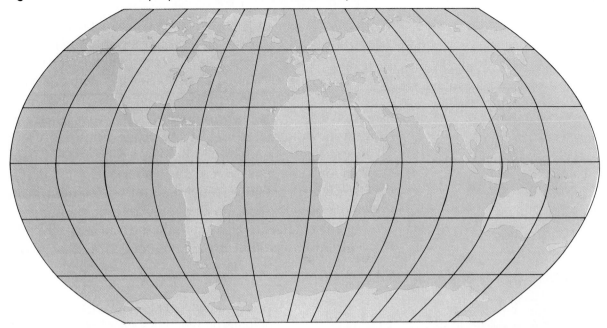

make map projections. But all types of projections have some sort of distortion in either the shapes of land masses or their areas.

One type is a Mercator (mur KAYT ur) projection. A **Mercator projection** has correct shapes of continents, but their areas are distorted. Lines of longitude are projected onto the map parallel to each other. As you learned earlier, only latitude lines are parallel. Longitude lines meet at the poles. When longitude lines are projected parallel, areas near the poles are exaggerated. Look at Greenland in the Mercator projection in Figure 8-11. It appears larger than South America. Greenland is actually much smaller than South America. Mercator projections are mainly used on ships and airplanes.

A map that has accurate continent shapes and shows accurate land areas is the **Robinson projection.** Here, lines of latitude remain parallel, and lines of longitude are curved as they would be on a globe. This results in less distortion near the poles.

A third type of projection is a conic projection. You use this type of projection whenever you look at a road map or a weather map. A **conic projection** is used to produce a map of small areas. They're made by projecting points and lines from a globe onto a cone.

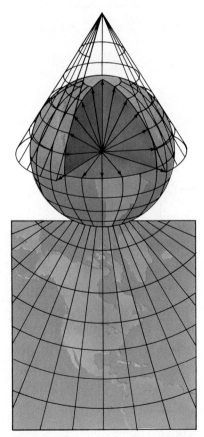

Figure 8-13. A conic projection is very accurate for small areas of Earth.

Topographic Maps

What does a topogaphic map show?

After you used a conic map projection to get to the mountain, you would also want a detailed map showing the hills and valleys of that specific area. A **topographic map** shows the changes in elevation of Earth's surface. With this map, you could tell how steep the mountain trail is. It also shows natural features such as mountains, hills, plains, lakes, and rivers and cultural features such as roads, cities, dams, and other structures built by people. Thus, topographic maps are models of a small part of Earth's surface.

If you were starting your hike up the mountain, you would look at the contour lines on your topographic map to see the changes in elevation that the trail goes through. A **contour line** is a line on a map that connects points of

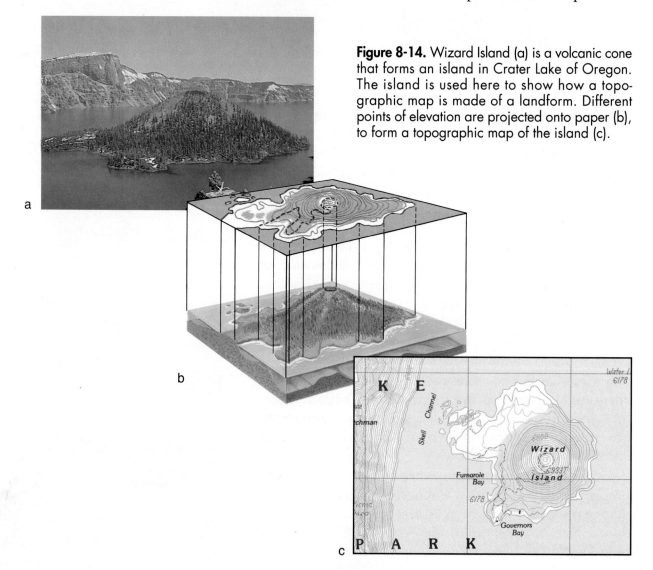

Figure 8-14. Wizard Island (a) is a volcanic cone that forms an island in Crater Lake of Oregon. The island is used here to show how a topographic map is made of a landform. Different points of elevation are projected onto paper (b), to form a topographic map of the island (c).

a

b

c

Rocks in 3-D!

You have learned that topographic maps are two-dimensional models of Earth. On such maps, contour lines connect points of equal elevation. Topographic maps are used to study features on Earth's surface.

To unravel Earth's complex structure, however, geologists also need to know what the rock beds "look like" in three dimensions. Using computers, topographic maps are digitized to get the "top layer" of data for the 3-D maps. Digitizing is a process by which points are located on a coordinate grid. Geologists then use data from wells drilled into the crust to obtain information about other "layers" of rocks beneath the surface. The computer analyzes all the data and generates a 3-dimensional map that shows what the rocks of an area look like. The map shown in the photograph shows how the drainage basin of an ancient river system was changed when forces at Earth's surface and forces within Earth acted on the river in Montana.

Think Critically: List one advantage a 3-D map has over a 2-D map.

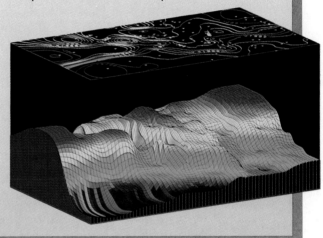

equal elevation. As you know, elevation refers to the distance above or below sea level. The difference in elevation between two side-by-side contour lines is called the **contour interval**. If the contour interval was 10 meters, then you would know that when you walked between those two lines on the trail, you would have climbed 10 meters.

The size of the contour interval can vary. If the land is very steep like in mountains, the contour lines might be very close and the contour interval might be as great as 100 meters. This would tell you that the land is very steep there because there is a large change in elevation between lines. However, if there isn't a great change in elevation and the contour lines are far apart, your map might have a contour interval of 5 meters.

Some contour lines, called index contours, are marked with their elevation. If you know the contour interval, you can tell the elevation of other lines around the index contour by adding or subtracting the known contour interval from the elevation indicated on the index contour.

What does a small contour interval tell you about land?

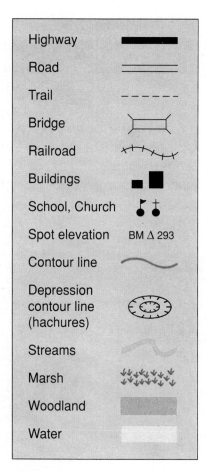

Highway	
Road	
Trail	
Bridge	
Railroad	
Buildings	
School, Church	
Spot elevation	BM △ 293
Contour line	
Depression contour line (hachures)	
Streams	
Marsh	
Woodland	
Water	

Figure 8-15. Here are some typical symbols used on topographic maps.

What is the purpose of a legend?

Here are some rules to remember when using topographic maps.

1. **Contour lines close around hills and basins or depressions.** To decide whether you're looking at a hill or basin, you can either read the elevation numbers or look for hachures (ha SHOORZ). Hachures are short lines at right angles to the contour line that are used to show depressions. These lines point toward lower elevations.

2. **Contour lines never cross.** If they did, it would mean that the spot where they cross would have two different elevations.

3. **Contour lines form Vs that point upstream whenever they cross streams.** This is because streams flow in depressions that are beneath the elevation of the surrounding land surface. When the contour lines follow the depression, they appear as Vs pointing upstream on the map.

Map Scale and Legends

Another thing you would want to know before you set out on your hike is, "How far is it to the top of the mountain?" Since maps are small models of Earth's surface, distances and sizes of things on a map should be proportional to the real thing on Earth. This is accomplished using "scale" distances. The **map scale** is the relationship between the distances on the map and actual distances on Earth's surface. For example, a topographic map of the Grand Canyon may have a scale that reads "1 : 80 000 ." This means that one unit on the map represents 80 000 units on land. If the unit you wanted to use was a centimeter, then one cm on the map would equal 80 000 cm on land. A map scale may also be in the form of a small bar graph that's divided into a number of units. The units are the scaled-down equivalent distances to real distances on Earth.

Topographic maps and most other maps have a legend. As you can see in Figure 8-15, topographic maps are covered with different colored lines, dots, letters, and odd shapes. A map's legend explains what the symbols used on the map mean. Some frequently used symbols for topographic maps are shown in Figure 8-15 and Appendix H on page 672.

A Climb to the Top

The map below is a topographic map of an area in California. One sunny day, three hikers started from the point marked with the + in the center of the map. One hiker headed for the peak of Cedar Mountain, another for the peak of Orr Mountain, while the third intended to climb to the top of Garner Butte.

All three would travel at the same rate on flat or gentle slopes. The climb would be slower on the steeper slope. If each hiker could choose any route to take to the top of the intended goals, which one do you think would reach the top first? Explain.

Think Critically: Could the three hikers see each other at the top? Why or why not?

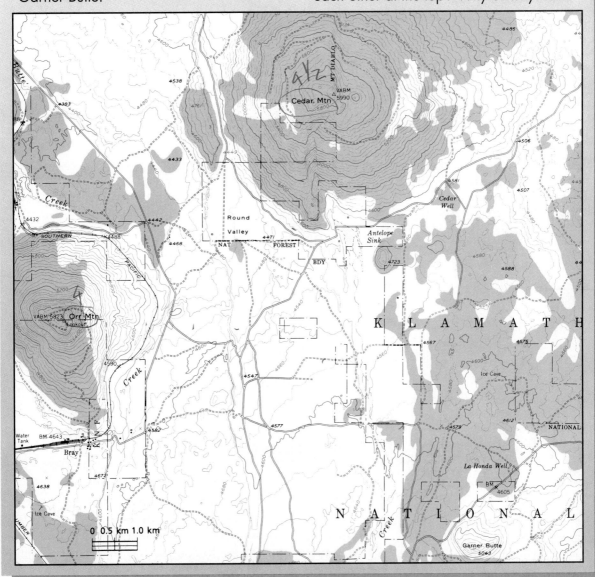

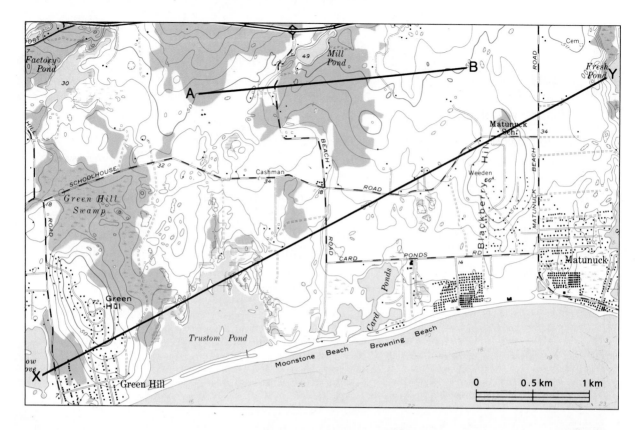

Figure 8-16. This topographic map of Kingston, Rhode Island shows many common features of topographic maps.

SECTION REVIEW

1. Why does Greenland appear larger on a Mercator projection than it does on a Robinson projection?
2. What does a map scale tell you?
3. Why can't contour lines cross?
4. **Apply:** Suppose you have a topographic map with a contour interval of 50 m. The scale is 1 cm on the map equals 1 km on Earth. The distance between point A and point B on the map is 8 cm. Four contour lines lie between points A and B. How far apart are the points and what is the change in elevation between them?

Skill Builder

☑ **Measuring in SI**

Use Figure 8-16 to practice measuring in SI.
1. How long is Matunuck Beach Road?
2. How far is it from Factory Pond to Mill Pond?
3. How big is Trustom Pond at its widest place?
If you need help, refer to Measuring in SI in the **Skill Handbook** on page 684.

ACTIVITY 8-1
Determining Elevation

Problem: *How is elevation indicated on a topographic map?*

Materials

- plastic model landform
- water
- transparency
- clear plastic storage box with lid
- beaker
- metric ruler
- tape
- transparency marker

Procedure

1. Using the ruler and the transparency marker, make marks up the side of the storage box 2 cm apart.
2. Secure the transparency to the outside of the box lid with tape.
3. Place the plastic model in the box. The bottom of the box will be zero elevation.
4. Using the beaker, pour water into the box to a height of 2 cm. Place the lid on the box.
5. Use the transparency marker to trace the top of the water line on the transparency.
6. Using the scale 2 cm = 10 m, mark the elevation on the line.
7. Remove the lid and add water until a depth of 4 cm is reached.

8. Map this level on the storage box lid and record the elevation.
9. Repeat the process of adding water and tracing until you have the hill mapped.
10. Transfer the tracing of the hill onto a white sheet of paper.

Analyze

1. What is the contour interval of this topographic map?
2. How does the distance between contour lines on the map show the steepness of slope on the landform model?
3. What is the total elevation of the hill?
4. How was elevation represented on your map?

Conclude and Apply

5. How are elevations shown on topographic maps?
6. Must all topographic maps have a 0-m elevation contour line? Explain.
7. How would the contour interval of an area of high relief compare to one of low relief on a topographic map?

8-4 Secret Maps

New Science Words

sonar
Sea Beam

Objectives

▶ Explain why some maps have been intentionally distorted.
▶ Recognize why some maps of the ocean floor have been classified as secret and why these maps would be valuable to some people.

Intentional Distortion of Maps

Over the years, several countries in the world have intentionally distorted maps. Early Romans designed maps to greatly exaggerate the size of the Roman Empire. This made them appear even more powerful than they actually were to their enemies. The Soviet Union has also distorted and falsified public maps. Rivers, mountains, roads, and towns were misplaced. The purpose of distorting their maps was to confuse spies from other countries. Throughout history, countries have tried to keep some maps secret for security reasons. Even today, many maps are classified "secret."

Sea Beam

Using a new technology called Sea Beam, scientists are making detailed, accurate maps of the ocean floor in the coastal areas around the United States.

Figure 8-17. Sea Beam sonar, shown at left, can make very accurate maps of the ocean floor—right.

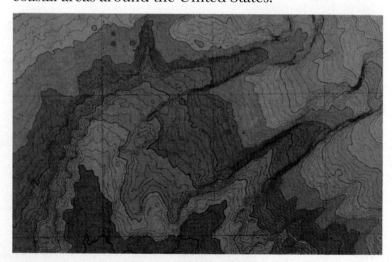

Sea Beam is a new type of sonar technology. **Sonar** refers to the use of sound waves to detect ocean bottom structures. First a sound wave is sent from the bottom of a ship toward the ocean floor. A receiving device then picks up the returning echo when it bounces off the bottom. The distance to the bottom is calculated by a computer on the ship using the speed of sound in water and the time it takes for the sound to be reflected.

A ship with **Sea Beam** sonar has 16 of these sonar devices. The sonar devices are each "aimed" at different parts of the seafloor, gathering depth readings from a wide swath as the ship moves. As the ship goes back and forth across the seafloor, readings of depth overlap. Computers take this information and make a detailed continuous map of the ocean floor.

These new Sea Beam maps are very useful. For example, fishing companies can use them to locate underwater canyons where certain fish might be found. Petroleum engineers use them to find oil-bearing deposits. Oceanographers use them to study parts of the ocean floor that previously they didn't know existed.

At first, all of the new Sea Beam maps were classified as secret. Because Sea Beam maps are so accurate, government officials didn't want other countries to have detailed maps of the ocean floor around the United States. They feared that enemy submarines could use the maps to navigate in United States coastal areas. Now most of the Sea Beam maps have been released to the public.

Science and MATH

Sea Beam sends a sonar signal toward the ocean floor. The sound wave travels at 1454 meters per second, reflects off the ocean floor, and returns to the sonar receiver in 2.25 seconds. How deep is the ocean at that point?

Why are Sea Beam maps so desirable?

SECTION REVIEW

1. Why are some maps intentionally distorted?
2. How do Sea Beam's maps aid people who fish and look for oil?

You Decide!

There are Sea Beam maps of the ocean floor near navy bases that are still classified secret. The government wants to keep this area of the ocean floor a secret because submarines navigate in these areas. This means that fishing companies, petroleum engineers, and oceanographers can't benefit from these maps. What do you think? Should all Sea Beam maps be released to the public?

SCIENCE & SOCIETY

ACTIVITY 8-2
Reading Topographic Maps

Problem: *How can distances and features be determined on a topographic map?*

Materials
- Figure 8-16
- paper
- Appendix H

NOTE: The contour interval on Figure 8-16 is expressed in feet above sea level.

Procedure
1. Lay a piece of paper along a straight line between Matunuck and Green Hill. Use the first letter of each name for the measurement.
2. Make a mark on the paper where the two towns are located.
3. Move the paper to the scale and determine the distance.

Analyze
1. What is the distance between the two towns? Is this measurement the same distance you would cover if you traveled by car between the two cities? Explain.
2. How would you measure this same distance using a ratio scale?
3. What is the contour interval of this map?
4. What is the approximate elevation of the Matunuck School?
5. What is the distance between the Matunuck School and the intersection of Moonstone Beach Road and Schoolhouse Road?
6. What is the approximate elevation of Mill Pond?
7. What is the approximate elevation of Green Hill Swamp?
8. What is the elevation of Schoolhouse Road where it intersects Green Hill Road?

Conclude and Apply
9. How can you determine the distance between two points on a topographic map?
10. How many closed contour lines would Green Hill have if the contour interval were 50 feet?
11. Would a contour interval of 50 feet give more or less detail? Explain.
12. If sea level rose 50 feet, would the State Trout Hatchery be covered by water?
13. What is the relief of the area south of Post Road?
14. Locate the closed contour line just northeast of the intersection of Moonstone Beach Road and Card Ponds Road. Is this feature a hill or a depression? Explain.

CHAPTER
REVIEW

SUMMARY

8-1: Landforms

1. Plains are large, flat areas that cover much of the United States. Plateaus are high, relatively flat areas next to mountains.

2. Folded mountains are formed when rocks are squeezed from opposite sides. Upwarped mountains form when Earth's crust is pushed up and then eroded. Fault-block mountains are tilted blocks that are bounded by at least one fault. Volcanic mountains are made of layers of molten material that pile up to form cone-shaped structures.

8-2: Viewpoints

1. Latitude refers to the distance in degrees north or south of the equator. Longitude refers to distance in degrees east or west of the prime meridian.

2. Lines of latitude and longitude form an imaginary grid that enables points on Earth to be located exactly.

3. Earth is divided into 24 time zones, each one hour ahead or behind the adjacent zone.

8-3: Maps

1. On a Mercator projection, landmasses near the poles are distorted, appearing larger than they actually are. Robinson projections have curved lines of longitude resulting in less distortion near the poles. Conic projections are used for maps of small areas. Road maps and weather maps are conic projections.

2. A contour line on a topographic map connects points of equal elevation. The difference in elevation between contour lines is the contour interval.

3. Because maps are small models of Earth's surface, a scale is used to show the relationship between map distances and the actual distances on Earth's surface.

8-4: Science and Society: Secret Maps

1. Maps are sometimes distorted to exaggerate the size of a country.

2. Some maps of the ocean floor are secret even though people would benefit from them.

KEY SCIENCE WORDS

a. conic projection
b. contour interval
c. contour line
d. equator
e. fault-block mountains
f. folded mountains
g. International Date Line
h. latitude
i. longitude
j. map scale
k. Mercator projection
l. plains
m. plateaus
n. prime meridian
o. Robinson projection
p. Sea Beam
q. sonar
r. topographic map
s. upwarped mountains
t. volcanic mountains

UNDERSTANDING VOCABULARY

Match each phrase with the correct term from the list of Key Science Words.

1. high, flat areas next to mountains
2. mountains formed when Earth's crust is squeezed from opposite sides
3. imaginary line parallel to the equator
4. 0° longitude
5. projections used mainly for navigation
6. map that shows changes in elevation
7. line connecting points of equal elevation
8. change in elevation between adjacent contour lines
9. instrument that uses sound waves to detect features
10. system using 16 sonar devices

CHAPTER

REVIEW

Choose the word or phrase that completes the sentence.

1. _____ make up about 50 percent of all land areas in the United States.
   a. Plateaus
   b. Plains
   c. Folded mountains
   d. Volcanoes

2. The Grand Canyon is part of the _____.
   a. Great Plains   c. Appalachians
   b. Rocky Mountains   d. none of these

3. _____ mountains form when Earth's crust is pushed up into a dome shape by internal forces.
   a. Fault-block   c. Volcanic
   b. Upwarped   d. Folded

4. Lines parallel to the equator are _____.
   a. lines of latitude   c. lines of longitude
   b. prime meridians   d. contour lines

5. Earth can be divided into 24 time zones that are _____ degrees apart.
   a. 10   c. 15
   b. 34   d. 25

6. _____ projections are distorted at the poles.
   a. Conic   c. Robinson
   b. Topographic   d. Mercator

7. A _____ map shows changes in elevation at Earth's surface.
   a. conic   c. Robinson
   b. topographic   d. Mercator

8. _____ is measured with respect to sea level.
   a. Contour interval   c. Conic projection
   b. Elevation   d. Sonar

9. _____ are used to show depressions.
   a. Vs   c. Hachure lines
   b. Scales   d. Legends

10. Sea Beam sonar can be used to find _____.
    a. schools of fish
    b. submarine hiding places
    c. oil deposits
    d. all of these

UNDERSTANDING CONCEPTS

Complete each sentence.

11. Lines east or west of the prime meridian are lines of longitude

12. The equator is an imaginary line halfway between the North and South Poles.

13. The North Pole is located at 90° latitude.

14. The Hawaiian Islands are _____ mountains.

15. Mountains, tilted and bounded by faults, are _____ mountains.

THINK AND WRITE CRITICALLY

16. Compare and contrast plains and plateaus.

17. Compare and contrast lines of latitude and lines of longitude.

18. Why would Antarctica be larger on a Mercator map than it actually is?

19. Would a topographic map of the Great Plains have a large or small contour interval? Explain.

20. How does the information gathered by ships using Sea Beam sonar differ from that collected with standard methods which use one sonar device?

21. How would a topographic map of the Atlantic Coastal Plain differ from a topographic map of the Rocky Mountains?
22. If it was Wednesday and you were flying east across the Soviet Union, what day would it be when you reached Alaska?
23. If you were flying directly south from the North Pole and reached 70° north latitude, how many more degrees of latitude would be left to pass over before reaching the South Pole?
24. Why can't two contour lines overlap?
25. What does a map scale of 1 : 50 000 mean?

2. **Measuring in SI:** What is the area in square kilometers of the topographic map in the Problem Solving feature on page 211?
3. **Outlining:** Outline the major points in Section 8-2, Viewpoints.
4. **Sequencing:** Arrange these cities in order from the city with the earliest time to that with the latest time on a given day: Anchorage, AK; San Francisco, CA; Bangor, ME; Columbus, OH; Houston, TX.
5. **Interpreting Data:** If a map has a scale of "1 cm = 80 000 cm," how far on the map would two cities be if they were 300 km apart on Earth's surface?

MORE SKILL BUILDERS

If you need help, refer to the Skill Handbook.

1. **Concept Mapping:** Make a network tree concept map that explains how topographic maps are used. Use the following terms: *topographic maps, mountains, rivers, natural features, contour lines, changes in elevation, equal elevation, hills, plains.*

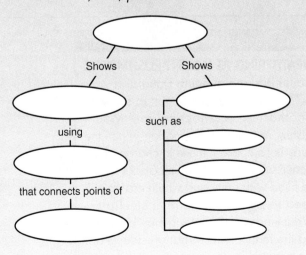

Shows   Shows

using

such as

that connects points of

PROJECTS

1. Use modeling clay to construct a physiographic map to scale of the United States. Be sure to include all the landforms shown in Figure 8-2.
2. Determine the actual area of each continent. Then, compute the difference in size between the actual size of each and its size on a Mercator, Robinson, and a conic projection. Make a table to display your results. Which projection is the most accurate for each of the continents?
3. Find out what daylight savings time is and why it was implemented. Also find out why some states do not use this plan.

UNIT 3
GLOBAL CONNECTIONS

The Changing Surface of Earth

In this unit, you studied processes that change Earth's surface. Now find out how these processes are connected to other subjects and places around the world.

120°   60°

60°

60°

CHEMISTRY

CARLSBAD CAVERNS
Carlsbad, New Mexico
Water percolating through soil picks up carbon dioxide, forming a weak acid capable of dissolving limestone. When a droplet with limestone reaches the air-filled chamber of a cave, the limestone is precipitated from the water and left on the ceiling, wall, or floor, as calcite crystals. These grow to form stalactites or stalagmites. Are the crystal formations the result of weathering or deposition?

HISTORY

WEATHERING AT MOUNT RUSHMORE
Mount Rushmore, South Dakota
In 1989, a study was begun to see how weathering is affecting the Mount Rushmore National Memorial. When the study is completed, those in charge of the monument will decide which cracks should be filled with putty and which cracks will need to be supported with steel pins. What kinds of weathering may be affecting the monument? What presidents are represented by the monument?

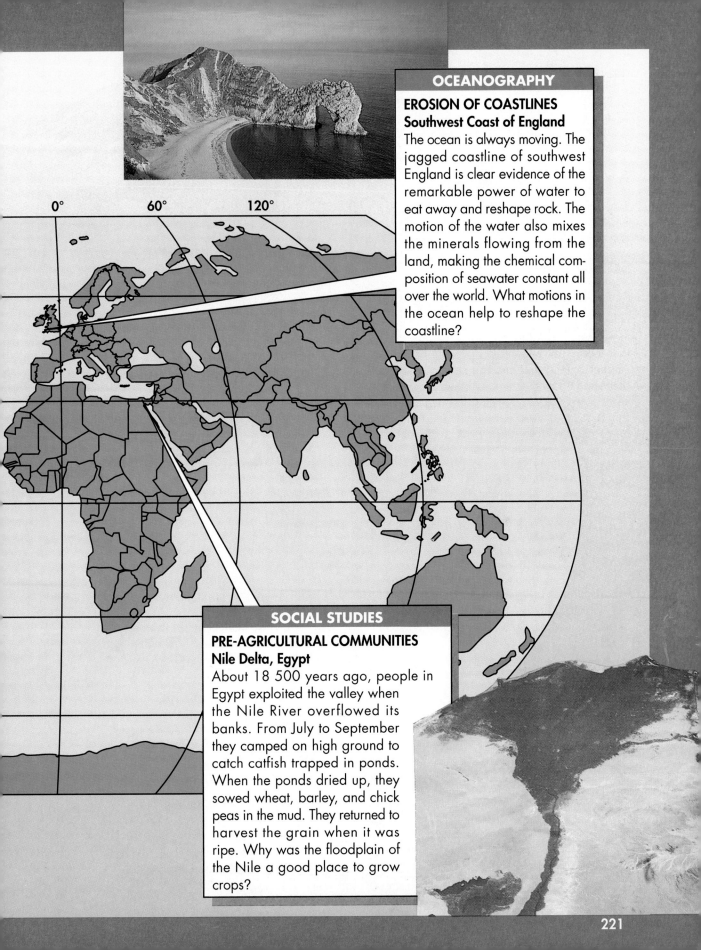

0°   60°   120°

EROSION OF COASTLINES
Southwest Coast of England
The ocean is always moving. The jagged coastline of southwest England is clear evidence of the remarkable power of water to eat away and reshape rock. The motion of the water also mixes the minerals flowing from the land, making the chemical composition of seawater constant all over the world. What motions in the ocean help to reshape the coastline?

SOCIAL STUDIES

PRE-AGRICULTURAL COMMUNITIES
Nile Delta, Egypt
About 18 500 years ago, people in Egypt exploited the valley when the Nile River overflowed its banks. From July to September they camped on high ground to catch catfish trapped in ponds. When the ponds dried up, they sowed wheat, barley, and chick peas in the mud. They returned to harvest the grain when it was ripe. Why was the floodplain of the Nile a good place to grow crops?

221

CAREERS

SOIL ENGINEER

A *soil engineer* tests the soil during every stage of excavation for buildings, roads, tunnels, and bridges. In areas of the country where there is a danger of earthquakes, the importance of a soil engineer is greatly increased. At each level during the excavation, a sample of the soil is taken. Every sample is subjected to several tests: a hammer is used to pound the soil. A soil that has a density of 1.8 g/cm^3 may be compacted to a density of 0.2 g/cm^3. The tests help the soil engineer to decide whether or not it's safe to build on the land. They may prevent a later disaster.

A soil engineer usually obtains a degree as a civil engineer and then specializes in geotechnical subjects. A student interested in becoming a soil engineer should take courses in mathematics and physics.

For Additional Information

Contact the American Society of Civil Engineers, 345 E. 47th Street, New York, NY 10017.

FOREST TECHNICIAN

A *forest technician* may assist forest rangers in the work of preserving our national parks. Sometimes the work involves protecting the national monuments in the parks. For example, the technicians may check that no visitor to the Mount Rushmore National Memorial causes any harm to the monument. They also monitor damage done to the monuments by acid rain.

A forest technician usually has a two-year associate degree. In some states, a high school diploma followed by extensive on-the-job training is sufficient to become a forest technician.

For Additional Information

Contact the Society of American Foresters, 5400 Grovenor Lane, Bethesda, MD 20814.

UNIT READINGS

▶Albright, Horace M., Russ Dickenson, and William Penn Mott, Jr. *National Park Service: The Story Behind the Scenery 1916-1986.* Las Vegas, Nevada: KC Publications, 1986.
▶"Saving Face: Mount Rushmore National Memorial." *Life,* February 1990, pp. 50-52.

Los Angeles, A Mobile Society

by Art Buchwald

The excerpt that follows gives Art Buchwald's humorous account of life in Los Angeles.

Los Angeles—I came to Los Angeles last week for rest and recreation, only to discover that it had become a rain forest.

I didn't realize how bad it was until I went to dinner at a friend's house. I had the right address, but when I arrived there was nothing there. I went to a neighboring house where I found a man bailing out his swimming pool.

"I beg your pardon," I said. "Could you tell me where the Cables live?"

"They used to live above us on the hill. Then about two years ago, their house slid down in the mud, and they lived next door to us. I think it was last Monday, during the storm, that their house slid down there. We were sorry to see them go—they were really nice neighbors."

I thanked him and slid straight down the hill to the new location of the Cables' house....

"Cable," I said, "You and your wife are intelligent people, why do you build your house on the top of a canyon, when you

know that during a rainstorm it has a good chance of sliding away?"

"It's hard for people who don't live in California to understand how we people out here think. Sure we have floods, and fire and drought, but that's the price you have to pay for living the good life. When Esther and I saw this house, we knew it was a dream come true. It was located right on the tippy top of the hill, way up there. We would wake up in the morning and listen to the birds, and eat breakfast out on the patio and look down on all the smog.

"Then, after the first mudslide, we found ourselves living next to people. It was an entirely different experience. But by that time we were ready for a change. Now we've slid again and we're in a whole new neighborhood. You can't do that if you live on solid ground. Once you move into a house below Sunset Boulevard, you're stuck there for the rest of your life."

In Your Own Words

▶ Why do you think Art Buchwald wrote a humorous article about such a serious topic? Write an essay to explain your reasoning.

UNIT
4
EARTH'S AIR AND WATER

224

What's Happening Here?

Hurricanes, the largest and most powerful storms in Earth's atmosphere, form over tropical regions of the oceans. As long as they remain over water, they gain energy and become stronger. Satellite photographs from space enable scientists to track these storms. When hurricanes reach land, they can cause tremendous destruction. People can be warned to evacuate, but their homes and businesses often can't be saved. As you read the chapters in Unit 4, you'll discover how Earth's atmosphere and oceans interact to generate storms and other weather.

UNIT CONTENTS

How do these hot-air balloons float in the atmosphere? How is the atmosphere inside a giant balloon different from the atmosphere outside of it? Heat makes molecules of air inside the balloon move away from each other. Therefore, the air inside the balloon has less density than the colder air around it. The cold air pushes the balloon up into the atmosphere.

FIND OUT!

Your teacher will perform this simple activity to demonstrate how temperature affects the density of air.

Your teacher will pour a small quantity of water into a metal can. Then, with the cap still off, he or she will heat the can over a hot plate or other burner. When the water begins to boil, the heat source is turned off and the cap is screwed on the metal can. Watch what happens as the can cools. Why does the can collapse in on itself?

Gearing Up
Previewing the Chapter

Use this outline to help you focus on important ideas in this chapter.

Previewing Science Skills

► In the **Skill Builders,** you will make and use graphs, make concept maps, and compare and contrast.
► In the **Activities,** you will record and analyze data and observations and draw conclusions.
► In the **MINI-Labs,** you will measure in SI, observe, and infer.

What's next?

Now that you've seen how the density of air increases and decreases because of changes in its temperature, you can see how this affects air pressure within our atmosphere. You'll also explore the composition and structure of Earth's atmosphere and how air pressure changes within it.

New Science Words

troposphere
ionosphere

Objectives

▶ Name the common gases in Earth's atmosphere.
▶ Describe the structure of Earth's atmosphere.
▶ Explain what causes air pressure.

Composition of the Atmosphere

It's early morning and you're getting dressed for work. As you eat breakfast, you read the weather report coming over the computer screen. The report says "Smog levels are higher than normal, temperatures will near 38°C, and the ozone layer in the stratosphere is thinner than yesterday." You realize you'll need your filter mask to protect your lungs from the smog. Pollution in the atmosphere has raised the temperature, so you'll have to wear clothes designed to keep you cool. The thin ozone layer means you'll have to use a strong sunblock lotion to protect yourself from skin cancer. It's an average day in the city.

Does this sound like your future? It's one possible future you may face. Your life depends on the air you breathe and the condition of the atmosphere that you live in. But what do you know about the atmosphere? You

Figure 9-1. This graph illustrates the percentages of gases in our atmosphere.

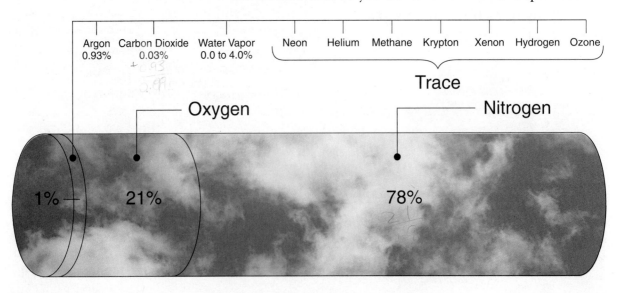

Argon 0.93%　Carbon Dioxide 0.03%　Water Vapor 0.0 to 4.0%　Neon　Helium　Methane　Krypton　Xenon　Hydrogen　Ozone

Trace

Oxygen　　　　　Nitrogen

1%　　21%　　78%

Figure 9-2. When pollution levels are high, it's necessary to protect ourselves from the harmful side effects of breathing smog.

learned in Chapter 2 that the atmosphere is a mixture. What types of substances make up this mixture? Learning about the composition and structure of the atmosphere will help you make decisions to protect it for your future.

The atmosphere surrounding Earth is a mixture of solids, liquids, and gases. In Figure 9-1 you see a graph of the gases in Earth's atmosphere. Nitrogen is the most common gas. Water vapor can make up from zero to four percent of the atmosphere. When the volume of water vapor is high, the percentages of other gases is slightly lower.

The smog in the atmosphere is a mixture of compounds that include sulfur, nitrogen, and oxygen. When we burn coal, gasoline, and other fossil fuels, we produce sulfur and nitrogen. The sulfur and nitrogen combine with oxygen in the atmosphere, and sunlight then reacts with these gases to produce smog.

Smog is a type of pollution. It's visible as a smoke-like haze hanging over cities and towns. One component of smog is called ozone. As you'll learn in Section 9-2, ozone is a compound that occurs naturally higher up in the atmosphere. But when it's present where plants and animals come in contact with it, it can be very harmful.

Gases aren't the only thing making up Earth's atmosphere. Dust and ice are two common solids found in the atmospheric mixture. Dust gets into the atmosphere when wind picks it up off the ground and erodes it. Ice is common in the form of hailstones and snowflakes.

Did You Know?

Earth's original atmosphere had almost no oxygen. Organisms called cyanobacteria, living about 3.5 billion years ago, produced oxygen as part of their life processes. Eventually, enough oxygen existed in the atmosphere that lifeforms that use oxygen could evolve.

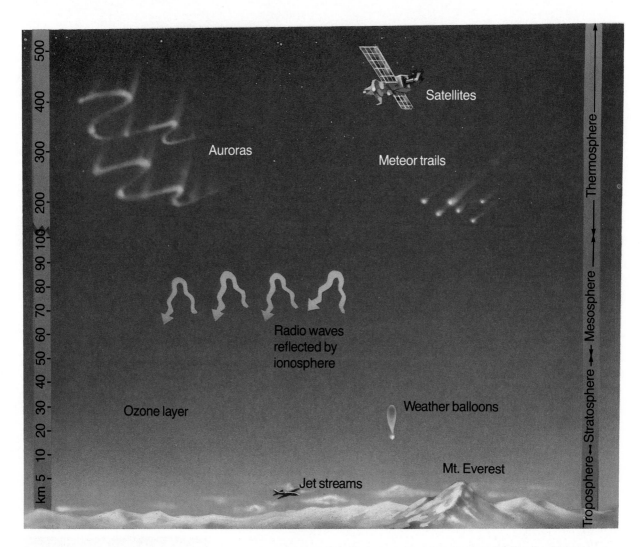

Figure 9-3. Although Earth's atmosphere extends nearly 700 kilometers upward, 75 percent of all its gases are in the lowest 15 kilometers.

The other components of the atmosphere are liquids. The most common liquid in the atmosphere is water. Water is the only substance that exists as a solid, liquid, and gas in Earth's atmosphere.

Structure of the Atmosphere

The weather forecast on this morning in your future said that the smog was heavy and the ozone layer in the stratosphere was thin. Both will affect how you're able to spend your day. But what do you know about smog and the ozone layer? Where do each of these occur in the atmosphere?

Earth's atmosphere has four main layers, each with its own unique characteristics. In Figure 9-3 you see that the names of these layers are troposphere, stratosphere, mesosphere, and thermosphere.

You live in the troposphere. It's the layer closest to the ground. The **troposphere** contains 75 percent of all the atmosphere's gases, as well as dust, ice, and liquid water. This layer is where weather and clouds occur. It's also where smog is found.

Above the troposphere lies the stratosphere. Within the stratosphere a layer of ozone exists. It's this ozone layer that was mentioned in this morning's forecast. As you already know, the ozone layer in the stratosphere is important because it directly affects your health. You'll learn more about this layer in Section 9-2 later in this chapter.

Beyond the stratosphere are the mesosphere and thermosphere. One important layer of the thermosphere is the **ionosphere.** It's a layer of electrically charged particles. When these particles are bombarded by energy from

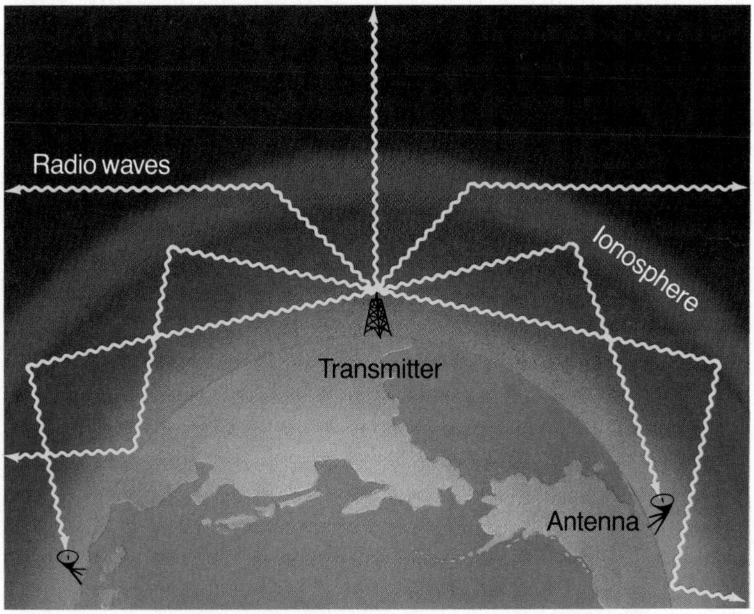

Where is the ozone layer located?

Figure 9-4. Radio waves that strike the ionosphere at sharp angles pass through to space. Some strike at lower angles and are reflected. These may be received by antennas around the globe.

space, ions and free electrons are created. These particles are useful for communications because they reflect radio waves. Radio transmissions from one side of the globe can be received on the other side of the globe because they bounce off the ionosphere. Figure 9-4 illustrates how this is possible.

When particles of matter from the sun strike the ionosphere, the ions glow in different colors. The result is visible bands of shimmering light called auroras. The famous Northern and Southern Lights are auroras.

The thermosphere is the uppermost part of Earth's atmosphere. Beyond it lies space. There's no clear boundary between the thermosphere and space. If you were an astronaut, you would encounter fewer and fewer molecules and ions as you traveled upward through the thermosphere. Eventually, you would find so few molecules and ions that, for all practical purposes, you would be out of Earth's atmosphere.

Temperatures in the Atmosphere

The division of Earth's atmosphere into layers is based on temperature differences. Figure 9-5 illustrates the temperature changes throughout the layers.

Earth's atmospheric gases heat up when they absorb energy from the sun. For example, the molecules of ozone in the stratosphere absorb the sun's ultraviolet radiation, heating the stratosphere. While some layers contain gases that easily absorb the sun's energy, other layers do not. As a consequence, the various layers have different amounts of thermal energy.

Figure 9-5. The division of the atmosphere into layers is based primarily on temperature variations.

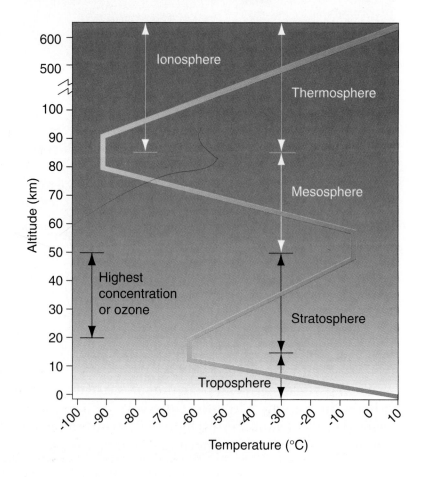

Atmospheric Pressure

Gases in the atmosphere, like all matter, have mass. The gravitational attraction between Earth and the atoms and molecules of gas causes the gas to be pulled toward Earth's surface. Atoms and molecules of the gas are pushed together because of the weight of the atmosphere above them. This increase in density causes the molecules to collide more often, causing pressure on each other.

Where do you hypothesize that pressure is greater: at the top of a mountain or at sea level? The pressure is greater at sea level because there are more molecules of air pushing down from above. In general, atmospheric pressure is greatest near Earth's surface and decreases as you move out toward space. But pressure can vary from one location to another even if the locations are at the same elevation. This happens because the density of air varies from one location to another.

How does pressure change with altitude?

TECHNOLOGY

Barometers

A barometer is an instrument used by scientists and weather forecasters to measure air pressure. One common type of barometer is pictured here. Aneroid barometers often consist of a sealed metal can with an attached pen. All of the air is removed from the can, leaving a vacuum inside. As air pressure outside of the vacuum changes, the can expands and contracts, which causes the pen to rise or fall.

A record of the changing air pressure is made as the pen marks on a chart attached to a spinning drum. Usually the drum turns one full turn in a 24-hour period.

You may be familiar with mercurial barometers. They consist of a long tube closed at one end. The tube is partially placed in a dish of mercury. As air pushes down on the mercury in the

dish, more mercury is forced into the tube. The level of mercury in the tube is measured in centimeters and rises with rising air pressure.

Think Critically: How can barometers be used to measure elevation?

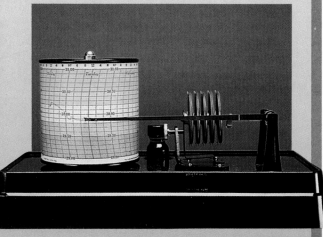

When the density of air is high, there are more molecules above a particular location exerting their weight on those below. Cold air is more dense than warm air and, therefore, has higher pressure. At any one time, one area of the United States may be covered by a high-pressure air while areas surrounding it are covered by low-pressure air. Because these masses of air are almost always moving, scientists measure the pressure changes in an area to make weather forecasts. In the Technology section of this chapter and in Chapter 10, you'll read how we measure air pressure and make forecasts based on those measurements.

Forecasting the weather allows us to plan how we will spend our day. We know whether to bring an umbrella or to plan a picnic. Understanding the composition and structure of Earth's atmosphere also helps us know when we are making changes to it. In the next section, you will read how we may be changing Earth's atmosphere and how it may affect how we all live.

SECTION REVIEW

1. What are the two most common gases in our atmosphere?
2. What are some characteristics of the troposphere?
3. Why doesn't the temperature in the atmosphere steadily increase or decrease as you move from Earth's surface toward space?
4. **Apply:** Imagine you're a football player running with the ball. You're tackled and, soon, six other players pile on top of you. Relate the pressure that you and each player above you feels to the pressure in the layers of the atmosphere.

Skill Builder

☒ Making and Using Graphs

Use Figure 9-1 to answer the following questions. If you need help, refer to Making and Using Graphs in the **Skill Handbook** on page 691.

1. What is the most abundant gas in Earth's atmosphere?
2. What percentage of the total volume of gases is argon?
3. What percentage of the total volume is nitrogen and oxygen? Argon and carbon dioxide?

ACTIVITY 9-1
Air Pressure

Problem: *How does a barometer work?*

Materials

- small coffee can
- drinking straw
- rubber balloon
- heavy paper (28 cm × 21.5 cm)
- transparent tape
- scissors
- metric ruler
- rubber band

Data and Observations

Date	Barometric readings (high or low)	Weather conditions

Procedure

1. Using the figure below as a guide, draw a line 8 cm from the right edge of the paper. Draw a second line lengthwise through the center of the paper. The second line should extend 20 cm from the left edge to the 8-cm line.
2. Cut the paper along the 20-cm line. Cut away the section shown in blue.
3. Fold the paper along the 8-cm line.
4. Wrap the section shown in dark blue around the can and fasten with tape. The long edge of the paper should stick up above the can to form a gauge.
5. Cover the top of the coffee can with the rubber balloon. The balloon must be stretched tightly over the top of the can in order for the barometer to function correctly. Secure the balloon with a rubber band.
6. Trim one tip of the straw to a point. Position the straw so that the pointed end is alongside the gauge. Tape the other end of the straw to the balloon. DO NOT tape the straw to the gauge.
7. Make a horizontal mark on the gauge showing the position of the straw. Write "high pressure" above this mark, and write "low pressure" below this mark.
8. Keep track of the movement of the straw over a period of a week. Also record the weather conditions each day. Record your observations in a data table similar to the one shown.

Analyze

1. Explain how your barometer works.
2. What type of barometric readings would you expect if you brought your barometer to the top of a mountain? The mesosphere?

Conclude and Apply

3. What type of weather is usually associated with high pressure? With low pressure?
4. How can a weather forecaster use the barometric reading to help formulate a forecast?

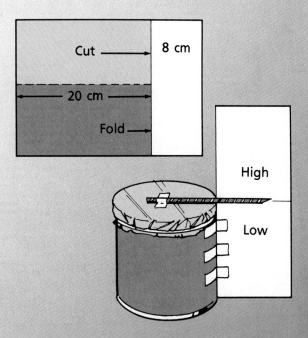

9-2 The Ozone Layer

New Science Words

ozone layer
ultraviolet radiation
chlorofluorocarbons

Objectives

▶ Explain why exposure to ultraviolet radiation can be a problem for plants and animals.
▶ Describe how chlorofluorocarbons destroy ozone molecules.

Do We Need to Protect the Ozone Layer?

About 24 kilometers above your head lies the ozone layer. You can't see, feel, smell, or observe it in any way. It's out of reach and unobservable, yet your life depends on it. The ozone layer is a shield between you and harmful energy coming from the sun.

Ozone is a compound whose molecules are composed of three oxygen atoms bonded together. The **ozone layer** is a layer in the stratosphere where concentrations of ozone are high. Ozone absorbs most of the ultraviolet radiation that enters the atmosphere. **Ultraviolet radiation** is one of the many types of energy that comes to Earth from the sun. Ultraviolet radiation can cause you to tan or sunburn. Too much exposure to this radiation, however, causes people to develop skin cancer. It causes cancer and other health problems in many types of plants and animals.

What would happen if the ozone layer disappeared? Already, about 27 000 Americans develop skin cancer annually, and 6000 die from it. If the ozone layer disappeared, these numbers would probably

Figure 9-6. What's causing the ozone layer to disappear?

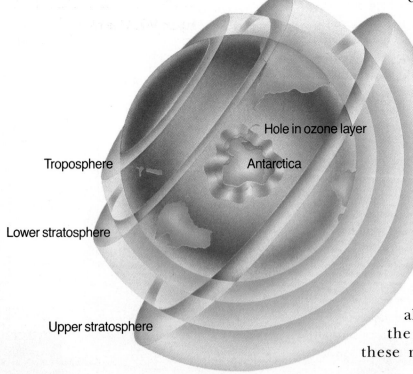

Troposphere

Lower stratosphere

Upper stratosphere

Hole in ozone layer

Antarctica

increase. But that may be exactly what's happening. In 1986, scientists found areas in the stratosphere where almost no ozone existed. One very large hole was over Antarctica. A smaller hole was discovered over the North Pole. Since that time, every year, these holes appear during certain seasons, and disappear during others. Not only is the ozone layer missing over the poles, but the entire ozone layer has become thinner around the world.

We don't know for sure why the ozone layer is disappearing, but some scientists hypothesize that pollutants in the environment are the cause. Chlorofluorocarbons are a group of chemicals that are being blamed. **Chlorofluorocarbons** are used in making refrigerants, some aerosol sprays, and some foam products. They enter the atmosphere when these products are manufactured and used.

Chlorofluorocarbon molecules destroy ozone molecules when they come in contact with each other. Recall that an ozone molecule is composed of three oxygen atoms bonded together. When a chlorine atom from a chlorofluorocarbon molecule comes near a molecule of ozone, the ozone molecule breaks apart. It forms the same type of oxygen that you breathe in the troposphere. This oxygen can't absorb ultraviolet radiation. The result is that more ultraviolet radiation reaches the plants and animals of Earth's surface.

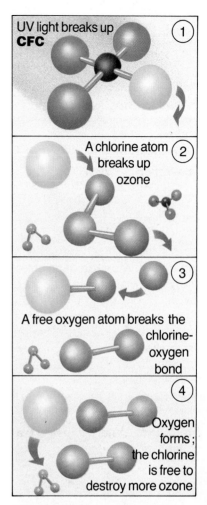

Figure 9-7. One atom of chlorine can destroy 10 000 ozone molecules.

SECTION REVIEW

1. Why is exposure to too much ultraviolet radiation a problem?
2. How do chlorofluorocarbons destroy ozone molecules?
3. Why do people other than those living near the poles need to be concerned about the ozone layer?

You Decide!

The use of chlorofluorocarbons has provided us with many conveniences including refrigerators, air conditioners, spray paints, and foam cups and fast food containers. However, when we use these products, we may be destroying the ozone layer. Is the risk worth it? Which of these conveniences would you be willing to give up if it were proven that they cause holes in the ozone layer?

Energy from the Sun

New Science Words

radiation
conduction
convection

Objectives

▶ Describe three things that happen to the energy Earth receives from the sun.
▶ Contrast radiation, conduction, and convection.

Energy Transfer in the Atmosphere

After returning from work, you eat dinner and sit down to read the evening news as it's transmitted on the computer network. You see that the Space Agency is still trying to create a hospitable atmosphere on Mars. It's studying the atmospheres of Earth and Venus to understand how they work and how an Earthlike atmosphere might be produced on Mars. The atmosphere on Mars is currently too thin to support life or to hold much heat from the sun. As a result, Mars is a cold, lifeless world. Venus' atmosphere is so dense that almost no heat coming in from the sun can escape. Venus is so hot that a living thing would instantly melt if put on its surface.

After finishing the story, you decide to go for a walk. You think about Mars and Venus and how Earth is different from them. In our solar system, there are many planets circling the star we call the sun, but Earth is the

Figure 9-8. Most radiation entering Venus' atmosphere is trapped by thick gases and clouds. On Mars, a thin atmosphere allows much radiation to escape. Earth's atmosphere creates a delicate balance between energy received and energy lost.

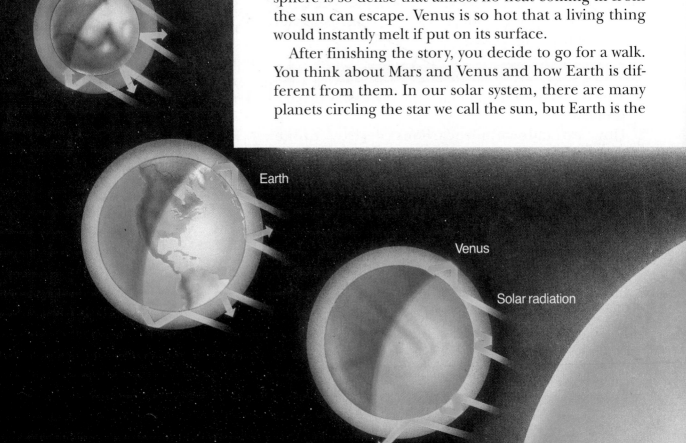

only one known to support life. Why is this the case? How does the interaction between Earth's atmosphere and the sun provide an environment suitable for life?

The sun is the source of all energy on Earth. Three different things happen to the energy Earth receives from the sun. Some of it escapes back into space, some is absorbed by the atmosphere, and some is absorbed by land and water surfaces. The balance among these three events controls the characteristics of the atmosphere and the life that it supports. Let's take a look at what happens to the energy that reaches Earth.

What three things may happen to energy from the sun?

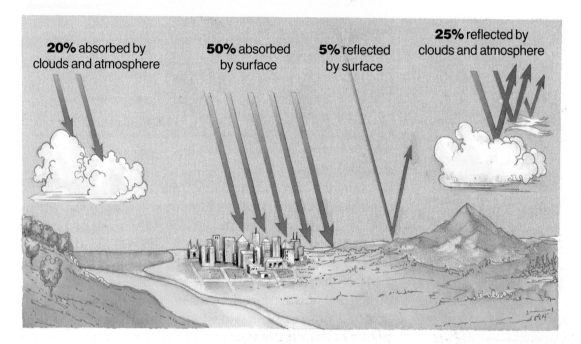

20% absorbed by clouds and atmosphere

50% absorbed by surface

5% reflected by surface

25% reflected by clouds and atmosphere

Radiation

Energy from the sun reaches our planet in the form of radiant energy, or radiation. **Radiation** is the transfer of energy by electromagnetic waves. Radiation from the sun travels through empty space as well as through our atmosphere. You experience radiation when you sit by a campfire and the side of your body facing the fire becomes warm. You aren't in direct contact with the fire, but its energy still reaches you.

When radiation from the fire reaches you, the molecules of your skin absorb the energy and you feel heat. Heat is the transfer of energy from an object with a higher temperature to an object with a lower temperature. You know that the ozone layer absorbs ultraviolet

Figure 9-9. Thirty percent of the incoming radiation is reflected back into space. Only 20 percent is absorbed by the atmosphere directly. Most atmospheric heating is from heat radiated from the surface back to the atmosphere.

Figure 9-10. Pollution can change the proportions of radiation that enter and leave the atmosphere. Some types of pollution prevent radiation from escaping back into space, possibly causing Earth's temperature to rise.

radiation. When ozone and other gases absorb radiation, the temperature of the atmosphere rises. Vegetation, rocks, and surfaces such as asphalt also absorb radiation.

Once objects at Earth's surface have absorbed radiation, they can transfer heat back to the atmosphere. Heated surfaces give off radiation, but the radiation they give off is slightly different than that coming from the sun. Much of the radiation coming from the sun can pass through the atmosphere, whereas most radiation coming from Earth's surface can't pass back out into space.

On Venus, even less radiation is able to escape back to space. As a result, Venus is extremely hot. On Earth, there is a delicate balance between heat received from the sun and heat escaping back to space. In your future weather forecast this morning, you read that temperatures were going to be very high. This may be because smog and other pollutants in the atmosphere keep radiation from returning to space. You'll learn more about this one-way flow of energy in Chapter 10.

Some radiation from the sun isn't absorbed by Earth's atmosphere or surface objects. Instead, it simply reflects off the atmosphere and surface, like a ball bouncing off a wall. Figure 9-9 illustrates the percentages of radiation absorbed and reflected by Earth's surface and atmosphere.

Conduction

When you walk barefoot on asphalt during a hot summer day, your feet heat up because of conduction. The asphalt was heated by radiation from the sun, but your feet are heated because they're in direct contact with the asphalt. In a similar way, objects on Earth's surface transfer energy directly to the atmosphere. As air moves over hot land, oceans, and roads, it's heated by conduction.

Conduction is the transfer of energy that occurs when molecules bump into one another. Molecules are always in motion, but molecules in heated objects move more rapidly than those in cooler objects. Energy is transferred from the fast-moving molecules to slow-moving molecules until all molecules are moving at about the same rate.

Convection

After the atmosphere is warmed by radiation or conduction, the heat is transferred throughout the atmosphere by a third process. This process is convection. **Convection** is the transfer of heat that occurs because of density differences in the air. Let's see how this works.

When air is warmed, the air molecules move apart. This increases the volume of the air, which, in turn, reduces its density. With lower density, there is less air

How is air heated by conduction?

Figure 9-11. Heat is transferred within Earth's atmosphere by the processes of radiation, conduction, and convection.

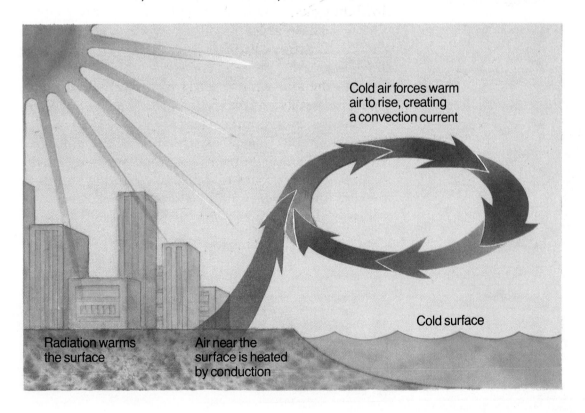

Cold air forces warm air to rise, creating a convection current

Cold surface

Radiation warms the surface

Air near the surface is heated by conduction

Science and WRITING

Mars and Venus are similar to Earth in size and structure, but have atmospheres very different from Earth's. Write a report about how the atmospheres of these three planets differ. Include in your report a discussion of the possibility of "terra-forming," or creating an Earthlike atmosphere, on Mars.

pressure because there are fewer molecules pressing in on each other. Cold temperatures affect the air density in just the opposite way. Molecules move closer together and the density and air pressure increase.

Because warm air has low density, it rises as cold air moves in and pushes it up. A circular movement of air, called a convection current, results.

Our Unique Atmosphere

Convection currents and other processes that transfer energy control the environment that we all live in. As you have seen, radiation from the sun can escape back into space, be absorbed by the atmosphere, or be absorbed by bodies on Earth's surface. Once it's been absorbed, heat can be transferred by radiation, conduction, or convection. Just how much and what type of radiation is absorbed determines the type of life, if any, that can exist on this planet. Other planets in the solar system similar to Earth, such as Venus and Mars, don't absorb and lose radiation like Earth does. Their atmospheres aren't able to support life as we know it. Many factors determine whether a planet will have an atmosphere capable of supporting life. But one thing is for certain, learning about our atmosphere will help us protect it so it can support life for years to come.

SECTION REVIEW

1. Why doesn't the sun transfer energy to Earth through the process of conduction?
2. What is a convection current?
3. Pollution may be making our atmosphere more like Venus'. How might this affect temperatures on Earth?
4. **Apply:** Suppose you fill a balloon with air, and then put it into a freezer. Will the balloon shrink, expand, or stay the same size? Why?

Skill Builder

☑ Concept Mapping

Make a cycle concept map that explains what happens to energy that reaches Earth as radiant energy. If you need help, refer to Concept Mapping in the **Skill Handbook** on pages 688 and 689.

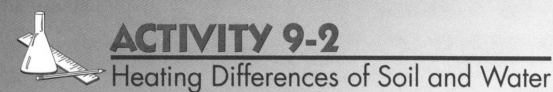

ACTIVITY 9-2
Heating Differences of Soil and Water

Problem: *How do soil and water compare in their abilities to absorb and release heat?*

Materials
- ring stand
- soil
- metric ruler
- graph paper
- clear plastic boxes (2)
- overhead light with reflector
- thermometers (4)
- water
- masking tape
- colored pencils (4)

Procedure
1. Fill one box two-thirds full of soil.
2. Place one thermometer in the soil with the bulb barely covered. Use masking tape to fasten the thermometer to the side of the box as shown.
3. Position a second thermometer in the box with its bulb about 1 cm above the soil. Tape the thermometer in place.
4. Fill the second box two-thirds full of water.
5. Position the remaining two thermometers the same way as you did in the soil box.
6. Attach the light source to the ring stand. Place the two boxes about 2 cm apart below the light. The light should be about 25 cm from the tops of the boxes.
7. Record the temperature of all four thermometers with the light turned off.
8. Turn on the light. Check to make sure that the bulbs of the thermometers are shielded from direct light.
9. Take temperature readings every two minutes for 14 minutes and record.
10. Turn off the light. Take temperature readings every two minutes for 14 minutes and record.
11. Using temperature units on the vertical axis and time in minutes on the horizontal axis, graph your data. Use a different colored pencil to plot the data from each different thermometer.

Analyze
1. Did the air heat up faster over water or soil?
2. When the light was turned off, which lost heat faster, water or soil?
3. Compare the temperatures of the air above the water and above the soil after the light was turned off.

Conclude and Apply
4. Explain how the information you gathered relates to land and sea breezes.

Data and Observations

Light on				
Time (minutes)	Temperature (°C)			
	1	2	3	4
0				
2				
Light off				
Time (minutes)	Temperature (°C)			
	1	2	3	4
0				
2				

Movement of Air

New Science Words

Coriolis effect
doldrums
trade winds
prevailing westerlies
polar easterlies
jet streams
sea breezes
land breezes

Objectives

▶ Explain why different latitudes receive different amounts of solar energy.
▶ Describe causes of the Coriolis effect, sea breezes, and land breezes.
▶ Locate the positions of the doldrums, trade winds, prevailing westerlies, and polar easterlies.

The Coriolis Effect

Have you ever watched a tree swaying in the breeze and wondered where wind comes from? Wind is the movement of air molecules from an area of high pressure to an area of lower pressure. In this section, you'll learn how temperature differences on Earth's surface create areas of different pressure and the winds that circulate the air on our planet.

What causes temperature differences at Earth's surface? Because Earth's surface is curved rather than flat, not all areas receive the same amount of radiation. Figure 9-12 illustrates why more radiation is received at the equator than at any other latitude. Thus, the air above the

Figure 9-12. Near the poles, the sun's rays are spread out more than at the equator. So, equal amounts of energy don't heat equally—each square meter of land at the poles receives less energy than each square meter at the equator.

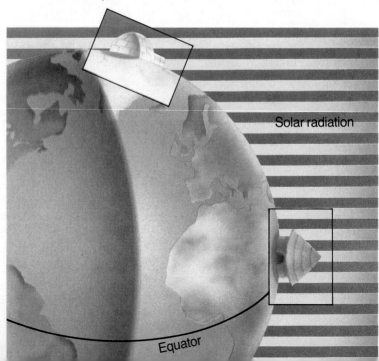

Solar radiation

Equator

equator is heated more than at any other place on Earth. As you know, heated air has low density and low pressure, so it rises.

Because less radiation is received at the poles, air there is much cooler. This dense, high pressure air sinks and moves along the surface.

Because Earth rotates, the **Coriolis** (kohr ee OH lus) **effect** is created. This effect causes air masses moving in the northern hemisphere to be turned westward from their original paths. Imagine a volume of cold, dense air from the North Pole moving toward the equator. To someone standing at the equator, the southbound air appears to be turning to the west because Earth is moving to the east. Just the opposite is true in the southern hemisphere. When seen from space, overall air movement appears to be from northeast to southwest in the northern hemisphere, whereas airflow in the southern hemisphere is from southeast to northwest. The flow of air caused by differences in heating and by the Coriolis effect has created distinct wind patterns on Earth's surface. Not only do these wind systems determine the weather, but they also determine when and where ships and planes can travel.

Name two things that are responsible for Earth's major wind patterns.

PROBLEM SOLVING

The Coriolis-go-round

Ricardo and Sam were playing on a merry-go-round when they made an interesting observation. Sam sat in the middle of the spinning merry-go-round and threw a rubber ball to Ricardo. To Ricardo, the ball appeared to travel in a straight line from Sam to him. But to Sam, the ball appeared to be curving as it traveled from him to Ricardo.

Think Critically: Was the ball actually curving as it traveled to Ricardo? Why did it appear to Sam, on the spinning merry-go-round, to follow a curved path?

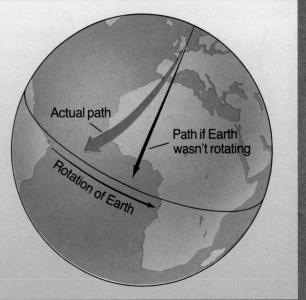

Actual path

Path if Earth wasn't rotating

Rotation of Earth

Wind Systems

Earlier, you read a possible forecast from your future. Now, let's venture into the past. Suppose you're sailing the oceans during the time of Christopher Columbus and the explorers who followed him.

You don't have any motors to propel your ship. You depend entirely on the winds for energy. As an experienced explorer of the oceans, you know you must avoid getting into the doldrums. The **doldrums** are the windless zone at the equator. There, the air seems motionless. Actually, the air in the doldrums is rising almost straight up. Do you remember why this happens?

A better place to sail is 15° north or south of the equator. There, air that has descended to Earth's surface creates steady winds that blow to the southwest. In the southern hemisphere, they blow toward the northwest. You know these winds as the **trade winds.** The northern trade winds provide a route for ships sailing from Europe to the Americas.

Between 30° and 60° north and south of the equator, winds blow in the opposite direction from the trade winds. These winds are called the **prevailing westerlies.** As a sailor, you use the prevailing westerlies to go east from the Americas to Europe. The prevailing westerlies blow from the southwest to the northeast in the northern hemisphere, and they are responsible for much of the movement of weather across the United States and Canada. In the southern hemisphere, the prevailing westerlies blow from the northwest to the southeast.

The last major wind systems at Earth's surface are the **polar easterlies.** These winds blow from the northeast to the southwest near the North Pole and from the southeast to the northwest in the southern hemisphere.

The trade winds, prevailing westerlies, and polar easterlies are the major wind systems at Earth's surface. There are also winds at higher altitudes. Narrow belts of winds, called **jet streams,** are located near the top of the troposphere. Flowing from west to east, they occur over locations where the trade winds and polar easterlies meet the prevailing westerlies. Thus, there are two jet streams in each hemisphere. These streams of air resemble very fast-moving, winding rivers. Their speeds range between 8 and 200 km/h, and their positions in latitude and altitude change from day to day and season to season.

What are the names of the major wind systems?

Just as sailors seek the trade winds, prevailing westerlies, and polar easterlies to help propel their ships, jet pilots take advantage of the jet streams when flying east. They save both time and fuel by using the energy of these winds.

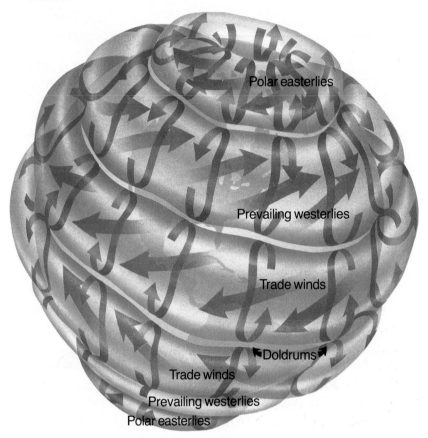

Figure 9-13. The purple arrows show the many convection currents resulting from differential heating of the latitudes. The blue arrows show the world's major wind systems created when air moving across the surface is deflected eastward or westward due to the Coriolis effect.

Sea Breezes and Land Breezes

The wind systems you've just read about determine weather patterns for the entire globe. But there are much smaller wind systems that determine local weather. If you live near a large body of water, you're familiar with two such wind systems—land breezes and sea breezes.

Convection currents over areas where the land meets the sea cause sea breezes and land breezes. **Sea breezes** are created during the day because solar radiation warms the land more than the water. Air over the land is heated by conduction. This heated air becomes less dense and is forced upward by cooler denser air moving inland from the ocean. A convection current results.

How are sea breezes and land breezes similar?

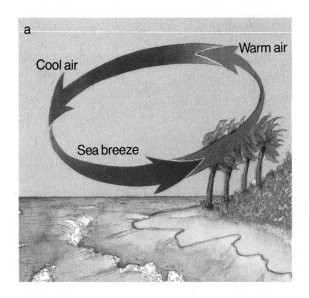

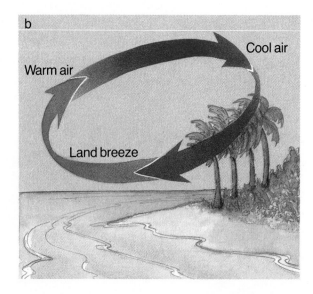

Figure 9-14. Cool air forces warm air to rise, creating a sea breeze during the day (a) and a land breeze at night (b).

At night, the land cools much more rapidly than the ocean water. Air over the land becomes cooler than the air over the ocean. The cool, dense air from the land moves out over the water, pushing the warm air over the water upward. Movements of air toward the water are called **land breezes.** Figure 9-14 illustrates sea breezes and land breezes.

SECTION REVIEW

1. Why do latitudes differ in the amount of solar energy they receive?
2. Why would a sailing ship take one route as it traveled from America to Europe and a different route on its return voyage?
3. Explain why a passenger jet that first flies from South Carolina to Arizona uses more fuel and takes longer to complete its journey than when it returns from Arizona to South Carolina.
4. **Apply:** Explain why the direction of the wind changes during a 24-hour period near the beaches of San Diego, California.

Skill Builder

☒ **Comparing and Contrasting**

Compare and contrast land and sea breezes. If you need help, refer to Comparing and Contrasting in the **Skill Handbook** on page 683.

CHAPTER
REVIEW

9-1: Earth's Atmosphere

1. Nitrogen and oxygen are the two most common gases in Earth's atmosphere.

2. Earth's atmosphere can be divided into layers based on temperature differences, which in turn cause differences in pressures among the layers.

3. Because the gases in Earth's atmosphere have mass, they push against one another creating air pressure.

9-2: Science and Society: The Ozone Layer

1. Exposure to too much ultraviolet radiation can cause cancer and other health problems in living things.

2. When ozone reacts with chlorofluorocarbons, the molecules of ozone break apart, changing the ozone into oxygen.

9-3: Energy from the Sun

1. Some of the sun's energy that reaches Earth escapes back into space, while some of the energy is absorbed by Earth's air, land, and water.

2. Radiation is the transfer of energy by waves. Conduction is the transfer that occurs when molecules bump into one another. Convection is the transfer of heat due to density differences in the air.

9-4: Movement of Air

1. Earth's surface is curved, thus not all areas receive the same amount of solar radiation.

2. The Coriolis effect is due to Earth's rotation. Land and sea breezes are due to convection currents that form where land areas are next to bodies of water.

3. The doldrums are the windless zone at the equator. The trade winds lie between the equator and 30° north or south of the equator. The prevailing westerlies blow between 30° and 60° north and south of the equator. The polar easterlies blow near the poles.

KEY SCIENCE WORDS

a. **chlorofluorocarbons**
b. **conduction**
c. **convection**
d. **Coriolis effect**
e. **doldrums**
f. **ionosphere**
g. **jet streams**
h. **land breezes**
i. **ozone layer**
j. **polar easterlies**
k. **prevailing westerlies**
l. **radiation**
m. **sea breezes**
n. **trade winds**
o. **troposphere**
p. **ultraviolet radiation**

UNDERSTANDING VOCABULARY

Match each phrase with the correct term from the list of Key Science Words.

1. layer of atmosphere closest to Earth
2. absorbs ultraviolet radiation
3. transfer of energy by waves
4. transfer of heat that occurs due to density differences in air
5. air that turns from its original path experiences this
6. occurs when cold air over water moves inland
7. windless zone at the equator
8. are used by ships sailing from Europe
9. blow in opposite directions from the trade winds
10. winds that blow near the poles

CHAPTER
REVIEW

CHECKING CONCEPTS

Choose the word or phrase that completes the sentence.

1. _____ is the most abundant gas in the air.
   a. Oxygen   **c.** Argon
   b. Water vapor   **d.** None of these

2. Smog is a mixture of compounds of sulfur, nitrogen, and _____.
   a. water vapor   **c.** oxygen
   b. carbon   **d.** argon

3. The _____ is the uppermost layer of the atmosphere.
   a. troposphere   **c.** mesosphere
   b. stratosphere   **d.** thermosphere

4. The coldest layer of air is the _____.
   a. troposphere   **c.** mesosphere
   b. stratosphere   **d.** thermosphere

5. _____ protects living things from too much ultraviolet radiation.
   a. Ozone   **c.** Nitrogen
   b. Oxygen   **d.** Argon

6. _____ is the transfer of energy from a warmer object to a cooler object.
   a. Absorption   **c.** Radiation
   b. Heat   **d.** Convection

7. Air in contact with hot surfaces is heated by _____.
   a. absorption   **c.** radiation
   b. conduction   **d.** convection

8. Differences in _____ cause wind.
   a. pressure   **c.** radiation
   b. conduction   **d.** convection

9. Movement of air toward water is a _____.
   a. sea breeze   **c.** land breeze
   b. doldrum   **d.** prevailing wind

10. _____ are near the top of the troposphere.
    a. Doldrums   **c.** Polar easterlies
    b. Jet streams   **d.** Trade winds

UNDERSTANDING CONCEPTS

Complete each sentence.

11. Air pressure is greatest in the _____.

12. _____ may be adding to the increase in health hazards by destroying ozone molecules.

13. When objects are in contact, energy is transferred by _heat_.

14. The _____ receives more radiation from the sun than the poles.

15. The _Trade Wind_ is an area that sailors avoid because air there is moving vertically.

THINK AND WRITE CRITICALLY

16. Compare and contrast the troposphere and the thermosphere.

17. Why have some countries banned the use of chlorofluorocarbons in manufacturing?

18. How does radiation differ from conduction?

19. Explain why air rises at the equator and sinks near the poles.

20. Why do ships take one route from Europe to the Americas and a different route on the return voyage?

APPLY

21. Why are there few or no clouds in the stratosphere?

22. It is thought that life could not exist on land until the ozone layer formed, about 2 billion years ago. Why did life on land require an ozone layer?

23. Explain how a pan of soup on a stove is heated by conduction and convection.

24. Why do land breezes occur during the night and sea breezes during the day?

25. How would a southward-moving air mass appear to move to an observer at 30° south latitude?

MORE SKILL BUILDERS

If you need help, refer to the Skill Handbook.

1. **Concept Mapping:** Make a cycle concept map that explains how air moves to form a convection current.

2. **Making and Using Graphs:** Does air pressure increase more rapidly at high or low altitudes? Why doesn't the air pressure drop to zero on the graph? At what altitude would it drop to zero?

Air pressure changes with altitude

3. **Observing and Inferring:** Suppose you measured the air temperature one meter above the ground on a sunny afternoon and again one hour after sunset. You observed that your second reading was lower than the first. What can you infer from this?

4. **Hypothesizing:** Trees use carbon dioxide to photosynthesize. Carbon dioxide in the atmosphere blocks radiation from Earth's surface from escaping to space. Hypothesize how the temperature on Earth would change if many trees were cut down.

5. **Using Variables, Constants, and Controls:** Describe how you could compare the abilities of soil and water to absorb and release heat. What are your variables? Your constants? Your controls?

PROJECTS

1. Use a metal sinker, a piece of string, water, and a beaker to determine the volume of air in a small, inflated balloon.

2. Design and conduct an experiment to find out how different surfaces such as aspalt, soil, sand, and water absorb and reflect solar energy.

10 Weather and Climate

A tornado is one type of severe weather that you will learn about in this chapter. Most weather conditions, however, are not destructive. How does a tornado move and what forces make it destructive?

FIND OUT!

Do this simple activity to find out more about tornadoes.

Obtain two 2-liter plastic bottles. Fill one about ¾ full of water and add one drop of dishwashing soap. Tape the mouth of the empty bottle to the mouth of the bottle with water in it. Make sure the tape has secured the bottles together. Now, flip the bottles so the one with the water is on top, and move the top bottle in a circular motion. What is forming in the bottle? How is this model of a tornado similar to a real tornado?

Gearing Up
Previewing the Chapter

Use this outline to help you focus on important ideas in this chapter.

Section 10-1   What Is Weather?
▶ Factors of Weather
▶ Clouds and Precipitation

Section 10-2   Weather Patterns
▶ Changes in Weather
▶ Severe Weather

Section 10-3   Forecasting and Climate
▶ Forecasting the Weather
▶ Climate

**Section 10-4   Science and Society
Can We Slow Down Global Warming?**
▶ The Greenhouse Effect
▶ Global Warming

Previewing Science Skills

▶ In the **Skill Builders,** you will make a concept map, recognize cause and effect, and compare and contrast.
▶ In the **Activities,** you will observe, infer, measure, predict, and read a scientific diagram.
▶ In the **MINI-Labs,** you will make a model, and observe and infer.

What's next?

You know that weather affects you every day. Luckily, severe weather such as a tornado doesn't occur very often. But weather does constantly change. In this chapter, you'll learn about weather and about the factors that determine our weather.

10-1 What Is Weather?

Objectives

▶ Explain the role of water vapor in the atmosphere and how it affects weather.
▶ Compare the origins of rain, hail, sleet, and snow.
▶ Describe how clouds form.

Factors of Weather

What's one of the very first things you want to know every morning when you get up? You probably ask, "What's the weather going to be like today?" You depend on information about the weather for a variety of reasons. You need to decide what to wear to school, and you need to plan after-school activities if they're outdoors.

Although you probably use the word *weather* every day, can you really explain what it is? **Weather** refers to the present state of the atmosphere and describes the current conditions. Some of the important factors that determine the present state of the atmosphere are air pressure, wind, temperature, and the amount of moisture in the air.

In Chapter 7, you learned how water moves around the hydrosphere in the water cycle. With the sun providing the energy, water evaporates into the atmosphere. There, it forms clouds and eventually falls back to Earth.

What are some factors that determine weather?

Figure 10-1. The weather influences what you do and what clothes you wear.

The water cycle forms the basis of our weather. But the sun does more than just evaporate water. It also heats air, causing it to rise and form the winds that you read about in Chapter 9. The interaction of air, water, and the sun cause our weather.

Humidity

You know from studying the water cycle that the sun evaporates water into the atmosphere. How can air hold water? Air is somewhat like a sponge. A sponge has holes in it that allow it to hold water. Air molecules in the atmosphere have spaces between them too. Like a sponge holds water, the atmosphere holds water vapor molecules. The amount of water vapor in the air is humidity. You've probably heard this term used before. People often comment on the high humidity on hot summer days when the air seems damp and sticky. The amount of water vapor in the air varies from day to day. What factors cause it to change?

The amount of water vapor that air can hold depends on the temperature of the air. At cooler temperatures, air and water vapor molecules are moving slowly. This slow movement makes it easier for the water vapor molecules to join together (condense). At warmer temperatures, air and water vapor molecules are moving quickly. Water vapor molecules can't join together easily. Condensation doesn't occur easily, so this air can hold more water vapor than air with cooler temperatures.

What does the amount of water vapor that air can hold depend on?

Figure 10-2. This chart shows that the amount of water vapor that air can hold increases with an increase in temperature.

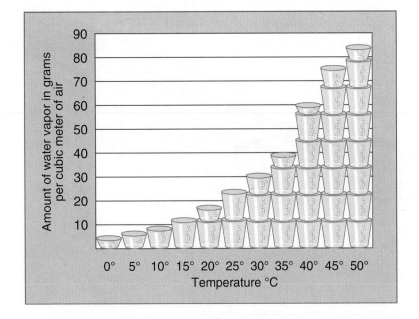

Figure 10-3. Condensation forms on a glass when the air next to it is cooled to its dew point.

What will happen to water vapor added to air that is already saturated?

For example, air can hold a maximum of 22 grams of water vapor at 25°C. On the other hand, the same air cooled down to 15°C can only hold about 13 grams of water vapor. This is how temperature affects humidity.

Have you ever heard a weather forecaster speak of relative humidity? **Relative humidity** is a measure of the amount of water vapor in air, compared to the total amount of water vapor it has room for at a particular temperature. It is stated as a percent. If you hear the weather forecaster say that the relative humidity is 50 percent, that means that the air on that day is holding only 50 percent of the water vapor it is capable of holding. Weather forecasters measure humidity because change in humidity often indicates a change in weather. Meteorologists use a psychrometer (si KRAH muh tur) as seen in Figure 10-4 to measure relative humidity. You'll use a home-made psychrometer in Activity 10-1 to measure the relative humidity of your classroom.

When air is holding all of the moisture it possibly can at a particular temperature, it's said to be **saturated** (SACH uh rayt id). Saturated air has 100 percent relative humidity. Any more water vapor will condense back to a liquid or freeze depending on its temperature. The temperature at which air is saturated and condensation takes place is the **dew point.**

You've probably experienced the water droplets that form on the outside of a glass of ice water. Why does this occur? The cold glass cools the air next to it. When the air reaches its dew point, the water vapor condenses and forms water droplets on the glass. Dew on grass in the early morning forms

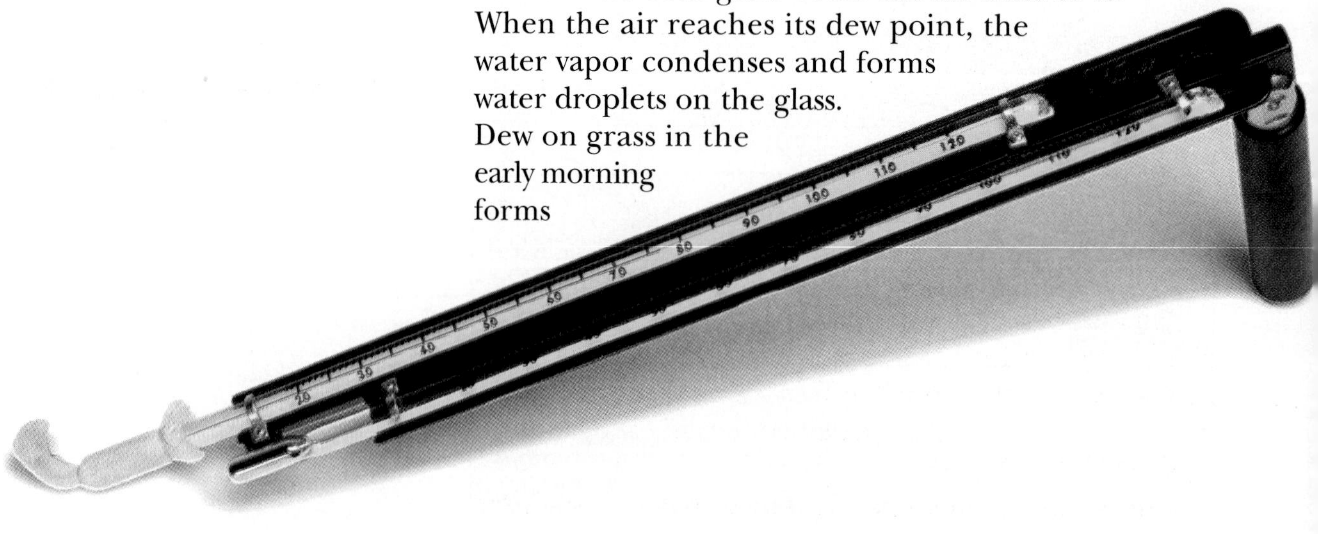

Figure 10-4. The humidity of air is measured with a psychrometer.

the same way. When air near the ground is cooled to its dew point, water vapor condenses and forms droplets on the grass.

Clouds and Precipitation

Have you ever wondered what clouds are made of? Would you believe that clouds are made of millions of tiny drops of water? These drops of water are so small that they are suspended in the air. Why are there clouds in the sky? Clouds form as humid air is cooled to its dew point and condenses. The condensing water vapor forms tiny drops of water around dust particles in the atmosphere. When millions of these drops form together, a cloud forms.

MINI-Lab

How can dew point be determined?

Partially fill a shiny metal container, such as a cup or can, with room temperature water. While slowly stirring the water with a thermometer, carefully add small amounts of ice. Note the exact temperature at which a thin film of moisture first begins to form on the outside of the metal can. Repeat the procedure two more times, making sure that the outside of the can is dry and the water begins at room temperature each time. The average of the three temperature readings at which the moisture begins to appear is the dew point temperature of the air around the container. What factors determine the dew point temperature? Will a change in air temperature cause the dew point temperature to change also? Explain.

Figure 10-5. Fog is a cloud formation near the ground.

You've probably seen many different types of clouds. They vary in shape and in the altitude at which they form in the atmosphere. Some clouds stack up vertically reaching high into the sky, while others are low and flat. Some dense clouds bring rain or snow, while other thin clouds appear on mostly sunny days. In Table 10-1 you'll find the major types of clouds, a description of each, and the type of weather associated with each.

Some stratus clouds form right next to the ground. Air that is cooled to its dew point near the ground condenses and forms a stratus cloud called **fog.** This also occurs when warm, moist layers flow across a cold surface.

What type of cloud is fog?

Table 10-1

CLOUD TYPES

VERTICAL CLOUDS 500 to 18 000 meters

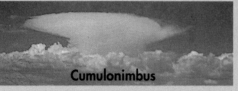
Cumulonimbus

Cumulus

- Towering clouds, may spread out at top to form an anvil shape
- Associated with thunderstorms, heavy rain, hail

- Dense, billowy clouds
- Associated with fair weather, but may produce precipitation if vertical development is great

HIGH CLOUDS above 6000 meters

Cirrostratus

Cirrocumulus

Cirrus

- Veil-like clouds, may cause halos around the moon or sun
- Associated with fair weather, may indicate approaching storm

- Thin, white clouds, may look like ripples, waves, or rounded masses
- Associated with fair weather, but may indicate approaching storm

- Thin, white, feathery clouds of ice crystals
- Associated with fair weather, may indicate approaching storms

MIDDLE CLOUDS 2000 to 6000 meters

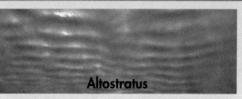
Altostratus

Altocumulus

- Gray fibrous clouds; sun or moon appears as a "bright" spot
- May produce light, continuous precipitation

- Light gray clouds in patches or rolls
- Often precede rain or thunderstorms

LOW CLOUDS below 2000 meters

Nimbostratus

Stratus

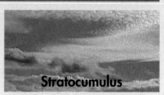
Stratocumulus

- Thick layer of dark clouds that blocks out the sun
- Associated with steady, long precipitation

- Low layer of gray clouds that may cover the entire sky
- Associated with light drizzle

- Soft gray clouds, may form a continuous layer
- Occasionally produce light rain or snow

As long as the water drops remain small, they stay suspended in the air. However, when droplets reach 0.2 millimeters, they're too heavy to remain suspended and fall out of the clouds. Falling water drops form **precipitation.** Precipitation can have many different forms depending on the temperature of the air the water drop falls through. Air temperature determines whether the water droplets form rain, snow, sleet, or hail—the four main types of precipitation. Drops of water that fall in temperatures above freezing fall as rain. Snow forms when the temperature is so cold that water vapor changes directly to a solid—snow. Temperatures in the air must be below freezing for snow to form.

Hail forms when drops of water freeze in layers around a small nucleus of ice. Hail forms in thunderstorms. Hailstones grow larger as they're tossed up and down by rising and falling air currents in the storm. Sleet forms when snow passes through a layer of warm air, melts, and then refreezes near the ground.

PROBLEM SOLVING

Where's the Water?

Jason and Kim decided that they would help their father fix spaghetti for dinner, so that he could have time to work in the garden. The sauce was already cooking, and it was time to cook the noodles. Jason filled a large pot 3/4 full with water and turned the burner to the highest temperature setting. After a few minutes of watching the pot, Kim and Jason could see that it was still not boiling. So they decided to watch TV while they were waiting.

They got so interested in the program they were watching, they lost track of the time. All at once, Jason remembered the water on the stove and bolted toward the kitchen. Much to his surprise, the pot was only 1/2 full of boiling water. On the wall above the stove were droplets of water.

After a minute, Jason understood what had happened. He put the noodles in the water and returned to the TV room to explain to Kim what had happened.

Think Critically: What did Jason tell Kim?

Table 10-2

Dry Bulb Temperature	Dry Bulb Temperature Minus Wet Bulb Temperature, °C									
	1	2	3	4	5	6	7	8	9	10
10°C	88	77	66	55	44	34	24	15	6	
11°C	89	78	67	56	46	36	27	18	9	
12°C	89	78	68	58	48	39	29	21	12	
13°C	89	79	69	59	50	41	32	22	15	7
14°C	90	79	70	60	51	42	34	26	18	10
15°C	90	80	71	61	53	44	36	27	20	13
16°C	90	81	71	63	54	46	38	30	23	15
17°C	90	81	72	64	55	47	40	32	25	18
18°C	91	82	73	65	57	49	41	34	27	20
19°C	91	82	74	65	58	50	43	36	29	22
20°C	91	83	74	67	59	53	46	39	32	26
21°C	91	83	75	67	60	53	46	39	32	26
22°C	92	83	76	68	61	54	47	40	34	28
23°C	92	84	76	69	62	55	48	42	36	30
24°C	92	84	77	69	62	56	49	43	37	31
25°C	92	84	77	70	63	57	50	44	39	33
26°C	92	85	78	71	64	58	51	46	40	34
27°C	92	85	78	71	65	58	52	47	41	36
28°C	93	85	78	72	65	59	53	48	42	37
29°C	93	86	79	72	66	60	54	49	43	38
30°C	93	86	79	73	67	61	55	50	44	39

SECTION REVIEW

1. How do clouds form?
2. When does water vapor in air condense?
3. What two factors determine relative humidity?
4. **Apply:** Explain why cold air can hold less moisture than warm air.

Skill Builder

☑ Concept Mapping

Make a network tree concept map that compares four cloud types. Use these terms: *cirrus, cumulus, stratus, nimbostratus, feathery, fair weather, puffy, layered, precipitation, cloud types, dark,* and *steady precipitation.* If you need help, refer to Concept Mapping in the **Skill Handbook** on pages 688 and 689.

ACTIVITY 10-1
Relative Humidity

Problem: *How is relative humidity determined?*

Materials

- identical Celsius thermometers (2)
- piece of gauze, 2 cm^2
- tape
- string
- cardboard
- beaker of water

Procedure

1. Attach the gauze to the bulb of one thermometer with string as shown.
2. Tape both thermometers side by side on the cardboard with the bulbs hanging over the edge of one end. You have created a psychrometer.
3. Thoroughly wet the gauze on the thermometer by dipping it into the beaker of water. This is called a wet bulb thermometer.
4. Create air motion across the thermometer bulbs by gently fanning them with a sheet of paper.
5. Wait until the alcohol stops moving in this thermometer and record the temperature.
6. Record the temperature of the dry bulb thermometer.
7. Subtract the wet bulb temperature from the dry bulb temperature.
8. Determine relative humidity using Table 10-2. Find the temperature difference you determined in Step 7 by reading across the top of the table. Keep one finger on this number. Find the dry bulb temperature in the first column of the table. Look across this row until you find the column you marked with your finger. The number at the point where the row and column intersect is the percent relative humidity.
9. Repeat Steps 3-8 at another location inside your school building. Be sure to resoak the wet bulb thermometer at your new test location. Also, wait at least 5 minutes in order to let the thermometers adjust to the new location.
10. Repeat Step 9 at a test site outside of your school building.

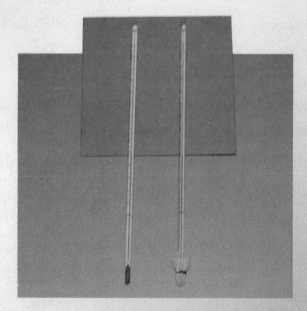

Analyze

1. What was the relative humidity at your three different test sites?

Conclude and Apply

2. Why did the wet bulb thermometer record a temperature lower than that recorded by the dry bulb thermometer?
3. What would be the relative humidity if the wet bulb and dry bulb thermometers recorded the same temperature?
4. How could the relative humidity in your classroom be decreased?
5. Why did the relative humidity vary at your three test sites?
6. How is relative humidity determined?

Weather Patterns

New Science Words

air mass
front
tornado
hurricane

Objectives

▶ Describe the weather associated with fronts and high and low pressure areas.
▶ Explain how low pressure systems form at fronts.
▶ Relate thunderstorms to tornadoes.

Changes in Weather

Why do you ask about the weather in the morning when you get up? Isn't it safe to assume that the weather is the same as it was the day before? Of course not! Weather is always changing because of the constant movement of air and moisture in the atmosphere. These changes are generally related to the development and movement of air masses.

What is an air mass?

An **air mass** is a large body of air that has the same properties as the surface over which it develops. For example, an air mass that develops over land is dry compared to one that develops over water and is moist. Also, an air mass that develops in the tropics is warmer than one that develops at a higher latitude.

Fronts

When you witness a change in the weather from one day to the next, it is due to the movement of air masses.

Figure 10-6. These are the six major air masses that affect the United States. Each has the same characteristics of temperature and moisture content as the area over which it forms.

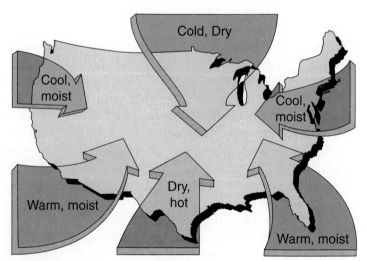

Cold, Dry

Cool, moist

Cool, moist

Dry, hot

Warm, moist

Warm, moist

When an air mass moves, it collides with another air mass, and a boundary forms between the two masses called a **front.** Most changes in weather occur at one of the four types of fronts.

A warm front develops when a warm air mass meets a cold air mass. The warm air, because it is less dense, slides up over the cold air. The first sign of this front is the presence of high cirrus clouds that form as rising water vapor condenses. Later, stratus clouds form as the front continues to move. Nimbostratus clouds may develop and produce rain or snow.

A cold front forms when a cold air mass invades a warm air mass. The cold air forces the warm air rapidly aloft along the steep front. Cumulus and cumulonimbus clouds form along the front, producing rain and thunderstorms.

A stationary front results when pressure differences cause a warm front or a cold front to stop moving forward. This type of front may remain in the same place for several days. Weather conditions include light winds and precipitation across the entire frontal region.

An occluded front results when two cool air masses merge, forcing the warmer air between them to rise. Strong winds and heavy precipitation may occur in an occluded front.

Precipitation is associated with each type of front. Do you know why? You learned earlier that when air is cooled, its ability to hold water is reduced. All along each of these fronts, warm air is being cooled. The air becomes saturated and water is precipitated.

What causes a front to develop?

Figure 10-7. These diagrams show the structure of a cold front, a warm front, and an occluded front.

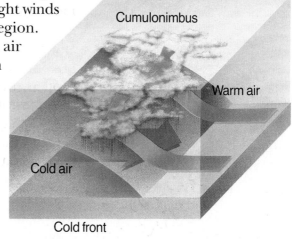

Cumulonimbus

Warm air

Cold air

Cold front

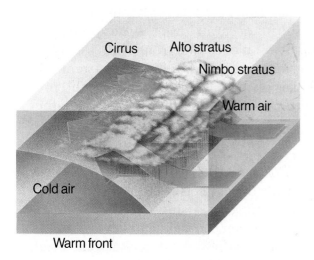

Cirrus   Alto stratus

Nimbo stratus

Warm air

Cold air

Warm front

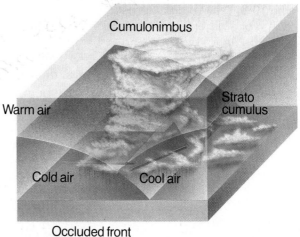

Cumulonimbus

Strato cumulus

Warm air

Cold air   Cool air

Occluded front

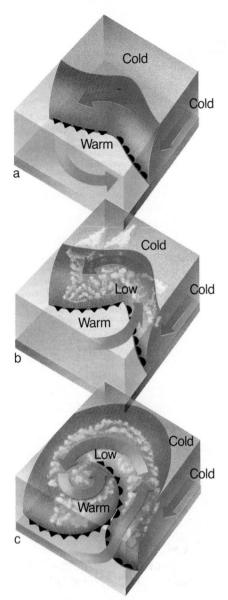

Figure 10-8. When a disturbance occurs along a front (a), the air masses begin to rotate around the disturbance forming a cold front and a warm front, with low pressure at the center (b). Eventually, the cold air forces all of the warm air up, forming an occluded front (c).

Pressure Systems

You've probably heard about low and high pressure systems in weather forecasts. Differences in pressure have a great effect on the weather. High pressure usually means clear weather and low pressure means cloudy weather.

As you learned in Chapter 9, air molecules have mass and cause air molecules to exert pressure on each other. When air molecules are densely packed, high pressure occurs. Barometers on Earth record high pressure on Earth as a result of cold, dense air that is sinking. As it descends, molecules heat up as more and more of them bump into each other. The warming of the air decreases its relative humidity and water vapor is evaporated. That's why high pressure means good weather. Moisture in the air is evaporated before it can form clouds.

Because of winds in Earth's atmosphere, pressure systems don't usually stay in one place for very long. Sooner or later they move, and another pressure system follows. Barometers record low pressure on Earth as warm, less dense air rises. One place where low pressure forms is along fronts where warm air meets cold air. These low pressure systems cause most of the weather changes in the United States. Thunderstorms are one result of these low pressure systems.

As stated earlier, different air masses don't mix together when they meet and form a front. Due to the Coriolis effect, air at this boundary sometimes begins to swirl counterclockwise in the northern hemisphere, as seen in Figure 10-8. The rising air in this swirling front forms a low pressure system. As the air in a low pressure system rises, it cools. At a certain point, the air reaches its dew point and condenses, forming clouds. Several different types of precipitation and storms occur in low pressure systems.

After several days, an occluded front evolves from the two swirling air masses in the low pressure system. The warm, moist air is pushed above cold air and the pressure begins to rise, bringing another change in weather.

Severe Weather

You know that weather affects you every day. Usually, you can still go about your business regardless of the weather. If it's raining, you can still go to school, and if it snows a little, you can still get to the store. But some weather conditions prevent you from going about your normal routine. Severe weather is weather conditions that pose danger to humans.

Thunderstorms

Have you ever experienced a thunderstorm? Heavy rain fell, lightning flashed, thunder roared, and maybe hail even fell. What forces cause such extreme weather conditions? Thunderstorms result from the rapid upward movement of warm, moist air. They can occur inside warm, moist air masses and at fronts. As the warm, moist air moves upward, it cools, condenses, and forms cumulonimbus clouds that can reach heights of 10 km. As the rising air reaches its dew point, water droplets and ice form and begin falling the long distance through the clouds toward Earth's surface. As the droplets fall, they collide with other droplets and become larger. The falling droplets create a downdraft of air that spreads out at Earth's surface and causes strong winds associated with thunderstorms.

Thunder and lightning are also associated with thunderstorms. During the rapid uplift of air, electric charges build up in the clouds. Some places in the clouds have a positive electrical charge and some have a negative electrical charge. Lightning occurs when current flows between regions of opposite electrical charge. Bolts of lightning can leap from cloud to cloud and from clouds to Earth.

What causes lightning?

Figure 10-9. A thunderstorm may include heavy rain, strong winds, thunder, lightning, and hail.

Thunder results from the rapid heating of the air around a bolt of lightning. Lightning can reach temperatures of about 28 000°C. That's more than five times the temperature of the surface of the sun! This extreme heat causes the air around the lightning to expand rapidly, forming a sound wave we hear as thunder.

Thunderstorms can cause a lot of damage. The rain sometimes causes flooding, and the lightning can strike objects and set them on fire. Strong winds generated by thunderstorms can also cause damage. If a thunderstorm has winds traveling faster than 80 kilometers per hour and hail more than two centimeters in diameter, it is classified as a severe thunderstorm. Hail can make dents in cars and the siding on houses. Even though the rain from thunderstorms helps crops grow, hail can flatten and destroy a crop in a matter of minutes.

Tornadoes

Some of the most severe thunderstorms produce tornadoes. A **tornado** is a violent, whirling wind that moves in a narrow path over land. In very severe thunderstorms, warm air is forced upward at great speed, causing very low pressure at Earth's surface. Strong winds approaching the center of the low pressure system collide from

What causes thunder?

Figure 10-10. The diagram on the left shows how wind forms funnel clouds like the one on the right.

Tailing a Tornado

A tornado can develop in less than an hour and can destroy property and kill people within a matter of minutes.

Next Generation Weather Radar, or NEXRAD, is a system of radar stations that uses Doppler radar to track severe weather such as tornadoes. Doppler radar sends out radio waves toward the storms. The waves reflect off of the storm clouds and are recorded at the radar station. The shift in frequency of the reflected signals allows meteorologists to determine the position, strength, and wind speed of the storm. Doppler radar helps scientists to detect tornadoes before they touch down.

Think Critically: Suppose a tornado were moving toward your town at 100 km/h. If Doppler radar spotted the storm 160 km from your town, how much time would you have to prepare for the storm?

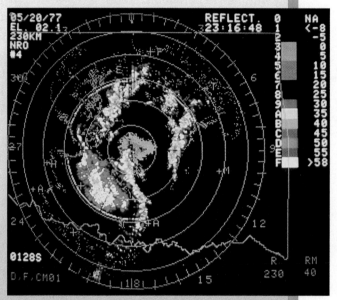

different directions and begin to rotate violently. When this happens, the air pressure inside drops rapidly, and a funnel cloud appears at the base of the cloud. Water vapor condenses in the funnel as it picks up dirt and debris from the ground. This gives a funnel its dark gray or black color.

When tornado funnels touch the ground, buildings and trees are ripped apart by the destructive winds that can reach up to 500 kilometers per hour. The pressure in the center of a tornado is so low that when it passes over buildings, the buildings actually explode because their inside pressure is higher than the tornado's pressure. The updraft in the center of a tornado can be so strong, it can lift animals, cars, and even houses into the air and move them. Even though tornadoes average only 200 meters in diameter, and last for a period of a few minutes, they are one of the most destructive types of storms.

Why are tornadoes usually dark gray or black?

Science and READING

Go to the library and get a book on weather experiments. Read about how you can make a model hurricane. You may want to consider the project for class. You might also find information about a model hurricane in an encyclopedia.

Figure 10-11. In this hurricane cross section, the red arrows indicate rising warm, moist air forming cumulus and cumulonimbus clouds in bands around the eye. The blue arrows indicate cool, dry air sinking in the eye and between the cloud bands. The purple arrows indicate the circular motion of the spiral cloud bands.

Hurricanes

The largest and most powerful severe storm is the hurricane. A **hurricane** is a large, swirling, low pressure system that forms over tropical oceans. A storm must have winds of at least 120 km/hour to be called a hurricane.

Hurricanes are similar to low pressure systems on land, but are much larger. They form over tropical oceans where two opposing winds meet and begin to swirl. For example, in the North Atlantic the southeast trade winds and the northeast trade winds sometimes meet. A low pressure area develops in the middle of the swirl and begins rotating counterclockwise in the northern hemisphere. This usually happens between 5° and 20° north latitude where the water is quite warm. Around the middle of the low pressure area, warm, moist air is forced up. As it rises to higher elevations, it cools and moisture condenses.

As long as a hurricane is over water, the warm, moist air will rise and provide energy for the storm. When a hurricane reaches land, however, its supply of warm, moist air is gone and the storm loses power.

A hurricane can create a lot of damage when it reaches land. High winds, tornadoes, heavy rains, high waves, and floods occur. As a result, crops are destroyed, buildings are demolished, and people and other animals are

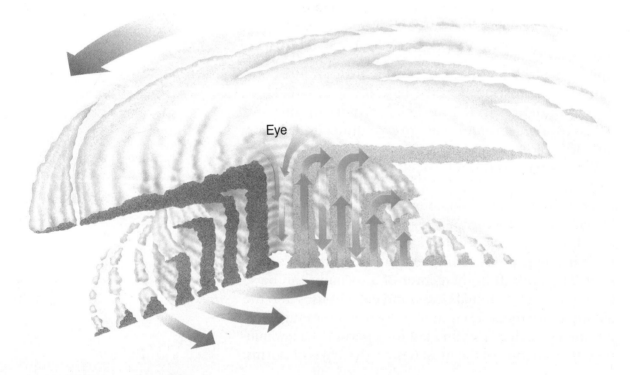

Eye

killed. In 1989, Hurricane Hugo hit the east coast of the United States, killing several people and causing about six billion dollars in damage.

Figure 10-12. Hurricanes can be very destructive.

You can see how changes in weather affect your life. The interaction of air and water vapor cause constant change in the atmosphere. Air masses meet and fronts form, causing changes in weather. Severe weather can affect human lives and property.

SECTION REVIEW

1. How can a low pressure system form at a front?
2. What weather is associated with a cold front?
3. Why do high pressure areas usually have clear skies?
4. Explain how a tornado evolves from a thunderstorm.
5. **Apply:** What would happen to a balloon in a tornado? Would it expand or contract? Why?

⊠ Recognizing Cause and Effect

Skill Builder

Use your knowledge of weather to answer the following questions. If you need help, refer to Recognizing Cause and Effect in the **Skill Handbook** on page 683.

1. What effect does a warm, dry air mass have on the area over which it forms?
2. What causes a cold front? What effect does a cold front produce?
3. Describe the cause and effect of an occluded front that might form over your city.

10-3 Forecasting and Climate

New Science Words

meteorologist
station model
isotherm
isobar
temperate zones

Objectives

▶ Explain how weather maps are made.
▶ Contrast tropical, temperate, and polar climates.
▶ Explain how large bodies of water and mountains affect climate.

Forecasting the Weather

You can easily tell what current weather conditions are by simply making observations. You can feel the temperature and you can see if clouds are in the sky. You also have a general idea of the weather because you are familiar with the climate you live in. For example, if you live in Florida, you probably won't have to worry about snow in the forecast. But what weather concerns do you have in your own climate?

A **meteorologist** is a person who studies the weather. Meteorologists make measurements of temperature, air pressure, winds, humidity, and precipitation. In addition to these, radar, computers, and instruments in balloons are also used to gather data. Meteorologists make observations to include on weather maps. They use weather maps to make weather forecasts, and they warn people of severe weather.

Figure 10-13. A station model shows the weather conditions at one specific location.

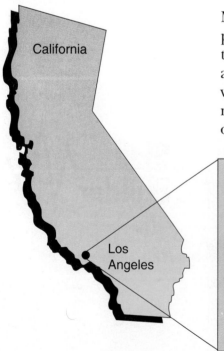

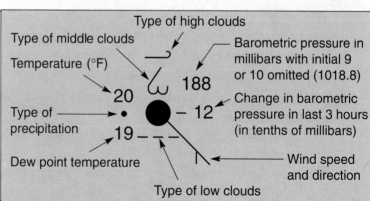

Type of high clouds
Type of middle clouds
Temperature (°F)
Barometric pressure in millibars with initial 9 or 10 omitted (1018.8)
188
20
Change in barometric pressure in last 3 hours (in tenths of millibars)
Type of precipitation
— 12
19 – – –
Dew point temperature
Wind speed and direction
Type of low clouds

Because storms like hurricanes, tornadoes, blizzards, and thunderstorms can be very dangerous, meteorologists at the National Weather Service issue advisories when severe weather has been observed, or when the conditions are such that severe weather could occur. When a watch is issued, you should prepare for severe weather. Watches are issued for severe thunderstorms, tornadoes, floods, blizzards, and hurricanes. During a watch, stay tuned to a radio or television station that is reporting weather updates. When a warning is issued, severe weather conditions exist, and you should take immediate action. Take shelter during a severe thunderstorm warning. During a tornado warning, go to the basement or a room in the middle of the house away from windows.

How do you suppose the National Weather Service knows when to issue weather advisories? It depends on two sources for its information: meteorologists from around the world and satellites.

Once meteorologists have made their measurements in their specific location, they communicate their findings to the National Weather Service. The Weather Service uses this information to make weather maps that are used to warn of severe weather and to forecast the weather.

Weather maps for large areas show the information collected by meteorologists in specific locations. This information is expressed using combined symbols, forming a **station model.** Figure 10-13 shows a station model and the information it contains.

Besides station models, there are also lines on weather maps that indicate atmospheric pressure and temperature. A line that connects points of equal temperature is called an **isotherm.** *Iso* means "same" and *therm* means "temperature." You've probably seen isotherms on weather maps on TV. An **isobar** is a line drawn to connect points of equal atmospheric pressure. Isotherms and isobars are like the contour lines you learned about in Chapter 8. But instead of connecting points of equal elevation, they connect locations of equal temperature or pressure.

Isobars indicate the locations of highs and lows on a map. These areas are drawn as circles with an *H* or an *L* in the middle. You can tell how fast the wind is blowing by looking at how close the isobars are to one another. When isobars are close together, there's a great pressure difference over a small area. That means there are strong winds. If isobars are spread apart, there's less of a difference in pressure, and winds are more gentle.

Figure 10-14. This person is collecting data, such as temperature and atmospheric pressure, for a weather forecast.

How are isobars and isotherms similar to, yet different from contour lines?

Climate

You know that weather conditions vary from day to day in the area where you live. If you live in Montana, you know that you can expect snow in the winter. But what's the weather like in other places around the world like Australia or Greenland? The climate there might be quite different from the one you live in now. As you recall from Chapter 5, climate is the average of all weather conditions of an area over a long period of time. These conditions include the average temperatures, air pressure, humidity, and days of sunshine for a period of 30 years. Greenland is generally cold and damp, whereas much of Australia is hot and dry.

Meteorologists classify climates in several different ways. One way is by the average yearly temperature of different regions. As you learned in Chapter 9, the amount of solar energy received at a particular location on Earth depends on the angle at which the sunlight strikes Earth.

Areas in the tropics ($23\text{-}1/2°$ north latitude to $23\text{-}1/2°$ south latitude) receive the most direct rays. Year-round temperatures in these areas are always hot, except at high elevations.

The polar zones extend from the poles to $66\text{-}1/2°$ north and south latitudes. Solar energy hits these regions at a low angle and is distributed over a large area. Also, some of the heat is lost when it's reflected by the polar ice. Therefore, the polar regions are never very warm.

Between the tropics and the polar zones are the **temperate zones.** Those of us living in the continental United States live in a temperate zone. Here, weather generally changes with the seasons. Winters are cold and summers are hot. Spring and fall usually have mild temperatures.

Actually, climates are more complex than the three general divisions of polar, temperate, and tropical. Within each zone, a number of factors affect weather patterns. As you already know, large bodies of water influence the weather. Coastal areas are warmer in the winter and cooler in summer than inland areas. Mountains, too, influence the climate. They act as barriers over which winds must flow. On the side of a mountain facing the wind, air rises, cools, and drops its moisture as precipitation. On the other side of the mountain, the air descends, heats up, and dries out the land. Deserts are common on this side of a mountain.

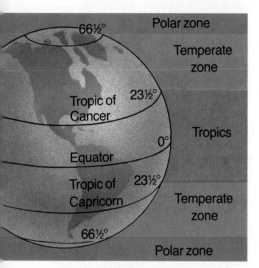

Figure 10-15. Climate zones are determined by the amount of solar energy received at different parts of Earth. The northern boundary of the tropics is called the Tropic of Cancer, and the southern boundary is called the Tropic of Capricorn.

EcoTip

Save energy this winter. During cold weather, close doors and turn off vents to unused rooms that don't need heating.

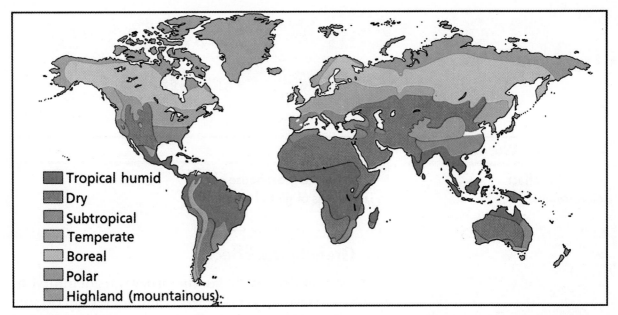

Tropical humid
Dry
Subtropical
Temperate
Boreal
Polar
Highland (mountainous)

Even though some weather patterns are predictable because of known factors of climate, some weather events are hard to predict. As you've learned in this chapter, weather is constantly changing. Sometimes the conditions that affect weather are unpredictable and can change very quickly. The next time you see a weather report for the United States, look at the weather in a different climate than your own. Imagine how your day would be different with that weather forecast.

Figure 10-16. This world climate map is based on the average temperature, rainfall, and other measurements over a period of 30 years.

SECTION REVIEW

1. How are weather maps made?
2. What are differences between tropical and temperate climates?
3. How do mountains affect climate?
4. **Apply:** Use Appendix K to analyze the station model—Figure 10-13 on page 270. What is the temperature, type of clouds, wind speed and direction, and the type of precipitation at that location?

☑ Comparing and Contrasting

Contrast Earth's three climate zones. If you need help, refer to Comparing and Contrasting in the **Skill Handbook** on page 683.

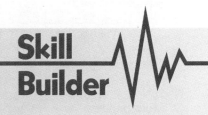

Skill Builder

10-4

Can We Slow Down Global Warming?

New Science Words

greenhouse effect
deforestation

Objectives

▶ Describe the greenhouse effect.
▶ List causes of global warming.

The Greenhouse Effect

Do you remember the last sunny day you got into a car that had the windows up? It was really hot inside. Do you know why? When sunlight shines through the car windows, it is absorbed by the seats and other materials inside the car. Some of this energy is then radiated from the seats as heat. Heat radiation cannot pass through glass, so the temperature inside the car got hotter and hotter. This also happens in glass greenhouses. Sunlight penetrates the glass and heat that is reflected by the plants in the greenhouse can't escape back through the glass. This warms the air in greenhouses.

Why does it get hot in a green-house?

This process of warming also happens to Earth. As you learned in Chapter 9, much of the heat radiated from Earth's surface is reflected back down to Earth by gases in the atmosphere. This causes Earth's atmosphere to warm up. This process by which heat is trapped by gases

Figure 10-17. In the greenhouse effect, heat from the sun is trapped next to Earth's surface by greenhouse gasses from many sources.

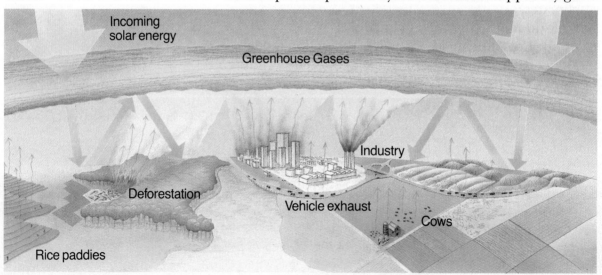

Incoming solar energy

Greenhouse Gases

Industry

Deforestation

Vehicle exhaust

Cows

Rice paddies

in Earth's atmosphere is called the greenhouse effect. Some of the gases that increase the **greenhouse effect** are carbon dioxide, water vapor, methane, nitrous oxide, and chlorofluorocarbons.

Global Warming

During this century, average temperatures on Earth have risen 0.5°C. Although you may think this is a very small temperature change, it indicates that Earth is warming. Some people blame human activities during the past 150 years for contributing to global warming.

One cause of this global warming is the burning of natural gas, petroleum, and coal to get energy. When these fuels are burned, carbon dioxide is released into the atmosphere. Carbon dioxide is one of the main gases that increases the greenhouse effect.

Another cause of global warming is deforestation. **Deforestation** is the removal of forests. Forests around the world are being cleared so that people can use the land for mining, drilling for oil, raising cattle, roads and buildings.

What does deforestation have to do with global warming? There are two problems created when trees are removed. First of all, trees take in carbon dioxide naturally as they grow. When trees are removed, the carbon dioxide they would have removed from the atmosphere is left to cause problems. Secondly, many of the trees that are removed are burned. This burning produces carbon dioxide that goes into the atmosphere.

Figure 10-18. Deforestation contributes to global warming.

Why does deforestation contribute to global warming?

SECTION REVIEW

1. What is the greenhouse effect?
2. How do human activities contribute to global warming?

You Decide!

SCIENCE & SOCIETY

As more regions of the world become industrialized, the amounts of greenhouse gases added to the atmosphere will increase. Global warming will cause the ice caps to melt, sea level to rise, and rainfall patterns to change. Regulations to reduce greenhouse gases will raise the prices of goods and put some companies out of business. What do you think? How can we reduce global warming without affecting prices and companies?

ACTIVITY 10-2
Reading a Weather Map

Problem: *How do you read a weather map?*

Materials
- hand lens
- Appendix K

Procedure
Use the information provided in the questions below and Appendix K to learn how to read a weather map.

Analyze
1. Find the station models on the map for Tucson, Arizona, and Albuquerque, New Mexico. Find the dew point, cloud coverage, pressure, and temperature at each location.
2. After reviewing information about the spacing of isobars and wind speed in Section 10-3, determine whether the wind would be stronger at Roswell, New Mexico, or at Fort Worth, Texas. Record your answer. What is one other way to tell the wind speed at these locations?
3. Determine the type of front near Key West, Florida. Record your answer.
4. The triangles or half circles on the weather front symbol are on the side of the line that indicates the direction the front is going. Determine the direction that the cold front, located over Colorado and Kansas, is going. Record your answer.

Conclude and Apply
5. Locate the pressure system over Winslow, Arizona. After reviewing Section 10-3, describe what would happen to the weather of Wichita, Kansas, if this pressure system should move there.
6. The prevailing westerlies are the winds responsible for the movement of weather across the United States and Canada. Based on this, would you expect Charleston, South Carolina, to continue to have clear skies? Explain your answer.
7. The line on the station model that indicates wind speed shows from which direction the wind is coming, and the wind is named accordingly. What is the name of the wind at Jackson, Mississippi?

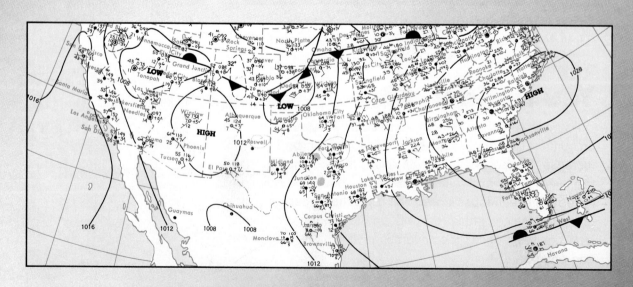

SUMMARY

10-1: What Is Weather?

1. Water vapor forms most clouds and the precipitation that falls from them. Water vapor also determines the relative humidity at a given time.

2. Rain, hail, sleet, and snow are types of precipitation that fall from clouds. The state of the precipitation depends on air temperature.

3. Clouds form when air is cooled to its dew point and water vapor condenses around dust.

10-2: Weather Patterns

1. Warm fronts may produce rain or snow. Cold fronts produce rain showers and thunderstorms. A stationary front produces slow winds and precipitation. Occluded fronts are associated with high winds and heavy precipitation. Clear skies and fair weather are due to high pressure areas, whereas low pressure areas are stormy.

2. Low pressure systems form when air at a front begins to swirl, rises and cools, and forms clouds.

3. Tornadoes are small, intense, whirling wind storms that can result from extreme conditions of strong winds and low pressure in thunderstorms.

10-3: Forecasting and Climate

1. Weather maps are made using information collected by meteorologists in their local areas.

2. Areas in the tropics receive the most direct solar rays and thus are hot all year round. Polar regions receive solar energy at low angles and are cold most of the year. Temperate regions usually have four seasons that include hot summers, cold winters, and mild falls and springs.

3. Coastal areas are warmer in the winter and cooler in the summer than inland areas. Mountains tend to also affect climate by making land on the side facing the wind cool and wet and the land on the opposite side of the mountain hot and dry.

10-4: Science and Society: Can We Slow Down Global Warming?

1. Much of the energy radiated from Earth's surface is absorbed and reflected back toward Earth by gases in the atmosphere. This trapping of heat is called the greenhouse effect.

2. The burning of fossil fuels and deforestation contribute to global warming.

KEY SCIENCE WORDS

a. air mass
b. deforestation
c. dew point
d. fog
e. front
f. greenhouse effect
g. hurricane
h. isobar
i. isotherm
j. meteorologist
k. precipitation
l. relative humidity
m. saturated
n. station model
o. temperate zones
p. tornado
q. weather

UNDERSTANDING VOCABULARY

Match each phrase with the correct term from the list of Key Science Words.

1. temperature at which condensation occurs
2. falling water droplets
3. air that can't hold any more water vapor
4. boundary between air masses
5. violent swirling storm moving in a narrow path
6. large, swirling tropical storm
7. person who studies the weather
8. symbols on a weather map describing weather
9. line on a weather map that indicates points of equal pressure
10. stratus cloud next to the ground

CHAPTER

REVIEW

Choose the word or phrase that completes the sentence.

1. Weather depends on _____.
   a. air temperature   c. air pressure
   b. amount of moisture   d. all of these

2. Cool air can hold _____ water vapor as an identical amount of warm air.
   a. the same   c. less
   b. more   d. almost the same

3. Air condenses at its _____.
   a. dew point   c. front
   b. station model   d. temperate zone

4. _____ forms when water vapor changes directly into a solid.
   a. Rain   c. Sleet
   b. Hail   d. Snow

5. _____ clouds are low, layered clouds that may produce precipitation.
   a. Cirrus   c. Cumulus
   b. Stratus   d. Nimbus

6. A(n) _____ front forms when two cool air masses merge.
   a. warm   c. stationary
   b. cold   d. occluded

7. Tornadoes are destructive because they _____.
   a. have high winds   c. cause updrafts
   b. have low pressures   d. all of these

8. A _____ is issued when severe weather conditions exist and immediate action should be taken.
   a. front   c. station model
   b. watch   d. warning

9. The poles receive_____solar energy.
   a. the most direct   c. no
   b. the least direct   d. a lot of

10. The burning of coal releases _____ into the air.
    a. oxygen   c. methane
    b. nitrous oxide   d. carbon dioxide

UNDERSTANDING CONCEPTS

Complete each sentence.

11. Water vapor will condense from air when it is _____.

12. The climate region north of 66-1/2° latitude is the _____.

13. A large body of air that has the same properties as the area over which it formed is a(n) _____.

14. Places near the equator have _____ climates.

15. A(n) _____ contains weather information for one local area.

THINK AND WRITE CRITICALLY

16. Explain how temperature affects humidity.
17. Describe the characteristics of an air mass that forms over central Canada in December.
18. What are isobars and how are they used to describe weather conditions?
19. Why do tropical areas have the warmest climates?
20. Describe how water and the sun interact to cause our weather.

APPLY

21. If you hear a weather observation that there is 79 percent relative humidity, what does that mean?
22. What weather conditions would very tall, thick clouds indicate?
23. Why doesn't hail form if rain falls through a freezing layer of air?
24. Why don't hurricanes form in polar regions?
25. If a barometer showed that the air pressure was dropping, what general weather prediction could you make?

3. **Observing and Inferring:** After letting your cold iced tea sit outside on a hot day, you observe that water droplets have formed on the outside of the glass. What can you infer?
4. **Making and Using Tables:** Use the cloud descriptions in Table 10-1 to describe the weather at your location today. Then try to predict tomorrow's weather.
5. **Hypothesizing:** You observe that a weather map of the United States shows a cold front and a low pressure system to the west of where you live. Hypothesize what the weather in your area will be like in a day or two.

MORE SKILL BUILDERS

If you need help, refer to the Skill Handbook.

1. **Comparing and Contrasting:** Compare and contrast tornadoes and hurricanes.
2. **Interpreting Scientific Illustrations:** Describe the weather conditions shown on the station model below.

PROJECTS

1. Design and construct an anemometer and a rain gauge. Use them for one week. Compare the accuracy of your instruments with reported data from radio or TV weather reports.
2. Use reference books to compare and contrast the climates of each of the seven continents. Summarize your findings in a table.

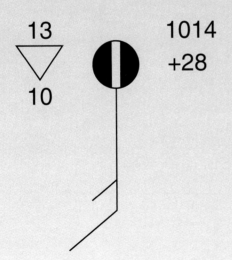

11 Ocean Water

Windsurfing looks like a lot of fun, doesn't it! But what makes this sport possible? This wind-surfer is making use of wind and waves, two aspects of the ocean environment that you will study in this chapter. How do the mighty forces of ocean waves, currents, and tides work? How are currents formed in the ocean?

FIND OUT!

Do this simple activity to discover how currents work.

Fill a large beaker with warm water. You could also use a pan of water instead of a beaker. Gently add a drop of food coloring at the center. Now carefully float an ice cube at the center. After a minute, what happens to the food coloring? Add two drops of food coloring directly on the ice cube to help you see what is happening. You have just made a density current.

Previewing Science Skills

▶ In the **Skill Builders,** you will make a concept map, classify, and compare and contrast.
▶ In the **Activities,** you will observe, interpret data, experiment, and hypothesize.
▶ In the **MINI-Labs,** you will experiment and make a model.

What's next?

Now that you've made your own and currents, you'll learn how these things happen in Earth's oceans. You'll also learn about the tides and why the oceans are salty.

Origin and Composition of Ocean Water

New Science Words

basins
salinity

Objectives

▶ Learn the origin of the water in Earth's oceans.
▶ Explain how dissolved salts and other substances get into seawater.
▶ Describe the composition of seawater.

The Ocean and You

You probably think the ocean doesn't affect you unless you live on a coastline. But actually, the ocean is influencing you right now, no matter where you live. If it is raining or snowing today, most of that water came from the ocean. If today is sunny, it is partly due to weather systems that developed over the ocean. If you eat fish today, it most likely will have come from the ocean.

Oceans also affect the prices charged for clothing, cars, and gasoline. The price includes the cost of shipping those materials across a great barrier, the ocean. If you live near a stream or river that is polluted, that pollution eventually will travel to the ocean. The ocean greatly affects your life.

Figure 11-1. We get some of our oil from rock under the oceans and some of our food from the oceans.

Origin and Composition of Oceans

In the first billion years after Earth was formed, its surface was much more volcanically active than it is today. As you'll learn in Chapter 15, volcanoes not only spew lava and ash, but give off water vapor as well. About 4 billion years ago, this water vapor began to accumulate in Earth's early atmosphere. It eventually cooled enough to condense. Precipitation began to fall onto Earth. Earth's oceans were formed over millions of years as this water filled low areas on Earth called **basins.**

Where did the water come from that formed the oceans?

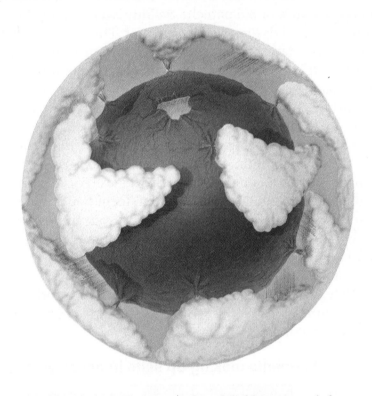

Figure 11-2. Earth's oceans formed from water vapor originally released in the atmosphere by volcanoes.

You learned in Chapter 7 that drinking water is becoming scarce in some states and countries. If Earth's surface is 70 percent ocean, why can't we use this water?

Taste water from the ocean, and you can immediately tell that it is different from the water you drink. It tastes salty. Oceanographers have learned that the ocean contains many dissolved elements, including sodium, chlorine, silica, and calcium.

Where do these elements come from? One source is groundwater, which very slowly dissolves elements such as calcium from rocks and minerals. The calcium is then carried by rivers into the ocean. Another source is volcanoes that erupt, releasing gases into the ocean.

What is one source of the dissolved elements found in ocean water?

The two most abundant dissolved elements are sodium and chlorine. Sodium is dissolved in river water that flows into the ocean. Chlorine gas is added by volcanoes. When sodium and chlorine atoms combine in the seawater, they form a salt called halite. You may recall from Chapter 3 that halite is the salt you use to season food. In the ocean, halite remains dissolved in the seawater. It's this compound, and a few similar compounds, that make ocean water taste salty. Nearly 90 percent of the salt in seawater is made of sodium and chlorine.

Every 1000 L of ocean water contains about 35 L of dissolved salts, or 3.5 percent. **Salinity** is a measure of the amount of solids dissolved in seawater. The salinity of the ocean has stayed about the same for hundreds of millions of years. This tells us that the ocean's composition is in balance.

Although substances are added constantly by rivers, volcanoes, and the atmosphere, they are being used at the same rate by plants and animals, or are forming solids on the ocean bottom. Sea animals and plants use the dissolved substances in their life processes. For example, some marine animals use calcium to form bones. Others use silica and calcium to form shells. Even some plants have silica shells. Because there are so many sea plants and animals, calcium and silica are removed very quickly from seawater.

Now you know where the ocean came from and what it contains. Next we'll see how the ocean is constantly stirred by currents.

Why does the salinity of ocean water stay balanced?

Figure 11-3. Ocean water contains about 3.5 percent salts, as shown at the left. The main elements that make up the salts in ocean water are shown at the right.

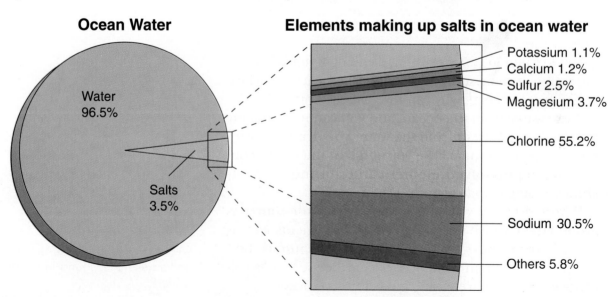

Ocean Water

Water 96.5%

Salts 3.5%

Elements making up salts in ocean water

Potassium 1.1%
Calcium 1.2%
Sulfur 2.5%
Magnesium 3.7%

Chlorine 55.2%

Sodium 30.5%

Others 5.8%

TECHNOLOGY

Desalting Ocean Water

In some areas that have little fresh water, salt is removed from ocean water. Saudi Arabia, which borders the Red Sea and the Persian Gulf, for example, makes fresh water from salt water using a desalination system.

Desalting ocean water can be done in several ways. In one method, salt water is boiled and the steam is piped into a container where it cools. As the steam forms, the salts are left behind and fresh water is produced.

In another method, permeable membranes and an electric current are used to separate the salt from the water. Membranes that allow positive ions to pass through are placed between membranes that allow only negative ions to pass. The electric current is then used to further separate the ions to produce fresh water.

In a third method of desalination, ocean water is frozen. The salt crystals are separated from the ice crystals by washing the salt from the ice with fresh water. The ice is then melted to produce fresh water.

Think Critically: Why wouldn't desalination be a good way to get fresh water for use in the center of a continent?

SECTION REVIEW

1. How do scientists think Earth's oceans formed?
2. Why does ocean water taste salty?
3. What are three ways that dissolved substances get into seawater? Give an example of each.
4. **Apply:** Why does the salinity of Earth's oceans remain balanced?

☑ Concept Mapping

Make a cycle concept map that explains how water from Earth's atmosphere can move to Earth's oceans and back. Use these terms: *evaporates, condenses, falls as precipitation,* and *collects in basins.* If you need help, refer to Concept Mapping in the **Skill Handbook** on pages 688 and 689.

Skill Builder

ACTIVITY 11-1
Desalination

Problem: How does desalination produce fresh water?

Materials

- pan balance
- table salt
- water
- 500-mL beakers (2)
- 1000-mL flask
- 1-hole rubber stopper
- rubber tubing
- hot plate
- cardboard

- ice
- shallow pan
- glass tubing bent at right angle
- glycerine
- towel
- scissors
- washers
- goggles

Procedure

1. Dissolve 18 g of table salt in a beaker containing 500 mL of water. Carefully taste the solution. **CAUTION:** *Be sure the glassware is clean.*
2. Put the solution into the flask. Place the flask on the hot plate. Do not turn on the hot plate.
3. Assemble the stopper, glass tubing, and rubber tubing as shown in the photo. To do this, rub a small amount of glycerine on both ends of the glass tubing. Hold the tubing with a towel, and gently slide it into the stopper and rubber tubing.
4. Insert the stopper into the flask. Make sure the glass tubing is above the surface of the solution.
5. Use the scissors to cut a small hole in the piece of cardboard. Insert the free end of the rubber tubing through the hole. Be sure to keep the tubing away from the hot plate.
6. Place the cardboard over a clean beaker. Add several washers to the cardboard to hold it in place.
7. Set the beaker in a shallow pan filled with ice.
8. Turn on the hot plate. Bring the solution to a boil. Observe what happens in the flask and in the beaker.

9. Continue boiling until the solution is almost, but not quite, boiled away.
10. Turn off the hot plate and let the water in the beaker cool.

Analyze

1. What happened to the water in the flask as you boiled the solution?
2. What happened inside the beaker? Explain your answer.
3. Taste the water in the beaker. Is it salty?
4. What remains in the flask?
5. Is the combined water in the flask and in the beaker the same volume you placed in the flask at the beginning of the activity? Explain.
6. Examine the sides of the flask and describe what you see.

Conclude and Apply

7. How might the desalination process be used to extract minerals from seawater?
8. How does desalination produce fresh water?

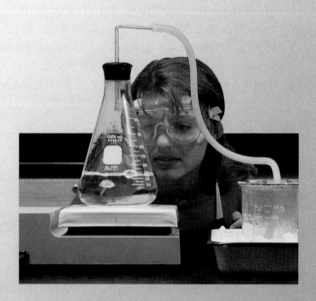

Ocean Currents

Objectives

▶ Determine how surface currents are influenced by winds, the Coriolis effect, and continents.
▶ Explain why waters off the western coasts of continents are usually colder than waters off the eastern coasts of continents.
▶ Describe how density currents cause ocean water below the surface to circulate.

New Science Words

surface current
density current
upwelling

Surface Currents

When you stir chocolate flavoring into milk, or stir a pot of soup, you make currents with the spoon. The currents are what does the mixing. In the ocean, currents move water from place to place. There are two kinds of currents—surface currents and density currents.

In the late 1760s, the American colonies depended on sailing ships to carry mail back and forth between America and England. But a constant complaint was that it took the mail two weeks longer to travel from England to America than it did to travel the other direction. The Deputy Postmaster General of the colonies, Benjamin Franklin, decided to investigate.

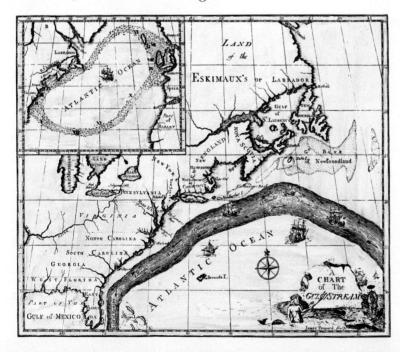

Figure 11-4. Benjamin Franklin completed this map of the Gulf Stream in about 1770.

The Gulf Stream, called "a river in the ocean," is bigger than any river on land. It is 800 m deep, flows at an average of 6.5 km/hr, and transports 1000 times as much water as the Mississippi River.

Figure 11-5. This diagram shows the major surface currents of Earth's oceans.

Franklin learned that a strong current flowed in the ocean from America toward England. On their way to England, the ships would travel with the current and it added to their speed. However, when the ships traveled the opposite direction, back toward America, they ran against the current and lost speed. This is what made them two weeks late on the trip back from England. Franklin had a cousin named Timothy Folger who was a ship captain. It was actually Folger who told Franklin about the Gulf Stream, and led to the map on page 287.

The current was only 100 km wide, so with a good map, ships could avoid the current on their way to America. To help them, Franklin drew the first map of the current. He called it the Gulf Stream because it flowed out of the Gulf of Mexico.

The Gulf Stream is still flowing. It is one of several surface currents in Earth's oceans seen in Figure 11-5. It's called a **surface current** because it affects only the upper few hundred meters of seawater. Most surface currents are caused by winds. Friction between the windblown air and the water surface causes the water to move. For

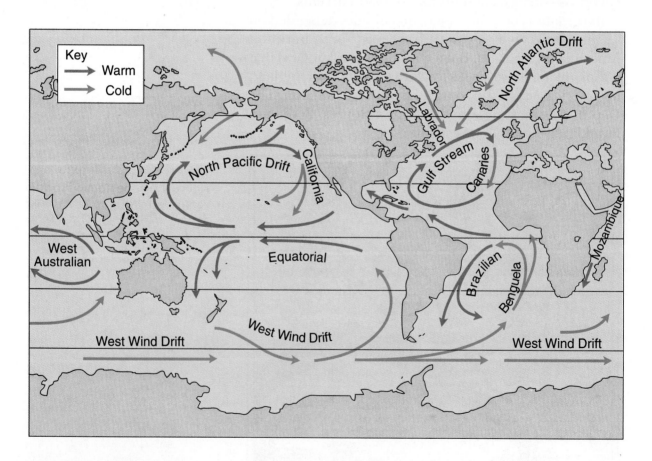

example, surface currents in the tropics are pushed by the energy of the trade winds, which you learned about in Chapter 9.

Surface ocean currents, just like surface winds, are influenced by the Coriolis effect, which you also learned about in Chapter 9. The Coriolis effect causes most currents north of the equator to move in a clockwise direction, as the Gulf Stream does. Most currents south of the equator always move in a counterclockwise direction.

Another factor that controls currents is the continents that deflect currents. For example, in the Pacific Ocean, currents moving toward the west are deflected northward by Asia and southward by Australia. These currents then move eastward until they meet North and South America, which deflect them toward the equator.

In Figure 11-5, note that many currents on the western coasts of continents are cold, whereas currents on the eastern coasts are warm. The reason is that currents on the western coasts generally originate far from the equator, in the cooler latitudes. Currents on the eastern coasts originate near the equator.

Surface currents are important because they affect the climate of places they pass by. Iceland is on the Arctic Circle, so you would expect it to have a very frigid climate. But the Gulf Stream flows past Iceland. The current's warm water heats the surrounding air. Because of the Gulf Stream, Iceland has a surprisingly mild climate. If you lived near a seacoast, how do you think the warm or cold currents off your coastline would affect your climate?

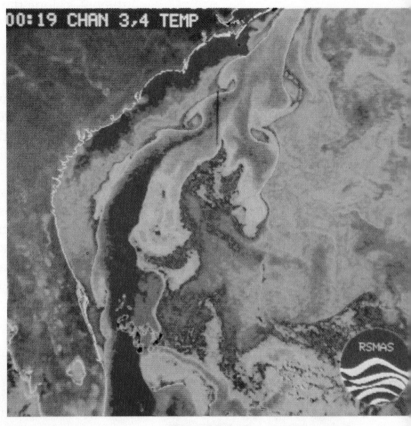

Figure 11-6. Ocean temperature data collected by a satellite were used to make this surface temperature image of the Atlantic Ocean. The warm Gulf Stream waters appear orange and red, and cooler water appears blue and green.

Density Currents

Some currents aren't caused by winds. A **density current** occurs when denser seawater moves toward an area of less dense seawater.

As you learned in Chapter 2, dense materials sink below less dense materials. In the ocean, denser water around the North Pole and the South Pole sinks and travels along the ocean floor toward the equator. At the same time, less dense water at the equator rises and moves toward the poles along the surface. These two events form a continuous cycle that circulates ocean water.

What can make seawater denser and sink? The cold air near the poles chills the water, causing its molecules to be less active and closer together. This decreases the volume of the water and makes it denser, so it sinks. Also, the cold climate freezes some of the water. This concentrates the salts in the remaining unfrozen water, which increases its mass, makes it denser, and causes it to sink. Once this happens, the colder, saltier, denser water moves as a mass along the ocean bottom.

You made a density current in the Find Out activity at the beginning of this chapter. As the ice cube melted, its cold water was denser than the warm water in the pan, so the cold water sank to the bottom. This created a density current which moved the food coloring.

What is one reason that cold ocean water is more dense than warm ocean water?

PROBLEM SOLVING

Testing the Water

Parul decided that her dog, Grover, needed a bath. She got a metal washtub and began filling it with water from the garden hose. She filled it three-fourths full. When she tested the temperature with her hand, she thought it was just too cold to put Grover into. So, she decided to heat some water on the stove and add that to the washtub. She did this, then retested the water. To her surprise, the surface of the water was very hot, but the bottom three-fourths of the water was still quite cold.

Think Critically: Why wasn't all the water in the tub the same warm temperature?

At the same time these deep density currents are flowing toward the equator, water at the equator is heated by the sun. It flows on the surface toward the poles to replace the cold water heading toward the equator in the deep ocean. As this heated water leaves the area near the equator, water below it rises, warms, and continues the density current cycle.

In some places, cold water from the deep ocean rises all the way to the surface. This occurs where strong wind-driven surface currents carry water away from an area. An **upwelling** occurs when cold water from deep in the oceans rises to the surface in an area. Upwellings bring high concentrations of nutrients to the surface. This water contains nutrients from organisms that died and sank to the bottom. Because of these nutrients, upwellings are usually good fishing areas. The coasts of Oregon, Washington, and Peru have good fishing because of upwellings.

Our knowledge has come a long way since Benjamin Franklin investigated the Gulf Stream. Today we can track the positions of currents by satellite. We use this information to help ships navigate and to help fishing fleets locate upwellings.

MINI-Lab

How can you make a density current model?

Fill a clear plastic storage box or a glass pie plate or baking dish with water at room temperature. Mix several teaspoons of table salt into a glass of water of the same temperature as the water in the container. Add a few drops of food coloring to the saltwater solution and pour it very gently and slowly into the clear water in the large container. Describe what happens. What conditions in large bodies of water, such as lakes or the ocean, all can create currents caused by density differences?

SECTION REVIEW

1. How does the energy from wind affect the behavior of surface currents?
2. What does the Coriolis effect do to surface currents in the Northern Hemisphere?
3. How do density currents affect the circulation of water in deep parts of the oceans?
4. What type of current is the Gulf Stream?
5. **Apply:** The latitudes of San Diego, California, and Charleston, South Carolina, are exactly the same. However, the average yearly water temperature in the ocean off Charleston is much higher than the water temperature off San Diego. Explain why.

☑ Classifying

How would an ocean current that forms at a depth of one kilometer be classified? If you need help, refer to Classifying in the **Skill Handbook** on page 680.

Ocean Waves and Tides

New Science Words

crest
trough
wave height
wavelength
breaker
tides
tidal range

Objectives

▶ Describe the parts of a wave.
▶ Differentiate between the movement of water particles in a wave and the movement of wave energy.
▶ Describe how waves are created by the energy of wind and the gravitational force of the moon and sun.

Waves

If you've been to the seashore, you have watched the waves roll in. If not, you have seen pictures of waves on TV. Waves are caused by winds, earthquakes, and the gravitational force of the moon and sun. You'll find out about waves caused by earthquakes in Chapter 14. But first, what are waves?

What are waves?

Waves are movements in which water alternately rises and falls. Several terms are used to describe waves. As shown in Figure 11-7, the **crest** is the highest point of the wave. The **trough** is the lowest point. **Wave height** is the vertical distance between crest and trough. **Wavelength** is the horizontal distance between the crests of two successive waves or the troughs of two successive waves.

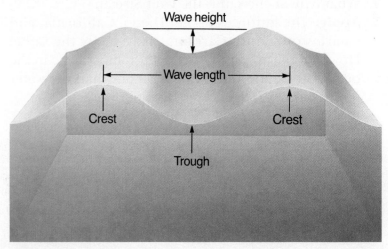

Figure 11-7. Parts of a Wave.

When you watch a wave, it looks like the water moves forward. But it doesn't. The water actually stays in about the same place. An object floating on water will rise and fall as a wave passes, but the object will not move otherwise. Each particle of water in a wave moves around in a circle. Energy moves forward while water particles remain in the same place.

When waves move into a shallow area, water at the bottom of a wave is slowed down by friction with the ocean bottom. This causes them to change shape. As they slow, their crests and troughs become closer together. Their wave heights also increase. The waves continue to grow higher as the water depth decreases. The tops of waves move faster than the bottoms, so when a wave becomes tall enough, it collapses, creating a **breaker.** Then, as the crest falls, the water tumbles over on itself. After a wave breaks onto shore, gravity pulls the water back into the sea.

Now let's look at two very different types of waves: (1) the common sea waves caused by the wind and (2) the long waves of the tides.

Why do waves slow down in shallow water?

Figure 11-8. In water, individual particles of water move in circles as a wave passes, as seen in diagram (a) below. Energy in waves is transferred like falling dominoes (b). Like water particles, individual dominoes remain near where they were standing as they fall and transfer energy.

Direction of wave movement

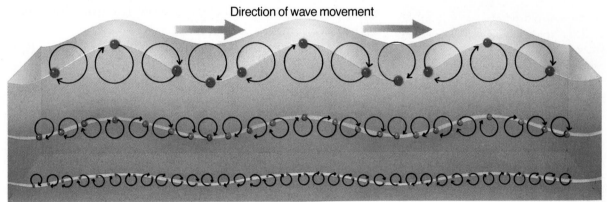

a

b

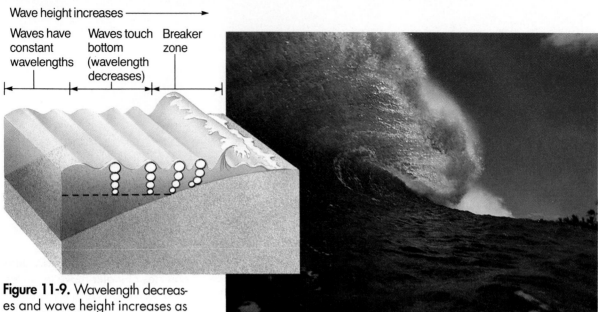

Wave height increases ⟶

| Waves have constant wavelengths | Waves touch bottom (wavelength decreases) | Breaker zone |

Figure 11-9. Wavelength decreases and wave height increases as waves approach the shore, as shown in diagram at left. This leads to breakers.

Waves Caused by Wind

When wind blows across a body of water, friction causes the water to be moved along with the wind. If the speed is great enough, the water begins to pile up, forming a wave. As the wind continues to blow, the wave increases in height.

Waves stop forming when the wind stops blowing. But, once set in motion, waves continue moving for long distances. Waves you might see at a seashore originated many kilometers away. The height of waves depends on the speed of the wind, the distance over which the wind blows, and the length of time the wind blows.

Tides

Besides the waves caused by wind, waves also are created by the gravitational force of the moon, the sun, and Earth. These long waves that result in a periodic change in the surface level of the oceans are called **tides.** Along most seashores, tides make the sea level slowly rise and fall by a few meters twice a day. The **tidal range** is the difference between high tide and low tide.

You learned about gravitational force in Chapter 6 when you learned that gravity causes loose materials to move down a slope. Gravitational force is an attractive force that exists between all objects. The strength of gravity is affected by the masses of objects and the distances between them. The bigger the objects and the closer they are to one another, the greater the gravitational attraction between them.

The moon and Earth are relatively close together in space, so the moon's gravity exerts a strong pull on Earth. The gravitational force of the moon is stronger on the side of Earth that is facing the moon. The moon's gravity pulls on water particles in the ocean and causes the water to bulge on the side toward the moon and on the side opposite the moon.

These bulges of water on both sides of Earth actually are waves that we call high tides. When high tides form, water is drawn away from the areas between the bulges, creating low tides at those places.

As Earth rotates, different locations on Earth's surface pass through the high and low positions. Many coastal locations, such as the Atlantic and Pacific Coasts of the United States, experience two high tides and two low tides each day. Ocean basins vary in size and shape, so some coastal locations, such as many along the Gulf of Mexico, have only one high and one low tide each day.

The sun also affects tides. The sun can strengthen or weaken the moon's effects. When the moon, Earth, and sun are lined up, high tides are higher and low tides are lower than normal. These are called spring tides. When the sun, Earth, and moon form a right angle, high tides

Figure 11-10. The difference between high and low tide is easily seen at Mt. Saint Michel off the northwestern coast of France.

Figure 11-11. When the sun, moon, and Earth are aligned, spring tides occur. When the sun, moon, and Earth form a right angle, neap tides occur.

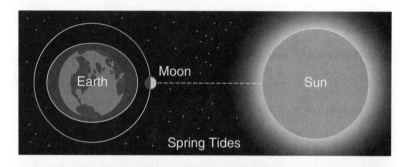

Spring Tides

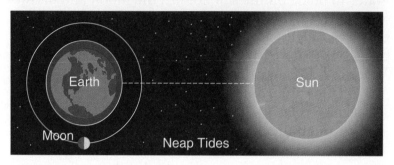

Neap Tides

What are neap tides?

are lower and low tides are higher than normal. These are called neap tides.

In this section, you've learned how the energy of the wind and gravity causes waves. Now when you go to the beach, you'll understand the various movements of the water. In the next lesson, you'll see a valuable way that people use the energy of waves.

SECTION REVIEW

1. What do the terms *wavelength* and *wave height* mean?
2. One day at the ocean, you spot a large wave about 200 meters from shore. A few seconds later, the wave breaks on the beach. Why is the breaker composed of different water than the wave was made of when you first saw it?
3. How does wind cause waves?
4. **Apply:** You're walking along a beach on a clear night and you notice that the tide is really high, but the moon is nowhere in sight. Where must the moon be? Why?

Skill Builder

☒ **Comparing and Contrasting**

Compare and contrast the effects of the sun and moon on Earth's tides. If you need help, refer to Comparing and Contrasting in the **Skill Handbook** on page 683.

ACTIVITY 11-2
Air Motion and Waves

Problem: **What is the effect of wind on waves?**

Materials

- white paper
- electric fan (3-speed)
- light source
- clock or watch
- clear plastic shoe or storage box
- ring stand
- water
- metric ruler
- protractor

Procedure

1. Place the light source on the ring stand. Position the plastic box on top of the paper under the ring stand.
2. Arrange the light source so that it shines directly on the box.
3. Pour water into the box to almost fill it.
4. Place the fan at one end of the box as shown in the photo. Start it on slow. **CAUTION:** *Do not allow any part of the fan or cord to come in contact with the water.*
5. After three minutes, measure the height of the waves caused by the fan. Record your observations in a table similar to the one shown. Observe the shadows of the waves on the white paper through the plastic box.
6. After five minutes, measure the waves and record your observations in your table.
7. Repeat Steps 4 to 6 with the fan on medium, and then with the fan on high.
8. Turn off the fan and observe what happens.

Data and Observations

Fan Speed	Time	Wave height	Observations
Low			
Medium			
High			

Analyze

1. From your data sheet, is the wave height affected by the length of time that the wind blows? Explain.
2. Is the height of the waves affected by the force (velocity) of the wind? Explain.
3. How does an increase in fan speed affect the pattern of the shadows of waves on the white paper?
4. What caused shadows to appear on the paper below the plastic storage box?
5. What was the effect when you turned off the fan?

Conclude and Apply

6. What three factors cause the wave height to vary in the oceans?
7. Where does the energy that generates waves come from? How could this energy be used to reduce Earth's dependence on its decreasing supply of fossil fuels?

11-4 Tapping Tidal Energy

New Science Words

turbine

salt marsh

Objectives

▶ Explain why Nova Scotia's Bay of Fundy is a good place to build a tidal power plant.
▶ Relate how a tidal dam converts energy from tides into electricity.
▶ Consider the consequences of building a power plant at the Bay of Fundy.

Science and WRITING

Every year on September 23, the Center for Marine Conservation sponsors a 3-hour beach cleanup to help save the water, birds, and fish. If you'd like to help, write to the center for information on adopting a local beach. The mailing address is 1725 DeSales St., NW, Washington, DC 20036.

Tidal Power

Imagine having a constant supply of nonpolluting energy that you could use to generate electricity. You wouldn't be burning fossil fuels or polluting the air. You wouldn't be worried about running out of electricity for heat, air conditioning, and appliances. In areas where there is a large difference between the water level of high and low tide, tides can be used to generate electricity.

Electric power generating plants that use tidal energy already have been built in France, Russia, and China. The Bay of Fundy in Nova Scotia is a perfect location for tapping energy from tides because the tidal range there reaches 16 m, the greatest on Earth. At the Bay of

Figure 11-12. This is the LaRance Tidal Power Plant at Saint Malo, France.

Fundy, the water moves through a narrow opening into a funnel-shaped bay. The power of the incoming tide has been calculated to have more force than 8000 freight locomotives or 25 000 000 horses. At high tide, the water is kept in the bay by the force of the incoming tide. Then, at low tide it flushes out of the bay.

The Canadian government is building a dam at this site. It will have large gates to let water enter the bay at high tide. Then the gates will be closed, and water will be stored behind the dam. As the tide goes out, the dammed water will pass over turbines in the dam. A **turbine** is similar to a fan blade. When the water pushes the blades, the turbine spins. The spinning turbine turns a generator to produce electricity.

When this power plant is completed, it will provide electrical power to cities in Canada and the United States. Because there will be no expenses of buying fuel, pollution control, or waste disposal, the cost of the power will be relatively low. New jobs will also be created.

Figure 11-13. This diagram shows the basic concept of a tidal dam power plant. As the tide rises, it flows into the bay and becomes trapped by the dam (b). Then as the tide goes down, the water is released through the dam (c) and spins the turbine generator to make electricity.

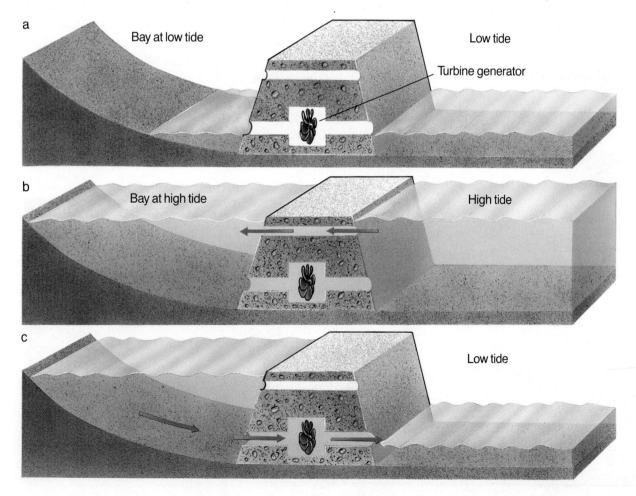

a Bay at low tide   Low tide
Turbine generator

b Bay at high tide   High tide

c   Low tide

Figure 11-14. Some salt marshes like this one will be flooded if a tidal power plant is built at the Bay of Fundy.

Science and READING

In Isaac Asimov's *New Guide to Science,* he gives a great perspective on the oceans. Report to the class some of the interesting statistics he cites.

However, this dam will create some problems. Shores as far south as Boston, Massachusetts, 600 km away, will have greater tidal ranges than they do now. At low tide, some Boston harbor channels will become too shallow to use. At high tide, some farmlands and towns will be flooded. Water wells will become contaminated with salt water, and valuable salt-marsh habitats will be ruined. A **salt marsh** is the breeding ground of many ocean organisms. If these habitats are destroyed, these organisms will die.

Environmentalists fear that other problems will be created at the dam site. Many fish will be killed by the dam's turbines. Also, the mud flats at the Bay of Fundy, where many migrating birds feed on mud shrimp, will be flooded by the water retained behind the dam. The birds may not be able to find a substitute food source, and could starve to death.

SECTION REVIEW

1. Why was the Bay of Fundy picked as a site to build a tidal power plant?
2. How does a tidal dam convert energy from tides into electricity?

SCIENCE & SOCIETY

You Decide!

When we make changes in our environment, we must consider the consequences. This certainly is the case with the building of a tidal dam at the Bay of Fundy. Consider the benefits and problems involved with the building of this dam. Do you think this tidal dam should be built?

CHAPTER
REVIEW

SUMMARY

11-1: Origin and Composition of Ocean Water

1. Water that fills Earth's oceans started as water vapor released from volcanoes. The water vapor condensed, and rain fell, forming the oceans over millions of years.

2. Groundwater and rivers weather rocks and cause some elements to dissolve. The dissolved elements are carried by rivers to the oceans. Volcanoes also add elements to seawater.

3. Nearly 90 percent of the salt in seawater is halite. Ocean water also contains calcium, silica, and many other substances.

11-2: Ocean Currents

1. Friction between air and the ocean's surface causes surface currents. Surface currents are affected by the Coriolis effect. Currents are also deflected by landmasses.

2. Currents off western coasts originate far from the equator and are cooler than currents on eastern coasts, which begin near the equator.

3. Differences in temperatures and densities between water masses in the ocean set up circulation patterns called density currents.

11-3: Ocean Waves and Tides

1. The crest is the highest point of a wave. The trough is the lowest point. Wave height is the vertical distance between crest and trough. Wavelength is the horizontal distance between two successive wave crests or troughs.

2. Particles of water in ocean waves move in circles, whereas the energy transmitted by the wave moves forward.

3. Wind can cause water to pile up and form waves. Waves called tides are due to the attraction among Earth, the moon, and the sun.

11-4: Science and Society: Tapping Tidal Energy

1. The Bay of Fundy is a good place for tapping tidal energy from tides.

2. A tidal dam has gates that are opened and closed to let water in and out of a bay. The water passes over turbines, which turn generators.

3. Energy from tides is essentially nonpolluting but can cause problems in tidal ranges at other locations. Flooding, contamination of freshwater wells, and damage to habitats are also drawbacks to using energy from tides.

KEY SCIENCE WORDS

a. basins
b. breaker
c. crest
d. density current
e. salinity
f. salt marsh
g. surface current
h. tidal range
i. tides
j. trough
k. turbine
l. upwelling
m. wave height
n. wavelength

UNDERSTANDING VOCABULARY

Match each phrase with the correct term from the list of Key Science Words.

1. low area that collects water
2. nutrient-rich water that comes to surface
3. a current at or near the surface
4. the lowest point of a wave
5. vertical distance between crests and troughs
6. horizontal difference between crests
7. the highest part of a wave
8. difference between high and low tide
9. spun by falling water to generate electricity
10. breeding place of many sea organisms

OCEAN WATER **301**

CHAPTER
REVIEW

CHECKING CONCEPTS

Choose the word or phrase that completes the sentence.

1. Water in Earth's oceans came from _____.
   a. salt marshes   c. basins
   b. volcanoes   d. surface currents

2. Calcium is carried into the ocean by _____.
   a. rivers   c. volcanoes
   b. groundwater   d. all of these

3. _____ is the most common ocean compound.
   a. Oxygen   c. Silica
   b. Calcium   d. None of these

4. Most surface currents are caused by _____.
   a. density differences   c. temperature
   b. the Gulf Stream   d. wind

5. The highest point on a wave is the _____.
   a. wave height   c. crest
   b. trough   d. wavelength

6. Ocean _____ are movements in which water alternately rises and falls.
   a. currents   c. crests
   b. waves   d. none of these

7. As waves move into shallow areas, _____.
   a. they slow down
   b. crests and troughs come together
   c. wave height increases
   d. all of these

8. Tides are due to _____ gravitational force.
   a. Earth's   c. the sun's
   b. the moon's   d. all of these

9. Tidal power plants use energy from _____.
   a. Earth's oceans   c. the sun
   b. salt marshes   d. floods

10. Tidal power plants have _____.
    a. no fuel expenses
    b. no waste to get rid of
    c. no pollution
    d. all of these

UNDERSTANDING CONCEPTS

Complete each sentence.

11. The depressions that hold ocean water are called _____.

12. The Coriolis effect causes _____ currents to be deflected.

13. _____ is the distance between two successive wave crests.

14. The force of _____ causes tides.

15. _____ tides occur when the sun, Earth, and the moon are lined up.

THINK AND WRITE CRITICALLY

16. How are spring tides different from high tides?

17. Compare and contrast surface and density currents.

18. Describe the effects of temperature on density currents.

19. What happens to a wave when it enters shallow water?

20. How can surface currents affect climate?

APPLY

21. Describe the position of the moon and sun if a low tide is higher than normal.

22. Halite makes up 90 percent of the salt in ocean water. How much halite is found in 1000 L of ocean water?

23. Why is ocean water low in silica and calcium?

24. A deep-water wave is one in which the depth is greater than one-half the wavelength. Would a wave with a 10-m wavelength in 8 m of water be a deep-water wave? Explain.

25. How can a tidal power plant in the Bay of Fundy prevent flooding in the area?

If you need help, refer to the Skill Handbook.

1. **Recognizing Cause and Effect:** What causes an upwelling?
2. **Comparing and Contrasting:** Compare and contrast wave height and wavelength.
3. **Graphing:** Plot the data provided in the table below on a sheet of graph paper. Label the vertical axis "Tide in Meters" and use a scale running upward from −0.6 m to 2.4 m. The horizontal axis should show days 1 to 30. Plot each data point for high tide and connect with a red pencil. Connect each data point for low tide with a blue pencil. Describe any pattern that you observe in the graphed data.

4. **Outlining:** Make an outline that discusses the pros and cons of tidal power.
5. **Interpreting Data:** Based on the information in this chapter, is there more sodium or calcium in the oceans? Explain your answer.

PROJECTS

1. Design an experiment to test the density of water at different temperatures. Make a table to record your observations and measurements.
2. Design a way to desalinate salt water without using a heat source.

Day	Height of high tide (meters)	Height of low tide (meters)	Day	Height of high tide (meters)	Height of low tide (meters)
1	1.4	0.5	16	1.6	0.2
2	1.5	0.4	17	1.7	0.1
3	1.7	0.2	18	1.7	−0.1
4	1.8	−0.1	19	1.8	−0.2
5	2.1	−0.3	20	1.9	−0.2
6	2.2	−0.5	21	1.9	−0.2
7	2.3	−0.6	22	1.9	−0.2
8	2.3	−0.6	23	1.9	−0.2
9	2.3	−0.6	24	1.8	−0.2
10	2.1	−0.5	25	1.7	−0.1
11	1.9	−0.2	26	1.6	0.0
12	1.6	−0.1	27	1.4	0.1
13	1.6	0.2	28	1.3	0.3
14	1.6	0.4	29	1.5	0.4
15	1.6	0.4	30	1.5	0.5

12 Exploring Oceans

The deep oceans have been a mystery for many years. Submarines called submersibles now allow humans to venture and observe deep into the ocean. How can submersibles dive and rise in the oceans?

FIND OUT!

Do this simple activity to find out how submersibles work.

Fill a 2-liter plastic bottle with water. Draw water into an eye dropper so that there is a small amount of air in the bulb of the dropper. Place the dropper in the plastic bottle. The bulb should be up and the dropper should float in the bottle. Now seal the bottle with its cap. By squeezing on the sides of the bottle, you can cause the dropper to "dive" to the bottom. By squeezing the sides of the bottle, you have compressed the tiny air bubble inside the bulb of the dropper. This decreased the volume of the air and let just enough water into the dropper to make it sink.

Gearing Up

Previewing the Chapter

Use this outline to help you focus on important ideas in this chapter.

Previewing Science Skills

- ▶ In the **Skill Builders**, you will make a concept map, compare and contrast, and use variables, constants, and controls.
- ▶ In the **Activities**, you will observe, classify, measure, infer, predict, use numbers, and hypothesize.
- ▶ In the **MINI-Labs**, you will observe and make a model.

What's next?

In this chapter, you'll first look at seashores and how the waves carve them. Then you'll discover that there are mountains and trenches on the seafloor much larger than ones on Earth's land masses. Finally, you'll meet the plants and creatures that live in the ocean and learn how they are threatened by pollution.

12-1 Shorelines

New Science Words

shore zone
longshore current
beaches
barrier islands

Objectives

▶ Describe three forces that affect all shore zones.
▶ Contrast steep shore zones and flat shore zones.
▶ List some origins of sand.

Shore Zones

Picture yourself sitting on a beautiful white sand beach. Palm trees sway in the breeze above your head, and small children play in the quiet waves lapping at the water's edge. It's hard to imagine a place more peaceful than this shore. Now picture yourself sitting along another shore. You're on a high cliff, overlooking waves crashing onto huge boulders below.

Both of these settings are shore zones. A **shore zone** is the land area between the water's edge at high tide and the water's edge at low tide. You learned in Chapter 11 that tidal range is the difference in height between high and low tides, a few meters in most places. This produces a shore zone that often is hundreds of meters wide.

The two shore zones we just described are very different. Why are they so different? Both are subjected to the same forces. Both experience the same surface waves, tides, and currents. These cause both shore zones to con-

What determines a shore zone?

Figure 12-1. Waves cause shore zones to constantly change.

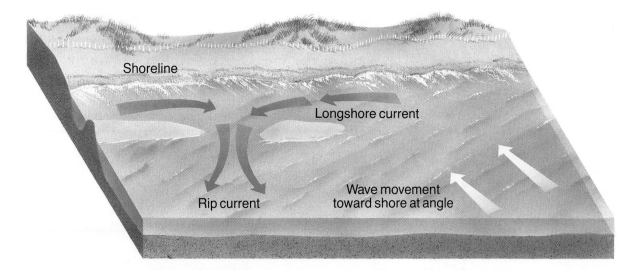

Shoreline

Longshore current

Rip current

Wave movement
toward shore at angle

stantly change. Sometimes you can see these changes from hour to hour. We'll look at why these shore zones are different, but first, let's learn about the forces that carve shores.

Along all shore zones, surface waves constantly move sediments. These waves move sediments back and forth across the shore zone. The waves shape shore zones by eroding them and by depositing sediments. The tides also shape shore zones. Every day they raise and lower the place on the shore zone where surface waves erode and deposit sediment.

Waves usually collide with a shore at slight angles. This creates a **longshore current** of water that runs parallel to the shore. Longshore currents carry many metric tons of loose sediments and act like rivers of sand in the ocean. What do you suppose happens if a longshore current isn't carrying all of the sand it has the energy to carry? It will use this extra energy to erode more shore zone sediments.

You've seen the forces that affect all shore zones. Now we'll look at the differences that make one shore a flat, sandy beach and another shore a steep, rocky cliff.

Steep Shore Zones

Along steep shore zones, rocks and cliffs are the most common features. Waves scour the rocks to form hollows or notches. Over time, these enlarge and become caves. Rock fragments broken from the cliffs are ground up by the endless motion of waves. These fragments act like the sand on sandpaper.

Figure 12-2. Waves approaching the shoreline at an angle cause a longshore current. Rip currents form where longshore currents meet and flow in a swift, narrow current out to sea.

Softer rocks are eroded away before harder rocks, leaving islands of harder rocks. This takes many years, but remember that the ocean never sleeps. In your lifetime, more than 200 million waves will crash onto any shore.

The rock fragments produced by eroding waves are sediment. When steep shore zones are being eroded away, where do you think the sediment goes? Waves carry it away and deposit it where water is quieter. If you want to go to a beach, you probably won't find one where the shore zone is steep.

Figure 12-3. A steep, rocky shore zone.

Flat Shore Zones

Flat shore zones are quite different from steep shore zones. Beaches are the main feature here. **Beaches** are deposits of sediment that run parallel to the shore. They extend inland as far as the tides and waves are able to deposit sediment. Beaches also extend out under the water to a depth of 9 to 40 m below the water surface.

What defines the area of a beach?

Beaches are made of different materials. Some are made of rock fragments from the shore zone, and others consist of seashell fragments. These fragments range from pebbles large enough to fill your hand to fine sand. Sand grains are 1/16 to 2 mm in diameter. Why do most beaches have sand-size particles? This is because waves break rocks and seashells down to sand-size particles. The constant wave motion bumps sand grains together and, in the process, rounds their corners.

Figure 12-4. Sand varies in size and composition. This sand is made of shell fragments.

What kinds of materials do you think are in most beach sands? Most are made of resistant minerals such as quartz. However, sands in some places are composed of other things. For example, Hawaii's black sands are made of basalt, and green sands are made of the mineral olivine. Jamaica's white sands are made of coral and shell fragments.

Sand constantly is carried down beaches by longshore currents. When a longshore current loses velocity, it drops its load of sediment to form structures that you can see in Figure 12-5. Sand is also moved by storms and the wind. Thus, beaches are fragile, temporary features that are easily damaged by storms and human activities such as construction.

How does sediment get deposited to form barrier islands?

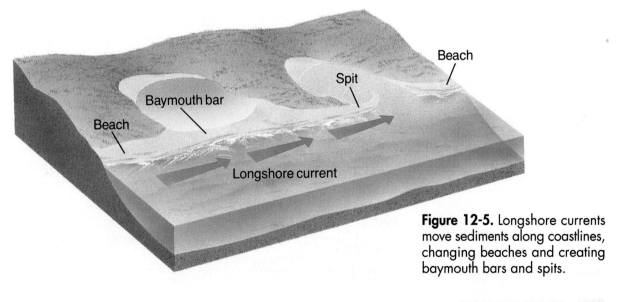

Figure 12-5. Longshore currents move sediments along coastlines, changing beaches and creating baymouth bars and spits.

Figure 12-6. The size and shape of barrier islands constantly change due to wave action.

How does a barrier island remain above sea level?

Barrier islands are sand deposits that parallel the shore but are separated from the mainland. North America's Atlantic Coast and the Gulf of Mexico have many barrier islands. These islands start as underwater sand ridges, formed by breaking waves. Hurricanes and storms add sediment to them, raising some to sea level. Once a barrier island is exposed, the wind blows its loose sand into dunes, keeping the island above sea level. As with all seashore features, barrier islands are temporary, lasting from a few years to a few centuries.

Shore zones of all types change constantly due to erosion and deposits from waves, tides, and longshore currents. Storms can alter a shore zone in only minutes. Our beautiful beaches are fragile, temporary features.

SECTION REVIEW

1. What three forces affect all shore zones?
2. Contrast the features you'd find in a steep shore zone with the features you'd find in a flat shore zone.
3. List some origins of sand.
4. **Apply:** Why is there no sand on many of the world's shorelines?

Skill Builder

☑ **Concept Mapping**

Make a cycle concept map that discusses how the sand from a barrier island that is currently in place can become a barrier island 100 years from now. Use these terms: *barrier island, breaking waves, wind, longshore currents,* and *new barrier island.* If you need help, refer to Concept Mapping in the **Skill Handbook** on page 688.

ACTIVITY 12-1
Beach Sand

Problem: *What are some characteristics of beach sand?*

Materials
- 3 samples of different types of beach sand
- stereomicroscope
- magnet

Procedure
1. Use the stereomicroscope to examine the sand samples. Copy the data table and record your observations of each sample.
2. Describe the color of each sample.
3. Describe the average roundness of the grains in each sample.
4. Place sand grains from one of your samples in the middle of the circle of the sand gauge shown below the table. Use the upper half of the circle for dark-colored particles, and the bottom half of the circle for light-colored particles. Determine the average size of the grains.
5. Repeat Steps 2-4 for the other two samples.
6. Pour a small amount of sand from one sample into your hand. Describe its texture as "smooth," "rough," or "sharp." Repeat for the other two samples.
7. Describe the luster of the grains as "shiny" or "dull."
8. Determine if a magnet will attract grains in any of the samples.
9. Try to identify the types of fragments that make up your samples. Record the compositions in a table like the one shown.

Analyze
1. Were the grains of a particular sample generally the same size? Explain.
2. Were they generally the same shape?

Conclude and Apply
3. What are some characteristics of beach sand?
4. Why are there differences in the characteristics of different sand samples?

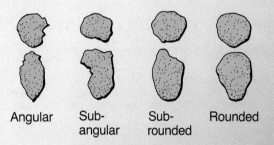

Angular   Sub-angular   Sub-rounded   Rounded

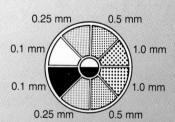

Data and Observations

Sample	Color	Roundness	Grain Size	Texture	Luster	Composition
1						
2						
3						

New Science Words

continental shelf
continental slope
abyssal plain
rift zone
mid-ocean ridges
ocean trench

Objectives

▶ Differentiate among the continental shelf, the continental slope, and the abyssal plain.
▶ Describe rift zones, mid-ocean ridges, and ocean trenches.

Continental Shelf, Slope, and Abyssal Plain

Where can you find the biggest mountains, the deepest valleys, and the flattest plains on Earth? They are at the bottom of the ocean. But the mountains, valleys, and plains there are different from those on the continents.

Beyond every shoreline, out under the ocean, extends a flat part of the continent called the **continental shelf.** Along some coasts the continental shelf is wide. For example, on North America's East Coast and Gulf Coast, it's 100-200 km wide. But on coasts where mountains are close to shore, as in California, the shelf is 10-30 km wide. The continental shelf slopes gently out into the ocean. But at the end of the shelf, it dips steeply, forming the **continental slope.**

Think of a large swimming pool. It is much like an ocean basin. The side of the pool is like the continental slope, and the bottom of the pool is the seafloor. The

What is the ocean floor called closest to the shoreline?

Figure 12-7. This illustration shows some of the features of the ocean floor.

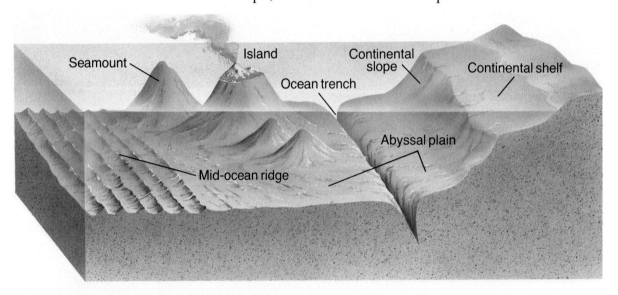

seafloor is where you find the flattest areas on Earth. This is because currents deposit sediments from the continental shelves and slopes onto the bottom. These deposits fill in valleys, creating a flat seafloor in the deep ocean called an **abyssal** (a BIHS uhl) **plain.**

Figure 12-8. This map shows that ocean basins have mountains, valleys, and plains.

Rifts, Ridges, and Trenches

Study the ocean floor map shown in Figure 12-8. Down the middle of some oceans, you can see a system of cracks in the seafloor. These cracks form a **rift zone,** where the seafloor is spreading apart. One rift zone extends southward from Iceland through the center of the Atlantic Ocean. From these cracks, hot lava oozes from Earth's interior. This lava is quickly chilled by the seawater and becomes solid rock, forming new seafloor.

Alongside rift zones you can see underwater mountain chains called **mid-ocean ridges.** They form because forces within Earth spread the seafloor apart at rifts, causing the seafloor to buckle. Along the mid-ocean ridges you'll find volcanoes. They build up mountains underwater, just as they do on land. A volcano forms an island if it rises above sea level. If it doesn't break the surface, it's called a seamount. The rift zone extending southward from Iceland runs through the Mid-Atlantic Ridge, which is 500 to 5000 km wide and 65 000 km long.

Did You Know?

Until 1977 only five percent of the ocean floor had been charted. NASA's Seasat measured the other 95 percent in only three months in 1978.

Figure 12-9. If Earth's tallest mountain, Mt. Everest, was set in the bottom of the Marianas Trench, it would still be covered with more than 2000 meters of water.

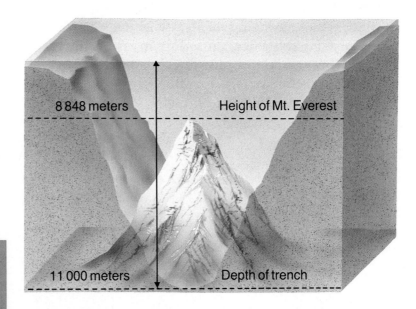

8 848 meters   Height of Mt. Everest

11 000 meters   Depth of trench

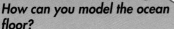
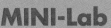

MINI-Lab

How can you model the ocean floor?

Use clay, or plaster of paris and newspaper, to make a model of coastal features and the ocean floor. Use Figures 12-7 and 12-8 as examples and label all of the features. You could also make the model realistic by painting it. What are the features located close to the shorelines?

While forces spread the seafloor apart at rift zones, in other places these forces are shoving pieces of the seafloor against each other. Where one piece of seafloor is pushed beneath another one, a deep **ocean trench** may form. Many oceanic trenches are longer and deeper than any valley you can see on the continents. For example, the Marianas Trench is the Pacific Ocean's deepest place, almost 11 km deep. By contrast, the Grand Canyon is about 1.6 km deep.

You'll learn more about these features of the seafloor in Chapter 13 when you study plate tectonics. Plate tectonics explains how many of the features on land and underwater are formed.

SECTION REVIEW

1. How do the continental shelf and the continental slope differ?
2. What happens at a rift zone?
3. **Apply:** What's the difference between an island and a seamount?

Skill Builder

☑ Comparing and Contrasting

Compare and contrast the continental shelf, the continental slope, and the abyssal plain. If you need help, refer to Comparing and Contrasting in the **Skill Handbook** on page 683.

ACTIVITY 12-2
Ocean-Floor Profile

Problem: *How can you make a profile of the ocean floor?*

Materials
- graph paper

Procedure
1. Set up a graph as shown.
2. Examine the data listed in the data table. This information was collected at 29 oceanographic locations in the Atlantic Ocean. Each station was along the 39° north latitude line from New Jersey to Portugal.
3. Plot each data point listed on the table. Then connect the points with a smooth line.

Analyze
1. What ocean-floor structures occur between 160 and 1050 km from the coast of New Jersey? Between 2000 and 4500 km? Between 5300 and 5600 km?
2. You have constructed a profile of the ocean floor along the 39°N latitude line. If a profile is drawn to represent an accurate scale model of a feature, both the horizontal and vertical scales of the profile will be the same. What is the vertical scale of your profile? What is the horizontal scale?
3. Does the profile you have drawn give an accurate picture of the ocean floor? Explain.

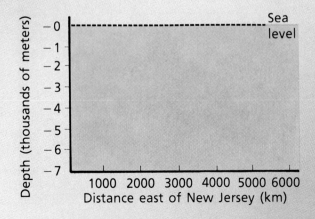

Data and Observations

Station Number	Distance from New Jersey (km)	Depth to Ocean Floor (m)
1	0	0
2	160	165
3	200	1800
4	500	3500
5	800	4600
6	1050	5450
7	1450	5100
8	1800	5300
9	2000	5600
10	2300	4750
11	2400	3500
12	2600	3100
13	3000	4300
14	3200	3900
15	3450	3400
16	3550	2100
17	3600	1330
18	3700	1275
19	3950	1000
20	4000	0
21	4100	1800
22	4350	3650
23	4500	5100
24	5000	5000
25	5300	4200
26	5450	1800
27	5500	920
28	5600	180
29	5650	0

12-3 Life in the Ocean

New Science Words

photosynthesis
respiration
chemosynthesis
plankton
nekton
benthos
reef

What makes you buoyant?

Objectives

▶ List six things that the ocean provides for organisms.
▶ Describe the relationship between photosynthesis and respiration.
▶ List the key characteristics of plankton, nekton, and benthos.

Life Processes in the Ocean

What would it be like to be a sea creature? In some ways life would be easier than on land. This is because the ocean provides many things that organisms need to survive. You've experienced one of these things if you've gone swimming. Did you feel lighter in the water? This feeling was created because your density is less than water's density, making you buoyant. Buoyancy (BOY un see) allows for easy movement. Therefore, organisms in the ocean use less energy in moving around than you do.

Seawater also protects against sudden temperature changes. Temperature changes very slowly in the ocean. Marine organisms don't experience the stresses you feel when the air temperature suddenly changes.

Water is a basic compound used in all life processes. The tissues of most plants and animals are mostly water. Organisms that live in the ocean have no problem finding water!

Figure 12-10. These life-forms live at shorelines and are sometimes exposed during low tide.

The ocean provides the liquid in which male and female reproductive cells can join. In the ocean, many organisms have external fertilization. This means that the male and female reproductive cells unite outside of the bodies of the parents. The reproductive cells are released by both parents, float to the surface of the water, and unite to form new individuals.

Another way that ocean water helps organisms is in getting rid of wastes. Their wastes dissolve in seawater and are then used as nutrients by other organisms. Seawater also contains other important nutrients and gases that organisms need. Let's see why these materials are so important.

How does ocean water help organisms with their external fertilization?

TECHNOLOGY

Submersibles

Submersibles are small submarines that enable scientists to study parts of the ocean that are too deep and dangerous for divers. One of the most famous submersibles, *Alvin,* was used to discover the wreck of the *Titanic* in 1985. *Alvin* is equipped with cameras and a manipulator arm. New submersibles called ROVs (Remotely Operated Vehicles) or minirovers are smaller, less expensive to operate, and have many of the same capabilities as *Alvin.* ROVs can stay underwater for any length of time because they have no crew. They are remotely controlled by a scientist on board a ship. Some are connected to the ship on the surface with a cable. Scientists communicate with the ROV by sending signals through the cable. Other ROVs are not attached to the ship and are controlled by radio signals. ROVs have lights, a video camera, and manipulator arms.

Minirovers have a variety of uses. One ROV was dropped through an eight-foot hole in the Arctic ice to explore ice formations. Other ROVs are being used to study sea life and to inspect ship hulls and pipelines.

Think Critically: What advantages does an ROV have over a submersible with a crew?

Photosynthesis and Respiration

One of the important dissolved gases in seawater is carbon dioxide. Plants use carbon dioxide, nutrients in the water, and sunlight to produce food and oxygen. The food and oxygen are then available to other organisms. The process plants use to make food is called **photosynthesis** (foh toh SIHN thuh sihs). *Photo* refers to light; *synthesis* means to make.

All organisms, including you, perform a process called respiration. During **respiration,** oxygen is combined with food so that the energy in food can be used. The process produces water and carbon dioxide, which plants use in photosynthesis.

Throughout the ocean, energy is transferred through food chains. Energy moves in this order: from plants, to plant-eating animals, to animal-eating animals. In these food chains, sunlight is very important because plants can perform photosynthesis only in the presence of light.

Chemosynthesis

Another type of food chain in the ocean does not depend on sunlight, however. This food chain depends on bacteria performing a process called **chemosynthesis** (kee moh SIHN thuh sihs). *Chemo* means chemical. This process takes place in rift zones where hot lava oozes from the crust. In these areas, bacteria produce food and oxygen by using dissolved sulfur compounds that escape from the lava. Organisms then feed on the bacteria.

How does respiration help photosynthesis?

Figure 12-11. Sulfur compounds escaping from a "black smoker" deep sea vent, at left, provide the energy for chemosynthesis. Tube worms, at right, feed on bacteria at the vents.

Ocean Life

More animals and plants live in the ocean than anywhere else. Some simply drift with the surface currents. Others swim through the water on their own power or crawl over the sediments. Still others are permanently attached to the ocean bottom.

Plankton

Imagine what it would be like to drift in the currents all of your life. Drifting plants and animals are called **plankton.** You can see most plankton only with a microscope. One plant plankton is the diatom (DI uh tahm). Diatoms are one-celled, yellow-green algae. Although diatoms are tiny, they're very important as the main food for many sea animals.

Examples of animal plankton include eggs, very young fish, jellyfish and crabs, and tiny adults of some organisms. Most animal plankton depend on surface currents to move them, but some can swim.

Nekton

Larger animals that swim are called **nekton** (NEK tuhn). Examples are fish, turtles, whales, and seals. Nekton can move from one depth and place to another. Some prefer cold water, whereas others like warm regions. Some, like whales, roam the entire ocean. Many nekton come to the surface at night to feed on plankton, while others remain in deeper parts of the ocean where sunlight does not reach.

How are nekton different from plankton?

Figure 12-12. Swimming animals are nekton.

How is the viperfish specially adapted to deep water?

Some of these deep-dwelling creatures have special light-generating organs for attracting live food. The angler fish dangles a luminous lure over its forehead. When small animals bite at the lure, the angler fish swallows them whole. The viperfish has luminous organs in its mouth. It swims with its mouth open, and small organisms swim right into the viperfish's mouth.

Bottom-Dwellers

Plants and animals also live on the seafloor. In fact, many live on the sunlit continental shelf. In shallow water, forests of kelp grow. Kelp is a large brown algae that likes cool water near shore. A special organ holds each kelp plant to the bottom, and gas-filled organs on its stems keep the plant upright in the water. Did you know that kelp is the fastest growing plant in the world? It can grow up to 0.6 m each day and reach lengths of 60 m.

Many animals called **benthos** (BEN thohs) live on the ocean bottom. Benthos include corals, snails, clams, sea urchins, and bottom-dwelling fish. How do you suppose these animals get food? Many of them eat the partially decomposed matter that sinks to the ocean bottom. Some prey on other benthos, eating them whole. Others are permanently attached to the bottom and filter food particles from water currents. Still others have specialized organs that sting prey that comes near. An attached benthos that stings its prey is coral. Let's learn more about this fascinating animal.

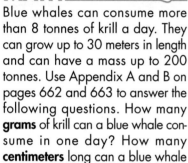

Science and MATH

Blue whales can consume more than 8 tonnes of krill a day. They can grow up to 30 meters in length and can have a mass up to 200 tonnes. Use Appendix A and B on pages 662 and 663 to answer the following questions. How many **grams** of krill can a blue whale consume in one day? How many **centimeters** long can a blue whale become? What can a blue whale's mass get up to in **kilograms**?

Figure 12-13. This angler fish is adapted to living in the deep ocean.

Figure 12-14. Coral reefs are found in warm water near the equator.

Corals live in warm waters close to the equator. Each coral animal builds a hard, boxlike capsule around its body from the calcium it removes from seawater. Each capsule is cemented to others to form a colony called a **reef.** As a coral reef forms, other benthos and nekton begin living on it.

If you could swim quietly through a coral reef, you'd see many ocean organisms interacting. Fish, crabs, sea urchins, and many others congregate in reefs. Nutrients, food, carbon dioxide, and oxygen are cycled among these organisms, although you can't actually see this happening. Plankton, nekton, and benthos all depend on each other for survival, not only in coral reefs, but throughout the entire ocean. It's been this way for millions of years.

SECTION REVIEW

1. What six things does the ocean provide for organisms?
2. Describe the relationship between photosynthesis and respiration.
3. List the key characteristics of plankton, nekton, and benthos.
4. How do benthos get food?
5. **Apply:** In walking along a beach, you find many seashells. Are they the shells of plankton, nekton, or benthos? How can you tell?

☑ **Using Variables, Constants, and Controls**

Skill Builder

Describe how you can test the effects of salinity on marine organisms. If you need help, refer to Using Variables, Constants, and Controls in the **Skill Handbook** on page 686.

12-4 Pollution and Marine Life

New Science Words

pollution
thermal pollution

Objectives

▶ List seven human activities that pollute the ocean.
▶ Explain how ocean pollution affects the entire world.
▶ Determine how we can live on this planet without destroying its oceans.

Ocean Pollution

How would you feel if someone came into your bedroom while you were asleep, spilled oil on your carpet, littered your room with plastic bags, cans, bottles, and newspapers, sprayed bug killer all over, scattered sand, and then poured hot water all over you? Organisms in the ocean experience these very things when people pollute seawater.

Pollution occurs whenever harmful substances are introduced into an environment. Most ocean pollution caused by humans is concentrated along the coasts of continents. Let's see what some of the pollutants are.

Figure 12-15. Ocean pollution has many sources.

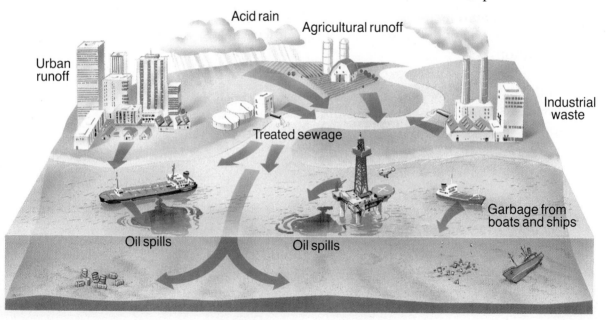

Acid rain

Agricultural runoff

Urban runoff

Industrial waste

Treated sewage

Garbage from boats and ships

Oil spills

Oil spills

Industrial wastes sometimes get into seawater. Often, these contain concentrations of metals and chemicals that harm organisms. Solid wastes, such as plastic bags and fishing line left lying on beaches, can entangle animals. Medical waste such as needles, plastic tubing, and bags are a threat to both humans and animals.

Pesticides (insect killers) and herbicides (weed killers) used in farming reach the ocean as runoff. They become concentrated in the tissues of marine organisms.

Crop fertilizers and human sewage create a different kind of problem. They fertilize the water. This causes some types of plant plankton to reproduce very rapidly. When these plants die, they're decomposed by huge numbers of bacteria. The problem is that the bacteria use up much of the oxygen in the water during respiration. Therefore, other organisms such as fish can't get the oxygen they need, and they die.

Oil spills also pollute the ocean. You've heard in the news about major oil spills caused by tanker collisions, and leaks at offshore oil wells. Another source of oil pollution is oil mixed with wastewater that's pumped out of ships. In addition to these sources, oil discarded from cars and industries is sometimes dumped into groundwater and streams. It, too, eventually reaches the ocean.

How does an abundance of bacteria cause other life-forms to die?

PROBLEM SOLVING

Washed Ashore

A chemical plant and a nuclear power plant are both located along Barney Beach. The chemical plant produces electricity by burning coal. The nuclear power plant generates power using nuclear fission, a process that produces vast amounts of energy. The chemical plant is located about 20 kilometers north of Hometown. The nuclear power plant is about 10 kilometers south of the city. Recently, many of the fish along the beaches in the area were washed ashore. Many of the organisms in the shallow waters have also died as a result of thermal pollution.

Think Critically: What do you think is the source of the pollution? Explain.

Figure 12-16. Pollution kills marine animals.

Science and READING

In this chapter, several types of water pollution are mentioned, but there is much more to learn about the cause of each of them. Go to the library and read about one specific type of pollution and its causes.

Thermal pollution results when power plants and other industries pump warm water into the ocean. Organisms adapted to cooler water are killed by this warm water.

Did you realize that even natural sediments such as silt and clay can pollute? Human activities such as agriculture, deforestation, and construction tear up the soil. Rain washes the soil into streams and eventually into the ocean. This causes huge amounts of silt to accumulate in some coastal areas. Filter-feeding benthos such as oysters and clams become clogged up and die. Also, when saltwater marshes are filled for land development, marine habitats are destroyed.

When the ocean becomes polluted, it isn't just the resident animals and plants that are affected. Food chains are disrupted and Earth's oxygen supply is affected. Many organisms on Earth depend on the oxygen produced by plant plankton. If the plankton dies, so will many organisms on Earth.

SECTION REVIEW

1. List seven human activities that pollute the ocean.
2. How does pollution of the ocean affect the entire world?

SCIENCE & SOCIETY

You Decide!

In this section, you learned how many human activities are severely polluting our ocean. However, many of these activities are part of the systems that provide your food, home, energy, transportation, and recreation. As Earth's population increases, the problem can only grow worse. How can we maintain our quality of life without destroying life in the ocean? What are your ideas?

SUMMARY

12-1: Shorelines

1. Shore zones are subjected to waves, tides, and currents.

2. Rocks and cliffs are common along steep shore zones, whereas sandy beaches are found near flat shore zones.

3. Sand forms when rocks, coral, and seashells are broken into small particles by wave action.

12-2: The Seafloor

1. The continental shelf is a gently sloping part of the continent that extends out under the water along coastlines. The continental slope is the steeply sloping part of the ocean floor extending beyond the continental shelf. The continental slope extends down to the ocean floor.

2. Rift zones are cracks that form where seafloor is spreading apart. Along rift zones, mid-ocean ridges form from buckled seafloor. Ocean trenches form where seafloor is forced under another section of seafloor.

12-3: Life in the Ocean

1. Buoyancy, constant temperatures, water, nutrients, and a method of reproduction are provided to marine organisms by their habitat.

2. Photosynthesis and respiration are two processes that complement one another to recycle nutrients and gases needed by living things.

3. Plankton are microscopic plants and animals that drift in ocean currents. Nekton are marine organisms that swim. Benthos are plants and animals that live on the ocean floor.

12-4: Science and Society: Pollution and Marine Life

1. Industrial, solid, and medical wastes; pesticides, herbicides, and fertilizers; and oil spills and hot water all pollute Earth's ocean.

2. Because all Earth's oceans are interconnected, ocean pollution is a worldwide problem.

3. Careful disposal of wastes, limited usage of agricultural chemicals, and careful construction are only a few ways to reduce ocean pollution.

KEY SCIENCE WORDS

a. **abyssal plain**
b. **barrier islands**
c. **beaches**
d. **benthos**
e. **chemosynthesis**
f. **continental shelf**
g. **continental slope**
h. **longshore current**
i. **mid-ocean ridges**
j. **nekton**
k. **ocean trench**
l. **photosynthesis**
m. **plankton**
n. **pollution**
o. **reef**
p. **respiration**
q. **rift zone**
r. **shore zone**
s. **thermal pollution**

UNDERSTANDING VOCABULARY

Match each phrase with the correct term from the list of Key Science Words.

1. water that flows parallel to the shore
2. any kinds of sediments that are deposited parallel to a shore
3. steep seafloor beyond the continental shelf
4. mountains formed where seafloor is spreading apart
5. plant process that produces oxygen
6. drifting marine plants and animals
7. animals that live on the ocean floor
8. colony made of many coral
9. occurs whenever harmful substances are introduced to the environment
10. when hot water is added to a body of water

REVIEW

CHECKING CONCEPTS

Choose the word or phrase that completes the sentence.

1. Longshore currents _____.
   a. flow parallel to shore
   b. carry loose sediments
   c. erode shores
   d. all of these

2. Beaches are most common along _____.
   a. steep shore zones   c. flat shore zones
   b. abyssal plains   d. rift zones

3. Beach sands are moved by _____.
   a. longshore currents   c. wind
   b. storms   d. all of these

4. _____ are formed along rift zones.
   a. Mid-ocean ridges   c. Continental slopes
   b. Oceanic trenches   d. None of these

5. Organisms that live on the surface are called _____.
   a. nekton   c. benthos
   b. fish   d. plankton

6. The ocean provides organisms with _____.
   a. nutrients   c. a constant temperature
   b. water   d. all of these

7. Certain bacteria in the ocean perform _____ to provide food for other organisms.
   a. photosynthesis   c. respiration
   b. chemosynthesis   d. rifting

8. Ocean swimmers are _____.
   a. benthos   c. kelp
   b. nekton   d. coral

9. Most human-made ocean pollution _____.
   a. is near shore   c. is thermal pollution
   b. is solid waste   d. harms only plants

10. Fertilizers cause some _____ to reproduce rapidly, resulting in the lack of oxygen.
    a. benthos   c. plant plankton
    b. animal plankton   d. coral

UNDERSTANDING CONCEPTS

Complete each sentence.

11. Waves, currents, and tides constantly change _____.

12. New ocean crust forms at _____.

13. The ocean basin is flattest at the _____.

14. The force that allows organisms to "float" in the ocean is called _____.

15. If hot water from manufacturing processes isn't cooled before it leaves the plant, it can cause _____ in a body of water.

THINK AND WRITE CRITICALLY

16. Explain why shorelines are constantly being changed.

17. Compare and contrast the continental shelf with the continental slope.

18. Where would you expect to find the most marine organisms—closer to continents or in deeper waters? Explain.

19. Why is pollution an international problem?

20. Discuss how agricultural chemicals can kill marine organisms.

APPLY

21. A stack is an island of rock along certain shores. Along what kind of shorelines would you find stacks? Explain.

22. Describe an ocean food chain.

23. The distance to the ocean bottom can be calculated using the equation: $D = (1/2 \text{ time} \times v)$, where D is the depth, and v is the velocity of a sound wave. If the velocity is 1500 m/s, what is the depth of the ocean if the wave takes 8 seconds to get back to the ship?

24. Would you expect to find coral reefs growing around the bases of volcanoes off the coast of Alaska? Explain your answer.

25. Some oil spills in the ocean are natural. Where does the oil come from?

MORE SKILL BUILDERS

If you need help, refer to the Skill Handbook.

1. Inferring: What is the most common rock on Hawaii?

2. Comparing and Contrasting: Compare and contrast mid-ocean ridges and trenches.

3. Measuring in SI: If a certain kelp grows at a steady rate of 0.6 m/day, how long would it take to reach a height of 60 m?

4. Classifying: Classify each of the following sea creatures according to how they move: shrimp, dolphins, and sea lions.

5. Concept Mapping: Make an events chain concept map that describes how crop fertilizers can harm marine fish.

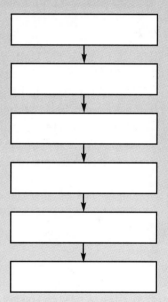

PROJECTS

1. Use a stream table and wooden blocks to make and observe the effects of longshore currents on a coastline.

2. Research the oil spill that occurred in Prince William Sound, Alaska. Then, design a method to clean up an oil spill from a sandy beach. Keep in mind that detergents may cause additional harm to the environment.

UNIT 4
GLOBAL CONNECTIONS

Earth's Air and Water

In this unit, you studied about Earth's atmosphere, weather, and oceans. Now find out how the atmosphere, weather, and oceans are connected to other subjects and places around the world.

120°   60°

60°

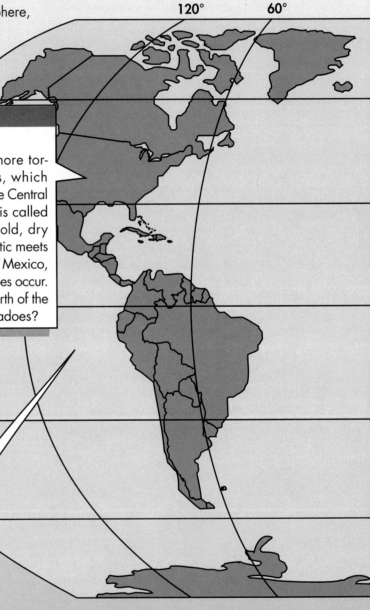

METEOROLOGY

TORNADO BELT, USA
No country in the world has more tornadoes than the United States, which averages about 700 annually. The Central Plains from Texas to Nebraska is called the Tornado Belt. When very cold, dry polar air from the Canadian Arctic meets warm, humid air from the Gulf of Mexico, severe thunderstorms and tornadoes occur. How would a mountain range north of the Gulf of Mexico affect these tornadoes?

BIOLOGY

ANIMALS AT WARM-WATER VENTS
Galapagos Rift, E. Pacific Ocean
Scientists have found places on the ocean floor where the water is warm enough for several kinds of deep-sea animals to live. Clams and tube worms are found in large numbers near these warm-water vents. How do you think scientists found out about these creatures?

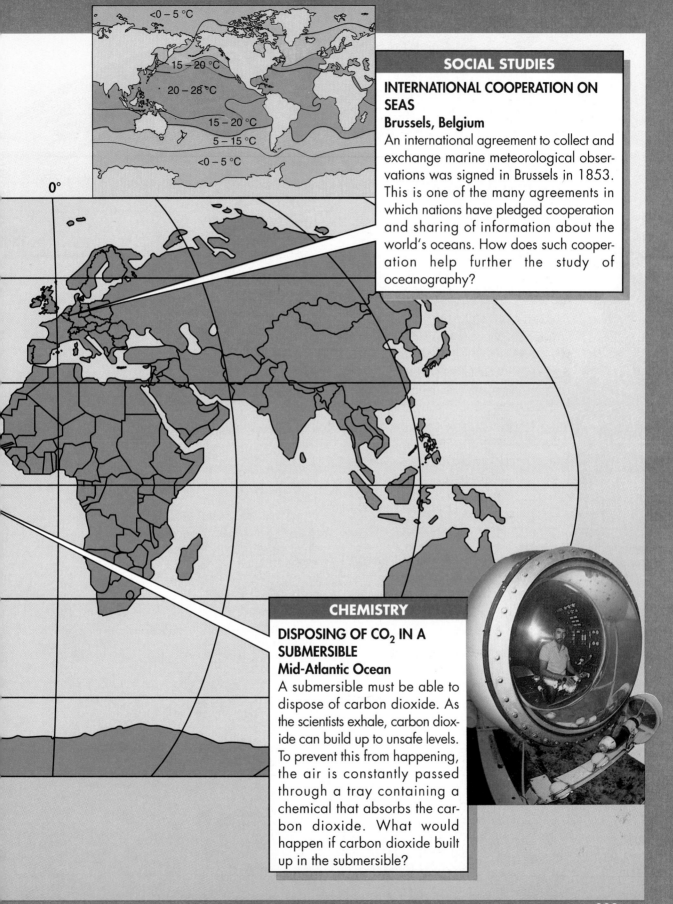

<0 – 5 °C

15 – 20 °C

20 – 28 °C

15 – 20 °C

5 – 15 °C

<0 – 5 °C

0°

SOCIAL STUDIES

INTERNATIONAL COOPERATION ON SEAS
Brussels, Belgium
An international agreement to collect and exchange marine meteorological observations was signed in Brussels in 1853. This is one of the many agreements in which nations have pledged cooperation and sharing of information about the world's oceans. How does such cooperation help further the study of oceanography?

CHEMISTRY

DISPOSING OF CO_2 IN A SUBMERSIBLE
Mid-Atlantic Ocean
A submersible must be able to dispose of carbon dioxide. As the scientists exhale, carbon dioxide can build up to unsafe levels. To prevent this from happening, the air is constantly passed through a tray containing a chemical that absorbs the carbon dioxide. What would happen if carbon dioxide built up in the submersible?

CAREERS

OCEANOGRAPHER

An *oceanographer* is a geologist who studies Earth's surface beneath the oceans. Some oceanographers use sound waves to explore the ocean floor. Instruments plot each measurement on a chart. All the measurements together produce an accurate picture of the ocean floor over which the ship is traveling. Oceanographers also study the composition and temperature of ocean water all over the world. They have found all the known substances in Earth's crust in ocean water. They study the constant exchange of gases between the ocean and the atmosphere. Their studies show that the amount of carbon dioxide in the atmosphere is increasing.

Oceanographers require a college degree. A student interested in becoming an oceanographer should take courses in chemistry, physics, and languages such as German and Russian.

For Additional Information
Contact the Scripps Institution of Oceanography, La Jolla, CA 92093.

METEOROLOGICAL TECHNICIAN

A *meteorological technician* assists a meteorologist in collecting information about the weather and climate. Technicians use instruments such as thermometers, barometers, and hygrometers to measure different conditions of the atmosphere. They collect data on the wind, temperature, precipitation, air pressure, and other atmospheric conditions. They also assist in measuring chemical substances in the atmosphere, such as carbon dioxide and ozone. The information that meteorological technicians gather helps in making weather forecasts.

Most meteorological technicians have at least an associate degree from a community college in meteorology. A student planning to become a meteorological technician should take courses in mathematics and physics.

For Additional Information
Contact the American Meteorological Society, 45 Beacon Street, Boston, MA 02108.

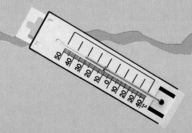

UNIT READINGS

▶Barton, Robert. *The Oceans.* New York: Facts on File, Inc., 1980.
▶Jones, Philip D. and Tom, M.L. "Global Warming Trends." *Scientific American,* August 1990, pp. 84-91.
▶White, Robert. "The Great Climate Debate." *Scientific American,* July 1990, pp. 36-43.

In Times of Silver Rain

by Langston Hughes

In this unit, you studied how rain forms and its effect on the environment. You've explored rain from the viewpoint of an earth scientist. Now read how one poet, Langston Hughes, described rain.

In time of silver rain
        The earth
        Puts forth new life again,
Green grasses grow
And flowers lift their heads,
And over the plain
The wonder spreads
        Of life,
        Of life,
        Of life!

In time of silver rain
The butterflies
Lift silken wings
To catch a rainbow cry,
And trees put forth
New leaves to sing
In joy beneath the sky
As down the roadway
Passing boys and girls
Go singing, too.
In time of silver rain
        When spring
        And life
        Are new.

Most people would agree that rain is of vital importance. Without it, Earth would be parched, food supplies would dwindle, and water would be extremely scarce. This is the practical side of rain.

To a poet such as Langston Hughes, rain is filled with beautiful images to inspire poetry. His image of "silver rain" evokes the idea of a shimmering cascade of raindrops—each like a silvered mirror reflecting the effect of rain on the plants growing on the plain.

What do you think the poet means by the phrase in the second stanza "To catch a rainbow cry?" How do you think Langston Hughes feels about rain?

In Your Own Words

▶ What images does rain evoke for you? Write a poem or an essay that reveals how you feel when it rains.

What's Happening Here?

We aren't always able to protect our homes and other possessions from the engulfing lava of an erupting volcano. People living in Pompeii, Italy, in 79 A.D. had little warning that Mt. Vesuvius was about to erupt. Many were trapped in the ash that covered their town. Their bodies decayed, leaving molds in the solidified ash. Today, archeologists fill the molds with plaster to produce casts of the long-dead residents of Pompeii. As you read the chapters in Unit 5, you'll discover how volcanoes are generated by Earth's internal processes and how these processes affect your world.

UNIT CONTENTS

13 Plate Tectonics

This photo of Earth is unique because the clouds have been removed using a computer. You can see the shapes of the continents just like on a map. Are their shapes related?

FIND OUT!

Do this simple activity to find out how the shapes of the continents are related.

Using thin white paper, trace the outline of the continents using the world map on page 668— Appendix F. Carefully cut each continent out of the paper you traced them on. Using the shapes of the continents as you would pieces of a puzzle, try fitting all continents together into one landmass. Did some continents fit together better than others? Did the shapes of the continents enable you to guess how continents once may have fit together?

Gearing Up
Previewing the Chapter
Use this outline to help you focus on important ideas in this chapter.

Previewing Science Skills
▶ In the **Skill Builders,** you will outline, make a concept map, and recognize cause and effect.
▶ In the **Activities,** you will analyze and interpret data, make a model, observe, and infer.
▶ In the **MINI-Labs,** you will experiment, compare and contrast, observe, and record observations.

What's next?

You've seen that the shapes of the continents can be used to determine if they all fit together at one time in the past. Now you will learn how this and other evidence enabled scientists to draw maps of what ancient Earth may have been like. You will also learn that sections of Earth's crust and mantle move in relation to one another, causing earthquakes, volcanoes, and mountain building.

New Science Words

inner core
outer core
mantle
crust

What does soil evolve from?

Objectives

▶ Diagram Earth's structure.
▶ Describe each layer inside Earth.

Structure of Earth

When you go into school in the morning, what are you walking on? You probably walk on a sidewalk built on top of the soil. You learned in Chapter 5 how soil evolves from weathered rock that lies under the soil. But what lies beneath that? Is the whole interior of Earth solid rock?

Earth's interior is made mostly of rock, but it's not all solid. These different forms of rock form four main layers inside Earth. A peach cut in half can be used as a model showing the layers of Earth's interior.

The innermost layer of a peach is the seed inside the pit. Around the seed is a rough oval shaped pit with a very irregular surface. Above the pit is the thick, juicy part of the peach that tastes so good. The outermost layer of a peach is the fuzzy skin. This layer is very thin in comparison to the whole peach. Earth has a similar layered arrangement of different forms of rock.

At the very center of Earth is its **inner core.** The inner core is solid and is composed of very dense iron and nickel. Pressure from the layers above the inner core causes the iron and nickel to be solid. This layer can be compared to the seed inside the pit of a peach.

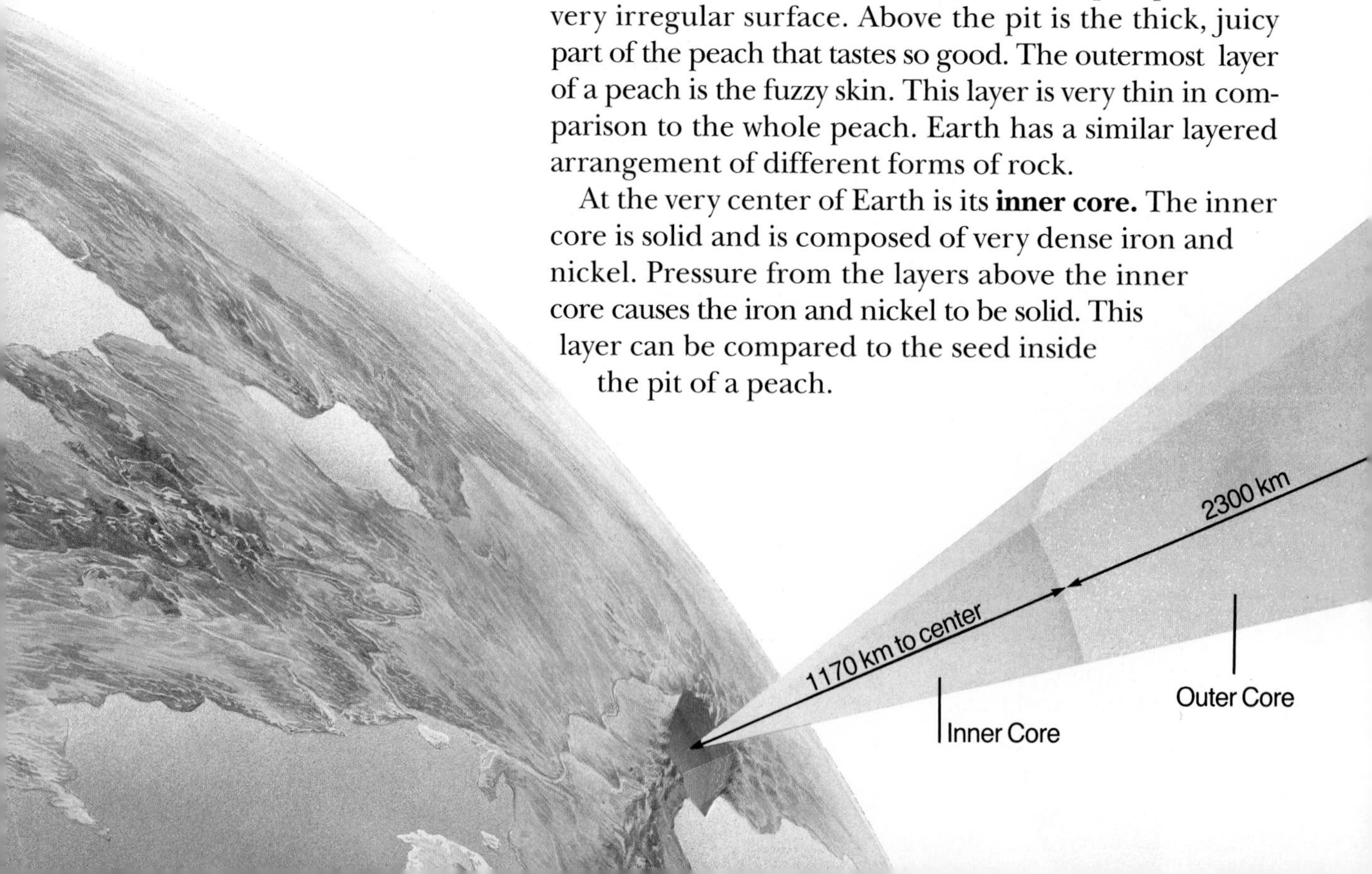

2300 km

1170 km to center

Inner Core

Outer Core

Above the solid inner core lies the liquid **outer core.** Like the inner core, the outer core is also made of iron and nickel. This layer can be compared to the pit of a peach that covers the seed.

Is the outer core solid or liquid?

The **mantle** is the largest layer inside Earth, lying directly above the outer core. It is made mostly of silicon, oxygen, magnesium, and iron. The rock material in the upper mantle is described as "plasticlike." It has characteristics of a solid, but also flows like a liquid when under pressure. Some kinds of hard taffy have this plasticlike characteristic. The taffy can be pulled apart slowly, but if you hit it on the edge of a table it would break. This layer can be compared to the juicy, thickest part of the peach that you eat.

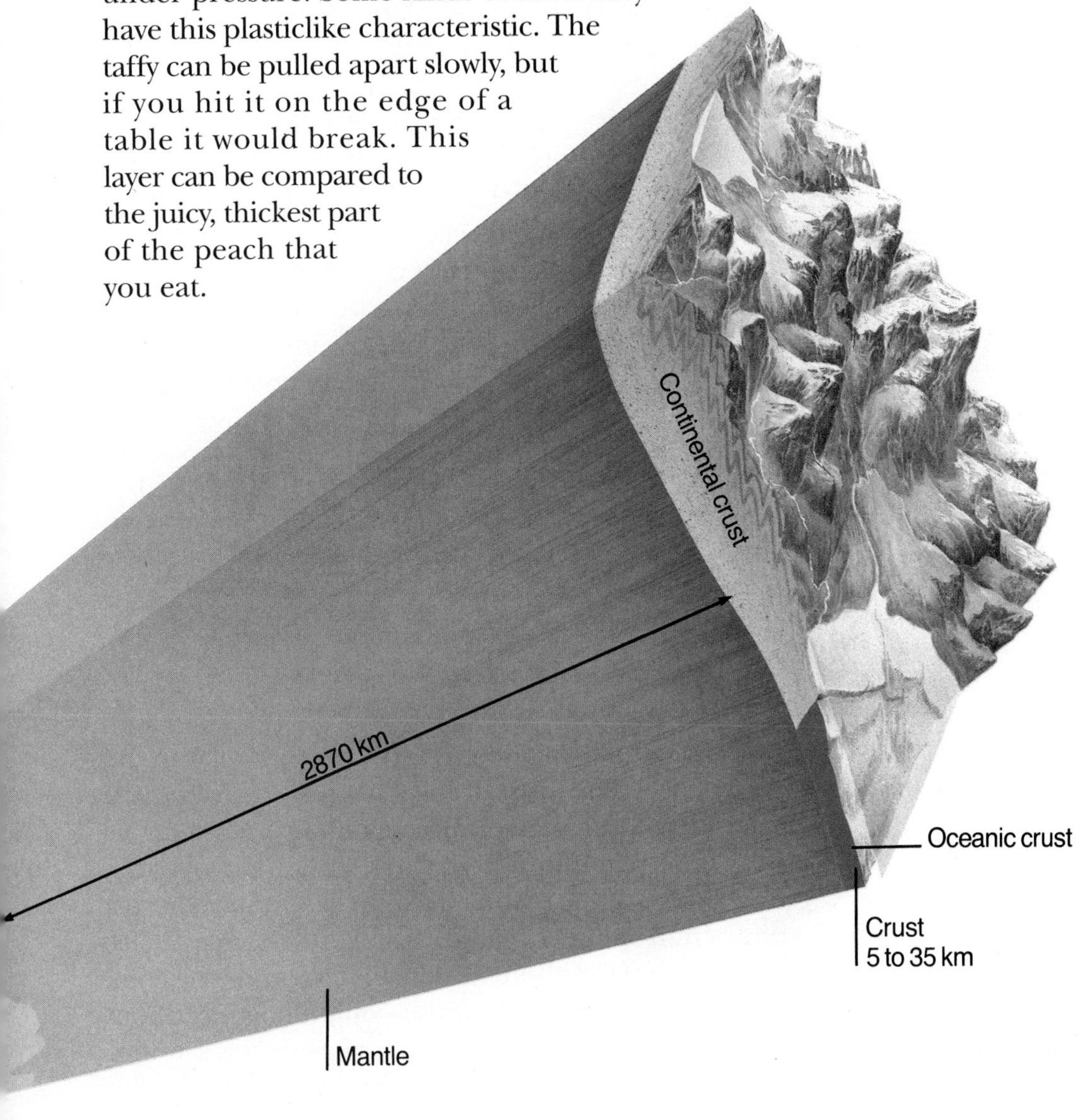

Continental crust

2870 km

Oceanic crust

Crust
5 to 35 km

Mantle

Figure 13-1. This wedge shows the layers inside Earth from the inner core. The inner core, outer core, and mantle are shown at the correct scale, but the crust is shown much thicker than it actually is.

A New Picture of Earth's Interior

What does the interior of Earth look like? Since the early 1900s, scientists have been using earthquakes to create models of the

structure of Earth's interior. When an earthquake occurs, it generates an energy wave that travels through Earth. By measuring the speed of the wave, scientists constructed a model of Earth's interior that was like an onion. They thought Earth's interior was made of separate layers like an onion's.

Using a new technique called travel-time tomography (TTT), scientists have made a new model of Earth's interior. TTT uses new technology in which a computer combines data from thousands of earthquakes around the world. The models from the computer have shown hot blobs of mantle material rising from the core-mantle boundary in some places and cooler blobs sinking from the upper mantle in other places.

Think Critically: How is this new model using travel-time tomography different from the old model of Earth's interior?

Did You Know?

The temperature at the center of Earth is about 6600 degrees C, or 1100 degrees hotter than the surface of the sun.

The outermost layer of Earth is the **crust,** similar to the skin of a peach. The crust of Earth varies in thickness. It is greater than 70 kilometers in some mountainous regions and less than five kilometers thick under the oceanic regions. Data from earthquakes indicated that the crust was different from the oceanic crust. Until the late 1960s, scientists had only earthquake data to determine the composition of oceanic crust. Scientists couldn't be sure about the composition of the oceanic crust because it was under up to three kilometers of water and hundreds of meters of sediments. The deep-sea drilling ship *Glomar Challenger* made the recovery of actual ocean floor samples possible. The rock samples proved to be basaltic, as the earthquake data had indicated. Features such as mountains and valleys are part of the crust.

MINI-Lab

Is it solid or liquid?

Use hard taffy or silicon putty to model the rock in the mantle. Apply differing amounts of force to change its shape. Apply this force in different directions and at different rates. Describe how the taffy or putty reacts when a steady force is applied over several seconds. What happens to the taffy or putty when a greater force is applied rapidly? Describe how the taffy or putty reacts to the different forces. In what ways might the taffy or putty and rock material in Earth's mantle be similar? What causes material in the Earth's mantle to display properties similar to those of the putty and taffy?

When you use a peach as a model, you can see that the crust that we live on is very thin in comparison to the other layers inside Earth. Even in Figure 13-1, the thickness of the crust is exaggerated so it can be seen easily. The *Glomar Challenger* couldn't even drill through the crust where it is the thinnest. As you read on, you'll see that unlike the skin of a peach, Earth's crust is always changing and moving.

SECTION REVIEW

1. Why is the inner core solid?
2. Which part of Earth is comparable to the skin on a peach?
3. Why can the mantle be compared to taffy?
4. **Apply:** Explain why a peach is a good model of Earth's interior.

☑ Outlining

Make an outline that shows the characteristics of each layer of Earth and answer the question below. If you need help, refer to Outlining in the **Skill Handbook** on page 681.

1. What is the inner core composed of?
2. What is the outer core composed of?
3. What is the mantle composed of?

Skill Builder

13-2 Science and New Ideas

New Science Words

continental drift
Pangaea

Objectives

▶ Explain the idea of continental drift.
▶ Recognize that new ideas require careful consideration.

Are New Ideas Sometimes Laughed At?

When you look at a map of Earth's surface, one thing is very obvious. The edges of some continents look as if they would fit together like a puzzle. In the early 1800s, as accurate maps of Earth's surface were first being developed, others also noticed this fact.

Alfred Wegener thought that the fit of the continents wasn't just a coincidence. He believed that all the continents were joined together in the past, and in 1915, proposed the idea of continental drift. **Continental drift** states that continents have moved horizontally to their current locations. Wegener believed that all continents were once connected as one large landmass that broke apart about 200 million years ago. When the continents broke apart, they drifted to their present positions. He called this large landmass **Pangaea** (pan JEE uh), which means "all Earth."

What is continental drift?

Figure 13-3. The coastlines of South America and Africa look like they would fit together as puzzle pieces.

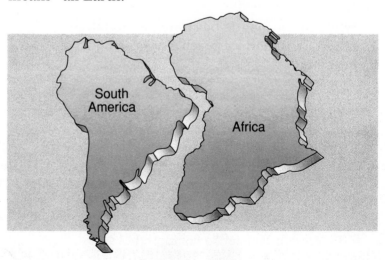

Although the basic idea of continental drift is now widely accepted, it wasn't always that way. Wegener couldn't explain how, when, or why these changes in the position of the continents had taken place. Because other scientists at that time could not provide these explanations either, Wegener's idea of continental drift was rejected. The idea was so different that most people closed their minds to it. In fact, some people laughed and made fun of Wegener's idea. Today, some people are having similar experiences with their new ideas.

One topic that is currently being debated is how the dinosaurs died. Walter and Luis Alvarez have proposed that a large rocky object from space collided with Earth. The collision threw tons of dust into the atmosphere. Sunlight was blocked for several years, eventually causing the death of the dinosaurs.

Figure 13-4. These computer models show the probable course that continents have taken. On the far left is their position 200 million years ago, in the middle is their position 100 million years ago, and at right is their current position.

SECTION REVIEW

1. Explain how Pangaea fits into Wegener's idea of continental drift.
2. State one reason why Wegener's ideas about continental drift were not believed.

You Decide!

Because the idea proposed by Walter and Luis Alvarez is so different, many scientists have rejected it completely. What do you think about this issue? Would you accept their idea as a way that the dinosaurs might have been killed? How can you decide which new ideas to reject and which ones to accept?

SCIENCE & SOCIETY

Evidence for Continental Drift

New Science Words

sea-floor spreading
magnetometer

Objectives

▶ Discuss four pieces of evidence for the idea of continental drift.
▶ Describe sea-floor spreading.
▶ Relate how age and magnetic clues confirm sea-floor spreading.

Early Evidence

Since Wegener's death in 1930, much of his basic idea that the continents drift has been accepted as fact. But the evidence he had at that time to support his idea wasn't enough to convince many. Wegener's early evidence has since been joined by other important proofs. Let's explore both Wegener's clues and some newer ones.

Fossil and Climate Clues

Besides the puzzle-like fit of the continents, other clues were found in fossils. Fossils of the reptile *Mesosaurus* have been found in South America and Africa. This swimming reptile lived in fresh water and on land. How could fossils of the *Mesosaurus* be found so far apart? It's very unlikely that it could have swum between the continents. Wegener thought this reptile lived on both continents when the continents were connected.

Another fossil that helps support continental drift is *Glossopteris*. This fossil fern was found in Africa, Australia, India, South America, and later in Antarctica. Finding this fern in so many areas with widely different climates led Wegener to believe all of these areas were once connected and had a similar climate.

Fossils of warm weather plants were found in Greenland, which has a cold climate. Wegener believed Greenland drifted through the ocean floor from a warmer to a colder climate. He also found glacial clues. Glacial deposits and grooved bedrock found in southern areas of South America, Africa, India, and Australia

Figure 13-5. Alfred Wegener

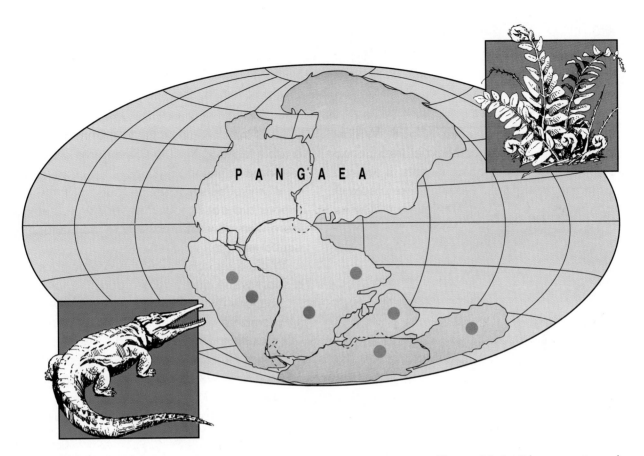

P A N G A E A

indicated that these continents were once covered with glaciers. How could you explain why glacial deposits were found in these areas where no glaciers exist today? Wegener thought that these continents were all connected and covered with ice near Earth's South Pole at one time.

Figure 13-6. *Glossopteris* and *Mesosaurus* lived in many areas of Pangaea. Their fossils are now found on separate continents that have since drifted apart.

Rock Clues

If the continents were connected at one time, then wouldn't rocks that make up the continents be the same? Yes, similar rock structures are found on different continents. Parts of the Appalachian Mountains of the eastern United States are similar to those found in Greenland and western Europe. If you were to travel to South America and western Africa, you would find rock structures that are very similar. If the continents were connected when the rock structures formed, you would expect them to be the same.

Why are matching rock structures evidence for continental drift?

Rock, fossil, and climate clues were the main points of evidence for continental drift. Later, after Wegener's death, more clues were found and new ideas related to continental drift were discovered.

A Perfect Fit?

While looking at a map of Earth, William noticed what many others before him had suggested about the continents. It seemed that they might all fit together like pieces of a puzzle. One day he took an old map and cut out each of the continents. He laid them all on a table top and tried to fit them into a single large continent.

Much to his surprise, he found that the pieces did not fit together very well. Yet there were several areas where the fit was almost perfect.

William thought about this problem for a short while and had an idea. He took one look at another map and made one small adjustment in his procedure. Cutting another old map, he found that almost all of the pieces would fit together with the one slight change in what he had done.

Think Critically: How do you suppose William solved this problem?

Sea-floor Spreading

What did echo sounding discover about the ocean floor?

Up until the early 1950s, little was known about the ocean floors. Scientists didn't have the technology needed to explore the deep oceans. But echo sounding devices allowed scientists to begin making accurate maps of the ocean floor. Soon, scientists discovered a complex ocean floor that had mountains and valleys just like continents had above water. They also found a system of ridges and valleys extending through the center of the Atlantic and in other oceans around the world. The mid-ocean ridges form an underwater mountain range that extends through the center of much of Earth's oceans. This discovery raised the curiosity of many scientists. What formed these mid-ocean ridges?

In the early 1960s, Princeton scientist Harry Hess suggested an explanation. His now famous and accepted theory is known as **sea-floor spreading.** Hess proposed that molten material in the mantle rises to the surface at a mid-ocean ridge. Then it turns and flows sideways, carrying the seafloor away from the ridge in both directions as seen in Figure 13-7. New seafloor is then created in the middle of the mid-ocean ridge by the rising magma. The seafloor that is carried away from the ridge is forced down into the mantle at the edges of the oceans, forming trenches. Sea-floor spreading was later shown to be true by the two following pieces of evidence.

Age Evidence

In 1968, scientists aboard the research ship *Glomar Challenger* began gathering information about the rocks in the seafloor. The *Challenger* is equipped with a drilling rig that allows scientists to drill into the seafloor to obtain rock samples. The scientists began drilling to study the age of rocks in the seafloor and made a remarkable discovery. They found no rocks older than 200 million years. In contrast, some continental rocks are more than three billion years old. Why were these seafloor rocks so young?

Scientists also found that the youngest rocks were located at the mid-ocean ridges. The age of the rocks became increasingly older farther from the ridges on both sides. The evidence for sea-floor spreading was getting stronger.

Magnetic Clues

The final bit of evidence in support of sea-floor spreading came with magnetic clues found in the iron-bearing basalt rock in the ocean floor.

What did the *Glomar Challenger* discover about the ocean floor?

Figure 13-7. As the seafloor spreads apart at a mid-ocean ridge, new seafloor is created. The older seafloor moves away from the ridge in both directions.

Age of ocean floor in millions of years

| 150-200 | 100-150 | 50-100 | 0-50 | 50-100 | 100-150 | 150-200 |

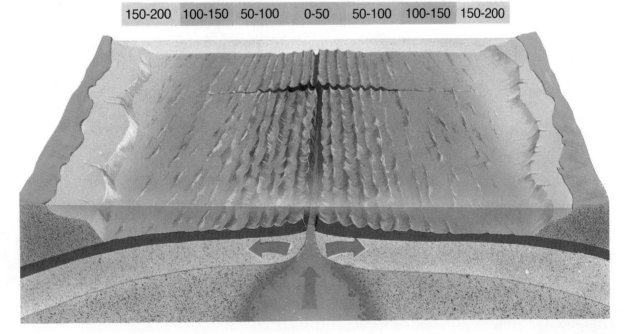

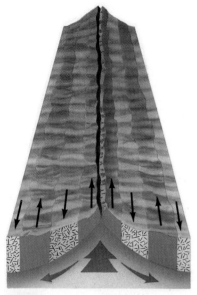

↑ Normal polarity   ⬛ Reversed polarity

Figure 13-8. Changes in magnetic polarity of the rock on both sides of mid-ocean ridges reflect the past reversals of Earth's magnetic poles. This is evidence for sea-floor spreading.

Scientists know that Earth's magnetic field has reversed itself several times in its past. In other words, the north magnetic pole becomes the south magnetic pole. Iron minerals in rocks such as basalt align themselves according to the magnetic orientation at the time that they form. If Earth's magnetic field is reversed, new iron minerals being formed would reflect that magnetic reversal.

Scientists found that rocks on the ocean floor showed many magnetic reversals. Scientists used a magnetometer to record magnetic data about the rocks in the ocean floor. A **magnetometer** is a sensitive instrument that records magnetic fields. The magnetic alignment of the rocks reversed back and forth in strips parallel to the mid-ocean ridge. These magnetic reversals were found to match with known reversals of Earth's magnetic pole.

This discovery proved that sea-floor spreading was indeed happening. The magnetic reversals showed that new rock was being formed at the mid-ocean ridges.

The ideas of Alfred Wegener and Harry Hess changed the way people think about Earth's crust. Fossil, rock, and climate evidence supporting continental drift is too strong to be discounted. Sea-floor spreading proves that ocean floors change too. You'll see in Section 13-4 how these two ideas are closely related.

SECTION REVIEW

1. How did the magnetic alignment of iron minerals help to prove sea-floor spreading?
2. What continental drift clue did Wegener first use?
3. How were fossils used as clues for continental drift?
4. What eventually happens to seafloor that is carried away from a mid-ocean ridge?
5. **Apply:** How is sea-floor spreading different from continental drift?

Skill Builder

☑ Concept Mapping

Make a concept map that discusses the evidence for continental drift using the following terms and phrases: *continental edges, same fossils, climate, rock structures, on different continents, mountains with similar features, continental ice sheets,* and *puzzle pieces.* If you need help, refer to Concept Mapping in the **Skill Handbook** on page 688.

ACTIVITY 13-1
Sea-floor Spreading

Problem: *How does magnetic evidence confirm sea-floor spreading?*

Materials

- metric ruler
- paper
- tape
- small magnetic compasses (2)
- bar magnets
- pen or marker

Procedure

1. Tape several sheets of paper together to produce a strip from 40 to 60 cm in length.
2. Fold the strip of paper and place it between two close desks or piles of books as shown. The paper represents oceanic crust on either side of a mid-ocean ridge.
3. Place the magnets as shown.
4. Place the two compasses next to each other on either side of the space between the desks.
5. Draw a line along each side of the space to represent the edges of the ocean ridge.
6. Beside the line, draw arrows showing the direction the compass needles are pointing.
7. Split the "seafloor" by moving the paper away from the center 3 cm on each side. Reverse the magnets by turning them 180°.

8. Return the compasses to their original positions along the side of the space between the desks. Draw new arrows on the paper to represent the direction that the compass needles are now pointing.
9. Repeat this procedure several times.

Analyze

1. Where are the "oldest" marks on the strip of paper?
2. Compare your completed strip to the patterns in Figure 13-8. What are the similarities and differences?

Conclude and Apply

3. How does this activity compare to the movement of crustal and mantle material?
4. How do the plates move?
5. What is a magnetic reversal?
6. How does this model answer the question of why the ocean basins have younger crustal rocks than the continents?

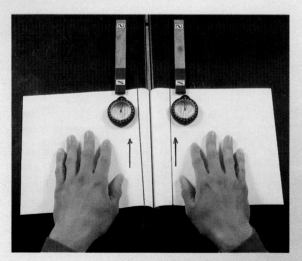

13-4 Theory of Plate Tectonics

New Science Words

plate tectonics
plates
lithosphere
asthenosphere
divergent boundary
convergent boundary
subduction zone
transform fault
convection current

Objectives

▶ Compare and contrast divergent, convergent, and transform plate boundaries.
▶ Describe how convection currents might be the cause of plate tectonics.

Science and READING

There were many scientists besides Alfred Wegener and Harry Hess who contributed ideas that led to plate tectonics. Some of them include A. L. Du Toit, S. K. Runcorn, Bruce Heezen, Arthur Holmes, J. Tuzo Wilson, Jack Oliver, and Lynn R. Sykes. Get a book on plate tectonics and read about contributions made by these scientists.

Plate Tectonics

With the discovery of sea-floor spreading, scientists began to understand what was happening to Earth's crust and upper mantle. The idea of sea-floor spreading showed that more than just continents were moving as Wegener had thought. It was now evident to scientists that sections of the seafloor and continents move around in relation to one another.

By 1968, scientists had developed a new theory that combined the main ideas of continental drift and sea-floor spreading. The theory of **plate tectonics** states that Earth's crust and upper mantle are broken into sections called **plates.** These plates move around on the mantle.

The continents can be thought of as "rafts" that float and move around on the mantle. Plates are composed

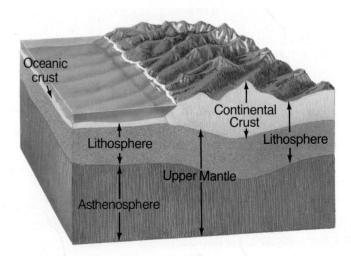

Figure 13-9. The less dense plates of the lithosphere move on the asthenosphere.

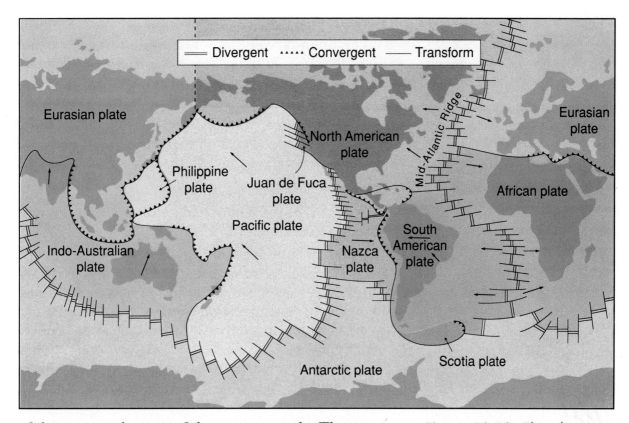

Divergent ⸺ Convergent ⸺ Transform

Eurasian plate

Philippine plate

Juan de Fuca plate

North American plate

Mid-Atlantic Ridge

Eurasian plate

African plate

Indo-Australian plate

Pacific plate

Nazca plate

South American plate

Antarctic plate

Scotia plate

Figure 13-10. This diagram shows the major plates of the lithosphere, their direction of movement, and the type of boundary between them.

of the crust and a part of the upper mantle. These two parts together are called the **lithosphere** (LITH uh sfihr). This rigid layer is about 100 km thick and is less dense than material underneath. This plasticlike layer below the lithosphere is called the **asthenosphere** (as THEN uh sfihr). The less dense plates of the lithosphere "float" and move around on the denser asthenosphere. The interaction of the plates on the asthenosphere is like large flat stones placed in wet cement. You can move the stones around in the cement before it dries.

What happens when plates move? They can interact in three ways. They can move toward each other and collide, they can pull apart, or they can simply move past one another. When the plates interact, the result of their movement is seen at the plate boundaries. Movement along any plate boundary requires that adjustments be made at the other boundaries. Here, mountains are formed, volcanoes erupt, or earthquakes occur. For example, the Pacific Plate moves past the North American Plate, causing earthquakes in California. And it causes volcanoes in Alaska where it collides with the North American Plate. Mountain building, earthquakes, and volcanoes are known as tectonic activities.

What are the three ways in which plates interact?

Divergent Boundaries

The boundary between two plates that are moving apart from one another is called a **divergent boundary.** You learned about divergent boundaries when you read about seafloor spreading. In the Atlantic Ocean, the North American Plate is moving away from the Eurasian and the African plates as seen in Figure 13-10 on page 349. That divergent boundary is called the Mid-Atlantic Ridge. The Great Rift Valley in eastern Africa is another good example of a diverging plate boundary. Here, a valley has formed where two continental plates have separated.

Convergent Boundaries

If new crust is being added at one location, why doesn't Earth's crust keep getting thicker? As new crust is added in one place, it disappears at another. The disappearance of crust can occur where two plates collide at a **convergent boundary.**

There are three types of convergent boundaries. When an ocean floor plate collides with a less dense continental plate, the denser ocean plate sinks under the continental plate. The area where an oceanic plate descends into the upper mantle is called a **subduction zone.** Volcanoes occur at subduction zones.

Figure 13-11. As Earth's plates pull apart at some boundaries, they collide at others, forming mountains and volcanoes.

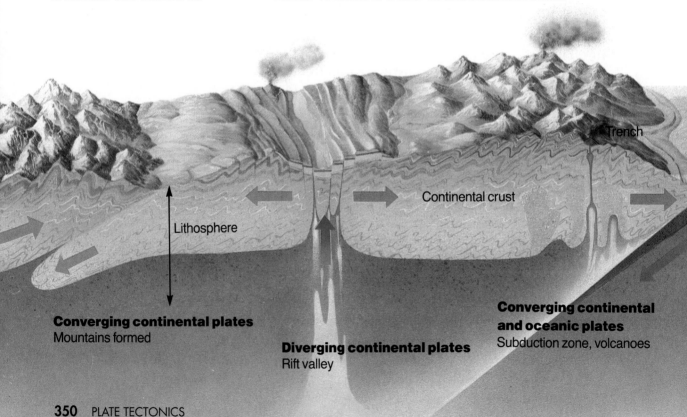

Lithosphere

Continental crust

Trench

Converging continental plates
Mountains formed

Diverging continental plates
Rift valley

Converging continental and oceanic plates
Subduction zone, volcanoes

Figure 13-11 shows how this type of convergent boundary creates a deep-sea trench where one plate is subducting under the other. High temperatures and pressures cause the subducted plate to melt as it descends under the other plate. The newly formed magma rises toward the surface along these plate boundaries, forming volcanic mountains. The Andes Mountains of South America contain many volcanoes. They were formed at the convergent boundary of the Nazca and the South American plates.

The second type of convergent boundary occurs when two ocean plates collide. Like the first type of boundary, when two ocean plates collide, one bends and slides under the other, forming a subduction zone. A deep-sea trench is formed, and the new magma that is produced rises to form an island arc of volcanoes. The islands of Japan are volcanic island arcs formed when two oceanic plates collided.

The third type of convergent boundary occurs when two continental plates collide. Because both of these plates are less dense than the material in the asthenosphere, usually no subduction occurs. The two plates just collide and crumple up, forming mountain ranges. Earthquakes are common at these convergent boundaries. The Himalaya Mountains in Asia were formed when the Indian Plate crashed into the Eurasian Plate.

What kinds of plates collided to form the Himalaya Mountains?

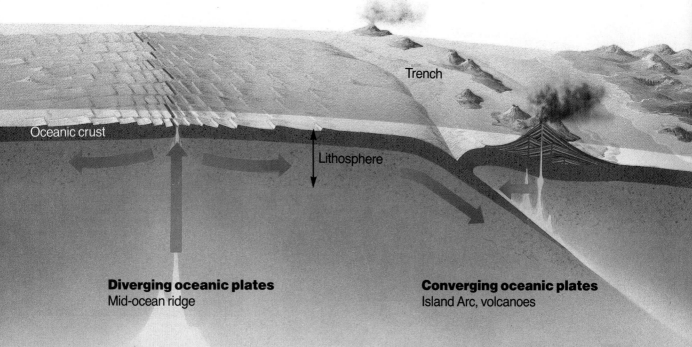

Oceanic crust

Lithosphere

Trench

Diverging oceanic plates
Mid-ocean ridge

Converging oceanic plates
Island Arc, volcanoes

Transform Fault Boundaries

The third type of plate boundary is called a **transform fault.** Transform faults occur when two plates slide past one another. This occurs when two plates are moving in opposite directions or in the same direction at different rates. As one plate slides past another, earthquakes occur. The famous San Andreas Fault is a transform fault plate boundary. It has been the site of many earthquakes. The Pacific Plate is sliding past the North American Plate, forming the San Andreas Fault.

Causes of Plate Tectonics

There have been many new discoveries about Earth's crust since Wegener's day. But one question still remains. What causes the plates to move and the seafloor to spread? Scientists now think they have a pretty good idea. They think that plates are moved by the same basic process that is used in heating some buildings. In a forced air heating system, air is warmed in the furnace and a blower forces it into each room of the building. The air rises from the register and releases its heat to surrounding air. The cooler air, which is now denser, sinks to the floor of the room. It returns to the furnace through the cold air return, to be reheated. This entire cycle of heating, rising, cooling, and sinking is called a **convection current.** This same process is thought to be the force behind plate tectonics.

Figure 13-12. The San Andreas Fault forms a transform fault boundary where the Pacific Plate is sliding past the North American Plate.

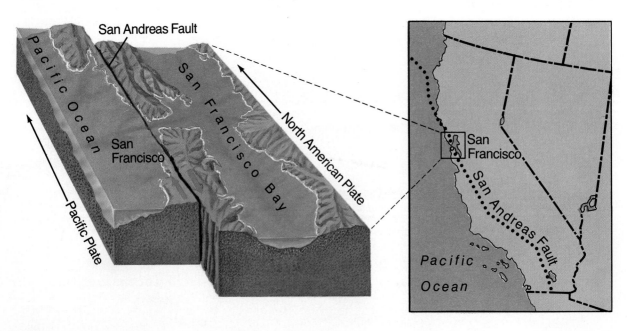

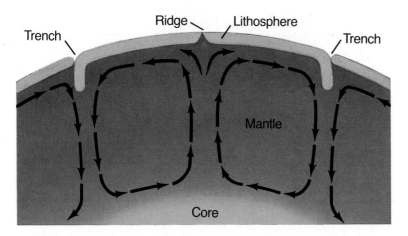

Figure 13-13. Convection currents (see arrows) are the driving force of plate tectonics.

Scientists believe differences in density cause hot plasticlike rock in the asthenosphere to rise toward the surface. When this plasticlike rock reaches Earth's lithosphere, it moves horizontally and carries plates of the lithosphere with it as described earlier. As it cools, the plasticlike rock becomes denser. It then sinks into the mantle, taking overlying crust with it.

These huge convection cells provide the energy to move plates in the lithosphere. Plate tectonics shows how activity inside Earth causes changes on Earth's crust.

SECTION REVIEW

1. What happens to plates at a transform fault boundary?
2. What type of plate boundary is associated with sea-floor spreading?
3. What happens when a denser ocean plate collides with a less dense continental plate?
4. Island arcs form at what type of plate boundary?
5. **Apply:** Looking at Figure 13-10 on page 349 and Appendix F on page 668 if necessary, determine why Iceland could be a dangerous place to live.

MINI-Lab

How do convection currents form?

Fill a metal pan with water to 5 cm from the top. Center the pan on a hot plate and heat. **CAUTION:** *Wear thermal mitts to protect your hands as the pan becomes hot.* Add a few drops of food coloring to the water directly above the hot plate. Watch for currents to form in the water. What do you think causes these currents?

☑ Recognizing Cause and Effect

What causes a divergent boundary to form? What is the effect of collision on the edges of continental plates? Use your knowledge of cause-and-effect relationships to answer the questions. Then, write a cause-and-effect statement explaining the relationship between convection currents and plate movement. If you need help, refer to Recognizing Cause and Effect in the **Skill Handbook** on page 683.

Skill Builder

ACTIVITY 13-2
Rates of Sea-floor Spreading

Problem: *How can you determine the rate of sea-floor spreading?*

Materials

- metric ruler
- pencil

Procedure

1. Study the magnetic field profile below. You will be working with six major peaks east and west of the Mid-Atlantic Ridge for both normal and reversed polarity.
2. Place the ruler through the first peak west of the main rift. Determine and record the distance in km to the Mid-Atlantic Ridge.
3. Repeat Step 2 for each of the six major peaks east and west of the main rift, for both normal and reversed polarity.
4. Find the average distance from peak to ridge for each pair of corresponding peaks on either side of the ridge. Record these values.
5. Use the normal polarity readings to find the age of the rocks at each average distance.
6. Using normal polarity readings, calculate the rate of movement in cm/year. Use the formula (distance = rate × time) to calculate the rate. You must convert km to cm.

Data and Observations

Peak	1	2	3	4	5	6
Distance west normal polarity						
Distance east normal polarity						
Average distance						
Distance west reversed polarity						
Distance east reversed polarity						
Average distance						
Age from scale (millions of years)						
Rate of movement (cm/year)						

Analyze

1. Compare the age of the igneous rock found near the mid-ocean ridge to that of the rock found farther away from the ridge.
2. In what way does the information shown in the graph relate to the procedure in Activity 13-1?

Conclude and Apply

3. On your paper, draw a line that would represent the amount of total movement that would occur between a point east of the Mid-Atlantic Ridge and a point west of the ridge in one year.
4. If the distance from a point on the coast of Africa to the Mid-Atlantic Ridge is approximately 2400 km, how long ago was that point in Africa at or near that mid-ocean ridge?

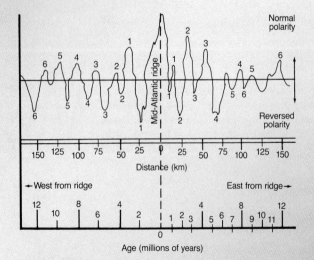

CHAPTER
REVIEW

13-1: Structure of Earth

1. Earth has four main layers: a solid, inner core; a liquid, outer core; the mantle; and the crust.

2. The inner core is solid and is composed of iron and nickel. The outer core is liquid. The upper mantle is plasticlike rock made of silicon, oxygen, magnesium, and iron. The crust is the outermost layer of Earth.

13-2: Science and Society: Science and New Ideas

1. The theory of continental drift states that continents have moved to their present positions on Earth.

2. Some ideas are not taken seriously when first proposed. New ideas should be given careful consideration.

13-3: Evidence for Continental Drift

1. The puzzle-like fit of the continents, fossils, climatic evidence, and similar rock structures support Wegener's idea of continental drift.

2. Sea-floor spreading states that the seafloor is spreading apart at the mid-ocean ridges.

3. Sea-floor spreading is supported by magnetic evidence in rocks and in the age of rocks on the ocean floor.

13-4: Theory of Plate Tectonics

1. Plates move away from each other at divergent boundaries. Plates collide at convergent boundaries. At a transform fault, two plates move horizontally past each other.

2. Hot, plasticlike material from the mantle rises to the lithosphere moves horizontally, cools, and then sinks back into the mantle. The movement of this material sets up convection currents, the driving force of plate tectonics.

KEY SCIENCE WORDS

a. asthenosphere
b. continental drift
c. convection current
d. convergent boundary
e. crust
f. divergent boundary
g. inner core
h. lithosphere
i. magnetometer
j. mantle
k. outer core
l. Pangaea
m. plates
n. plate tectonics
o. sea-floor spreading
p. subduction zone
q. transform fault

UNDERSTANDING VOCABULARY

Match each phrase with the correct term from the list of Key Science Words.

1. innermost part of Earth
2. Earth's thick, plasticlike layer
3. idea that continents moved to their current positions on Earth
4. large landmass made of all continents
5. Earth's uppermost layer
6. process that forms new seafloor
7. large sections of Earth's crust and upper mantle
8. boundary where plates move apart from each other
9. boundary at which plates collide
10. place where plates slide past one another

CHAPTER
REVIEW

Choose the word or phrase that completes the sentence.

1. Earth's _____ can be compared to the seed of a peach.
   a. crust   c. outer core
   b. mantle   d. inner core

2. The San Andreas Fault is a _____.
   a. divergent boundary
   b. subduction zone
   c. convergent boundary
   d. none of these

3. _____ states that continents moved to their present positions.
   a. Subduction
   b. Sea-floor spreading
   c. Continental drift
   d. None of these

4. Evidence supporting continental drift includes _____.
   a. fossils   c. rock structures
   b. continental margins   d. all of these

5. Evidence from _____ indicates that many continents were near Earth's South Pole.
   a. glaciers   c. rock structures
   b. mid-ocean ridges   d. plates

6. _____ of iron in rocks confirmed continental drift.
   a. Plate movement
   b. Subduction
   c. Magnetic alignment
   d. All of these

7. The theory of _____ states that plates move around on the asthenosphere.
   a. continental drift
   b. sea-floor spreading
   c. subduction
   d. none of these

8. The Great Rift Valley is a _____ margin.
   a. convergent   c. transform fault
   b. divergent   d. lithosphere

9. A _____ forms when a plate slides under another.
   a. transform fault   c. subduction zone
   b. divergent boundary d. mid-ocean ridge

10. When two oceanic plates collide, _____ form.
    a. folded mountains   c. transform faults
    b. island arcs   d. all of these

Complete each sentence.

11. Plates move because of _____.
12. Earth's _____ is its thinnest layer.
13. Plates "float" on the _____.
14. Both the inner and the outer core are composed of _____ and _____.
15. Echo sounding led to the discovery of the _____.

THINK AND WRITE CRITICALLY

16. Compare and contrast continental drift and plate tectonics.

17. Why was continental drift initially not accepted by many scientists?

18. Explain the relationship between a mid-ocean ridge and sea-floor spreading.

19. Compare and contrast divergent, convergent, and transform fault boundaries.

20. Explain how island arcs form.

APPLY

21. Why are there few volcanoes in the Himalayas, but many earthquakes?

22. Glacial deposits often form at high latitudes near the poles. Explain why glacial deposits have been found in Africa.

23. How is magnetism used to support the theory of sea-floor spreading?

24. Explain why no volcanoes are forming along the San Andreas Fault.

25. Why wouldn't the fossil of an ocean fish found on two different continents be good evidence of continental drift?

MORE SKILL BUILDERS

If you need help, refer to the Skill Handbook.

1. Hypothesizing: Mount St. Helens in the Cascade Mountain Range is a volcano. Use Figure 13-10 on page 349 and Appendix F on page 668 to hypothesize how it may have formed.

2. Measuring in SI: Movement along the African Rift Valley is about 2.1 cm per year. If plates continue to move apart at this rate, how large will the rift be (in meters) in 1000 years? 15 500 years?

3. Outlining: Outline the major points in Section 13-3.

4. Comparing and Contrasting: Compare and contrast the formation of the Andes Mountains and the Himalayas.

5. Concept Mapping: Make an events chain concept map that describes sea-floor spreading.

PROJECTS

1. Use modeling clay to construct three-dimensional scale models of each type of plate boundary. Make sure to show the boundaries to a depth of at least a few hundred kilometers. Also show the features that form at each type of boundary.

2. Research the normal and reversed magnetic bands that cover the seafloors. Use the magnetic data to compute the rates of spreading during each magnetic period.

You may have seen pictures of the October 1989 earthquake that occurred in the San Francisco Bay area. Have you ever thought about what caused this and other earthquakes? As you read this chapter, you will explore how movement and changes in Earth's lithosphere produce earthquakes.

FIND OUT!

Do this simple activity to find out how forces in Earth cause rocks to deform.

Place two pieces of clay flat on a table. Place your hands on opposite ends of one of the pieces of clay. Begin pushing your hands together, compressing the clay. What do you notice about the clay? Draw a picture of the clay on a sheet of paper. Now hold the other piece of clay in your hands. Begin to apply tension by gradually pulling the clay apart. What happens as you pull on the clay? What do you think will happen if you continue to apply tension to the clay? Draw a picture of what you observe.

Gearing Up

Previewing the Chapter

Use this outline to help you focus on important ideas in this chapter.

Previewing Science Skills

► In the **Skill Builders,** you will make concept maps, use graphs, and make tables.
► In the **Activities,** you will measure, construct and interpret graphs, analyze data, and draw conclusions.
► In the **MINI-Labs,** you will interpret graphs and apply skills in a role-playing exercise.

What's next?

Now that you've seen how the forces of compression and tension affect a layer of clay, you can relate this to how forces in Earth might affect rock. As you read this chapter, you will learn what causes earthquakes, how their point of origin is located, and what we learn from them.

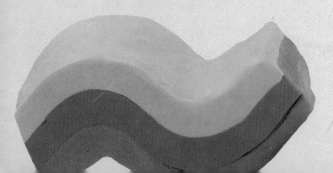

Earthquakes and Plate Tectonics

New Science Words

faults
earthquakes
normal fault
reverse fault
strike-slip fault

Objectives

▶ Explain how earthquakes result from the buildup of stress in Earth's crust.
▶ Contrast normal, reverse, and strike-slip faults.

Did You Know?

The 1989 San Francisco earthquake was caused by the Pacific plate slipping past the North American plate by only 2 m.

Causes of Earthquakes

Think about the last time you used a rubber band to hold a roll of papers together. You knew you could stretch the rubber band only so far before it would break. Rubber bands bend and stretch when force is applied to them. Because they are elastic, they return to their original shape once the force is released.

There is a limit to how far a rubber band will stretch. Once it passes this elastic limit, it breaks. Rocks act in much the same way. Up to a point, applied forces cause rocks to bend and stretch. Once their elastic limit is passed, the rocks break. Rocks break and move along surfaces called **faults**. The rocks on either side of a fault move in different directions.

What produces the forces that cause faults to form? Obviously, something must be causing the rocks to move, otherwise, the rocks would just rest quietly without any stress building up in them. As you know, Earth's crust is in constant motion because of tectonic forces. When plates move, stress is put on rocks. To relieve this stress, the rocks tend to bend, compress, and stretch like rubber bands. But if the force is great enough, the rocks break. This breaking produces vibrations in Earth, called **earthquakes.**

Types of Faults

Compare Figure 14-1 with Figure 13-10 on page 349. You will see that most earthquakes occur along tectonic plate boundaries. In fact, 80 percent of all earthquakes occur along the edges of the Pacific plate.

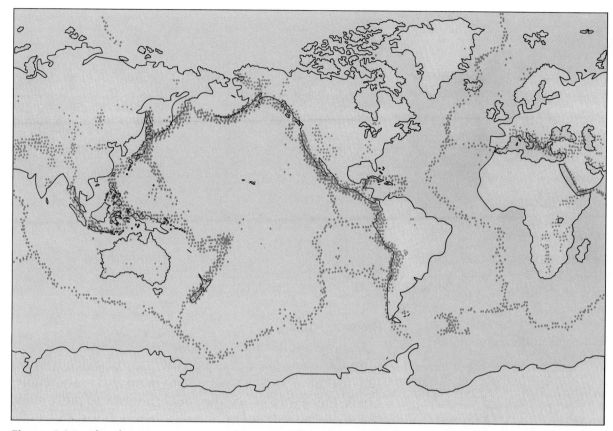

Figure 14-1. The dots represent the epicenters of the major quakes over a ten-year period. Eighty percent of earthquakes occur along the edges of the Pacific plate. This ring of seismic and volcanic activity is called the Pacific Ring of Fire.

Rocks experience several types of forces at the different types of plate boundaries. In the Find Out activity at the beginning of this chapter, you experimented with two of these forces—compression and tension. As you read on, you will discover that rocks also experience a force called shearing. Let's take a look at these three forces and the types of faults they create.

Normal Faults

At divergent plate boundaries, the plates and the rocks that compose them are moving apart. The rocks are subjected to the force of tension. Tension can pull rocks apart and create a **normal fault.** Along a normal fault, rock above the fault surface moves downward in relation to rock below the fault surface. A model of a normal fault is shown in Figure 14-2.

Many normal faults occurred during the formation of the Sierra Nevadas. The continental crust was subjected to tension as it spread apart. The resulting mountains are a series of fault blocks.

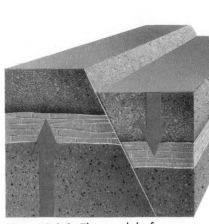

Figure 14-2. The model of a normal fault shows the relative movement of rocks on either side of the fault line. The Sierra Nevadas consist of a series of fault blocks.

Figure 14-3. The relative movement of rocks in a reverse fault results from applied pressure. Why do the Himalaya Mountains exhibit so many reverse faults?

Reverse Faults

Compression forces are generated at convergent plate boundaries. Compression pushes on rocks from opposite directions and causes them to bend and to sometimes break. Once they break, the rocks continue to move along the reverse fault surface. At a **reverse fault,** the rocks above the fault surface are forced up and over the rocks below the fault surface.

The Himalaya Mountains of India contain many reverse faults. The continental crusts of India and Asia are still being subjected to compressional forces as two tectonic plates continue to converge.

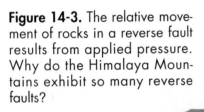

Strike-slip Faults

Recall the transform fault boundaries you studied in Chapter 13. The most famous example of this type of plate boundary is the San Andreas Fault of California. A transform fault, like the San Andreas, is a type of strike-slip fault. At a **strike-slip fault,** rocks on either side of the fault surface are moving past each other without much upward or downward movement. Compare the fault in Figure 14-4 with those on the previous page. How do they differ?

Rocks along strike-slip faults are subjected to shearing forces. Shearing forces push on rocks from different, but not opposite, directions. As the rocks move past each other, their irregular surfaces snag each other, and the

What type of force is generated at a strike-slip fault boundary?

Figure 14-4. There is very little vertical movement along a strike-slip fault such as the San Andreas Fault shown here.

rocks are twisted and strained. Not only are they deformed, but the snagging of the irregular surface hinders the movement of the plates. As tectonic forces keep driving the plates to move, the stress builds up and the rocks reach their elastic limit. They break and an earthquake results.

Earthquakes can be dramatic events. Some have devastating effects, others go almost unnoticed. Regardless of their magnitudes, most earthquakes are the result of plates moving over, under, and around each other. If these plates simply slid smoothly past each other, the

Figure 14-5. These railroad tracks along Mexico's Pacific coast were twisted during an earthquake. They illustrate the damage that can occur from seismic waves and fault movements.

tension, compression, and shear forces would not build up stress. But in actuality, rocks do experience these forces and stress builds up in them. When rocks break because of the stress, energy is released along the fault surfaces and we observe the effects in the form of earthquakes.

SECTION REVIEW

1. How is plate tectonics related to earthquakes?
2. What type of force is usually generated at strike-slip fault boundaries? What type of force causes reverse faults to form?
3. The surfaces of normal faults and reverse faults look very similar. Why do rocks above the fault surface slide down at a normal fault and up at a reverse fault?
4. The Appalachian Mountains formed when two plates collided. What type of fault do you think is most common in these mountains?
5. **Apply:** Why is it easier to predict where an earthquake will occur than it is to predict when it will occur?

Skill Builder

☑ **Concept Mapping**

Make a cycle concept map that shows why many earthquakes occur along the San Andreas fault. Use these terms and phrases: *rocks, stress, bend and stretch, elastic limit reached, earthquakes.* If you need help, refer to Concept Mapping in the **Skill Handbook** on pages 688 and 689.

ACTIVITY 14-1
Earthquake Depths

Problem: *What do earthquakes tell us about plate boundaries?*

Materials
- graph paper
- Figures 13-10 and 13-11

Procedure

1. The data table below shows the depths and locations of earthquake foci near the coast of a continent. Use the table to construct a line graph. Place "Distance from the coast" on the horizontal axis. Begin labeling at the far left with 100 km west. To the right of it should be 0 km then 100 km east, 200 km east, 300 km east, and so on through 700 km east. The coast of the continent is represented by 0 km.

2. Label the vertical axis "Depth below Earth's surface." Label the top of the graph 0 km to represent Earth's surface. Label the bottom of the vertical axis −800 km.

3. Plot the focus depth against the distance and direction from the coast for each earthquake in the table below.

Analyze

1. What is the relationship between distance from the coast to the epicenters and the depth of the earthquake?

2. Is this a converging plate boundary or a strike-slip plate boundary? How do you know?

Conclude and Apply

3. Is the continent located east or west of the plate boundary? How do you know?

4. Why don't earthquakes occur below a depth of 700 km? (HINT: Think about the structure of the asthenosphere compared to the lithosphere.)

5. What do earthquakes tell us about plate boundaries?

Data and Observations

Quake	Focus Depth	Distance of Epicenter from Coast (km)	Quake	Focus Depth	Distance of Epicenter from Coast (km)
A	− 55 km	0	L	− 45 km	95 east
B	− 295 km	100 east	M	− 305 km	495 east
C	− 390 km	455 east	N	− 480 km	285 east
D	− 60 km	75 east	O	− 665 km	545 east
E	− 130 km	255 east	P	− 85 km	90 west
F	− 195 km	65 east	Q	− 525 km	205 east
G	− 695 km	400 east	R	− 85 km	25 west
H	− 20 km	40 west	S	− 445 km	595 east
I	− 505 km	695 east	T	− 635 km	665 east
J	− 520 km	390 east	U	− 55 km	95 west
K	− 385 km	335 east	V	− 70 km	100 west

14-2 Earthquake Information

New Science Words

seismic waves
focus
primary waves
secondary waves
epicenter
surface waves
Moho discontinuity

Objectives

▶ Compare and contrast primary, secondary, and surface waves.
▶ Explain how an earthquake epicenter is located using seismic wave information.
▶ Describe how seismic wave studies indicate the structure of Earth's interior.

Types of Seismic Waves

Have you ever seen a coiled-spring toy? When children play with a coiled-spring toy, they send energy waves through it. **Seismic waves,** generated by an earthquake, are similar to the waves of the toy. Where are seismic waves formed? How do they move through Earth and how can we use the information that they carry? Let's investigate how scientists have answered these questions.

As you have learned, when rocks move along a fault surface, energy is released. The point in Earth's interior where this release occurs is the **focus** of the earthquake. Seismic waves are produced and travel outward from the earthquake focus.

Figure 14-6. Primary waves cause the ground to compress and stretch. Secondary waves cause the ground to move perpendicular to the direction of the wave. Surface waves cause the most damage by creating vertical motion at the surface.

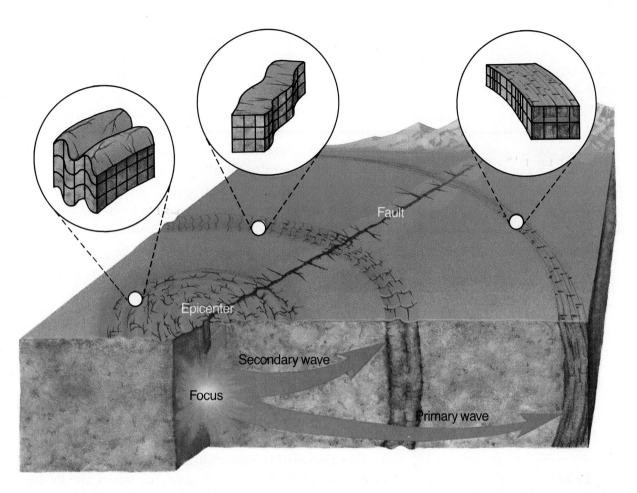

Figure 14-7. Primary and secondary waves travel outward from the focus. Surface waves move outward from the epicenter. The enlarged blocks show how the waves deform rock and soil as they pass by.

How do primary and secondary waves differ?

Waves that move through Earth by causing particles in rocks to move back and forth in the same direction the wave is moving are called **primary waves.** If you squeeze one end of a coiled-spring toy and then release it, you cause it to compress and then stretch as the primary wave travels through it. Particles in rocks also compress together and stretch apart, transmitting primary waves through the rock.

Now, if you and a friend stretch the coiled-spring toy between you, and then move one end up and down, a different type of wave will pass through the toy. The spring will move up and down as the wave moves along it. **Secondary waves** move through Earth by causing particles in rocks to move at right angles to the direction of the wave.

The point on Earth's surface directly above an earthquake's focus is the **epicenter.** Energy that reaches the surface of Earth generates waves that travel outward from the epicenter. These waves, called **surface waves,** move by giving particles a circular motion.

MINI-Lab

How do you use a travel time graph?

Use Figure 14-9 to determine the difference in arrival times for primary and secondary waves at the distances listed in the data table below. Two examples are provided for you. What happens to the difference in arrival times as the distance from the earthquake increases?

Distance (km)	Difference in arrival time
1500	2 min 45 sec
2250	
3000	
4000	5 min 35 sec
7000	
9000	

Figure 14-8. This system of lasers monitors the movement along the San Andreas Fault. It's mounted on a hilltop in Parkfield, CA. Lasers bounce off a series of 18 reflectors positioned several kilometers away. Any change in a reflector's position is measured. Movements of less than one millimeter along the fault can be detected.

If you've ever floated on an innertube in a wave pool, you've experienced this type of wave. The wave lifts you and your innertube, moves you in a circle, and places you back down.

Surface waves cause most of the destruction during an earthquake. Because most buildings are very rigid, they begin to fall apart when surface waves pass. The waves cause one part of the building to move up while another part moves down.

Locating an Epicenter

Primary, secondary, and surface waves don't travel through Earth at the same speed. Primary waves are the fastest; surface waves are the slowest. Can you think of a way this information could be used to determine how far away an earthquake epicenter is? Think of the last time you and two friends rode your bikes to the store. You were fastest so you arrived first. In fact, the longer you rode, the farther ahead of your friends you became.

You'll learn in the next section that seismic waves are measured at seismograph stations. Primary waves arrive first, secondary waves second, and surface waves last. This enables scientists to determine the distance to an earthquake epicenter. The farther apart the waves, the farther away the epicenter is. When epicenters are far from the seismograph station, the primary wave has more time to put distance between it and the secondary and surface waves.

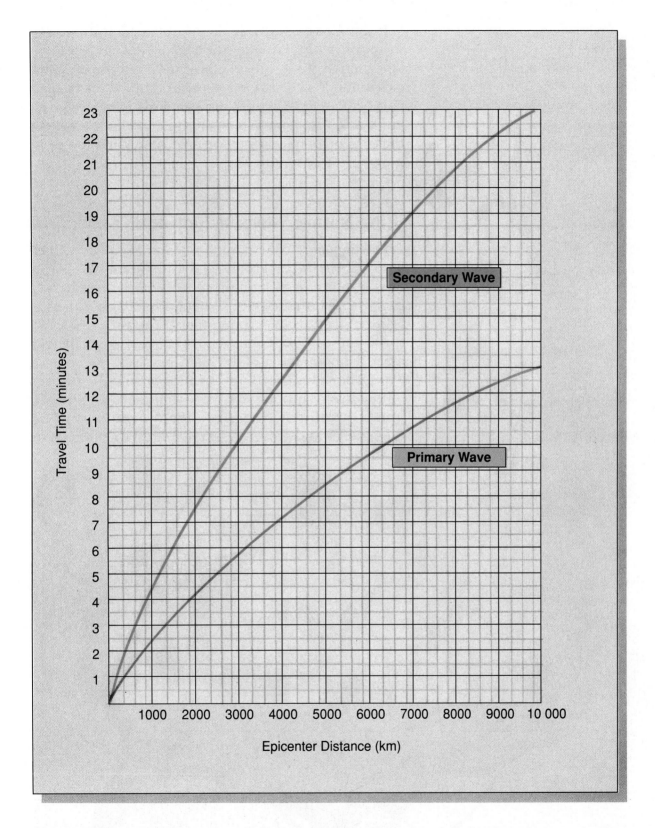

Figure 14-9. This graph shows the distance the primary and secondary waves travel with time. By measuring the difference in arrival times, a seismologist can determine the distance to the epicenter.

If seismic wave information is obtained at three seismograph stations, the location of the epicenter can be determined. To locate an epicenter, scientists draw circles around each station on a map. The radius of each circle equals that station's distance from the earthquake epicenter. The point where all three circles intersect is the location of the earthquake epicenter. Why is one seismograph station not enough?

Using Seismic Waves to Map Earth's Interior

In Chapter 13, you learned that Earth is divided into layers. These layers are the crust, upper mantle, lower mantle, outer core, and inner core. Without ever having been there, how do scientists know what Earth's interior is like? Scientists have found that at certain depths, the speed and path of seismic waves change. These changes mark the boundaries of the layers in Earth.

Seismic waves speed up when they reach the bottom of the crust. This boundary between the crust and the upper mantle is called the **Moho discontinuity.** The boundary was discovered by the Yugoslavian scientist,

Figure 14-10. The radius of each circle is equal to the distance to the epicenter from each seismograph station. The intersection of the three circles is the location of the epicenter.

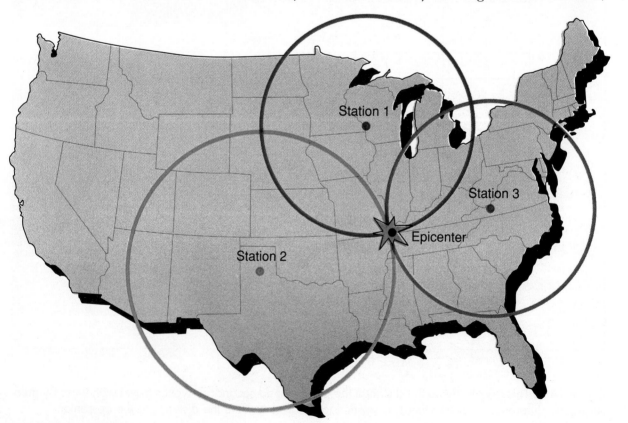

What's in the Box?

Maria returned home from school one day to find a box, approximately 30 cm × 18 cm × 12 cm, sitting on the kitchen table. Her aunt had come to visit and brought Maria a present. In order for Maria to get the present, she had to be able to tell her aunt at least three facts about it. Maria could do anything she needed to do to the box except open it to look at the gift directly. Of course, Maria would be careful not to damage the gift.

Think Critically: How many facts do you think Maria can learn about the gift? How is Maria's challenge related to earthquakes and mapping Earth's interior?

Andrija Mohorovičić (moh hoh ROH vuh chihch), who inferred that seismic waves speed up because they're passing into a denser layer of the lithosphere.

Primary and secondary waves slow down when they hit the plasticlike asthenosphere and then speed up again as they're transmitted through the solid lower mantle.

There's an area on Earth, between 105° and 140° from the focus, where no waves are detected. This area is called the shadow zone. Secondary waves aren't transmitted through liquid, so they're stopped completely when they hit the liquid outer core. Primary waves are slowed and deflected but not stopped by the liquid outer core. The deflection of the primary waves and the stopping of the secondary waves create the shadow zone. These primary waves again speed up as they travel through the solid inner core.

The boundaries between layers in Earth not only cause seismic waves to change in speed, but they also cause the waves to bend. Figure 14-11 shows how all of this information has led to the model we now have for Earth's interior.

Why is a shadow zone produced?

Figure 14-11. Primary waves bend when they contact the outer core, and secondary waves are stopped completely. Primary waves that are transmitted through the outer and inner cores are detected beyond the shadow zone.

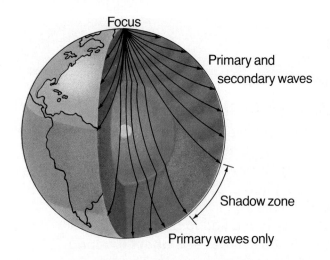

Focus

Primary and secondary waves

Shadow zone

Primary waves only

SECTION REVIEW

1. Which type of seismic wave does the most damage to property?
2. Draw a diagram of what would happen to a row of evenly spaced utility poles as a primary wave traveled parallel to the row.
3. Why is a seismic record from three locations needed to determine the position of an epicenter?
4. **Apply:** Suppose an earthquake occurs at the San Andreas Fault. What area on Earth would experience no secondary waves? Would China experience primary and secondary waves from the earthquake? Explain your answers.

Skill Builder

☑ Making and Using Graphs

Use the data table below to make a graph of some travel times of earthquake waves. Which line represents primary waves? Which line represents secondary waves? If you need help, refer to Making and Using Graphs in the **Skill Handbook** on page 691.

Distance from earthquake (km)	1 500	2 000	5 000	5 500	8 600	10 000
Time (minutes)	5.0	2.5	14.0	7.0	11.0	23.5

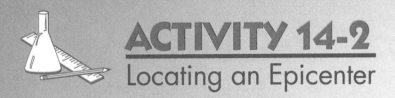

ACTIVITY 14-2
Locating an Epicenter

Problem: How are epicenters located?

Materials
- Figure 14-9
- string
- metric ruler
- globe
- paper
- chalk or water-soluble marker

Procedure
1. Determine the difference in arrival time between the primary and secondary waves at each station for each quake from the data table below.
2. Use Figure 14-9 to determine the distance in kilometers of each seismograph from the epicenter of each earthquake. Record these data in the Data and Observations table. An example has been done for you. The difference in arrival times in Paris for earthquake B is 10.0 minutes. On the graph, the primary and secondary waves are separated along the vertical axis by 10.0 minutes at 9750 km.

Data and Observations

	Calculated distance from epicenter (km) from each seismograph location				
Quake	(1)	(2)	(3)	(4)	(5)
A					
B				9750	

3. Using the string, measure the circumference of the globe. Determine a scale of centimeters of string to kilometers on Earth's surface. (Earth's circumference = 40 000 km.)
4. For each earthquake, A and B, place one end of the string at each seismic station location. Use the chalk or marker to draw a circle with a radius equal to the distance to the epicenter of the quake.
5. Identify the epicenter for each earthquake.

Analyze
1. How is the distance of a seismograph from the earthquake related to the arrival time of the waves?
2. What is the location of the epicenter of each earthquake?
3. How many stations were necessary in order to accurately locate each epicenter?

Conclude and Apply
4. Predict why some seismographs didn't receive secondary waves from some quakes?
5. How are epicenters located?

Data and Observations

Location of Seismograph	Wave	Wave Arrival Times	
		Earthquake A	Earthquake B
(1) New York	P	2:24:05 PM	1:19:00 PM
	S	2:28:55 PM	1:24:40 PM
(2) Seattle	P	2:24:40 PM	1:14:37 PM
	S	2:30:00 PM	1:16:52 PM
(3) Rio de Janeiro	P	2:29:00 PM	———
	S	2:38:05 PM	———
(4) Paris	P	2:30:15 PM	1:24:05 PM
	S	2:40:29 PM	1:34:05 PM
(5) Tokyo	P	———	1:23:30 PM
	S	———	1:33:05 PM

14-3 Destruction by Earthquakes

New Science Words

seismologists
seismograph
magnitude
tsunamis

Objectives

▶ Define magnitude and the Richter Scale.
▶ List ways to make your classroom and home more earthquake safe.

Measuring Earthquakes

On October 17, 1989, an earthquake shocked the San Francisco Bay area. Surface waves moved through the area in less than 20 seconds, but their effects will be felt for years to come. The quake killed 67 people and damaged billions of dollars of property. In 1988, more than 45 000 people died when an earthquake struck Armenia. More than 50 000 died in the June 1990 earthquake that struck Iran. What determines the amount of damage done by an earthquake, and what can you do to protect yourself from the effects?

Figure 14-12. Most of the damage that resulted during the 1989 San Francisco earthquake was caused by surface waves.

Scientists who study earthquakes and seismic waves are **seismologists.** They use an instrument called a **seismograph** to record primary, secondary, and surface waves from earthquakes all over the world. As you learned earlier, an earthquake's epicenter can be located by studying the record from three seismograph stations.

One type of seismograph has a drum holding a sheet of paper on a fixed frame. A pendulum with an attached pen is suspended from the frame. When seismic waves occur at the station, the drum vibrates but the pendulum remains at rest. The pen on the pendulum traces a record of the vibrations on a sheet of paper. The height of the lines traced on the paper is a measure of the energy released, or **magnitude** of the earthquake. Seismologists use the Richter (RIHK tur) Scale to describe earthquake magnitudes. The scale describes how much energy is released by the earthquake. Thirty times as much energy

Science and MATH

Calculate the difference in energy released between an earthquake of magnitude 8 and one of magnitude 5.5.

Table 14-1

STRONG EARTHQUAKES			
Year	Location	Richter Value	Deaths
1556	Shensi, China	?	830 000
1737	Calcutta, India	?	300 000
1755	Lisbon, Portugal	8.8	60 000
1811-12	New Madrid, MO	8.3	few
1886	Charleston, SC	?	60
1906	San Francisco, CA	8.3	700
1908	Messina, Italy	7.5	120 000
1920	Kansu, China	8.5	180 000
1923	Tokyo, Japan	8.3	143 000
1939	Concepcion, Chile	8.3	30 000
1960	Southern Chile	8.6	5 700
1964	Prince William Sound, AK	8.5	117
1970	Peru	7.8	66 000
1975	Liaoning Province, China	7.5	few
1976	Tangshan, China	7.6	240 000
1985	Mexico City, Mexico	8.1	7 000
1988	Armenia	6.9	45 000
1989	San Francisco Bay, CA	7.1	67
1990	Iran	7.7	50 000

Predicting Earthquakes

In 1990, a climate consultant predicted that a major quake would strike New Madrid, Missouri, on December 3, 1990. A parade scheduled for that date was postponed and businesses announced they would be closed. But most scientists weren't surprised when it didn't strike on the predicted date. Today, seismologists review the earthquake history of a region to predict when one might strike in the future. Scientists hope that a new approach to predicting earthquakes will be more reliable. A series of satellites developed for use in navigation may provide the answer. The satellites emit radio signals that are picked up by radio receivers on Earth's surface. When Earth's crust deforms, by as little as a few centimeters, it can be detected because the radio receivers move along with it.

Think Critically: Both seismographs and satellites detect movement in Earth's crust. Why aren't seismographs very useful for predicting quakes?

is released for every increase of 1.0 on the scale. For example, a magnitude 8.5 earthquake releases about 30 times as much energy as a magnitude 7.5 earthquake. Table 14-2 shows how often earthquakes of the various magnitudes are expected to occur.

Tsunamis

Most earthquake damage happens when surface waves cause buildings, bridges, and roads to collapse. People living near the seashore, however, have another concern. An earthquake under the sea causes abrupt movement of the ocean floor. The movement pushes against the water, generating a powerful wave that travels to the surface. After reaching the surface, the wave can travel thousands of kilometers in all directions.

Table 14-2

EARTHQUAKE OCCURRENCES	
Richter Magnitude	**Number Expected per Year**
1.0 to 3.9	> 100 000
4.0 to 4.9	6 200
5.0 to 5.9	800
6.0 to 6.9	120
7.0 to 7.9	20
8.0 to 8.9	< 1

An earthquake wave has a wavelength of several kilometers. Therefore, such a wave stirs a tremendous amount of water in a circular motion as it passes. Far from shore, an earthquake-generated wave is so long that a large ship may ride over it without anyone noticing. But when one of these waves breaks on a shore, it forms a towering crest that can reach 30 meters high.

Ocean waves generated by earthquakes are called seismic sea waves, or **tsunamis** (soo NAHM eez). Tsunamis engulf people and entire towns in huge walls of water, causing great destruction and loss of life.

Figure 14-13. A tsunami begins over the earthquake focus. The height of the wave increases dramatically as it approaches the shore.

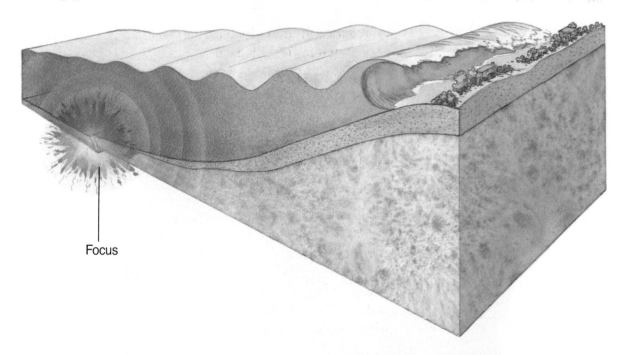

Focus

Earthquake Safety

You've seen the destruction that earthquakes can cause. But, there are ways to minimize the damage and loss of life.

One of the first steps in earthquake safety is to study the earthquake history of a region. If you live in an area that's had earthquakes in the past, you can expect them to occur there in the future. As you know, most earthquakes happen along plate boundaries. Figure 14-1 shows that severe earthquakes can happen in other places. Being prepared is an important step in earthquake safety.

Make your home as earthquake safe as possible. Take heavy objects down from high shelves and place them on lower shelves. To reduce the chance of fire from broken gas lines, see that hot-water heaters and gas appliances are held securely in place. During an earthquake, keep away from windows and avoid anything that could fall on you. Watch for fallen power lines and possible fire hazards. Stay clear of rubble that could contain many sharp edges. In the Science and Society section that follows, you will see how practicing earthquake safety and preparing for an earthquake make a difference in the amount of damage done by an earthquake.

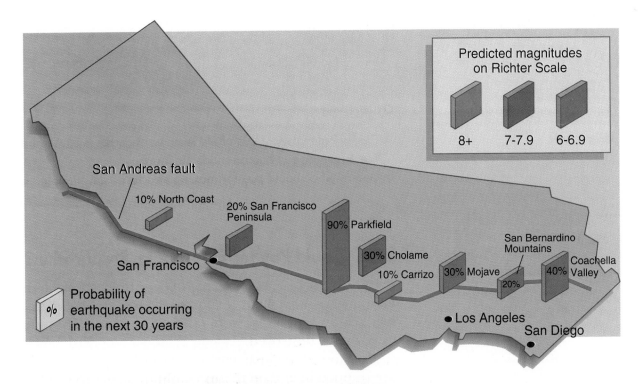

Predicted magnitudes on Richter Scale

8+   7-7.9   6-6.9

San Andreas fault

10% North Coast

20% San Francisco Peninsula

90% Parkfield

30% Cholame

San Bernardino Mountains

San Francisco

10% Carrizo

30% Mojave

20%

40% Coachella Valley

Probability of earthquake occurring in the next 30 years

Los Angeles

San Diego

Figure 14-14. The bars on the map show the probabilities that an earthquake of the specified magnitude will strike within the next 30 years. Many residents of California are preparing for the major earthquakes predicted to hit their areas.

SECTION REVIEW

1. How often might you expect a magnitude 6.0 earthquake to occur?
2. What is the magnitude of an earthquake that releases 30 times as much energy as the one that hit Armenia?
3. A friend of yours moves to southern California, near the San Andreas Fault. What can you tell her to help her prepare for an earthquake?
4. **Apply:** Explain why a seismograph wouldn't work if the pen vibrated along with the rest of the machine.

☑ Making and Using Tables

Skill Builder

Use Table 14-1 to answer the following questions.

1. Which earthquake listed resulted in the greatest number of deaths? The fewest?
2. Which quake listed had the highest magnitude?
3. Hypothesize why the 1920 China quake resulted in fewer deaths than the 1976 quake.

If you need help, refer to Making and Using Tables in the **Skill Handbook** on page 690.

14-4 Living on a Fault

New Science Words

seismic-safe

Objectives

▶ Recognize that most loss of life in an earthquake is caused by the destruction of human-made structures.
▶ Decide who should pay for making structures seismic safe.

Who Should Pay for Earthquake Preparation?

In Section 14-3, you saw pictures of the aftermath of earthquakes. What kind of damage did you see? Buildings, bridges, and highways were cracked and broken. Some were totally destroyed.

Most loss of life in an earthquake occurs when people are trapped in and on these crumbling structures. What can be done to reduce loss of life? Who should be responsible for the cost of making structures seismic safe?

Seismic-safe structures are resistant to vibrations that occur during an earthquake. You can see the advantage of seismic safety by watching a young child play with blocks. He or she builds them up and becomes very upset

Figure 14-15. Research has led to new technologies that can help buildings withstand earthquake waves.

rubber

steel

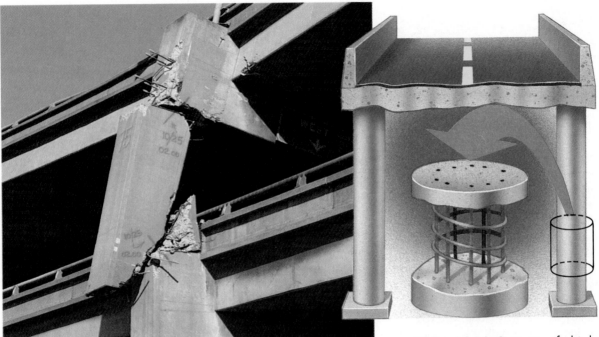

Figure 14-16. Seismic-safe highways are supported by vertical steel rods wrapped with reinforcing rods encased in concrete. The major highway that collapsed in San Francisco in 1989 lacked the seismic-safe construction shown at the right.

when the dog walks by and knocks them down. What do you think would happen if rubber bands were wrapped around the columns of blocks? The block structure would be more resistant to falling. When making seismic-safe highways, cement pillars have spiral reinforcing rods wrapped around them. These rods act the same as rubber bands do on the blocks.

Will making structures seismic safe reduce the loss of life in an earthquake? Look again at Table 14-1. Notice that earthquakes in Armenia (December 1988), in the San Francisco Bay area (October 1989), and in Iran (June 1990) are all close in magnitude. However, the loss of life in these earthquakes were quite different. Why were so many more lives lost in Armenia and Iran than in the San Francisco Bay area?

The San Francisco Bay area, as well as much of the Pacific Coast, is very susceptible to earthquakes. People living in the California area have been getting ready for big earthquakes for many years. Since 1971, stricter building codes have been enforced and older buildings have been reinforced. In other parts of the world, such seismic-safe structures are rare or don't exist at all.

Today in California, some new buildings are anchored to flexible, circular moorings made of steel plates filled with alternating layers of rubber and steel. When an earthquake occurs, the lower portion of the mooring stretches back and forth with the waves. The rubber portions of the moorings absorb most of the wave motion of the quake. The building itself only sways gently. Tests have shown that buildings supported with these moorings should be able to withstand an earthquake measuring up to 8.3 on the Richter scale without major damage.

One structure severely damaged in the San Francisco Bay area earthquake was Interstate Highway 880. The collapsed highway, shown in Figure 14-16, was due to be renovated to make it seismic safe. Built in the 1950s, it didn't have spiral reinforcing rods in its concrete columns. When the surface waves hit, the upper highway went in one direction; the lower one went in the opposite direction. The columns collapsed and the upper highway came crashing down onto the lower one.

Highways and buildings in earthquake-prone areas can be made seismic safe. Lives and property can be saved by replacing underground water and gas pipes with ones that will bend, but not break, during an earthquake. But who should pay for these renovations? In some parts of the United States and of the world, people can afford to build seismic-safe structures. In other cases, people can't even afford food and shelter. In these areas, seismic-safe structures can be constructed only if people outside of the region are willing to help.

SECTION REVIEW

1. Why did more people die in the earthquakes in Armenia and Iran than in San Francisco?
2. What conditions can exist that cause greater loss of life during one earthquake than during another of the same magnitude?

You Decide!

Suppose you are living in an area that's never had a severe earthquake. Would you be willing to pay an earthquake safety tax to help others in other parts of the United States? In other parts of the world? Some people think you should. Others think only those living in the area should pay. What do you think?

CHAPTER REVIEW

14-1: Earthquakes and Plate Tectonics

1. Plate movements put stress on rocks. To a point, the rocks bend and stretch. But if the force is great enough, rocks will break and produce earthquakes.

2. Normal faults form when rocks undergo tension. Compressional forces produce reverse faults. Strike-slip faults result from shearing forces.

14-2: Earthquake Information

1. Primary waves compress and stretch rock particles as the waves move. Secondary waves move by, causing particles in rocks to move at right angles to the direction of the waves. Surface waves move by, giving rock particles a circular motion.

2. By measuring the speeds of seismic waves, scientists are able to locate the epicenter of an earthquake.

3. By observing the speeds and paths of seismic waves, scientists are able to determine the boundaries among Earth's layers.

14-3: Destruction by Earthquakes

1. The magnitude of an earthquake is a measure of the energy released by the quake. The Richter Scale describes how much energy is released by an earthquake.

2. Removing objects from high shelves and securing hot-water heaters and gas appliances are ways to prevent damage due to earthquakes.

14-4: Science and Society: Living on a Fault

1. Most lives lost during an earthquake are due to the destruction of human-made structures.

2. Money for seismic-safe structures might come from people who live in the earthquake-prone area or from people in other parts of the country or the world.

KEY SCIENCE WORDS

a. earthquakes
b. epicenter
c. faults
d. focus
e. magnitude
f. Moho discontinuity
g. normal fault
h. primary waves
i. reverse fault
j. secondary waves
k. seismic-safe
l. seismic waves
m. seismograph
n. seismologists
o. strike-slip fault
p. surface waves
q. tsunamis

UNDERSTANDING VOCABULARY

Match each phrase with the correct term from the list of Key Science Words.

1. a fault formed due to tension on rocks
2. fault due to shearing forces
3. point where earthquake energy is released
4. point on Earth's surface directly above the origin of an earthquake
5. waves that produce a circular motion of particles
6. boundary between the crust and mantle
7. instrument that records seismic waves
8. measure of energy released by a quake
9. seismic sea waves
10. refers to structures that are resistant to seismic vibrations

CHAPTER
REVIEW

Choose the word or phrase that completes the sentence.

1. Most earthquakes occur along _____.
   a. normal faults
   b. tsunamis
   c. plate boundaries
   d. all of these

2. A _____ fault forms when the rock above the fault surface moves down relative to the rock below the fault surface.
   a. normal
   b. strike-slip
   c. reverse
   d. shearing

3. Seismic waves move outward from the _____.
   a. epicenter
   b. focus
   c. Moho discontinuity
   d. tsunami

4. _____ waves stretch and compress rocks.
   a. Surface
   b. Primary
   c. Secondary
   d. All of these

5. _____ waves are the slowest.
   a. Surface
   b. Primary
   c. Secondary
   d. Tsunami

6. At least _____ seismograph stations are needed to locate the epicenter of an earthquake.
   a. two
   b. three
   c. four
   d. five

7. Primary waves _____ when they go through solids.
   a. slow down
   b. speed up
   c. stay the same
   d. quit moving

8. The _____ of a seismograph remains still.
   a. sheet of paper
   b. pen
   c. drum
   d. pendulum

9. An earthquake of magnitude 7.5 has _____ energy than a quake of 6.5.
   a. 30 times more
   b. 30 times less
   c. twice as much
   d. about half as much

10. Most lost lives during a quake are due to _____.
    a. tsunamis
    b. primary waves
    c. collapse of buildings
    d. broken gas lines

UNDERSTANDING CONCEPTS

Complete each sentence.

11. Earthquakes occur when the _____ of rocks is passed.

12. _____ waves cause rock particles to move parallel to the direction of wave movement.

13. _____ and _____ determine the amount of damage an earthquake causes.

14. The height of the lines traced by a(n) _____ is directly related to the amount of energy released.

15. _____ structures, such as highways with reinforcing bands wrapped around their pillars, save lives.

THINK AND WRITE CRITICALLY

16. Contrast normal faults with reverse faults.
17. How are primary and secondary waves alike? How are they different?
18. Explain how seismic records were used to determine that Earth's outer core is liquid.
19. What is the relationship between earthquakes with magnitudes on the Richter Scale of 1.0 and 3.0?
20. In 1906, an earthquake with a magnitude of 8.6 struck San Francisco. Most of the damage done was due to fire. Hypothesize why this is so.

21. What kind of faults would you expect to be most common along the mid-Atlantic Ridge? Explain.
22. Where is earthquake damage greater—nearer the focus or nearer the epicenter? Explain.
23. Explain why the pendulum of a seismograph remains at rest.
24. Tsunamis are often called tidal waves. Explain why this is incorrect.
25. Which would probably be more stable during an earthquake—a single-story wood-frame house or a brick building? Explain.

MORE SKILL BUILDERS

If you need help, refer to the Skill Handbook.

1. **Interpreting Scientific Illustrations:** The illustration below is a typical record of earthquake waves made on a seismograph. How many minutes passed between the arrival of the first primary wave and the first secondary wave? The last primary wave and the first surface wave?
2. **Interpreting Scientific Illustrations:** Suppose another seismograph station were located in the shadow zone of the same earthquake from Question 1. How would the record of the seismograph located in the shadow zone compare to the record shown below?

3. **Outlining:** Make an outline of the material presented in Section 14-1.
4. **Measuring in SI:** Use an atlas and metric ruler to answer the following. Primary waves travel at about 6 km/s in continental crust. How long would it take a primary wave to travel from San Francisco, CA to Reno, NV?
5. **Using Variables, Constants, and Controls:** Leah investigated how waves are reflected from curved and flat surfaces using water, a dropper, and flexible cardboard. She filled two flat pans half full of water and produced ripples with water from the dropper. One pan held the flat cardboard; the other the curved piece. What are her variables? What should she keep constant?

PROJECTS

1. Make a simple seismograph. Experiment with different "seismic" sources such as pounding your fist, hammering, and dropping a brick to see how they affect the height of the lines produced on the drum of your device.
2. Research how magnetometers, tiltmeters, and radon detectors are used to help predict the possibility of earthquakes.

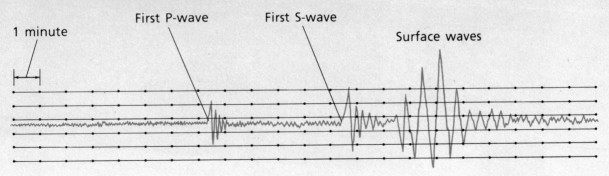

1 minute First P-wave First S-wave Surface waves

15 Volcanoes

This explosive eruption is ejecting tonnes of volcanic ash into the atmosphere. Volcanoes can be spectacular and dangerous. They also can be useful. How do volcanoes erupt?

FIND OUT!

Do this simple activity to discover how volcanoes erupt.

Use clay to make a small model volcano with a crater at the top. Place a small amount of baking soda and a drop of red food coloring in the crater. After putting on safety goggles to protect your eyes, add approximately 20 mL of vinegar to the baking soda in the crater and observe what happens. Describe how your model eruption is similar to a real volcanic eruption. In what ways is it different?

Gearing Up

Previewing the Chapter

Use this outline to help you focus on important ideas in this chapter.

Section 15-1 Volcanoes and Plate Tectonics
▶ Volcanoes and You
▶ What Causes Volcanoes?
▶ Where Do Volcanoes Occur?

Section 15-2 Science and Society Geothermal Energy from Volcanoes
▶ Electricity from Geothermal Energy?

Section 15-3 Eruptions and Forms of Volcanoes
▶ Types of Eruptions
▶ Forms of Volcanoes

Section 15-4 Volcanic Features
▶ Intrusive Features
▶ Other Features

Previewing Science Skills

▶ In the **Skill Builders,** you will make a concept map, sequence events, and compare and contrast.
▶ In the **Activities,** you will hypothesize, measure, observe, predict, classify, infer, and interpret data.
▶ In the **MINI-Labs,** you will observe and compare and contrast.

What's next?

You've seen that gases and other materials flow out of a volcano as it erupts. Now you'll learn about some famous volcanoes and what caused them to form. You also will learn where on Earth volcanoes occur and how this relates to plate tectonics.

15-1 Volcanoes and Plate Tectonics

New Science Words

volcano
vent
crater
Pacific Ring of Fire
hot spots

Objectives

▶ Describe how volcanoes can affect people.
▶ Describe conditions that cause volcanoes.
▶ Describe the relationship between volcanoes and plate tectonics.

Science and READING

The events involving many famous volcanic eruptions around the world have been recorded. Go to the library and read a book about famous eruptions such as the 1902 eruption of Mount Pelée and read how it affected the people there.

Volcanoes and You

If you live near the Pacific Ocean, you may have seen a volcano. If not, you've probably seen pictures of them. A **volcano** is a mountain that forms when layers of lava and volcanic ash erupt and build up. Most of Earth's volcanoes are dormant, which means that they are not currently active, but more than 600 are active. Active volcanoes sometimes spew smoke, steam, ash, cinders, and flows of lava. Here are stories of some famous volcanoes. Read them and notice the fact that all volcanoes are not the same.

In 1902, Mount Pelée (puh LAY) on the Caribbean island of Martinique erupted. A very hot gas cloud from the volcano flowed over a nearby city and killed almost all of the 30 000 people there. One survivor was a prisoner who was protected by the dungeon he was in. In 1980, Mount Saint Helens in Washington State erupted. It was one of the largest recent volcanic eruptions in North America. Geologists warned people to leave the area surrounding the mountain. Most people left, but a few stayed. About 60 were killed as a result of Mount Saint Helens exploding. Heat from the eruption melted snow, which caused flooding in the area also.

For centuries, Kilauea (kee law WAY uh) volcano in Hawaii has been erupting, but not explosively. Every few years lava flows out for a while. The lava covered a town and burned houses in 1990, but no one was hurt because the lava moved slowly. Kilauea is the world's most active volcano.

Figure 15-1. The often-erupting Kilauea volcano in Hawaii destroyed homes with this lava flow.

What Causes Volcanoes?

What happens inside Earth to create volcanoes? Why are some areas of Earth more likely to have volcanoes than others?

You learned in Chapter 4 that rock deep inside Earth melts to form magma and that magma is called lava when it flows out onto Earth's surface. You also learned that heat and pressure cause rock to melt and form magma. Some deep rocks already are molten. Others are hot enough that a small rise in temperature can melt them to form magma.

Magma is less dense than the rock around it, so it very slowly rises toward Earth's surface. You can see this process if you turn a bottle of cold syrup upside down. Watch the less-dense air bubbles push the syrup aside and slowly rise to the top.

After many thousands or even millions of years, some magma reaches Earth's surface and flows out through an opening called a **vent.** As lava flows out, it cools quickly and becomes solid, forming layers of igneous rock around the vent. The opening at the top of a volcano's vent is the **crater.**

Why does magma rise?

Why is there volcanic activity in Iceland?

Where Do Volcanoes Occur?

Volcanoes form in three kinds of places that are directly related to plate tectonics. You learned about two of these places in Chapter 13 when you studied plate tectonics. Volcanoes occur at divergent plate boundaries, at convergent plate boundaries, and at locations not at plate boundaries called hot spots. There are many examples of volcanoes around the world at the three different types of locations related to plate tectonics. Let's explore Iceland, Hawaii, and Mount Saint Helens.

Divergent Boundaries

Iceland is a large island in the North Atlantic Ocean. It is near the Arctic Circle and has some glaciers. But it also has many volcanoes. Iceland has volcanic activity because it sits on top of the Mid-Atlantic Ridge.

You learned in Chapter 13 that the Mid-Atlantic Ridge is a divergent plate boundary. Where plates separate, they form long, deep cracks called rifts. Magma flows from rifts as lava and is instantly cooled by the seawater. As more lava flows, it builds up from the seafloor. Sometimes the volcanoes rise above sea level, forming islands such as Iceland.

Figure 15-2. Volcanic ash covered these buildings in Iceland.

Convergent Boundaries

Mount Saint Helens is not an island. It is one of several volcanoes that make up the Cascade Mountain Range in Oregon and Washington in the northwestern United States. Why are there volcanoes here?

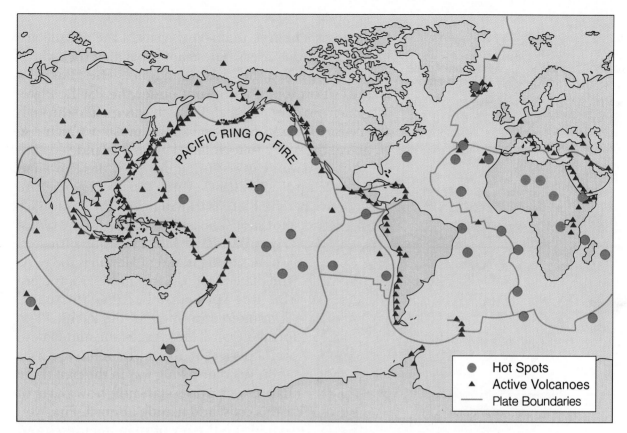

Figure 15-3. This diagram shows the active volcanoes and hot spots around the world. Note their relationship to plate boundaries you learned about in Chapter 13.

Mount Saint Helens and the other volcanic peaks in the Cascade Range formed because of a convergent plate boundary. Here, the Juan de Fuca Plate is converging with the North American Plate. Magma that is created in the subduction zone works its way to the surface, forming the volcanoes of the Cascades.

Such volcanoes have formed all around the Pacific Plate where it collides with other plates. This area around the Pacific Plate where earthquakes and volcanoes are common is called the **Pacific Ring of Fire.** All of the earthquakes and volcanoes in the Pacific Ring of Fire can be attributed to tectonic movement at the boundary of the Pacific Plate. Mount Saint Helens is just one volcano in the Pacific Ring of Fire. Can you list others?

What causes volcanic activity around the Pacific Ring of Fire?

Hot Spots

Like Iceland, the Hawaiian Islands also are volcanic islands. But unlike Iceland, they haven't formed at a plate boundary. The Hawaiian Islands are in the middle of the Pacific Plate, far from its edges. What process could be forming them?

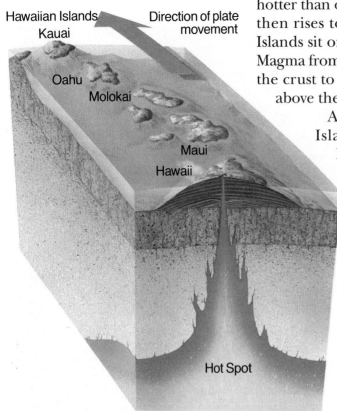

Hawaiian Islands
Kauai

Oahu

Molokai

Maui

Hawaii

Direction of plate movement

Hot Spot

Figure 15-4. The Hawaiian Islands have formed as the Pacific Plate moves over a hot spot.

Geologists believe that some areas in the mantle are hotter than other areas. These **hot spots** melt rock which then rises toward the crust as magma. The Hawaiian Islands sit on top of a hot spot under the Pacific Plate. Magma from deep in Earth's mantle has melted through the crust to form several volcanoes, most of which rise above the water to form an Hawaiian Island.

As you can see in Figure 15-4, the Hawaiian Islands are all in a line. This is because the Pacific Plate is moving over the stationary hot spot. The island of Kauai is the oldest Hawaiian island and was once located where the big island of Hawaii is today. As the plate moved, Kauai moved away from the hot spot and became dormant. Continued movement of the Pacific Plate formed Oahu, Molokai, Maui, and Hawaii over a period of about five million years.

You've come a long way in the past three chapters in understanding how parts of Earth's crust and mantle interact. First, you learned the theory of plate tectonics and how Earth's lithosphere is divided into plates that move on the asthenosphere. Then you learned that these movements cause earthquakes that affect people all over the world. Now you can see that tectonic activity can also lead to the formation of volcanoes at diverging or converging plate boundaries and at hot spots.

SECTION REVIEW

1. How do volcanoes affect people?
2. How does magma deep inside Earth cause volcanoes?
3. How is plate tectonics related to volcanoes?
4. **Apply:** Do you think that any more Hawaiian islands may be created? How could it happen?

Skill Builder

☒ Concept Mapping

Make a concept map that shows how the Hawaiian Islands formed over a hot spot. Use these terms and phrases: *volcano forms, plate moves, volcano becomes dormant, new volcano forms.* If you need help, refer to Concept Mapping in the **Skill Handbook** on pages 688 and 689.

ACTIVITY 15-1
Locating Active Volcanoes

Problem: *Where do active volcanoes occur?*

Materials
- world map (Appendix F)
- tracing paper
- Figure 13-10 on page 349

Procedure
1. Use tracing paper to outline the continents on the world map in Appendix F. Include the lines of latitude and longitude on your tracing.
2. Listed at right are the latitudes and longitudes of 20 active volcanoes around the world. Locate them on the world map. Mark and name their locations on your tracing.
3. Compare your tracing to Figure 13-10 in Chapter 13, which shows the major plate boundaries around the world.
4. On a data table like the one shown, list the location of each volcano. Then, place a check in the column that best describes the type of tectonic process (divergent plate boundary, convergent plate boundary, or hot spot) that is causing the volcano in that location.

Analyze
1. Describe the patterns of distribution that the volcanoes form on Earth.
2. From looking at these patterns and the locations of the active volcanoes, is there a relationship between plate tectonics and volcanoes? What is it?

Conclude and Apply
3. Is there a relationship between the locations of the active volcanoes and areas of earthquake activity described in Chapter 14? Explain.

Data and Observations

Volcano	Volcano location	Convergent	Divergent	Hot Spot
# 1				
# 2				
#19				
#20				

Volcano	Latitude	Longitude
#1	64° N	19° W
#2	28° N	34° E
#3	43° S	172° E
#4	35° N	136° E
#5	18° S	68° W
#6	25° S	114° W
#7	20° N	155° W
#8	54° N	167° W
#9	16° N	122° E
#10	28° N	17° W
#11	15° N	43° E
#12	6° N	75° W
#13	64° S	158° E
#14	38° S	78° E
#15	21° S	56° E
#16	38° N	26° E
#17	7° S	13° W
#18	2° S	102° E
#19	38° N	30° W
#20	54° N	159° E

15-2 Geothermal Energy from Volcanoes

New Science Words

geothermal energy

Objectives

▶ List the pros and cons of using geothermal energy to produce electricity.
▶ Form an opinion as to whether the geothermal energy under the Hawaiian Islands should be used to generate electricity.

Electricity from Geothermal Energy?

Because of destructive eruptions like that at Mount Saint Helens, we usually think of igneous activity as destructive. But some people in Hawaii want to use the heat from igneous activity to generate electricity. You learned that Kilauea is the most active volcano on Earth. The magma underneath volcanoes holds tremendous thermal energy. This **geothermal energy** can be used to generate electricity. The heat from magma can be used to heat water and produce steam in a power plant on the surface. The steam is pressurized and then spins generators that make electricity.

Right now, Hawaii depends on oil to generate 87 percent of its electricity. Government officials hope that Hawaii will stop using fossil fuels by the year 2007. They hope to generate all of Hawaii's electricity by using geothermal energy. If this happened, Hawaii could stop burning fossil fuels. This would reduce air pollution, and Hawaii would have to buy less oil. This would also reduce the danger of oil spills from tankers.

Geothermal energy is a proven energy technology. It is used in more than 20 foreign countries including Iceland. Geothermal energy supplies about 5 percent of California's electricity.

But what problems might be caused by using the geothermal energy beneath Kilauea? Some people worry that using geothermal energy might harm the rain forest. To tap the energy, roadways must be cleared, power plants must be built, and drilling rigs must be moved in.

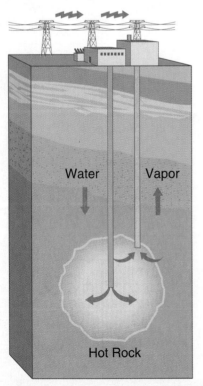

Figure 15-5. Heat from volcanic activity is used to heat water and make steam, which is used to generate electricity.

Water

Vapor

Hot Rock

You see why they are concerned. If you have watched a road or a large factory being built, you may have seen the damage to the environment that construction can cause. Another concern is that drilling might release harmful gases from the magma. People who are against the project say that solar energy and wind energy should be used instead of geothermal energy.

Those who favor the project claim that only small areas of rain forest would be cleared. They say harmful gases are not significant, because Kilauea already releases huge amounts of them.

Figure 15-6. These people protested geothermal energy development in Hawaii.

SECTION REVIEW

1. What are two advantages and two disadvantages of using geothermal energy to generate electricity in Hawaii?
2. How will the use of geothermal energy on Hawaii reduce the danger of oil spills from oil tankers in the ocean?

You Decide!

SCIENCE & SOCIETY

Using geothermal energy from hot magma beneath Hawaii's volcanoes is very controversial. Is damage to rain forests offset by the advantages of geothermal energy? Is it better to destroy some rain forest than to continue releasing pollution into the air from burning fossil fuels? What do you think about geothermal energy use in Hawaii?

Eruptions and Forms of Volcanoes

New Science Words

shield volcano
tephra
cinder cone
composite volcano

Objectives

▶ Relate the explosiveness of a volcanic eruption to the silica and water vapor content of its lava.
▶ Describe three forms of volcanoes.

Types of Eruptions

Some volcanic eruptions are explosive and violent, like those from Mount Pelée and Mount Saint Helens. But in others, the lava quietly flows from a vent, as in the Kilauea volcano eruptions. What causes this difference?

There are two important factors that determine whether an eruption will be explosive or quiet. One is the amount of water vapor and other gases that are trapped in the magma. The other factor is whether the magma is basaltic or granitic as you learned about in

Chapter 4. Let's look first at the gas content of the magma.

Have you ever shaken a soft drink container and then quickly opened it? The pressure from the gas in the drink builds up and is released suddenly when you open it, spraying the drink. In the same way, gases such as water vapor and carbon dioxide are trapped in magma by the pressure of the surrounding magma. As the magma nears the surface, the pressure is reduced. This allows the gas to escape the magma. Gas escapes easily from some magma during quiet eruptions. Gas that gets trapped under high pressure eventually escapes, causing explosive eruptions.

The second major factor that affects the type of eruption is the composition of the magma. Basaltic magma contains little silica, is very fluid, and produces quiet, nonexplosive eruptions like those at Kilauea. This type of lava pours from volcanic vents and runs down the side of the volcano. These quiet eruptions form volcanoes over mid-ocean rift zones like Iceland and hot spots like Hawaii. You may have seen on TV that people can walk right up to some lava flows on Kilauea volcano. Because the magma is very fluid when it rises in a vent, trapped gases can escape easily in a nonexplosive manner. Sometimes gas causes lava fountains during quiet eruptions.

What happens if gas cannot escape easily from magma?

Figure 15-7. A calm day in Washington was suddenly interrupted when Mount Saint Helens erupted on May 18, 1980.

Granitic magma, on the other hand, produces explosive, violent eruptions like those at Mount Saint Helens. It often forms in the subduction zones at convergent plate boundaries. Granitic magma, as you learned in Chapter 4, is very thick and contains a lot of silica. Because it is thick, it gets trapped in vents, causing pressure to build up beneath it. When an explosive eruption occurs, the gases expand rapidly, often carrying pieces of lava in the explosion.

Why does granitic magma cause explosive eruptions?

Another factor that causes granitic magma to erupt explosively is its high water content. This magma at subduction zones contains a lot of water vapor. This is because of the wet oceanic crust that is carried into the subduction zone. The trapped water vapor in the thick magma causes explosive eruptions. Different types of eruptions form different types of volcanic cones.

TECHNOLOGY

Volcanic Eruptions

On November 13, 1985, Colombia's volcano Nevado del Ruiz erupted. On that day, nearly 23 000 people lost their lives not from the exploding mountain or from lava flows, but from mudflows. Mudflows are another hazard of volcanoes. Many volcanic peaks have a high enough elevation that they are covered with snow fields and glaciers. The heat from volcanic activity melts this snow and ice during an eruption. This can mean disaster for people living below such a volcano. The melted snow mixes with ash from the eruption and soil from the mountain and flows rapidly downhill as it did in Colombia.

The Japanese have developed mudflow control technology to protect populated areas below active volcanoes. Their technology is designed to slow down mud as it flows down valleys. They have installed concrete and steel damlike structures in valleys where mudflows have occured before. This will give the villagers below time to evacuate the area. The Japanese also use television cameras as earthquake sensors to help them detect eruptions.

Think Critically: Why would earthquake sensors be used to detect volcanic eruptions?

Forms of Volcanoes

A volcano's form depends on whether it is the result of a quiet or an explosive eruption and the type of lava it is made of—basaltic or granitic. Volcanoes are of three basic forms—shield volcanoes, cinder cone volcanoes, or composite volcanoes.

Figure 15-8. Quiet eruptions with fluid lava form shield volcanoes such as this Hawaiian island.

Magma

Shield Volcano

Quiet eruptions spread out basaltic lava in flat layers. The buildup of these layers forms a broad volcano with gently sloping sides called a **shield volcano.** Examples of shield volcanoes are the Hawaiian Islands and volcanoes in rift zones like Iceland.

Cinder Cone Volcano

Explosive eruptions throw lava high into the air. The lava cools and hardens into different sizes of volcanic material called **tephra.** Tephra varies from volcanic ash—the smallest—to cinders, to larger rocks called bombs.

When tephra falls to the ground, it forms a steep-sided, loosely consolidated **cinder cone** volcano. A Mexican farmer learned about cinder cones one morning when he went to his cornfield. He discovered a long crack in the ground, with ash, cinders, and lava around the opening. In just a few days, a cinder cone several hundred meters high covered his cornfield. It is the volcano named Parícutin (puh REE kuh teen).

MINI-Lab

How are the shapes of volcanic cones different?

Make models of a cinder cone and a shield volcano. First, pour a granulated substance such as a cereal or sand onto one spot on a paper plate, forming a cinder cone volcano. Use a protractor to measure the slope angle of the sides of the volcano. Then mix a batch of plaster of paris and pour it onto one spot on another paper plate, forming a shield volcano. Allow it to dry before measuring the slope angle of the sides. Which type of volcano has steeper sides? Why is this so?

Figure 15-9. A cinder cone volcano is composed of layers of tephra and has steep sides.

Figure 15-10. A composite volcano is made up of alternating layers of tephra and lava.

Composite Volcano

Some volcanic eruptions can vary between quiet and violent. An explosive period can release gas and ash, forming a tephra layer. Then, the eruption can switch over to a quiet period, erupting lava over the top of the tephra. When this cycle of lava and tephra is repeated over and over in alternating layers, a **composite volcano** is formed. Composite volcanoes are found mostly at convergent plate boundaries, above subduction zones. Mount Saint Helens is an example.

The Rock Star

Janet is an avid rock and mineral collector. Because her earth science class was studying volcanoes, Janet thought she would trick the class using two igneous rock samples from her collection.

The next day Janet explained to the class that both rock samples were extrusive volcanic rocks. She then asked the class to predict what would happen if she dropped the samples into a glass of water. Most classmates predicted that the rocks would sink. The class watched closely as she dropped the first rock into a glass of water. It sank as predicted. She then dropped the second rock into a glass of water. But, the second rock floated. Why did one rock sink and the other rock float?

Think Critically: Explain how each rock was formed by volcanic activity. What enabled the second rock to float?

As you can see, there are many factors that affect volcanic eruptions and the form of a volcano. Mount Saint Helens was formed as the Juan de Fuca Plate was subducted under the North American Plate. Silica-rich magma rose toward the surface. Successive eruptions of lava and tephra produced the composite volcano that towers above the surrounding landscape. Magma inside the volcano solidified, blocking the opening to the surface. But as the magma continued to rise, it caused the pressure to build up in the volcano. In May of 1980, Mount Saint Helens released the pressure in a series of explosive eruptions as seen in Figure 15-7 on page 397.

The same forces that caused the Mount Saint Helens volcanic activity have also caused other eruptions. In 1991, Mount Unzen in Japan and Mount Pinatubo in the Philipines violently erupted after lying dormant for 300 and over 600 years respectively. The islands of Japan and the Philippines are volcanic island arcs, formed as the Pacific and the Philippine Plates converged with the Eurasian Plate.

What tectonic activity caused Mount Saint Helens to erupt?

Table 15-1

15 SELECTED ERUPTIONS IN HISTORY							
Volcano and Location	Year	Type	Eruptive Force	Magma Content Silica	Magma Content H₂O	Ability of Magma to Flow	Products of Eruption
Etna, Sicily	1669	composite	moderate	high	low	medium	lava, ash
Tambora, Indonesia	1815	cinder	high	high	high	low	cinders, gas
Krakatoa, Indonesia	1883	cinder	high	high	high	low	cinders, gas
Pelée, Martinique	1902	cinder	high	high	high	low	gas, ash
Vesuvius, Italy	1906	composite	moderate	high	low	medium	lava, ash
Lassen, California	1915	composite	moderate	high	low	low	ash, cinders
Mauna Loa, Hawaii	1933	shield	low	low	low	high	lava
Parícutin, Mexico	1943	cinder	moderate	high	low	medium	ash, cinders
Surtsey, Iceland	1963	shield	moderate	low	low	high	lava, ash
Kelut, Indonesia	1966	cinder	high	high	high	low	gas, ash
Arenal, Costa Rica	1968	cinder	high	high	low	low	gas, ash
Helgafell, Iceland	1973	shield	moderate	low	high	medium	gas, ash
Saint Helens, WA	1980	composite	high	high	high	low	gas, ash
Laki, Iceland	1983	shield	moderate	low	low	medium	lava, ash
Kilauea Iki, Hawaii	1989	shield	low	low	low	high	lava

SECTION REVIEW

1. Some volcanic eruptions are quiet and others are violent. What causes this difference?
2. Name and describe the three forms of volcanoes and give examples.
3. **Apply:** In 1883, an island volcano named Krakatoa (krak uh TOH uh) erupted explosively. The island is in Indonesia, in the Pacific Ring of Fire. Which kind of lava did Krakatoa erupt—basaltic or granitic? How do you know?

Skill Builder

☑ Sequencing

Arrange these events of the history of Mount Saint Helens in correct order. If you need help, refer to Sequencing in the **Skill Handbook** on page 680.

Erupts in 1980   Composite volcano formed
Subduction zone formed   Silica-rich magma rises
Pressure builds   Magma in volcano solidifies

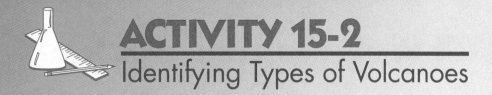

ACTIVITY 15-2
Identifying Types of Volcanoes

Problem: *How are the properties of magma related to volcano type?*

Materials
- Table 15-1
- paper
- pencil

Procedure
1. Copy the graph shown at right.
2. Using the information from Table 15-1, plot the magma content data for each of the volcanoes listed by writing the name of the basic type of volcano in the appropriate spot on the graph. The data for the 1669 eruption of Mount Etna has already been plotted for you on the diagram.
3. When the plotting of all 15 volcanoes has been completed, analyze the patterns of volcanic types on the diagram to answer the questions.

Data and Observations

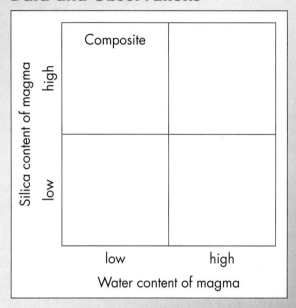

Analyze
1. What relationship appears to exist between the ability of the magma to flow and the eruptive force of the volcano?
2. Which would be more liquid in its properties, a magma that flows easily or one that flows poorly or with difficulty?
3. What relationship appears to exist between the silica or water content of the magma and the nature of the material ejected from the volcano during the eruptions?

Conclude and Apply
4. How is the ability of the magma to flow related to its silica and water content?
5. Which of the two variables (silica or water content) appears to have the greater effect on the eruptive force of the volcano?
6. What relationship appears to exist between the silica and water content of the magma and the type of volcano that is produced?

15-4 Volcanic Features

New Science Words

batholiths
dike
sill
laccolith
volcanic neck
caldera

Objectives

▶ Give examples of intrusive igneous features and how they form.
▶ Explain how a volcanic neck and a caldera form.

Intrusive Features

We can observe volcanoes because they are examples of igneous activity on the surface of Earth. But there is far more igneous activity underground because most magma never reaches the surface to form volcanoes. As you learned in Chapter 4, magma that cools underground forms intrusive igneous rock. What forms do intrusive igneous rocks take on? You can look at some of these features in Figure 15-12.

The largest intrusive igneous rock bodies are **batholiths.** They can be many hundreds of kilometers wide and long and several kilometers thick. Batholiths form when huge bodies of magma cool underground and stop rising. Not all of them are hidden in Earth, though. Some batholiths have been exposed at Earth's surface by erosion. The

Figure 15-11. Most of the bare rock visible in Yosemite National Park is a batholith that was exposed by erosion.

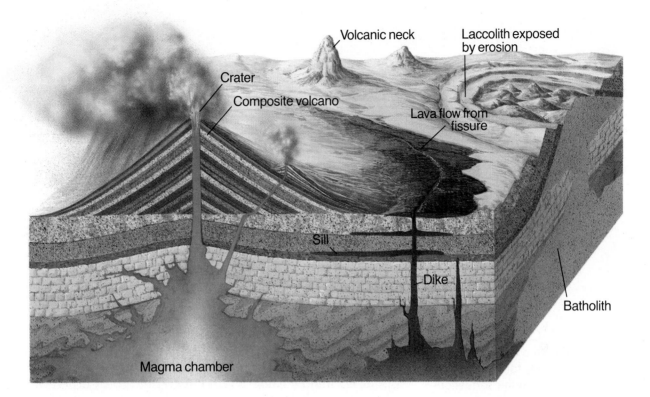

Volcanic neck

Laccolith exposed by erosion

Crater

Composite volcano

Lava flow from fissure

Sill

Dike

Batholith

Magma chamber

granite domes of Yosemite National Park, as seen in Figure 15-11, are exposed parts of a huge batholith that extends much of the length of California.

Magma sometimes squeezes into cracks in rock below the surface. This is like squeezing toothpaste into the spaces between your teeth. Magma that is squeezed into a vertical crack and hardens is called a **dike.** Magma that is squeezed into a horizontal crack and hardens is called a **sill.** You can remember the difference between a dike and a sill because a sill forms horizontally like a windowsill. Dikes and sills run from a few meters to hundreds of meters long. Some magma that forms a sill may continue to push the rock layers upward. This forms a dome of rock called a **laccolith.**

Other Features

When a volcano stops erupting, the magma hardens inside the vent. Erosion begins to wear away the volcano. The cone is much softer than the solid igneous rock in the vent. So, the cone erodes away first, leaving behind the solid igneous core as a **volcanic neck.** Ship Rock, New Mexico, is a volcanic neck. It is just one of many volcanic necks in the southwest United States.

Figure 15-12. This diagram shows intrusive and other features associated with volcanic activity.

MINI-Lab

What are some properties of volcanic materials?

If your teacher is able to provide you with some products of volcanic eruptions, take the time to observe their physical properties closely. Use a pin or dissecting probe to scratch away particles of volcanic rock. Rub these particles, volcanic ash, and beach sand from volcanic areas slowly between your fingers. Observe the volcanic material brightly illuminated under a microscope. Describe what you see and feel. What physical properties of these materials might be used to identify them as having a volcanic origin?

Figure 15-13. Crater Lake (right), formed when the top of the volcano collapsed, forming a caldera as shown in the sequence (left).

Sometimes after an eruption, the top of a volcano collapses down into the vent. This produces a very large opening called a **caldera** (kal DARE uh). You studied the topography of a caldera in Chapter 8. Crater Lake in Oregon is a caldera that is now a lake.

Chapter 15 has shown one way that Earth's surface is continually built up and worn down. The surface is built up by volcanoes. Igneous rock is also formed when magma hardens below ground. Eventually, the processes of erosion wear down the rock, exposing batholiths and forming volcanic necks. Plate tectonics ensures that the processes that cause volcanoes will continue.

SECTION REVIEW

1. What is the difference between a dike and a sill?
2. What's the difference between a caldera and a crater?
3. What is a volcanic neck and how does it form?
4. **Apply:** Why are the dome features of Yosemite National Park actually intrusive volcanic features when they are exposed at the surface in the park?

Skill Builder

☑ Comparing and Contrasting

Compare and contrast dikes, sills, batholiths, and laccoliths. If you need help, refer to Comparing and Contrasting in the **Skill Handbook** on page 682.

CHAPTER
REVIEW

15-1: Volcanoes and Plate Tectonics

1. Volcanoes can be dangerous to people, causing deaths and destroying property.

2. Rocks in the mantle melt to form magma, which rises and eventually reaches Earth's surface. When the magma flows through vents, it becomes lava and forms volcanoes.

3. Volcanoes along rift zones form when magma from the rift flows to the seafloor. The lava builds up from the seafloor to form a volcanic island. Volcanoes over hot spots form when the rising magma breaks through the crust and forms a mountain. Volcanoes also form when an ocean plate is subducted under a continental plate. Here, the ocean plate melts to form volcanic mountains.

15-2: Science and Society: Geothermal Energy from Volcanoes

1. Geothermal energy can reduce the dependence on oil and thus reduce air pollution and the risk of oil spills. Developing geothermal energy in Hawaii would destroy some of the rain forests. Also, drilling might release harmful gases into the air.

2. You may think geothermal energy should be developed on Hawaii, or you may think it would be too environmentally harmful.

15-3: Eruptions and Forms of Volcanoes

1. Basaltic lavas, because they are thin and flow easily, produce quiet eruptions. Silica-rich lavas are thick and stiff, and thus produce very violent eruptions. Water vapor in magma adds to its explosiveness.

2. Shield volcanoes are mountains made of basaltic lava and have gently sloping sides. Cinder cones are steep-sided and are made of tephra. Composite volcanoes, made of silica-rich basalt and tephra, are steep-sided mountains.

15-4: Volcanic Features

1. Batholiths, dikes, sills, and laccoliths form when magma solidifies underground.

2. A caldera forms when the top of a volcano collapses, forming a very large depression.

KEY SCIENCE WORDS

a. batholiths
b. caldera
c. cinder cone
d. composite volcano
e. crater
f. dike
g. geothermal energy
h. hot spots
i. laccolith
j. Pacific Ring of Fire
k. shield volcano
l. sill
m. tephra
n. vent
o. volcanic neck
p. volcano

UNDERSTANDING VOCABULARY

Match each phrase with the correct term from the list of Key Science Words.

1. mountain made of lava and/or volcanic ash
2. large depression formed by the collapse of a volcano
3. solid magma core of a volcano
4. volcano with gently sloping sides
5. ash and cinders thrown from a volcano
6. steep-sided volcano of lava and tephra
7. the largest igneous intrusion
8. an opening through which lava flows
9. a horizontal igneous intrusion
10. energy that comes from magma

CHAPTER
REVIEW

CHECKING CONCEPTS

Choose the word or phrase that completes the sentence.

1. Volcanoes form near _____.
   a. diverging plates   c. converging plates
   b. hot spots   d. all of these
2. Hawaii is made of volcanoes due to _____.
   a. diverging plates   c. converging plates
   b. a hot spot   d. all of these
3. Lavas _____ produce violent volcanic eruptions.
   a. rich in silica   c. made of basalt
   b. that are fluid   d. none of these
4. Magma rich in silica produces _____ eruptions.
   a. flowing   c. quiet
   b. caldera   d. explosive
5. A _____ is made of tephra.
   a. shield volcano   c. cinder cone
   b. caldera   d. composite volcano
6. Kilauea is a _____.
   a. shield volcano   c. cinder cone
   b. composite volcano d. rift zone
7. Magma that squeezes into a vertical crack then hardens is a _____.
   a. sill   c. volcanic neck
   b. dike   d. batholith
8. A _____ is a dome-shaped igneous intrusion body.
   a. dike   c. sill
   b. laccolith   d. none of these
9. Geothermal energy comes from _____.
   a. fossil fuels   c. the sun
   b. electricity   d. magma
10. Using geothermal energy in Hawaii might _____.
   a. release volcanic gases
   b. replace fossil fuels
   c. harm forests
   d. all of these

UNDERSTANDING CONCEPTS

Complete each sentence.

11. Magma that reaches Earth's surface is called _____.
12. Openings in Earth's crust through which lava flows to form volcanoes are _____.
13. A volcano that is not currently active is _____.
14. If a volcano doesn't form at a plate boundary, it forms over a(n) _____.
15. _____ could be used in Hawaii to convert water into steam, which would be used to generate electricity.

THINK AND WRITE CRITICALLY

16. Why do volcanoes differ in shape?
17. Contrast volcanoes that form along rift zones with those that form along subduction zones.
18. Compare and contrast basaltic lava with granitic lava.
19. Explain how these terms are related: vent, caldera, and crater.
20. What is geothermal energy?

APPLY

21. Explain how glaciers and volcanoes can exist on Iceland.
22. What kind of eruption is produced when basaltic lava flows from a volcano? Explain.
23. How are volcanoes related to earthquakes?
24. A mountain called Misti is a volcano in Peru. Peru is on the western border of South America. How might this volcano have formed?
25. In addition to Iceland and Hawaii, where else on Earth do you think could people use geothermal energy?

MORE SKILL BUILDERS

If you need help, refer to the Skill Handbook.

1. **Concept Mapping:** Make a network tree concept map that compares quiet eruptions to explosive eruptions. Use the following words and phrases: *type of eruption, high silica, quiet, flows easily, granitic, explosive, non-flowing, cinder cone, Parícutin, Hawaii, shield, low silica, basaltic.*

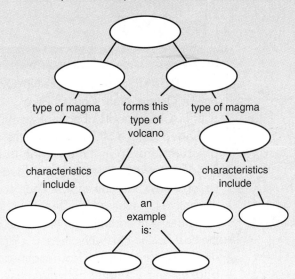

2. **Observing and Inferring:** A volcano violently erupted in Indonesia in 1883. What can you infer about the magma's composition? If people saw the eruption, what were they able to observe about the flow of the lava?
3. **Comparing and Contrasting:** Compare and contrast batholiths and laccoliths.
4. **Classifying:** Mount Fuji is a volcano in Japan. Its steep sides are made of layers of silica-rich lava and ash. Classify Mount Fuji.
5. **Measuring in SI:** The base of the volcano Mauna Loa is about 5000 meters below sea level. The total height of the volcano is 9560 m. What percentage of the volcano is above sea level? Below sea level?

PROJECTS

1. Use reference books to prepare a short report explaining the relationship between plate tectonics and volcanoes. Make a simple map of the world that shows plate boundaries and the locations of major volcanoes.
2. Find out how the eruption of Mount Saint Helens affected plants and animals in the area. Find photos that show what the area looked like shortly after the eruption and what it looks like now. How long did it take the area to "recover" from the eruption?

GLOBAL CONNECTIONS

Change and Earth's Internal Processes

In this unit, you studied about plate tectonics, earthquakes, and volcanoes. Now find out how these subjects are connected to other subjects and places around the world.

120°   60°

PHYSICS

EARTHQUAKE REFLECTED
San Francisco, California

If a diver underwater holds a flashlight at an angle to the surface, the surface acts like a mirror, reflecting the light back into the water. Physicists say a similar thing happened during the 1989 San Francisco earthquake. Seismic waves hit the Moho discontinuity at an angle and were redirected, causing more damage at San Francisco than would have been expected. What information do reflected waves give scientists about Earth?

OCEANOGRAPHY

EARTHQUAKES: CAUSE OF EL NINO?
Pacific Ocean, Near Coastal Peru

El Niño, the periodic abnormal warming of the sea surface off Peru, causes the air pressure to drop in the east, the trade winds to reverse directions, and warm water to flow back to Peru. El Niño occurs every five to seven years. This cycle also coincides with earthquakes that occur on the East Pacific Rise when there is a great deal of volcanic activity. How might earthquakes and volcanic activity cause El Niño?

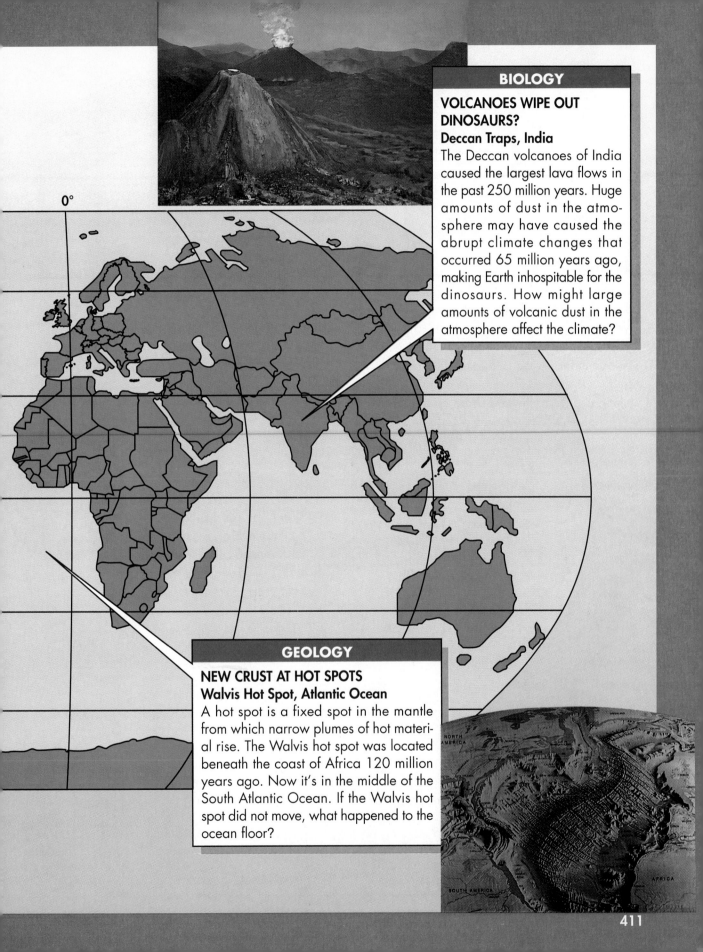

0°

BIOLOGY

VOLCANOES WIPE OUT DINOSAURS?
Deccan Traps, India
The Deccan volcanoes of India caused the largest lava flows in the past 250 million years. Huge amounts of dust in the atmosphere may have caused the abrupt climate changes that occurred 65 million years ago, making Earth inhospitable for the dinosaurs. How might large amounts of volcanic dust in the atmosphere affect the climate?

GEOLOGY

NEW CRUST AT HOT SPOTS
Walvis Hot Spot, Atlantic Ocean
A hot spot is a fixed spot in the mantle from which narrow plumes of hot material rise. The Walvis hot spot was located beneath the coast of Africa 120 million years ago. Now it's in the middle of the South Atlantic Ocean. If the Walvis hot spot did not move, what happened to the ocean floor?

411

CAREERS

SEISMOLOGIST

A *seismologist* studies the seismic waves produced by earthquakes. To record seismic waves, they use an instrument called a seismograph. Seismologists also try to predict when an earthquake will occur. To do this, they may study radon measurements in certain wells, which change at the time of an earthquake.

Seismologists require a college degree in geology, with an emphasis on seismology. Many seismologists have an advanced degree.

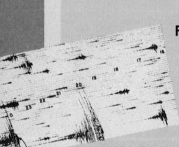

For Additional Information

Contact the American Geological Institute, 4220 King Street, Alexandria, VA 22302.

GEOPHYSICAL TECHNICIAN

A *geophysical technician* assists a geophysicist by collecting data from seismic waves. The data may be used to locate oil and natural gas. Geophysical technicians may also collect meteorological data or oceanographic data. They may be involved in any field related to the study of Earth or other planets.

Geophysical technicians require an associate degree in geophysics or a related field.

For Additional Information

Contact the Society of Exploration Geophysicists, P.O. Box 70240, Tulsa, OK 74170.

UNIT READINGS

▶Erickson, Jon. *Volcanoes and Earthquakes*. Blue Ridge Summit, Pennsylvania: Tab Books, Inc., 1988.
▶Weiner, Jonathan. *Planet Earth*. New York: Bantam Books, Inc., 1986, pp. 5-49.
▶White, Robert S. and Dan P. McKenzie. "Volcanism at Rifts." *Scientific American*, July 1989, pp. 62-71.

Mount Fuji: Woodcuts by Hokusai

Mount Fuji is the highest mountain in Japan, located on the island of Honshu about 97 kilometers west of Tokyo. An inactive volcano crater is located at its summit.

Because Mount Fuji is a sacred mountain to many, thousands of Japanese pilgrims climb it every year. It is no wonder that artists have featured the mountain in many works of art. The great artist Katsushika Hokusai made woodcuts showing thirty-six different views of Mount Fuji. Beautiful ink prints were made using the woodcuts.

The prints were made from one block of wood. The artist drew a design on paper in ink, which was then glued onto a block of hardwood. Then, a carver cut away the wood between the lines of the drawing. The design itself was left on the block. A printer then applied a water-based ink to the block, which was then transferred to absorbent paper. The block could be used to make many prints.

Hokusai critiqued his own work in the following translation by Richard Lane, which shows the artist's humility and sense of humor.

"From the age of fifty I produced a number of designs, yet of all I drew prior to the age of seventy there is truly nothing of any great note. At the age of seventy-three, I finally came to understand somewhat the nature of birds, animals, insects, fishes—the vital nature of grasses and trees. Therefore, at eighty I shall have made great progress, at ninety I shall have penetrated even further the deeper meaning of things, and at one hundred I shall have become truly marvelous, and at one hundred and ten, each dot, each line shall surely possess a life of its own." (Unfortunately, Hokusai lived to be only eighty-nine!)

After Hokusai's death in 1849, some of his prints were shown in other parts of the world. Artists outside of Japan, including James A. M. Whistler of the United States, Edgar Degas, Paul Gauguin, and Henri de Toulouse-Lautrec of France, and Vincent van Gogh of the Netherlands were all influenced by the work of Hokusai.

Write

▶ Look up information about the artists that were influenced by Hokusai. What characteristics of Hokusai do you think most influenced artists of the West? Write an essay supporting your view.

What's Happening Here?

When people think of extinctions, they often think of life-forms that lived long ago. Humans, however, are causing the extinction of many present-day life-forms. Although hunting elephants for their ivory tusks is illegal in many African countries, poachers continue to kill the large animals. Elephants are becoming an endangered species because their ivory is valued for carvings and jewelry. In Unit 6, you'll learn more about extinctions and how the fossil record indicates when extinctions occurred throughout Earth's past. You will also learn more about how people may affect the rate of extinctions.

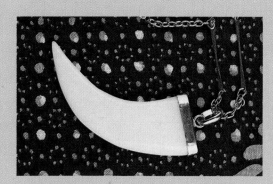

UNIT CONTENTS

16 Clues to Earth's Past

These remains of a crinoid are a fossil. Crinoids are still living in today's oceans, but we have fossils of ancient crinoids dating back more than 450 million years. How do such fossils form? What evidence of past life do we have?

FIND OUT!

Do this simple activity to see how some fossils are formed.

Cut the top off of a small milk carton and add enough plaster of Paris to fill it halfway. Mix enough water with the plaster of Paris so that it's smooth and thick. Coat a leaf, shell, or bone with petroleum jelly. Press it into the plaster of Paris. Allow the plaster of Paris to dry at least 24 hours and then remove the leaf, shell, or bone. Compare the shapes of the objects with the imprints they left in the plaster. Look at the imprints made by others in your class. Can you determine, from the imprints alone, what type of objects made them? How do you think imprints of once-living organisms are made in nature?

Gearing Up

Previewing the Chapter

Use this outline to help you focus on important ideas in this chapter.

Previewing Science Skills

- ▶ In the **Skill Builders,** you will make concept maps, interpret data, and use tables.
- ▶ In the **Activities,** you will interpret illustrations, analyze data, and draw conclusions.
- ▶ In the **MINI-Labs,** you will apply previous knowledge and make inferences.

What's next?

Now that you've seen how imprints of plant and animal remains can be made in plaster of Paris, you can relate this to the formation of fossils in Earth's rocks. As you read this chapter, you'll learn about different types of fossils and how they form. You will also learn how fossils and other evidence are used to measure the age of a rock.

16-1 Fossils

Objectives

▶ List the conditions necessary for fossils to form.
▶ Describe processes of fossil formation.
▶ Explain how fossil correlation is used to determine rock ages.

Traces from Our Past

The dense forest thunders as the *Tyrannosaurus rex* charges forward in pursuit of her evening meal. On the other side of the swamp, a herd of apatosaurs moves slowly and cautiously onward. The adults surround the young to protect them from predators. Soon, night will fall on this prehistoric day, 70 million years ago.

Does this scene sound familiar to you? It's likely that you've read about dinosaurs and other past inhabitants of Earth before. But how do you know they really existed? What evidence do we have of past life on Earth?

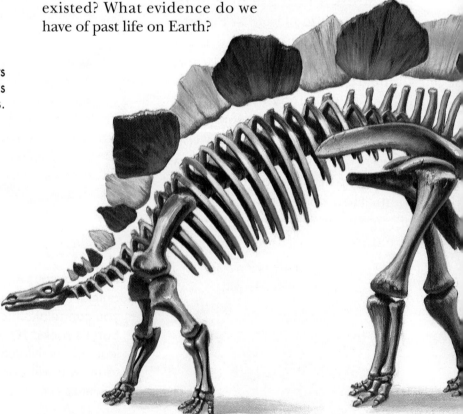

Figure 16-1. Scientists and artists can reconstruct what dinosaurs looked like using fossil remains. Pictured here is *Stegosaurus.*

In the Find Out activity, you made imprints of parts of organisms. The imprints were records, or evidence, of life. If they had been evidence of life that once existed, but no longer exists, then they would be fossils. **Fossils** are the remains or traces of once-living organisms. By studying fossils, geologists help solve mysteries of Earth's past. Fossils have helped geologists and biologists determine approximately when life began, when plants and animals first lived on land, and when certain types of organisms, such as the dinosaurs, disappeared. Fossils tell us not only *when* and *where* organisms once lived, but also *how* they lived.

How Fossils Form

Usually the remains of dead plants and animals are quickly destroyed. Scavengers eat the dead organisms, or bacteria cause them to decay. If you've ever left a banana on the shelf too long, you've seen this process begin. Compounds in the banana cause it to become soft and moist, and bacteria move in and cause it to quickly decay. What keeps some plants and animals from decaying so they can become fossils?

First of all, to become a fossil the body of a dead organism must be protected from scavengers and bacteria. One way this can occur is when the body is quickly covered by sediments. If a fish dies and sinks to the bottom of a pond, sediments carried into the pond by a stream will rapidly cover the fish. As a result, no animals or bacteria can get to it. Quick burial, however, isn't enough to make a fossil.

Organisms have a better chance of being preserved if they have hard parts such as bones, shells, teeth, or wood. As you know, these hard parts are less likely to be eaten by other organisms and are less likely to weather away. Most fossils that have been found are the hard parts of organisms.

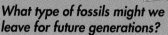

MINI-Lab

What type of fossils might we leave for future generations?

Suppose you are to decide on five items to be placed in a plastic "time capsule." The capsule will be buried in soil so that some future generation might dig it up and learn about their ancestors and how they lived. List the five items you would bury in the plastic container. Keep in mind that they might have to endure the natural weathering and erosion processes if the container is damaged. Explain what you expect the future generation to be able to learn from each item. Can they learn about our average size and weight? Can they learn about the environment we live in? What other things can they learn?

Figure 16-2. Much of the original matter in these petrified plant remains has been replaced by quartz and other minerals.

How do petrified remains differ from original remains?

EcoTip

Will the fossils you leave behind pollute the environment? Plastic foam cups and plates last up to 500 years in a landfill. Reduce waste by washing and reusing cups and plates whenever possible.

Petrified Remains

You have some idea of what *Tyrannosaurus rex* looked like because you've seen illustrations of this dinosaur. The artists who draw *Tyrannosaurus rex* base their illustrations on fossils. One type of fossil they use is petrified bone. Perhaps you've seen skeletal remains of dinosaurs towering above you in museums. These bones are usually petrified.

Petrified remains are hard and rocklike. Some or all of the original materials in the remains have been replaced by minerals. For example, a solution of water and dissolved quartz may flow through the bones of a dead organism. The water dissolves the calcium in the bone and deposits quartz in its place. Quartz is harder than calcium, so the petrified bone is rocklike.

We learn about past life-forms from bones, wood, and other remains that become petrified. But there are also many other types of fossils to consider.

Carbonaceous Films

The tissues of most organisms are made of compounds that contain carbon. Sometimes the only fossil remains of a dead plant or animal is this carbon. As you know, fossils usually form when a dead organism is buried in sediments. When more and more sediments pile up, the organism is subjected to pressure and heat. These conditions force gases and liquids from the body. A thin film of carbon residue is left, forming an outline of the original plant part. This process of chemically changing plant material is called carbonization, and it produces a fossil called a **carbonaceous film.**

In swamps and deltas, large volumes of plant matter accumulate. Over millions of years, these deposits can be completely carbonized, forming the sedimentary rock coal. Coal is more important as a source of fuel than as a fossil because the structure of the original plant is lost when the coal forms.

Molds and Casts

Think again about the impressions in plaster of Paris you made earlier. In nature, such impressions are made when seashells or other hard parts of organisms fall into soft sediments such as mud and beach sand. The object and sediments are then covered by more sediments. Compaction and cementation turn the sediments into rock. Cracks in the rock let water and air reach the shell or hard part and it then decays, leaving behind a cavity in the rock called a **mold.** Later, other sediments may fill in the cavity, harden into rock, and produce a **cast** of the original object.

How are molds and casts related?

Figure 16-3. A cast resembling the original organism forms when a mold fills with sediments.

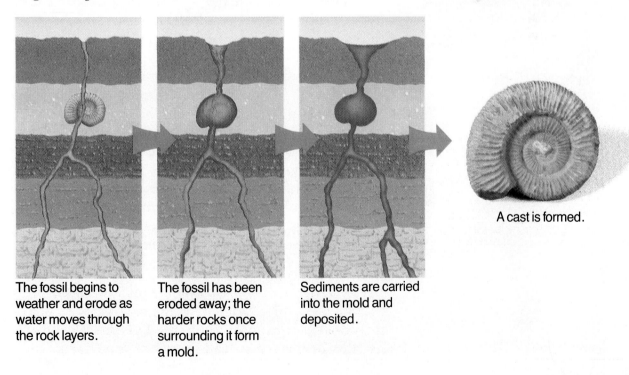

A cast is formed.

The fossil begins to weather and erode as water moves through the rock layers.

The fossil has been eroded away; the harder rocks once surrounding it form a mold.

Sediments are carried into the mold and deposited.

Figure 16-4. This 40 million year old grasshopper was trapped in the sticky resin produced by a plant. Over time, the resin crystallized into amber, preserving the insect inside.

Figure 16-5. Tracks in solidified mud indicate that adult apatosaurs protected their young by surrounding them as they traveled in herds.

Original Remains

Sometimes the actual organism or parts of organisms are found. Figure 16-4 shows an insect trapped in amber, a crystallized form of the sticky resin produced by some trees. The amber protects the insect's body from decay and petrification. Other organisms, such as woolly mammoths, have been found preserved in frozen ground. Some woolly mammoths have been found with their skin and hair intact.

Trace Fossils

It's not only from body parts that we learn about organisms. We also learn from the tracks and traces they leave behind. Fossilized tracks and other evidence of animal activity are called trace fossils. Perhaps your parents made your handprint or footprint in plaster of Paris when you were born. If so, it's a record that tells something about you. From it, we can guess your approximate size and maybe your weight. Animals walking on Earth long ago have left similar tracks. In some cases, tracks can tell us more about how an organism lived than any other type of fossil.

From a set of tracks at Davenport Ranch, Texas, we have learned something about the social life of *Apatosaurus*, one of the largest dinosaurs. The tracks were made by a traveling herd. The largest tracks are on the outer edges and the smallest are on the inside. This suggests that the adult apatosaurs surrounded the young as they traveled—probably to protect them from enemies, such as allosaurs. In fact, a nearby set of allosaur tracks indicates that one was stalking the herd, following alongside waiting for a chance to attack.

Other trace fossils include worm holes and burrows made by sea creatures. These, too, tell us something about the life-style of these animals. As you can see, a combination of fossils can tell us a great deal about the individuals that inhabited Earth before us.

List several examples of trace fossils.

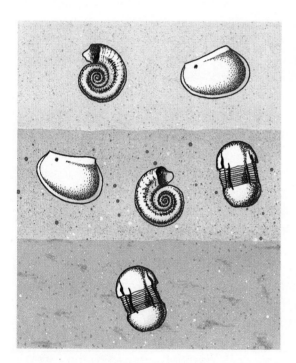

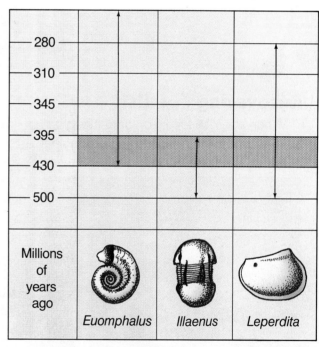

Figure 16-6. The chart on the right shows when each organism inhabited Earth. The middle layer of rock had to be deposited between 430 and 395 million years ago—the only time all three types of organisms in the layer were alive.

Index Fossils

One thing we've learned by studying fossils is that organisms are constantly changing, or evolving. A species inhabits Earth for only a certain period of time before it evolves into a new species or dies out completely. Some species of organisms inhabit Earth for very long periods of time without changing much. Others remain unchanged for only a short time. It's these organisms that produce index fossils.

How do index fossils differ from other fossils?

Index fossils are fossils from species that existed on Earth for short periods of time and were widespread geographically. Scientists use index fossils to determine the age of rock layers. For example, suppose you find a rock layer containing fossils of an organism that lived only between 100 and 145 million years ago. You can conclude that the rock layer must have formed during that time.

Fossils and Ancient Environments

Fossils can also be used to determine what the environment of an area was like long ago. For example, rocks in Antarctica contain fossils of tropical plants. The environment of Antarctica today certainly isn't tropical, but we know that it was when the fossilized plants were living.

T E C H N O L O G Y

Recovering Fossils

When scientists locate an area thought to have fossils, large earth-moving equipment or explosives are used to remove overlying

rocks and soil. Smaller and smaller tools are then used as the excavation draws nearer to the fossils. In the final phases of fossil recovery, tiny picks and brushes are used to remove soil from the fossils.

In order for the fossils to be removed or transported, they must be strengthened and protected. Large, brittle bones, such as dinosaur remains, are first covered with a layer of shellac. Then, strips of wet newspaper are molded onto the fossils. Finally, a plaster mixture is used to coat burlap straps, which are then applied to the fossils. This final step produces a kind of cast that protects and supports the fossils. The cast can be made even stronger with wooden sticks. The reinforced fossils are now ready to be transported to a museum, where they will undergo final preparations before being placed on exhibit.

Think Critically: Why are remains such as dinosaur bones so fragile?

How would you explain the presence of fossilized brachiopods, animals that once lived in shallow seas, in the rocks of the midwest United States? The central portion of North America was covered by a shallow sea when the brachiopods were living.

Fossils tell us not only about past life on Earth, but about the history of the rock layers that contain them.

Today

425 million years ago

514 million years ago

Figure 16-7. The position and environment of Antarctica, shown in red, have changed through time. Fossils found in its rocks indicate Antarctica once had a tropical environment.

SECTION REVIEW

1. What conditions are needed for most fossils to form?
2. What type of fossil forms when the organism decays leaving a cavity in the rock?
3. What can be said about the ages of two widely separated layers of rock that contain the same type of fossil?
4. **Apply:** Why would dinosaur bones be considered useful index fossils?

☑ Concept Mapping

Make a concept map that compares and contrasts petrified remains and original remains. Use these terms and phrases: *original remains, evidence of former life, petrified remains, replaced by minerals,* and *actual parts of organisms.* If you need help, refer to Concept Mapping in the **Skill Handbook** on pages 688 and 689.

Skill Builder

16-2 Extinction of Dinosaurs

New Science Words

extinct

Objectives

▶ Discuss the meteorite-impact theory of dinosaur extinction.
▶ Describe several theories on why dinosaurs became extinct.

What Killed the Dinosaurs?

In layers of sedimentary rock in the western United States rest the remains of thousands of dinosaurs. The bones tell us that dinosaurs were fast, agile, intelligent animals who ruled the land longer than any other organism before or since. Why are they no longer a dominant life-form on Earth? What happened to the dinosaurs, and what can we learn from their disappearance?

The last species of dinosaurs became extinct about 65 million years ago. When a species becomes **extinct,** there are no longer any living members of its kind. Before their extinction, species of dinosaurs had dominated the land

Figure 16-8. Evidence in the rock record indicates a large meteorite may have struck Earth at about the same time the dinosaurs became extinct.

for 130 million years. Mammals have ruled the land for only the last 65 million years, and humans and their direct ancestors have been around for less than 6 million. The dinosaurs are no longer on Earth, but we learn from them by investigating what caused their extinction.

One theory of dinosaur extinction is that a large meteorite collided with Earth. The collision threw dust and debris into Earth's upper atmosphere. The collision may have also caused large forest fires that would have added smoke to the atmosphere.

If enough dust and smoke were released into Earth's upper atmosphere, the sun would have been completely blocked out. If the sun's energy remained blocked off for a long time, plants couldn't have carried on photosynthesis and would have died. With no food, plant-eating dinosaurs also would have died. With no plant-eating dinosaurs to prey on, meat-eating dinosaurs would have starved as well.

Luis and Walter Alvarez, whom you first learned about in Chapter 13, may have found evidence to support the theory that a meteorite collided with Earth. They found a layer of clay in a column of sedimentary rock that was deposited at about the same time the dinosaurs became extinct. The layer contained small deformed grains of quartz very much like those found near meteorite craters elsewhere on Earth. But more importantly, the clay layer is rich in the element iridium. Iridium is rare on Earth's surface but found in greater amounts in meteorites.

The iridium in the clay layer may have come from the meteorite when it broke apart on impact. As the dust from the meteorite and the impact crater settled, the Alvarezes believe it formed the clay layer.

Some scientists believe the Alvarez theory is too complex and look for simpler explanations for the dinosaur extinction. Perhaps the iridium-rich clay layer can be explained by large amounts of volcanic activity. The iridium may have been brought up from deep inside Earth. The volcanic activity could have caused large amounts

Did You Know?

Earth is losing about three species every day. That number is expected to increase as we destroy natural environments such as grasslands, wetlands, and rain forests.

Figure 16-9. The dinosaurs were well adapted to their environments. When their environments changed, they perished. Are we headed for the same fate?

of dust to enter Earth's atmosphere. The rock record indicates that global temperatures started to go down about 65 million years ago. Perhaps with colder temperatures, the dinosaurs could not produce offspring and eventually died.

It's difficult to know for sure what caused Earth's environment to change 65 million years ago. But one thing that we have learned from the dinosaurs is that all organisms are dependent on their environment.

SECTION REVIEW

1. How long ago did dinosaurs become extinct?
2. What evidence indicates that a meteorite collided with Earth and may have caused the extinction of the dinosaurs?
3. Discuss two theories that explain how iridium could have gotten into the clay layer deposited about 65 million years ago.

SCIENCE & SOCIETY

You Decide!

Compared to dinosaurs, humans have inhabited Earth for a very short time. As you read in Chapters 9 and 10, we face possible changes in our environment because of the destruction of the ozone, the greenhouse effect, and other pollution. Do we need to worry about disappearing like the dinosaurs did? Is it possible that our environment is changing enough to cause the extinction of our own species?

ACTIVITY 16-1
Determining Relative Ages

Problem: *How can the relative order of events be determined in layers of rock?*

Procedure

1. Study Figures a and b below. The legend provided will help you interpret the figures.
2. Determine the relative ages of the rock layers, unconformities, igneous dikes, and fault in each figure.
3. Answer the questions in the Analyze and Conclude and Apply sections that follow.

Analyze

Figure A

1. Were any layers of rock deposited after the igneous dike formed? Explain.
2. What type of unconformity is shown? Is it possible that there were originally more layers of rock than are shown here? Explain.
3. What type of fault is shown?
4. Based on the figure alone, do you know whether the shale was deposited before or after the fault occurred? Assume that the layers have not been overturned.

5. Is it possible to determine if the igneous dike formed before or after the fault occurred? Explain.

Figure B

6. What type of fault is shown?
7. Is the igneous dike on the left older or younger than the unconformity nearest the surface? Explain.
8. Are the two igneous dikes shown the same age? How do you know?
9. Which two layers of rock may have been much thicker at one time than they are now?

Conclude and Apply

10. Make a sketch of Figure a. Indicate on it the relative age of each rock layer, igneous dike, fault, and unconformity. For example, the shale layer is the oldest, so mark it with a "1." Mark the next oldest feature with a "2" and so on.
11. Repeat the procedure in Question 10 for Figure b.

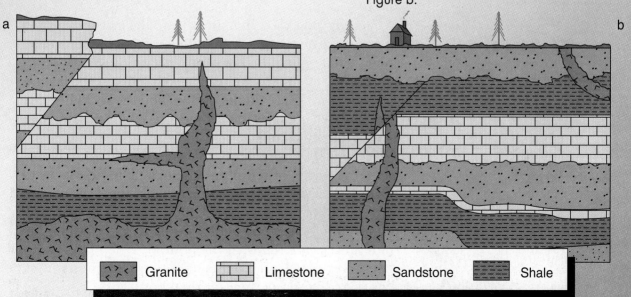

Granite Limestone Sandstone Shale

Relative Ages of Rocks

New Science Words

law of superposition
relative dating
unconformities

Objectives

▶ Describe several methods used to date rock layers relative to other rock layers.
▶ Interpret gaps in the rock record.
▶ Give an example of how rock layers may be correlated with other rock layers.

How is the law of superposition used by geologists?

The Law of Superposition

It's a hot summer day in July and you're getting ready to meet your friends at the local park. You put on your helmet and pads and grab your skateboard. But the bearings in one of the wheels are worn, and the wheel isn't spinning freely. You remember reading an article in a skateboarding magazine about how to replace wheels, and you decide to look it up. In your room is a stack of magazines from the past year. You know that the article came out in the January edition, so it must be near the bottom of the pile. As you dig downward, you find the March issue then the February issue. January must be next.

How did you know that the issue of the magazine would be on bottom? To find the older edition under newer ones, you applied the law of superposition.

The **law of superposition** states that in a layer of rock, the oldest rocks are on the bottom and the rocks become progressively younger toward the top. Why is this the case, and is it always true?

As you know, sediments are often deposited in layers, forming layers of sedimentary rock. The first layer to form is usually on the bottom. Each additional layer forms on top of the previous one. Unless forces, such as those generated by tectonic activity, overturn the layers, the oldest rocks are found at the bottom. When layers have been overturned, geologists use other clues in the rock layers to determine their original positions.

Relative Dating

Suppose you now want to look for another issue of your skateboarding magazine. You're not sure exactly how old it is; all you know is that it arrived after the January issue. You can find it in the stack by using relative dating.

Relative dating is used in geology to determine the order of events and the relative age of rocks by examining the position of rocks in a sequence. For example, if layers of sedimentary rock have a fault running through them, you know that the layers had to be there first before a fault could form in them. The relative age of the rocks is older than the relative age of the fault.

Relative dating doesn't tell you anything about the exact age of rock layers. You don't know if a layer is 100 million or 10 000 years old, only that it's younger than the layers below it and older than the fault running through it.

Relative dating works well if rocks haven't been folded or overturned by tectonic processes. For example, look at Figure 16-10. Which layer is the oldest? In cases where rock layers have been disturbed, you may have to look for fossils and other clues to date the rocks. If you find a fossil in the top layer that's older than a fossil in a lower layer, you can hypothesize that the layers have been overturned.

How are relative dating and the law of superposition related?

Figure 16-10. Starting with layer 1, can you tell if the layers become progressively older or younger? Methods other than using the law of superposition must be used to date overturned or disturbed layers.

Unconformities

As you have seen, a layer of rock is a record of past events. But some rock records are incomplete—there are layers missing. These gaps in rock layers are called **unconformities.**

Unconformities develop when agents of erosion remove existing rock layers. They also form when a period of time passes without any new deposition occurring to form new layers of rock.

Figure 16-11 illustrates one way an unconformity can form. Horizontal layers of sedimentary rock are tilted and uplifted above the surface of the water, where agents of erosion and weathering wear them down. Eventually, the tilted layers are again underwater where new sediments are deposited on them in horizontal layers. The rock record records the event as tilted layers of rock meeting horizontal ones. Such an unconformity is called an angular unconformity.

Name and describe two types of unconformities.

Figure 16-11. An angular unconformity results when horizontal and tilted layers contact each other.

Rocks formed as horizontal layers

The rock layers are tilted as they're lifted above the water surface

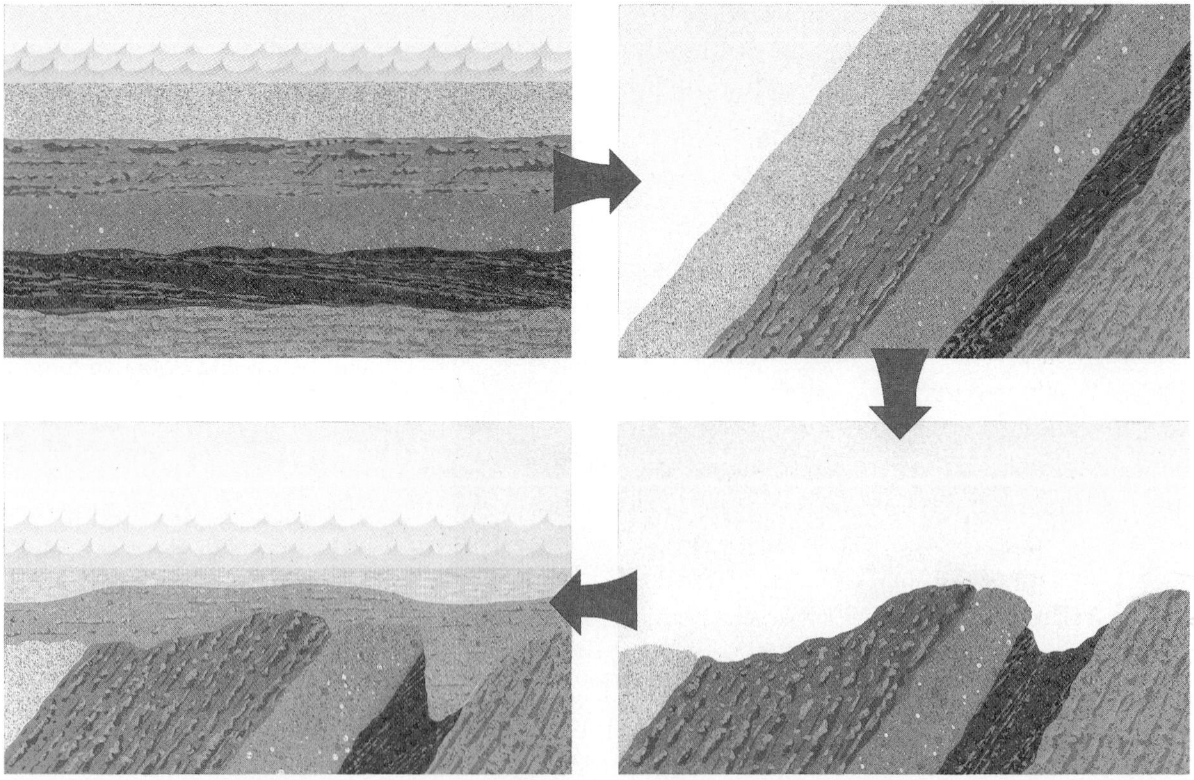

An angular unconformity results when new horizontal layers form on the tilted layers

The tilted layers are eroded above the water surface

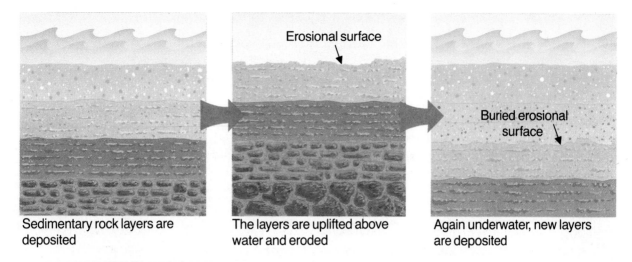

| Sedimentary rock layers are deposited | The layers are uplifted above water and eroded | Again underwater, new layers are deposited |

Erosional surface

Buried erosional surface

Suppose you're standing before a great wall of sedimentary rock layers. Here, layers of sandstone, shale, and limestone are stacked neatly on top of each other in horizontal layers. The rock record looks complete, but in actuality, there are layers missing. If you look closely you may find an old erosional surface in one of the layers. This records a time when the rocks were lifted above the water surface and eroded. Then new sedimentary rocks formed above the eroded surface when it was again lowered beneath the water surface. Even though all the layers are horizontal, there's still a gap in the record. This type of unconformity, called a disconformity, is illustrated in Figure 16-12.

Figure 16-12. The buried erosional surface in the far right illustration is a disconformity.

Correlating Rock Layers

Suppose you're a geologist working in Utah near Canyonlands National Park and Bryce Canyon National Park. You're studying a layer of sandstone in Bryce Canyon. Later, when you visit the Canyonlands, you notice that a layer of sandstone there looks just like the sandstone in Bryce Canyon, 250 kilometers away. Above the sandstone in the Canyonlands is a layer of limestone and then another sandstone layer. You return to Bryce Canyon and find the same sequence—sandstone, limestone, and sandstone. What do you conclude?

It's likely that you're actually looking at the same rocks at the two locations. These rocks are parts of huge deposits that covered this whole area of Utah. The sandstones and limestone you found at the two parks are the exposed surfaces of the same rock layers.

Closing the Gap

Lana and Geoff spent part of their summer vacation on a field trip through Colorado and Utah. They observed many rock outcrops and recorded what they saw in notebooks. The geologic column on the left was drawn by Lana from observations made in Green River, Utah. The column on the right was made by Geoff from the data he collected in Westwater, Colorado. Help them reconstruct the geologic history of the area by answering the following. What type of rock is found at the base of each column? How many unconformities occur in each column? Describe the locations of these unconformities.

Think Critically: Explain the geologic history of the Green River area in terms of erosion and deposition. Why are some formations missing from the Westwater column?

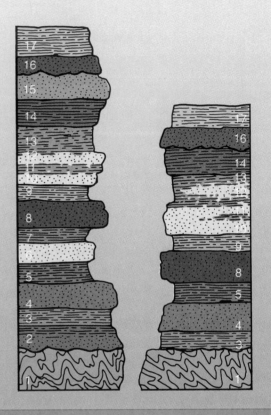

Why is it more difficult to correlate some layers than others?

Geologist match up, or correlate, layers of rocks over great distances. It's not always easy to say that rock exposed in one area is the same rock exposed in another area. Sometimes it's possible to simply walk along the layer for kilometers and prove that it's one continuous formation. In other cases, such as at the Canyonlands and Bryce Canyon, the rock layers are exposed only where rivers have cut down through overlying layers of rock and sediment. How can you prove that the limestone sandwiched between the two sandstones in the Canyonlands is the same limestone at Bryce Canyon? One way is to use fossil evidence. If the same types of fossils are found in both exposures of limestone, it's a good indication that the limestone at each location is the same age, and therefore, one continuous deposit.

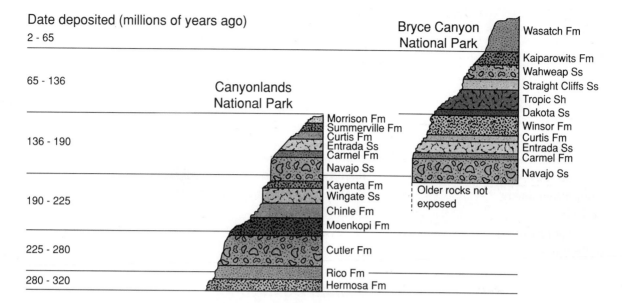

Date deposited (millions of years ago)

2 - 65	
65 - 136	Canyonlands National Park
136 - 190	Morrison Fm, Summerville Fm, Curtis Fm, Entrada Ss, Carmel Fm, Navajo Ss
190 - 225	Kayenta Fm, Wingate Ss, Chinle Fm, Moenkopi Fm
225 - 280	Cutler Fm
280 - 320	Rico Fm, Hermosa Fm

Bryce Canyon National Park — Wasatch Fm, Kaiparowits Fm, Wahweap Ss, Straight Cliffs Ss, Tropic Sh, Dakota Ss, Winsor Fm, Curtis Fm, Entrada Ss, Carmel Fm, Navajo Ss, Older rocks not exposed

Are there other ways to correlate layers of rock? Is there a way to say that two rocks are the same age? Sometimes relative dating isn't enough, and absolute dating must be used. In the next section, you will see how the actual age of rocks can be determined and how we've been able to determine the age of Earth from dating rocks.

Figure 16-13. The many rock layers, or formations, in Canyonlands and Bryce Canyon have been dated and named. Some formations have been correlated between the two canyons. Which layers are present at both canyons? (NOTE: Fm = formation, Ss = sandstone, Sh = shale.)

SECTION REVIEW

1. Suppose you haven't cleaned out your locker all year. Where would you expect to find papers from the beginning of the year? What principle in geology would you use to find these old papers?
2. Why is it more difficult to recognize a disconformity than an angular unconformity?
3. **Apply:** What is the relative age of an igneous intrusion that is forcing overlying sedimentary rock layers to dome upward?

☑ Interpreting Data

A geologist finds a series of rocks. The sandstone contains a trilobite that is 400 million years old. The shale contains some graptolites, which are between 550 and 500 million years old. The limestone, which lies under the sandstone, contains fossils that are between 500 and 400 million years old. Which rock bed is oldest? Explain. If you need help, refer to Interpreting Data in the **Skill Handbook** on page 687.

Skill Builder

16-4 Absolute Ages of Rocks

New Science Words

absolute dating
radioactive decay
half-life
radiometric dating
uniformitarianism

Objectives

▶ Identify how absolute dating differs from relative dating.
▶ Describe how the half-lives of isotopes are used to determine a rock's age.

Absolute Dating

As you continue to shuffle through your stack of skateboarding magazines looking for articles about wheels and bearings, you decide you need to restack them into a neat pile. By now, they're a jumble and no longer in order of their relative ages. How can you stack them so the oldest are on bottom and the newest on top? Fortunately, magazines have their dates printed on their covers. So, stacking magazines in order is a simple process. Unfortunately for geologists, rocks don't have their ages stamped on them. Or do they?

Absolute dating is a method used by geologists to determine the age, in years, of a rock or other object. Absolute dating is a process that uses the properties of atoms in rocks and other objects to determine their ages.

Contrast absolute and relative dating.

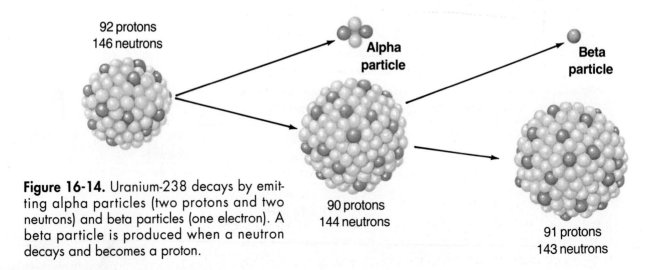

92 protons
146 neutrons

Alpha particle

Beta particle

90 protons
144 neutrons

91 protons
143 neutrons

Figure 16-14. Uranium-238 decays by emitting alpha particles (two protons and two neutrons) and beta particles (one electron). A beta particle is produced when a neutron decays and becomes a proton.

Radioactive Decay

In Chapter 2, you learned that an element can have atoms with different numbers of neutrons in their nuclei. Some of these isotopes undergo a process called radioactive decay. When an atom of an isotope decays, one of its neutrons breaks down into a proton and and an electron. The electron leaves the atom as a beta particle. The nucleus loses a neutron, but gains a proton. Some isotopes give off two protons and two neutrons in the form of an alpha particle. As you know, when the number of protons in an atom is changed, as it is in **radioactive decay,** a new element is formed. For example, when an atom of the radioactive isotope uranium-238 decays, it eventually forms an atom of lead-206. Lead-206 isn't radioactive, so it doesn't decay any further.

In the case of uranium decaying to lead, uranium-238 is known as the parent material and lead-206 as the daughter product. Another example of a parent material is carbon-14, which decays to its daughter, nitrogen-14. Each radioactive parent material has a certain rate at which it decays to its daughter product. This rate is known as its half-life.

The **half-life** of an isotope is the time it takes for half of the atoms in the isotope to decay. For example, the half-life of carbon-14 is 5730 years. So, it will take 5730 years for half of the carbon-14 atoms in an object to decay to nitrogen-14. You might guess that in another 5730 years, all of the remaining carbon-14 atoms will have decayed to nitrogen-14. However, this is not the case. Only half of the atoms of carbon-14 remaining after the first 5730 years will decay during the second 5730 years. So, after two half-lives, one-fourth of the original carbon-14 atoms still remains. Half of them will decay after another 5730 years. After three half-lives, one-eighth of the original carbon-14 atoms still remains. After many half-lives, such a small amount of the parent material remains that it all decays to its daughter product.

Radiometric Dating

To a geologist, the decay of radioactive isotopes is like a clock ticking away, keeping track of time that's passed since rocks have formed. As time passes, the concentration of parent material in a rock decreases as the

MINI-Lab

What are some of the relative and absolute dates of events in Earth's history?

Listed below are several events in Earth's history. List them in the relative order in which you think they occurred. Make a time line using the following dates: 4.6 billion years, 3.5 billion years, 1.0 billion years, 630 million years, 410 million years, 360 million years, 210 million years, 65 million years, and 5 million years. Match each event on your list with the absolute date on your time line. Check your time line with your teacher or other reference source.

Events: *Earth forms, first multicellular plants evolve, first plants move onto the land, first mammals evolve, first multicellular animals evolve, dinosaurs become extinct, first animals move onto the land, first human ancestors evolve, formation of oldest known fossils.*

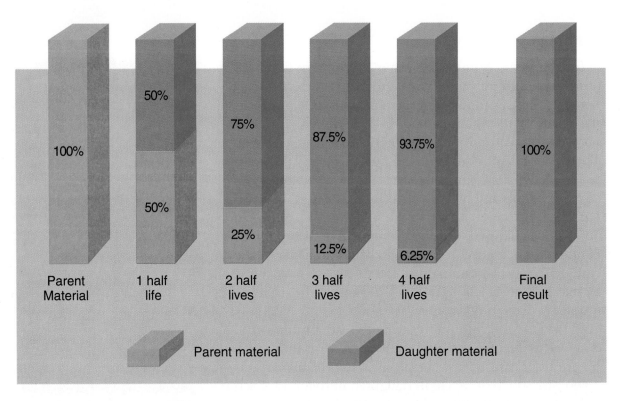

100%

50%
50%

75%
25%

87.5%
12.5%

93.75%
6.25%

100%

Parent Material | 1 half life | 2 half lives | 3 half lives | 4 half lives | Final result

Parent material   Daughter material

Figure 16-15. After each half-life, one-half the amount of parent material remains. Eventually, such a small amount of the parent material is left that it all decays to daughter material.

Did You Know?

The half-life of rubidium–87 is 500 billion years. That's more than ten times the age of Earth.

concentration of daughter product increases. By measuring the amounts of parent and daughter materials in a rock and by knowing the half-life of the parent, a geologist can calculate the absolute age of the rock. This process is called **radiometric dating.**

A scientist must decide which parent and daughter materials to measure when dating a rock or fossil. If the object to be dated is very old, then an isotope with a long half-life must be used. For example, if a fossil is 1 billion years old, there would be no carbon-14 left to measure. However, the half-life of uranium-238 is 4.5 billion years. Enough of the parent and daughter would still be present to measure.

Carbon-14 is useful for dating fossils up to 75 000 years old. Organisms take in carbon from the environment to build tissues in their bodies. When the organism dies, some of the carbon-14 decays and escapes as nitrogen-14 gas. The amount of carbon-14 remaining can be measured to determine the age of the fossil.

Radiometric dating has been used to date the oldest rocks found on Earth. These rocks are 3.96 billion years old. Scientists have determined that the oldest known fossils are 3.5 billion years old and have estimated the age of Earth at 4.6 billion years.

Before radiometric dating was available, many people had estimated the age of Earth to be only a few thousand years old. But in the 1700s, Scottish scientist James Hutton estimated that Earth was much older. He used the principle of **uniformitarianism.** This principle states that Earth processes occurring today are similar to those that occurred in the past. He observed that the processes that changed the rocks and land around him were very slow, and he inferred that they had been just as slow throughout Earth's history. Hutton hypothesized that it took much longer than a few thousand years to form the layers of rock around him and to erode mountains that once towered kilometers high.

Hutton and others concluded that Earth was millions of years old, not thousands. Since their time, geologists have established that Earth is indeed very old. But only by observing the processes occurring around us today have we been able to unlock the mysteries of our past. As you read the next chapter, you will see how observing life on Earth today has allowed us to understand how organisms have evolved through time.

Science and MATH

The half-life of radium-226 is 1600 years. How old is an object in which 1/32 of the original radium-226 is present?

SECTION REVIEW

1. Suppose you discover three layers of rock that have not been overturned. You measure the absolute age of the middle layer to be 120 million years old. What can you say about the ages of the layers above and below it?

2. Suppose you now date an igneous dike running through only the bottom two layers. The dike is cut off by the upper rock layer. The dike is 70 million years old. What can you say about the absolute age of the upper layer?

3. **Apply:** How old would a fossil be if it had only one-eighth of its original carbon-14 remaining?

☑ Making and Using Tables

Skill Builder

Make a table that shows the amounts of parent and daughter materials left of a radioactive element after four half-lives if the original parent material had a mass of 100 g. If you need help, refer to *Making and Using Tables* in the **Skill Handbook** on page 690.

ACTIVITY 16-2
Radioactive Decay

Problem: How can absolute age be determined by radioactive decay?

Materials
- shoe box with lid
- paper clips (100)
- pennies (100)
- brass fasteners (100)
- graph paper
- colored pencils (2)

Procedure
1. Place 100 pennies into the shoe box with all heads up.
2. Place the lid on the box and shake it one time.
3. Remove the lid. Replace the pennies that are now tails up with paper clips. Record the number of pennies remaining in the box in a data table similar to the one shown.
4. Repeat Steps 2 and 3 until all the pennies have been removed.
5. Remove the paper clips from the box. Put an "X" on one of the shorter sides of the box. Place 100 fasteners in the box.
6. Repeat Steps 2 and 3 until all the fasteners have been removed. Remove only the fasteners that point toward the "X." Be sure to replace them with paper clips.
7. Plot both sets of data on the same graph. Graph the "shake number" on the horizontal axis and the "number of pennies or fasteners remaining" on the vertical axis. Be sure to use a different colored pencil for each set of data.

Data and Observations

Shake number	Number Remaining	
	Pennies	Fasteners
0	100	100
1		
2		
12		
13		
14		
15		

Analyze
1. In this model of radioactive decay, what do the coins and fasteners represent? The paper clips? The box? Each shake?
2. What was the half-life of the pennies? The fasteners?
3. How does the difference between the two objects affect the half-life? Compare the objects to the differences among radioactive elements.

Conclude and Apply
4. Suppose you could make only one shake in 100 years. How many years would it take to have 25 coins and 75 paper clips remaining? 25 fasteners and 75 paper clips remaining?
5. How can absolute age of rocks be determined?

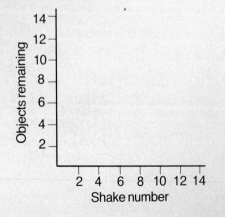

CHAPTER
REVIEW

SUMMARY

16-1: Fossils

1. In order for fossils to form, hard parts of the dead organisms must be covered quickly.

2. Some fossils form when original materials that made up the organisms are replaced with minerals. Other fossils form when remains are subjected to heat and pressure, leaving only a carbonaceous film behind. Some fossils are the actual remains of once-living organisms. Some fossils are merely the tracks or traces left by former organisms.

3. In nearly all situations, a rock layer can be no older or younger than the age of the fossils embedded in it.

16-2: Science and Society: Extinction of the Dinosaurs

1. The meteorite-impact theory of dinosaur extinction states that a large object from space collided with Earth and caused vast climate changes. Dinosaurs weren't able to adapt and eventually became extinct.

2. Another theory suggests that volcanic activity led to the extinction of the dinosaurs.

16-3: Relative Ages of Rocks

1. The law of superposition states that older rocks lie underneath younger rocks in areas where the rocks haven't been disturbed. Faults are always younger than the rocks they crosscut. These two concepts can be used to determine relative ages of rocks.

2. Unconformities, or gaps in the rock record, are due to erosion, nondeposition, or both.

3. Fossils and rock types are often helpful when correlating similar rock bodies.

16-4: Absolute Ages of Rocks

1. Relative dating of rocks, unlike absolute dating, doesn't provide an exact age for the rocks.

2. The half-life of a radioactive isotope is the time it takes for half of the atoms in the isotope to decay. Because half-lives are constant, absolute ages of rocks containing radioactive elements can be determined.

KEY SCIENCE WORDS

a. **absolute dating**
b. **carbonaceous film**
c. **cast**
d. **extinct**
e. **fossils**
f. **half-life**
g. **index fossils**
h. **law of superposition**
i. **mold**
j. **petrified remains**
k. **radioactive decay**
l. **radiometric dating**
m. **relative dating**
n. **unconformities**
o. **uniformitarianism**

UNDERSTANDING VOCABULARY

Match each phrase with the correct term from the list of Key Science Words.

1. thin film of carbon preserved as a fossil
2. rocklike fossils made of minerals
3. fossils of species that existed for a short time
4. states that older rocks lie under younger rocks
5. states that natural processes occur today as they did in the past
6. gaps in the rock record
7. method that gives actual rock ages
8. neutrons break down during this process
9. the time it takes for half of the atoms of a radioactive isotope to decay
10. this process measures the amounts of parent and daughter materials to determine age

CHAPTER
REVIEW

Choose the word or phrase that completes the sentence.

1. Remains of organisms in rocks are _____.
   - a. half-lives
   - b. fossils
   - c. unconformities
   - d. extinctions

2. Fossils may form when dead organisms are _____ .
   - a. buried quickly
   - b. kept from bacteria
   - c. made of hard parts
   - d. all of these

3. _____ are cavities left in rocks when a shell or bone decays.
   - a. Casts
   - b. Petrified remains
   - c. Molds
   - d. None of these

4. Dinosaurs lived _____.
   - a. about 1000 years ago
   - b. about 10 000 years ago
   - c. before humans
   - d. with humans

5. Extinction of dinosaurs may have been due to _____.
   - a. changes in climate
   - b. volcanoes
   - c. hunting by humans
   - d. both a and b

6. A fault can be used to find the _____ age of a group of rocks.
   - a. absolute
   - b. radiometric
   - c. index
   - d. relative

7. An unconformity between horizontal rock layers is a(n) _____.
   - a. angular unconformity
   - b. fault
   - c. disconformity
   - d. none of these

8. Rocks can be correlated using _____.
   - a. fossils
   - b. rock types
   - c. absolute ages
   - d. all of these

9. In one type of radioactive decay, a(n) _____ breaks down.
   - a. alpha particle
   - b. proton
   - c. beta particle
   - d. neutron

10. Radiometric dating indicates that Earth is _____ years old.
    - a. 2000
    - b. 5000
    - c. 3.5 billion
    - d. 4.6 billion

UNDERSTANDING CONCEPTS

Complete each sentence.

11. In a mold and cast fossil, the _____ might be mistaken for a petrified fossil.

12. Another way to state the principle of _____ is to say "the present is the key to the past."

13. Determining ages of rocks by using a fault that cuts across the rocks is an example of _____ dating.

14. During _____, new elements are formed.

15. The _____ of carbon-14 is 5730 years.

THINK AND WRITE CRITICALLY

16. How do relative and absolute dating methods differ?

17. Compare and contrast fossil molds and casts.

18. Why did James Hutton and others infer that Earth had to be much older than a few thousand years?

19. Explain why a clay layer rich in iridium might explain why the dinosaurs became extinct.

20. How many half-lives have passed in a rock containing 1/8 of the original radioactive material and 7/8 of the daughter product?

APPLY

21. We don't have a complete fossil record of life on Earth. Give some reasons why.

22. Suppose a lava flow were found between two sedimentary rock layers. How could the lava flow be used to date the rocks? (HINT: Most lava contains radioactive isotopes.)

23. Mammals began to evolve on Earth shortly before the dinosaurs became extinct. Suggest a hypothesis explaining how the mammals may have caused the dinosaurs to become extinct.

24. Suppose you're correlating rock layers in the western United States. You find a layer of shale that contains volcanic dust deposits. How can this layer help you in your correlation over a large area?

25. Why is carbon-14 not suitable for dating fossils formed about 2 million years ago?

MORE SKILL BUILDERS

If you need help, refer to the Skill Handbook.

1. **Making and Using Graphs:** Copy and complete the graph below to show the radioactive decay of an element with a half-life of 1 million years.

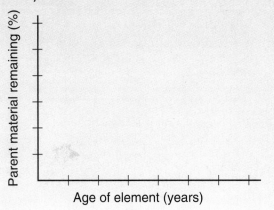

2. **Observing and Inferring:** Suppose you found a rock containing brachiopods. What can you infer about the environment in which the rock formed?

3. **Recognizing Cause and Effect:** Explain why some woolly mammoths have been found intact in frozen ground.

4. **Classifying:** Suppose you were given a set of ten fossils to classify. Make a table to classify each specimen according to the type of fossil it is.

5. **Outlining:** Make an outline of Section 16-1 that discusses the ways in which fossils form.

PROJECTS

1. Start your own fossil collection. Label each find as to type, approximate age, and the place where it was found. Most state geological surveys can provide you with reference material that explains the types of fossils you are apt to find in your area.

2. Find out about other extinctions that occurred at about the same time as the dinosaur extinctions. Were these extinctions caused by the same events that may have killed the dinosaurs?

Dinosaurs had to compete with each other and other organisms to survive. They were successful animals because they were well-adapted to their environments.

FIND OUT!

Do this activity to observe how traits determine whether an individual survives in an environment.

Cut green, orange, and blue yarn into 3-cm lengths. You should have 15 pieces of each color when you're done. Place all of the pieces on a sheet of green construction paper. Use a pair of tweezers to pick up as many pieces of yarn as you can in 15 seconds. How many pieces of each color did you pick up? Suppose the construction paper represents green grass, each piece of yarn represents an insect, and your tweezers represent a bird preying on the insects. Would you expect many orange or blue insects to survive over a long period of time? What advantage would the green insects have over the others?

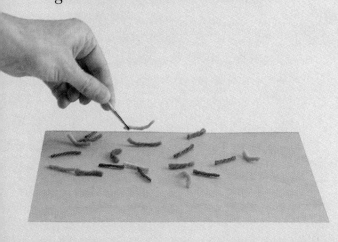

Gearing Up
Previewing the Chapter

Use this outline to help you focus on important ideas in this chapter.

Section 17-1   Evolution and Geologic Time
▶ The Geologic Time Scale
▶ Organic Evolution
▶ The Effect of Plate Tectonics on Earth History

Section 17-2   Science and Society
Present-Day Rapid Extinctions
▶ Can Humans Slow the Rate of Extinctions?

Section 17-3   Early Earth History
▶ The Precambrian Era
▶ The Paleozoic Era

Section 17-4   Middle and Recent Earth History
▶ The Mesozoic Era
▶ The Cenozoic Era

Previewing Science Skills

▶ In the Skill Builders, you will recognize cause and effect, make and use tables, and sequence events.
▶ In the Activities, you will measure in SI, hypothesize, formulate models, make mathematical calculations, and make inferences.
▶ In the MINI-Labs, you will measure in SI and make mathematical calculations.

What's next?

In the Find Out activity, you demonstrated that some individuals are better suited to survive in a particular environment. They often survive, reproduce, and pass on their traits while other individuals do not. This is the process of evolution by natural selection, and you'll learn more about it in this chapter.

17-1 Evolution and Geologic Time

New Science Words

geologic time scale
eras
periods
epochs
organic evolution
species
natural selection

Objectives

▶ Explain how geologic time is divided into units.
▶ Relate organic evolution to divisions on the geologic time scale.
▶ Describe how plate tectonics affects organic evolution.

The Geologic Time Scale

It's a rainy day in the prairie lands of the central United States. A herd of horses is roaming toward a local stream where they can find fresh drinking water. Their large, powerful muscles easily carry them across several kilometers of open grassland. Along the way, they occasionally stop to feed on the grass.

The horses are well suited for this environment. Their hoofed feet allow them to run at great speeds to protect themselves from predators. The males use their speed and power to compete with other males for territory and mates. The teeth of the horses allow them to grind up grass.

The characteristics of the horses allow them to survive in the demanding environment in which they live. These same characteristics are what you would use to describe a horse—a large, powerful, hoofed animal with teeth made for grinding up grasses and grains.

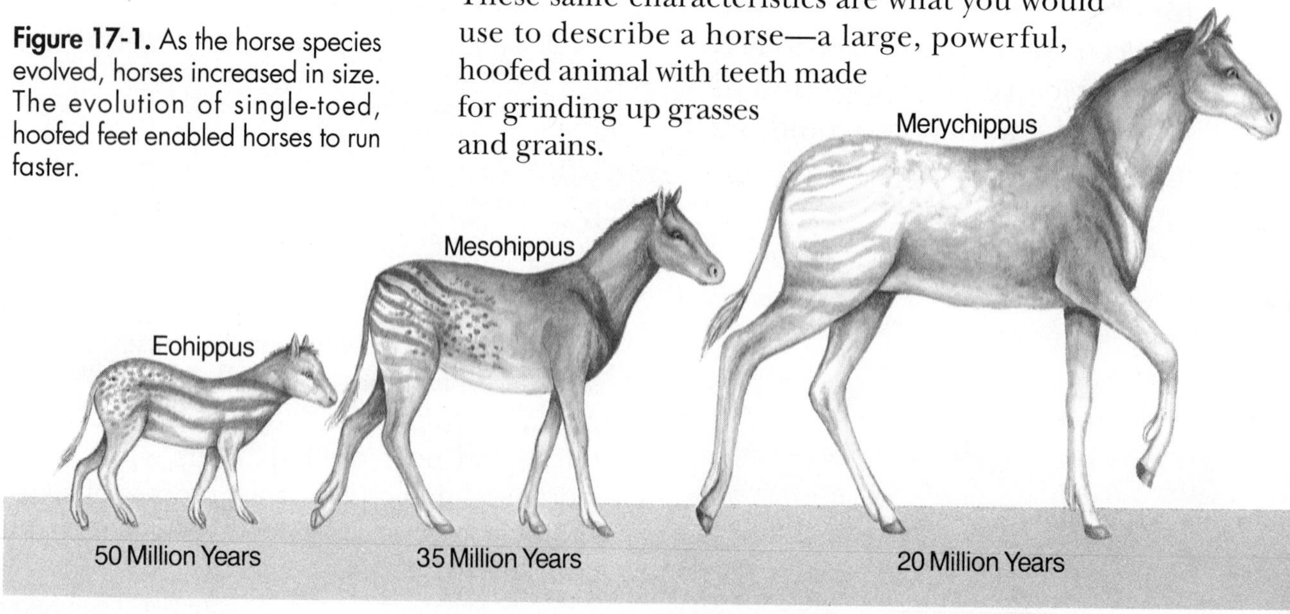

Figure 17-1. As the horse species evolved, horses increased in size. The evolution of single-toed, hoofed feet enabled horses to run faster.

Merychippus

Mesohippus

Eohippus

50 Million Years   35 Million Years   20 Million Years

Suppose you found a fossil of an animal that was the size of a dog. The animal had four toes on its front feet and three toes on its hind feet. Its teeth were sharp—well suited for eating shrubs and bushes, but not for grinding grass. Would you classify this as a fossil of a horse? In fact, it may be just that.

At one time in Earth's history, horses were small, they had several toes and no hoofs, and they had teeth much different from the teeth of today's horses. Before that time, there were no animals we would classify as horses. Before that, there weren't even mammals. If you look far back into time, there were no animals and no plants. At one point, there were only the molecules that combine to make life, but not life itself. The appearance and disappearance of types of organisms throughout Earth's history give us markers in time. We can divide up Earth's history into smaller units based on the types of life-forms living during certain periods. The division of Earth's history into smaller units makes up the **geologic time scale.** Some of the divisions in the geologic time scale are also based on geologic changes occurring at the time.

The geologic time scale is a record of Earth's history, starting with Earth's formation about 4.6 billion years ago. Each period of time is named. When fossils and rock layers are dated, scientists can assign them to a specific place on the geologic time scale. As you can see in Figure 17-2, the time scale is divided into subunits.

What are the divisions of the geologic time scale based on?

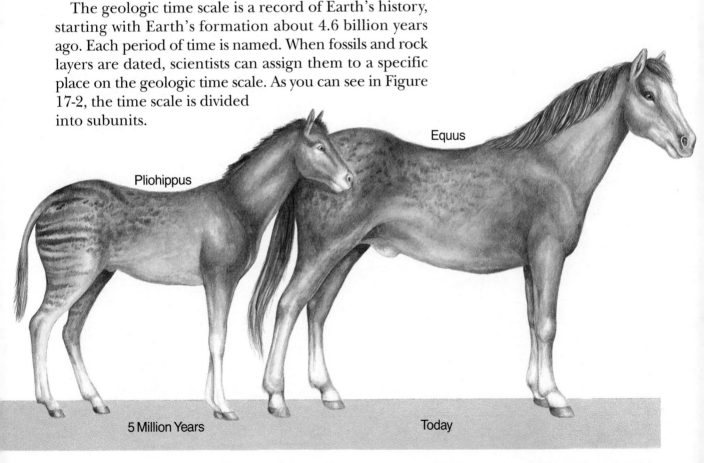

Pliohippus

Equus

5 Million Years

Today

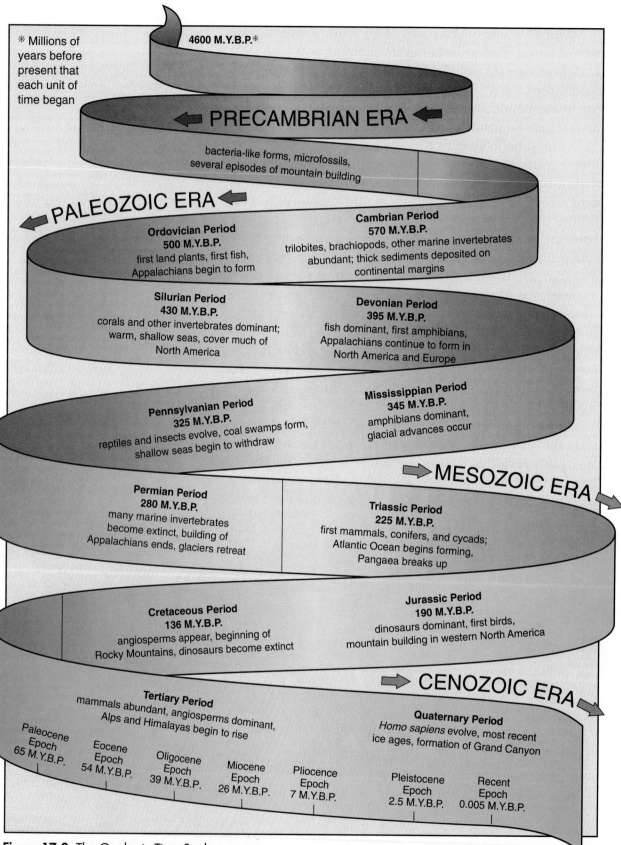

4600 M.Y.B.P.*

PRECAMBRIAN ERA

bacteria-like forms, microfossils, several episodes of mountain building

PALEOZOIC ERA

Cambrian Period
570 M.Y.B.P.
trilobites, brachiopods, other marine invertebrates abundant; thick sediments deposited on continental margins

Ordovician Period
500 M.Y.B.P.
first land plants, first fish, Appalachians begin to form

Silurian Period
430 M.Y.B.P.
corals and other invertebrates dominant; warm, shallow seas, cover much of North America

Devonian Period
395 M.Y.B.P.
fish dominant, first amphibians, Appalachians continue to form in North America and Europe

Pennsylvanian Period
325 M.Y.B.P.
reptiles and insects evolve, coal swamps form, shallow seas begin to withdraw

Mississippian Period
345 M.Y.B.P.
amphibians dominant, glacial advances occur

MESOZOIC ERA

Permian Period
280 M.Y.B.P.
many marine invertebrates become extinct, building of Appalachians ends, glaciers retreat

Triassic Period
225 M.Y.B.P.
first mammals, conifers, and cycads; Atlantic Ocean begins forming, Pangaea breaks up

Cretaceous Period
136 M.Y.B.P.
angiosperms appear, beginning of Rocky Mountains, dinosaurs become extinct

Jurassic Period
190 M.Y.B.P.
dinosaurs dominant, first birds, mountain building in western North America

CENOZOIC ERA

Tertiary Period
mammals abundant, angiosperms dominant, Alps and Himalayas begin to rise

Quaternary Period
Homo sapiens evolve, most recent ice ages, formation of Grand Canyon

Paleocene Epoch
65 M.Y.B.P.

Eocene Epoch
54 M.Y.B.P.

Oligocene Epoch
39 M.Y.B.P.

Miocene Epoch
26 M.Y.B.P.

Pliocence Epoch
7 M.Y.B.P.

Pleistocene Epoch
2.5 M.Y.B.P.

Recent Epoch
0.005 M.Y.B.P.

Figure 17-2. The Geologic Time Scale

There are three types of subdivisions of geologic time—eras, periods, and epochs. **Eras** are the major subdivision of the geologic time scale. As you can see, the Mesozoic Era began about 225 million years ago and ended with the extinction of the dinosaurs and other organisms about 65 million years ago.

Eras are subdivided into **periods.** Periods are based on the types of life existing at the time and on geologic events, such as mountain building and plate movements, occurring at the time.

Periods may be divided into smaller units of time called **epochs.** Figure 17-2 shows that only the Cenozoic Era is broken into epochs. Why would this be true? The fossil record and geologic history is more complete in recent rock layers. As a result, geologists have more markers to divide the time with.

Which periods make up the Paleozoic Era?

Organic Evolution

Based on the fossil record, organisms appear to have followed an ordered series of changes. This gradual change in life-forms through time is known as **organic evolution.** Most theories describing the processes of organic evolution state that changes in the environment result in changes in species of organisms.

A **species** is a group of organisms that normally reproduce only among themselves. For example, dogs are a species of animals because they mate and reproduce only with other dogs. Within one species, individual organisms possess certain traits that give them a better chance to survive.

Figure 17-3. In some cases, animals of different species can breed and produce offspring. A horse (a) and a donkey (c) can produce a mule (b). Mules possess characteristics of both horses and donkeys, making them desirable work animals. Mules are sterile—they can't reproduce.

a

b

c

Figure 17-4. Before pollution darkened tree bark, light-colored members of the peppered moth species were abundant. Their light color hid them from birds in search of a meal. When pollution covered the trees, the dark members of the species began to survive and reproduce more often than the lighter members. The evolution of the peppered moths demonstrates how nature selects for certain characteristics.

Evolution within a Species

Suppose a species of bird exists on an island. A few of the individuals have a very hard beak, but most have soft beaks. Now suppose most of the food the birds rely on has a hard shell around it. Which of the birds will be better suited, or more fit, to survive? The birds with the harder beaks will be better able to break the hard shell on the food and, therefore, have an advantage over the soft-beaked individuals in the species. Some of the soft-beaked birds may die from lack of food. The hard-beaked birds have a better chance of surviving and producing offspring. Their offspring will inherit the trait of having a hard beak. Gradually the number of hard-beaked birds becomes greater, and the number of soft-beaked birds decreases. The species has evolved so that nearly all of its members have hard beaks.

Because the selection of the hard-beaked birds was a natural process, this process is called natural selection. Charles Darwin, a naturalist who sailed around the world to study wildlife, developed the theory of evolution by natural selection. He proposed that **natural selection** is the process by which organisms with traits that are suited to a certain environment have a better chance of survival than organisms whose traits are not suited to it.

Notice in the example of the birds that individual soft-beaked birds didn't change into hard-beaked birds. A species only evolves a new trait if some members already possess that trait. If no bird in the species had possessed a hard beak, the species would not have been able to evolve into a species of hard-beaked birds. The birds may have been able to survive, if they could find soft food to eat, or they may have died out completely.

Embryology

Evidence for evolution has come from studying the embryos of organisms of different species. It's difficult to tell the difference between the embryos of a reptile (left) and a human (right) just by looking at them. The embryos of each of these animals have tails and gill pouches during periods in their development. In fact, at some point during their growth, both of these embryos develop many features that are found in adult fish. Why are fishlike features present in the embryos of reptiles, mammals, and birds?

Because reptiles, mammals, and birds evolved from early fish, they go through the same basic development as fish. As the embryos of these animals develop, they undergo the pattern of changes that their fish ancestors underwent. As they continue to develop, they undergo the changes that have evolved in their species.

By studying the similarities between the embryos of different species, we have discovered clues about which species are most closely related. Those species with similar embryo development probably shared a common ancestor in relatively recent geologic history.

Think Critically: Humans didn't evolve from dinosaurs, yet a human embryo would probably have several features and developmental patterns in common with a dinosaur embryo. Explain why this would be the case.

The Evolution of New Species

Natural selection explains not only how characteristics develop within a species, but also how new species arise. For example, if the soft-beaked birds in our example would have moved to a different part of the island where soft food was available, they may have survived. The soft-beaked birds would continue to reproduce apart from the hard-beaked birds on a different part of the island. Over time, the soft-beaked birds would develop characteristics that were different from those of the hard-beaked birds. At some point, the birds would no longer be breeding with each other. They would have evolved into two different species.

Think again of the horses discussed at the beginning of this section. Why did they change over time? You have learned that fossil evidence shows that early horses were small, multi-toed animals adapted to grazing on shrubs and bushes. As environments on Earth changed from brushy fields to open grasslands, the horse species became bigger and developed hoofs and complex molars. Over millions of years, horses became adapted to open grasslands by the process of natural selection. As the environment changed, the horse species adapted and survived.

Many species that lived on Earth during its long history couldn't adapt to changing environments. Such species became extinct. What processes on Earth could cause environments to change so much that species must adapt or become extinct?

Figure 17-5. These ten species of finches on Isle Santa Cruz in the Galapagos archipelago evolved from one ancestral species. Small groups of the ancestral species became isolated when they began to specialize in the types of food they ate. These groups eventually evolved into different species.

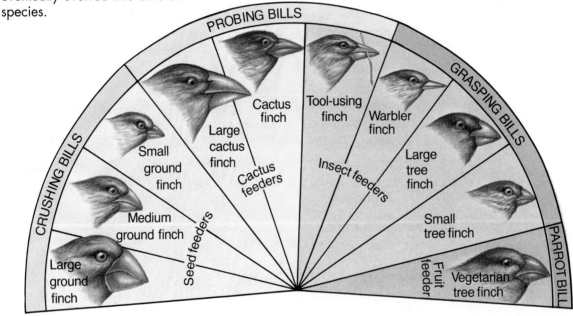

The Effect of Plate Tectonics on Earth History

Plate tectonics is one process that causes changing environments on Earth. As plates on Earth's surface move about, continents collide with and separate from each other many times. Collisions cause mountain building and the draining of seas. Separations cause deeper seas to develop between continents. This rearranging of land and sea causes changes in climates. How might these changes affect organisms?

If species adapt to the changes, or evolve, they survive. If a species doesn't have individuals with characteristics needed to survive in the changing environment, the species becomes extinct. Look again at Figure 17-2. Note that during the Silurian Period, warm, shallow seas covered much of North America. Corals, which are sea animals, were a dominant life-form on Earth. But as plate tectonic processes changed Earth's surface, climates also changed. Glaciers started to form during the Permian Period. Some species of corals weren't able to adapt to the cooler climate. Thus, corals became less and less abundant. Certain other sea creatures, like the trilobites, couldn't adapt to the changes and eventually became extinct.

Figure 17-6. During the Silurian Period, most of North America was covered by warm, shallow seas. Coral thrived in this environment.

SECTION REVIEW

1. What are the types of subdivisions of geologic time?
2. What is organic evolution?
3. How does organic evolution relate to the geologic time scale?
4. How does plate tectonics affect organic evolution?
5. **Apply:** Today, the peppered moth species shown in Figure 17-4 has many light-colored individuals. How can this be attributed to recent anti-pollution laws?

☑ Recognizing Cause and Effect

Skill Builder

Answer the questions below. If you need help, refer to Recognizing Cause and Effect in the **Skill Handbook** on page 683.

1. If there had been no horses with fewer than three toes, could the species have evolved into a single-toed, hoofed species? Explain.
2. Is natural selection a cause or effect of organic evolution?
3. How could the evolution of a trait within one species affect the evolution of a trait within another species? Give an example.

17-2 Present-Day Rapid Extinctions

New Science Words

endangered
habitat

Objectives

▶ Recognize how humans have caused extinctions.
▶ Predict what might happen to the diversity of life on Earth if land is developed without protection of natural habitats.
▶ Decide what can be done to stop or slow down the rate of species extinction.

Can Humans Slow the Rate of Extinctions?

For years you've watched and listened to a beautiful species of bird near your home. Now you learn that a new mall is to be built just down the road. The birds live in the trees that need to be cut down to make room for the mall. The mall is important to the community's economy, but the birds are important to the community's environment. What can be done to allow the economic development without destroying the area where the birds live?

You've learned that extinctions have occurred throughout Earth history. They were caused by changes in environments or competition with other species for resources. Some of these extinctions may have been caused by the appearance of early humans. Present-day humans are causing extinctions at a much greater rate.

How do humans cause extinctions? When humans kill organisms faster than they can reproduce, the number of members in their species decreases. Such species can become endangered. A species becomes **endangered** when only a small number of its members are living. If the number of members of a species continues to dwindle, the species can become extinct. A species becomes extinct when no more of its members are living. Once a species is extinct, it will never again exist on our planet.

Humans cause extinctions by hunting, carelessness, and by making changes in the environment. Often, we take over the natural habitats of other species, leaving

Figure 17-7. The dodo bird became extinct approximately 300 years ago.

them with no food or space in which to live. Pollution also causes extinctions.

You may have heard about problems caused by the cutting or burning of tropical rain forests. During the past decade, people have cleared much of these forests for farming, logging, and other industries. In doing so, many habitats have been destroyed. A **habitat** is where organisms live, grow, and interact with each other and with the environment. Many species on Earth can live in only one type of habitat. If the habitat is destroyed, so are all members of the species.

The tropical rain forest habitat covers only about seven percent of Earth's surface, but contains 50 to 80 percent of Earth's species. Think of what would happen to these species if the tropical rain forests were destroyed. Nearly all would become extinct.

Several possible solutions have been proposed to slow the rate of extinctions. Governments could restrict construction to allow both development and preservation. Projects could be planned so that habitats are disturbed as little as possible. When clearing land, some could be left in its natural state.

Figure 17-8. This African mountain gorilla makes its home in Rwanda. However, the expansion of human settlements into the habitat of mountain gorillas has led to their endangerment.

SECTION REVIEW

1. List three ways humans cause extinctions.
2. How does developing land reduce the diversity of life on Earth?
3. How might humans work to slow the rate of present-day extinctions?
4. Why is the loss of rain forest habitats of great concern to environmentalists?

You Decide!

Many of the medicines and other products used by people come from organisms. In some cases, the substances in these products are produced in only one species of organism. Some people fear that by causing the disappearance of species before we have even discovered their existence, we will miss opportunities to invent new medicines that could be derived from the organisms. Do you think this is a good enough reason to restrict development so that species aren't eliminated? Are there other reasons to prevent extinctions?

ACTIVITY 17-1
Evolution within a Species

Problem: *How does a trait evolve within a species?*

Materials
- Deck of playing cards

Procedure
1. Remove all of the Kings, Queens, Jacks, and Aces from a deck of playing cards.
2. Each remaining playing card represents an individual in a population of animals called "varimals." The number on each card represents the height of the individual. For example, the "5 of diamonds" is a varimal that's 5 units tall.
3. Calculate the average height of the population of varimals represented by your cards.
4. Suppose varimals eat grass, shrubs, and leaves from trees. A drought causes many of these plants to die. All that's left are a few tall trees. Only varimals at least 6 units tall can reach the leaves on these trees.
5. All the varimals under 6 units leave the area to seek food elsewhere or die from starvation. Discard all of the cards with a number value less than 6. Calculate the new average height of the population of varimals.
6. Shuffle the deck of remaining cards.
7. Draw two cards at a time. Each pair represents a pair of varimals that will mate and produce offspring.
8. The offspring of each pair reaches a height equal to the average height of his or her parents. Calculate and record the height of each offspring.
9. Now suppose all the varimals under 8 units tall die or migrate because of another shortage of food. Discard all of the parents that are under 8 units tall. On your data table, mark out all of the offspring under 8 units tall.

10. Calculate the new average height of varimals. Include both the parents and offspring in your calculation.

Analyze
1. How did the average height of the population change over time?
2. If you hadn't discarded the shortest varimals in Step 5, would the average height of the population have changed as dramatically? Explain.
3. What trait was selected for in this activity?

Conclude and Apply
4. Why didn't every member of the original population reproduce?
5. If there had been no varimals over 6 units tall in Step 5, what would have happened to the population?
6. Did any individual varimal increase in height because of natural selection? Explain.
7. If there had been no variation in height in the population before the droughts occurred, would the species have been able to evolve into a taller species than it started as?
8. How does this activity demonstrate that traits evolve in species?

Early Earth History

Objectives

▶ Identify dominant life-forms in the Precambrian and Paleozoic Eras.

▶ Draw conclusions about how organisms adapted to changing environments in the Precambrian and Paleozoic Eras.

▶ Describe changes in Earth and its life-forms at the end of the Paleozoic Era.

New Science Words

Precambrian Era
cyanobacteria
Paleozoic Era
amphibians
reptiles

The Precambrian Era

Look again at Figure 17-2. Which part of Earth's history is the longest? The **Precambrian** (pree KAM bree un) **Era** makes up about 90 percent of Earth's history. This time lasted from 4.6 billion to about 570 million years ago. Although the Precambrian Era is the longest unit of geologic time, relatively little is known about Earth and the organisms that lived during this time. Why is the fossil record from the Precambrian Era so sparse?

Precambrian rocks have been deeply buried and changed by heat and pressure. They have also been eroded more than more recent rocks. These changes affect

Figure 17-9. Lightning or the sun may have provided the energy necessary to build amino acids out of the simple compounds in Earth's Precambrian atmosphere. Amino acids are the "building blocks of life." These amino acids reacted with each other and combined to form the compounds from which life evolved.

not only the rocks but the fossil record as well. Most fossils can't withstand the metamorphic and erosional processes that Precambrian rocks have experienced.

It wasn't until fossilized cyanobacteria, called stromatolites, were found that scientists could begin to unravel Earth's complex history. **Cyanobacteria** are bacteria thought to be one of the earliest forms of life on Earth. Cyanobacteria first appeared on Earth about 3.5 billion years ago. As these organisms evolved, they helped to change Earth's atmosphere. During the few billion years following the appearance of cyanobacteria, oxygen became a major gas in Earth's atmosphere. The ozone layer in the stratosphere also began to develop, shielding Earth from ultraviolet rays. These major changes in the air allowed species of single-celled organisms to evolve into more complex organisms.

What role did cyanobacteria play in the evolution of Earth's atmosphere?

Figure 17-10. Cyanobacteria produce mound-shaped layers of calcium carbonate called *stromatolites.* Stromatolites were common about 2.8 billion years ago and are still being formed by some cyanobacteria today.

Animals without backbones, called invertebrates, developed near the end of the Precambrian. Imprints of jellyfish and marine worms have been found in late Precambrian rocks. Because invertebrates were soft, they weren't easily preserved as fossils. This is another reason the Precambrian fossil record is so sparse.

The Paleozoic Era

In Chapter 16, you discovered that fossils are more likely to form if organisms have hard parts. When organisms developed hard parts, the **Paleozoic** (pay lee uh ZOH ihk) **Era** began. Fossils were more easily preserved.

Figure 17-11. This model recreates a Paleozoic sea. Trilobites, brachiopods, mollusks, and other organisms were common marine animals of the time.

The Paleozoic Era, or era of ancient life, began about 570 million years ago. Warm, shallow seas covered much of Earth's surface during early Paleozoic time. Because of this, most of the life-forms were marine, meaning they lived in the ocean. Trilobites (TRI luh bites) were very common. Brachiopods (BRAY kee uh pahdz) and crinoids (KRI noyds), which still exist today, were also very common. Although these animals may not be familiar to you, one type of animal you are familiar with—the fish—also evolved during this era.

The Paleozoic Era is broken into seven periods. The beginning of the Ordovician Period is marked by the beginning of the Appalachian Mountain building process. This was probably caused by the collision of the Eurasian or African continental plate with the North American Plate.

The first vertebrates, animals with backbones, developed during the Ordovician Period. Plant life moved from the oceans onto land during the Silurian Period. Fish became dominant in the Devonian Period. By this time plant life had developed on land, and animals began to move onto land as well.

One type of fish evolved a lung that enabled it to survive out of water. This fish had fins that allowed it to move across land. The fact that lung fish could move across the land and breathe air has led scientists to theorize that lung fish evolved into amphibians (am FIHB ee unz). **Amphibians** live on land and breathe air, but must return to water to reproduce. Their eggs must be kept moist in water. They first appeared during the Devonian Period and became the dominant form of vertebrate life on land by the Mississippian Period.

MINI-Lab

How can fossils be used to date rock layers?

Suppose you find a layer of sedimentary rocks containing fossils. You number the layers 1 through 5, from bottom to top. The bottom layer, layer 1, contains fossils C and A. Layer 2 contains fossils A, B, and C. Layer 3 contains fossils A, B, and D. Layer 4 contains fossils B and D. The top layer, layer 5, contains only fossil D. You know the geologic periods during which each type of organism producing the fossils lived. Fossil A lived from the Cambrian through the Devonian Periods. Fossil B lived from the Ordovician through the Pennsylvanian. Fossil C lived from the Cambrian through the Ordovician. Fossil D lived from the Devonian through the Permian. Construct illustrations to help you determine the ages of each rock layer. It's possible to date only two of the layers to one specific period. Which layers are they? Why isn't it possible to determine during which specific period the other layers formed? What is the age or possible ages of each layer?

Paleozoic Puzzle

Neila enjoyed finding and collecting fossils. She had investigated many of the rock outcrops in her city and had begun an

excellent collection of local fossil types. Her favorite fossil was a particular species of brachiopod known as a *Mucrospirifer*. She identified her fossil using pictures and descriptions from a book on Paleozoic fossils.

While on a trip with her family to visit relatives in another state, Neila found what seemed like the same type of *Mucrospirifer* fossil in a rock formation on her aunt's farm. **Think Critically:** What could Neila say about the rocks in which she found both fossils?

EcoTip

Oil forms from the decay of dead plant material. It takes millions of years for it to form. All the oil we use today formed during the time of the dinosaurs. Because oil is a nonrenewable resource, we need to conserve it. Call a garage in your area to find out how you can recycle used motor oil.

Over time, one species of amphibian evolved an egg with a membrane that protected it from drying out. Because of this, the species no longer needed to return to water to reproduce. By the Pennsylvanian Period, some species of amphibians had evolved into reptiles. **Reptiles** do not need to return to water to reproduce. They have a skin composed of hard scales that prevent loss of body fluids. Their skin enables them to survive farther from water. They can survive in the relatively dry climates where amphibians cannot.

Many of the coal deposits mined today in the United States began forming during the Pennsylvanian Period. Inland seas were cut off from the oceans. Swamps similar to those found in the Florida Everglades formed. When the swamp vegetation died, it was deposited in layers and quickly buried. This material later changed to the coal beds of today.

Mass extinctions of many land and sea animals occurred to signal the end of the Paleozoic Era. The cause of these extinctions may have been changes in the environment caused by plate tectonics. Near the end of the Permian Period, all continental plates came together to form the single landmass Pangaea.

Figure 17-12. Reptile egg shells prevent developing embryos from drying out. Unlike frogs, salamanders, and other amphibians, reptiles can lay their eggs on land. This allows them to survive in relatively dry environments.

The slow, gradual collision of continental plates caused mountain building. Mountain building processes caused seas to drain away, and interior deserts spread over much of the United States and parts of Europe. Climates changed from mild and warm to cold and dry. The areas of oceans and landmasses changed. Many species, especially sea creatures, weren't able to adapt to these and other changes and became extinct.

Why did many sea creatures become extinct at the end of the Permian Period?

SECTION REVIEW

1. What major change in life-forms occurred to separate Precambrian time from Paleozoic time?
2. What geologic events occurred at the end of the Paleozoic Era?
3. **Apply:** How might geologic events at the end of the Paleozoic Era have caused the mass extinctions that occurred?

☑ Making and Using Tables

Skill Builder

Use Figure 17-2 to answer these questions about the Paleozoic Era. If you need help, refer to Making and Using Tables in the **Skill Handbook** on page 690.
  1. When did the Paleozoic Era begin? When did it end?
  2. How long did the Silurian Period last?
  3. When did the Appalachian Mountains start to form?
  4. When did the first insects appear on Earth?

Middle and Recent Earth History

New Science Words

Mesozoic Era
Cenozoic Era

Objectives

▶ Compare and contrast dominant life-forms in the Mesozoic and Cenozoic Eras.
▶ Explain how changes caused by plate tectonics affected the evolution of life during the Mesozoic Era.
▶ Identify when humans first appeared on Earth.

The Mesozoic Era

Some of the most distinctive life-forms ever to live on Earth evolved during the Mesozoic Era. One group of organisms you're familiar with—the dinosaurs—appeared during this geologic era.

The **Mesozoic** (mez uh ZOH ihk) **Era,** or era of middle life, began about 225 million years ago. At the beginning of the Mesozoic Era, all continents were joined as a single landmass. Recall from Chapter 13 that this landmass was called Pangaea. Pangaea separated into two large landmasses during the Triassic Period. The northern mass was *Laurasia,* and *Gondwanaland* was in the south. As the Mesozoic Era continued, *Laurasia* and *Gondwanaland* broke up and formed the present-day continents.

Species that survived the mass extinctions of the Paleozoic Era adapted to new environments. Recall that the hard scales of a reptile's skin help to retain body fluids. This trait, along with the hard shell of their eggs, enabled them to readily adapt to the drier climate of the Mesozoic Era. They became the dominant animal life-form in the Jurassic Period. Some reptiles evolved into dinosaurs.

Figure 17-13. Fossil evidence suggests that some dinosaurs, such as *Maiasaura* and *Protoceratops* (shown above), may have nurtured their young.

Dinosaurs

What were the dinosaurs like? Dinosaurs ranged in height from less than one meter to enormous creatures like *Apatosaurus* and *Tyrannosaurus*. One species of tyrannosaur stood as tall as a two-story building. Some dinosaurs ate meat, whereas others ate only plants.

The first small dinosaurs appeared during the Triassic Period. Larger species of dinosaurs appeared during the Jurassic and Cretaceous Periods. Throughout the Mesozoic Era, new species of dinosaurs evolved as other species became extinct.

Recent studies indicate that dinosaurs may not have been cold-blooded like present-day reptiles. Tracks left in the mud by reptiles are usually close together. This indicates that reptiles generally moved very slowly. Dinosaur tracks have been found that indicate a much faster speed than that of most cold-blooded reptiles. This faster speed would be expected of warm-blooded animals. They need the faster speed to be successful in hunting. *Orodromeus* was three meters long and could reach speeds of 30 km/h.

The fossil record indicates that some dinosaurs nurtured their young and traveled in herds with adults surrounding the young. One such dinosaur is *Maiasaura*. This dinosaur built nests in which it laid its eggs and raised the offspring. Nests have been found in clusters, indicating that more than one family of dinosaurs built in the same area. Some fossils have been found of hatchlings located very close to the adult animal. This has led

What evidence is there that some dinosaurs nurtured their young?

some scientists to hypothesize that some dinosaurs nurtured their young. In fact, *Maiasaura* hatchlings may have stayed in the nest while they grew in length from about 35 cm to more than one meter.

Other evidence that leads scientists to think that dinosaurs may have been warm-blooded has to do with their bone structure. The bones of cold-blooded animals exhibit rings similar to growth rings in trees. The bones of dinosaurs don't show this ring structure. Instead, they are similar to bones found in birds and mammals. These observations indicate that dinosaurs may have been warm-blooded, fast-moving, nurturing animals somewhat like present-day mammals and birds. They might have been quite different from present-day reptiles.

Figure 17-14. Fossils of *Archaeopteryx* about 150 million years old show both birdlike features, such as feathers, and dinosaur-like features, such as claws and teeth.

During which era and period did mammals evolve?

Birds

The first birds appeared during the Jurassic Period of the Mesozoic Era. You've learned that the fossil record shows how some traits of the dinosaurs are similar to present-day birds. Scientists think that birds evolved from dinosaurs. The animal *Archaeopteryx* had wings and feathers like a bird, but teeth and claws like a meat-eating dinosaur. It was an ancestor of the birds. Whether it should be classified as a bird or a dinosaur is debatable.

Mammals

Mammals first appeared in the Triassic Period. Mammals are warm-blooded vertebrates that have hair or fur covering their bodies. The females produce milk to feed their young. These traits enabled mammals to survive in many changing environments.

Angiosperms

During the Cretaceous Period, seas moved inland and species of plants, animals, and other organisms continued to adapt to new environments. Gymnosperms (JIHM nuh spurmz), which first appeared in the Paleozoic Era, continued to adapt to their changing environment. Gymnosperms are called naked seed plants because they have no fruit covering their seeds. Pines, sequoias, and ginkgos are gymnosperms.

A new classification of plant, called angiosperms (AN jee uh spurmz), evolved from existing plants. Angiosperms, or flowering plants, produce seeds with hard, outer coverings. Common angiosperms were magnolias and willows.

Many angiosperms survived while other organisms did not because their seeds had hard coatings that protected them and allowed them to develop in varied environments. Angiosperms are so adaptive, they remain the dominant land plant today. Present-day angiosperms that evolved during the Mesozoic Era include maple and oak trees.

The end of the Mesozoic Era was a time when landmasses were breaking up and seas were draining from the land. There was also increased volcanic activity. Many life-forms, including the dinosaurs, became extinct. These extinctions were caused by changing environments. What caused the environments to change is still actively investigated by scientists. As discussed in Chapter 16, one event that may have caused a drastic change was a meteorite impact at the very end of the Cretaceous Period.

MINI-Lab

How old is the Atlantic Ocean?

Geologists have measured the rate of seafloor spreading at the Mid-Atlantic Ridge at approximately 3.5 to 4.0 centimeters per year. The continents on each side of the Atlantic Ocean are moving away from each other at that rate. On a globe or world map, measure the distance in kilometers between a point near the east coast of North or South America and a corresponding point on the west coast of Europe or Africa. Making the assumption that the rate of motion listed above has been relatively constant through time, calculate how many years it took to create the present Atlantic Ocean if the continents on either side were once joined. Make several other measurements and take the average of your results. Check your predictions with the information provided to you in the geologic time scale in Figure 17-2. How close did you come to the accepted estimate for the beginning of the breakup of Pangaea?

Figure 17-15. Angiosperms and pollinating insects co-evolved. The sweet nectar produced by many flowers attracts insects in search of food. The pollen of the flower sticks to the insect, which then carries it to a new flower. There, the pollen drops off the insect and produces sperm, which fertilizes an egg in the new flower. Some angiosperms wouldn't be able to reproduce without a particular species of insect on which they rely.

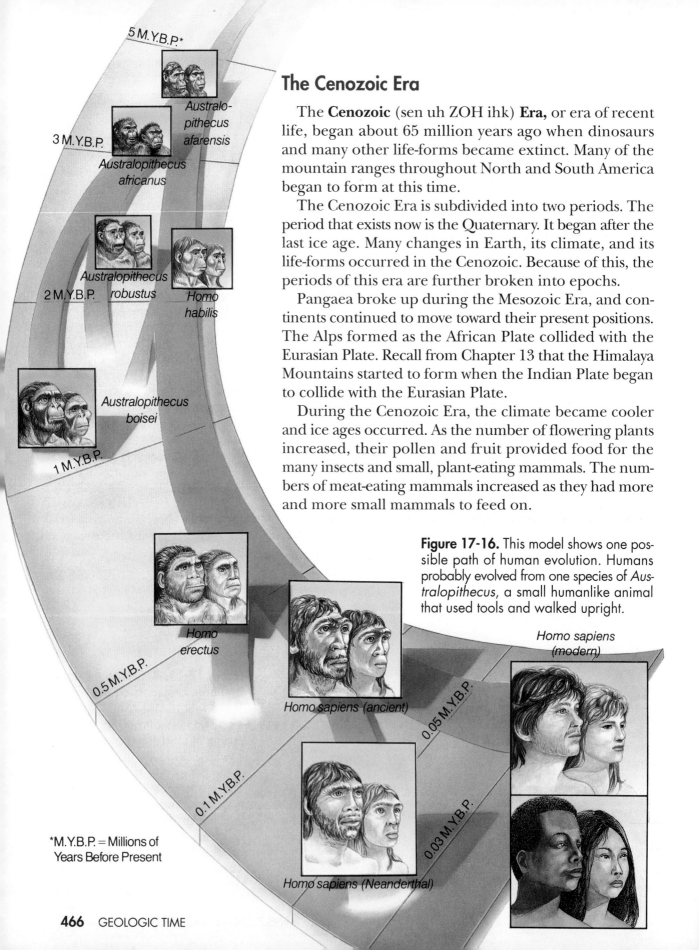

Australo-
pithecus
afarensis

3 M.Y.B.P.

Australopithecus
africanus

Australopithecus
robustus

Homo
habilis

2 M.Y.B.P.

Australopithecus
boisei

1 M.Y.B.P.

Homo
erectus

0.5 M.Y.B.P.

0.1 M.Y.B.P.

Homo sapiens (ancient)

Homo sapiens (Neanderthal)

0.05 M.Y.B.P.

0.03 M.Y.B.P.

Homo sapiens
(modern)

*M.Y.B.P. = Millions of
Years Before Present

The Cenozoic Era

The **Cenozoic** (sen uh ZOH ihk) **Era,** or era of recent life, began about 65 million years ago when dinosaurs and many other life-forms became extinct. Many of the mountain ranges throughout North and South America began to form at this time.

The Cenozoic Era is subdivided into two periods. The period that exists now is the Quaternary. It began after the last ice age. Many changes in Earth, its climate, and its life-forms occurred in the Cenozoic. Because of this, the periods of this era are further broken into epochs.

Pangaea broke up during the Mesozoic Era, and continents continued to move toward their present positions. The Alps formed as the African Plate collided with the Eurasian Plate. Recall from Chapter 13 that the Himalaya Mountains started to form when the Indian Plate began to collide with the Eurasian Plate.

During the Cenozoic Era, the climate became cooler and ice ages occurred. As the number of flowering plants increased, their pollen and fruit provided food for the many insects and small, plant-eating mammals. The numbers of meat-eating mammals increased as they had more and more small mammals to feed on.

Figure 17-16. This model shows one possible path of human evolution. Humans probably evolved from one species of *Australopithecus*, a small humanlike animal that used tools and walked upright.

Mammals evolved into larger life-forms. Recall how horses have evolved from small, multi-toed animals into the much larger, hoofed animals of today. Not all mammals remained on land. Ancestors of the present-day whales and dolphins began to make their lives in the sea.

As Australia and South America separated from Antarctica, many life-forms became isolated. They evolved separately from life-forms in other parts of the world. Evidence of this can be seen today with the dominance of marsupials (mar SEW pee ulz) in Australia. Marsupials are mammals that carry their young in a pouch. Kangaroos, wallabies, wombats, and koalas are marsupials that exist only in Australia.

Our species, *Homo sapiens*, probably appeared about 500 000 years ago, but became a dominant land animal only about 10 000 years ago. As the climate remained cool and dry, many larger mammals became extinct. Some scientists think the appearance of humans may have led to the extinction of other mammals. As their numbers grew, humans competed for food that other animals relied on. Also, fossil records indicate early humans were hunters. They may have hunted some animals, such as the woolly mammoth, into extinction.

SECTION REVIEW

1. In which era, period, and epoch did *Homo sapiens* first appear? According to Figure 17-16, which human ancestor existed 5 million years ago?
2. Did mammals become more or less abundant after the extinction of the dinosaurs? Why do you think this is the case?
3. What characteristic of angiosperms allowed them to adapt to changing environments?
4. **Apply:** Why are the periods of only the Cenozoic Era divided into epochs?

⊠ Sequencing

Arrange these organisms in sequence according to when they first appeared on Earth: *mammals, reptiles, dinosaurs, fish, angiosperms, birds, insects, amphibians, first land plants,* and *bacteria.* If you need help, refer to Sequencing in the **Skill Handbook** on page 680.

Skill Builder

ACTIVITY 17-2
Geologic Time Line

Problem: *How is an absolute time line constructed?*

Materials

- adding machine tape
- meterstick
- pencil
- scissors

Procedure

1. Using a scale of 1 millimeter equals 1 million years (1 mm = 1 000 000 years), measure and cut a piece of adding machine tape equal to the approximate age of Earth (4.6 billion years).
2. Mark one end of the tape "today" and the other end "4.6 billion years."
3. Using the table shown as a reference, measure and mark the places on the tape that represent the time when each era began.
4. Examine the events and ages listed in the data table. Measuring carefully, include each event on your adding machine tape in the proper place in time. Note that the dates are provided in years B.P. (before present).

Analyze

1. Which events were most difficult to plot?
2. How does the existence of humans on Earth compare with the duration of geologic time?
3. Approximately what percent of geologic time occurred during the Precambrian?

Conclude and Apply

4. Form a hypothesis as to why more is known about recent history than about the Precambrian. How could you test this hypothesis?
5. What can be determined from your time line about the rate at which events have occurred on Earth's surface? Does this rate reflect what has actually happened on Earth? Explain.

Data and Observations

Earth History Events	
Event	**Years B.P.**
1. today	0
2. astronauts land on moon	25
3. American Civil War	135
4. Columbus lands in America	500
5. Pompeii destroyed	1 900
6. Eratosthenes calculates Earth's circumference	2 100
7. continental ice retreats from North America	10 000
8. beginning of most recent ice age	1 million
9. early human ancestors	5 million
10. first elephants	40 million
11. first horse	50 million
12. dinosaurs become extinct; beginning of Paleocene	65 million
13. Rocky Mountains begin to rise	80 million
14. beginning of Cretaceous	136 million
15. first birds	150 million
16. beginning of Jurassic	190 million
17. first mammals and dinosaurs	225 million
18. beginning of Permian	280 million
19. first reptiles	325 million
20. coal forests; Appalachians rise	330 million
21. beginning of Mississippian	345 million
22. first amphibians	390 million
23. beginning of Silurian	430 million
24. first land plants and vertebrates	480 million
25. beginning of Ordovician	500 million
26. Animals evolve hard parts	570 million
27. early sponges	600 million
28. oldest microfossils (algae)	3 300 million
29. oldest known rocks	3 800 million

CHAPTER
REVIEW

17-1: Evolution and Geologic Time

1. Geologic time is divided into eras, periods, and epochs.

2. Divisions within the geologic time scale are based on major evolutionary changes in organisms and on geologic events such as mountain building and plate movements.

3. Plate movements cause changes in Earth's climates that affect organic evolution.

17-2: Science and Society: Present-Day Rapid Extinctions

1. Humans cause extinctions primarily by eliminating natural habitats of organisms.

2. As land is developed by humans, the diversity of life on Earth is reduced.

3. Careful planning, concern for all organisms, and strict laws can help prevent extinctions.

17-3: Early Earth History

1. Cyanobacteria were an early form of life that evolved during the Precambrian Era. Trilobites, brachiopods, fish, and corals were abundant during the Paleozoic Era.

2. By the process of natural selection, bacteria evolved into higher life-forms which evolved into many marine invertebrates during the early Paleozoic. Plants and animals began to move onto land once a protective ozone layer had been established.

3. During the Paleozoic Era, glaciers advanced, and seas withdrew from the continents. Many marine invertebrates became extinct.

17-4: Middle and Recent Earth History

1. Reptiles and gymnosperms were dominant land life-forms in the Mesozoic Era. Mammals and angiosperms began to dominate the land in the Cenozoic.

2. Changes caused by plate tectonics affect the evolution of life.

3. *Homo sapiens* evolved during the Pleistocene.

KEY SCIENCE WORDS

a. **amphibians**
b. **Cenozoic Era**
c. **cyanobacteria**
d. **endangered**
e. **epochs**
f. **eras**
g. **geologic time scale**
h. **habitat**
i. **Mesozoic Era**
j. **natural selection**
k. **organic evolution**
l. **Paleozoic Era**
m. **periods**
n. **Precambrian Era**
o. **reptiles**
p. **species**

UNDERSTANDING VOCABULARY

Match each phrase with the correct term from the list of Key Science Words.

1. change in the hereditary features of a species over a long period of time
2. record of events in Earth history
3. largest divisions of geologic time
4. geologic era with weakest fossil record
5. process by which the best-suited individuals survive in their environment
6. evolved directly from amphibians
7. group of individuals that normally breed only among themselves
8. the geologic era in which we live
9. a species in which only a relatively small number of members exists
10. a place where organisms live and grow

CHAPTER
REVIEW

CHECKING CONCEPTS

Choose the word or phrase that completes the sentence.

1. The era in which you live began about _____ million years ago.
   - **a.** 650
   - **b.** 225
   - **c.** 2.5
   - **d.** 65

2. Process by which better suited organisms survive and reproduce is called _____.
   - **a.** endangerment
   - **b.** extinction
   - **c.** gymnosperm
   - **d.** none of these

3. The next smaller division of geologic time after the era is a(n) _____.
   - **a.** period
   - **b.** era
   - **c.** epoch
   - **d.** none of these

4. Plate movement can affect _____.
   - **a.** geography
   - **b.** organisms
   - **c.** climate
   - **d.** all of these

5. One of the earliest forms of life on Earth was the _____.
   - **a.** gymnosperm
   - **b.** cyanobacterium
   - **c.** angiosperm
   - **d.** dinosaur

6. Amphibians evolved from _____.
   - **a.** reptiles
   - **b.** fish
   - **c.** angiosperms
   - **d.** gymnosperms

7. Dinosaurs lived during the _____ Era.
   - **a.** Mesozoic
   - **b.** Paleozoic
   - **c.** Precambrian
   - **d.** Cenozoic

8. _____ have seeds without protective coverings.
   - **a.** Angiosperms
   - **b.** Flowering plants
   - **c.** Gymnosperms
   - **d.** All of these

9. _____ evolved to become the dominant land plant during the Cenozoic Era.
   - **a.** Gymnosperms
   - **b.** Angiosperms
   - **c.** Ginkgos
   - **d.** Algae

10. A key factor in preserving many species is _____.
    - **a.** poaching
    - **b.** law enforcement
    - **c.** construction
    - **d.** changing habitats

UNDERSTANDING CONCEPTS

Complete each sentence.

11. New _____ evolve from common ancestors.

12. The beginning of the _____ Period was marked by the most recent ice age.

13. The direct ancestors of birds may have been the _____.

14. Our species, _____, may have hunted woolly mammoths into extinction.

15. Some species of elephants are illegally hunted, making them a(n) _____ species.

THINK AND WRITE CRITICALLY

16. How is natural selection related to evolution?
17. Briefly describe the major geologic and biological changes that took place during the Paleozoic Era.
18. Compare and contrast the traits of reptiles and amphibians.
19. Describe several causes for extinctions throughout geologic time.
20. Contrast the animal life of the Paleozoic with that of the early Cenozoic.

APPLY

21. Why couldn't plants move onto land prior to the establishment of an ozone layer?
22. Why do trilobites make excellent index fossils?
23. What is the most significant difference between Precambrian and Paleozoic life-forms?
24. How might the extinction of an edible species of plant from a tropical rain forest affect animals that live in the forest?
25. In the early 1800s, a naturalist proposed that the giraffe species has a long neck because the animals stretched their necks to reach tall tree leaves. Explain why this isn't true.

MORE SKILL BUILDERS

If you need help, refer to the Skill Handbook.

1. **Observing and Inferring:** Use the outlines of the present-day continents to make a sketch of the Mesozoic supercontinent Pangaea.
2. **Hypothesizing:** Why did trilobites become extinct at the end of the Paleozoic Era?
3. **Interpreting Data:** Benjamin found what he thought was a piece of coral in a chunk of coal. Was he right? Explain.

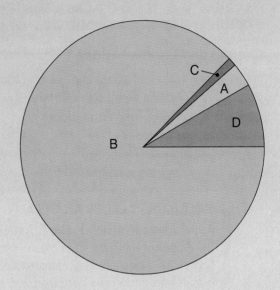

4. **Interpreting Scientific Illustrations:** The pie graph above represents geologic time. Determine which era of geologic time is represented by each portion of the graph.
5. **Interpreting Scientific Illustrations:** The Cenozoic Era has lasted 65 million years. What percentage of Earth's 4.6 billion year history is that? How many degrees on the pie graph represent the Cenozoic Era?

PROJECTS

1. Choose one of Earth's present-day continents and find out how it has changed through geologic time. Include drawings of the different geographic positions it had through time and summaries of the ancient climates, environments, and topography.
2. Research the most recent theories on mass extinctions that occurred at the end of both the Paleozoic and Mesozoic Eras. Compare and contrast the most accepted theories. Form your own hypothesis as to why the extinctions occurred. Support your position with facts.

GLOBAL CONNECTIONS

Change and Earth's History

In this unit, you studied about change and Earth's history. Now find out how Earth's history is connected to other subjects and places around the world.

120°   60°

60°

GEOLOGY

MOUNTAINS ACROSS AN OCEAN

Appalachian Mountains, North America

The Appalachian Mountains extend north-eastward into Nova Scotia and Newfoundland. They reappear on the other side of the Atlantic on the coasts of Ireland, Scotland, and Scandinavia. The relationship of the mountains on both sides of the Atlantic is established by fossils. How can fossils prove that the mountains on both sides are the same range?

30°

GEOGRAPHY

CHANGES IN ANTARCTICA

Antarctica

The most dramatic changes of any place on Earth have occurred in Antarctica. Fossils show that Antarctica once had dense forests that later became large coal deposits. Antarctica also has fossils of a mammal-like land reptile, *Lystrosaurus*. Similar fossils have been found in Africa and India. How might the fossils of *Lystrosaurus* help prove that Antarctica was once connected to Africa and India?

TROPICAL PARADISE IN THE NORTH
Scandinavian Peninsula

The climate during the late Paleozoic Era was recorded by the distribution of two fossil plants—the tropical lycopods in the north and the seed ferns in the cool, temperate south. Lycopods had scar patterns over their trunks and grew over 30 meters high. They flourished even to the northern tip of Scandinavia. The seed ferns grew as far south as Antarctica. How can scientists know what the climate was like in these places 230 million years ago?

ADAPTING TO A HIGHER LIFE
Himalayan Mountains, Tibet

Tibet, once at sea-level on the southern coast of Asia, now has a mountainous terrain. When India began colliding with Asia, the Himalayas began to rise. The animal species already present in both Asia and India had to adapt in order to colonize the mountainous territory. The snow leopard species evolved to have thicker fur and a paler color. How did a change of color help the leopard as it moved to higher land?

THE SEA THAT DISAPPEARED
Tethys Sea

The Tethys Sea began to close when Africa and India migrated northward. By 50 million years ago, the Tethys Sea was completely closed off by the Arabian Peninsula. The Saudi Arabian oil fields produce petroleum from limestone formed in the Tethys Sea during the Jurassic Period. What other countries have oil that may have formed offshore in the Tethys Sea?

Tethys Sea

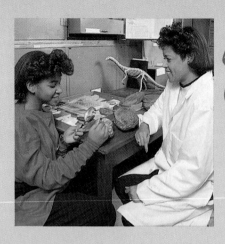

CAREERS

PALEONTOLOGIST

A *paleontologist* studies fossils to find out what kinds of organisms lived during each of the geologic periods. Fossils help paleontologists and geologists determine the age of the rocks in which the fossils are found. Paleontologists can tell from fossils whether the rocks were formed underwater or on land. From this, geologists can form a better picture of how Earth has changed.

Paleontologists usually obtain an advanced degree after college. A student wishing to become a paleontologist should study biology, earth science, and mathematics.

For Additional Information

Contact the Paleontological Society, U.S. Geological Survey, E/501 National Museum Building, Smithsonian Institution, Washington, DC 20506.

MUSEUM WORKER

A *museum worker* may perform any of several functions to keep a museum running smoothly. Since a museum is constantly acquiring new materials, a museum worker may assist the curator in placing these objects in their proper locations. He or she may also assist in preparing an exhibit or caring for the materials once they have been placed on display.

Museum workers usually receive on-the-job training after high school. A student wishing to become a museum worker should study biology and earth science.

For Additional Information

Contact the Museum of Natural History, Smithsonian Institution, Washington, DC 20506.

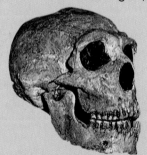

UNIT READINGS

▶Gould, Stephen Jay. *Time's Arrow Time's Cycle*. Cambridge, Massachusetts: Harvard University Press, 1987.
▶Norman, David. *The Illustrated Encyclopedia of Dinosaurs*. New York: Crescent Books, 1985.
▶Weiner, Jonathan. *Planet Earth*. New York, Bantam Books, 1986.

The Origin
A Biographical Novel of Charles Darwin

by Irving Stone

T he following passage reveals Darwin's understanding of how Earth's changing surface was linked to the evolution of living things:

He cruised the bay with Captain FitzRoy and Sulivan. When they reached Punta Alta, Darwin's attention was attracted to low cliffs about a mile in length. At the striking of his geological hammer on the lowest bed, he discovered stratified gravel.

"Captain, look what's showing through! Bones! Fossils! The first I've ever seen *in situ*. Come and help me dig them out."

The conglomerate gave easily. Soon Charles had in his hands the bones of gigantic, ancient mammifers. . . .

Punta Alta was a gold mine of ancient bones. He found the lower jaw of a large animal with a quantity of its teeth; the bones of two or three gnawing animals, bones of the extremities of some great megatherioid quadruped.

"How did these animals get trapped up here in a cliff?" Covington asked.

"They didn't. From the presence of the marine shells and the fact that there are barnacles attached to some of the bones, we can feel certain that these remains were embedded in the bottom of a shallow sea."

"And something pushed that sea bottom up in the air to become cliffs?"

"Yes. Not a volcano, there's no lava here. Probably not an earthquake either, or they might have been sucked down and disappeared. What then? I don't know. Some mysterious boiling force. I wish I had Professor Sedgwick or Charles Lyell here to tell us."

. . . Almost as welcome as the letters from his family was the package containing the second volume of Lyell's *Principles of Geology,* in which Lyell turned his attention to the changes in progress in the animate creations. Lying in his hammock in the stillness of the chart room, he read Lyell's germinal question: ". . . whether there be proofs of the successive extermination of species in the ordinary course of nature, and whether there be any reason for conjecturing that new animals and plants are created from time to time, to supply their place?"

He lay quietly thinking forward to the day when he could show Charles Lyell the fossil bones he had discovered in Punta Alta.

In Your Own Words

▶In an essay, explain how Darwin showed a reasonable knowledge of changes that occur on Earth.

7 EARTH'S RESOURCES

What's Happening Here?

Could you build a scale model of Earth? Biosphere II, located near Oracle, Arizona, is a glass-enclosed structure covering 10 000 m^2 of land. It encases a human habitat and five connected biomes. Teams of humans, living in Biosphere II, conduct research on bio-farming and recycling techniques. Biosphere II is shown in the larger photograph. Biosphere I, Earth, is shown in the smaller photograph below. As you study the chapters in this unit, you'll learn about some of the environmental problems that we face and what you can do to help save Biosphere I.

UNIT CONTENTS

18 Energy

Why is energy so important? We use energy for things we do every day, as you'll see when you do the Find Out activity below. There are many different sources of energy. One way is to use solar panels to collect the energy from the sun as shown at the left. Some solar collectors are used to heat water, while solar cells convert energy from the sun into electricity. You probably use hot water and electricity all the time and don't think about where this energy comes from.

FIND OUT!

Do this simple activity to find out how many kinds of energy you will use today.

Make a list of ten things you will do today. Examples might be eat breakfast, travel, be in school, listen to a radio, watch TV, take a bath. Beside each item, write where you think the energy comes from for doing each activity. For example, if your dinner will be cooked on a gas range, the energy comes from gas.

Gearing Up

Previewing the Chapter

Use this outline to help you focus on important ideas in this chapter.

Section 18-1   Nonrenewable Energy Sources
▶ Fossil Fuels
▶ Conserving Fossil Fuels

Section 18-2   Renewable Energy Sources and Others
▶ Renewable Energy
▶ Solar Energy
▶ Energy from Wind
▶ Energy from Water
▶ Synfuel and Biomass Fuel

Section 18-3   Science and Society Nuclear Energy
▶ Nuclear Energy
▶ Nuclear Power Accidents

Previewing Science Skills

▶ In the **Skill Builders,** you will make a concept map and hypothesize.
▶ In the **Activities,** you will observe, classify, infer, communicate, predict, and interpret data.
▶ In the **MINI-Labs,** you will learn about conservation and nuclear reactor safety.

What's next?

Now that you've thought about where the energy comes from for your everyday activities, you'll learn about different energy sources. Then you'll explore alternative sources of energy and look at where energy will come from in the future.

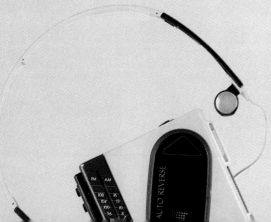

18-1 Nonrenewable Energy Sources

New Science Words

energy
fossil fuels
peat
lignite
bituminous coal
anthracite
nonrenewable energy sources

Objectives

▶ Describe the evolution of fossil fuels—coal, oil, and natural gas.
▶ Explain why fossil fuels are called nonrenewable energy sources.
▶ Discuss how you can help conserve fossil fuels.

Fossil Fuels

You learned in the Find Out activity how much you depend on energy. Our world depends on energy. **Energy** is the ability to do work. An object has energy if it is able to exert a force or move something. We use energy for heating buildings, running car engines, lighting, farming, making clothes, building roads, cooking—just about everything we do. Where do we get the energy? Right now, we get most of it from fossil fuels.

Fossil fuels include coal, oil, and natural gas. They're called fossil fuels because they actually are fossils, the remains of plants and animals that died and decayed over millions of years. We use fossil fuels to make gasoline for cars, to heat our homes, and for many other uses.

Figure 18-1. Gasoline is one product from fossil fuels we depend on.

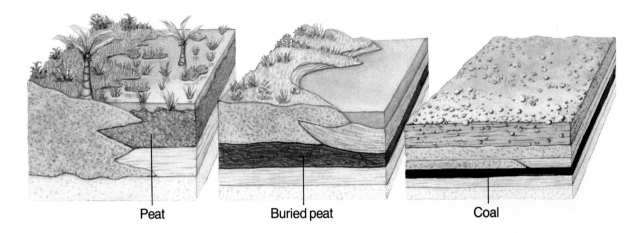

Peat   Buried peat   Coal

Coal

Coal begins forming when swamp plants die and partially decay. Plants are made up of molecules that contain atoms of carbon, hydrogen, and oxygen. Decay occurs when bacteria break apart these molecules, releasing oxygen and hydrogen gases and leaving solid carbon behind. When we burn coal, it is the carbon that releases heat.

The next step occurs when sediments begin piling up on top of the decaying plants. The mass of the sediments compresses the partially decayed plants, squeezing out the moisture. After the decaying plants become buried, coal evolves in the following stages.

The first stage is peat. **Peat** is composed of decaying twigs, leaves, and branches, but is 75 to 90 percent water. Peat is used to heat homes in some parts of the world such as the British Islands, but it is a very poor, smoky fuel that pollutes the air.

As peat becomes buried deeper under more sediment, it evolves into **lignite.** This soft brown coal has much less moisture and is about 30 percent carbon. Lignite is mined in North Dakota, South Dakota, Montana, and Germany. It's a better fuel for heating homes than peat, but is still very smoky and polluting.

As burial under sediments continues, **bituminous** (bi TOO mihn us) **coal**, or soft coal, forms. It's dense, black, brittle, and has lots of carbon, about 50 to 75 percent. It has lost all but 5 to 15 percent of its water. Bituminous coal is the coal used most often. It provides lots of heat energy when burned, but still pollutes the air. Most of it is mined in the Appalachian Mountains, the Midwest, and the Rocky Mountains of the United States, and in Europe, China, and Australia.

Figure 18-2. If peat becomes buried and compressed, coal may be formed.

Did You Know?

In one year, burning the coal to light one 100-watt light bulb for 12 hours a day creates more than 936 pounds of carbon dioxide and 7.8 pounds of sulfur dioxide.

What is the most commonly used coal?

Figure 18-3. Peat, shown at top, can eventually turn into coal.

If heat and intense pressure are applied to bituminous coal, it becomes **anthracite** (AN thruh site). Anthracite is the cleanest burning of all coals and is about 90 percent carbon. It produces less heat than bituminous coal, but industries like it because it burns cleaner and longer. It is mined mostly underground in Pennsylvania and Virginia.

Oil and Natural Gas

We burn vast quantities of oil and gas. In fact, every year we obtain twice the energy from oil and gas than we do from coal. Natural gas is used mostly for heating and cooking. Oil has many more uses.

Most oil is refined into fuels such as gasoline and air-craft fuel. Other oil is made into heating oil for furnaces, lubricants, and plastics. Did you realize that plastic is made from oil?

Both oil and natural gas form over millions of years from the decaying of tiny organisms in the ocean. The process begins when plankton organisms die, fall to the seafloor, and pile up. Later, other sediments are deposited over them, in the same way that coal is buried. They are compacted by the weight, and this pressure on the organic matter helps chemical reactions to occur. This creates the liquid we call oil, as well as gases we call natural gas.

Oil Uses

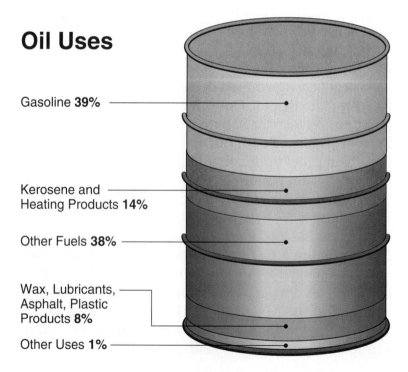

Gasoline **39%**

Kerosene and
Heating Products **14%**

Other Fuels **38%**

Wax, Lubricants,
Asphalt, Plastic
Products **8%**

Other Uses **1%**

Figure 18-4. This diagram shows what percentages of oil are used for different products. Most oil is used for fuel.

Because oil and natural gas are less dense than water, they migrate upward to get on top of water-saturated rock layers. Sometimes this movement is stopped by impermeable rock, such as shale. This rock traps the oil and gas below it. When this happens, a reservoir of oil or natural gas forms under the impermeable rock.

How do we remove oil and natural gas from these reservoirs? We drill wells down through the rocks until we reach the reservoirs. Wells are lined with pipe to keep them from caving in. Wells are often thousands of meters deep. But they are only centimeters in diameter because oil and natural gas are fluids that travel easily up the pipe to the surface.

Science and MATH

Four people living in the same neighborhood each drive 30 km roundtrip to work each day and pay $4/day to park. How much money could they each save if they car pool, assuming it costs $.15 per km to operate their cars and they work 5 days/week, 50 weeks/year?

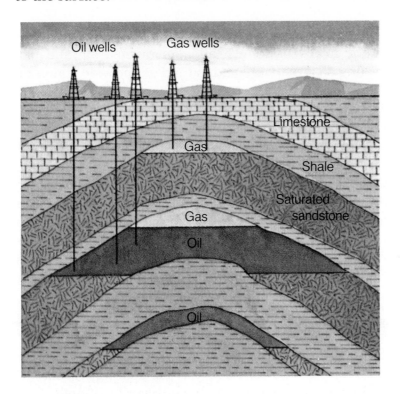

Figure 18-5. Oil and natural gas are often found together. Because gas is less dense than oil, it is found above the oil in the reservoir.

Conserving Fossil Fuels

Do you sometimes forget to turn off the lights when you walk out of a room? Many people waste energy this way. You may not realize that electricity to run our homes and industries will not always be as plentiful and cheap as it is today. Most of the energy sources we are using to generate electricity right now are nonrenewable. **Nonrenewable energy sources** are those that we are using up faster than Earth can replace them. Remember that fossil fuels take millions of years to form.

Is the majority of our current energy sources renewable or nonrenewable?

Figure 18-6. Caulking windows is one way to conserve energy.

Today, coal provides about 30 percent of worldwide energy needs for home heating, manufacturing, and generating electricity. Oil and natural gas provide almost 60 percent of our energy needs. At the rate we're burning it, we have enough to last several hundred years, but we will run out someday.

How can you conserve fossil fuels? There are many ways. Turn off lights in rooms as you leave. Do the same with TVs and radios. During cold weather, make sure doors and windows are tightly shut so heated air doesn't leak out of your home. If you have air conditioning, run it as little as possible. Ask adults in your home if more insulation could be added, or if an insulated jacket could be put on the water heater to save energy. All of these steps reduce energy used for heating and cooling.

SECTION REVIEW

1. Describe how coal evolves from plants.
2. Why are fossil fuels nonrenewable energy sources?
3. List five ways you can help conserve fossil fuels.
4. **Apply:** Why are you likely to find natural gas and oil deposits in the same location, but less likely to find coal and oil deposits at the same location?

Skill Builder

☒ **Concept Mapping**

Make a concept map that explains how peat forms. If you need help, refer to Concept Mapping in the **Skill Handbook** on pages 688 and 689.

ACTIVITY 18-1
Predicting Natural Gas Reserves

Problem: *At present rates of consumption, what will happen to the United States' known reserves of natural gas?*

Materials

- pencil
- paper

Procedure

1. Many times scientists must be able to predict outcomes. One way of predicting outcomes is to analyze trends. Trends are general movements or directions actions have taken in the past. In this activity, you will learn ways of predicting outcomes.

2. Examine the graph below. It shows the billions of cubic meters of natural gas in U.S. reserves (identified deposits) and in marketed production from 1925 to 1985.

3. Analyze the trends of both the proved reserves and marketed production to predict future outcomes based on present rates by answering the following questions.

Analyze

1. Which best describes the trend in reserves between 1925 and 1965? Between 1965 and 1985?
   a. Reserves increased.
   b. Reserves decreased.
   c. Reserves remained constant.

2. Which best describes the trend in marketed production between 1945 and 1975? Between 1975 and 1985?
   a. Marketed production increased.
   b. Marketed production decreased.
   c. It remained constant.

Conclude and Apply

3. Why do you think the U.S. gas reserves increased from 1925 to 1965, but have decreased since that time?

4. Why did marketed production increase between 1945 and 1975 and then drop?

5. In order to predict the future when examining a graph, a method called extrapolation is used. Extrapolation assumes that the slopes of the curves will not change a great deal and that the latest trend will continue. Use this method to answer the following question. If trends continue in reserves and marketed production, predict what will happen to the U.S. natural gas reserves by 1995.

6. Predict what could happen to the reserves if people really started conserving natural gas and the marketed production dropped to where it was in 1945.

Data and Observations

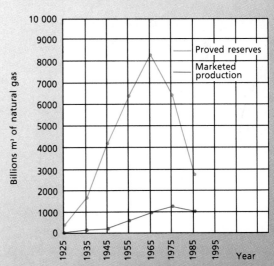

Renewable Energy Sources and Others

New Science Words

renewable energy sources
solar energy
solar cell
wind farm
hydroelectric energy
synfuel
biomass fuel

Objectives

▶ List the advantages of using solar power, wind power, and hydroelectric power.
▶ List the disadvantages of using solar power, wind power, and hydroelectric power.

Renewable Energy

Do you think we will we ever run out of fossil fuels? We will, although it will take many decades. Fortunately, we also have **renewable energy sources.** These sources are constant and will not run out in the future as coal will. Renewable energy sources include the sun, wind, water, and geothermal energy that you learned about in Chapter 15.

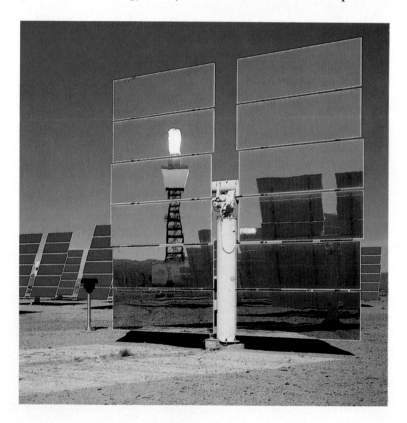

Figure 18-7. Energy from the sun can be used to make electricity.

Solar Energy

When you sit in the sun, walk into the wind, or swim against an ocean current, you are feeling the power of solar energy. As you learned in Chapters 9 and 10, the sun's energy not only heats Earth, but it causes Earth's atmosphere and oceans to circulate. Thus, we indirectly use solar energy when we use the wind and moving water to do work.

Many of the nonrenewable energy sources we use today are actually stored solar energy. Plants that formed coal grew using solar energy. Organisms that formed oil and natural gas ate plants, so they also used solar energy. When fossil fuels are burned, stored solar energy is released. These are indirect uses of solar energy.

How is oil indirectly a solar energy?

 **PROBLEM SOLVING**

Hot Spot

It was a hot summer day. Christie decided she wanted to make iced tea. She had heard that "sun tea" was really good. Her friend, Will, had told her that you use a large glass jar with a lid, tea bags, water, and the sun. She decided to make some.

She filled the jar up to the brim with water and put in four small tea bags. Then she screwed the lid tightly on the jar and placed the jar on the patio in the sun. She had forgotten to ask Will how long it took to make it, so she decided to check the jar in a half hour. At the end of the half hour, Christie found that only the top one-fourth of the jar had become tea-colored. Also, she noticed when she touched the jar that the top was warmer than the bottom. She checked it again 30 minutes later to find that the top one-half was tea-colored, but the bottom was still clear. Finally, at the end of one more hour, the whole jar was tea-colored.

Christie added ice cubes to the warm tea and drank a tall glass. As she sipped the long-awaited beverage, she was puzzled by several questions.

Think Critically: Why did only the top part of the water become tea at first? What made the tea so warm? Why was the top part of the jar warm before the bottom part?

TECHNOLOGY

Solar-Powered Plane

Researchers for NASA have designed a solar plane that is able to stay aloft for an entire year. Although the plane will have a wingspan of 98 meters and a 12-meter propeller, it will be made of lightweight wood, and thus will have a low mass.

Energy from the sun will be collected by nearly 4000 square meters of solar cells that will cover the wing tips of the plane and vertical arrays on the wings. During the day, the wing tips will swing to 90-degree angles to receive maximum solar radiation. Excess electricity produced by the cells will be channeled to a fuel cell. The fuel cell will then be used to provide electricity.

Think Critically: Study the photograph. The wing tips are at 90 degrees. Do you think the wing tips stay in this position during take-off? Explain.

Solar energy is energy from the sun. Enough energy from the sun reaches Earth in one hour to supply all the energy we need for a whole year! The problem is that we can't collect and store all this energy. We can collect part of it, though. One way of doing this is to use solar cells. A **solar cell** collects energy from the sun and transforms it into electricity. Solar energy is free and doesn't create any pollution. Solar cells were invented to generate electricity on satellites, but now they're used to power calculators, TVs, streetlights, and experimental cars.

Solar energy also is used to heat and cool homes and buildings and to heat water. One way this is done is with thermal collectors. Solar energy heats air or water inside the collectors, and then the hot air or water is piped to where the heat is needed.

Solar energy does have some disadvantages. Solar energy can be received only when the sun is shining. That means solar cells work less well on cloudy days, and they don't work at all at night. When seasons cause days to be shorter, solar cells generate less electricity. The closer a

What are two advantages of solar energy?

Figure 18-8. Technology being developed and tested in this experimental solar car will be used to improve solar energy for common use.

solar cell is to the equator, the more direct solar radiation it receives. Solar cells closer to the North Pole or the South Pole receive less solar radiation.

Where would solar energy work best, near the North Pole or near the equator?

Energy From Wind

Have you ever flown a kite on a windy day? Then you know how much energy wind can have. It lifts the kite high in the sky and whips it around.

People have long used the wind for power. As you learned in Chapter 9, one of its first uses was to power sailing ships. The Dutch have used windmills to grind corn and pump water. In the United States during the early 1900s, windmills pumped water on farms. Today, windmills again are capturing energy from wind.

Figure 18-9. Wind has been used as an energy source for many centuries.

A **wind farm** is a location where a number of windmills are placed to gather wind and generate electricity. Wind farms usually are on ridges where the wind is strong and steady. The energy from the spinning windmill turns a generator that makes electricity. If the wind changes direction, computers control motors that keep the blades facing into the wind.

Can you think of advantages and disadvantages of using wind energy? Wind is nonpolluting and free. It produces no waste and causes no environmental harm. But only a few regions have winds strong enough to generate electricity. The best locations in the United States are the Great Plains, mountainous areas, and some coastal regions. Also, the wind isn't steady, sometimes stopping and other times blowing too hard. Storing and transporting electricity generated by wind is very expensive.

Figure 18-10. The energy from all these windmills is combined to generate electricity.

Energy from Water

You learned in Chapter 11 how the energy of tides can be used to generate electricity. Obtaining energy from moving water is not new. Mills turned by tidal energy ground grain in England, France, and Spain a thousand years ago. Today, energy from running water is used to turn turbines to make electricity. The production of electricity by water power is called **hydroelectric energy.** We've built dams on many large rivers to generate hydroelectric power.

Hydroelectric dams on rivers work much the same way as the tidal power dam described in Chapter 11. As seen in Figure 18-11, a large concrete dam holds water and forms a lake behind it. As water passes by turbines at the base of the dam, the turbines turn generators that make electricity.

The advantages of hydroelectric energy are that it doesn't make any pollution and the water used is free of cost. However, when dams are built, upstream lakes fill with sediment and downstream erosion increases. Land above the dam is flooded, and wildlife habitats are disturbed.

What are advantages of hydro-electric power?

Synfuel and Biomass Fuel

A **synfuel** is a human-made energy source. Most synfuel products are made by changing fossil fuels into a different form. Coal gasification makes natural gas from coal. This is done by mixing coal with steam and oxygen in a complex process. Some rocks called oil shales contain a waxy oil material. The oil can only be removed in a complex process of crushing and heating.

If you have ever built a campfire with wood, you have used a biomass fuel. **Biomass fuel** is organic matter used as fuel. Some power plants burn wood to generate electricity. Other power plants add trash and garbage to coal to generate electricity.

Gasohol is a biomass fuel used in cars and trucks. It is 90 percent gasoline and 10 percent alcohol. The alcohol is made from corn or sugarcane.

How can energy be obtained from shale?

Figure 18-12. This trash-burning power plant generates electricity by burning trash and coal.

How have solar cells been improved?

Although these renewable energy sources are limited at the present time, they might become more effective in replacing fossil fuels in the future. Recent advances in solar cell technology have reduced the price of solar cells and increased their efficiency. Other advances in the development of electric cars will help us to be less dependent on oil for transportation. Further improvements in solar and wind technology may enable the sun and wind to be major energy sources in the future.

SECTION REVIEW

1. Why is wind energy limited to certain geographic regions?
2. What are the limitations of solar energy?
3. What are the advantages of hydroelectric power?
4. **Apply:** Why would it be accurate to say that solar energy and wind energy have the same source? What is that source?

Skill Builder

☒ Hypothesizing

You have read that energy from the wind is essentially nonpolluting. Yet, some people claim that there *is* pollution from wind farms. Hypothesize how windmills can cause pollution. If you need help, refer to Hypothesizing in the **Skill Handbook** on page 686.

ACTIVITY 18-2
Solar Energy

Problem: *How does the color of a material affect its ability to absorb energy?*

Materials

- dry black soil
- dry brown soil
- dry white sandy soil
- clear glass or plastic dishes (3)
- thermometers (3)
- 200-watt lamp with reflector and clamp
- watch or clock with second hand
- ring stand
- glass marker
- graph paper
- colored pencils (3)
- metric ruler

Procedure

1. Use the glass marker to label the dishes A, B, and C.
2. Arrange the dishes close together on your desk.
3. Fill dish A with dry black soil to a depth of 2.5 cm.
4. Fill dish B to the same depth with dry brown soil.
5. Fill dish C to the same depth with dry white sandy soil.
6. Place a thermometer in each dish. Be sure to cover the thermometer bulb in each dish completely with the material.
7. Record the temperature of each dish in a table similar to the one shown.
8. Clamp the lamp to the ring stand and position over all three dishes.
9. Turn on the lamp. Be sure the light shines equally on each dish.
10. Read the temperature of each material every 30 seconds for 20 minutes and record in your data table.

11. Use the data to construct a graph. Time should be plotted on the horizontal axis and temperature on the vertical axis. Use a different colored pencil to plot the data and draw the line for each material.

Data and Observations

Time minutes	Temperature °C		
	Dish A	Dish B	Dish C
0			
0.5			

Analyze

1. Which material had the greatest temperature change?
2. Which material had the least change?

Conclude and Apply

3. Why do the curves on the graph flatten?
4. Why do you think flat-plate solar collectors have black plates behind the water pipes?
5. How does the color of a material affect its ability to absorb energy?

18-3 Nuclear Energy

New Science Words

nuclear energy
fission

Objectives

▶ Describe how nuclear energy is made.
▶ List the drawbacks and the advantages of nuclear energy.

Nuclear Energy

Does your electricity come from a nuclear power plant? It may, because about 20 percent of electricity in the United States comes from nuclear energy.

Nuclear energy is energy produced by fission. **Fission** is the splitting of nuclei of atoms in heavy elements such as uranium. The fuel used in fission power plants is a uranium isotope, uranium-235. You learned about radioactive elements in Chapter 16. Uranium-235 is a radioactive element. It occurs in ore in some sandstones in the Rocky Mountains. After the ore is mined, the uranium is concentrated and then placed in long metal pipes called fuel rods.

A nuclear power plant has a large chamber called a nuclear reactor. In it, the uranium fuel rods sit in a pool of cooling water. Neutrons are fired into the fuel. When the uranium-235 atoms are hit, they break apart, firing out neutrons that hit other atoms. This begins a chain reaction. As each atom fissions, it not only fires neutrons, but also releases heat. This heat is used to boil water to make steam. The steam drives a turbine, which turns a generator, producing electricity.

How is fission used to make electricity?

Figure 18-13. Fission occurs when a neutron hits the nucleus of a uranium atom, and the uranium atom splits and releases heat.

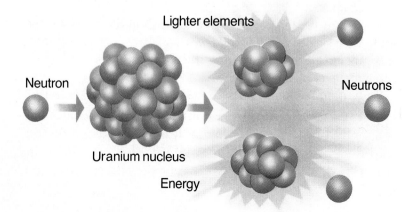

Lighter elements

Neutron

Neutrons

Uranium nucleus

Energy

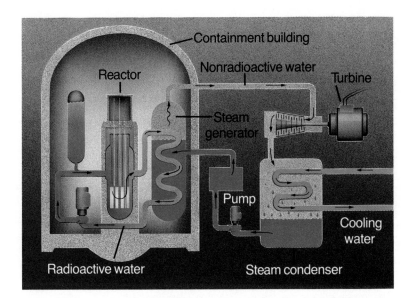

Figure 18-14. In a nuclear power plant, the boiling radioactive water from the reactor is piped into a steam generator. There, it changes nonradioactive water into steam. This steam spins a turbine before it is condensed back into water to repeat the cycle.

Do you know the advantages of fission energy? Fission reactors are very efficient. One kilogram of nuclear fuel can yield the energy of 3000 metric tons of coal! A fission reactor uses 100 tons of fuel each year, compared to millions of tons of fossil fuel needed to produce the same amount of electricity.

Nuclear Power Accidents

What do you think would happen if a nuclear chain reaction in a power plant got out of control? You know that it can't explode like a bomb because the fuel is too weak. But you also know that the used fuel is dangerously radioactive.

We learned what could happen in 1979, when something went wrong in a reactor at Three Mile Island near Harrisburg, Pennsylvania. Part of the uranium-235 fuel melted when most of its cooling water was drained away. The accident was caused by operator confusion and equipment failure. Fortunately, the reactor's walls held all the radioactive materials inside. Only a little radioactive gas was released. Nobody was injured, but thousands of people were very frightened.

A much more serious accident happened at the Chernobyl reactor in the Ukraine in 1986. Operators at the plant ignored warnings that temperatures inside the fuel were getting too high. Steam pressure built up in the pipes and exploded, sending pieces of fuel rods through the roof.

Figure 18-15. Many people fear nuclear energy because of accidents that have released radiation in the past. This photo shows the Chernobyl reactor after it exploded.

The roof caught fire, sending radioactive materials into the air. The wind carried this radioactivity for many kilometers over neighboring countries such as Poland. As a result, 135 000 people were evacuated from nearby towns, more than 200 suffered severe radiation injury, and at least 30 died. More may die from sickness and cancer caused by the radiation exposure.

Another hazard is the waste products from reactors. The United States has operated nuclear power plants since 1957. Many metric tons of used fuel have piled up. It will remain intensely radioactive for thousands of years before it decays into harmless isotopes. Yet even now, our country still does not have a permanent disposal place ready for this waste.

SECTION REVIEW

1. Describe how nuclear energy is produced.
2. What are the advantages of nuclear energy?
3. What are the drawbacks of nuclear energy?

SCIENCE & SOCIETY

You Decide!

America's energy demands are rising five percent each year, and we're running out of fossil fuels. Nuclear power may be the only alternative energy source that can produce the large amounts of energy we need very soon. The uranium needed for fuel is plentiful. However, nuclear power plants have the potential for accidents. The problem of disposing of radioactive fuel rods has not been solved. Should we continue to develop and build more nuclear power plants? Or should we place our emphasis on improving renewable energy sources and developing new energy sources?

CHAPTER
REVIEW

SUMMARY

18-1: Nonrenewable Energy Sources

1. Coal forms as plants become buried and decay over millions of years. Oil and natural gas form when marine plants and animals die and accumulate on the ocean floor. Over millions of years, pressure from overlying sediments changes these remains into oil and natural gas.

2. Fossil fuels are nonrenewable energy sources because they take millions of years to form.

3. Turning off lights, radios, and TVs in unoccupied rooms; insulating homes; limiting the use of an air conditioner; recycling; using public transportation; and car pooling are only a few ways to conserve fossil fuels.

18-2: Renewable Energy Sources and Others

1. Solar, wind, and hydroelectric energy are free and don't create the direct pollution that fossil fuels emit.

2. Solar cells are expensive and don't work when the sky is cloudy or dark. Wind energy can be used only where there is constant wind. Hydroelectric dams change the environment.

18-3: Science and Society: Nuclear Energy

1. Nuclear energy is produced by fission, which is the splitting of uranium atoms. Fission produces heat which is used to make steam that drives a turbine, which turns a generator, producing electricity.

2. Releasing radioactive materials into the air, releasing and disposing of wastes, and meltdowns are potential dangers of nuclear energy.

KEY SCIENCE WORDS

a. **anthracite**
b. **biomass fuel**
c. **bituminous coal**
d. **energy**
e. **fission**
f. **fossil fuels**
g. **hydroelectric energy**
h. **lignite**
i. **nonrenewable energy sources**
j. **nuclear energy**
k. **peat**
l. **renewable energy sources**
m. **solar cell**
n. **solar energy**
o. **synfuel**
p. **wind farm**

UNDERSTANDING VOCABULARY

Match each phrase with the correct term from the list of Key Science Words.

1. the ability to do work
2. first stage in coal formation
3. sources of energy that are being used quicker than it takes to replace them
4. collects solar energy and converts it into electricity
5. area with many windmills used to generate electricity
6. energy derived from running water
7. process of splitting of uranium-235 atoms
8. energy sources that won't run out in the near future
9. soft brown coal
10. the cleanest burning coal

CHAPTER
REVIEW

CHECKING CONCEPTS

Choose the word or phrase that completes the sentence.

1. _____ is a fossil fuel.
   a. Natural gas   c. Coal
   b. Oil   d. All of these

2. Coal forms when _____ die, decay, and become buried for millions of years.
   a. swamp animals   c. swamp plants
   b. marine plants   d. marine animals

3. _____ contains the most carbon.
   a. Peat   c. Bituminous coal
   b. Lignite   d. Anthracite

4. Oil is used to make _____.
   a. coal   c. solar energy
   b. nuclear energy d. none of these

5. A _____ uses moving water to generate electricity.
   a. wind farm   c. nuclear reactor
   b. hydroelectric plant d. solar cell

6. The most used coal is _____.
   a. peat   c. bituminous
   b. lignite   d. anthracite

7. Abundant sunshine is needed for _____.
   a. wind power   c. hydroelectric power
   b. solar power   d. all of these

8. The Three Mile Island accident was caused by _____.
   a. too little water
   b. equipment failure
   c. operator confusion
   d. all of these

9. The ability to do work is _____.
   a. solar cell   c. peat
   b. fission   d. energy

10. Gas is found in deposits under _____ rock.
    a. permeable   c. porous
    b. impermeable   d. unconsolidated

UNDERSTANDING CONCEPTS

Complete each sentence.

11. Today, _____ are burned to provide most of the energy in the United States.

12. _____ is the second stage in coal formation.

13. _____ causes flooding and erosion of nearby land areas.

14. Coal is converted to natural gas in a process called _____.

15. _____ are used to power some satellites, calculators, and street lights.

THINK AND WRITE CRITICALLY

16. Compare and contrast peat and lignite.

17. Describe two ways in which oil and natural gas differ from coal.

18. Explain how energy from the sun becomes trapped in plants and is later released when fossil fuels are burned.

19. Discuss the problems associated with obtaining energy from nuclear fission.

20. What precautions are used in nuclear power plants to prevent accidents?

APPLY

21. Mary found what she thought was a small piece of coral in a chunk of coal. Benjamin thought the fossil was a twig. Who was right? Explain.

22. Why is anthracite a better fuel than bituminous coal?

23. Describe how the windows of a building that uses solar energy should be designed so that the building is most efficient.

24. Which city would be bettter suited for the development of solar energy: a city that has cloud cover 55 percent of the time or a city that has cloud cover 45 percent of the time? Explain.

25. Why are most radioactive wastes so dangerous?

MORE SKILL BUILDERS

If you need help, refer to the Skill Handbook.

1. Sequencing: If a well were drilled into a rock containing oil and natural gas, which substance would be encountered first? Explain.

2. Comparing and Contrasting: Compare and contrast solar energy with power from the wind.

3. Interpreting Scientific Illustrations: Refer to Figure 18-5 on page 483. What lies above gas and oil in this diagram? Why does the gas seem to be trapped directly below this layer?

4. Making and Using Tables: Make a table showing the advantages and disadvantages of each energy source discussed in the chapter.

5. Concept Mapping: Make a network tree concept map that compares and contrasts the stages of coal formation.

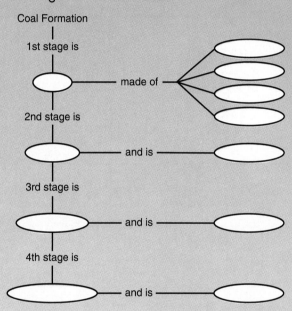

PROJECTS

1. Go to the library to find out about energy-efficient buildings that currently exist in the United States. Then, design and make a three-dimensional model of a futuristic building that is energy efficient.

2. Design and conduct an experiment using a silicon solar cell and a milliammeter to measure the available solar energy.

The landfill shown is one of many that holds the garbage produced by people. We're running out of space to build new landfills. At the same time, the human population is increasing. Is there enough land and resources to support more people?

FIND OUT!

Do this simple activity to illustrate human population growth.

Draw a square that's 10 cm on each side. This represents one square kilometer of Earth's land surface. In 1977, the average number of people for every square kilometer of land was 28. Draw 28 small circles inside your square to represent this. In 1990, the average rose to 35. Add seven circles to illustrate this increase. It's predicted that in 2075, there will be 98 people per square kilometer. Add circles to represent an average square kilometer of land in 2075. Why is the human population increasing so rapidly? How does the increased population growth affect the environment?

Previewing Science Skills

▶ In the **Skill Builders,** you will use a table and outline.
▶ In the **MINI-Labs,** you will collect data, apply previous knowledge, and make inferences.
▶ In the **Activities,** you will experiment, analyze data, make and use tables and graphs, and draw conclusions.

What's next?

You've seen that the population is rapidly increasing and that land is becoming more and more valuable as a limited resource. In this chapter, you'll discover how the increasing population threatens the environment all over Earth. Most importantly, you'll learn about things you can do to protect the environment.

19-1 Population Impact on the Environment

New Science Words

population
population explosion

Objectives

▶ Interpret data from a graph that shows human population growth.
▶ List reasons for Earth's rapid increase in population.
▶ List several ways each person in an industrialized nation affects the environment.

The Human Population Explosion

At one time, people thought of Earth as a world with unlimited resources. They thought Earth could provide them with whatever materials they needed. It seemed they would always have enough space to live and to grow food. Earth had an endless supply of metals, fossil fuels, clean water and air, and rich soils. Today, we know this isn't true. Earth's resources are limited. Unless we treat those resources with care, they will disappear. Why have attitudes toward Earth's resources changed? Why have we only recently realized that we need to conserve resources and care for the environment?

When there were fewer people on Earth, it seemed that only a few hundred million people could never use up all of the resources. And, at that time, each individual used fewer resources and produced less waste than people do today. Since that time, the number of people on Earth has increased at an alarming rate. The increase in the world population has changed the way we must view our world and how we care for it.

A **population** is the total number of individuals of a particular species in a particular area. The area can be small or large. For example, we can talk about the human population of one particular community, such as Los Angeles, or about the human population of the entire Earth.

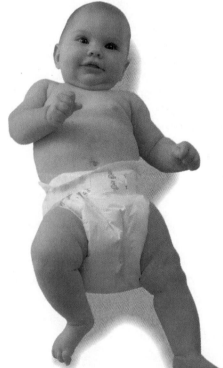

Figure 19-1. The human population is growing at an alarming rate. Will we be able to manage Earth's resources so our species, as well as others, can survive?

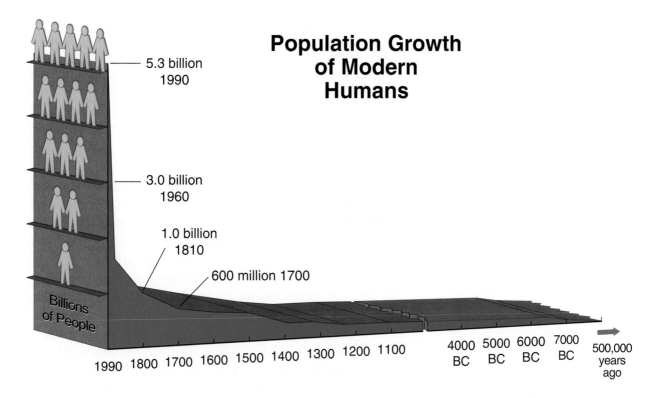

Population Growth of Modern Humans

5.3 billion 1990

3.0 billion 1960

1.0 billion 1810

600 million 1700

Billions of People

1990 1800 1700 1600 1500 1400 1300 1200 1100

4000 BC 5000 BC 6000 BC 7000 BC 500,000 years ago

Figure 19-2. The human species, *Homo sapiens,* may have appeared about 500 000 years ago. Our population numbers remained relatively steady until about 200 years ago. Since that time, we have experienced a sharp increase in growth rate.

Have you ever wondered how many people live on Earth? The global population in 1990 was 5.3 billion. Each year, almost 90 million new people are added. Earth is experiencing a **population explosion.** The word *explosion* is used because the rate at which people are reproducing has rapidly increased in recent history.

Look at Figure 19-2. You can see that it took hundreds of thousands of years for Earth's population to reach 1 billion people. After that, the population increased much faster. Why do you think the population has increased so rapidly in recent years?

The death rate has been slowed by modern medicines, better sanitation, and better nutrition. This means that more people are living longer and remaining in the population. Also, births have increased because more people are at the age where they can have children. The result is that Earth's population is increasing fast.

Earth's increasing population has seriously changed the environment. Scientists predict even greater changes as more people use Earth's limited resources. By the year 2075, the population is predicted to be 14 billion, nearly three times what it is now. Are there enough natural resources to support such a large population? How will such a large human population affect our environment?

What factors have led to an increase in population?

Did You Know?

The United States makes up only 5 percent of the world's human population, yet it consumes 25 percent of the world's natural resources.

How does the energy consumed by a person in the U.S. compare with that used by other people?

How People Affect the Environment

By the time you're 75 years old, you will have produced enough garbage to equal the mass of 16 African elephants (47 000 kilograms). You will have consumed enough water to fill 662 000 bathtubs (163 000 000 liters). And because you live in the United States, you will have used five times as much energy as an average person living elsewhere in the world.

Let's take a look at how your daily activities affect the environment. You use electricity, which is generated by burning fuels. The environment is changed when the fuels are mined, and it's further harmed when the fuels are burned. The water that you use is polluted and must be made as clean as possible before being returned to the environment. Sometimes cleaning the water adds substances such as chlorine to the environment. You eat food which takes land to grow. Farming causes huge volumes of topsoil to be eroded and lost each year. Much of the food you eat is grown using pesticides and herbicides—poisonous substances. How else do you and other people affect the environment?

Many of the products you buy are packaged in plastic and paper. Plastic is refined from oil. The process of refining oil produces many pollutants. The environment is

Table 19-1

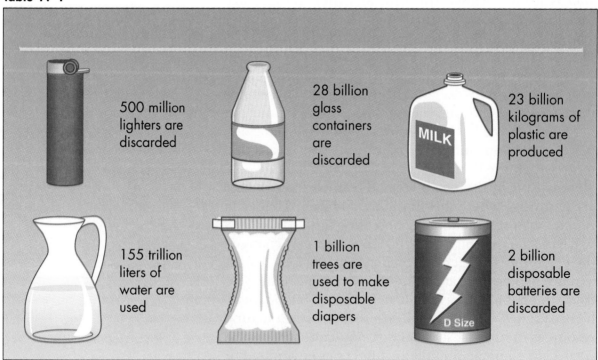

500 million lighters are discarded

28 billion glass containers are discarded

23 billion kilograms of plastic are produced

155 trillion liters of water are used

1 billion trees are used to make disposable diapers

2 billion disposable batteries are discarded

changed to produce the clean, shiny piece of plastic you buy in the store. Producing paper requires cutting down trees, using gasoline to transport them to a paper mill, and producing pollutants to transform the trees into paper.

We change the land when we remove resources from it, and we further harm the environment when we shape those resources into usable products. The effect on the environment doesn't end there, however. Once we've produced and consumed products, we have to dispose of them. In the next section, you will read about the problems associated with disposal of waste.

As the population continues to grow, more demands will be made on our environment. Becoming all too common are traffic-choked highways, overflowing garbage dumps, shrinking forests, and vanishing wildlife. What can we do? People are the problem, but we also are the solution. As you learn more about how we affect the environment, you'll discover what you can do to make the future world one that everyone can live in.

Figure 19-3. People are beginning to act to protect the environment. For example, egg cartons are made of recycled paper or plastic. Because of consumer demands, grocery stores began selling "environment friendly" materials.

SECTION REVIEW

1. Using Figure 19-2 calculate approximately how many years it took for the *Homo sapiens* population to reach 1 billion. How long did it take to double to 2 billion? to 4 billion?
2. List at least three reasons for Earth's rapid increase in population.
3. **Apply:** In nonindustrialized nations, such as Ethiopia, individuals have less negative impact on the environment than do citizens in industrialized nations. Why do you think this is the case?

☑ **Making and Using Graphs**

Skill Builder

Use Figure 19-2 on page 503 to answer the questions below. If you need help, refer to Making and Using Graphs in the **Skill Handbook** on pages 691 and 692.
1. Early humanlike ancestors existed more than 4 million years ago. Why does the graph indicate that it should extend back only 500 000 years?
2. How would the slope of the graph change if, in the near future, the growth rate were cut in half?

ACTIVITY 19-1
Human Population Growth Rate

Problem: *What is the mathematical nature of human population growth?*

Materials

- beaker (250 or 400 mL)
- paper cups or 50-mL beakers (11)
- small objects of uniform shape (dried beans, corn kernels, glass or plastic beads, paper clips, wooden markers)

Procedure

1. Place two of the small objects into the large beaker on your desk or table. Place each of the 11 smaller containers in a row beside the larger one. Number each of these containers from 1 to 11.
2. Place two of the objects into the first small container. In each succeeding container, from 2 through 11, place *twice* as many objects as in the one before it (four objects in 2, eight objects in 3, and so on). Record the number of objects in each of the small containers.
3. Estimate the percentage of empty space in the large beaker. Record this estimate in the first line of your data table.
4. Add the contents of container 1 to the large beaker. Record the total "population" (number of objects) and the approximate percentage of empty space in the large beaker.
5. Repeat the procedure for container 2 thirty seconds later. Add the contents of containers 3 through 11 at 30-second intervals. Record your results each time.
6. When the small objects in all of your containers have been added to the large container, make a graph of your results. Place the number of objects (population) on the vertical axis and the time intervals (0 through 11) on the horizontal axis.

Data and Observations

Time interval	Population	Percent of empty volume
0		
1		
2		
10		
11		

Analyze

1. Indicate what you think the large beaker and the smaller objects represent.
2. After 11 thirty-second intervals, what is the total number of small objects and percentage of empty space in the large beaker?
3. How does the graph of your data for this activity compare to the graph in Figure 19-2?

Conclude and Apply

4. The radius of Earth is about 6400 kilometers. Approximately 70 percent of its surface is covered by water. Given the present planet population of about 5.5 billion, what is the current population density in people per square kilometer of land surface? (Area of a sphere $= 4\pi r^2$)
5. The present world population is thought to be doubling about every 35 years. Assuming no change in that rate, what will the population density per square kilometer be 35 years from now? 105 years? 1000 years?
6. Identify and describe some "limiting factors" that might determine a maximum population for planet Earth?

Using the Land

Objectives

▶ List ways that we use land.
▶ Discuss environmental problems created because of land use.
▶ List things you can do to help protect the environment.

New Science Words

landfill
sanitary landfill
hazardous wastes
conservation
composting

Land Usage

You may not think of land as a natural resource. Yet, it is as important to people as oil, gold, clean air, and clean water. Through agriculture, logging, refuse disposal, and urban development, we not only use land, we often abuse it.

Farming

Earth's continents have about 130 million square kilometers of land. We use 15 million square kilometers as farmland. Even so, about 20 percent of the people living in the world live in poverty and hunger. Millions starve to death each year. Unfortunately, advanced farming techniques that produce large volumes of food also create serious environmental problems. To reduce weeds and insects in a field where crops are growing, herbicides and pesticides are often applied. These chemicals

Figure 19-4. Contour plowing is one way farmers reduce erosion. Water follows the natural contour of the land, along the plowed rows, instead of running straight downslope.

Figure 19-5. Herbicides and pesticides applied to crops run off into streams and poison the environment.

Did You Know?

Bacteria living in the intestines of cows and other herbivores break down plant material called cellulose. The cows and other animals can then use the cellulose as an energy source. It's the bacteria, not the animals, that produce methane gas.

make their way to the waterways where they contaminate the environment. People and other animals can get cancers from consuming food and water polluted by runoff from farmlands.

Perhaps the greatest damage caused by farming is excessive topsoil erosion. When croplands are tilled, there's no vegetation covering the soil to prevent it from being carried away by running water. Two or three centimeters of topsoil may be removed in one year. It can take more than 300 years for new topsoil to evolve and replace the eroded topsoil.

Grazing Livestock

Some land is used for grazing livestock. The animals eat the plants on the land and are then often used as food for humans. Two problems associated with grazing livestock include losing land that could be used to grow crops and the production of methane gas.

Figure 19-6. One-third of the land in North America is used to graze livestock. One-half of all croplands is used to grow feed for livestock.

A square kilometer of vegetable crops can feed many more people than a square kilometer used to raise livestock. Also, cows and other vegetarian animals produce methane. Methane is thought to contribute to the greenhouse effect.

Cutting Trees

Some land is used for a source of wood. Trees are cut down and used for lumber, fuel, and paper. Often new trees are planted to take their places. In some cases, especially in the tropical regions, whole forests are cut down without being replaced. Each year an area of rain forest the size of Pennsylvania disappears. It's not just the trees and soil that are destroyed when the trees are cut down. Scientists estimate that 17 500 species die each year because of this loss of habitat.

Organisms living outside of the tropics also suffer because of the lost vegetation. Plants remove carbon dioxide from the air and produce oxygen when they photosynthesize. Organisms all over the globe need oxygen to breathe. Reduced vegetation could also result in higher levels of carbon dioxide in the atmosphere. As you know, carbon dioxide is one of the gases that contributes to the greenhouse effect.

How large of an area of rain forest is lost each year?

How do organisms outside of the rain forest suffer from the loss?

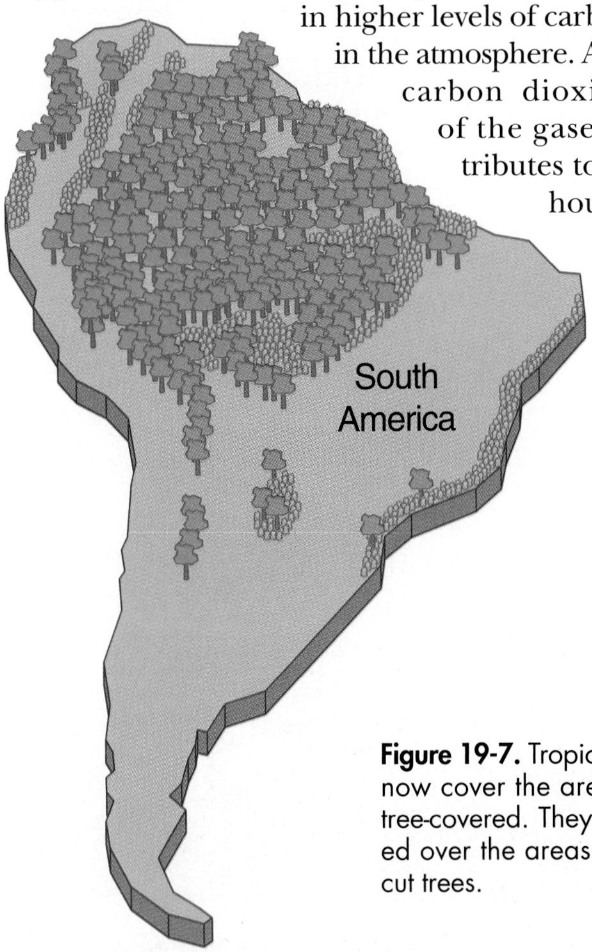

South America

Figure 19-7. Tropical rain forests now cover the areas shown as tree-covered. They once extended over the areas indicated by cut trees.

Read the following situation and answer the questions at the end. After you've answered in your own words, compare your responses with those of other students. Suppose you've just purchased a house with a small yard. The yard has many weeds growing among the grass, and the flower beds are overgrown with weeds. You're considering hiring a lawn-care service to come and spray your yard with herbicides and fertilizer. You know that these substances are toxic. Do you decide to have the chemicals applied to your yard? If a neighbor complained that he didn't like the chemicals being sprayed so close to his home, how would you respond?

Landfills

So far, we've discussed ways land is used to produce products we use. Land is also used when we dispose of those products. Eighty percent of all our garbage goes into landfills. A **landfill** is an area where waste is deposited. In a **sanitary landfill,** each day's deposit is covered with dirt. The dirt prevents it from blowing away in the wind, and it reduces the odor produced by the decaying waste. Sanitary landfills are also designed to prevent liquid wastes from draining into the soil and groundwater below. A sanitary landfill is lined with plastic or concrete, or it's located in clay-rich soils that trap the liquid waste.

Some of the wastes we put into landfills are dangerous to organisms. These poisonous, cancer-causing, or radioactive wastes are called **hazardous wastes.** Large quantities of hazardous wastes are put into landfills by industries. But this isn't the only source of these toxic substances. Every year, each person in the United States throws away enough hazardous waste to equal the mass of a small car. Examples of these wastes are insect sprays, fingernail polish removers, batteries, drain cleaners, bleaches, medicines, and paints.

Sanitary landfills greatly reduce the chance that hazardous substances will leak into the surrounding soil and groundwater. However, some of it does find its way into the environment.

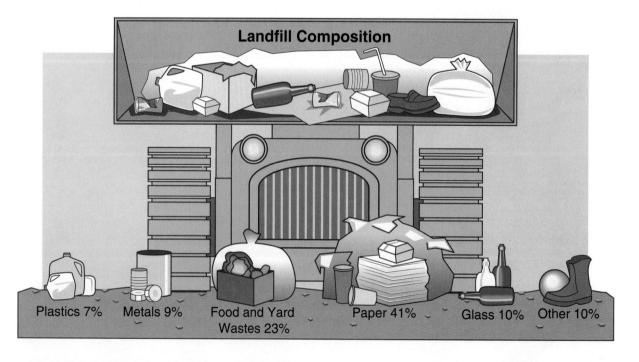

Landfill Composition

Plastics 7% Metals 9% Food and Yard Wastes 23% Paper 41% Glass 10% Other 10%

Will the Landfill be in Your Backyard?

Anthony was on his way home from school when he passed a group of people outside the local government building. They were carrying signs to protest the proposed landfill going up on the edge of their neighborhood. They carried signs that said "NIMBY," or "*Not In My Backyard*."

The protestors were concerned that the landfill would be bad for their neighborhood. They were hoping to prevent it from being built there. Instead, they thought it should be placed elsewhere.

That evening, Anthony saw a news report on the landfill controversy. The report said that the landfill had to be located within city limits. No matter where it was located, it would be in someone's neighborhood. The report went on to say that the current

city landfill had to close within the next year because it was almost full. Construction on the new landfill would have to begin soon.

Think Critically: Most people don't want a landfill in their "backyard." Yet, it's their garbage and the garbage of others in the community that must be disposed of. How can people prevent landfills from filling up in the first place? Why would a community refuse to pick up grass clippings if its landfill space were limited?

Another problem is that we're filling up our landfills. We're running out of good areas to build new ones. Many materials placed into landfills don't rot. Instead, they just stay there, taking up space.

The figure on page 510 illustrates the materials commonly put into landfills. Some of these materials decompose rapidly, whereas others do not. It may seem that when we throw something in the garbage can that it's gone and we don't need to be concerned with it anymore. But as you know, our garbage doesn't disappear. It can stay around for hundreds of years. In the case of radioactive waste, it may be around for thousands of years, troubling future generations.

Structures, Mines, and Natural Environments

Another way we change the land is by building structures on it. Concrete and asphalt are quickly replacing grass and woodlands in our communities. The impact on the environment is easy to observe. Asphalt and concrete

You use16 liters of water if you let
the water run while brushing your
teeth. Only 2 liters are used if the
water is turned off until it's time to
rinse. How much water could you
save per year by not letting the
water run? Base your calculations
on brushing your teeth three times
a day. How much water could be
saved by the entire U.S. population
(250 million people)?

Why is paving the land a
problem?

absorb a lot of solar radiation. The atmosphere is then
heated by conduction, and the air temperature rises. You
may have observed this if you've ever traveled from a
rural area to the city and noticed a rise in temperature.

Another effect of paving over the land is that less water
is able to soak into the soil. Instead, it either makes its
way to sewer lines or it evaporates. This greatly reduces the
amount of water that makes its way to groundwater
aquifers. Many communities rely on groundwater for
drinking water. At the same time, they're covering more
and more of the land with roads, sidewalks, and parking
lots that prevent the water from reaching the aquifers.

In previous chapters, you've read about mining and
how it adversely affects the environment. As more and
more people populate Earth, increased demands for fossil fuels and mineral ores will result in more and more
mining operations.

Not all land on Earth is being used to produce usable
materials or for storing waste. Some land remains unin-
habited by people. National Parks in the United States
are protected from much of the pollution and destruction that you've read about in this section. In many
countries throughout the world, land is set aside as natural preserves. As the world population continues to
increase, the strain on our environment is likely to
increase. Let's hope that we will be able to continue preserving some land as natural environments.

Figure 19-8. As we increase our
demands for energy, we must find
new resources. There are many
on-going debates about whether
we should mine our national
parks and wildlife reserves. One
such debate rages over whether
to drill for oil here, at the Arctic
National Wildlife Reserve in
Alaska.

Conserving Resources

People are the cause of our environmental problems, and we also are the solution. What can you do to help? In the United States and other industrialized countries, people have a throwaway life-style. When we are done with something, we throw it away. This means more products have to be produced to replace what we've thrown away; more land is used, and landfills overflow. You can help by conserving resources. **Conservation** is the careful use of resources that reduces damage to the environment. Two ways to conserve resources are by reusing and recycling materials. You'll read more about recycling in the Science and Society section that follows.

Reusing an item means finding another use for it instead of throwing it away. You can reuse old clothes by giving them to someone else, or by cutting them up into

What is a "throwaway" lifestyle?

T E C H N O L O G Y

Recycling Paper

What happens to the newspaper you recycle? After the paper is taken to a plant where it is to be recycled, the paper is put into a device called a pulper. The pulper contains water and other substances that remove any ink from the paper. The paper then becomes part of a soggy mixture called pulp.

Pulp is run through a machine that removes any solid objects such as rubber bands, paper clips, or staples that may have been fastened to the paper. Another device then squeezes the water from the paper mixture. The final stage of processing includes sifting and washing the pulp to remove any unwanted debris.

Water is added to the clean pulp to make a thick, pasty substance. This substance is rolled into thin sheets and dried to form sheets of recycled paper.

Think Critically: If 17 trees are saved when one tonne of paper is recycled, how many trees could be saved in a year if a community recycled 150 000 kilograms of paper each month?

Can one person make a difference?
This text identifies a number of things people can do to reduce environmental problems. Select at least one and do it. After a length of time that your class has agreed upon, report back on what it was that you did as your part in helping to conserve resources and protect the environment. The population of the United States is about 250 million. What do you suppose would be the result if each person in your country did his or her part in helping save planet Earth also?

rags. The rags can be used in place of paper towels for cleaning jobs around your home.

Reusing plastic and paper bags is another way to reduce waste. Plastic grocery bags are handy for carrying other things. Some grocery stores even pay a few cents when you return and reuse paper grocery bags. Out-of-doors, there are things you can do, too. If you cut grass or rake leaves, compost the leaves and grass clippings instead of putting them into the trash. **Composting** means to pile them up where they can gradually decompose. The decomposed matter can be used in gardens or flower beds to fertilize the soil. Some cities no longer pick up yard waste to take to the landfills. In those places, composting is common. If everyone composted, it would reduce the trash put into landfills by 20 percent.

The human population explosion has already had devastating effects on the environment and the organisms that inhabit Earth. It's unlikely that the population will begin to decline in the near future. To compensate, we must use our resources wisely. Conserving resources by reusing and recycling are two important ways that you can make a difference.

SECTION REVIEW

1. List at least five ways we use land.
2. Discuss environmental problems that are created by agriculture, mining, and trash disposal.
3. List at least five things you can do to help save the environment.
4. **Apply:** Why do you think there is less landfill space left in the northeastern United States than in other areas of the country?

Skill Builder

☑ Outlining

Make an outline of Section 19-2. Use your outline to answer the questions below. If you need help, refer to Outlining in the **Skill Handbook** on page 681.

1. How many uses of land are described in this section?
2. How does farming negatively impact the environment? How does grazing livestock negatively impact it?
3. An open landfill doesn't have many of the characteristics of a sanitary landfill. What do you think an open landfill is like?

ACTIVITY 19-2
A Model Landfill

Problem: *What materials rapidly decompose in a landfill?*

Materials

- 2-liter bottle
- soil
- thermometer
- plastic wrap
- rubber band
- graph paper
- garbage (including food scraps, yard waste, a plastic item, a metal item, a foam cup, and notebook paper or newsprint)

Procedure

1. Cut the top off of the 2-liter bottle.
2. Add soil to the bottle until it is half filled.
3. On graph paper, trace the outline of all the garbage items that you will place into the bottle. Label each outline. Keep the graph paper as a record of the original sizes of the items.
4. Place the items, one at a time, in the bottle. Completely cover each item with soil.
5. Add enough water to the "landfill" until the soil is slightly moist. Place a thermometer in the bottle and seal it up with the plastic wrap and a rubber band.
6. Check the temperature of the "landfill" each day for two weeks. Record the temperatures in your data table.
7. After two weeks, remove all of the items from the soil. Trace the outlines of each on a new sheet of graph paper. Compare the sizes of the items with their original sizes.
8. Wash your hands thoroughly after cleaning up your lab space. Be sure to properly dispose of each item as instructed by your teacher.

Analyze

1. Which items decomposed the most? Which showed the least decomposition?
2. Most decomposition in a landfill is due to the activity of microorganisms. The organisms can live only under certain temperature and moisture conditions. Why was it necessary to add moisture to the soil? How do you think the decomposition rates would have differed if the soil had been completely dry?
3. Compare your results with the results of a bottle that was stored in cold temperatures. What could explain the differences you observe?

Conclude and Apply

4. Why do some items decompose more rapidly than others?
5. What problems are created in landfills by plastics?
6. Yard wastes will eventually decompose, but they take up a lot of space in landfills. What alternatives are there to putting yard wastes in landfills?
7. Why do you think many people buy paper egg cartons instead of foam ones? Why have many stores begun selling only those eggs that come in paper cartons?

19-3 Recycling

New Science Words

recyclable
market
container law

Objectives

▶ List the advantages of recycling.
▶ Describe ways to promote recycling.
▶ Express your feelings about government control of recycling.

Should We Require Recycling?

If you recycle, you may be reducing the trash you will generate in your lifetime by 60 percent. If you don't recycle, you'll generate trash equal to 600 times your mass.

When an object is **recyclable,** it's suitable to be processed and used again. When you recycle, you help the environment in many ways. You save landfill space, energy, and natural resources. You reduce the damage caused by mining, cutting trees, and manufacturing. Let's see how.

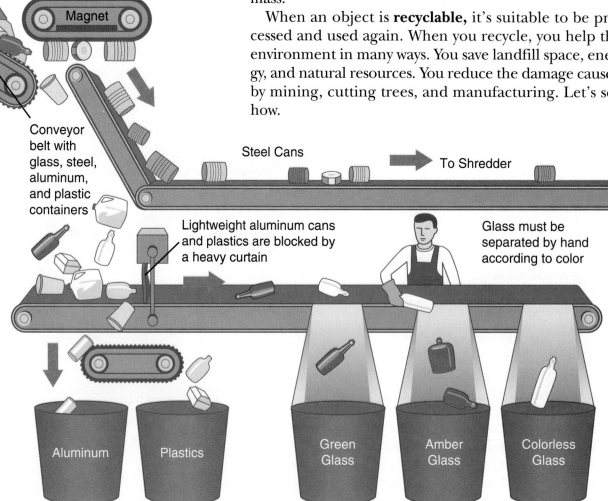

A magnet separates steel cans from the rest of the garbage

Magnet

Conveyor belt with glass, steel, aluminum, and plastic containers

Steel Cans

To Shredder

Lightweight aluminum cans and plastics are blocked by a heavy curtain

Glass must be separated by hand according to color

Aluminum

Plastics

Green Glass

Amber Glass

Colorless Glass

Paper makes up more than 40 percent of our trash. If you recycle paper, you save lots of landfill space. Making brand-new paper from trees uses lots of water and pollutes the air. But recycled paper takes 61 percent less water and produces 70 percent fewer air pollutants.

Paper isn't the only thing that can be recycled. How much energy is saved by recycling one aluminum can? Enough to keep a TV running for about three hours. Twenty aluminum cans can be recycled with the energy needed to produce a single brand-new can from ore.

Why do you suppose more things aren't recycled? One reason is that some people haven't gotten into the habit of recycling. Another is that many areas still do not have recycling centers. But there is a business reason, too. Like anything else, recycling requires money to pay for workers, trucks, buildings, and energy. Recycling businesses have to make a profit, or they can't exist. The only way to make a profit in recycling is to sell the recycled material. This means there must be a market for the material. A **market** is the people and businesses that want to purchase the recycled material. In many cities, old newspapers aren't recycled because there's no market for the recycled paper. Businesses in the community can often buy new paper cheaper than paper that's been recycled.

In the United States, only 10 percent of our garbage is recycled. In countries with mandatory recycling, like

Did You Know?

It takes more than 500 000 trees to make the newspapers that people in the United States read each Sunday.

Why is a market necessary to the survival of recycling efforts?

Japan and Germany, 50 percent of the garbage is recycled. Many state and city governments are now promoting and even requiring recycling.

Some cities encourage people to recycle by providing curbside collection or convenient drop-off facilities. Other cities get even more involved. In Seattle, Washington, people who recycle pay lower trash-collection fees. People who reduce their weekly trash from two bags to one pay a lower fee.

In some places, if you are caught throwing away things that should be recycled, you'll be warned the first time. The next time, your garbage will no longer be picked up. Other governments fine you if you don't recycle.

To provide a market for recycled items, some states require local businesses to use recycled products. For example, the Ohio congress proposed a law to require newspaper publishers in Ohio to use some recycled paper.

Our federal government in Washington, DC, is becoming involved in recycling. A good example is the **container law,** which requires at least a five-cent refundable deposit on most beverage containers nationwide. This means paying five cents extra at the store for a drink, but getting your nickel back if you take the container back to the store. If everyone in the nation would participate in this program, we would save enough energy to light a large city for four years.

EcoTip

Many items on grocery store shelves are packaged in *recyclable* containers. However, these packages are not always made of *recycled* materials. Buying recyclable packages only helps the environment if you make sure they go to a recycling center rather than a landfill.

SECTION REVIEW

1. List at least four advantages of recycling.
2. List at least four ways that governments encourage recycling.
3. Are all recyclable products made of recycled materials? Explain.

You Decide!

The container law saves energy, natural resources, and landfill space. However, it means that store owners must spend time handling the containers and storing them. It forces each of us to recycle, so we can get back our deposits.

Although some new jobs are created by this recycling, some miners and people who make brand-new containers will lose their jobs. Do you think the government should pass laws requiring people to recycle materials? Do you think people will do it without such laws?

REVIEW

SUMMARY

19-1: Population Impact on the Environment

1. Each year, almost 90 million people are added to Earth's population.

2. The rapid increase in Earth's human population in recent years is due to an increase in the birth rate, advances in medicine, better sanitation, and better nutrition.

3. People in industrial nations strongly impact the environment when they use electricity, burn fossil fuels, contaminate water, and use food that's been grown with pesticides and herbicides.

19-2: Using the Land

1. Land is used for farming, grazing livestock, cutting trees, and mining coal and mineral ores. We also build structures and landfills on the land. Some land is preserved as natural environments.

2. Land becomes polluted by hazardous wastes thrown away by industries and individuals.

Fertilizers and pesticides used by farmers pollute groundwater and soil. Mining can leave scars in the landscape and pollute underlying groundwater when the water comes in contact with certain minerals.

3. Recycling and reusing materials are important ways we can conserve natural resources.

19-3: Science and Society: Recycling

1. Recycling saves energy, natural resources, and the much-needed space in landfills.

2. Recycling is encouraged by curbside collection or convenient drop-off facilities. People who recycle may pay lower trash-collection fees. Container laws require a refundable deposit on containers.

3. Some people feel that laws are the only way to get people to recycle and conserve resources. Some people think that recycling should be an individual decision.

KEY SCIENCE WORDS

a. **composting**
b. **conservation**
c. **container law**
d. **hazardous wastes**
e. **landfill**
f. **market**
g. **population**
h. **population explosion**
i. **recyclable**
j. **sanitary landfill**

UNDERSTANDING VOCABULARY

Match each phrase with the correct term from the list of Key Science Words.

1. total number of individuals of a particular species in an area
2. describes the rapid increase in birth rate and decrease in death rate
3. area used to deposit garbage
4. trash that's dangerous to organisms
5. piling up organic material to decompose
6. careful use of resources
7. businesses or people that want to purchase a product or process
8. requires a deposit on containers
9. area lined with plastic, concrete, or clay where garbage is dumped
10. items that can be processed and used again

REVIEW

CHECKING CONCEPTS

Choose the word or phrase that completes the sentence.

1. Each year, almost _____ people are added to Earth.
   - **a.** 90 billion
   - **b.** 90 million
   - **c.** 90 000
   - **d.** 900 000 000

2. The population explosion is caused by _____.
   - **a.** modern medicine
   - **b.** increased birth rate
   - **c.** better nutrition
   - **d.** all of these

3. The United States uses about _____ percent of Earth's resources.
   - **a.** 5
   - **b.** 10
   - **c.** 25
   - **d.** 50

4. Forests are cleared in the U.S. for _____.
   - **a.** agriculture
   - **b.** mining
   - **c.** roads
   - **d.** all of these

5. Fertilizers and pesticides _____.
   - **a.** don't harm Earth
   - **b.** pollute groundwater
   - **c.** are nontoxic
   - **d.** fill up landfills

6. Some paper isn't recycled because _____.
   - **a.** there's no market
   - **b.** there's no profit
   - **c.** it goes to landfills
   - **d.** all of these

7. In a _____, garbage is covered with soil.
   - **a.** recycling center
   - **b.** surface mine
   - **c.** sanitary landfill
   - **d.** coal mine

8. An empty _____ fruit juice container causes the least harm to the environment.
   - **a.** clear plastic
   - **b.** glass bottle
   - **c.** paper
   - **d.** foam

9. Planting trees helps _____.
   - **a.** reduce erosion
   - **b.** slow global warming
   - **c.** remove atmospheric carbon dioxide
   - **d.** all of these

10. Recycling paper saves _____.
    - **a.** energy
    - **b.** trees
    - **c.** water
    - **d.** all of these

UNDERSTANDING CONCEPTS

Complete each sentence.

11. A rapid growth in the number of individuals of a certain species is a(n) _____.

12. Most of the trash in the United States is disposed of in _____.

13. Recycling leaves, grass cuttings, and other organic debris is _____.

14. Using less water is one example of the _____ of Earth's resources.

15. Imposing a(n) _____ that would require a deposit on motor oil cans could help reduce pollution.

THINK AND WRITE CRITICALLY

16. On average, how many people are added to Earth's population each minute?

17. What is the relationship between the number of people living on Earth and the rate at which resources are used?

18. Why is raising vegetable crops more efficient than raising livestock?

19. What relationship would you expect between increased cattle populations and methane in the atmosphere?

20. Discuss why recycling paper is good for the environment.

21. A ten-minute shower uses 190 liters of water. If a person takes one shower a day and reduces the time to five minutes, how much water would be saved in a year?
22. Oxygen is considered a renewable resource. Explain why.
23. Although land is farmable in many developing countries, hunger is a major problem in many of these countries. Give some reasons why this might be so.
24. Forests in Germany are dying due to acid rain. What effects might this loss have on the environment?
25. Describe how you could encourage your neighbors to recycle their newspapers.

MORE SKILL BUILDERS

If you need help, refer to the Skill Handbook.

1. **Recognizing Cause and Effect:** Suppose a city decided to pave over a large, grassy lot. What effects will this have on the local environment?
2. **Measuring in SI:** If each person in your class produced 47 174 kg of trash in a lifetime, how much trash would be produced by this small population?
3. **Classifying:** Analyze the garbage you throw away in one day. Classify each piece of garbage.
4. **Making and Using Graphs:** In a population of snails, each snail produces two offspring each month. Each offspring also produces two offspring. Using the graph (above right), determine how many snails would be present after five months if the initial population was only two snails.

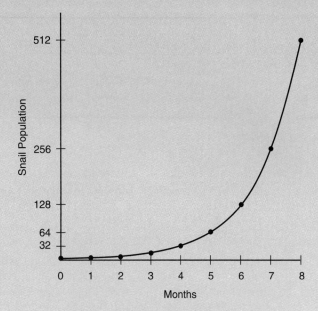

5. **Interpreting Scientific Illustrations:** Why does the curve of the line graph in Question 4 change its slope over time? Suppose half of the snails died after six months and draw a new graph to illustrate the effect.

PROJECTS

1. Use reference books and your knowledge of the environment to determine some of the problems you think will arise as the human population continues to increase. Discuss the problems and some possible solutions in a report.
2. Design an experiment to determine the factors that decrease the time it takes for newspapers or yard wastes to decompose.

20 You, Air, and Water

Most sources of drinking water are polluted. The water has to be treated with chemicals or filters before it's safe to use. Are any streams in your community severely polluted? What about the air in your area? Does it ever have a hazy appearance or unpleasant odor?

FIND OUT!

Do this simple activity to think about how the air and water are polluted.

Find a high shelf or the top of a tall cabinet—some place that hasn't been cleaned for a while. Run a cloth over the top and look at the dirt. This dirt was carried there by the air. This means that you are breathing in dirt like that all the time. Now, wash your hands. The dirt and the soap you used just went down the drain. It's on its way to a stream. Does your drinking water come from a nearby stream? Perhaps it's taken from underground aquifers. Either way, it's water that's been recycled by humans and nature after having been used before. Find out where the water that you use comes from and where it ends up.

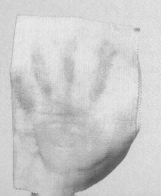

Gearing Up
Previewing the Chapter
Use this outline to help you focus on important ideas in this chapter.

Previewing Science Skills
▶ In the **Skill Builders,** you will make a concept map and make and use tables.
▶ In the **Activities,** you will collect and analyze data, make calculations, make inferences, and draw conclusions.
▶ In the **MINI-Labs,** you will experiment, observe, and infer.

What's next?

You've started thinking about how our air an water become polluted. Now you'll learn how pollutants get into air and water and what you can do to reduce pollution.

20-1 Air Pollution

New Science Words

photochemical smog
sulfurous smog
acid rain
pH scale
acids
bases
Clean Air Act

Objectives

▶ Identify the sources of pollutants that cause photochemical smog, sulfurous smog, holes in the ozone layer, and acid rain.
▶ Describe how air pollution affects people and the environment.
▶ Explain how air pollution can be reduced.

What Causes Air Pollution?

Have you ever noticed that the air looks hazy on some days? Do you know what causes this haziness? Air is everywhere, but its quality varies from place to place and day to day. Industries generate dust and chemicals. So, the more industries there are in a region, the more dust and chemicals there are in the air. Other human activities add pollutants to the air, too. For example, cars, buses, trucks, trains, and planes all burn fossil fuels for energy. Their exhaust—the waste products from burning the fossil fuels—adds polluting chemicals to the air. Other sources include smoke from burning trash and dust from plowed fields, construction sites, and mines.

Natural sources add pollutants to the air, too. Examples are volcanic eruptions, forest fires, and grass fires.

Both pollutants produced by human activities and those produced by natural processes cause the haze you sometimes see in the air. Around cities, polluted air is called smog, a word made by combining the words *smoke* and *fog*. Two types of smog are common—photochemical smog and sulfurous smog.

Smog

In areas such as Los Angeles, Denver, and New York, a hazy, brown blanket of smog is created when sunlight reacts with pollutants in the air. This brown smog is called **photochemical smog** because it forms with the aid of light. The pollutants get into the air when fossil fuels are burned. Coal, natural gas, and gasoline are burned by factories, airplanes, and cars. Heat from burning fossil

Figure 20-1. Cars are the main source of air pollution in the United States.

fuels causes nitrogen and oxygen to chemically combine to form nitrogen compounds. These compounds react with sunlight and produce other substances.

One of the substances created when sunlight reacts with waste gases is ozone. Recall that ozone in the stratosphere protects us from the sun's ultraviolet radiation. But ozone that forms in smog near Earth's surface causes health problems.

A second type of smog is called **sulfurous smog.** It's created when fossil fuels are burned in electrical power plants and home furnaces. The burning releases sulfur compounds, dust, and smoke particles into the air. Sulfurous smog forms when these substances collect in an area where there's little or no wind. The stagnant air fills with a blanket of gray smog. It may hang over a city for several days and is hazardous to breathe.

Nature plays an important role in creating smog. Sunlight helps form photochemical smog. Sulfurous smog forms when weather systems are calm and the air is not being moved around. Also, sometimes a layer of warm air lies on top of cooler air. Normally, the warmer air is near Earth's surface. But in cases where the warm air is above, it becomes a barrier that prevents the cool air below from rising. The result is that cool, dense air full of pollutants is trapped near the ground. Eventually, the weather changes and cleaner air is blown in, dispersing the polluted air.

Science and MATH

Cars emit about 20 pounds of carbon dioxide for each gallon of gas they use. How much more carbon dioxide will a car that gets 20 miles per gallon emit than one that gets 30 miles per gallon if they both drive 18 000 miles per year? Convert your answer from pounds to kilograms.

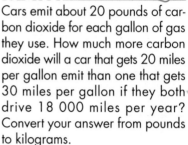

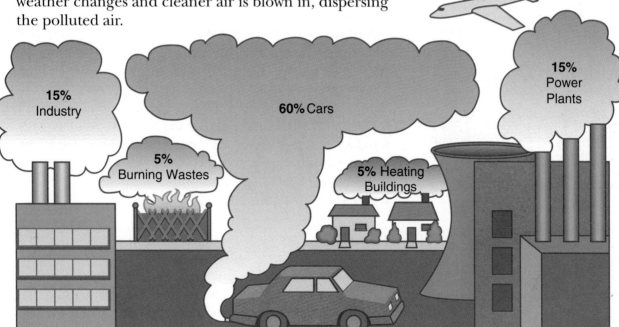

Figure 20-2. Proportions of Smog Caused by the Major Sources of Air Pollution

Figure 20-3. Fraser firs on Mt. Mitchell, North Carolina, are dying from the effects of acid rain.

What forms of precipitation can be acidic?

Figure 20-4. The natural pH of rainwater is about 5.0 in the eastern states. In the west, natural pH levels range between 5.3 and 6.5. Acid rain can have a pH of less than 3.0.

Landforms also affect smog development. For example, mountains may help cause smog by restricting the movement of air. Los Angeles has this problem because of nearby mountains. So does the city of Denver, in the Rocky Mountains. Some cities are in valleys, where dense, dirty air tends to stay.

Smog isn't the only air pollution problem we have. Recall from Chapters 9 and 10 that chlorofluorocarbons from air conditioners, refrigerators, and spray cans are destroying the ozone layer in the stratosphere. Carbon dioxide from burning coal, oil, natural gas, and forests is worsening the greenhouse effect.

Acid Rain

Another major pollution problem is acid rain. It has two sources. Acid rain is created when sulfur dioxide from coal-burning power plants combines with moisture in the air to form sulfuric acid. Acid rain also is created when nitrogen oxide from car exhausts combines with moisture in the air to form nitric acid. The moisture becomes so acidic that when it falls to the ground, we call it **acid rain.**

Actually, acid rain can fall as rain, snow, sleet, mist, or fog. As you might suspect, acid rain is very harmful to the environment.

What do you think would happen if you watered a plant with lemon juice instead of water? As you might guess, it would die. Lemon juice is a strong acid. Acid rain sometimes is as strong as lemon juice. Thus, acid rain can be strong enough to kill plants. To understand this, let's learn how the strength of an acid is measured.

We describe how acidic a solution is by using the **pH scale.** Figure 20-4 illustrates the pH scale. Substances with a pH lower than seven are considered **acids.** The lower the pH number, the stronger the acid. The higher the number, the weaker the acid. Substances with a pH above seven are considered **bases.**

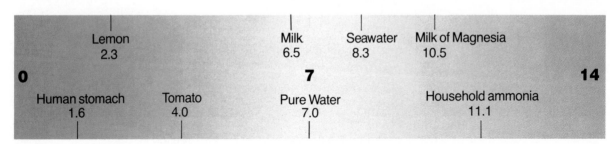

| Lemon 2.3 | Milk 6.5 | Seawater 8.3 | Milk of Magnesia 10.5 |

0   7   14

Human stomach 1.6   Tomato 4.0   Pure Water 7.0   Household ammonia 11.1

When acids get into soil, they remove essential nutrients. Acids also lower a plant's resistance to diseases, insects, and bad weather. This explains why many of Earth's forests are dying. Acid rain also increases the acidity of streams, rivers, and lakes, killing organisms that live in the water. It even damages the surfaces of buildings and cars.

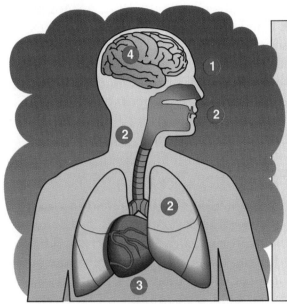

Effects of Air Pollution on the Body

1 Eyes
Compounds found in smog cause the eyes to water and sting. If conditions are bad enough, vision may be blurred.

2 Nose, throat, and lungs
Ozone irritates the nose and throat, causing burning. It reduces the ability of the lungs to fight infections.

3 Heart
Inhaled carbon monoxide is absorbed by red blood cells, rendering them incapable of transporting oxygen throughout the body. Chest pains result because of low oxygen levels.

4 Brain
Motor functions and coordination are impaired because oxygen levels in the brain are reduced when carbon monoxide is inhaled.

How Air Pollution Affects Our Health

Suppose you're an athlete in a large city and you're training for the big, upcoming competition. You have to get up at 4:30 A.M. to exercise. Later in the day, the smog levels will be so high that it won't be safe for you to do strenuous exercise. In southern California, Denver, and other areas, athletes adjust their training schedules to avoid exposure to ozone and other smog. Schools schedule football games for Saturday afternoons when the smog levels are low. Parents are warned to keep their children indoors when smog levels exceed certain levels. Breathing dirty air, especially taking deep breaths of it when you're actively exercising, causes health problems.

How hazardous is dirty air? Every year, between 40 000 and 100 000 people in the United States die from diseases related to air pollution. Breathing ozone and other smog damages people's lungs, making them more susceptible to diseases like pneumonia, flus, and asthma. Less severe symptoms of breathing ozone include a stinging chest, burning eyes, dry throat, and headache.

What are the physical symptoms of breathing ozone?

Name two substances that compose photochemical smog.

Substances other than ozone make up photochemical smog. One is carbon monoxide, a colorless, odorless gas. Even in small concentrations carbon monoxide makes people ill. When the concentration rises, people can die. You've probably heard of people who died from carbon monoxide poisoning when they left their car running in a garage or when their car's exhaust leaked into the car.

Sulfurous smog also kills people. In 1952, a smog in London, England, killed more than 4000 people. In 1953, a New York City smog caused about 200 deaths.

What do you suppose happens when you inhale the humid air from acid rain? Acid is deposited deep inside your lungs. This causes irritation, reduces your ability to fight respiratory infections, interferes with oxygen circulation, and puts stress on your heart.

Reducing Air Pollution

Why does pollution in one state affect other states?

Pollutants moving through the atmosphere don't stop when they reach the borders between states and countries. They float wherever the winds carry them. This makes them very difficult to control. Even if one state or country reduces its production of air pollutants, those from another state or country can blow in. However, cooperation among states and nations can help. So can controls by governments. Let's examine what's being done.

In 1987, officials from more than 30 countries wrote a treaty to reduce the use of chlorofluorocarbons (CFCs). These nations agreed to cut the production of CFCs in half by the year 2000.

Table 20-1

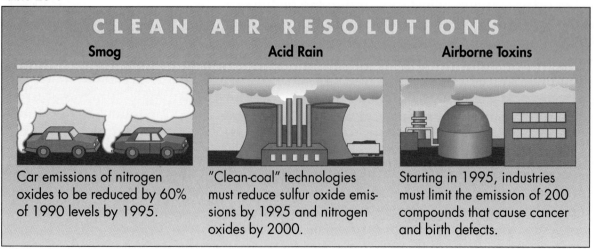

CLEAN AIR RESOLUTIONS

Smog	Acid Rain	Airborne Toxins
Car emissions of nitrogen oxides to be reduced by 60% of 1990 levels by 1995.	"Clean-coal" technologies must reduce sulfur oxide emissions by 1995 and nitrogen oxides by 2000.	Starting in 1995, industries must limit the emission of 200 compounds that cause cancer and birth defects.

The Congress of the United States passed several laws to protect the air. The 1990 **Clean Air Act** attacks the problems of automobile exhaust, factory pollution, destruction of ozone, and acid rain. In the figure on page 528, you can see some of the goals of the Clean Air Act.

Governments are passing laws to make everyone achieve the goals. The role of the federal Environmental Protection Agency is to check on progress toward the goals. The role of taxpayers and consumers is to pay the $50 billion or more each year to make the changes in industry and products necessary to clean up the air.

Governments are starting to do their part to protect our environment, but it's up to all of us to do what we can. The Clean Air Act can work only if you and everyone else cooperates. In Chapters 18 and 19 you discovered several ways you can save energy and reduce trash, such as using less electricity, recycling, and sharing rides. When you do these things, you also are reducing air pollution. We all must do our share to clean up the air.

MINi-Lab

Do we have acid rain?

The next time it rains or snows, use a glass or plastic container to collect a sample of several milliliters or centimeters of the rain or snow. Use pH ion paper to determine the acidity level of your sample. If you have collected snow, melt it before measuring its pH. Record the indicated pH of your sample and compare it to the results of other classmates who have followed the same procedure. What is the average pH of the samples obtained from this precipitation? How does the level of acidity in the samples compare to those shown on the pH scale in Figure 20-4 on page 526?

SECTION REVIEW

1. List the air pollutants, and their sources, that cause photochemical smog, sulfurous smog, holes in the ozone layer, and acid rain.
2. In what ways does air pollution affect the health of people?
3. How can you help reduce air pollution?
4. **Apply:** An earlier Clean Air Act, passed in 1970, required that coal-burning power plants use very tall smokestacks so that air pollutants would be injected high in the sky, where high-altitude winds would disperse them. Power plants in the midwestern states complied with the new law, but people in eastern Canada began complaining about acid rain. Explain the connection.

☑ Concept Mapping

Make a concept map that explains how sulfurous smog forms and how weather affects how long it persists. If you need help, refer to Concept Mapping in the **Skill Handbook** on pages 688 and 689.

Skill Builder

20-2 Acid Rain

New Science Words

scrubber

Objectives

▶ Describe the effects of acid rain on people, plants, water, and materials.
▶ Describe activities that help reduce acid rain.
▶ Decide who should pay the cost of reducing sulfur dioxide emissions.

How Soil Type Determines Acid Rain Damage

You may live in an area where there is very little acid rain. The amount of acid rain in an area depends on the number of factories and cars in the area. They are the sources of the sulfur and nitrogen gases that become acid rain. Whether acid rain falls where you live also depends on patterns of precipitation and wind direction where you are. Even if industry and cars are producing a lot of pollution near you, much of it may be carried away by the wind before it falls back down as acid rain.

It's not just the volume of acid rain that falls that determines how much damage is done in an area. There's another important factor: the soil. Different types of soil react differently to acid rain. Some soils already are acidic, and acid rain makes them even more acidic. But other soils are basic. If you mix an acidic solution with a basic solution, they neutralize each other. Therefore, if acid rain falls on basic soil, the acid rain becomes partly neutralized and causes less damage.

Soils in the midwestern states are basic. So, when acid rain falls in the Midwest, it's neutralized in the soil. But some areas, such as the northeastern states and eastern Canada, don't have basic soils. In these places, acid rain makes the ground and groundwater even more acid. Plants and fish have evolved to live in the naturally acidic soil and water. The additional acidity from acid rain injures them.

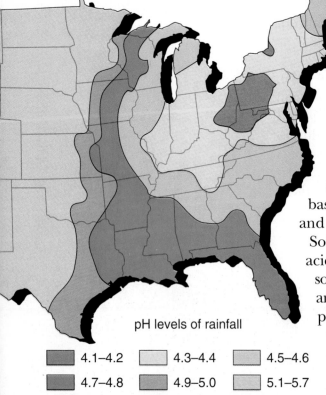

Figure 20-5. pH levels of rainfall in the eastern states and Canada are dangerously low.

pH levels of rainfall

4.1–4.2	4.3–4.4	4.5–4.6
4.7–4.8	4.9–5.0	5.1–5.7

What Can Be Done about Acid Rain?

The main source of the nitric acid in acid rain is car exhaust. Better emission control devices on cars will help reduce acid rain. So will car pooling and public transportation, because they reduce the number of trips, and thus the amount of fuel used.

Coal-burning power plants can help correct the problem. Some coal has lots of sulfur in it. When the coal is burned, the sulfur combines with moisture in the air to form sulfuric acid. Power plants can wash coal to remove some sulfur before the coal is burned. This way, burning produces less sulfur in the smoke. And they can run the smoke through a scrubber. A **scrubber** sprays the exhaust with basic compounds that increase the pH to a safe level.

Washing sulfur from the coal and using a scrubber lower sulfur emissions from coal-burning plants up to 90 percent. Unfortunately, taking these steps also raises the cost of generating electricity.

How does burning coal create acid rain?

T E C H N O L O G Y

Degradable Plastics

Plastics are used by nearly every major industry in the world. The United States alone produces close to 17 million tonnes of plastics each year. Plastics are used to make everything from appliance parts to packaging materials. The use of plastics is so widespread because they are waterproof, durable, and chemically stable. However, after plastics are used, they create a tremendous environmental problem. They don't decompose when buried in landfills. Burning them produces toxic smoke that pollutes the air.

Concerns for these problems have caused a company in Switzerland to invent a new type of plastic that repels water during use, but decomposes into harmless residues when it is discarded. A computer is used to choose the proper processing methods that will produce the plastic as pellets, films, tubes, adhesives, or sheets.

Think Critically: How can these new plastics be used in areas that suffer from acid rain?

Figure 20-6. Pressure from environmental groups and the government is forcing coal-burning power plants to make expensive changes to reduce emissions. How much are we willing to pay for cleaner air?

Another thing we could do is switch to other fuel sources. However, recall from Chapter 18 that these have disadvantages, too. And even if everyone agreed to make fuel changes, it would take many years for some areas to change. This is because many people, especially in the midwestern states, depend on coal for home heating and generating electricity. Changing the kind of fuel used costs money, because furnaces and boilers must be replaced.

As you read in the last section, the 1990 Clean Air Act requires great reductions in auto exhaust and sulfur dioxide emissions by the year 2003. This will cost all of us billions of dollars. It especially affects the Midwest, where thousands of people will lose their jobs. These include miners, workers in coal-burning power plants, and people who work for factories. The economy where these people live will suffer.

SECTION REVIEW

1. How does soil type determine the amount of damage done by acid rain?
2. How can acid rain be reduced?

SCIENCE & SOCIETY

You Decide!

Much of the acid rain problem comes from coal-burning power plants in the Midwest. Some people think that these midwestern states should pay to clean up the problem. But others propose that everyone in the nation should pay for the cleanup. This would reduce the financial burden on the midwestern states. They also propose a job-protection program to help coal miners and others who might lose their jobs. Is this fair to everyone? Why or why not?

ACTIVITY 20-1
What's in the Air?

Problem: *What types of dust or particles are in the air in your area?*

Materials

- small box of plain gelatin
- hot plate
- pan of water
- plastic lids (4)
- hand lens
- binocular microscope
- marker
- refrigerator
- thermal mitt

Procedure

1. Follow the mixing directions on the box of gelatin. Pour a thin layer of gelatin into each lid. **CAUTION:** *Wear a thermal mitt while working with a hot plate and while pouring the gelatin from the pan into the lids.*
2. Place the lids in a refrigerator until the gelatin is set.
3. Place the lids in four different locations in your community. Make sure that you choose places where the gelatin will not be disturbed.
4. After one week, collect the lids. Label each lid with its location.
5. Examine each lid with a hand lens.

6. Record your observations in a data table similar to the one shown in Data and Observations. Record whether the material on each lid is dust, large particles, or other materials.
7. Sketch some of the material found on each of your lids.
8. Sort the particulate matter (large pieces of dust, plant pieces, seeds, parts of insects, and so on) from each sample site.
9. Arrange these materials on microscope slides for each location.
10. Label the slides with the location from which each sample came.
11. Examine each slide with the microscope.
12. Try to identify what type of particulate matter you have collected.

Analyze

1. What sort of materials collected on each lid?
2. Rank the lids in order from the most solid particles to the least solid particles.
3. Which of the materials that were collected might be a result of human activities?
4. Explain why some areas had more and larger particles in the air.

Conclude and Apply

5. How does your body filter solid particles from the air you breathe?
6. Do any of the seeds that you might have collected suggest how some plants migrate from one area to another? Explain.
7. Try to identify what plants are responsible for the plant material on your slides. Try to identify the insect material. Were there any particles you could not identify?
8. Do you think any of the material you collected might be harmful to humans? Explain your answer.

Data and Observations

Location	Type of material	Description of material
1		
2		
3		
4		

20-3 Water Pollution

New Science Words

Safe Drinking Water Act
Clean Water Act

Objectives

▶ List five water pollutants and their sources.
▶ Describe ways that international agreements and U.S. laws are designed to reduce water pollution.
▶ Relate ways you can help reduce water pollution.

Causes and Effects of Water Pollution

Suppose you were hiking along a stream or lake and became very thirsty. Do you think it would be safe to drink the water? In most cases, it wouldn't. Many streams and lakes in the United States are quite polluted.

You learned in Chapter 12 how pollutants get into the oceans. Groundwater, streams, and lakes are polluted by similar sources. These pollutants cause health problems such as cancer, dysentery, birth defects, and liver damage in humans and other animals.

Our water is being contaminated from many sources. How do you think these pollutants get into the water? Bacteria and viruses get into the water because some cities illegally dump raw sewage directly into the water. Underground septic tanks can leak, too. Radioactive materials can get into the water from leaks at nuclear power plants and radioactive waste dumps.

Figure 20-7. Your drinking water comes from nearby streams, lakes, or underground aquifers. In most cases, pollutants have to be removed before the water is safe to drink.

Pesticides and herbicides from farms and lawns are picked up by rainwater and carried into streams. Oil and gasoline spilled on city streets and highways are carried through storm sewers, or they run over the ground and into the nearest stream. Some people dump motor oil into sewers after they've changed the oil in their cars. Water running through mines also carries pollutants to streams and underground aquifers. Industrial chemicals get into the water because some factories illegally dump toxic materials directly into the water. Waste from landfills and hazardous waste dumps leaks into the surrounding soil and groundwater.

It may seem as if the greatest causes of water pollution are illegal dumping, carelessness, and accidents. However, this isn't the case. Most pollution is caused by legal, everyday activities. Water is polluted when we flush our toilets, wash our hands, brush our teeth, and water our lawns. It's also polluted when oil and gas run off of pavement into streams. We all contribute to polluting Earth's waters.

Figure 20-8. Before our wastewater can be safely returned to the environment, it must be cleaned. The plant known as water hyacinth removes many pollutants from water. Water hyacinths can be used at wastewater treatment facilities to clean up water before it flows back into streams and aquifers.

Reducing Water Pollution

Several countries have worked together to reduce water pollution. Let's look at one example. Lake Erie is on the border between the United States and Canada. In the 1960s, Lake Erie was so polluted by phosphorus from sewage, soaps, and fertilizers that it was turning into a green, soupy mess. Large areas of the lake bottom had no oxygen and, therefore, no life. Some people said the whole lake was dead.

What's Happening to the Fish?

Joe and Scott had been fishing the same pond for seven years. However, they had noticed that they seemed to be catching fewer fish during the past two years than they had when they first started fishing there. They were also aware that the algae cover seemed to be getting thicker each year.

Joe and Scott were learning about air and water pollution in their science class.

They learned that high levels of phosphates and nitrates in water can cause an increase in algae populations. As these algae populations die, they sink to the bottom of the body of water. Then, the decomposer populations increase. Oxygen in the water is used up by the large numbers of decomposers. Fish and other aquatic populations do not have enough oxygen to survive.

Joe and Scott decided to make some careful observations near their fishing spot. They found that a nearby farm had a septic tank system for waste disposal. They questioned the owners about the types of soaps and detergents that were used for doing laundry. They also asked if fertilizers were being used on the crops.

Think Critically: Why were Joe and Scott interested in this information? If they determine that the pond is being polluted, what could be done to decrease the pollution?

How has the U.S. government helped to reduce water pollution?

In the 1970s, the United States and Canada made two water quality agreements. The two countries spent $15 billion to stop the sewage problem. Today, the green slime is gone, and the fish are back. However, more than 300 human-made chemicals still are in Lake Erie, and some of them are very hazardous. The United States and Canada now are studying ways to get them out of the lake.

The U.S. Congress also has reduced water pollution by passing several laws. Two important laws are the 1986 Safe Drinking Water Act and the 1987 Clean Water Act.

The 1986 **Safe Drinking Water Act** is a law to ensure that drinking water in our country is safe. Most cities have been able to comply with this law. In fact, 87 percent of the 58 000 public water systems met the government standards in 1986. However, some cities still don't meet these standards. In 1990, about 30 million U.S. citizens still drank from potentially unsafe water supplies.

The 1987 **Clean Water Act** gives money to the states for building sewage and wastewater treatment facilities. It also is for controlling runoff from streets, mines, and farms. Runoff caused up to half of the water pollution in the United States before 1987. This act also requires states to develop quality standards for all their streams.

The U.S. Environmental Protection Agency (EPA) makes sure that cities comply with both the Safe Drinking Water Act and the Clean Water Act. Most cities and states are working hard to clean up their water. Many streams that once were heavily polluted by sewage and industrial wastes are now safe for swimming and fishing. However, there is still much more to be done.

For example, the EPA discovered that one-half of the 5000 disposal sites for hazardous wastes are leaking into the groundwater. Also, mineral residues from 10 000 abandoned mines are killing aquatic life in streams in the Rocky Mountains. At least ten percent of the nation's lakes are contaminated with enough toxic chemicals and metals to make them dangerous to aquatic life. Worst of all, much of the groundwater in the United States is polluted. Groundwater provides drinking water for more than 50 percent of the nation's population.

What is one function of the EPA?

Figure 20-9. This water purification plant in Chicago provides drinking water for millions of people. Water taken from Lake Michigan is pumped into a tank where alum, chlorine, lime, and other compounds are added to kill microorganisms. It's thoroughly mixed and the large particles of matter settle out. Some smaller particles are filtered by sand and gravel. Clean water is then pumped to consumers.

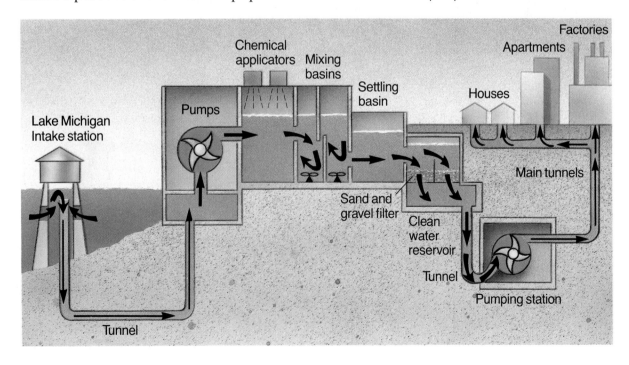

How hard is your water?

When minerals such as calcium carbonate, magnesium carbonate, or sulfates are dissolved in water, the water is said to be "hard." This is a type of natural "pollution" that occurs in some areas. Test the hardness of the water in your area by placing samples of water from the tap, a nearby pond or well, and a local stream into a small container such as a baby food jar. Place an equal amount of distilled water into another container. Add one drop of liquid soap to each, cap each container tightly and shake each rapidly. Observe how many soapsuds are produced. Repeat the procedure several times with each container. The container with the most suds contains the softest water. What was the source of the hardest water in your experiment? What problems might be caused by having a hard-water supply in your home or community?

How Can You Help?

As you discovered in Chapter 19, we are the cause of our environmental problems. We also are the solution. What can you do to help? You can help by following some simple steps. For example, if you dispose of household chemicals such as paints and motor oil, don't pour them down the drain or onto the ground. Also, don't put them out with your other trash. Why not?

If you pour hazardous wastes directly onto the ground, they move through the soil and reach the groundwater below. When you pour them down the drain, they flow through the sewer, through the wastewater treatment plant, and into wherever the wastewater is drained, usually into a stream. This is how rivers become polluted. If you put wastes out with the trash, they end up in landfills, where they may leak out.

What should you do with these wastes? First, read the label on the container for instructions on disposal. Don't throw the container into the trash if the label specifies a different method of disposal. Recycle if you can. Many cities have recycling facilities for metal, glass, and plastic containers. Store chemical wastes so that they can't leak. If you live in a city, call the sewage office, water office, or garbage disposal service and ask them how to safely dispose of the others.

Another way you can reduce water pollution is to conserve energy. With less use of fuels there will be less acid rain falling into forests and streams. And with less nuclear power, there will be a reduced risk of radioactive materials leaking into the environment.

Another way you can help is to conserve water that comes from your tap. How much water do you use every

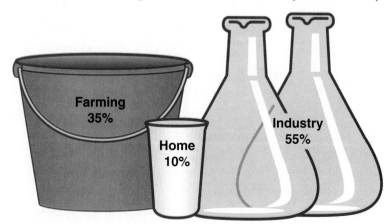

Figure 20-10. The industries that produce the products you use each day consume more than half of the freshwater used in the United States.

day? Think of all the ways you depend on water. How many times do you flush a toilet each day? How much water do you use every day for taking a bath or cleaning your clothes? How much water do you use when you wash dishes, wash a car, or use a hose or lawn sprinkler? Typical U.S. citizens like you use between 265 and 568 liters every day.

All of this water must be purified before it reaches your home. Then it must be treated as wastewater after you use it. It takes a lot of energy to treat this water and pump it to your home. Remember, when you use energy, you add to the pollution problem. Therefore, when you reduce the amount of water you use, you prevent pollution. Simple things you can do to use less water include taking a shower instead of a bath and turning off the water while brushing your teeth. Can you think of other things you can do?

Water pollution is everybody's problem, and we must do our part to help reduce it. Consider changes you can make in your life that will make a difference.

EcoTip

After obtaining an adult's permission, fill a two-liter soft-drink bottle with water and seal it. Place it in your toilet tank. You can save more than ten percent of the water used to flush the toilet.

SECTION REVIEW

1. List five water pollutants and their sources.
2. Describe how the United States and Canada reduced pollution in Lake Erie.
3. What is the purpose of the 1987 Clean Water Act?
4. What are three things you can do to help reduce water pollution?
5. **Apply:** Southern Florida is home to nearly 5 million people, many dairy farms, and sugarcane fields. It's also the location of Everglades National Park—a shallow river system with highly polluted waters that are drying up. Why do you think they're drying up? What kinds of pollutants do you think are in the Everglades?

☑ Interpreting Scientific Illustrations

Skill Builder

Use Figure 20-9 to answer the following questions: *Why are mixing basins needed? What's the purpose of the sand and gravel filter? Gravity forces the water through the system until it reaches the reservoir. Why is a pump needed after this point?* If you need help, refer to Interpreting Scientific Illustrations in the **Skill Handbook** on page 693.

ACTIVITY 20-2
Water Use

Problem: *How much water does your family use?*

Materials
• home water meter

Background
There are several different types of water meters. Meter *a* has six dials. As water moves through the meter, the pointers on the dials rotate. To read a meter similar to *a*, find the dial with the lowest denomination indicated. The bottom dial is labeled 10. Record the last number that the pointer on that dial has passed. Continue this process for each dial. Meter *a* shows 18 853 gallons. Meter *b* is read like a digital watch. It indicates 1959.9 cubic feet. Meter *c* is similar to meter *b,* but indicates water use in cubic meters.

Procedure
1. Record your home water meter reading at the same time of the day for eight days.
2. Subtract the previous day's reading to determine the amount of water used each day.
3. Record how much water is used in your home each day. Also, record the activities in your home that used water each day.
4. Plot your data on a graph like the one shown. Label the vertical axis with the units used by your meter.

Analyze
1. During which day is the most water used? Why?
2. Calculate the total amount of water used by your family during the week.
3. Calculate the average amount of water each person used during the week by dividing the total amount of water used by the number of persons. Calculate a monthly average.

Conclude and Apply
4. Why is your answer to Question 3 only an estimate of the amount of water used?
5. How might the time of year affect the rate at which your family uses water?
6. What are some things your family could do to conserve water?

One week's water usage

Water used (units)

1 2 3 4 5 6 7
Day

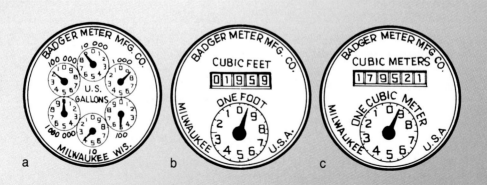

a   b   c

CHAPTER
REVIEW

20-1: Air Pollution

1. Photochemical smog forms when fossil fuels are burned. Sulfurous smog is created when fuels are burned in electrical power plants and home furnaces. CFCs cause holes in the ozone layer. Acid rain is the result of burning coal and gasoline, which produce gases that react to form acids in the air.

2. Air pollution causes health problems in people and other organisms.

3. Recycling and conservation of Earth's resources reduce pollution.

20-2: Science and Society: Acid Rain

1. Acid rain can lower a plant's resistance to disease, insects, and bad weather. It can also kill organisms that live in fresh water by increasing the acidity of the water.

2. Better emission control devices on cars, car pooling, and the use of public transportation can help reduce acid rain. Washing coal that contains a lot of sulfur and using scrubbers can also reduce acid rain.

3. The cost of reducing sulfur dioxide emissions could be shared by everyone or could be limited to the areas that produce the emissions.

20-3: Water Pollution

1. Bacteria and viruses from animal wastes, radioactive waste, pesticides and herbicides used in agriculture, fossil fuels from mines and wells, and industrial chemicals from manufacturing processes all pollute freshwater bodies.

2. The passing of laws and the enforcement of these laws by the EPA and other agencies has helped to reduce water pollution.

3. Safely disposing of hazardous wastes is one way to reduce water pollution. Recycling and conservation are also important.

KEY SCIENCE WORDS

a. **acid rain**
b. **acids**
c. **bases**
d. **Clean Air Act**
e. **Clean Water Act**
f. **photochemical smog**
g. **pH scale**
h. **Safe Drinking Water Act**
i. **scrubber**
j. **sulfurous smog**

UNDERSTANDING VOCABULARY

Match each phase with the correct term from the list of Key Science Words.

1. smog that forms with the aid of light
2. smog that forms when pollutants mix with a layer of stagnant air
3. acidic rain, snow, sleet, or hail
4. law passed to protect air in the U.S.
5. a scale used to measure the acidity or basicity of a solution
6. device that lowers sulfur emissions from coal-burning power plants
7. law assuring water is safe to drink
8. law that controls stormwater runoff
9. substances with low pH numbers
10. substances with high pH numbers

CHAPTER
REVIEW

CHECKING CONCEPTS

Choose the word or phrase that completes the sentence.

1. Dust gets into the air from _____.
   a. cars and buses   c. trucks and trains
   b. factories and farms d. all of these

2. _____ forms when chemicals mix with sunlight.
   a. pH   c. Sulfurous smog
   b. Photochemical smog   d. Acid rain

3. Smog development is controlled by _____.
   a. weather patterns   c. mountains
   b. sunlight   d. all of these

4. Acid rain can form when _____ combines with moisture in the air.
   a. ozone   c. carbon dioxide
   b. sulfur dioxide   d. none of these

5. Air pollution can be reduced by _____ .
   a. using less CFCs   c. recycling
   b. sharing rides   d. all of these

6. One goal of the _____ Act is to reduce the level of car emissions.
   a. Clean Water   c. Safe Drinking Water
   b. Clean Air   d. all of these

7. Acid rain has a pH _____.
   a. less than 5.5   c. greater than 7.0
   b. between 5.5 and 7.0 d. greater than 9.5

8. The damage done by acid rain depends on _____.
   a. the pH scale   c. soil type
   b. nitrogen emissions d. groundwater sources

9. Most water pollution is caused by _____.
   a. illegal dumping
   b. industrial chemicals
   c. everyday water use in the home
   d. wastewater treatment facilities

10. The _____ Act gives money to local governments to treat wastewater.
    a. Clean Water   c. Safe Drinking Water
    b. Clean Air   d. all of these

UNDERSTANDING CONCEPTS

Complete each sentence.

11. _____ forms when the gases produced by burning fossil fuels react with sunlight.

12. Weather plays an important role in the time it takes for _____ to disperse from an area.

13. Precipitation that forms when certain gases mix with the air is called _____.

14. A(n) _____ can prevent harmful substances from burning coal from getting into the air.

15. The _____ requires that water for human consumption be safe.

16. Compare and contrast photochemical smog and sulfurous smog.
17. Explain two ways in which acid rain can form.
18. Discuss the factors that affect the severity of the damage done by acid rain.
19. Which water pollutants are thought to cause cancer in humans?
20. Compare and contrast the Safe Drinking Water Act with the Clean Water Act.

APPLY

21. How might cities with smog problems lessen the dangers to people who live and work in the cities?
22. How are industries both helpful and harmful to humans?
23. How do trees help to reduce air pollution?
24. Thermal pollution occurs when heated water is dumped into a nearby water body. What effects does this type of pollution have on organisms in the water bodies?
25. What steps might a community in a desert area take to cope with the water supply problems?

MORE SKILL BUILDERS

If you need help, refer to the Skill Handbook.

1. **Hypothesizing:** Earth is nearly 75 percent water. Yet, much of this water is not available for many uses. Explain.
2. **Recognizing Cause and Effect:** What effect will an increase in the human population have on the need for fresh water?
3. **Classifying:** If a smog is brownish in color, is it sulfurous or photochemical smog?

4. **Concept Mapping:** Copy and complete the concept map of the water cycle. Indicate how humans interrupt the cycle. Use the phrases: *Evaporation occurs, Purified, Drinking water, Atmospheric water,* and *Wastewater.*

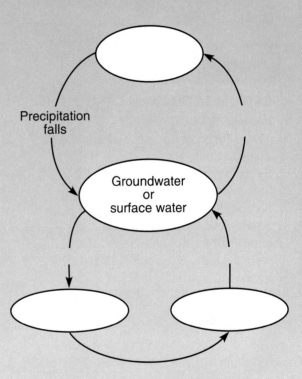

Precipitation falls

Groundwater or surface water

5. **Outlining:** Make an outline that summarizes what you personally can do to reduce air pollution.

PROJECTS

1. Design an experiment to test the effects of acid rain on various kinds of vegetation.
2. Design an experiment to determine which kind of sediment—gravel, sand, or clay—is most effective in filtering pollutants from water.

GLOBAL CONNECTIONS

Earth's Resources

In this unit, you studied about natural resources and conservation. Now find out how these topics are connected to other subjects and places around the world.

120°   60°

BIOLOGY

ORGANIC FARMING
Imperial Valley, California
When the citrus fruit in southern California was attacked by an insect called cottony cushion scale, organic farmers brought in ladybugs. These tiny beetles had the scale insects in check within two years. Why were the ladybugs a safer remedy than using pesticides?

HEALTH

RADIOACTIVE WASTE
Yucca Mountain, Nevada
When nuclear reactors produce energy, they generate radioactive waste. If this waste gets into groundwater, it can threaten the health of people who drink the water. How might radioactive waste get into groundwater from the Yucca Mountain nuclear-waste storage facility?

PHYSICS

CLEANER FUEL FOR CARS
Knoxville, Tennessee
Students at the University of Tennessee used M85, a mixture of 85 percent methanol—a kind of alcohol—and 15 percent gasoline, in the competition to find cleaner fuel. Tennessee took first place in fuel economy and the lowest pollutants. If a liter of methanol has one-half the energy of gasoline, what effect would this have on the design of a car?

CAUTION
TOXIC SUBSTANCES
CAUTION

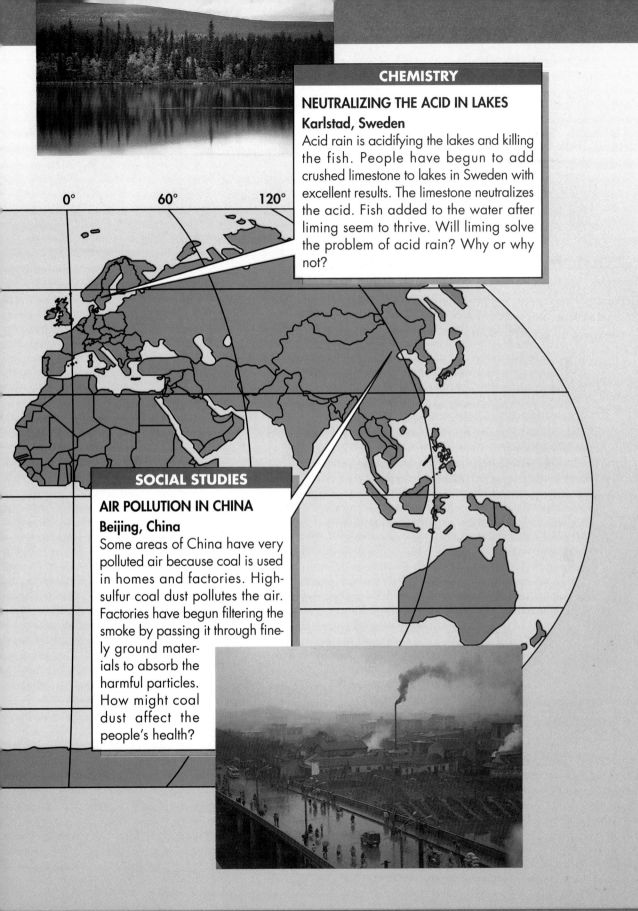

0°   60°   120°

NEUTRALIZING THE ACID IN LAKES
Karlstad, Sweden

Acid rain is acidifying the lakes and killing the fish. People have begun to add crushed limestone to lakes in Sweden with excellent results. The limestone neutralizes the acid. Fish added to the water after liming seem to thrive. Will liming solve the problem of acid rain? Why or why not?

AIR POLLUTION IN CHINA
Beijing, China

Some areas of China have very polluted air because coal is used in homes and factories. High-sulfur coal dust pollutes the air. Factories have begun filtering the smoke by passing it through finely ground materials to absorb the harmful particles. How might coal dust affect the people's health?

545

CAREERS

ECOLOGIST

An *ecologist* studies the relationships between living things and their habitats. One of the most important roles of ecologists is to help manage and control the environment. They study the effect of air and water pollution on living things. They also try to foresee the effect on wildlife of activities such as building dams or cutting down forests. Ecologists make people aware of the need to conserve natural resources.

An ecologist's job requires a college degree in ecology or related fields. A student interested in becoming an ecologist should take courses in biology and mathematics.

For Additional Information
Contact the American Institute of Biological Sciences, Office of Career Services, 730 11th Street NW, Washington, DC 20001-4584.

POLLUTION-CONTROL TECHNICIAN

Pollution-control technicians help improve the environment by monitoring the pollutants being released into the air or water. They may test the drinking water or the air quality to make certain it meets health standards. They may even check on noise pollution caused by cars and airplanes.

A pollution-control technician needs an associate degree from a community college. A student interested in a career as a pollution-control technician should study biology, chemistry, and mathematics.

For Additional Information
Contact the National Environmental Health Association, 720 S. Colorado Boulevard, Denver, CO 80222.

UNIT READINGS

►Berger, John J. *Restoring the Earth.* New York: Alfred A. Knopf, 1985.

►Seymour, John and Herbert Girardet. *Blueprint for a Green Planet: Your Practical Guide to Restoring the World's Environment.* New York: Prentice-Hall, 1987.

►Wild, Russel, ed. *The Earth Care Annual 1990.* Emmaus, Pennsylvania: National Wildlife Federation, Rodale Press, 1990.

Rachel Carson's *Silent Spring*

Rachel Carson was a scientist, a writer, and a lover of nature. She, like so many others, looked forward each year to the coming of spring with its songs of birds. She began to notice in the early 1960s that in some parts of America, spring was strangely silent because many of the birds were dead.

Her book *Silent Spring* tells about people's reckless attempt to control the environment by using large quantities of pesticides, particularly DDT. This effort was responsible for poisoning the birds in the air and the fish in the rivers. In *Silent Spring*, she writes:

Over increasingly large areas of the United States, spring now comes unheralded by the return of the birds, and the early mornings are strangely silent where once they were filled with the beauty of bird song. This sudden silencing of the song of birds, this obliteration of the color and beauty and interest they lend to our world have come about swiftly, insidiously, and unnoticed by those whose communities are as yet unaffected. From the town of Hinsdale, Illinois, a housewife wrote in despair to one of the world's leading ornithologists, Robert Cushman Murphy,

Curator Emeritus of Birds at the American Museum of Natural History.

"Here in our village the elm trees have been sprayed for several years. When we moved here six years ago, there was a wealth of bird life . . . After several years of DDT spray, the town is almost devoid of robins and starlings; chickadees have not been on my shelf for two years, and this year the cardinals are gone, too; the nesting population seems to consist of one dove pair and perhaps one catbird family."

Who has decided—who has the right to decide—for the countless legions of people who were not consulted that the supreme value is a world without insects, even though it is also a sterile world ungraced by the curving wing of a bird in flight?

In Your Own Words

▶ The use of DDT has been banned, but other pesticides still harm wildlife. Write a newspaper article to express your views about the use of pesticides.

UNIT

8 THE SOLAR SYSTEM

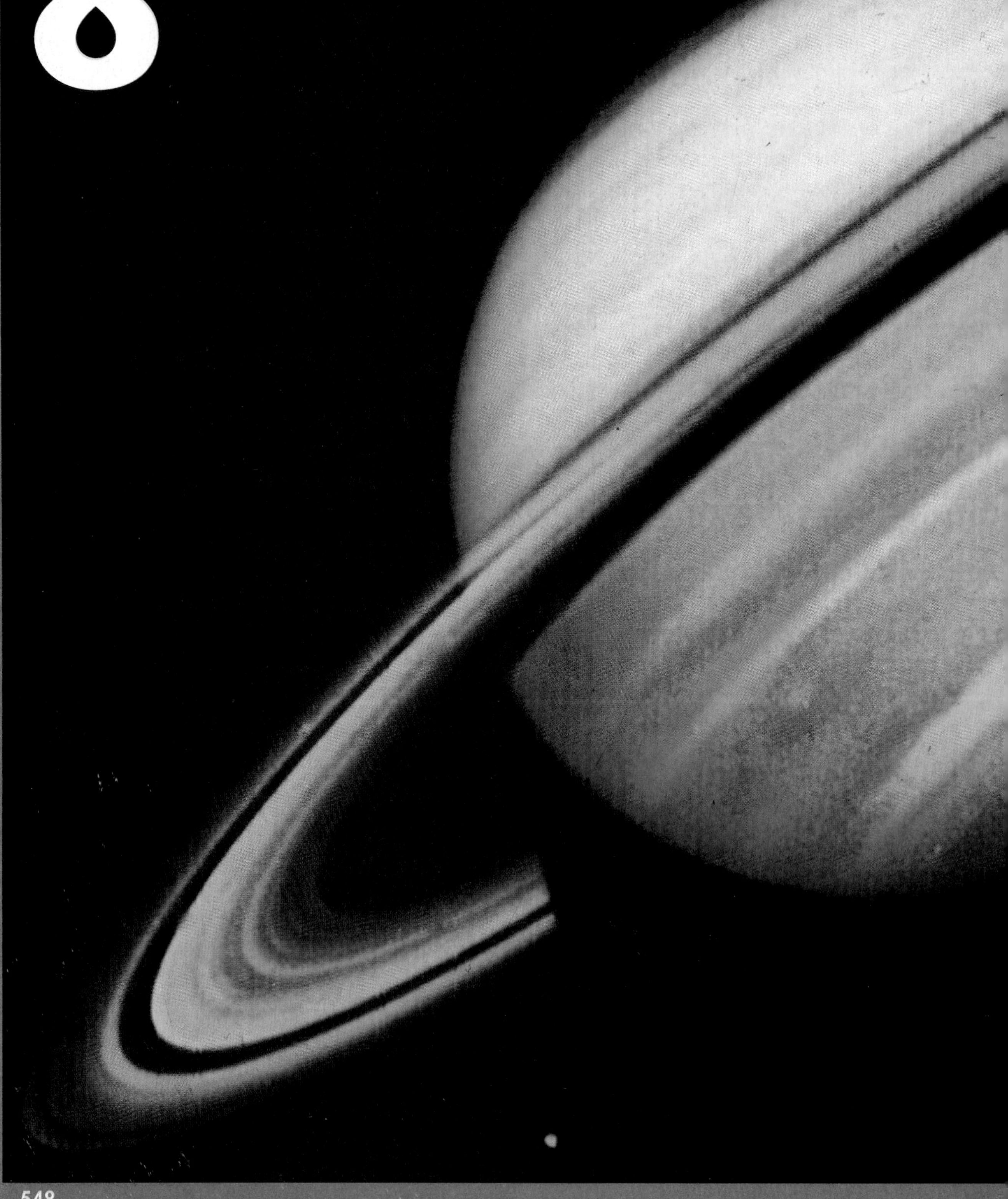

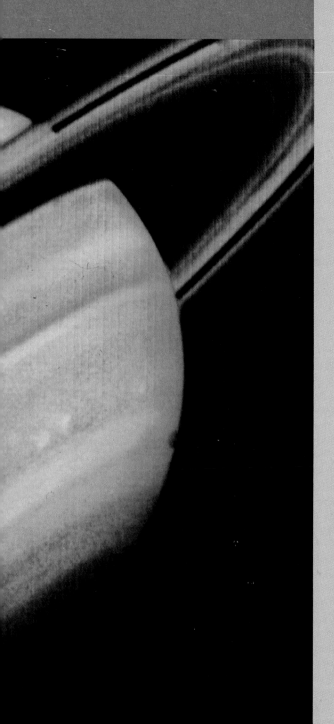

What's Happening Here?

In the 1980s, the *Voyager* space probes flew past Saturn and sent back photographs of its complex ring system. In the 1600s, when Galileo Galilei turned his telescope on Saturn, he saw what appeared to be a triple planet—one large planet with two smaller planets hidden behind it. Shown below is a sketch he made of his observation. People can study our universe by using telescopes, as Galileo did, or by launching spacecrafts, such as the *Voyager* probes. As you read the chapters that follow, you'll learn more about our universe and the instruments we use to study it.

UNIT CONTENTS

CHAPTER
21 Exploring Space

The radio telescopes shown detect energy from space that we can't see. But even visible energy holds information that isn't at first apparent. Some of the radiation we receive from stars is in the form of white light. White light is a mixture of the colors of the rainbow —red, orange, yellow, green, blue, indigo, and violet. By studying the visible light and invisible energy coming from objects in space, we have learned a great deal about the universe.

FIND OUT!

Do this simple activity to see how colors combine to form white light.

Cover the end of a flashlight with a green gelatin (or plexiglass) filter. Cover another flashlight with a blue filter and a third with a red filter. In a darkened room, shine the red light on a sheet of white paper. Then, keeping the red light on, shine the blue light at the same spot on the paper. What do you observe? Add the green light. What do you observe when all three lights are shining at the same spot?

Gearing Up

Previewing the Chapter

Use this outline to help you focus on important ideas in this chapter.

Previewing Science Skills

▶ In the **Skill Builders,** you will sequence events, make concept maps, and outline.
▶ In the **Activities,** you will observe, analyze data, make inferences, and draw conclusions.
▶ In the **MINI-Labs,** you will experiment, construct models, and draw conclusions.

What's next?

You've seen how colored light combines to form new colors and white light. But visible light is just one form of energy we receive from the sun and other stars in space. In Section 21-1, you'll read about the forms of energy radiated by objects in space and the tools we use to study that energy.

21-1 Radiant Energy from Space

New Science Words

electromagnetic spectrum
refracting telescope
reflecting telescope
observatories
radio telescope

Objectives

▶ Define the electromagnetic spectrum.
▶ Compare and contrast refracting and reflecting telescopes.
▶ Compare and contrast optical and radio telescopes.

Did You Know?

If it were possible for you to travel at the speed of light, you could travel around the world seven times in one second.

The Electromagnetic Spectrum

On this crisp autumn evening, you take a break from your homework to gaze out the window at the many stars filling the night sky. You think about your future and how humans might someday attempt to travel to one of those distant stars. Looking up at the night sky, it's easy to imagine future spaceships venturing through space and large space stations circling above Earth where people work and live. But when you look into the night sky, what you're really seeing is the distant past, not the future.

When you look at a star, you see the light that left it many years ago. The light that you see travels very fast, but the distances across space are so great that it takes years for the light to reach Earth—sometimes tens of thousands of years.

The light and other energy leaving a star are forms of radiant energy. Recall that radiant energy, or radiation,

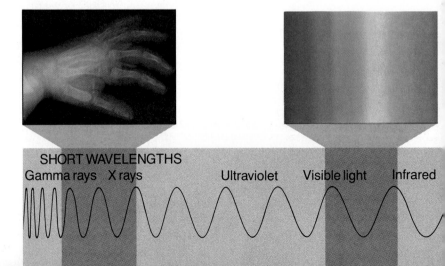

SHORT WAVELENGTHS
Gamma rays   X rays   Ultraviolet   Visible light   Infrared

is energy that's transmitted from one place to another by electromagnetic waves. Electromagnetic waves carry energy through empty space as well as through matter.

Recall what you learned about earthquake waves. Earthquake waves are mechanical waves and, unlike electromagnetic waves, they need matter to be transmitted. Sound waves, another type of mechanical wave, can't travel through empty space. How do we hear the voices of the astronauts while they're in space? When they speak into a microphone, the sound is converted into electromagnetic waves called radio waves. The radio waves travel through space and through our atmosphere. They are then converted back into sound waves by electronic equipment and audio speakers.

Radio waves and visible light from the sun are just two types of electromagnetic waves. The other types include gamma rays, X rays, ultraviolet waves, infrared waves, and microwaves. Figure 21-1 shows these forms of radiant energy arranged according to their wavelengths. This arrangement of radiant energy is called the **electromagnetic spectrum.**

Although the types of electromagnetic waves differ in their wavelengths, they all travel at the speed of 300 000 km/s in a vacuum. You're probably more familiar with this speed as the "speed of light." Visible light and other forms of radiant energy travel at this incredible speed, but the universe is so large that it takes billions of years for the light from some objects to reach Earth.

Once radiant energy from the stars and other objects reaches Earth, we can use it to learn about the objects. What tools and methods do scientists use to discover what lies beyond our planet?

Why aren't sound waves included in the electromagnetic spectrum?

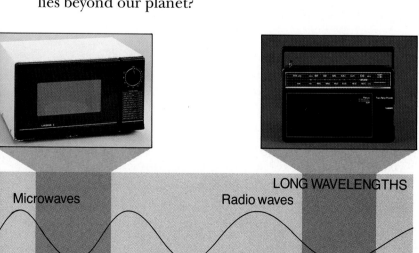

Microwaves   Radio waves   LONG WAVELENGTHS

Figure 21-1. The electromagnetic spectrum ranges from gamma rays with wavelengths of less than 0.000 000 000 01 meters to radio waves more than 100 000 meters long.

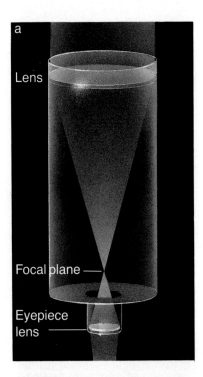

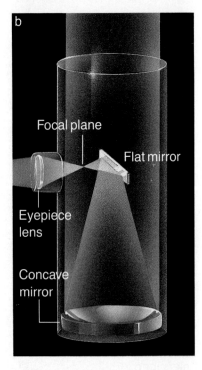

Figure 21-2. In a refracting telescope (a), a convex lense focuses light to form an image. In a reflecting telescope (b), a concave mirror focuses light to form an image. The image is then magnified by the eyepiece.

Optical Telescopes

Optical telescopes produce magnified images of objects. The two types of optical telescopes are refracting telescopes and reflecting telescopes. In a **refracting telescope,** the light from an object passes through convex lenses and is bent to converge on one plane called the focal plane. It is then bent again as it passes through another lens, the eyepiece, and a magnified image of the object forms in your eye.

A **reflecting telescope** uses mirrors to focus light from the object being viewed. At the end of the telescope tube is a concave mirror. When visible light strikes this mirror, it is reflected to the focal plane. A smaller mirror is often used to reflect the light into the eyepiece lens so the image can be viewed.

Most optical telescopes used by professional astronomers are housed in buildings called **observatories.** Observatories often have a dome-shaped roof that opens up so light can reach the telescopes. However, not all telescopes are in observatories. You've probably read about the *Hubble Space Telescope* launched in 1990 by the space shuttle *Discovery.*

Hubble was placed in space so scientists could avoid looking through our atmosphere. Earth's atmosphere absorbs and distorts some of the energy we receive from space. Because *Hubble* wouldn't have to view space through our atmosphere, it should have produced very clear images. Some images haven't been as clear as hoped. When the largest mirror of this reflecting telescope was being shaped, a mistake was made. Because of its distorted shape, about half of the programs scheduled for *Hubble* don't work as well as planned.

Radio Telescopes

Optical telescopes allow scientists to study the visible light coming from objects in space. But as you know, stars and other objects radiate more than visible light. They radiate energy throughout the electromagnetic spectrum. A **radio telescope** is used to study radio waves traveling through space. Unlike visible light, radio waves pass freely through Earth's atmosphere. Because of this, radio telescopes are useful under most weather conditions and at all times of day and night.

Radio waves reaching Earth's surface strike the large, curved dish of a radio telescope. This dish reflects the waves to a focal plane where a receiver is located. Computers record the waves picked up by the receiver. The recorded information allows us to map the universe, detect objects in space, and to search for intelligent life that might be broadcasting radio waves.

Since the early 1600s when the Italian scientist Galileo Galilei first turned a telescope toward the stars, people have been searching for better ways to study what lies beyond our atmosphere. Bigger and better mirrors and lenses have been constructed for use in optical telescopes. Today, the largest reflector has a segmented mirror ten meters wide, and the largest radio telescope is 300 meters wide. These telescopes are quite an improvement over Galileo's small, handheld model. Still, Galileo was able to see what others had not even dreamed of. He saw shadows in the craters of our moon and discovered four moons orbiting Jupiter. In the remainder of this chapter, you'll learn about the instruments we've sent into space to send back information that could never be collected through the eyepiece or radio receiver of a telescope.

PROBLEM SOLVING

A Homemade Antenna

Calid and Hiroshi had been looking forward to their camping trip for several weeks. They had just set up camp when some large clouds began to roll in and the wind began to stir.

Calid pulled out their radio to listen to the weather forecast. He thought a storm might be approaching and they would need to seek better shelter. The radio reception was poor and they could barely hear the weather report.

Hiroshi dug through their camping supplies and found some aluminum foil wrap, an umbrella, and some string. He suggested that they could use these items to improve the radio reception.

Think Critically: How could Calid and Hiroshi improve the radio reception with the items from their supplies? How are the parts of their radio and antenna like those of a radio telescope?

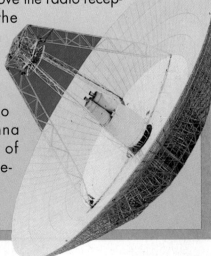

555

Figure 21-3. The *Hubble Space Telescope* was deployed from the cargo bay of the space shuttle *Discovery* on April 25, 1990. It's now orbiting Earth, sending back images and data about distant space objects.

SECTION REVIEW

1. What is the electromagnetic spectrum?
2. Which type of telescope reflects light from a mirror to form an image?
3. How are radio telescopes and optical telescopes different from one another?
4. Why should telescopes such as the *Hubble Space Telescope* produce more detailed images than Earth-based telescopes?
5. **Apply:** It takes light from the closest star to Earth (other than the sun) about four years to reach us. If there was intelligent life on a planet circling that star, how long would it take for us to send them a radio transmission and for us to receive their reply?

Skill Builder

☑ Sequencing

Sequence these electromagnetic waves from longest wavelength to shortest wavelength: *gamma rays, visible light, X rays, radio waves, infrared waves, ultraviolet waves,* and *microwaves.* If you need help, refer to Sequencing in the **Skill Handbook** on page 680.

ACTIVITY 21-1
Telescopes

Problem: *How do the paths of light differ in reflecting and refracting telescopes?*

Materials

- candle
- cardboard, white, 50 cm × 60 cm
- flashlight
- magnifying glass
- glass of water
- aluminum or silver spoon
- plane mirror
- convex mirror
- concave mirror
- empty paper towel roll
- masking tape

Procedure

1. Observe your reflection in a plane, convex, and concave mirror. Note differences in your image in the three mirrors.
2. Hold an object in front of each of the mirrors. Compare the images as to relative size and position.
3. Darken the room and hold the convex mirror at a 45° angle, slanting downward from your body. Direct the flashlight beam toward the mirror from right angles to your body. Note the size and position of the reflected light.
4. Repeat Step 3 using a plane mirror. Draw a diagram to show what happens to the beam of light.
5. Place the spoon in a glass of water. Diagram the shape of the spoon at the water line.
6. Attach the empty paper towel roll to the flashlight with masking tape so that the narrow beam of light will pass through the roll. Direct the light into a large glass of water, first directly from above, then from a 45° angle to the water surface. Compare the direction of the light rays when viewed from the side of the glass.

7. Light a candle and set it up some distance from the vertically held cardboard screen. **CAUTION:** *Keep hair and clothing away from the flame.* Using the magnifying glass as a convex lens, hold it between the candle and the screen until you have the best possible image.
8. Move the glass closer to the candle. Note what happens to the size of the image. Move the cardboard until the image is in focus.

Analyze

1. What is the purpose of the concave mirror in a reflecting telescope?
2. How did you determine the position of the focal plane of the magnifying glass in Step 7? What does this tell you about the position of all the light rays?
3. In one type of reflecting telescope, a plane mirror is in the tube near the eyepiece. What is the purpose of this mirror?
4. The eyepiece of a telescope is convex. What is its purpose?
5. What is the effect of the concave mirror on your reflection? Of the convex mirror? Of the plane mirror?
6. What effect did the convex mirror have on the beam of light in Step 3?

Conclude and Apply

7. Discuss your observations of the relationship of the distance between the object and lens and the clearest and largest image you could obtain in Steps 7 and 8.
8. How does the path of light differ in refracting and reflecting telescopes?

21-2 Light Pollution

New Science Words

light pollution

Objectives

▶ Explain how light pollution affects the ability to see dim objects in the sky.

▶ Discuss the controversy over light pollution as it relates to security and safety lighting.

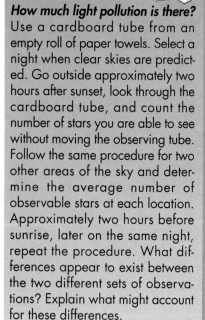

MINI-Lab

How much light pollution is there?
Use a cardboard tube from an empty roll of paper towels. Select a night when clear skies are predicted. Go outside approximately two hours after sunset, look through the cardboard tube, and count the number of stars you are able to see without moving the observing tube. Follow the same procedure for two other areas of the sky and determine the average number of observable stars at each location. Approximately two hours before sunrise, later on the same night, repeat the procedure. What differences appear to exist between the two different sets of observations? Explain what might account for these differences.

Should Light Pollution Be Controlled?

When you gaze out your window at the night sky, what do you see? Chances are, if you live in or near a city, you don't see a star-filled sky. Instead, you see only a few of the brightest stars scattered throughout a hazy, glowing sky. You're looking through a sky full of light pollution.

City lights cause a glow in the sky called **light pollution.** Light pollution makes the sky glow bright enough that dim stars can't be seen. What effect does light pollution have on your ability to stargaze? How do you think this affects astronomers working near large cities? Many people feel that their right to a dark night sky has been taken away.

Observing objects through Earth's atmosphere can be difficult even without light pollution. As you learned in Chapter 9, the atmosphere absorbs some of the radiant energy entering it. Visible light from objects in space can't pass through clouds or smog. Light pollution makes observing even more difficult. If an object is faint, it's difficult to distinguish between visible light from the object in space and visible light from the city.

Most people agree that lights are needed on city streets and parking lots for safety and security. What can be done to reduce light pollution without reducing public safety and security?

In several cities in the United States, work has begun to reduce light pollution. Tucson, Arizona, located only 80 km from Kitt Peak Observatory, has replaced its street lights with low-pressure sodium lamps. These lights shine at wavelengths that can be filtered out by astronomers. They produce better lighting for the streets and even cost

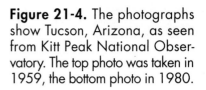

Figure 21-4. The photographs show Tucson, Arizona, as seen from Kitt Peak National Observatory. The top photo was taken in 1959, the bottom photo in 1980.

less to operate. Another solution is to put hoods on billboard, parking lot, and flood lights so they illuminate the object or the ground rather than the sky.

The problem of light pollution is not just a problem for the big cities. In some cases, even in rural towns security lighting at one home can cause light pollution. For example, suppose you decide to have a few friends over to sit outside and watch for meteors, or so-called "shooting stars." You set up your chairs and sit down for an evening of searching the skies. Soon you realize that the sky is too bright. Your neighbor's security lights are casting a glow into the sky. When you ask your neighbor to turn off the lights, he refuses. He is concerned about some recent robberies and wants to keep his yard completely lit up. He has a right to protect his property; you have a right to observe the skies unspoiled by glare. What's the solution to this problem?

SECTION REVIEW

1. Why does light pollution interfere with nighttime observations?
2. Why would it be difficult to pass laws that ban light pollution?

You Decide!

Security lighting causes light pollution that interferes with nighttime observations. What can be done to ensure the safety of people and also eliminate light pollution? Do you think people who are not interested in night-sky observing should be required to replace their lights with less-polluting types? Should they have to turn off all outside lights after a certain time?

21-3 Artificial Satellites and Space Probes

New Science Words

satellite
orbit
space probe
Project Mercury
Project Gemini
Project Apollo

Objectives

▶ Compare and contrast natural and artificial satellites.
▶ Differentiate between an artificial satellite and a space probe.
▶ Trace the history of the race to the moon.

The First Steps into Space

If you had your choice of watching your favorite team on television or from the stadium, which would you prefer? You would probably want to be as close as possible so you wouldn't miss any of the action. Some scientists feel the same way. Even though telescopes have taught them a great deal about the moon and planets, they want to learn more by actually going to those places, or by sending spacecraft where they can't go.

Space exploration began in 1957 when the former Soviet Union used a rocket to send *Sputnik I* into space. It was the first artificial satellite. A **satellite** is any object that revolves around another object. When an object enters space, it will travel in a straight line unless a force such

Figure 21-5. The combination of the satellite's forward movement and the gravitational attraction of Earth causes the satellite to travel in a curved path, or orbit.

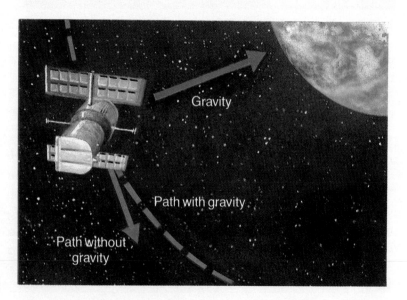

Gravity

Path with gravity

Path without gravity

as gravity deflects it. When Earth's gravity pulls on a satellite, it falls toward Earth. The result of the satellite traveling forward while at the same time falling toward Earth is that the satellite travels in a curved path around Earth. Such a path is called an **orbit.**

The moon is a natural satellite of Earth. It completes one orbit every month. *Sputnik I* orbited Earth for three months before gravity pulled it back into the atmosphere, where it burned up. *Sputnik I* was an experiment to show that artificial satellites could be made. Today, thousands of artificial satellites are in orbit around Earth.

Present-day communication satellites transmit radio and television programs to locations around the world. Other satellites gather scientific data that can't be obtained from Earth, and weather satellites constantly monitor Earth's global weather patterns.

Compare and contrast natural and artificial satellites.

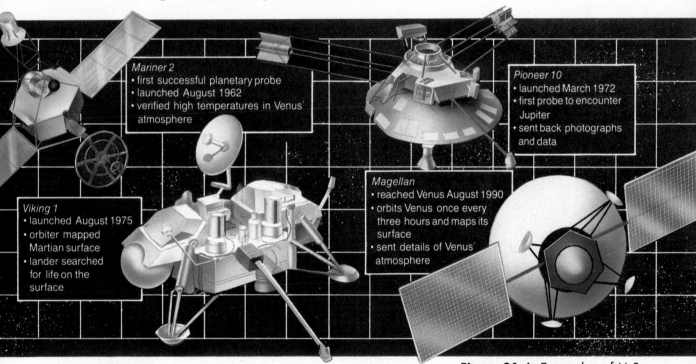

Mariner 2
• first successful planetary probe
• launched August 1962
• verified high temperatures in Venus' atmosphere

Pioneer 10
• launched March 1972
• first probe to encounter Jupiter
• sent back photographs and data

Viking 1
• launched August 1975
• orbiter mapped Martian surface
• lander searched for life on the surface

Magellan
• reached Venus August 1990
• orbits Venus once every three hours and maps its surface
• sent details of Venus' atmosphere

Figure 21-6. Examples of U.S. Space Probes

Space Probes

Not all objects carried into space by rockets become satellites. Rockets can also be used to send instruments far into space. A **space probe** is an instrument that gathers information and sends it back to Earth. Unlike satellites that orbit Earth, space probes travel far into the solar system. Some have even traveled out of the solar system. Space probes carry cameras and other data-gathering

Earth
- *Voyagers 1* and *2*. are launched in 1977

Jupiter
- July 1979 • found ring around Jupiter
- discovered three new moons and erupting volcanoes on Io

Saturn
- August 1981
- revealed the complexity of Saturn's rings

Figure 21-7. Major Discoveries of *Voyager 2*

Science and READING

The *Galileo* craft is scheduled to rendezvous with Jupiter after it first flies by Venus, circles the sun, and then comes past Earth. Research newspaper articles to find out why *Galileo* is taking such an indirect path to Jupiter. Research NASA's method of gravity-assisted space travel.

equipment as well as radio transmitters and receivers that allow them to communicate with scientists on Earth. Figure 21-6 is a timeline showing the space probes launched by NASA.

You've probably heard of the space probes *Voyager 1* and *Voyager 2*. These two probes were launched in 1977 and have now left our solar system. On their journeys, they flew past Jupiter, Saturn, Uranus, and Neptune. In Chapter 23, you will see many of the spectacular photographs obtained from the *Voyager* probes and read about what we've learned from them. Scientists expect these probes to continue to transmit data to Earth from beyond the solar system for at least 20 more years.

The *Voyager* probes didn't land on any of the planets they visited. Some probes, such as *Viking*, do land. *Galileo*, launched in 1989, will reach Jupiter in 1995 if all goes as planned. Once there, *Galileo* will drop a smaller probe into Jupiter's atmosphere. The small probe will take a parachute ride through Jupiter's violent atmosphere. Before being crushed by the atmospheric pressure, it will transmit information about Jupiter's composition, temperature, and pressure to the mother ship orbiting above. *Galileo* will then relay this information back to scientists eagerly awaiting it on Earth.

Neptune
- August 1989
- discovered Great Dark Spot—an Earth-sized cyclone
- discovered 6 new moons and rings that vary in density of particles
- found geysers on Triton

Uranus
- January 1986
- found "shepherding moons" in Uranus' rings that keep the rings from spreading out
- discovered 10 new moons

Voyager 2
- will pass Pluto's orbit by the year 2000

The Race to the Moon

It was quite a shock to people throughout the world when they turned on their radio and television sets and heard the radio transmissions from *Sputnik I* as it orbited over their heads. All that *Sputnik I* transmitted was a sort of "beeping" sound, but people quickly realized that putting a human into space wasn't far off.

In 1961, the Soviet cosmonaut Yuri A. Gagarin became the first human in space. He orbited Earth and then returned safely. Soon, President John F. Kennedy called for the United States to place people on the moon by the end of that decade. The "race for space" had begun.

The U.S. program to reach the moon began with **Project Mercury.** The goals of Project Mercury were to orbit a crewed spacecraft around Earth and to bring it safely back. The program provided data and experience in the basics of spaceflight. On May 5, 1961, Alan B. Shepard became the first U.S. citizen in space. In 1962, Mercury astronaut John Glenn became the first U.S. citizen to orbit Earth.

Project Gemini was the next step in reaching the moon. Teams of two astronauts in the same Gemini spacecraft orbited Earth. One Gemini team met and connected with

Who was the first human in space?

another spacecraft in orbit—a skill that would be needed on a voyage to the moon.

Along with the Mercury and Gemini programs, a series of probes was sent to the moon. Their mission was to take pictures of its surface that would be used to determine the best landing sites on the moon.

When did humans first reach the moon?

The final stage of the U.S. program to reach the moon was **Project Apollo.** On July 20, 1969, *Apollo 11* landed on the lunar surface. Neil Armstrong was the first human to set foot on the moon. His first words as he stepped onto its surface were: "That's one small step for a man, one giant leap for mankind." Edwin Aldrin, the second of the three *Apollo 11* astronauts, joined Armstrong on the moon and they explored its surface for two hours. Michael Collins remained in the Command Module

TECHNOLOGY

Spin-offs

The technology developed by NASA to achieve its goals in space has been remarkable. Much of it is now being used by people throughout the world. The technologies developed by NASA that are later used by the general public are called spin-offs.

NASA had to develop lightweight, compact breathing systems for the astronauts to carry as they ventured out of their spacecraft and onto the moon. Today, firefighters use these breathing systems as well as fire-resistant uniforms originally designed as flight suits for NASA pilots. The lightweight material in the suits won't burn or crack.

Another material, designed for boots worn by astronauts on the moon, is now found in some athletic shoes. Other materials have been incorporated into ski goggles, blankets, and bicycle seats.

Persons who are visually impaired have benefited from spin-offs too. They are able to use a device that vibrates ink on a printed page. This enables them to read materials that aren't in braille. Another device determines the denomination of currency and generates an audible signal.

Other spin-offs include pens that write without the help of gravity and sunglasses that adjust to various light levels.

Think Critically: How has the space program affected your life? You may need to look no farther than your wrist!

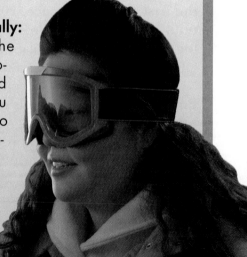
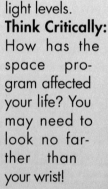

Figure 21-8. The Lunar Rover Vehicle was first used during the Apollo 15 mission. Riding in the "moon buggy," Apollo 15, 16, and 17 astronauts explored large areas of the lunar surface.

orbiting the moon, where Armstrong and Aldrin returned before beginning the journey home. A total of six lunar landings brought back more than 2000 samples of moon rock for study before the program ended in 1972.

During the past three decades, most missions in space have been carried out by individual countries, often competing to be the first or the best. Today, there is much more cooperation among countries of the world to work together and share what each has learned. Projects are now being planned for cooperative missions to Mars and elsewhere. As you read the next section, you'll see how the U.S. program has progressed since the days of Project Apollo, and where it may be going in the future.

SECTION REVIEW

1. Currently, no human-made objects are orbiting Neptune, yet Neptune has eight major satellites. Explain.
2. Galileo is considered a space probe as it travels to Jupiter. Once there, however, it will become an artificial satellite. Explain.
3. List the NASA projects that led to landing humans on the moon.
4. **Apply:** Is Earth a satellite of any other body in space? Explain your answer.

☑ Concept Mapping

Make a network-tree concept map that compares the first event in the U.S. space program to the first event in the former Soviet space program. If you need help, refer to Concept Mapping in the **Skill Handbook** on pages 688 and 689.

Skill Builder

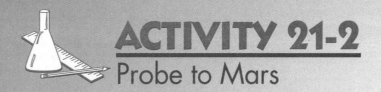
Problem: *How is a mission involving a robot surface probe to Mars organized and carried out?*

Materials

- portable screen
- remote controlled car
- bag to hold rock and mineral samples
- large rocks (30 cm)
- camera (instant), film
- stopwatch

Background

- During this activity, you and your classmates will conduct a role playing space camp mission to successfully land an exploration probe on the surface of Mars, retrieve samples, and return those samples to Earth for analysis.
- To achieve this goal, you must do what NASA does before, during, and after a mission.
- You and your classmates will perform individual and group tasks that will lead to a successful mission.

Procedure

1. **Mission Planning:** The entire class will plan the mission. Include methods to be used for observing, mapping, choosing a landing site, operating the robot surface probe (a battery operated remote control car), collecting samples, analyzing the success of the mission, and designing a mission emblem.

2. **Orbital Photographic Study of the Martian Surface:** Two students will photograph all parts of the martian surface to be studied.

3. **Mapping the Martian Surface:** Three students will use photographs from the orbital study and draw a map of the martian surface. Be sure to identify large boulders, craters, flat areas, locations of samples to be retrieved, and any other key surface features.

4. **Landing Site Selection:** Three students will study the maps of the surface and decide on a landing site and route for the robot surface probe.

5. **Design of RSR (Remote Sample Retrieval) System:** Three students will design a method of retrieving a container of rock samples from Mars' surface. Rock samples will be encased in a baglike container, so the retrieval system must be able to pick up the bag of samples. The retrieval system might also include a cart, attached to the rear of the robot surface probe, to hold the samples.

6. **Mission Control (part 1):** A team of five students will conduct the countdown, blast off, flight, and landing of the robot surface probe.

7. **Mission Control (part 2):** A mission specialist and assistant will operate remote controls that will enable the robot surface probe to move around on the martian surface. A second mission specialist will operate the RSR System and collect samples for study. A successful mission is one in which the lander explores all parts of the martian surface within range, without colliding with boulders or falling into craters. A successful mission also involves retrieving rock samples from the planet's surface and returning them to Earth for study. NOTE: AS THE MISSION SPECIALIST OPERATES CONTROLS FROM BEHIND A SCREEN, THE ASSISTANT WILL GIVE DIRECTIONS ON WHICH WAY TO MOVE THE SURFACE PROBE. THE ASSISTANT DOES THE JOB THAT SENSORS OR CAMERAS WOULD.

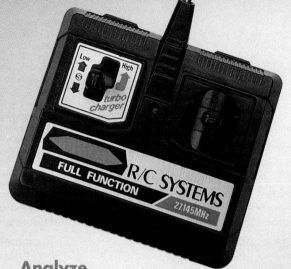

8. **Sample Analysis:** A team of eight students will conduct an analysis of the rocks brought back from Mars' surface. This team of students is to use methods of identifying minerals and rocks learned in Chapters 3 and 4.

▶ Separate all samples into two main groups. Group one will be those that are recognized as mineral samples. Group two will be those that are recognized as rocks.

▶ Four students are to complete Activity 3-2 on page 73 of Chapter 3 for the identification of the mineral samples in group one. Include a copy of this activity as part of the final mission report.

▶ Four students are to study the rock samples in group two.
- Determine the type of rocks present.
- Determine the mineral content of each rock sample.
- Look for any evidence of life on the surface of Mars by searching for fossils in the rocks brought back from the planet.

9. **Mission Debriefing:** A team of three students will:
▶ Observe the probe mission.
▶ Record the time required to conduct the surface probe mission.
▶ Judge when the mission is complete.
▶ Record the number of times the probe is delayed or hindered by various features.
▶ Review the reports of the sample analysis teams for general conclusions regarding the content of rocks on Mars' surface.

Analyze

1. What part of the mission did all other parts depend on?
2. What feature of the total project brought about a successful mission?
3. In an actual mission, how would photographs of possible landing sites be obtained?
4. What was the most common mineral found on the "martian" surface?
5. What types of rocks were found?

Conclude and Apply

6. What conclusion can be drawn from the mission about the past or present existence of life on Mars?
7. Why was the mission specialist placed behind a screen?
8. What task did the assistant perform when working with the mission specialist?
9. From your observations, list some likely sources of problems for an actual mission of this type.

Data and Observations

Time of Mission		Accuracy of Mission	
Mission start		Were all sites visited?	
Mission stop		List the number of times the mission was delayed by surface features.	
Mission length		Was the mission completed?	

The Space Shuttle and the Future

New Science Words

space shuttle
space station

Objectives

▶ Describe the benefits of the space shuttle.
▶ Evaluate the usefulness of orbital space stations.

The Space Shuttle: A Reusable Spacecraft

Imagine spending millions of dollars to build a machine, sending it off into space, and watching its 3000 tonnes of metal and other materials burn up after only a few minutes of work. That's exactly what NASA did for many years. The early rockets lifted into orbit a small capsule holding the astronauts. Sections of the rocket separated from the rest of the rocket body and burned as they re-entered the atmosphere.

NASA administrators, like many people, realized that it can be less expensive and less wasteful to reuse resources. Just as you may reuse a paper bag to pack your lunch, NASA has begun to reuse the spacecrafts that carry astronauts and cargo into space. The reusable spacecraft that transports astronauts, satellites, and other materials to and from space is the **space shuttle.**

At launch, the space shuttle orbiter stands on end and is connected to an external liquid-fuel tank and two solid-fuel booster engines. When the shuttle reaches an altitude of about 40 km, the emptied solid-fuel booster rockets drop off and parachute back to Earth. They are recovered and used again. The larger external liquid-fuel tank eventually separates and falls back to Earth. It isn't recovered.

Once the space shuttle orbiter reaches space, it begins to orbit Earth. There, astronauts perform many different tasks. The cargo bay can carry a self-contained laboratory where astronauts conduct scientific experiments and determine the effects of space flight on the human body. On missions in which the cargo bay isn't used as a laboratory, the shuttle can launch, repair, and retrieve satellites.

To retrieve a satellite, a large mechanical arm in the cargo bay is extended. An astronaut inside the shuttle orbiter moves the arm by remote control. The arm grabs the satellite and pulls it back into the cargo bay doors. It can then be returned to Earth.

Similarly, the mechanical arm can be used to lift a satellite or probe out of the cargo bay and place it into space. In some cases, a defective satellite can be pulled in by the mechanical arm, repaired while in the cargo bay, and then placed into space once more.

After the completion of each mission, the space shuttle orbiter glides back to Earth and lands like an airplane. A very large landing field is needed because the gliding speed of the orbiter is 335 km/hr.

Space Stations

Astronauts can spend only a short time in space in the space shuttle orbiter. Its living space is very small, and the crew needs more space to live, exercise, and work. A **space station** has living quarters, work and exercise space, and all the equipment and support systems needed for humans to live and work in space.

The United States had such a station in the past. The space station *Skylab* was launched in 1973. Crews of astronauts spent up to 84 days in it performing experiments and collecting data on the effects on humans living in space. In 1979, the abandoned *Skylab* fell out of orbit and burned up as it entered Earth's atmosphere.

Crews from the former Soviet Union have spent the most time in space aboard their space station, *Mir*. Two cosmonauts spent a record 365 days on board.

Presently, NASA is planning a space station that would be larger than *Skylab* or *Mir*. Construction of this space station is scheduled to begin in the late 1990s or early twenty-first century. Previous space stations have been assembled on Earth and then rocketed to space. If NASA

MINI-Lab

How can gravity be simulated in a space station?

Locate an LP record album you can use for this activity. Measure the circumference of the record. Now cut a piece of construction paper so it's the same length as the record's circumference and 8 cm wide. Fold the paper in half so that it is now 4 cm wide. Score the paper along the fold and then open it back up.

Wrap the paper around the record so the score line contacts the record all the way around. Fold the paper under one side of the record and tape it securely. Leave the other 4 cm of paper standing, so you have a wall around the outside of the record disc.

Place the record on a turntable and place three marbles at its center. Switch the turntable to its slowest setting, and turn it on.

Why do the marbles move to the wall of paper? How does this simulate gravity? How could a space station simulate gravity using the same method? Make a sketch of a space station that would be able to spin to simulate gravity.

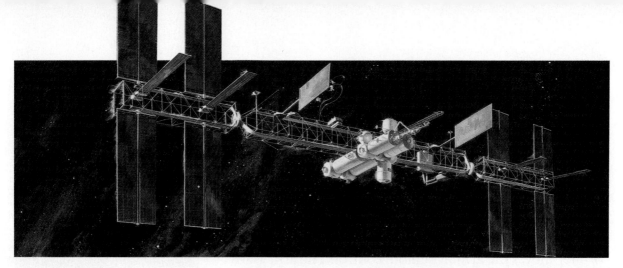

Figure 21-9. This is one proposal for the next space station. NASA will consider many models before deciding on a final plan for the new space station.

carries out its plan, the future space station will be assembled in orbit. The space shuttle will carry up the pieces and astronauts will connect them.

NASA plans for crews to stay on board the station for several months at a time. While there, researchers will make products that are returned for use on Earth. These products might include perfect crystals grown in the weightlessness of space that are useful in medical research. Robots may work in the vacuum and low temperatures of space to produce better and cheaper computer chips.

Another purpose for the space station is for it to serve as a refueling and repair station for satellites and other vehicles. In the future, plans call for it to be used as a construction site for ships to the moon and Mars.

Like many projects today, the future space station is planned as a cooperative effort of several countries. Japan, Canada, and the 13 countries of the European Space Agency may all contribute.

Science and WRITING

Suppose it's the year 2010 and you're in charge of assembling a crew for a new space station. Select the 100 people you want to fill the station. Remember, you will need people to do a variety of jobs, such as farming, maintenance, scientific experimentation, and so on. You will have to live with them and rely on them for the next year. Discuss, in writing, whom you would select and why.

SECTION REVIEW

1. What is the main advantage of the space shuttle?
2. Why is the space shuttle more versatile than earlier spacecraft?
3. **Apply:** *Skylab's* forward motion was slowed by friction caused by Earth's outer atmosphere. How could NASA prevent this from happening with a new space station?

☑ Outlining

Outline the possible uses of the mechanical arm of the space shuttle's cargo bay. If you need help, refer to Outlining in the **Skill Handbook** on page 681.

CHAPTER REVIEW

21-1: Radiant Energy from Space

1. The arrangement of radiant energy waves according to their wavelengths is the electromagnetic spectrum.

2. Optical telescopes produce magnified images of objects. A refracting telescope bends light to form an image. A reflecting telescope uses mirrors to focus light to produce an image.

3. Optical telescopes magnify visible light so that objects can be viewed. Radio telescopes collect and record radio waves given off by some space objects.

21-2: Science and Society: Light Pollution

1. City lights cause a glow in the night sky that obscures dim stars.

2. Lights are needed in towns and cities for safety and security reasons. However, light pollution can cause problems for amateur stargazers as well as professional astronomers.

22-3: Artificial Satellites and Space Probes

1. A satellite is an object that revolves around another object. The moons of the planets are natural satellites. Artificial satellites are those made by people.

2. An artificial satellite collects data as it orbits Earth. A space probe travels far out into the solar system, gathers data, and sends it back to Earth.

3. Early American space programs included the Mercury, Gemini, and Apollo projects.

21-4: The Space Shuttle and the Future

1. The space shuttle is a reusable spacecraft that carries astronauts, satellites, and other payloads to and from space.

2. Space stations provide the opportunity to do research not possible on Earth. Future space stations could also serve as refueling and repair stations for space vehicles.

KEY SCIENCE WORDS

a. **electromagnetic spectrum**
b. **light pollution**
c. **observatories**
d. **orbit**
e. **Project Apollo**
f. **Project Gemini**
g. **Project Mercury**
h. **radio telescope**
i. **reflecting telescope**
j. **refracting telescope**
k. **satellite**
l. **space probe**
m. **space shuttle**
n. **space station**

UNDERSTANDING VOCABULARY

Match each phrase with the correct term from the list of Key Science Words.

1. the arrangement of radiant energy waves according to their wavelengths
2. uses lenses to bend light toward a focal plane
3. uses mirrors to collect light and form an image
4. glow in the night sky caused by city lights
5. an object that revolves around another object
6. the path traveled by a satellite
7. the first crewed U.S. space program
8. space program that reached the moon
9. carries people and tools to and from space
10. a place in space to live and work

CHAPTER
REVIEW

Choose the word or phrase that completes the sentence.

1. _____ are electromagnetic waves.
   a. Gamma rays   c. Microwaves
   b. Visible light waves d. All of these

2. _____ telescopes use mirrors to collect light.
   a. Radio   c. Refracting
   b. Electromagnetic   d. Reflecting

3. A(n) _____ telescope can be used during the day or at night and during bad weather.
   a. radio   c. refracting
   b. electromagnetic   d. reflecting

4. _____ reduce light pollution.
   a. Radio telescopes c. Sodium lamps
   b. Observatories   d. All of these

5. *Sputnik I* was the first _____.
   a. telescope   c. observatory
   b. artificial satellite d. U.S. space probe

6. Goals of _____ were to put a spacecraft in orbit and bring it safely back.
   a. Project Mercury   c. Project Gemini
   b. Project Apollo   d. *Viking I*

7. The _____ of the space shuttle are reused.
   a. liquid-fuel tanks c. booster engines
   b. Gemini rockets   d. none of these

8. The _____ of the space shuttle can place a satellite into space and retrieve it.
   a. liquid-fuel tank c. mechanical arm
   b. booster rocket   d. carbo bay

9. *Skylab* was a(n) _____ that fell from its orbit.
   a. space probe   c. space shuttle
   b. space station   d. optical telescope

10. Microwaves are _____.
    a. invisible
    b. longer than visible waves
    c. shorter than gamma waves
    d. both a and b

UNDERSTANDING CONCEPTS

Complete each sentence.

11. A natural satellite of Earth is _____.

12. _____ use mirrors and lenses rather than radio receivers to gather electromagnetic waves.

13. _____ is caused by the use of many artificial lights.

14. The *Hubble Space Telescope* is a(n) _____ of Earth.

15. A(n) _____ provides astronauts with more living and working space than the space shuttle orbiter.

THINK AND WRITE CRITICALLY

16. How do electromagnetic waves differ from mechanical waves? Give an example to support your answer.

17. Compare and contrast two types of optical telescopes.

18. List one natural and two artificial sources that prevent clear observations of the night sky.

19. Explain what two motions keep a satellite in orbit around Earth.

20. If given the chance, would you choose to fly on a shuttle mission? Give reasons for your answer.

APPLY

21. How would a moon-based telescope have advantages over the Earth-based telescopes being used today?

22. Would a space probe to the sun's surface be useful? Explain.

23. Suppose NASA had to choose between continuing either the spaceflight programs with people aboard or the crewless space probes. Which do you think is the more valuable program? Explain your choice.

24. Suppose two astronauts were outside of the space shuttle orbiter while orbiting Earth. The audio speaker in the helmet of one of the astronauts quits working. The other astronaut is only one meter away, so she shouts a message to him. Can he hear her? Explain.

25. No space probes have visited the planet Pluto, the outermost planet of our solar system. Nevertheless, probes have crossed Pluto's orbit. Explain how this is possible.

MORE SKILL BUILDERS

If you need help, refer to the Skill Handbook.

1. **Sequencing:** Arrange these events in order from earliest to the most recent. Galileo discovered four moons orbiting Jupiter, *Sputnik I* orbited Earth, humans landed on the moon, *Galileo* began its journey to Jupiter, Yuri Gagarin orbited Earth, Project Apollo began, *Discovery* launched the *Hubble Space Telescope.*

2. **Measuring in SI:** Explain whether or not each of the following pieces of equipment could be used aboard the space shuttle as it orbits Earth: a balance, a graduated cylinder, a meterstick, and a thermometer.

3. **Concept Mapping:** Make an events chain map that explains what happens to different parts of the space shuttle including the orbiter, liquid fuel tank, and solid fuel booster engines, from takeoff to landing.

4. **Classifying:** Classify each of the following as a satellite or a space probe: Mercury spacecraft, *Sputnik I*, the *Hubble Telescope*, the space shuttle orbiter, and *Voyager 2.*

5. **Making and Using Tables:** Copy the table below. Use information in the chapter as well as news articles and other resources to complete your table.

Several U.S. Space Probes			
Probe	Launch Date	Destinations	Planets or objects visited
Mariner 4			
Vikings 1 & 2			
Pioneers 10 & 11			
Voyagers 1 & 2			
Magellan			
Galileo			

PROJECTS

1. Design and build a three-dimensional model of a space station. Be sure to include a way for people and equipment to be transported into and out of the station.

2. Construct working models of the two kinds of optical telescopes. Demonstrate their uses to your class.

CHAPTER

22 Earth-Moon System

You have experienced the changing of the seasons many times, but do you know what causes seasons? When it's winter in Earth's northern hemisphere, it's summer in the southern hemisphere and vice versa. Why is this the case?

FIND OUT!

Do this simple activity to see what causes the seasons to change.

Use a lamp without a shade to represent the sun. Turn the lamp on. Hold a globe of Earth about 2 m from the lamp. Tilt the globe slightly, so the northern half of it points toward the "sun." What season do you think this represents for Earth's northern hemisphere? What season would be occurring in the southern hemisphere? Now, keeping it tilted, walk the globe around the "sun." Don't turn or twist the globe as you walk. When you're halfway around the "sun," notice that the northern hemisphere is no longer pointing toward the "sun." What season is it in the northern hemisphere now?

Gearing Up
Previewing the Chapter
Use this outline to help you focus on important ideas in this chapter.

Previewing Science Skills
► In the Skill Builders, you will recognize cause and effect relationships and measure in SI.
► In the Activities, you will make models, analyze and interpret data, and make inferences.
► In the MINI-Labs, you will measure in SI, analyze data, interpret graphs, and draw conclusions.

What's next?

In the Find Out activity you learned that seasons on Earth change because Earth is tilted and sunlight hits it differently as Earth moves around the sun. As you read this chapter, you'll also learn what causes day and night, and how Earth and the moon interact.

Planet Earth

New Science Words

sphere
axis
rotation
revolution
ellipse
equinox
solstice

Objectives

▶ Describe Earth's shape and list physical data about Earth.
▶ Compare and contrast rotation and revolution of Earth.
▶ Demonstrate how Earth's revolution and tilt cause seasons to change on Earth.

Planet Earth Data

You rise early in the morning while it's still dark outside. You sit by the window and watch the sun come up. Finally, day breaks and the sun begins its journey across the sky. But is it the sun that's moving, or is it you?

Today, we know that the sun appears to move across the sky because Earth is spinning. You may take it for granted that Earth is traveling around the sun. But it wasn't long ago that people believed Earth was the center of the universe. They believed Earth stood still and the sun traveled around it.

As recently as the days of Christopher Columbus, there were people who also believed Earth was flat. They noticed the surface appeared to stretch out flat in all directions. They thought that if you sailed far out to sea, you would eventually fall off the edge of the world. How do you know this isn't true? How have scientists determined what Earth is shaped like?

Space probes and artificial satellites have sent back images that show Earth is sphere-shaped. A **sphere** is a round, three-dimensional object whose surface at all points is the same distance from its center. Tennis balls and basketballs are examples of spheres. But people had evidence of Earth's true shape long before cameras were sent into space.

In the 3rd century, B.C., Greek astronomer Aristotle reasoned that if Earth were flat, it would sometimes cast a shadow of a straight line on the moon. Because such a shadow is never observed, he concluded that Earth was spherical rather than flat.

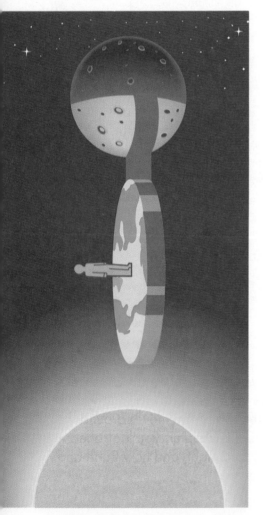

Figure 22-1. Aristotle's Proof That Earth Is Not Flat

Table 22-1

PHYSICAL PROPERTIES OF EARTH	
Diameter (pole to pole)	12 714 km
Diameter (equator)	12 756 km
Circumference (poles)	39 776 km
Circumference (equator)	39 843 km
Mass	5.98×10^{27} g
Density	5.52 g/cm^3
Average distance to the sun	149 600 000 km
Period of rotation (1 day)	23 hr, 56 min
Period of revolution (1 year)	365 day, 6 hr, 9 min

Axis

Rotation

Other evidence for Earth's shape was observed by early sailors. They watched ships approach from across the ocean and saw that the top of the ship would come into view first. As they continued to watch the ship, more and more of it would come into view. As the ship moved over the curved surface of Earth, they could see all of it.

Today, we know that Earth is sphere-shaped, but it's not a perfect sphere. It bulges slightly at the equator and is somewhat flattened at the poles. The poles are located at the north and south ends of Earth's axis. Earth's **axis** is the imaginary line around which Earth spins. The spinning of Earth on its axis, called **rotation,** causes day and night to occur.

What is Earth's axis?

As Earth rotates, the sun comes into view at daybreak. Earth continues to spin, making it appear that the sun moves across the sky until it sets at night. During night, the area of Earth that you're on has spun away from the sun. Because of this, the sun is no longer visible. Earth continues to steadily rotate, and the sun eventually comes into view the next morning. One complete rotation takes about 24 hours, or one day. How many rotations does Earth complete during one revolution around the sun? As you can see, it completes about 365 rotations during one year. Table 22-1 lists some other physical properties of Earth.

Solar winds

Solar winds

Solar winds

Figure 22-2. Particles streaming through space from the sun distort Earth's magnetic field. As a result, it doesn't have the same shape as a magnetic field surrounding a bar magnet.

Another physical property that you've observed the effects of is Earth's magnetic field. Recall from Chapter 13 that convection currents deep inside Earth's mantle power the movement of tectonic plates. Scientists hypothesize that movement of material inside Earth also generates a magnetic field.

The magnetic field of Earth is much like that of a bar magnet. Earth has a north and a south magnetic pole, just as a bar magnet has opposite magnetic poles at its ends. Figure 22-2 illustrates the effects of sprinkling iron shavings over a bar magnet. The shavings align with the magnetic field of the magnet. Earth's magnetic field is similar, almost as if Earth had a giant bar magnet in its core.

When you observe a compass needle pointing toward the north, you're seeing evidence of Earth's magnetic field. Earth's magnetic axis, the line joining its north and south magnetic poles, doesn't align with its rotational axis. The magnetic axis is inclined at an angle of 11.5° to the rotational axis. If you followed a compass needle pointing north, you'd end up at the magnetic north pole rather than the geographic (rotational) north pole.

You're now aware of some of Earth's physical properties. But how do these properties affect you? What everyday events can you explain in terms of Earth's physical properties and movement in space?

Seasons

Autumn is coming and each day it gets colder outside. The sun rises later each day and is lower in the sky. A month ago, it was light enough to ride your bike at 8:00 PM. Now it's dark at 6:30 PM. What is causing this change?

You learned earlier that Earth's rotation causes day and night to occur. Another important motion of Earth is its **revolution,** or yearly orbit around the sun. Just as the moon is a satellite of Earth, Earth is a satellite of the sun. If Earth's orbit were a circle, and the sun were at the center of the circle, Earth would maintain a constant distance from the sun. However, this isn't the case. Earth's orbit is an **ellipse,** an elongated closed curve. The sun is offset from the center of the ellipse. Because of this, the distance between Earth and the sun changes during Earth's yearlong orbit. Earth gets closest to the sun—about 147 million km away—on January 3. The farthest point in Earth's orbit is about 152 million km away from the sun and is reached on July 4. Is this elliptical orbit causing the changing temperatures on Earth? If it were, you would expect the warmest days in January. You know this isn't the case in the northern hemisphere. Something else is causing the change.

Why does Earth's distance from the sun change?

Figure 22-3. The northern hemisphere experiences summer when Earth is farthest from the sun. It experiences winter when Earth is closest to the sun. Earth's tilt on its axis causes the northern and southern hemispheres to be alternately tilted toward the sun. This diagram is drawn from a view below Earth's orbital plane.

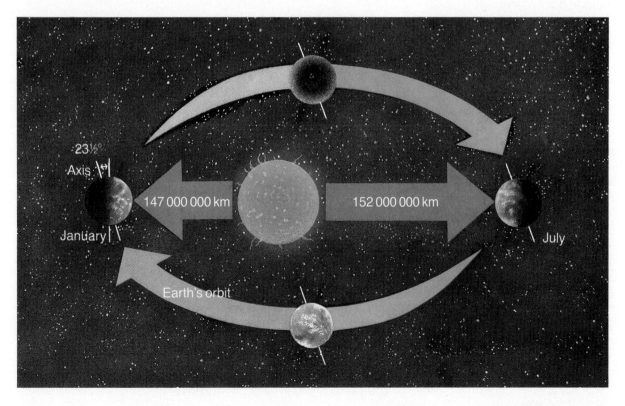

Clocks: The Old and the New

Atomic clocks measure time by recording the frequency of electromagnetic waves given off by atoms. Unlike conventional clocks, atomic clocks aren't affected by changes in temperature or the wearing of their parts. As a result, they gain or lose less than one second in 200 000 years.

Using atomic clocks, scientists have found that each successive day on Earth is get-

ting longer. Evidence indicates that Earth's rotation is slowing down.

Apparently, Earth's rotation has been slowing down for millions of years. By studying the growth lines on 375-million-year-old corals, scientists have determined that there were 440 days in a year at the time these corals were growing. Corals deposit monthly growth lines on their shells in much the same way trees develop yearly growth rings.

Atomic clocks and ancient corals have proven that Earth's rotation is slowing down. Scientist think that it's being "dragged" on by the gravitational attraction of the moon. **Think Critically:** As this drag continues, what will happen to the length of a day on Earth? To the length of a year?

Did You Know?

The slowing of Earth's rotation has been documented by Babylonian records of solar eclipses. The recorded dates of the eclipses only could have occurred if the Earth was rotating slightly faster in the past.

Even though Earth is closest to the sun in January, the overall amount of energy Earth receives from the sun changes very little throughout the year. However, the amount of energy any one place on Earth receives can vary quite a bit.

Recall the Find Out activity at the beginning of the chapter. You worked with a model of Earth revolving around the sun. Do you remember how you tilted the Earth slightly? Earth's axis is tilted 23.5° from a line perpendicular to its orbit. It's this tilt that causes the seasons.

Daylight hours are longer for the hemisphere tilted toward the sun. Think of how early it gets dark in the winter compared to in the summer. The hemisphere tilted toward the sun receives more hours of sunlight than the hemisphere tilted away from the sun.

Another effect of Earth's tilt is that the sun's radiation strikes the hemisphere tilted toward it at a higher angle than it does the other hemisphere. Because of this, the hemisphere tilted toward the sun receives more radiant energy per unit area than the hemisphere tilted away. In other words, if you measured the amount of radiation received in a one-square-kilometer area in the northern hemisphere and, at the same time, measured it for one-square-kilometer in the southern hemisphere, you would find a difference. The hemisphere tilted toward the sun would be receiving more energy.

A summer season results when the sun is in the sky longer and its radiant energy strikes Earth at a higher angle. Just the opposite occurs during winter. Figure 22-3 shows how Earth's tilted axis results in the change of seasons.

What causes the seasons to change?

Equinoxes and Solstices

Because of the tilt of Earth's axis, the sun's position relative to Earth's equator constantly changes. Most of the time the sun is north or south of the equator. Two times during the year, however, the sun is directly over the equator.

When the sun reaches an **equinox,** it is directly above Earth's equator, and the number of daylight hours equals the number of nighttime hours all over the world. At that

Figure 22-4. At summer solstice, the sun's rays directly strike the Tropic of Cancer, 23.5° north latitude. The sun is directly over the Tropic of Capricorn, 23.5° south latitude, at winter solstice. At both fall and spring equinoxes, the sun is directly over the equator.

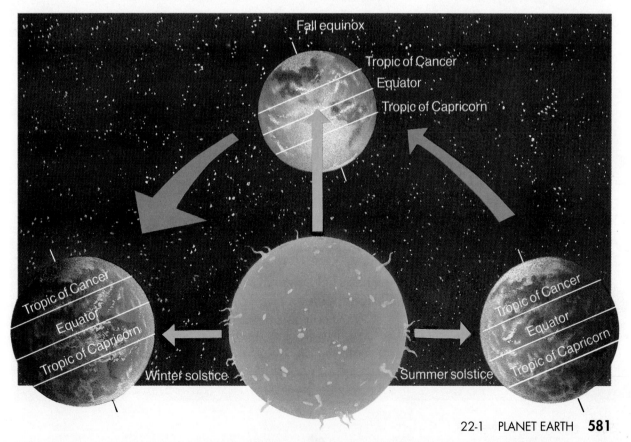

Fall equinox

Tropic of Cancer
Equator
Tropic of Capricorn

Tropic of Cancer
Equator
Tropic of Capricorn

Tropic of Cancer
Equator
Tropic of Capricorn

Winter solstice

Summer solstice

time, neither the northern nor the southern hemisphere is tilted toward the sun. Figure 22-4 shows how this happens. In the northern hemisphere, the sun reaches the spring equinox on March 20 or 21 and fall equinox on September 22 or 23. In the southern hemisphere, the equinoxes are reversed. These are the first days of spring and fall.

Solstice is where the sun reaches its greatest distance north or south of the equator. In the northern hemisphere, the sun reaches the summer solstice on June 21 or 22, and winter solstice occurs on December 21 or 22. Just the opposite is true for the southern hemisphere. When the sun is at the summer solstice, there are more daylight hours than during any other day of the year. When it's at the winter solstice, on the shortest day of the year, we have the most nighttime hours.

As you've seen, the rotation of Earth causes day and night. Earth's tilted axis is responsible for the seasons you experience, and our revolution around the sun marks the passing of a year. Earth is just one of many planetary bodies revolving around the sun. In the next section, you will read how Earth's nearest neighbor, the moon, is also in constant motion and how you observe this motion each day.

SECTION REVIEW

1. Why can't you give just one number to describe Earth's diameter?
2. Which Earth motion causes night and day?
3. What season occurs in Earth's northern hemisphere when Earth's north pole is tilted toward the sun?
4. **Apply:** How would a year on Earth be different if Earth's axis weren't tilted?

Skill Builder

☑ Recognizing Cause and Effect

Answer these questions about the Earth-moon relationship. If you need help, refer to Recognizing Cause and Effect in the **Skill Handbook** on page 683.

1. What causes seasons on Earth?
2. What causes winter?
3. What effect on seasons does the sun being closest to Earth in January have?

ACTIVITY 22-1
The Egg and the Equinox

Problem: *Is there any reason an egg would balance on end when the sun reaches equinox but not at other times?*

Materials
- raw egg

Procedure

1. Perform this activity on a day on which the sun is NOT at equinox.
2. The following article is similar to ones that appear in newspapers across the United States each year during the spring equinox. Read it before proceeding to Step 3.

   Believe it or not, spring arrived today. And because it's the first day of spring, you can balance a raw egg on its end. It sounds strange, but it's true. For centuries, people have been welcoming spring's arrival by balancing eggs on their large ends. In fact, several hundred people gathered in Bates Park this morning to watch as school children put 12 dozen eggs through their balancing acts. How does it work? Legends state that at the moment of spring equinox, the sun and Earth are in harmony, and everything is in balance—eggs included. Celebrate spring's arrival. Go balance an egg!

3. Hypothesize whether or not you would be able to stand an egg on end when the sun is at equinox. Hypothesize whether you will be able to today, when the sun is not at equinox.
4. Attempt to stand an egg on its large end. You may have to try many times, but it's probable that you will be able to do it.

Analyze

1. What is the position of the sun, relative to Earth's latitude, when it reaches equinox?
2. Is the sun directly overhead at the latitude at which you live?
3. On what days of the year does the sun reach equinox? How do those days differ from all others?
4. Is it possible to stand an egg on end on days other than when the sun is at equinox?

Conclude and Apply

5. Do you think that the gravitational attraction between the sun and Earth is significantly different during times of equinox and other days of the year?
6. Many people read articles such as the one on this page and then succeed in standing an egg on end on the day of equinox. Why would they believe that it's possible only on that day?
7. How does this activity prove that you shouldn't believe everything that you read?

New Science Words

moon phases
new moon
waxing
first quarter
full moon
waning
third quarter
solar eclipse
lunar eclipse
maria

Objectives

▶ Demonstrate how the moon's phases depend on the relative positions of the sun, the moon, and Earth.

▶ Describe why eclipses occur, and compare solar and lunar eclipses.

▶ Hypothesize what surface features of the moon tell us about its history.

Motions of the Moon

You have probably noticed how the moon's apparent shape changes from day to day. Sometimes, just after sunset, you can see a full, round moon low in the sky. Other times only half of the moon is visible and it's high in the sky at sunset. Sometimes the moon is visible during the day. Why does the moon look the way it does? What causes it to change its appearance and position in the sky?

Just as Earth rotates on its axis and revolves around the sun, the moon rotates on its axis and revolves around Earth. The moon's revolution causes changes in its appearance. If the moon rotates on its axis, why don't we see it spin around in space? The moon rotates on its axis once every 27.3 days. It takes the same amount of time to revolve once around Earth. Because these two motions take the same amount of time, the same side of the moon always faces Earth. The other side is never turned toward us.

You can demonstrate this by having a friend hold a ball in front of you. Instruct your friend to move the ball around you while keeping the same side of it facing you. Everyone else in the room will see all sides of the ball. You will see only one side. The ball rotated once as it revolved around you once.

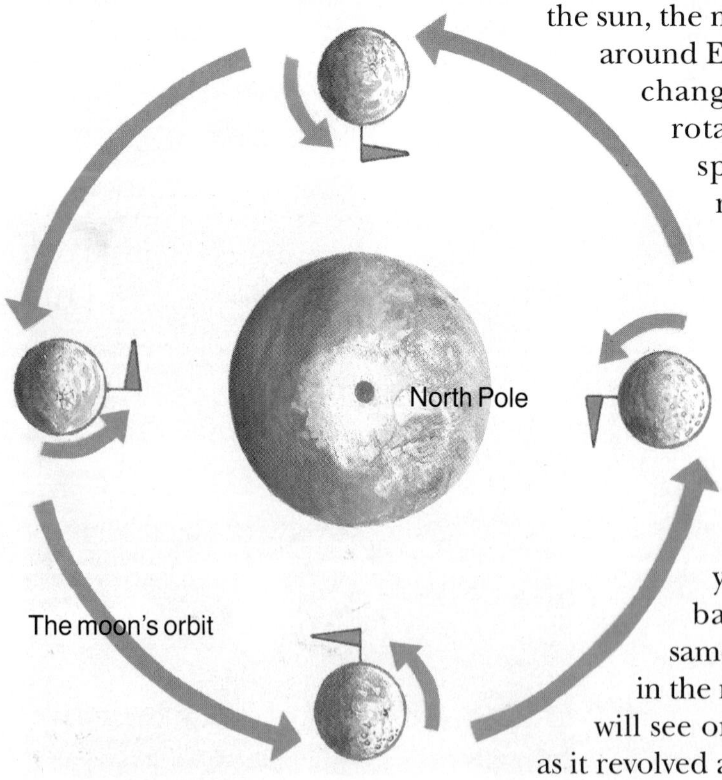

Figure 22-5. In about a one-month period, the moon orbits Earth. It also completes one rotation on its axis during the same period. As a result, the same side of the moon is always facing Earth.

North Pole

The moon's orbit

The moon shines by reflecting sunlight from its surface. Just as half of Earth experiences day as the other half experiences night, half of the moon is lighted while the other half is dark. As the moon revolves around Earth, you see different portions of its lighted side, causing the moon's appearance to change. **Moon phases** are the changing appearances of the moon as seen from Earth. The phase you see depends on the relative positions of the moon, Earth, and the sun.

Phases of the Moon

New moon occurs when the moon is between Earth and the sun. During **new moon**, the lighted half of the moon is facing the sun and the dark side faces Earth. The moon is in the sky, but it can't be seen.

Shortly after new moon, more and more of its lighted side becomes visible—the phases are **waxing.** About 24 hours after new moon, you can see a thin slice of the lighted side. This phase is called the waxing crescent. About a week after new moon, you can see half of the lighted side, or one-quarter of the moon's surface. This phase is **first quarter.**

The phases are continuing to wax—more and more of the lighted side can be seen. When more than one-quarter is visible, but less than half, it is called waxing gibbous. **Full moon** occurs when the half of the moon's surface facing Earth is lit up.

Define waxing and waning.

Figure 22-6. The Phases of the Moon: (a) New moon, (b) Waxing crescent, (c) First quarter, (d) Waxing gibbous, (e) Full moon, (f) Waning gibbous, (g) Third quarter, (h) Waning crescent

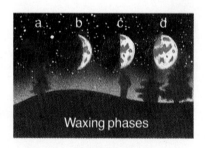

Waxing phases

Waning phases

After passing full moon, the amount of the lighted side that can be seen becomes smaller. The phases are said to be **waning.** Waning gibbous begins just after full moon. When you can see only half of the lighted side, the **third quarter** phase occurs. The amount of the moon that can be seen continues to become smaller. Waning crescent occurs just before another new moon. Once again you can see a small slice of the lighted side.

The complete cycle of the moon's phases takes about 29.5 days. During the span of a month, you can watch the moon pass through all of its phases. You may also notice that the moon rises about 50 minutes later each day. In the time that it takes Earth to rotate once, the moon has moved forward in its revolution. So it takes an extra 50 minutes for a location on Earth to "catch up" with the new position of the moon.

Eclipses

Imagine yourself as one of your ancient ancestors, living 50 000 years ago. You're out foraging for nuts and other fruit in the bright afternoon sun. Gradually, the sun disappears from the sky, as if being swallowed by a giant sky creature. You can see stars coming out, crickets begin to chirp to signal the nightfall, and birds return to the trees to settle down for the night. But the darkness lasts only a short time, and as quickly as the sun disappeared, it returns to full brightness. You realize something unusual has happened, but you don't know what caused it. It will be almost 48 000 years before anyone can explain the event that you just experienced.

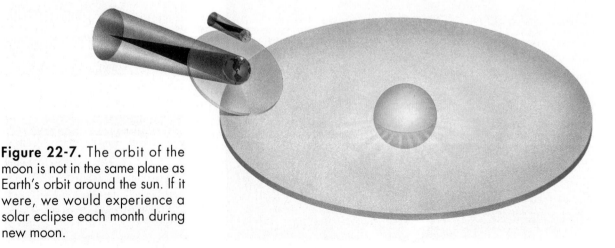

Figure 22-7. The orbit of the moon is not in the same plane as Earth's orbit around the sun. If it were, we would experience a solar eclipse each month during new moon.

The event just described was a total solar eclipse. Today, we know what causes such eclipses; but for our early ancestors, they must have been terrifying events. Many animals act as if night has come; cows return to their barns, and chickens go to sleep. But what causes the day to suddenly change into night and suddenly back into day?

Revolution of the moon causes more than just a change in its phases, it also causes eclipses. Eclipses occur when Earth or the moon temporarily blocks the sunlight reaching the other. Sometimes during new moon, a shadow cast by the moon falls on Earth and causes a solar eclipse. During full moon, a shadow of Earth can be cast on the moon, resulting in a lunar eclipse.

Eclipses can occur only when the sun, the moon, and Earth are perfectly lined up. Because the moon's orbit is not in the same plane as Earth's orbit around the sun, eclipses happen only a few times per year. If the moon's orbit were not inclined at an angle compared to Earth's, an eclipse would occur with every new and full moon.

Why don't solar eclipses occur with each new moon?

Solar Eclipses

A **solar eclipse** occurs when the moon moves directly between the sun and Earth and casts a shadow on part of Earth. The darkest portion of the moon's shadow is called the umbra. A person standing in an area of Earth within the umbra sees a total solar eclipse. The only portion of the sun that's visible is part of its atmosphere, which appears as a pearly white glow around the edge of the eclipsing moon.

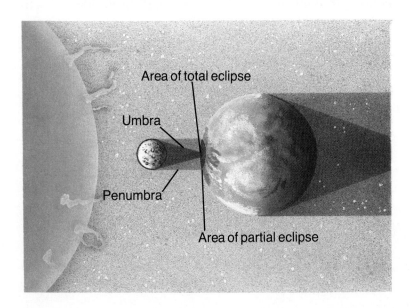

Area of total eclipse

Umbra

Penumbra

Area of partial eclipse

Figure 22-8. Only a small area of Earth experiences a total solar eclipse during the eclipse event. Only the outer portion of the sun's atmosphere is visible during a total solar eclipse.

Surrounding the umbra is a lighter shadow on Earth's surface called the penumbra. Persons standing in the penumbra see a partial solar eclipse. Photographs can be taken of the curved edge of the moon moving over a portion of the sun. **CAUTION:** *Never look directly at a solar eclipse. The light will permanently damage your eyes.*

Lunar Eclipses

When Earth's shadow falls on the moon, a **lunar eclipse** occurs. A lunar eclipse begins with the moon moving into Earth's penumbra. As the moon continues to move, it enters Earth's umbra and you see a curved shadow on the moon's surface. It was from this shadow that Aristotle concluded that Earth was a sphere. When the moon moves completely into Earth's umbra, the moon becomes very dark because light from the sun is blocked by Earth. A total lunar eclipse has occurred.

A partial lunar eclipse occurs when only a portion of the moon moves into Earth's umbra. The remainder of the moon is in Earth's penumbra and it therefore receives some direct sunlight.

A total solar eclipse occurs from zero to two times every year, yet most people live their entire lives never witnessing one. You may not be lucky enough to see a total solar eclipse, but it's almost certain you will have a chance to see a total lunar eclipse in your lifetime. Although total solar eclipses are more common than total lunar eclipses, only those people in the very small region where the moon's umbra strikes Earth can witness a total solar eclipse. In contrast, anyone on the nighttime side of Earth can see a total lunar eclipse.

Figure 22-9. During a total lunar eclipse, Earth's shadow blocks light coming from the sun.

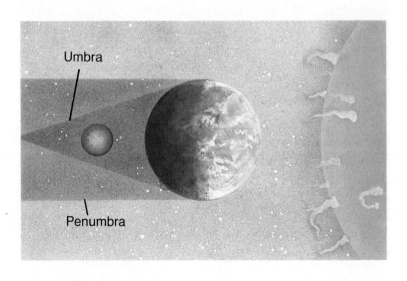

Umbra

Penumbra

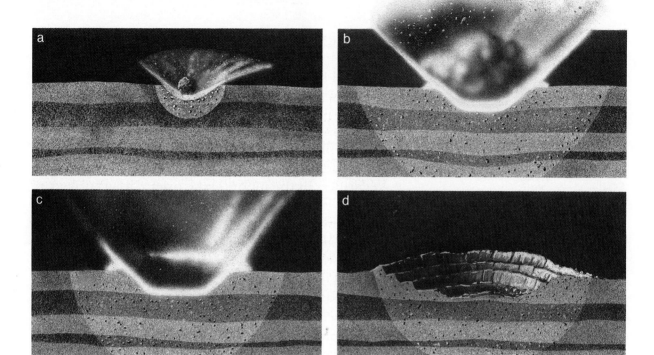

Structure of the Moon

When you look at the moon, you can see many of its larger surface features, especially if you use a telescope. The dark-colored, flat regions called **maria** are very easy to find. Maria were formed when lava from the moon's interior flooded over and filled large basins on the moon's surface. The basins formed early in the moon's history.

Many depressions on the moon were formed by meteorites, space objects that strike the surfaces of planets and their satellites. These depressions caused by meteorite impacts are called craters. During impact, cracks may have formed in the moon's crust, allowing lava to reach the surface and fill in the large craters. The igneous rocks of the maria are 3 to 4 billion years old. They are the youngest rocks found on the moon thus far.

Seismographs left on the moon by Apollo astronauts have enabled scientists to study moonquakes. Recall from Chapter 14 that the study of earthquakes allows scientists to map Earth's interior. Likewise, studying moonquakes has led to a model of the moon's interior. One model of the moon shows that its crust is about 60 km thick on the side facing Earth and about 100 km thick on the far side. Below the crust, a solid mantle extends to a depth of about 800 km. A partly molten zone of the mantle extends farther down. Below this is an iron-rich solid core.

Figure 22-10. A meteorite impact (a) sends shock waves through the moon's surface (b). Some of the moon's surface is ejected upward along with fragments from the exploding meteorite (c). Eventually, the crater stops growing as gravity overcomes the forces of expansion (d).

Did You Know?

The word *maria* comes from the Latin word for "sea." In the 17th century, astronomers thought the moon had oceans of water and named these areas maria. Today, we know the moon has little atmosphere and no water.

Origin of the Moon

A recent theory about the moon's origin states that in Earth's early history, a Mars-sized object collided with Earth, throwing gas and debris into orbit. Within about 1000 years the gas and debris condensed into one large mass, forming the moon. Figure 22-11 illustrates several theories of the moon's origin.

 List four theories of the moon's origin.

Regardless of the moon's true origin, it has played an important role in our history. It was the source of curiosity for many early astronomers. Studying the phases of the moon and eclipses led people to conclude that Earth and the moon were in motion around the sun. Earth's shadow on the moon proved that Earth wasn't flat. When Galileo first turned his telescope to the moon, he found a surface scarred by craters and maria. Before that time, many people believed that all planetary bodies were "perfect," without surface features.

By studying the moon, we have learned about ourselves and the planet we live on. As you will read in the next section, the moon is not only important as an object from our past, but it is important to our future as well.

PROBLEM SOLVING

Marooned on the Moon

You and your crew have crash-landed on the moon, far from your intended landing site at the moon colony. It will take you one day to reach the moon colony on foot. The side of the moon that you're on will be facing away from the sun during your entire trip back to the colony. You manage to salvage the following items from your wrecked ship: food, rope, solar-powered heating unit, battery operated heating unit, three 70-kilogram oxygen tanks, map of the moon's constellation, magnetic compass, oxygen-burning signal flares, matches, 8 liters of water, solar-powered radio receiver and transmitter, 3 flashlights and extra batteries, signal mirror, and binoculars.

Keep in mind that the moon's gravity is much less than that of Earth's, and it lacks a magnetic field.

Think Critically: Which of these items do you and the other two members of your crew decide to take? Why is each item useful or not useful?

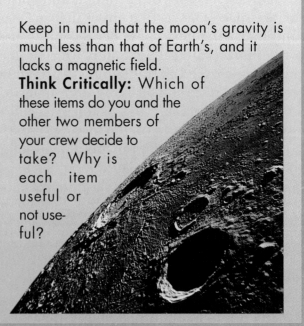

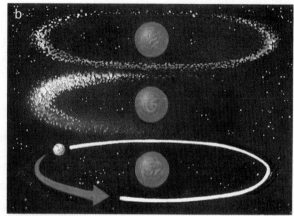

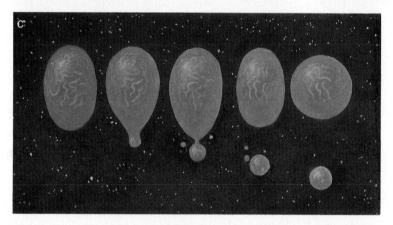

Figure 22-11. Three models of the moon's formation: (a) The moon is captured by Earth's gravity. The moon would have formed elsewhere and then "wandered" into Earth's vicinity. (b) The moon is condensed from loose material surrounding Earth during the early formation of the solar system. (c) A blob of molten material may have been ejected while Earth was still in its early, molten state.

SECTION REVIEW

1. What are the relative positions of the sun, moon, and Earth during a full moon?
2. Which type(s) of eclipse(s) can occur during full moon?
3. What caused the formation of maria on the moon?
4. **Apply:** Suppose the moon's diameter were one-half what it is now. Describe how a solar eclipse would differ from the solar eclipses that actually occur. Make a sketch of what would be observed.

☑ Measuring in SI

The moon's mass is 1/81 of Earth's mass. The moon's density is 3.3 g/cm³. Calculate the moon's volume using the formula: *volume = mass/density*. If you need help, refer to Measuring in SI in the **Skill Handbook** on pages 684 and 685.

22-3 Building a Moon Colony

New Science Words

moon colony

Objectives

▶ Describe how a moon colony might be constructed.
▶ List advantages and disadvantages of constructing a moon colony.

Should Humans Colonize the Moon?

NASA is now considering plans for a colony on the moon early in the twenty-first century. A **moon colony** would be a permanent structure on the moon in which scientists could live and work for extended periods of time. Would benefits of a moon colony outweigh the cost and dangers involved in building one? What would a moon colony be like? Where would the materials needed to survive on the moon come from?

One idea for a moon colony includes living quarters made of a high-strength, multiple-layer fabric. The fabric

would be supported by a framework inside, forming a dome about 15 m in diameter. At first, astronauts would take the supplies they needed with them. Eventually, the moon colony would become self-sufficient.

Oxygen can be extracted from moon rocks and soil. This oxygen could be used for breathing and to combine with hydrogen to produce water for the colony. Food could be grown in lunar soil that has been enclosed under protecting domes.

There are several advantages to building a moon colony. Scientists would learn more about the moon itself by studying it up close. The more we learn about the moon, the more we might learn about the evolution of our solar system.

Before astronauts travel into interplanetary space, many scientists want the opportunity to study how they will react to long missions. Mars missions may require three years to complete. A moon colony would provide the opportunity to study long-term exposure to a space environment.

The moon would make an excellent location from which to study the universe. The moon has almost no atmosphere. The sky is half as bright as the darkest Earth sky. Nighttime on the moon is two weeks long. These characteristics make the moon a great place to study objects in deep space.

Moon rocks may contain large deposits of usable resources. Although products from the moon may not be used on Earth, they could supply many of the needs of space exploration. Oxygen could be extracted from moon rocks to be used in spacecraft propellants. One of the goals of a moon colony would be to supply spacecraft with fuel and other materials.

Building a moon colony would have its problems. The cost of a colony on the moon could reach into the billions of dollars. Some people would rather see this money spent on Earth-based research. A second problem would be the danger to astronauts who live and work on the moon. They would spend long periods of time exposed to the dangers of possible radiation and no breathable atmosphere.

Science and MATH

It's the summer of 2025, and you're planning your family's vacation to the new resort on the moon. How long will it take you to get there if you cruise at 4000 km/h?

SECTION REVIEW

1. What is a moon colony?
2. What are the advantages and disadvantages of a moon colony?

You Decide!

SCIENCE & SOCIETY

Some scientists believe the economic cost and the risks of human space travel are too great. They believe that recent improvements in the use of robots show that humans are not needed in space. They want to see funds used to explore the solar system with noncrewed spacecraft.

Are the benefits humans would receive from such a colony worth the risks involved? Are there other missions in space that should be funded in place of a moon colony?

ACTIVITY 22-2
Moon Phases and Eclipses

Problem: *How do the motions and size of the moon cause moon phases and eclipses?*

Materials

- light source (unshaded)
- polystyrene ball on pencil
- globe
- Figure 22-6

Procedure

1. Study the positions of the sun, the moon, and Earth in Figure 22-6.
2. Use a polystyrene ball on a pencil as a model moon. Move the model moon around the globe to duplicate the exact position that would have to occur for a lunar eclipse to take place.
3. Move the model moon to the position that would cause a solar eclipse.
4. Place the model moon at each of the following phases: first quarter, full moon, third quarter, and new moon. Identify which, if any, eclipse could occur during each phase. Record you data.
5. Place the model moon at the location where a lunar eclipse could occur. Move it slightly toward and away from Earth. Note the amount of change in the size of the shadow causing the eclipse. Record this information.
6. Repeat Step 5 with the model moon in a position where a solar eclipse could occur.

Analyze

1. During which phase(s) of the moon is it possible for an eclipse to occur?
2. Describe the effect that a small change in the distance between Earth and the moon has on the size of the shadow causing the eclipse.
3. As seen from Earth, how does the apparent size of the moon compare to the apparent size of the sun? How can an eclipse be used to confirm this?

Data and Observations

Moon Phase	Observations
first quarter	
full	
third quarter	
new	

Conclude and Apply

4. Why don't a lunar and solar eclipse occur every month?
5. Suppose you wanted to more accurately model the movement of the moon around Earth. How would your model moon move around the globe? Would it always be in the same plane as the light source and the globe?

CHAPTER REVIEW

SUMMARY

22-1: Planet Earth

1. Earth is a sphere that is slightly flattened at its poles. Earth's mass is nearly 6.0×10^{27} grams and its density is 5.52 g/cm^3. Earth's magnetic field is due to convection currents in its mantle.

2. Earth rotates, or spins, on its axis once each day and revolves about the sun in a little more than 365 days.

3. Seasons on Earth are due to the amount of solar energy received by a hemisphere at a given time. The tilt of Earth on its axis causes the amount of solar energy to vary, thus causing changes in seasons.

22-2: Earth's Moon

1. Earth's moon goes through phases that depend on the relative positions of the sun, the moon, and Earth.

2. Eclipses occur when Earth or the moon temporarily blocks out the sunlight reaching the other. A solar eclipse occurs when the moon moves directly between the sun and Earth. A lunar eclipse occurs when Earth's shadow falls on the moon.

3. The moon's maria are the result of ancient volcanism. Craters on the moon's surface formed from impacts with meteorites.

22-3: Science and Society: Building a Moon Colony

1. One proposed moon colony would be made of layers of fabric supported by an inner, dome-shaped framework. Air and water could be obtained from gases in the moon's rocks. Food could be grown in lunar soil within the colony.

2. Advantages of a moon colony include learning more about Earth's natural satellite, learning how people would adapt to living in space, and learning more about the universe. Disadvantages include high costs, and risks of radiation and no breathable atmosphere.

KEY SCIENCE WORDS

a. axis
b. ellipse
c. equinox
d. first quarter
e. full moon
f. lunar eclipse
g. maria
h. moon colony
i. moon phases
j. new moon
k. revolution
l. rotation
m. solar eclipse
n. solstice
o. sphere
p. third quarter
q. waning
r. waxing

UNDERSTANDING VOCABULARY

Match each phrase with the correct term from the list of Key Science Words.

1. Earth's shape
2. causes day and night to occur on Earth
3. Earth's path around the sun
4. shape of Earth's orbit
5. the sun's position when it's directly above the equator
6. the moon can't be seen during this phase
7. moon phase in which all of the lighted side is seen
8. eclipse that occurs when the moon is between Earth and the sun
9. flat regions on the moon
10. a place to live and work on the moon

CHAPTER REVIEW

CHECKING CONCEPTS

Choose the word or phrase that completes the sentence.

1. The sun rises and sets because _____.
   a. Earth revolves
   b. it moves in space
   c. Earth rotates
   d. none of these

2. Earth's circumference at the _____ is greater than it is at the _____.
   a. equator, poles
   b. axis, mantle
   c. poles, equator
   d. mantle, axis

3. When the sun reaches equinox, the _____ is facing the sun.
   a. southern hemisphere
   b. northern hemisphere
   c. equator
   d. none of these

4. The moon rotates once every _____.
   a. 24 hours
   b. 365 days
   c. 27.3 hours
   d. 27.3 days

5. Moon phases depend on the position of _____.
   a. Earth
   b. the moon itself
   c. the sun
   d. all of these

6. As the moon appears to get larger, it is said to _____.
   a. wane
   b. wax
   c. rotate
   d. be crescent-shaped

7. During a _____ eclipse, the moon is directly between the sun and Earth.
   a. solar
   b. new
   c. full
   d. lunar

8. The _____ is the darkest part of the moon's shadow during a solar eclipse.
   a. waxing gibbous
   b. umbra
   c. waning gibbous
   d. penumbra

9. _____ are depressions on the moon.
   a. Maria
   b. Moonquakes
   c. Phases
   d. Craters

10. Oxygen for a moon colony could be obtained from the _____.
    a. lunar atmosphere
    b. lunar rocks and soil
    c. lunar water
    d. none of these

UNDERSTANDING CONCEPTS

Complete each sentence.

11. Even if you could view Earth from space, you wouldn't be able to see its _____ because it's an imaginary line about which Earth rotates.

12. The shape of the path Earth makes around the sun is a(n) _____.

13. In the _____ hemisphere, fall equinox is reached on March 20 or 21.

14. The moon's _____ formed from ancient lava flows.

15. A(n) _____ would make a great "observatory" from which to study space.

THINK AND WRITE CRITICALLY

16. Compare and contrast rotation and revolution. Give an example of each.
17. Why have observers on Earth never seen craters on one side of the moon?
18. How do equinoxes and solstices differ?
19. What causes umbras and penumbras?
20. What advantages would astronomers on the moon have over astronomers on Earth for studying the universe?

APPLY

21. How would the moon appear to an observer in space during its revolution? Would phases be observable? Explain.
22. Would you weigh more at Earth's equator or at the North Pole? Explain.
23. Recall that tides occur due to the gravitational attraction among the sun, moon, and Earth. During which phases of the moon are tides the highest? Explain.
24. If you were lost on the moon's surface, why would it be more beneficial to have a star chart rather then a compass?
25. Which of the moon's motions are real? Which are apparent? Explain why each occurs.

MORE SKILL BUILDERS

If you need help, refer to the Skill Handbook.

1. **Hypothesizing:** Hypothesize why locations near Earth's equator travel faster during one rotation than places near the poles.
2. **Using Variables, Constants, and Controls:** Describe a simple activity that would show that direct rays from the sun provide more energy than slanted rays.

3. **Inferring:** The moon doesn't produce its own light. Why can we see it in the night sky?
4. **Comparing and Contrasting:** Compare and contrast a waning moon with a waxing moon.
5. **Concept Mapping:** Copy and complete the cycle map below. Show the sequences of the moon's phases.

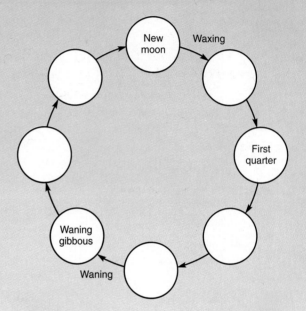

PROJECTS

1. Construct a model that demonstrates how all the phases of the moon are seen from Earth *and* from space.
2. Research the work done by a Greek mathematician named Eratosthenes. How does his circumference of Earth compare with the value used today?

23 The Solar System

Some of the planets in the solar system have systems of rings around them. The image at the left is a photo collage of several planets in the solar system. The rings of Saturn are seen in the center. From Earth, planetary rings look like solid bands that circle the planet. Actually, planetary rings are made up of millions of individual particles of dust, rock, and ice that are orbiting around some planets in bands.

FIND OUT!

Do this simple activity to find out about planetary rings.

Bring in some color comics from your local newspaper. First, examine the color while holding the comics at arm's length from your eyes. The colors of areas within the lines seem solid and made up of just one color, don't they? Now examine the comics up close with a magnifying glass. Try to observe tan or orange colors in the comics. What does the magnifying glass reveal? Are all of the colors really solid? What does this comparison help to explain about planetary rings?

Gearing Up
Previewing the Chapter
Use this outline to help you focus on important ideas in this chapter.

Previewing Science Skills
▶ In the **Skill Builders,** you will make a concept map and interpret a scientific illustration.
▶ In the **Activities,** you will measure, predict, interpret, and use numbers.
▶ In the **MINI-Labs,** you will make a model and plan for a trip to Mars.

What's next?

Many objects in the solar system are different than they appear from Earth. As you read this chapter, you'll learn about many new discoveries about the planets and their moons. You will also learn about other objects that are part of our solar system.

The Solar System

New Science Words

solar system
inner planets
outer planets

Objectives

▶ Compare and contrast the sun-centered and the Earth-centered models of the solar system.
▶ Describe the theory for the formation of the solar system.

Early Ideas about the Solar System

Imagine yourself lying in the grass on a warm, clear summer night gazing at the stars and the moon. The stars and the moon seem so still and beautiful. You may even have looked at other planets in the solar system thinking they were stars. Although the planets are very different from stars, they blend in with the stars and are usually hard to pick out.

As you learned in Chapter 22, the sun and the stars appear to move through the sky because Earth is moving. This wasn't always a known fact. Many early Greek scientists thought the planets, the sun, and the moon

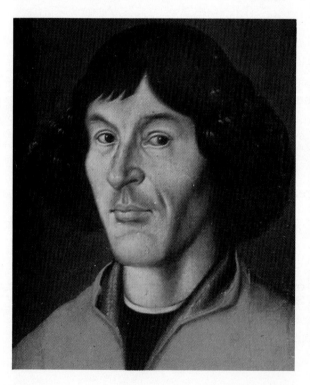

Figure 23-1. Nicholas Copernicus (at left) and Galileo Galilei

were each embedded in a separate sphere that rotated around Earth. The stars were embedded in another sphere that also rotated around Earth. Early observers described moving objects in the night sky using the term planet, which means "to wander." This model is called the Earth-centered model of the solar system. To the astronomers who believed in this model of the solar system, there were seven planets. They were Mercury, Venus, the moon, the sun, Mars, Jupiter, and Saturn.

This idea of an Earth-centered solar system was held for centuries until the Polish astronomer Nicholas Copernicus published a different view in 1543. Copernicus proposed that Earth was also a planet and that it, along with the other planets, revolved around the sun. He also stated that the movement of the planets and the stars was due to the rotation of Earth. This is the sun-centered model of the solar system.

Using his telescope, Galileo found evidence that supported the ideas of Copernicus. He did this by discovering that Venus went through phases like the moon's. These phases could only be explained if Venus and Earth were orbiting the sun. From this, he concluded that Venus revolves around the sun, and the sun is the center of the solar system.

We now know that Earth is one of nine planets and many smaller objects that orbit the sun, making up the **solar system.** The nine planets and the sun, at right, are shown here at the correct scale. The dark areas on the sun are sunspots that you will learn about in Chapter 24. You can see how small Earth is compared to some of the other planets and the sun, which is much larger than any of the planets.

The solar system includes a vast territory extending billions of kilometers in all directions from the sun. If all the matter in the solar system, excluding the sun, were combined, it would make up less than one percent of the sun's total mass. The sun contains 99.86 percent of the mass of the whole solar system. Because of its gravitational pull, the sun is the central object around which other objects of the solar system revolve.

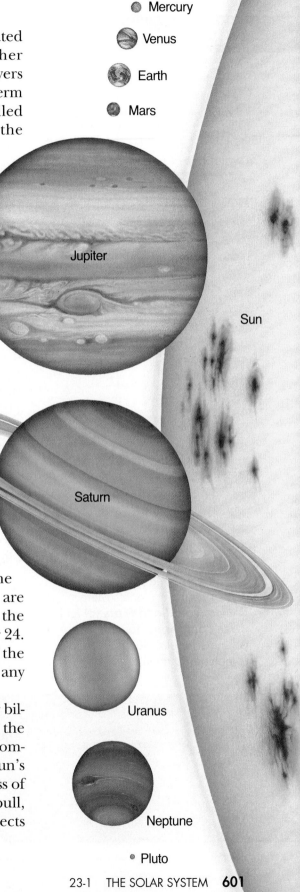

Mercury

Venus

Earth

Mars

Jupiter

Sun

Saturn

Uranus

Neptune

Pluto

What is fusion?

Why are the inner planets solid and rocky?

Figure 23-2. This diagram shows the relative distances between the planets. Notice how relatively close the inner planets Mercury, Venus, Earth, and Mars (at left) are compared to the outer planets Jupiter, Saturn, Uranus, Neptune, and Pluto.

Formation of the Solar System

Scientists hypothesize that the sun and the solar system formed more than 4.6 billion years ago from a cloud of gas and dust. Gravitational forces acting on the cloud probably caused it to begin to contract. Initially, the cloud was rotating very slowly. But, as the density of the cloud became greater, increased gravity pulled more gas and dust into the cloud center. This caused the cloud to rotate faster, which in turn caused it to flatten into a disk.

Eventually, the core of the cloud became so dense that nuclear fusion began. Fusion occurs when hydrogen atoms combine, forming helium. The new helium atom has less mass than that of the original hydrogen atoms. The lost mass is converted to energy. Once energy formed by fusion radiated into space, the cloud center formed into the sun.

Not all gas and dust was drawn into the core of the cloud. Remaining gas and dust particles combined, attracting more particles as they became larger. Because of the greater heat in the inner solar system, most of the elements with low atomic mass could not condense into solids. This accounts for the fact that planets close to the sun lack light elements and have formed into rocky planets with iron cores.

The **inner planets,** Mercury, Venus, Earth, and Mars, are the solid, rocky planets closest to the sun. The **outer planets,** Jupiter, Saturn, Uranus, Neptune, and Pluto, are those farthest from the sun and are made mostly of lighter elements such as hydrogen. You'll learn in Section 23-4, however, that Pluto is more like an inner planet.

Motions of the Planets

When Nicholas Copernicus developed his sun-centered model of the solar system, he thought that the

planets orbited the sun in circles. In the early 1600s, the German mathematician Johannes Kepler began studying the orbits of the planets. He discovered that the shapes of the orbits are not circular, but are elliptical. He also calculated that the sun is not at the center of the ellipse, but is offset from the center.

Kepler also discovered that the planets travel at different speeds in their orbits around the sun. The planets closer to the sun travel faster than planets farther away from the sun. Mercury orbits the sun at about 48 kilometers per second, whereas Neptune orbits the sun at about 5 kilometers per second. As a result, the outer planets take much longer to orbit the sun than the inner planets do.

Figure 23-3. The solar system may have formed from a rotating cloud of gas and dust.

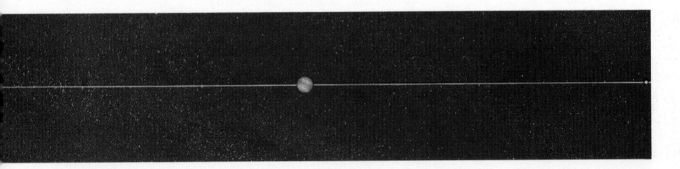

Figure 23-4. This device is an early model of the solar system.

Copernicus and his ideas, considered radical at the time, led to the birth of modern astronomy. Early scientists didn't have technology such as space probes to learn about the planets. Nevertheless, they discovered a great deal about our solar system and developed theories about the solar system that we use today.

SECTION REVIEW

1. What is the difference between the sun-centered and the Earth-centered models of the solar system?
2. How do scientists think the sun and the solar system formed?
3. Why are most of the outer planets made of lighter elements?
4. **Apply:** Would a year on the planet Uranus be longer or shorter than an Earth year?

Skill Builder

◻ Concept Mapping

Make a concept map that compares and contrasts the Earth-centered universe with the sun-centered model. If you need help, refer to Concept Mapping in the **Skill Handbook** on pages 688 and 689.

ACTIVITY 23-1
Planetary Orbits

Problem: *What is the most accurate model of the shape of a planet's orbit around the sun?*

Materials

- thumbtacks or pins
- string
- cardboard (21.5 cm × 28 cm)
- metric ruler
- pencil
- paper

Procedure
Part A

1. Place a blank sheet of paper on top of the cardboard and place two thumbtacks or pins about 3 cm apart.
2. Tie the string into a circle with a circumference of 15 to 20 cm. Loop the string around the thumbtacks. With someone holding the tacks or pins, place your pencil inside the loop and pull it taut.

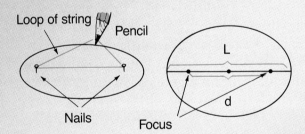

Loop of string
Pencil
Nails
L
d
Focus

3. Move the pen or pencil around the tacks, keeping the string taut, until you have completed a smooth, closed curve or an ellipse.
4. Repeat Steps 1 through 3 several times. First vary the distance between the tacks and then vary the circumference of the string. However, change only one of these each time. Note the effect on the size and shape of the ellipse with each of these changes.
5. Orbits are usually described in terms of eccentricity (*e*). The eccentricity of any ellipse is determined by dividing the distance (*d*) between the foci (here, the tacks) by the length of the major axis (*L*). See the diagram above.

6. Calculate and record the eccentricity of the ellipses that you constructed.

Part B

7. Refer to Appendix I to determine the eccentricities of planetary orbits.
8. Construct an ellipse with the same eccentricity as Earth's orbit.
9. Repeat Step 8 with the orbit of either Pluto or Mercury.

Data and Observations

Constructed Ellipse	d (cm)	L (cm)	e (d/L)
#1			
#2			
#3			
Earth's orbit			.017
Mercury's orbit			.206
Pluto's orbit			.248

Analyze

1. What effect does a change in the length of the string or the distance between the tacks have on the shape of the ellipse?
2. What must be done to the string or placement of tacks to decrease the eccentricity of a constructed ellipse?

Conclude and Apply

3. Describe the shape of Earth's orbit. Where is the sun located within the orbit?
4. Name the planets that have the most eccentric orbits.

The Inner Planets

New Science Words

Mercury
Venus
Earth
astronomical unit
Mars

Objectives

▶ List the inner planets in their relative order from the sun.
▶ Identify important characteristics of each inner planet.
▶ Compare and contrast Venus and Earth.

Inner Planets

We know much more about the solar system since the days of Copernicus and Galileo. Advancements in telescopes have allowed us to observe the planets from Earth. And space probes have explored much of our solar system, obtaining much of the knowledge we have about the planets. Let's take a tour of the solar system through the "eyes" of the space probes.

Mercury

Which planet is closest to the sun?

The closest planet to the sun is **Mercury.** It's also the second smallest planet. Our first close look at Mercury came in 1974, when *Mariner 10* flew by the planet and sent pictures back to Earth, as shown in Figure 23-5. The surface of Mercury has many craters and looks much like our moon. It also has cliffs as high as 3 km on its surface.

Figure 23-5. Mercury looks very much like Earth's moon.

PROBLEM SOLVING

The Hotter It Gets???

Carol and Salvatore were pretending to be a part of an astronaut team whose next mission was to land on the surface of one of the inner planets. In researching information about the surface conditions that they might expect to find on the inner planets, Carol and Sal were surprised to note that Mercury, which is the closest planet to the sun, does not have the highest average surface temperature. Venus, shown at right, which is almost twice as far from the sun, averages higher surface temperatures.

Think Critically: How can you explain this fact?

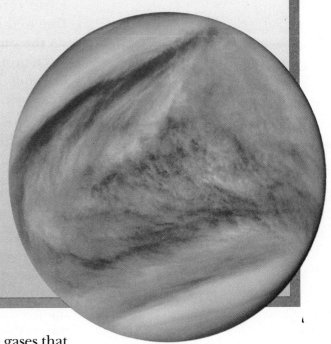

Because of a low force of gravity, most of the gases that could form an atmosphere have escaped the planet into space. Mercury has a very thin atmosphere composed mostly of sodium, helium, potassium, and hydrogen. Because it has almost no atmosphere and is very close to the sun, Mercury has great extremes in temperature. Because Mercury is a relatively dark object, it does not reflect much of the sunlight falling on it. Mercury's surface can reach temperatures of 450°C during the day—hot enough to melt lead. The very thin atmosphere allows heat to escape the surface rapidly and temperatures drop to −170°C at night.

Why does Mercury have great extremes in temperature?

Venus

The second planet outward from the sun is **Venus.** Venus is sometimes called Earth's twin because its size and mass are very similar to Earth's. One major difference is that the entire surface of Venus is blanketed by an atmosphere of dense clouds. The atmosphere of Venus, which has 90 times the pressure of Earth's, is mostly carbon dioxide. The clouds in the atmosphere contain droplets of sulfuric acid which give the clouds a slightly yellow color.

Why does Venus have a greenhouse effect?

Clouds on Venus are so dense that only two percent of the sunlight that strikes the top of the clouds reaches the planet's surface. This solar energy is trapped by the carbon dioxide gas and causes a greenhouse effect similar to Earth's greenhouse effect you read about in Chapter 10. Due to this intense greenhouse effect, the temperature on the surface of Venus is 470°C.

The former Soviet Union has led in the exploration of Venus. Beginning in 1970 with the first *Venera* probe, the Russians have photographed and mapped the surface of Venus using radar. But in 1990, the United States' *Magellan* probe began using its radar to make the most detailed maps yet of the surface of Venus. *Magellan* revealed huge craters, faultlike cracks, and volcanoes with visible lava flows.

Earth

Earth is the third planet from the sun. The average distance from Earth to the sun is 150 million km, or one **astronomical unit** (AU). Astronomical units are used to measure distances to objects in the solar system. Surface temperatures on Earth allow water to exist as a solid, liquid, and gas.

Mars

Mars is the fourth planet from the sun. It's referred to as the red planet because iron oxide in the weathered rocks on its surface gives it a reddish color. Mars actually appears red from Earth. Other features of Mars visible

Figure 23-6. Like Earth, Mars has ice caps at both poles.

from Earth are its polar ice caps which get larger during the Martian winter and shrink during the summer.

Most of the information we now have about Mars came from the *Viking* probes. *Viking 1* and *2* landed on Mars in 1976. The *Viking* probes sent back pictures of a reddish-colored, barren, rocky, and windswept surface. Mars also has many craters.

The *Viking* probes also discovered long channels on the planet that look like they were carved by flowing water at some time in Mars' past. Also discovered was the largest volcano in the solar system, Olympus Mons. Large rift zones have formed in the Martian crust. One such rift, Valles Marineras, is more than 4000 km long, up to 240 km wide in places, and more than 6 km deep.

Viking probes also discovered that Mars has ice caps at the north and south poles that change with the seasons. The southern polar ice cap changes little with the seasons and is made mostly of frozen carbon dioxide. The northern polar ice cap is much smaller in the summer and is made of water ice. Frozen carbon dioxide accumulates in the winter, enlarging the ice cap.

Mars has two small moons, both of which are highly cratered. Phobos is only 25 km in diameter and Deimos is 13 km in diameter.

As you toured the inner planets using the "eye" of the space probes, you saw how each planet is unique. Mercury, Venus, Earth, and Mars are quite different from the outer planets that you'll tour in the next section.

Why does Mars' northern ice cap get bigger in the winter?

SECTION REVIEW

1. List the inner planets in order from the sun.
2. How are Mercury and Earth's moon similar?
3. Why is Venus called Earth's twin?
4. List one important characteristic for each inner planet.
5. **Apply:** Why is the surface temperature of Venus higher than Mercury's, even though Mercury is closer to the sun?

☑ Interpreting Data

Skill Builder

Using the information given, explain how Mars is like Earth. If you need help, refer to Interpreting Data in the **Skill Handbook** on page 687.

23-3 Mission to Mars

New Science Words

data gloves

Objectives

▶ Recognize problems that astronauts will encounter during a trip to Mars.

▶ Decide if a crewed mission to Mars is necessary.

Who Should Explore Mars—Humans or Robots?

You learned about exploring space in Chapter 21. Scientists are currently developing plans to further explore Mars. Because Mars is 55 million kilometers at the closest, it will take about three years to get to Mars and back. Because of the long duration of the flight, astronauts would face much more danger than they currently do in space shuttle missions.

Because of the near zero gravity in outer space, bones lose calcium and weaken. Bones might fracture more easily once astronauts land on Mars or return to Earth. Also, muscles get weak because they don't have to hold the body up as they do under Earth's gravity.

In addition to these problems, body fluids move upward because no gravity is pulling them down. The movement of fluids could signal the kidneys to excrete more fluids, causing dehydration. Also, astronauts will be exposed to more radiation from the sun than during space shuttle flights. Some scientists are suggesting that advanced robots being developed can be used to explore Mars instead of humans. They say that robots could operate equipment, build space stations, make repairs, or carry out scientific experiments in space or on Mars.

This new technology uses video and artificial touch sense. The artificial senses of the robot are connected to the real senses of a human. The robot has video cameras

Figure 23-7. Fiber-optic sensors in data gloves transfer the movement of the operator to a robot.

for eyes and special touch sensors in its limbs. The human operator looks at tiny video screens worn as goggles and sees exactly what the robot sees. **Data gloves** worn by the operator have sensors connected to the robot's hands. Any movement performed by the operator is duplicated by the robot's hands.

One problem facing the robot technology is the long distance from Earth to Mars. Radio signals from the operator to a robot on Mars would take about 20 minutes—too long to be practical. Researchers would like to develop the robot technology for use on the moon or on a space station at first, then work on developing artificial intelligence for robots on Mars. A robot with artificial intelligence would be programmed to do a task and would have some ability to "think" on its own.

How might scientists deal with the problems of delayed radio signals to robots on Mars?

SECTION REVIEW

1. What are two problems astronauts will experience during extended space travel?
2. How could we benefit from a crewed mission to Mars?

You Decide!

Even with the drawback of crewed flight to Mars, scientists think that humans should go because of the challenge of human exploration. Also, humans might find more clues about the formation of the solar system and life on other planets. Should astronauts or robots explore Mars?

SCIENCE & SOCIETY

New Science Words

Jupiter
Great Red Spot
Saturn
Uranus
Neptune
Pluto

Objectives

▶ List the major characteristics of Jupiter, Saturn, Uranus, and Neptune.
▶ Recognize how Pluto differs from the other outer planets.

Outer Planets

You have learned that the inner planets are small, solid, rocklike bodies in space. By contrast, the outer planets, except for Pluto, are very large, gaseous objects.

You first heard of the *Voyager* probes in Chapter 21. Although they were not the first probes to the outer planets, they have discovered a wealth of new information about Jupiter, Saturn, Uranus, and Neptune. Let's follow the *Voyager* probes on their journeys to the outer planets of the solar system.

Jupiter

In 1979, *Voyager 1* flew by **Jupiter,** the largest planet and the fifth planet from the sun. *Voyager 2* flew by Jupiter later that same year. The major discoveries of the probes include new information about the motions of Jupiter's atmosphere and the discovery of three new moons. *Voyager* probes also discovered that Jupiter has a faint ring around it and that one of its moons has volcanoes on it.

Jupiter is composed mostly of gaseous and liquid hydrogen, helium, and some ammonia, methane, and water vapor. Scientists believe the atmosphere of hydrogen and helium gradually changes to a planetwide ocean of liquid hydrogen and helium toward the middle of the planet. Below this liquid layer, there is a solid core of ice and rock.

You've probably seen pictures from the *Voyager* probes of Jupiter's colorful clouds. Its atmosphere has bands of white, red, tan, and brown clouds. Continuous storms of swirling, high pressure

Figure 23-9. Jupiter's cloud bands are its most visible feature.

Table 23-1

LARGE MOONS OF JUPITER			
Io	**Europa**	**Ganymede**	**Callisto**
The most volcanically active object in the solar system. Sulfur lava gives it its distinctive red and orange color.	Rocky interior is covered by a 100 km thick ice crust, which has a network of cracks, indicating tectonic activity.	Has an ice crust about 100 km thick, covered with grooves. Crust surrounds a 900 km thick slushy mantle of water and ice. Has a rocky core.	Has a heavily cratered ice-rock crust several hundred km thick. Crust surrounds a water or ice mantle around a rocky core.

gas have been observed on Jupiter. The **Great Red Spot** is the most spectacular of these storms. Lightning has also been observed within Jupiter's clouds.

In orbit around Jupiter are 16 moons. Io is the closest of these moons to Jupiter. Jupiter's tremendous gravitational force pulls on Io, causing it to be the most volcanically active object in the solar system. The next moon out is Europa. it is composed mostly of rock with a thick coating of ice. Another significant moon of Jupiter is Ganymede, which is the largest satellite in the solar system. It's larger than the planet Mercury. Callisto is the fourth moon out, composed of ice and rock.

Saturn

The next planet for the *Voyager* probes was Saturn in 1980 and 1981. **Saturn** is the sixth planet from the sun, also known as the ringed planet. Saturn is the second largest planet in the solar system, but has the lowest density. Its density is so low that it would float on water.

Similar to Jupiter, Saturn is a large, gaseous planet with a thick outer atmosphere composed mostly of hydrogen and helium. Saturn's atmosphere also contains ammonia, methane, and water vapor. As you go deeper into Saturn, the gases gradually change to liquid hydrogen and helium. Below the atmosphere and liquid ocean, Saturn has a core of rock and ice.

Why do scientists think Io is so volcanically active?

Science and MATH

Voyager 2 traveled 7 billion km in 12 years. What was the average speed in km?

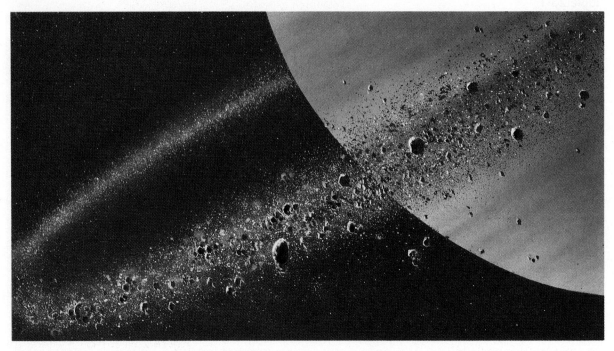

Figure 23-10. Saturn's rings are made of pieces of rock and ice.

MINI-Lab

How can you draw planets to scale?

To determine how the sizes of the planets in the solar system compare to each other, use the information on planet diameters in Appendix I. Select a scale diameter of Earth and draw a circle with this diameter on paper. Using Earth's diameter as 1.0, draw each of the other planets to scale also. At this scale, how far would your model Earth have to be located from the sun? What would 1 AU be for this model? Using a scale of 1 AU = 2 m, how large would the sun and Earth models have to be to remain in scale?

The *Voyager* probes gathered new information about Saturn's ring system and its moons. Scientists once believed that Saturn had only three rings around it. The *Voyager* probes showed that Saturn has several broad rings, each of which is composed of hundreds of thin ringlets. Each ring is composed of countless particles ranging from the size of a speck of dust to tens of meters across. This makes Saturn's ring system the most complex of all outer gaseous planets.

At least 18 moons orbit Saturn. That's more than any other planet in our solar system. The largest of these, Titan, is also larger than Mercury. It has an atmosphere of nitrogen, argon, and methane.

Uranus

After Saturn, *Voyager 2* flew by Uranus in 1986. **Uranus** is the seventh planet from the sun. It is a large, gaseous planet with 15 satellites and a system of thin, dark rings.

Voyager discovered numerous new thin rings and ten new moons that were not seen earlier. *Voyager* also detected that the magnetic field is tilted 60° from its rotational poles. This is odd because most magnetic fields are nearly aligned with a planet's poles. Scientists think Uranus may be undergoing a magnetic reversal.

The atmosphere of Uranus is composed of hydrogen, helium, and some methane. The methane gives the planet its blue-green color. Methane absorbs the red and yellow light, and the clouds reflect the green and blue. Under its atmosphere, scientists believe Uranus has a mantle of liquid water, methane, and ammonia surrounding a rocky core.

One of the most unique features of Uranus is that its axis of rotation is tilted on its side compared to the other planets. The axes of rotation of the other planets are nearly perpendicular to the planes of their orbits. Uranus, however, has a rotational axis nearly parallel to the plane of its orbit.

Neptune

From Uranus, *Voyager 2* traveled on to **Neptune,** a large, gaseous planet very similar to Uranus. Most of the time, Neptune is the eighth planet from the sun. However, Pluto's orbit crosses inside Neptune's during a part of its voyage around the sun. Currently, Pluto is closer to the sun than Neptune, and it will remain closer to the sun until 1999.

Neptune's atmosphere is very similar to that of Uranus. The methane content gives Neptune its distinctive blue-green color just as it does for Uranus. Neptune has dark-colored, stormlike features in its atmosphere that are similar to the Great Red Spot on Jupiter.

Under its atmosphere, Neptune is thought to have liquid water, methane, and ammonia. Neptune probably has a rocky core.

With *Voyager 2* discovering six new moons, the total for Neptune is now eight. Of these, Triton is most interesting. Triton has a diameter of 2700 km and has a thin atmosphere composed mostly of nitrogen. *Voyager* also discovered that Neptune also has rings that are thin in some places and thick in other places. At a certain distance, the thin places are not visible, and the rings seem broken.

Figure 23-11. Pictured here are the blue planets Uranus (above) and Neptune (below).

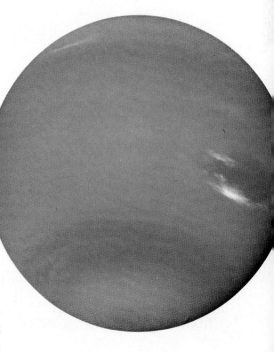

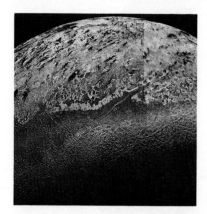

Figure 23-12. Neptune's Moon Triton

Why are Charon and Pluto considered a double planet?

Voyager ended its tour of the solar system with Neptune. Scientists were not able to direct *Voyager* to Pluto because Neptune's gravity deflected it toward Triton, away from the direction of Pluto. Both *Voyager* probes are now out of the solar system. They will continue into space searching for the extent of the sun's effect on charged particles.

Pluto

Because **Pluto** is farther from the sun during most of its orbit around the sun, it is considered the ninth planet from the sun. Pluto is not like the other outer planets. It's not surrounded by a dense atmosphere, and it's the only outer planet with a solid, rocky surface. Some scientists believe that Pluto may have been a moon that escaped from an orbit around Neptune.

Pluto's only moon, Charon, has a diameter equal to half of Pluto's. Charon orbits very close to Pluto. Because of their close size and orbit, Charon and Pluto are often considered a double planet.

With the *Voyager* probes leading the way, we have entered a new age of knowledge about the solar system. Other new probes such as the *Galileo* will continue to extend our understanding of the solar system.

SECTION REVIEW

1. What's the difference between the outer planets and the inner planets?
2. What causes the Great Red Spot on Jupiter?
3. Are there moons in the solar system that are larger than planets? What are they?
4. How is Pluto different from the other outer planets?
5. **Apply:** Why is Neptune sometimes the farthest planet from the sun?

Skill Builder

☑ Recognizing Cause and Effect

Answer the following questions about Jupiter. If you need help, refer to Recognizing Cause and Effect in the **Skill Handbook** on page 683.

1. What causes Jupiter's surface color?
2. How is the Great Red Spot affected by Jupiter's atmosphere?
3. How does Jupiter's size affect its gravitational force?

ACTIVITY 23-2
Solar System Distance Model

Problem: *How can you construct a scale model showing the distance between the sun and planets in the solar system?*

Materials

- adding machine tape
- meterstick
- scissors
- pencil

Procedure

1. Use Appendix I to obtain the mean distance from the sun in AUs for each planet. Record these data in the table.
2. Using 10 centimeters as the distance between Earth and the sun (10 cm = 1 AU), determine the length of adding machine tape you will need to do this investigation.
3. Calculate the scale distance that each planet would be from the sun on the adding machine tape. Record this information.
4. Cut the tape to the proper length.
5. Mark one end of the tape to represent the position of the sun.
6. Put a label at the proper location on the tape where each planet would be if the planets were in a straight line outward from the sun.

7. Complete the table by calculating the scale distance of each planet from the sun if 1 AU equals 2 meters on a model.

Analyze

1. Explain how the scale distance is determined.
2. How much adding machine tape would be required to construct a model with a scale distance 1 AU = 2 m?

Conclude and Apply

3. In addition to scale distances, what other information do you need before you can construct an exact scale model of the solar system?
4. Proxima Centauri, the next closest star to our sun, is 4.3 light-years from the sun. Using the scale of 10 cm = 1 AU, how long a piece of adding machine tape would you need to include this star on your scale model?

Data and Observations

Planet	Distance to sun (km)	Distance to sun (AU)	Scale distance (1 AU = 10 cm)	Scale distance (1 AU = 2 m)
Mercury	58×10^6			
Venus	108×10^6			
Earth	150×10^6			
Mars	228×10^6			
Jupiter	780×10^6			
Saturn	143×10^7			
Uranus	288×10^7			
Neptune	451×10^7			
Pluto	592×10^7			

Other Objects in the Solar System

New Science Words

comet
Oort Cloud
meteor
meteorite
asteroid

Objectives

▶ Explain where a comet comes from and describe how a comet develops as it approaches the sun.
▶ Differentiate between comets, meteoroids, and asteroids.

Other Objects in the Solar System

Although the planets and their satellites are the most noticeable members of the sun's family, there are many other objects that orbit the sun. Comets, meteors, and asteroids are other objects in the solar system.

You've probably heard of Halley's comet. It was last seen from Earth in 1986. English astronomer Edmund Halley realized that comet sightings that had taken place about every 76 years were really sightings of the same comet. This comet that takes about 76 years to orbit the sun was named after him. Halley's comet is just one example of the many other objects in the solar system beside the planets. Figure 23-13 describes comets.

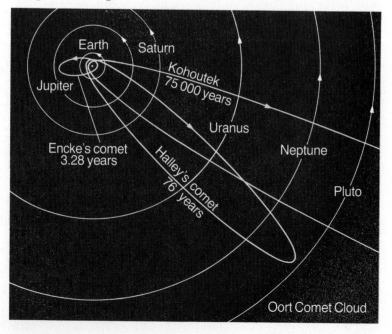

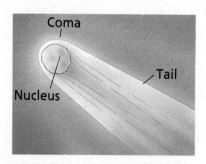

Figure 23-13. A comet consists of a nucleus, a coma, and a tail, as shown above. The orbits of three famous comets are shown at right.

Comets

A **comet** is composed of dust and rock particles mixed in with frozen water, methane, and ammonia. The Dutch astronomer Jan Oort proposed the idea that a large collection of comets lies in a cloud that completely surrounds the solar system. This cloud is located beyond the orbit of Pluto and is called the **Oort Cloud.** Scientists believe the gravity of nearby stars or another planet interacts with the Oort Cloud, changing the orbits of some comets. The sun's gravity then pulls the comet toward it. The comet then either escapes from the solar system or gets captured into a much smaller orbit.

The structure of a comet is like a large, dirty snowball, or a mass of frozen ice and rock. But as the comet approaches the sun, it develops a very distinctive structure. Ices of water, methane, and ammonia begin to vaporize because of the heat from the sun. The vaporized gases form a bright cloud called a coma around the nucleus, or solid part, of the comet. The solar wind, a stream of charged particles from the sun, pushes on the gases in the coma. These particles form a bright tail that always points away from the sun.

After many trips around the sun, most of the frozen ice in a comet has vaporized. All that is left are small particles which spread out in the orbit of the original comet.

Figure 23-14. This is a computer-enhanced image of Halley's comet.

Why do comets move toward the center of the solar system?

Did You Know?

There are about 25 comets visible to the naked eye every century.

Figure 23-15. This meteor was seen in the daytime sky over the Grand Tetons.

Meteoroids, Meteors, and Meteorites

You learned earlier that comets tend to break up after they have passed close to the sun many times. The small pieces of the comet nucleus spread out into a loose group within the original orbit of the broken comet. These small pieces of rock moving through space are then called meteoroids.

Where do meteroids come from?

If the path of a meteoroid crossed the position of Earth, it would enter our atmosphere at between 12 and 72 km/s. Most meteoroids are so small that they are completely vaporized in Earth's atmosphere. A meteoroid that burns up in Earth's atmosphere is called a **meteor.** People often see these and call them "shooting stars."

Figure 23-16. Meteor Crater in Arizona is 1.2 kilometers wide.

Each time Earth passes through the loose group of particles within the path of a broken-up comet, many small particles of rock and dust enter the atmosphere. Because more meteors than usual are seen, this is called a meteor shower. Some meteor showers will have more than 50 meteors per hour.

If the meteoroid is large enough, it may not completely burn up in Earth's atmosphere. When it strikes Earth, it is called a **meteorite.** Meteor Crater in Arizona was formed when a large meteorite struck Earth. Because meteorites originally come from comets or asteroids, scientists believe they are made of material that formed at the beginning of the solar system.

What happens to the smallest meteroids as they fall to Earth?

T E C H N O L O G Y

Garbage in Space

Since the 1950s, people have been exploring space. And since then, more than 3.5 million kilograms of garbage—from wrenches to satellites—has been dumped in space! Much of the space trash is only a few centimeters in size, but in the zero gravity environment of space, such particles could move at speeds that exceed 24 000 kilometers per hour and cause much damage to spacecraft!

NASA scientists are currently working on designs that would protect spacecraft and space station *Freedom,* in particular, from space debris. One proposed system is a collision warning system that would alert astronauts and ground controllers to potentially dangerous debris. The system would use infrared sensors mounted like headlights onto a spacecraft or space station to detect objects. Space-based radars would then determine the path of the object and allow the astronauts time to either avoid or prepare for the collision.

Think Critically: One estimate has 3.5 million particles of garbage in space. What is the average mass of each particle?

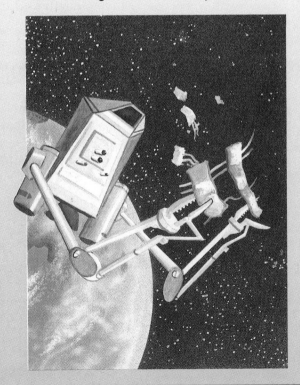

Asteroids

An **asteroid** is a piece of rock similar to the material that later formed into the planets. Most asteroids are located in an area between the orbits of Mars and Jupiter called the asteroid belt.

Why are they located there? One theory states that the gravity of Jupiter kept a planet from forming in the area where the asteroid belt is now located. In addition to this, some of the larger asteroids may have been thrown out of the belt and are probably scattered throughout the present-day solar system. Many have since been captured as moons around other planets.

The size of the asteroids in the asteroid belt range from tiny particles to almost 1000 km in diameter. The largest asteroid, and the first one ever discovered, is Ceres. Its diameter is 940 km.

Comets, meteoroids, and asteroids are probably composed of material that formed early in the history of the solar system. Scientists study the structure and composition of these space objects in order to better understand what the solar system may have been like long ago. Understanding what the early solar system was like could help scientists to better understand the formation of Earth and its relationship to other objects in the solar system.

Did You Know?

Venus rotates in the opposite direction from Earth. It also takes longer to rotate one complete turn than it does to complete one revolution around the sun. This means that a day on Venus is longer than its year.

SECTION REVIEW

1. Why does a comet's tail form as it approaches the sun?
2. How do a meteoroid, a meteor, and a meteorite differ?
3. What type of feature might be formed on Earth if a large meteorite reached its surface?
4. **Apply:** Describe differences among comets, meteoroids, and asteroids.

Skill Builder

☒ Interpreting Scientific Illustrations

Identify the coma and tail of the comet shown in Figure 23-14 on page 619. In which direction is the sun relative to the comet? If you need help, refer to Interpreting Scientific Illustrations in the **Skill Handbook** on page 693.

CHAPTER REVIEW

SUMMARY

23-1: The Solar System

1. The Earth-centered model proposed that Earth was inside a sphere and that the planets and the stars rotated around Earth. The sun-centered model states that the sun is the center of the solar system.

2. Our solar system formed about 4.6 billion years ago from a cloud of gas and dust. The cloud rotated and pulled much matter into its center. Eventually, the central part formed the sun and the remaining matter formed the planets.

23-2: The Inner Planets

1. The inner planets, in increasing distance from the sun, are Mercury, Venus, Earth, and Mars.

2. The moonlike Mercury has a very thin atmosphere. Venus has a dense atmosphere of carbon dioxide and sulfuric acid. On Earth, water exists in three states. Mars appears red due to weathering of its rocks.

3. Venus and Earth are similar in size and mass. Both have greenhouse effects.

23-3: Science and Society: Mission to Mars

1. Problems that astronauts to Mars would face include muscle and bone weakness and exposure to dangerous levels of radiation.

2. A crewed mission to Mars would be dangerous to the astronauts involved. Robots may be a better alternative than sending humans to Mars.

23-4: The Outer Planets

1. A faint ring and 16 moons orbit the gaseous Jupiter. Jupiter's Great Red Spot is a storm. Saturn is made of mostly gas and has rings. Uranus is a large, gaseous planet with many moons and several rings. Neptune is similar to Uranus in composition and has stormlike features similar to Jupiter.

2. Pluto doesn't have a dense atmosphere, and its surface is rocky.

23-5: Other Objects in the Solar System

1. As a comet approaches the sun, vaporized gases form a bright coma around the comet's nucleus. A tail that points away from the sun is formed by solar wind.

2. Meteoroids are small pieces of rock moving through space. An asteroid is a piece of rock that is a part of the asteroid belt.

KEY SCIENCE WORDS

a. asteroid
b. astronomical unit
c. comet
d. data gloves
e. Earth
f. Great Red Spot
g. inner planets
h. Jupiter
i. Mars
j. Mercury
k. meteor
l. meteorite
m. Neptune
n. Oort Cloud
o. outer planets
p. Pluto
q. Saturn
r. solar system
s. Uranus
t. Venus

UNDERSTANDING VOCABULARY

Match each phrase with the correct term from the list of Key Science Words.

1. solid, rocky planets closest to the sun
2. planet most like Earth in size and mass
3. planet with carbon dioxide ice caps
4. Ganymede and Io are two of its moons
5. planet that could float on water
6. large gaseous planets
7. currently the farthest planet from the sun
8. large group of comets beyond Pluto's orbit
9. a rock that enters Earth's atmosphere
10. a meteoroid that strikes Earth

CHECKING CONCEPTS

Choose the word or phrase that completes the sentence.

1. ____ proposed a sun-centered solar system.
   a. Ptolemy   c. Galileo
   b. Copernicus   d. Oort

2. _____ formed the sun.
   a. Rotation   c. Nuclear fusion
   b. Revolution   d. The greenhouse effect

3. Planets orbit the sun in _____.
   a. circles   c. rotation
   b. ellipses   d. none of these

4. _____ has very extreme temperatures because it has little atmosphere.
   a. Earth   c. Mars
   b. Jupiter   d. Mercury

5. Water is a solid, liquid, or gas on _____.
   a. Pluto   c. Saturn
   b. Uranus   d. Earth

6. The largest volcano in the solar system is on _____.
   a. Earth   c. Mars
   b. Jupiter   d. Uranus

7. A problem with living in space is _____.
   a. bones lose calcium   c. muscles weaken
   b. dehydration   d. all of these

8. _____ has a very complex ring system made of hundreds of ringlets.
   a. Pluto   c. Uranus
   b. Saturn   d. Mars

9. The magnetic pole of _____ is tilted 60°.
   a. Uranus   c. Jupiter
   b. Earth   d. Pluto

10. The tail of a comet always points _____.
    a. toward the sun   c. toward Earth
    b. away from the sun   d. away from the Oort Cloud

UNDERSTANDING CONCEPTS

Complete each sentence.

11. The object around which all planets and stars were once believed to have orbited is _____.
12. Although it is the ninth planet from the sun, Pluto is like a(n) _____ planet.
13. A greenhouse effect occurs on ____ and ____.
14. Robots imitate the motions made by _____.
15. In 2001, _____ will be the farthest planet from the sun.

THINK AND WRITE CRITICALLY

16. Contrast Copernicus' model of the solar system with Kepler's model.
17. Describe the general characteristics of the inner and outer planets.
18. Describe how the structure of a comet changes as it nears the sun.
19. How is Uranus different from the other eight planets?
20. Compare and contrast Mercury and Pluto.

21. Why is the surface temperature on Venus so much higher than that on Earth?

22. Describe the relationship between the mass of a planet and the number of satellites it has.

23. Why are probe landings on Jupiter or Saturn unlikely events?

24. What evidence suggests that water is or once was present on Mars?

25. An observer on Earth can watch Venus go through phases much like Earth's moon does. Explain why this is so.

MORE SKILL BUILDERS

If you need help, refer to the Skill Handbook.

1. Concept Mapping: Make a concept map that explains how a comet changes as it travels through space.

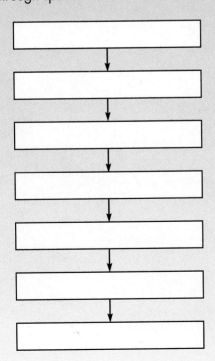

2. Hypothesizing: Mercury is the closest planet to the sun, yet it does not reflect much of the sun's light. What can you say about Mercury's color?

3. Measuring in SI: The Great Red Spot of Jupiter is about 40 000 km long and about 12 000 km wide. What is its area in km^2?

4. Sequencing: Arrange the following planets in order from the planet with the most natural satellites to the one with the least number: Earth, Jupiter, Saturn, Neptune, Uranus, and Mars.

5. Making and Using Tables: Make a table that summarizes the main characteristics of each planet in the solar system.

PROJECTS

1. Build a three-dimensional scale model of the solar system.

2. Mercury, Venus, Mars, Jupiter, and Saturn can be observed by the unaided eye. Research where in the sky these planets can be observed for the next five years. Construct a display with your findings.

Stars and Galaxies

The collection of stars, gas, and dust shown at left is a galaxy similar to the one that contains our solar system. There are countless galaxies in the universe, most of which are moving away from each other. Our universe is expanding.

FIND OUT!

Do this simple activity to model the expansion of the universe.

Partially inflate a balloon. Fold the neck and clip it shut with a clothespin so air doesn't escape. Draw six evenly spaced dots on the balloon with a felt-tip marker. Label the dots A through F. Use a string and ruler to measure the distance, in millimeters, from dot A to each of the other dots. Remove the clothespin and inflate the balloon some more. Measure the distance of each dot from A again. Inflate the balloon once more and take the new measurements. Which distances changed the most? The least? If each dot represents a galaxy, describe the motion of the galaxies relative to one another. Is the universe expanding?

Gearing Up
Previewing the Chapter

Previewing Science Skills

- ▶ In the Skill Builders, you will recognize cause and effect, sequence events, interpret scientific illustrations, and observe and infer.
- ▶ In the Activities, you will collect and analyze data and draw conclusions.
- ▶ In the MINI-Labs, you will interpret scientific illustrations and make inferences.

What's next?

You've discovered that the galaxies are moving away from each other. But what are galaxies, and why are they moving? In this chapter, you'll learn that galaxies are large groups of stars, and you'll discover how we know they are moving apart.

24-1 Stars

New Science Words

constellations
absolute magnitude
apparent magnitude
parallax
light-year

Objectives

▶ Explain why the positions of the constellations change throughout the year.
▶ Compare and contrast absolute magnitude and apparent magnitude.
▶ Describe how parallax is used to determine distances.

Constellations

Have you ever watched clouds drift by on a summer day? It's fun to look at the clouds and imagine they have shapes familiar to you. One may look like a face. You might see a cloud that resembles a rabbit or a bear. People long ago did much the same thing with patterns of stars in the sky. They named certain groups of stars, called **constellations,** after animals, characters in mythology, or familiar objects.

From Earth, a constellation looks like a group of stars that are relatively close to one another. In most cases, the stars in a constellation have no relationship to each other in space. Figure 24-1 illustrates how this is possible.

The position of a star in the sky can be given as a specific location within a constellation. For example, you can say that the star Betelgeuse (BEET ul joos) is in the

Figure 24-1. The star at the end of the "handle" of the Big Dipper is 210 light-years away. The star second from the end is only 88 light-years away, yet they appear next to each other in the sky.

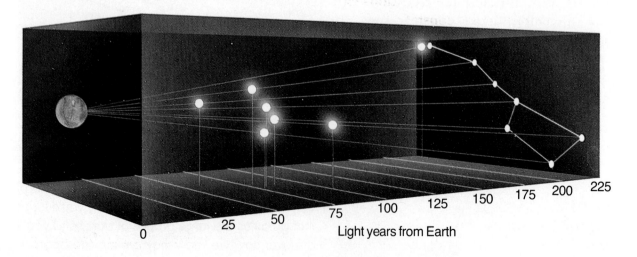

Light years from Earth

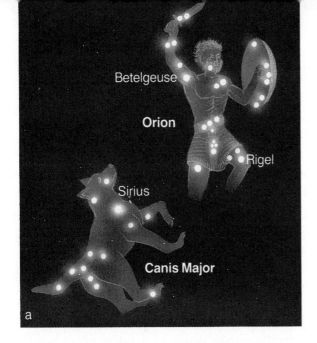

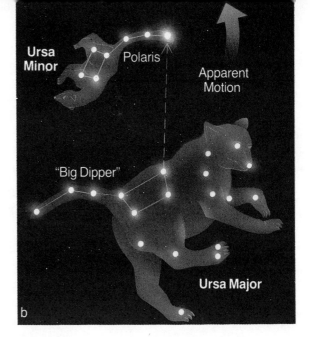

right shoulder of the mighty hunter Orion. Orion's faithful companion is his dog, Canis Major. The brightest star in the winter sky, Sirius (SIHR ee us), is in the constellation Canis Major.

Early Greek astronomers named many constellations, and today astronomers have divided the sky into 88 constellations. You may already know some of them. Have you ever tried to find the Big Dipper? It's part of the constellation Ursa Major. Notice how the front two stars of the Big Dipper point directly at the star Polaris. Polaris, also known as the North Star, is located at the end of the Little Dipper—part of Ursa Minor. Polaris is almost directly over Earth's north pole.

As Earth rotates, you can watch Ursa Major, Ursa Minor, and other constellations in the northern sky circle around Polaris. Because these constellations circle Polaris they are called circumpolar constellations.

All of the constellations appear to move because Earth is moving. The stars appear to complete one full circle in the sky in just under 24 hours as Earth rotates on its axis. The stars also appear to change positions in the sky throughout the year as Earth revolves around the sun.

Circumpolar constellations are visible all year long, but other constellations are not. As Earth orbits the sun, different constellations come into view while others disappear. Orion, which is visible in the winter, can't be seen in the summer because the daytime side of Earth is facing it. The various constellations visible each season are shown in Appendix J on pages 674 and 675.

Figure 24-2. Orion and Canis Major (a) are visible in the winter sky, but rest below the horizon during other seasons. Circumpolar constellations such as Ursa Major (b) are visible year-round.

Figure 24-3. This photograph shows the path of the circumpolar stars over a period of several hours. Because Polaris is almost directly over the North Pole, it doesn't appear to move much as Earth rotates.

Absolute and Apparent Magnitudes

When you look at constellations, you'll notice that some stars are brighter than others. Sirius looks much brighter than Rigel (RI juhl). But is Sirius actually a brighter star, or is it just closer to Earth, which makes it appear brighter? As it turns out, Sirius is 100 times closer to Earth than Rigel. If Sirius and Rigel were the same distance from Earth, Rigel would appear much brighter in the night sky than would Sirius.

When you refer to the brightness of a star, you can refer to either its absolute magnitude or its apparent magnitude. The **absolute magnitude** of a star is a measure of the amount of light it actually gives off. The amount of light received on Earth is called the **apparent magnitude.** A star that's actually rather dim can appear quite bright in the sky if it's close to Earth. A star that's actually bright can appear dim if it's far away.

PROBLEM SOLVING

Star Light, Star Bright

Mary conducted an activity to determine the relationship between distance and the brightness of stars. She used a meterstick, a light meter, and a light bulb. The bulb was mounted at the zero end of the meterstick. Mary placed the light meter at the 20-cm mark on the meterstick and recorded the distance and the light meter reading in the data table. Readings are in luxes, which are units for measuring light intensity. Mary doubled and tripled the distance and took more readings.

Distance (cm)	Meter Reading (luxes)
20	4150
40	1050
60	460
80	262.5

Think Critically: What is the relationship between light intensity and distance? What would it be at 100 cm?

Determining the Distances to Stars

How do we know when a star is close to our solar system? One way is to measure its parallax. **Parallax** is the apparent shift in the position of an object when viewed from two different positions. You can easily observe parallax. Hold your hand at arm's length and look at one finger first with your left eye and then with your right eye. Your finger appears to change position with respect to the background. Now try the same experiment with your finger closer to your face. What do you observe? The nearer an object is to the observer, the greater its parallax.

Why are parallax measurements useful only for nearby stars?

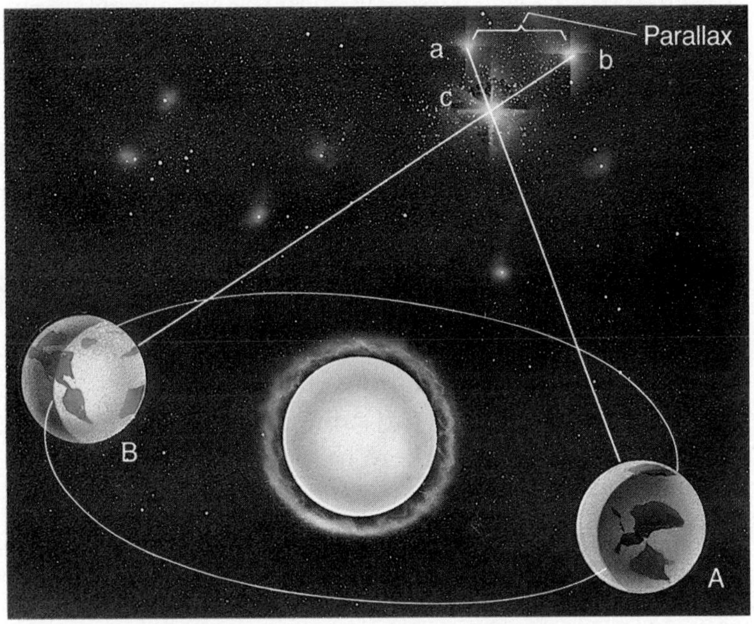

Figure 24-4. When Earth is in position A, the star appears to be in position a. The star appears to be in position b when Earth is in position B. This apparent shift in the star's position is its parallax. The actual position of the star is c.

We can measure the parallax of relatively close stars to determine their distances from Earth. When astronomers first realized how far away stars actually are, it became apparent that a new unit of measure would be needed to record their distances. Measuring star distances in kilometers would be like measuring the distance between cities in millimeters.

Distances in space are measured in light-years. A **light-year** is the distance that light travels in one year. Light travels at 300 000 km/s, or about 9.5 trillion kilometers in one year. The nearest star to Earth, other than the sun, is Proxima Centuri. Proxima Centuri is 4.2 light-years away, or about 40 trillion kilometers. It takes 4.2 years for its light to reach your eyes.

Determining a Star's Temperature and Composition

The color of a star indicates its temperature. For example, very hot stars are a blue-white color. A relatively cool star looks orange or red. Stars the temperature of our sun have a yellow color.

Astronomers learn about other properties of stars by studying their spectra. They use spectrographs to break visible light from a star into its component colors. If you look closely at the spectrum of a star, such as the one shown on page 650, you will see dark lines in it. The lines are caused by elements in the star's atmosphere. As light radiated from a star passes through the star's atmosphere, some of it is absorbed by elements in the atmosphere. The wavelengths of visible light that are absorbed appear as dark lines in the spectrum. Each element absorbs certain wavelengths, producing a certain pattern of dark lines. The patterns of lines can be used to identify which elements are in a star.

Figure 24-5. A triangle-shaped glass called a prism can be used to produce a spectrum. The various wavelengths making up white light bend at different angles when they pass through the prism. They separate from each other, and the colors of the spectrum become visible.

SECTION REVIEW

1. Explain how Earth's revolution affects constellations that are visible throughout the year.
2. If two stars give off the same amount of light, what might cause one of them to look much brighter than the other?
3. Measuring distances in space using parallax is only useful for relatively near stars. Explain why it can't be used for objects that are very far away.
4. **Apply:** Only about 700 stars have large enough parallaxes that their distances can be determined using parallax. Most of them are invisible to the naked eye. What does this indicate about their absolute magnitudes?

Skill Builder

☑ Recognizing Cause and Effect

Suppose you viewed Proxima Centuri through a telescope. How old were you when the light that you see left Proxima Centuri? Why might Proxima Centuri look dimmer than the star Betelgeuse, a very large star 489 light-years away? If you need help, refer to Recognizing Cause and Effect in the **Skill Handbook** on page 683.

Problem: *How does distance affect parallax?*

Material

- meterstick
- metric ruler
- masking tape

Procedure

1. Place a piece of masking tape next to the 20-, 40-, and 60-cm marks of the meterstick so that a pencil will stop at the tape and be aligned with the 20-, 40-, or 60-cm mark.
2. Use tape to attach the metric ruler to a bulletin board in the room. Make sure the metric ruler is in a horizontal position so that it reads left to right.
3. Carefully place the 1-cm end of the meterstick on the bridge of your nose. **CAUTION:** *Be sure to wear goggles to protect your eyes. Don't walk with the meterstick in this position.* Place the other end of the meterstick against the 1-cm mark on the ruler.
4. Move a pencil along the meterstick to where the first piece of tape is located.
5. Close your left eye. Align the pencil with the end of the meterstick and the 1-cm mark on the ruler. Close your right eye and open your left eye. Observe the number of centimeters from the metric ruler that the pencil shifted. Record the number in the data table.
6. Write a hypothesis stating how moving the pencil farther from the eye will affect the distance the pencil shifts.
7. Repeat Steps 5 and 6 with the pencil at the 40- and 60-cm marks.

Data and Observations

Distance of pencil from eye (cm)	Apparent movement (cm)
20	
40	
60	

Analyze

1. What happened to the pencil when the right eye was closed and the left eye was opened?
2. At what distance from the eye did the pencil shift the greatest distance?
3. What happened to the shift of the pencil as the distance of the pencil from the eye increased?

Conclude and Apply

4. How does your hypothesis compare with the results of the activity?
5. How does the distance of an object from an observer affect parallax?
6. How might astronomers use parallax?

24-2 Evolution of Stars

New Science Words

main sequence
nebula
giant
white dwarf
supergiant
neutron star
black hole

Objectives

▶ Diagram how stars are classified.
▶ Relate the temperature of a star to its color.
▶ Outline the evolution of a main sequence star.

The H-R Diagram

In the early 1900s, Ejnar Hertzsprung and Henry Russell noticed that for most stars, the higher their temperatures, the brighter their absolute magnitudes. They developed a graph to show this relationship.

Hertzsprung and Russell placed the temperatures of the stars across the bottom of the graph and the absolute magnitudes of the stars up one side. A graph that shows the relationship of a star's temperature to its absolute magnitude is called a Hertzsprung-Russell (H-R) diagram. Figure 24-7 shows a typical H-R diagram.

As you can see, stars seem to fit into specific areas of the chart. Most stars fit into a diagonal band that runs from the upper left to the lower right of the chart. This band, called the **main sequence,** contains hot, blue, bright

Figure 24-6. The Relative Sizes of Stars: (a) A supergiant can be 250 times as large as our sun. (b) The sizes of white dwarfs vary considerably, but a typical white dwarf is planet-sized, or about 100 times smaller than our sun. (c) A typical white dwarf is 700 times larger than a typical neutron star. (d) A black hole is about one-third the size of a neutron star.

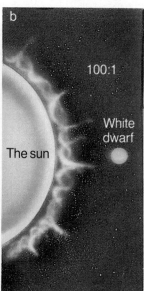

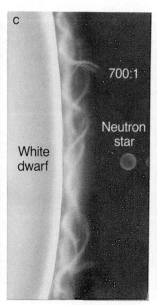

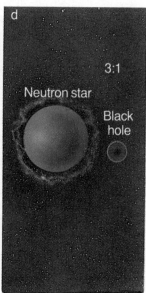

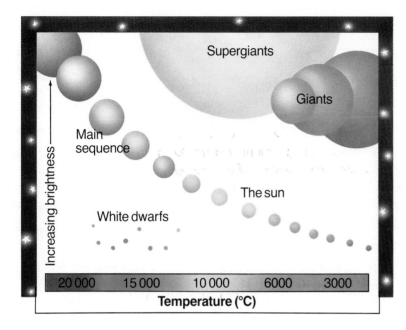

Figure 24-7. Hot, blue stars in the upper left of the main sequence are as large as giants but they are much hotter. Moderate, yellow stars are near the middle of the main sequence. Very dim, small red stars are in the lower right of the main sequence. Giants and supergiants are bright but cool and don't fall within the main sequence. White dwarfs are hot but not very bright.

stars in the upper left and cool, red, dim stars in the lower right. Yellow, medium temperature, medium brightness stars fall in between. The sun is a yellow main sequence star.

About 90 percent of all stars are main sequence stars. Among main sequence stars, the hottest stars generate the most light and the coolest generate the least. But what about the remaining ten percent? Some of these stars are hot but not very bright. These small stars are located on the lower left of the H-R diagram and are called white dwarfs. Other stars are extremely bright but not very hot. These large stars on the upper right of the H-R diagram are called giants, or red giants because they are usually red in color. The largest giants are called supergiants.

Fusion

When the H-R diagram was developed, scientists didn't know what caused stars to shine. Hertzsprung and Russell developed their diagram without knowing what produced the light and heat of stars.

For centuries, people had been puzzled by the question of what stars were and what made them shine. It wasn't until the early part of this century that scientists were forced to explain how a star could shine for billions of years. Until that time, many had estimated the age of Earth as only a few thousand years old. The

Did You Know?

In 1600, Giordano Bruno was burned at the stake for suggesting that the stars were like our sun. He thought perhaps they even had planets orbiting them as the sun of our solar system does. Bruno's beliefs are accepted today as common knowledge, but during his time they were unacceptable.

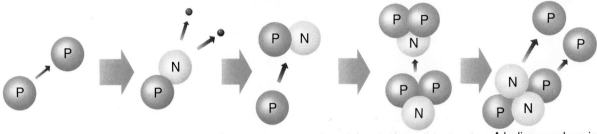

Two hydrogen nuclei (protons) are forced together in the core of a star.

One of the protons decays to a neutron, releasing subatomic particles.

Another proton fuses with the proton and neutron to form an isotope of helium.

Another helium isotope fuses with the previously formed isotope.

A helium nucleus is formed as two protons break away. Energy is released in the process.

sun could have been made of coal and shined for that long. But what material could possibly burn for billions of years?

In 1920, A. S. Eddington suggested that hydrogen atoms in the sun fused, or combined, to form helium atoms. Recall that the nucleus of a hydrogen atom is a single proton. A helium atom contains two protons and two neutrons in its nucleus. The diagram above illustrates how four hydrogen nuclei could combine to create one helium nucleus. The mass of one helium nucleus is less than the mass of four hydrogen nuclei, so some mass is lost in the reaction.

Years earlier, in 1905, Albert Einstein had proposed a theory stating that mass can be converted into energy. The mass "lost" when hydrogen atoms fuse to form a helium atom is converted to energy. Eddington concluded that hydrogen fusion powered the sun and other stars.

Fusion occurs in the cores of stars. Only there, are temperatures and pressures high enough to cause atoms to fuse. Normally, they would repel each other, but in the core of a star, atoms are forced close enough together that their nuclei attract.

The Evolution of Stars

The H-R diagram and Eddington's theory explained a lot about stars. But, they also led to more questions. Many wondered why some stars didn't fit in the main sequence group and what happened when a star exhausted its supply of hydrogen fuel. Today, we have a theory of how stars evolve, what makes them different from one another, and what happens when they die.

A star begins as a large cloud of gas and dust called a **nebula.** The particles of gas and dust exert a gravitational force on each other, and the nebula begins to contract. As the particles in the cloud move closer together, the temperatures in the nebula increase. When temperatures inside the nebula reach 10 000 000°C, fusion begins. The energy released radiates outward through the condensing ball of gas. As the energy radiates into space, a star is born.

What determines when fusion begins within a nebula?

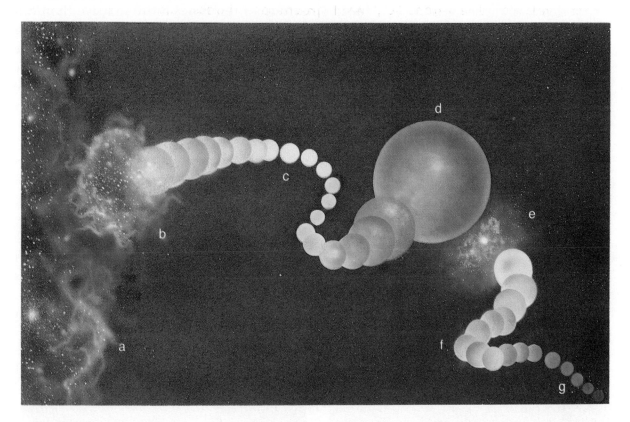

The heat from the fusion causes pressure that balances the attraction due to gravity, and the star becomes a main sequence star. It continues to use up its hydrogen fuel.

When the hydrogen in the core of the star is exhausted, there is no longer a balance between pressure and gravity. The core contracts, and the temperatures inside the star increase. This causes the outer layers of the star to expand. The star has evolved into a **giant.**

Unless a giant has a small mass, helium nuclei fuse to form carbon in its core. By this time, the star has expanded to an enormous size, and its outer layers are much cooler than they were when it was a main sequence star. In about 5 billion years, our sun will become a giant.

Figure 24-8. The Life of a Main Sequence Star the size of our sun: A nebula (a) condenses and stars begin to form within it as temperatures rise (b). A main sequence star forms (c). When its hydrogen fuel is exhausted, it expands and becomes a giant (d). The core collapses while the outer portions of the giant are blown away (e), forming a white dwarf (f). Eventually, the white dwarf uses up it fuel and becomes a cold, dead star (g). Note that stars are not shown to scale.

After the star's core uses up its supply of helium, it contracts even more. If the star has a large mass, its core uses up the carbon and other elements it previously created and produces even heavier elements. As the core of the star runs out of fuel, the outer layers become unstable and begin escaping into space. This leaves behind the hot, dense core. The burned-out core contracts under the force of gravity. At this stage in a star's evolution, it is a **white dwarf.**

In stars more than ten times more massive than our sun, the stages of evolution occur more quickly and more violently. The core heats up to much higher temperatures. Heavier and heavier elements form by fusion. The star expands into a **supergiant.** Eventually, iron forms in the core. Because fusion can no longer occur, the core collapses violently, sending a shock wave outward through the star. The outer portion of the star explodes, producing a supernova. A supernova can be millions of times brighter than the original star.

What determines whether a star becomes a giant versus a supergiant?

Figure 24-9. The photo on the left shows the star named Sanduleak−69°202 before it evolved into a supernova. The photo on the right was taken in 1987, when Sanduleak −69°202 entered a supernova stage.

The collapsed core shrinks to about the size of a large city. Only neutrons can exist in the dense core, which becomes a **neutron star.**

If the original star is more than 30 times more massive than the sun, probably nothing can stop the core's collapse. It quickly evolves into a **black hole**—an object so dense, nothing can escape its gravity field. In fact, not even light can escape a black hole. If you could shine a flashlight on a black hole, it wouldn't illuminate it. The light would simply disappear into it. As matter and energy are pulled toward a black hole, X rays are given off.

TECHNOLOGY

Studying Supernovas

Near Cleveland, Ohio, and in Kamioka, Japan, large tanks of water and sensitive radiation-detecting instruments rest underground. The instruments are capable of detecting the radiation given off when subatomic particles called neutrinos strike protons or electrons in the water. In February 1987, the instruments recorded the presence of neutrinos. The records of the neutrinos striking the tanks went unnoticed until astronomers in the southern hemisphere observed a supernova.

Astronomers had previously theorized that neutrinos are emitted when a star evolves into a supernova. When the supernova was spotted, astronomers asked researchers at the underground tanks to check records of activity in the tanks. Records from Cleveland and Kamioka verified that neutrinos had been emitted during the explosion of the star. The neutrinos had

traveled at the speed of light and arrived at Earth at about the same time as the visible light from the supernova.

Think Critically: The neutrinos that traveled through Earth in 1987 were created about 163 000 years ago when Sanduleak −69°202 evolved into a supernova. How far away was Sanduleak −69°202?

Astronomers have located X-ray sources around possible black holes. Extremely massive black holes may exist in the centers of galaxies.

A star begins its life as a nebula, but where does the matter in a nebula come from? Nebulas form partly from the matter that was once in other stars. A star ejects enormous amounts of matter during its lifetime. Millions or billions of years after a star dies, this matter condenses to form new nebulas, which then evolve into new stars. The matter in stars is recycled many times.

What about the matter created in the cores of stars? Are elements like carbon and iron recycled also? Some of these elements do become parts of new stars. In fact, spectrographs have shown that our sun contains carbon, iron,

Why haven't black holes been directly observed?

Figure 24-10. A thick collection of gas and dust makes up the Horsehead nebula. There's evidence that new stars are evolving from the matter and energy contained within this nebula.

What evidence is there that our sun evolved from material from a previous star?

and other such elements. Because the sun is a main sequence star, it is too young to have created these elements itself. Our sun condensed from material that was created in stars that died many billions of years ago.

Some elements condense to form planets and other bodies rather than stars. In fact, your body contains many atoms that were fused in the cores of ancient stars. Most scientists believe that the early universe contained only hydrogen and helium. The first stars formed from these two elements, and all other elements have formed in the cores of stars.

SECTION REVIEW

1. Explain why giants are not in the main sequence on the H-R diagram. How do their temperature and absolute magnitude compare to main sequence stars?
2. What can be said about the absolute magnitudes of two equal-sized stars whose colors are blue and yellow?
3. Outline the history and probable future of our sun, a main sequence star.
4. Why do some stars evolve into neutron stars but others do not?
5. **Apply:** Why doesn't the helium currently in the sun's core undergo fusion?

Skill Builder

☑ Sequencing

Sequence these stars in order of most evolved to least evolved: *white dwarf, main sequence star, giant, neutron star,* and *black hole.* If you need help, refer to Sequencing in the **Skill Handbook** on page 680.

ACTIVITY 24-2
Sunspots

Problem: *How can you trace the movement of sunspots?*

Materials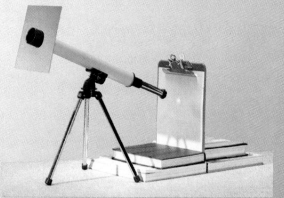

- several books
- clipboard
- small tripod
- small refracting telescope
- cardboard
- drawing paper
- scissors

Procedure

1. Find a location where the sun may be viewed at the same time of day for a minimum of five days. **CAUTION:** *Do not look directly at the sun. Do not look through the telescope at the sun. You could damage your eyes.*
2. Set up the telescope with the eyepiece facing away from the sun as shown. Set up the clipboard with the drawing paper attached.
3. Use the books to prop the clipboard upright. Point the eyepiece at the drawing paper.
4. Arrange a shield of heavy cardboard with the center cut out.
5. Move the clipboard back and forth until you have the largest possible image of the sun on the paper. Adjust the telescope to form a clear image.
6. Trace the outline of the sun on the paper.
7. Trace any sunspots that appear as dark areas on the sun's image. At the same time each day for a week, check the sun's image and trace the position of the sunspots.
8. Using the sun's diameter as approximately 1 400 000 km, estimate the size of the largest sunspots that are observed.

9. Calculate how many kilometers any observed sunspots appear to move each day.
10. At the rate determined in Step 9, predict how many days it will take for the same group of sunspots to return to about the same position in which you first observed them.

Analyze

1. Which part of the sun showed up in your image?
2. What are solar flares, and how can they be related to sunspots?
3. What was the average number of sunspots observed each day during this investigation?

Conclude and Apply

4. How can the movement of sunspots be traced?
5. How can sunspots be used to determine that the sun's surface is not solid like Earth's?

Data and Observations

Date of observation	Number of sunspot groups (approx.)	Estimated average sunspot diam. (km)	Approximate actual movement (km)	Predicted return time (Earth days)

The Sun

New Science Words

photosphere
chromosphere
corona
sunspots
binary system

Objectives

▶ Describe how energy is produced in the sun.
▶ Recognize that sunspots, prominences, and solar flares are related.
▶ Explain why our sun is considered an average star and how it differs from stars in binary systems.

The Layers of the Sun

More than 99 percent of all of the matter in our solar system is in the sun. It is the center of our solar system, and it makes life possible on Earth. To you and everyone else on Earth, the sun is a special object in the sky and one of the most important objects in your life. Nevertheless, our sun is just an average star.

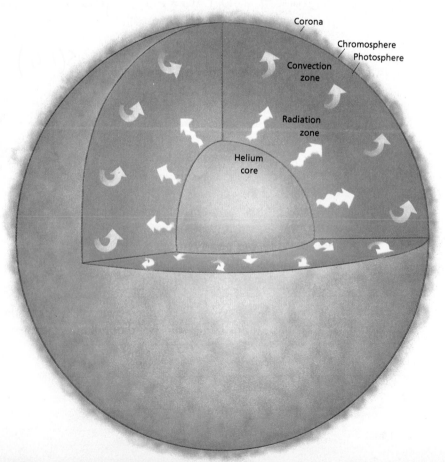

Figure 24-11. Energy produced by fusion in the sun's core travels outward by radiation and convection. The sun's atmosphere, composed of the photosphere, chromosphere, and corona, is illuminated by the energy produced in the core.

The sun is a main sequence star on the H-R diagram. Its absolute magnitude is about average and it shines with a yellow light. The sun is an enormous ball of gas, fusing hydrogen into helium in its core. Figure 24-11 is a model of the sun's interior.

The lowest layer of the sun's atmosphere and the layer from which light is given off is the **photosphere.** Temperatures there are around 6000°C. Above the photosphere is the **chromosphere.** This layer extends upward about 6000 km. Above the chromosphere is the **corona.** This is the largest layer of the sun's atmosphere and extends millions of kilometers into space. Temperatures in the corona are as high as 2 000 000°C. Charged particles continually escape from the corona and move through space as the solar wind.

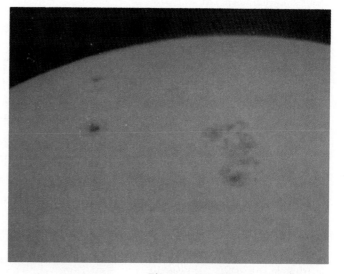

Figure 24-12. Sunspots are brighter than a full moon, but seen against the rest of the photosphere, they appear dark.

Sunspots

The sun's surface is not a smooth layer of gas. There are many features that can be studied. Dark areas of the sun's surface, which are cooler than surrounding areas, are called **sunspots.** Ever since Galileo first identified sunspots, scientists have been studying them. One thing we've learned by studying sunspots is that the sun rotates. We can observe individual sunspots moving across the surface as they are carried by the sun's rotation. The sun doesn't rotate as a solid body, as does Earth. It rotates faster at its equator than at its poles. Sunspots near the equator take about 25 days to go around the sun; at higher latitudes, they take a day or two longer.

Sunspots aren't permanent features on the sun. They appear and disappear over a period of several days or months. Also, there are times when there are many large sunspots—a sunspot maximum—and times when there are only a few small sunspots or none at all—a sunspot minimum. Sunspot maximums occur about every 11 years. The last maximum was in 1990. The next is expected in 2001.

Prominences and Flares

Sunspots are related to several features on the sun's surface. The intense magnetic field associated with sunspots may cause prominences, huge arching columns of gas. Some prominences are so eruptive that material from the sun is blasted into space at speeds approaching 1000 km/s. Others form into loops through which matter flows into and out of the corona.

Gases near a sunspot sometimes brighten up suddenly, shooting gas outward at high speed. These violent eruptions from the sun are called solar flares.

Ultraviolet light and X rays from solar flares can reach Earth and cause disruption of radio signals. This makes communication by radio and telephone very difficult at times. Solar flares can also interact with Earth's magnetic field, causing Earth's atmosphere to radiate light called the aurora borealis, or northern lights. In the southern hemisphere this light is called the aurora australis.

Figure 24-13. This photograph of a huge prominence was taken by astronauts on board *Skylab* in 1973. The prominence arches hundreds of thousands of kilometers into space and is large enough to contain several Earths.

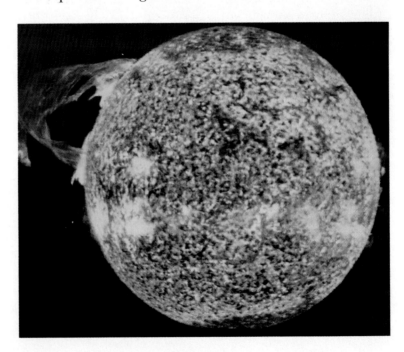

Our Sun: A Typical Star?

Although our sun is a main sequence star, it is somewhat unusual in one way. Most stars are in systems in which two or more stars orbit each other. When two stars orbit each other, it is called a **binary system.** In some cases, astronomers can detect binary systems because one star occasionally eclipses the other. The total amount of light from the star system becomes dim and then bright again, on a regular cycle.

In many cases, stars move through space together as a cluster. In a star cluster, many stars are relatively close to one another and are gravitationally attracted to each other. The Pleiades star cluster can be seen in the constellation of Taurus in the winter sky. On a clear, dark night, you may be able to make out seven of the stars of this cluster. Most star clusters are far from our solar system, and appear as a fuzzy patch in the night sky.

Figure 24-14. Pleiades is a cluster of stars gravitationally bound to each other. All of the stars in this cluster have only recently begun fusing hydrogen in their cores—becoming main sequence stars.

SECTION REVIEW

1. How does the sun generate energy? What will happen to the sun when it exhausts its supply of hydrogen?
2. How are sunspots, prominences, and solar flares related?
3. What properties of the sun make it a typical star? What property makes it different from most other stars?
4. **Apply:** In approximately 5 billion years, our sun's surface may expand beyond the orbit of Earth, engulfing Mercury, Venus, and Earth in its fiery gases. What evolutionary stage will the sun be in at this point? What type of star will it become after that?

☑ Interpreting Scientific Illustrations

Skill
Builder

Use Figure 24-11 to answer the questions below. If you need help, refer to Interpreting Scientific Illustrations in the **Skill Handbook** on page 693.

1. Compare Figure 24-11 with Figure 22-8 on page 587, showing a total solar eclipse. What part of the sun is visible in Figure 22-8?
2. Which layers make up the sun's atmosphere?
3. How does the diameter of the sun's core compare to the diameter of the core of a supergiant?

Galaxies and the Expanding Universe

New Science Words

galaxy
big bang theory

Objectives

▶ Describe a galaxy and list the three main types of galaxies.
▶ Identify several characteristics of the Milky Way Galaxy.
▶ Explain how the big bang theory explains observed Doppler shifts.

Galaxies

One reason to study astronomy is to learn about your place in the universe. Long ago, people thought they were at the center of the universe and everything revolved around Earth. Today, you know this isn't the case. But do you know where you are in the universe?

You are on Earth, and Earth orbits the sun. But does the sun orbit anything? How does it interact with other objects in the universe? The sun is one star in the Milky Way Galaxy. A **galaxy** is a large group of stars, gas, and dust held together by gravity. Our galaxy, the Milky Way,

Figure 24-15. Centaurus A is a peculiar elliptical galaxy 16 million light-years away.

contains about 200 billion stars. Galaxies are separated by huge distances—often millions of light-years.

Just as stars are grouped together within galaxies, galaxies are grouped into clusters. The cluster the Milky Way belongs to is called the Local Group. It contains about 25 galaxies of various types and sizes.

There are three major classifications of galaxies: elliptical, spiral, and irregular. The most common type of galaxy is the elliptical galaxy. These galaxies are shaped like large, three-dimensional ellipses. Many are football-shaped. Some elliptical galaxies are quite small, while others are so large that the entire Local Group of galaxies would fit inside one of them.

Spiral galaxies have spiral arms winding outward from inner regions. These spiral arms are made up of stars and dust. In between the arms, there are fewer stars. The fuzzy patch you can see in the constellation of Andromeda is actually a spiral galaxy. It's so far away that you can't see its individual stars. Instead, it appears as a hazy spot in our sky. The Andromeda galaxy is a member of the Local Group and is about 2 million light-years away.

Arms in a normal spiral start close to the center of the galaxy. Barred spirals have two spiral arms extending from a large bar that passes through the center of the galaxy. Figure 24-18 shows a barred spiral galaxy.

What is the Local Group?

In what ways are the Andromeda galaxy and the Milky Way related?

Figure 24-16. NGC 2997 is a spiral galaxy similar to our own. The scattered stars in the picture are in the foreground and belong to the Milky Way.

Figure 24-17. The Large Magellanic Cloud is an irregular galaxy. It's a member of the Local Group, and it orbits our own galaxy.

Figure 24-18. In a barred spiral, the spiral arms originate at the ends of a bar passing through the nucleus. This galaxy is named NGC 1365.

Figure 24-19. The Milky Way Galaxy is probably a normal spiral galaxy. Its spiral arms, composed of stars and gas, radiate out from an area of densely packed stars, the nucleus. Clusters of stars lie above and below the plane of the spiral arms.

The third class of galaxies, irregulars, includes most of those galaxies that don't fit into the other classifications. Irregular galaxies have many different shapes and are smaller and less common than the other types. Two irregular galaxies called the Clouds of Magellan orbit the Milky Way Galaxy at a distance of about 170 000 light-years.

The Milky Way Galaxy

The Milky Way contains more than 200 billion stars. It's about 100 000 light-years across, and the sun is located about 30 000 light-years out from its center. In our galaxy, all stars orbit around a central region. The sun orbits around the center of the Milky Way once every 200 million years.

A diagram of our galaxy is shown in Figure 24-19. The Milky Way is usually classified as a normal spiral galaxy. However, recent evidence suggests that it might be a barred spiral. It is difficult to know for sure because we can never see our galaxy from the "outside."

You can't see the normal spiral or barred shape of the Milky Way because you are located within one of its spiral arms. You can see the Milky Way stretching across the sky as a faint band of light. All of the stars you can see in the night sky belong to the Milky Way Galaxy.

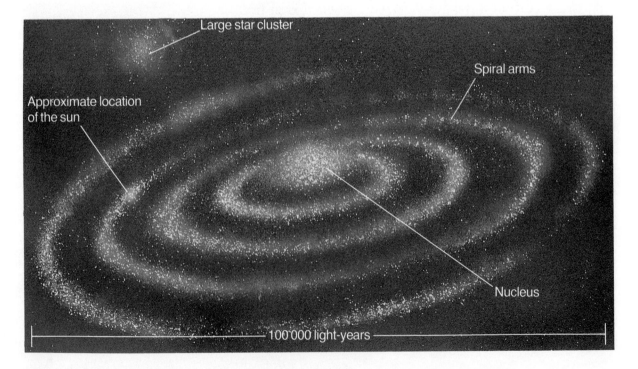

Large star cluster

Spiral arms

Approximate location of the sun

Nucleus

100 000 light-years

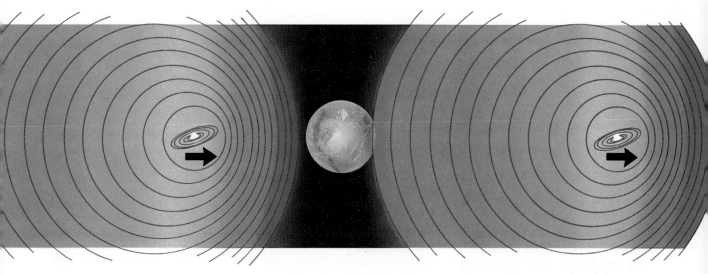

Expansion of the Universe

What does it sound like when a car is blowing its horn while it drives past you? The horn has a high pitch as the car approaches you, then the horn seems to change to a low pitch as the car drives away. This effect is called the Doppler shift. The Doppler shift occurs with light as well as with sound.

Look at the spectrum of a star containing sodium in Figure 24-21a. Note the position of the dark lines. How do they compare with the lines in Figures 24-21b and c? They have shifted in position. What caused this shift? When a star is moving toward you, its wavelengths of light are pushed together, just as the sound waves from the car's horn are. The dark lines in the spectrum shift toward the blue-violet. A red shift in the spectrum occurs when an object is moving away from you. In a red shift, the dark lines shift toward the longer wavelength, red end of the spectrum.

In 1924, Edwin Hubble noticed an interesting fact about the light coming from most galaxies. When a spectrograph is used to study light from galaxies beyond the Local Group, there is a red shift in the light. What does this red shift tell you about the universe?

Because all galaxies beyond the Local Group show a red shift in their spectra, they must be moving away from Earth. If all galaxies outside the Local Group are moving away from you, the entire universe must be expanding. Think of the Find Out activity at the beginning of the chapter. The dots on the balloon moved apart as the

Figure 24-20. The Doppler effect causes the wavelengths of light coming from galaxies to be compressed or stretched. When a galaxy is moving toward Earth, the wavelengths are forced together and the light shifts toward the blue-violet end of the spectrum. A galaxy shows a red shift when moving away from Earth.

EcoTip

Viewing the stars and galaxies is possible only when the sky is unpolluted by artificial lights. Help keep the sky dark and save energy by turning off unnecessary outdoor lights.

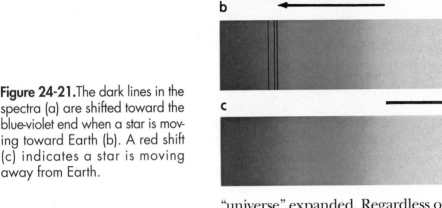

a

b ⟵

c ⟶

Figure 24-21. The dark lines in the spectra (a) are shifted toward the blue-violet end when a star is moving toward Earth (b). A red shift (c) indicates a star is moving away from Earth.

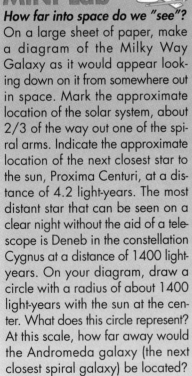

"universe" expanded. Regardless of which dot you picked, all the other dots moved away from it. Galaxies beyond the Local Group move away from us just as the dots moved apart on the balloon.

When scientists determined that the universe was expanding, they realized that galaxies must have been closer together in the past. The leading theory about the formation of the universe is based on this fact. The **big bang theory** states that between 15 and 20 billion years ago, the universe began expanding out of an enormous explosion.

At the beginning of the explosion, all matter in the universe was concentrated in a state of infinite density. The explosion of the big bang sent all matter moving apart. As matter cooled, hydrogen and helium gas formed. Matter began collecting in clumps and eventually formed into galaxies. There is evidence to support the big bang theory. Scientists have discovered radiation in space they believe was created by the explosion of the big bang.

Will the universe expand forever? Some scientists think that it will. Others think that the expansion will stop. Whether the universe expands forever or stops depends on how dense the matter is in the universe. All matter exerts a gravitational force. If there's enough matter, gravity will halt the expansion. In that case, the universe would contract until everything came to one point—a "big crunch" would result. It's not known if the universe is dense enough for this to happen.

Astronomers continue to study the structure of the known universe in hopes of learning its exact age, how it has evolved, and how it might end. You will learn in the next section that astronomers also search the galaxy in hopes of finding evidence that life exists elsewhere in our solar system and galaxy.

Figure 24-22. This 305-m dish at Arecibo, Puerto Rico is the world's largest telescope. On page 661 in the Science and Art feature, you will read how this telescope was used in an attempt to communicate with extraterrestrial life.

SECTION REVIEW

1. List the three major classifications of galaxies. What do they all have in common?
2. What is the name of the galaxy that you live in? What motion do the stars in this galaxy exhibit?
3. How does the big bang theory explain observations of galaxies made with spectrographs?
4. **Apply:** All galaxies outside the Local Group show a red shift in their spectra. What does this tell you about the galaxies in the Local Group?

☑ Recognizing Cause and Effect

Skill Builder

Current measurements and calculated densities of the universe show it's not dense enough to collapse on itself. Scientists are trying to prove the existence of so-called "dark matter," which is not directly observable. If the universe contains an abundance of dark matter, what could you infer about the true density and the future of the universe? If you need help, refer to Recognizing Cause and Effect in the **Skill Handbook** on page 683.

24-5 The Search for Extraterrestrial Life

New Science Words

extraterrestrial life

Objectives

▶ Name locations in our solar system where life may have existed in the past or could exist now.
▶ Describe methods used by astronomers to search for extraterrestrial life within and beyond our solar system.
▶ Decide if methods used by scientists might cause contamination of other worlds.

Can NASA Safely Explore Other Worlds?

On July 20, 1976, the first *Viking* probe landed on Mars. It conducted three different types of tests on Martian soil in searching for evidence of extraterrestrial life. **Extraterrestrial life** is life that exists beyond Earth. It could be microorganisms living in the rocks of a barren world or intelligent life living on a planet orbiting a distant star.

Figure 24-23. The *Viking* probes failed to find evidence of life on Mars.

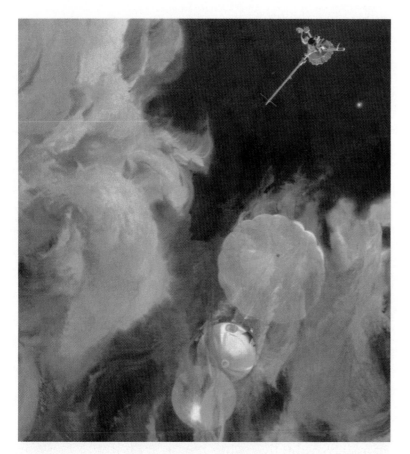

Figure 24-24. The *Galileo* probe will send a small probe parachuting into Jupiter's atmosphere. It will transmit data back to the orbiter above. Should the probe have been sterilized prior to launch?

Each test made by the *Viking* probes gave results that could have been caused by life or by chemical reactions with the Martian soil. However, analysis of the soil showed it lacked the types of molecules that appear to be necessary for life. It appears Mars doesn't contain life or the remains of life.

The *Viking* spacecrafts were carefully sterilized so the Martian soil would not be contaminated. The *Galileo* spacecraft, which should arrive at Jupiter in 1995, will send a probe down into the clouds of the planet. It was not sterilized before being launched. Is there a danger that microbes from Earth could contaminate the environment of Jupiter's clouds? NASA doesn't think so. *Galileo's* probe will be crushed and sterilized in the depths of Jupiter's atmosphere. Project scientists don't believe there is any chance for planetary contamination.

Triton, one of the satellites of Neptune, contains organic molecules. The molecules themselves aren't considered to be life, but they are thought to resemble the molecules from which life evolved on Earth. Given enough time, millions or billions of years, it's possible that the molecules

Why would Triton be a good place to look for extraterrestrial life?

will evolve into life as they did on Earth. Scientists hope to send a probe to Triton to further investigate the organic molecules there.

Cracks in the icy crust of Europa, one of Jupiter's moons, may allow sunlight into the ocean underneath. The sunlight could have helped start biological activity. If this is even remotely possible, what types of precautions should be taken before a probe is sent to Europa?

Are there perfectly safe ways to search for life? One method is to search the universe for sources of radio signals from intelligent life. This program is called SETI, the *S*earch for *E*xtra*t*errestrial *I*ntelligence. In 1974, astronomers used the large radio telescope in Arecibo, Puerto Rico, to beam a radio message to a star cluster more than 26 000 light-years away. Although more than 52 000 years will pass before a reply from intelligent life in the star cluster could arrive at Earth, the attempt was still made.

Maybe the wait won't be that long. Perhaps life elsewhere has already sent out a message. The program called SETI continues to listen for signs of intelligence in radio signals from space.

SECTION REVIEW

1. Where is life known to exist in the solar system? Name two other places in the solar system where life might be evolving.
2. Which program searches for evidence of intelligent life using radio telescopes?
3. The *Viking* probes were sterilized, but the *Galileo* probe wasn't? Why?

SCIENCE & SOCIETY

You Decide!

Scientists believe life could now exist or could someday evolve on several planets and moons in our solar system. A spacecraft from Earth studying these planets could carry organisms with it. Is it acceptable to sterilize only those probes going to Triton and other moons or planets felt to have a relatively good chance of having life on them? It's possible we could contaminate other worlds with microorganisms and organic molecules from Earth. Should we avoid going to those worlds where life may be evolving? Would it be better to search for intelligent life with radio telescopes only?

SUMMARY

24-1: Stars

1. The constellations seem to move because Earth rotates on its axis and revolves around the sun.

2. The magnitude of a star is a measure of the star's brightness. Absolute magnitude is a measure of the light emitted. Apparent magnitude is the amount of light received on Earth.

3. Parallax is the apparent shift in the position of an object when viewed from two different positions. The closer an object is to the observer, the greater its parallax.

24-2: Evolution of Stars

1. The H-R diagram illustrates the relationship between a star's temperature and its absolute magnitude.

2. Blue-white stars are very hot and bright. Red stars are relatively dim and cool. Yellow stars have brightnesses and temperatures in between those of blue and red stars.

3. A main sequence star uses hydrogen as fuel. When the hydrogen is used up, the core collapses and the star's temperature increases. The star becomes a giant or a supergiant, which use helium as fuel. As the star evolves, the outer layers escape into space. The core has no fuel left and the star becomes a white dwarf. Depending on the original mass of the star, it can evolve into a neutron star or a black hole.

24-3: The Sun

1. The sun produces energy by fusing hydrogen into helium in its core.

2. Sunspots, prominences, and flares are all probably caused by the intense magnetic field of the sun.

3. The sun is a main sequence star. Yet it's somewhat unusual because it isn't part of a binary system, which forms when two stars orbit each other.

24-4: Galaxies and the Expanding Universe

1. A galaxy is a large group of stars, gas, and dust held together by gravity. Galaxies can be elliptical, spiral, or irregular in shape.

2. The Milky Way is a spiral galaxy and contains over 200 billion stars. The sun is located about 30 000 light-years from the center of the galaxy.

3. Shifts toward red light suggest that all galaxies beyond the Local Group are moving away from our galaxy. This fact supports the big bang theory, which states that the universe began expanding out of an explosion 15 to 20 billion years ago.

24-5: Science and Society: The Search for Extraterrestrial Life

1. Organic molecules, similar to those that evolved into life on Earth, have been found on Triton, a satellite of Neptune.

2. Space probes and radio telescopes are used to determine whether or not life exists in other parts of the universe.

3. Spacecraft sent to other planets might contaminate the planets with organisms from Earth. Sterilization of spacecraft may eliminate the contamination.

CHAPTER
REVIEW

a. absolute magnitude
b. apparent magnitude
c. big bang theory
d. binary system
e. black hole
f. chromosphere
g. constellations
h. corona
i. extraterrestrial life
j. galaxy
k. giant
l. light-year
m. main sequence
n. nebula
o. neutron star
p. parallax
q. photosphere
r. sunspots
s. supergiant
t. white dwarf

UNDERSTANDING VOCABULARY

Match each phrase with the correct term from the list of Key Science Words.

1. groups of stars that resemble objects, animals, or mythological characters
2. amount of light given off by a star
3. distance light travels in one year
4. the beginning of a star's life cycle
5. star that uses helium as fuel
6. dense object that allows nothing to escape its field of gravity
7. our sun belongs to this group of stars
8. layer of the sun's atmosphere that emits light
9. formed when two stars orbit each other
10. supported by observed red shifts in the spectra of galaxies

CHECKING CONCEPTS

Choose the word or phrase that completes the sentence.

1. The stars of a constellation are _____.
   a. in the same cluster   c. equally bright
   b. all giants   d. none of these
2. _____ is a measure of the amount of a star's light received on Earth.
   a. Absolute magnitude   c. Fusion
   b. Apparent magnitude   d. Parallax
3. The closer an object is to an observer, the greater its _____.
   a. absolute magnitude   c. parallax
   b. red shift   d. all of these
4. As a nebula contracts, _____ begins.
   a. main sequencing   c. fusion
   b. supernova   d. a white dwarf
5. A _____ is about the size of a city.
   a. giant   c. black hole
   b. white dwarf   d. neutron star
6. Our sun _____.
   a. fuses hydrogen   c. emits yellow light
   b. is an average star   d. all of these
7. Loops of matter flowing from the sun are _____.
   a. sunspots   c. coronas
   b. auroras   d. prominences
8. Groups of galaxies are called _____.
   a. clusters   c. giants
   b. supergiants   d. binary systems
9. _____ galaxies are sometimes shaped like footballs.
   a. Spiral   c. Barred
   b. Elliptical   d. Irregular
10. A shift toward the _____ end of the spectra of stars indicates that galaxies are moving away from the Local Group.
    a. red   c. either a or b
    b. blue-violet   d. none of these

UNDERSTANDING CONCEPTS

Complete each sentence.

11. The _____ magnitude of a star depends on its distance from Earth.
12. Because they are so large, distances in space are measured in _____.
13. Temperatures in the sun's _____ are greater than those in the chromosphere.
14. Evidence indicates that the universe has been expanding ever since the _____.
15. _____ prove that the sun rotates.

THINK AND WRITE CRITICALLY

16. How can parallax be used to determine which of two stars is closer to Earth?
17. What variables determine a star's position on the H-R diagram?
18. Compare and contrast sunspots, solar flares, and prominences.
19. How do red shifts support the big bang theory?
20. What are the advantages and disadvantages of using radio telescopes and probes to search for life in the universe?

APPLY

21. Why have the first galaxies that formed not yet been observed by astronomers?
22. How do scientists know that black holes exist if these objects don't emit any visible light?
23. Use the autumn star chart in Appendix J to determine which constellation is directly overhead at 8 P.M. on November 21 for an observer in North America.
24. How are radio waves used to detect objects in space?
25. What kinds of reactions produce the energy emitted by stars?

MORE SKILL BUILDERS

1. **Making and Using Tables:** Astronomical objects are given numbers to represent their absolute and apparent magnitudes. The lower the number, the greater the object's brightness. What object listed in the table below has the brightest absolute magnitude? What object is the brightest as seen from Earth?
2. **Making and Using Tables:** How does the table show that apparent magnitude is dependent on both absolute magnitude and distance from an observer?

Star	Absolute Magnitude	Apparent Magnitude	Light-years from Earth
The sun	4.9	−26.7	0.000 002
Sirius	1.5	−1.5	8.70
Arcturus	−0.3	−0.1	35.86
Alpha Centauri	4.4	0.0	4.34
Betelgeuse	−5.5	0.8	489.0
Deneb	−6.9	1.3	1401.80

3. **Concept Mapping:** Make a concept map that shows the evolution of a main sequence star with a mass similar to that of the sun.
4. **Comparing and Contrasting:** Compare and contrast the sun with other stars on the H-R diagram.
5. **Measuring in SI:** The Milky Way is 100 000 light-years in diameter. What scale would you use if you were to construct a scale model of the Milky Way with a diameter of 20 cm?

PROJECTS

1. Design and construct scale models of a spiral and a barred Milky Way. Show the approximate position of the sun in each.

GLOBAL CONNECTIONS

Astronomy

In this unit, you studied astronomy including exploring space, the Earth-moon system, the solar system, and finally the stars and galaxies. Now find out how astronomy is connected to other subjects and places around the world.

120° 60°

60°

BIOLOGY

SEARCH FOR PLANETS
Pittsburgh, Pennsylvania

Planetary systems other than our own might be home to extraterrestrial life. Scientists at the Allegheny Observatory use an astrometric photometer to search for such planets. Gravity from a planet orbiting a star would pull the star slightly out of position. The star would appear to "wobble" back and forth as the planet orbited it. How might this motion be noted in still photographs?

30°

METEOROLOGY

SUNSPOTS AND DROUGHT
Tucson, Arizona

By studying annual rings of trees, climatologists at the University of Arizona have discovered that a pattern of widespread drought occurs over the western United States every 22 years. This pattern matches another 22-year cycle—more sunspots, followed by fewer sunspots on the sun—for over 250 years. How would drought affect a tree's annual rings?

PHYSICS

SOLAR POWER STATION IN SPACE
Cape Canaveral, Florida

Solar radiation does not reach a power station at night or on cloudy days. This problem could be overcome by placing a large array of solar cells in space. The array could orbit Earth at an altitude of 35 000 kilometers. What would be an advantage of a solar power station in space over one on Earth?

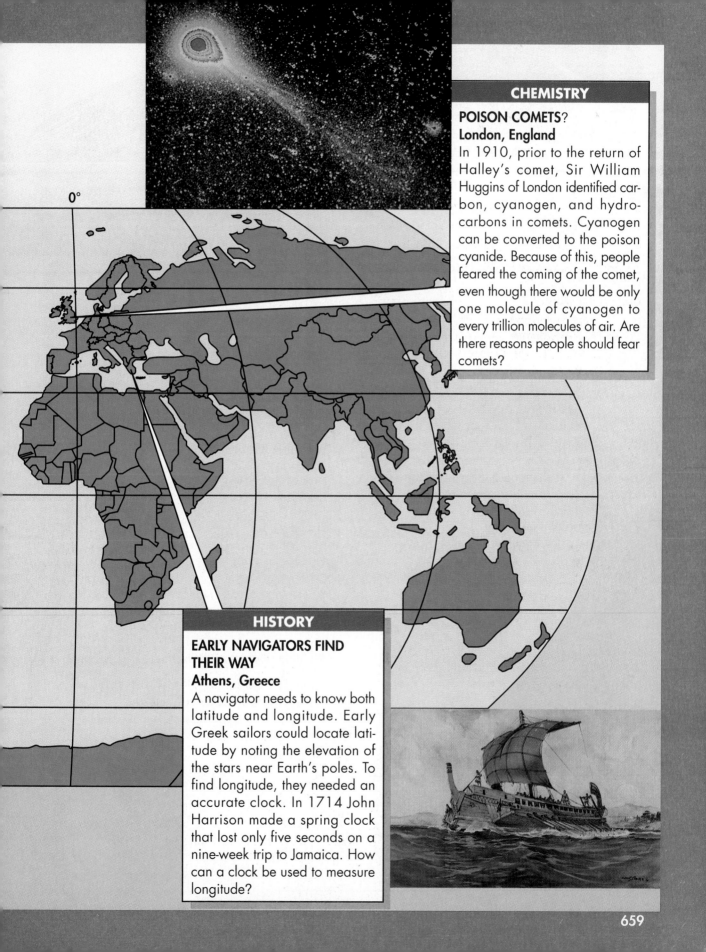

0°

CHEMISTRY

POISON COMETS?
London, England
In 1910, prior to the return of Halley's comet, Sir William Huggins of London identified carbon, cyanogen, and hydrocarbons in comets. Cyanogen can be converted to the poison cyanide. Because of this, people feared the coming of the comet, even though there would be only one molecule of cyanogen to every trillion molecules of air. Are there reasons people should fear comets?

HISTORY

EARLY NAVIGATORS FIND THEIR WAY
Athens, Greece
A navigator needs to know both latitude and longitude. Early Greek sailors could locate latitude by noting the elevation of the stars near Earth's poles. To find longitude, they needed an accurate clock. In 1714 John Harrison made a spring clock that lost only five seconds on a nine-week trip to Jamaica. How can a clock be used to measure longitude?

659

CAREERS

ASTRONOMER

An *astronomer* uses a telescope to locate objects in the sky. Some astronomers analyze light with a spectroscope to determine the chemical composition of the stars. Astronomers use computers to guide their telescopes and to measure the light from the star they observe.

An astronomer requires a college degree in astronomy. Most people in the field have advanced degrees. A student interested in becoming an astronomer should take courses in computer science, physics, and mathematics.

For Additional Information

Contact the Education Officer, American Astronomical Society, Sharp Laboratory, University of Delaware, Newark, DE 19716.

AEROSPACE WORKER

An *aerospace worker* is a skilled worker who may be involved in making, assembling, or repairing aircraft or spacecraft. To acquire these skills, aerospace workers may spend from four to six years as apprentices. They also take courses in blueprint reading and mechanical drawing.

Some aerospace manufacturers have trade schools in which the necessary skills are acquired while the student is working. Students who wish to prepare for the aerospace trades should take shop and mathematics courses in high school.

For Additional Information

Contact the International Association of Machinists and Aerospace Workers, 1300 Connecticut Avenue NW, Washington, DC 20036.

UNIT READINGS

▶Frazier, Kendrick. *Solar System.* Alexandria, Virginia: Time-Life Books, 1985.
▶Friedman, Herbert. *The Astronomer's Universe: Stars, Galaxies, and Cosmos.* New York: W.W. Norton and Company, 1990.
▶Sagan, Carl and Ann Druyan. *Comet.* New York: Random House, 1985.

Message ...ars

In this unit, ...oduced to radio telescopes as to...ying about the universe
that lies bey...but one radio telescope,
the largest ...has been used for another purpose...but how we used a tool of
astronomy...pt to communicate with life
among th...

...at some stars have planets revolv-
...n th...em and that those planets might
...in...lligent beings, the Arecibo radio
...h...erto Rico was used to
teles...tic interstellar message
send...cluster named M13.
to t...3 is located in the Milky
Cl...xy, 26 000 light-years from
W...probably consists of about
E...0 stars.

Much information is crammed
...each row of design. The top row
...s down the rules for counting in
...e message. It states that all num-
...ers are in the binary number system,
using just 0 and 1. The second row
states the atomic numbers of the elements hydrogen, carbon, nitrogen,
oxygen, and phosphorus, the elements that all known living things are
made of. The rows of green blocks
and blue blocks stand for substances
in DNA—molecules in the cells of living things that carry genetic
information. The vertical white design
gives information about human
genes. The red figure is that of a
human being. The white design to

the left shows how many people are on the planet Earth. The yellow figures represent our solar
system, with the sun and nine planets. The purple
design is the radio telescope in Arecibo.

The art of this message had to be rigidly controlled by the kind of radio signal being used.
Words couldn't be used in the signal going to
another planet because an intelligent being would
not understand what was being transmitted.

In Your Own Words
▶ Write an essay describing what
you would like any intelligent
beings in the M13 cluster to know
about you and your planet.

International System ⸢

The International System (SI) of Measurement ⸢ ⸢ the standard for measurement throughout most of the w⸢ ⸢ the stan-
in SI are the meter, kilogram, and second. Freque⸢base units
listed below.

Table A-1

FREQUENTLY USED SI UNITS	
LENGTH	1 millimeter (mm) = 1000 micrometers (μm) 1 centimeter (cm) = 10 millimeters (mm) 1 meter (m) = 100 centimeters (cm) 1 kilometer (km) = 1000 meters (m) 1 light-year = 9 460 000 000 000 kilometers (km)
AREA	1 square meter (m²) = 10 000 square centimeters (c⸢ 1 square kilometer (km²) = 1 000 000 square meters
VOLUME	1 milliliter (mL) = 1 cubic centimeter (cc) (cm³) 1 liter (L) = 1000 milliliters (mL)
MASS	1 gram (g) = 1000 milligrams (mg) 1 kilogram (kg) = 1000 grams (g) 1 metric ton = 1000 kilograms (kg)
TIME	1 s = 1 second

Temperature measurements in SI are often made in degrees Celsius.
Celsius temperature is a supplementary unit derived from the base unit
kelvin. The Celsius scale (°C) has 100 equal graduations between the
freezing temperature (0°C) and the boiling temperatue of water
(100°C). The following relationship exists between the Celsius and
kelvin temperature scales:

$$K = °C + 273$$

Several other supplementary SI units are listed below.

Table A-2

SUPPLEMENTARY SI UNITS			
Measurement	**Unit**	**Symbol**	**Expressed in base units**
Energy	Joule	J	$kg \cdot m^2/s^2$ or $N \cdot m$
Force	Newton	N	$kg \cdot m/s^2$
Power	Watt	W	$kg \cdot m^2/s^3$ (J/s)
Pressure	Pascal	Pa	$kg/(m \cdot s^2)$ (N $\cdot$ m)

Table B-1

SI/METRIC TO ENGLISH CONVERSIONS			
	When you want to convert:	**Multiply by:**	**To find:**
Length	inches	2.54	centimeters
	centimeters	0.39	inches
	feet	0.30	meters
	meters	3.28	feet
	yards	0.91	meters
	meters	1.09	yards
	miles	1.61	kilometers
	kilometers	0.62	miles
Mass and Weight*	ounces	28.35	grams
	grams	0.04	ounces
	pounds	0.45	kilograms
	kilograms	2.20	pounds
	tons	0.91	tonnes (metric tons)
	tonnes (metric tons)	1.10	tons
	pounds	4.45	newtons
	newtons	0.23	pounds
Volume	cubic inches	16.39	cubic centimeters
	cubic centimeters	0.06	cubic inches
	cubic feet	0.03	cubic meters
	cubic meters	35.31	cubic feet
	liters	1.06	quarts
	liters	0.26	gallons
	gallons	3.78	liters
Area	square inches	6.45	square centimeters
	square centimeters	0.16	square inches
	square feet	0.09	square meters
	square meters	10.76	square feet
	square miles	2.59	square kilometers
	square kilometers	0.39	square miles
	hectares	2.47	acres
	acres	0.40	hectares
Temperature	Fahrenheit	5/9 (°F – 32)	Celsius
	Celsius	9/5 °C + 32	Fahrenheit

*Weight as measured in standard Earth gravity

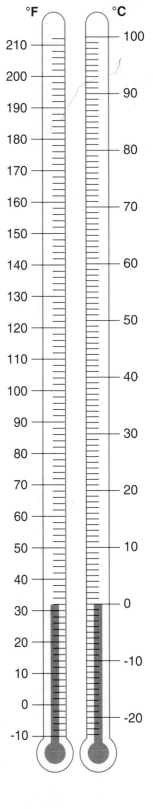

Safety in the Science Classroom

1. Always obtain your teacher's permission to begin an investigation.
2. Study the procedure. If you have questions, ask your teacher. Understand any safety symbols shown on the page.
3. Use the safety equipment provided for you. Goggles and a safety apron should be worn when any investigation calls for using chemicals.
4. Always slant test tubes away from yourself and others when heating them.
5. Never eat or drink in the lab, and never use lab glassware as food or drink containers. Never inhale chemicals. Do not taste any substances or draw any material into a tube with your mouth.
6. If you spill any chemical, wash it off immediately with water. Report the spill immediately to your teacher.
7. Know the location and proper use of the fire extinguisher, safety shower, fire blanket, first aid kit, and fire alarm.
8. Keep materials away from flames. Tie back hair and loose clothing.
9. If a fire should break out in the classroom, or if your clothing should catch fire, smother it with the fire blanket or a coat, or get under a safety shower. **NEVER RUN.**
10. Report any accident or injury, no matter how small, to your teacher.

Follow these procedures as you clean up your work area.

1. Turn off the water and gas. Disconnect electrical devices.
2. Return all materials to their proper places.
3. Dispose of chemicals and other materials as directed by your teacher. Place broken glass and solid substances in the proper containers. Never discard materials in the sink.
4. Clean your work area.
5. Wash your hands thoroughly after working in the laboratory.

Table C-1

FIRST AID	
Injury	**Safe response**
Burns	Apply cold water. Call your teacher immediately.
Cuts and bruises	Stop any bleeding by applying direct pressure. Cover cuts with a clean dressing. Apply cold compresses to bruises. Call your teacher immediately.
Fainting	Leave the person lying down. Loosen any tight clothing and keep crowds away. Call your teacher immediately.
Foreign matter in eye	Flush with plenty of water. Use eyewash bottle or fountain.
Poisoning	Note the suspected poisoning agent and call your teacher immediately.
Any spills on skin	Flush with large amounts of water or use safety shower. Call your teacher immediately.

APPENDIX D

Safety Symbols

	DISPOSAL ALERT This symbol appears when care must be taken to dispose of materials properly.		**ANIMAL SAFETY** This symbol appears whenever live animals are studied and the safety of the animals and the students must be ensured.
	BIOLOGICAL HAZARD This symbol appears when there is danger involving bacteria, fungi, or protists.		**RADIOACTIVE SAFETY** This symbol appears when radioactive materials are used.
	OPEN FLAME ALERT This symbol appears when use of an open flame could cause a fire or an explosion.		**CLOTHING PROTECTION SAFETY** This symbol appears when substances used could stain or burn clothing.
	THERMAL SAFETY This symbol appears as a reminder to use caution when handling hot objects.		**FIRE SAFETY** This symbol appears when care should be taken around open flames.
	SHARP OBJECT SAFETY This symbol appears when a danger of cuts or punctures caused by the use of sharp objects exists.		**EXPLOSION SAFETY** This symbol appears when the misuse of chemicals could cause an explosion.
	FUME SAFETY This symbol appears when chemicals or chemical reactions could cause dangerous fumes.		**EYE SAFETY** This symbol appears when a danger to the eyes exists. Safety goggles should be worn when this symbol appears.
	ELECTRICAL SAFETY This symbol appears when care should be taken when using electrical equipment.		**POISON SAFETY** This symbol appears when poisonous substances are used.
	PLANT SAFETY This symbol appears when poisonous plants or plants with thorns are handled.		**CHEMICAL SAFETY** This symbol appears when chemicals used can cause burns or are poisonous if absorbed through the skin.

Periodic Table

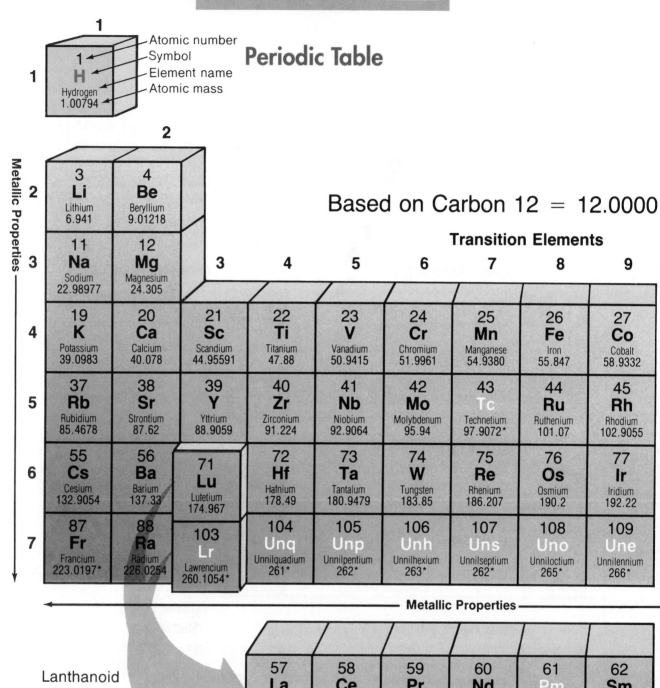

1
1
H
Hydrogen
1.00794

Atomic number
Symbol
Element name
Atomic mass

Based on Carbon 12 = 12.0000

Transition Elements

Metallic Properties

1	2	3	4	5	6	7	8	9

Row 2:
3 **Li** Lithium 6.941 | 4 **Be** Beryllium 9.01218

Row 3:
11 **Na** Sodium 22.98977 | 12 **Mg** Magnesium 24.305

Row 4:
19 **K** Potassium 39.0983 | 20 **Ca** Calcium 40.078 | 21 **Sc** Scandium 44.95591 | 22 **Ti** Titanium 47.88 | 23 **V** Vanadium 50.9415 | 24 **Cr** Chromium 51.9961 | 25 **Mn** Manganese 54.9380 | 26 **Fe** Iron 55.847 | 27 **Co** Cobalt 58.9332

Row 5:
37 **Rb** Rubidium 85.4678 | 38 **Sr** Strontium 87.62 | 39 **Y** Yttrium 88.9059 | 40 **Zr** Zirconium 91.224 | 41 **Nb** Niobium 92.9064 | 42 **Mo** Molybdenum 95.94 | 43 **Tc** Technetium 97.9072* | 44 **Ru** Ruthenium 101.07 | 45 **Rh** Rhodium 102.9055

Row 6:
55 **Cs** Cesium 132.9054 | 56 **Ba** Barium 137.33 | 71 **Lu** Lutetium 174.967 | 72 **Hf** Hafnium 178.49 | 73 **Ta** Tantalum 180.9479 | 74 **W** Tungsten 183.85 | 75 **Re** Rhenium 186.207 | 76 **Os** Osmium 190.2 | 77 **Ir** Iridium 192.22

Row 7:
87 **Fr** Francium 223.0197* | 88 **Ra** Radium 226.0254 | 103 **Lr** Lawrencium 260.1054* | 104 **Unq** Unnilquadium 261* | 105 **Unp** Unnilpentium 262* | 106 **Unh** Unnilhexium 263* | 107 **Uns** Unnilseptium 262* | 108 **Uno** Unniloctium 265* | 109 **Une** Unnilennium 266*

Metallic Properties

Lanthanoid Series

57 **La** Lanthanum 138.9055 | 58 **Ce** Cerium 140.12 | 59 **Pr** Praseodymium 140.9077 | 60 **Nd** Neodymium 144.24 | 61 **Pm** Promethium 144.9128* | 62 **Sm** Samarium 150.36

Actinoid Series

89 **Ac** Actinium 227.0278* | 90 **Th** Thorium 232.0381 | 91 **Pa** Protactinium 231.0359* | 92 **U** Uranium 238.0289 | 93 **Np** Neptunium 237.0482 | 94 **Pu** Plutonium 244.0642*

*Mass of isotope with longest half-life, that is, the most stable isotope of the element

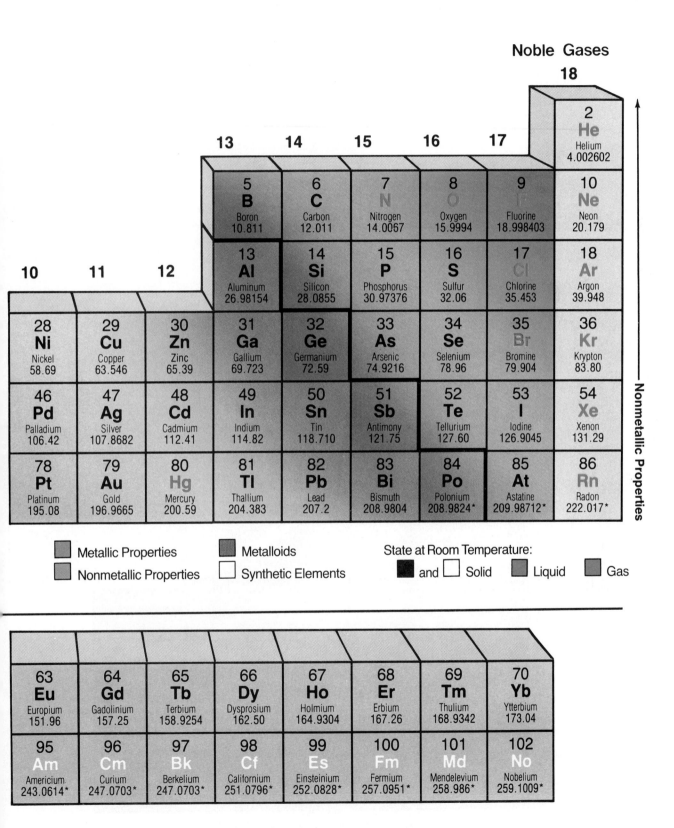

Noble Gases

18

13	14	15	16	17	2 **He** Helium 4.002602
5 **B** Boron 10.811	6 **C** Carbon 12.011	7 N Nitrogen 14.0067	8 O Oxygen 15.9994	9 F Fluorine 18.998403	10 **Ne** Neon 20.179
13 **Al** Aluminum 26.98154	14 **Si** Silicon 28.0855	15 **P** Phosphorus 30.97376	16 **S** Sulfur 32.06	17 Cl Chlorine 35.453	18 **Ar** Argon 39.948

10	11	12						
28 **Ni** Nickel 58.69	29 **Cu** Copper 63.546	30 **Zn** Zinc 65.39	31 **Ga** Gallium 69.723	32 **Ge** Germanium 72.59	33 **As** Arsenic 74.9216	34 **Se** Selenium 78.96	35 Br Bromine 79.904	36 **Kr** Krypton 83.80
46 **Pd** Palladium 106.42	47 **Ag** Silver 107.8682	48 **Cd** Cadmium 112.41	49 **In** Indium 114.82	50 **Sn** Tin 118.710	51 **Sb** Antimony 121.75	52 **Te** Tellurium 127.60	53 **I** Iodine 126.9045	54 **Xe** Xenon 131.29
78 **Pt** Platinum 195.08	79 **Au** Gold 196.9665	80 Hg Mercury 200.59	81 **Tl** Thallium 204.383	82 **Pb** Lead 207.2	83 **Bi** Bismuth 208.9804	84 **Po** Polonium 208.9824*	85 **At** Astatine 209.98712*	86 Rn Radon 222.017*

Nonmetallic Properties

■ Metallic Properties   ■ Metalloids   State at Room Temperature:
■ Nonmetallic Properties   ☐ Synthetic Elements   ■ and ☐ Solid   ■ Liquid   ■ Gas

63 **Eu** Europium 151.96	64 **Gd** Gadolinium 157.25	65 **Tb** Terbium 158.9254	66 **Dy** Dysprosium 162.50	67 **Ho** Holmium 164.9304	68 **Er** Erbium 167.26	69 **Tm** Thulium 168.9342	70 **Yb** Ytterbium 173.04
95 Am Americium 243.0614*	96 Cm Curium 247.0703*	97 Bk Berkelium 247.0703*	98 Cf Californium 251.0796*	99 Es Einsteinium 252.0828*	100 Fm Fermium 257.0951*	101 Md Mendelevium 258.986*	102 No Nobelium 259.1009*

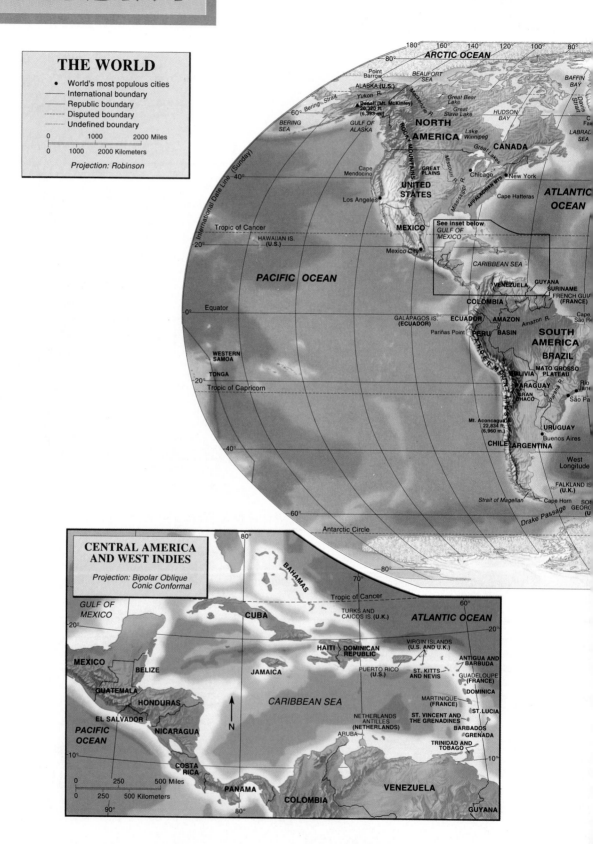

THE WORLD

- • World's most populous cities
- ——— International boundary
- ——— Republic boundary
- - - - Disputed boundary
- ...... Undefined boundary

| 0 | 1000 | 2000 Miles |
| 0 | 1000 | 2000 Kilometers |

Projection: Robinson

ARCTIC OCEAN

Point Barrow
BEAUFORT SEA
BAFFIN BAY
ALASKA (U.S.)
Yukon R.
Bering Strait
Mackenzie R.
Davis Strait
Denali (Mt. McKinley) 20,320 ft. (6,193 m.)
Great Bear Lake
BERING SEA
Great Slave Lake
HUDSON BAY
LABRADOR SEA
GULF OF ALASKA
NORTH AMERICA
Lake Winnipeg
CANADA
Cape Mendocino
ROCKY MOUNTAINS
GREAT PLAINS
Great Lakes
Missouri R.
Chicago
New York
UNITED STATES
Mississippi R.
APPALACHIAN MTS.
Cape Hatteras
ATLANTIC OCEAN
Los Angeles
Tropic of Cancer
MEXICO
See inset below
GULF OF MEXICO
HAWAIIAN IS. (U.S.)
Mexico City
CARIBBEAN SEA
VENEZUELA
GUYANA
SURINAME
COLOMBIA
FRENCH GUIANA (FRANCE)
PACIFIC OCEAN
Equator
GALÁPAGOS IS. (ECUADOR)
ECUADOR
AMAZON
Amazon R.
Cape São R.
Pariñas Point
PERU
BASIN
SOUTH AMERICA
BRAZIL
WESTERN SAMOA
MATO GROSSO PLATEAU
TONGA
BOLIVIA
Rio Jane
Tropic of Capricorn
PARAGUAY
GRAN CHACO
Paraná R.
São Pa
Mt. Aconcagua 22,834 ft. (6,960 m.)
URUGUAY
Buenos Aires
CHILE
ARGENTINA
West Longitude
FALKLAND IS. (U.K.)
Strait of Magellan
Cape Horn
SO GEORG (U
Drake Passage
Antarctic Circle
International Date Line (Sunday)
ANDES MOUNTAINS

CENTRAL AMERICA AND WEST INDIES

Projection: Bipolar Oblique Conic Conformal

BAHAMAS
Tropic of Cancer
GULF OF MEXICO
CUBA
TURKS AND CAICOS IS. (U.K.)
ATLANTIC OCEAN
VIRGIN ISLANDS (U.S. AND U.K.)
MEXICO
HAITI
DOMINICAN REPUBLIC
ANTIGUA AND BARBUDA
BELIZE
JAMAICA
PUERTO RICO (U.S.)
ST. KITTS AND NEVIS
GUADELOUPE (FRANCE)
GUATEMALA
DOMINICA
HONDURAS
CARIBBEAN SEA
MARTINIQUE (FRANCE)
ST. LUCIA
EL SALVADOR
N
NETHERLANDS ANTILLES (NETHERLANDS)
ST. VINCENT AND THE GRENADINES
PACIFIC OCEAN
NICARAGUA
ARUBA
BARBADOS
GRENADA
TRINIDAD AND TOBAGO
COSTA RICA

| 0 | 250 | 500 Miles |
| 0 | 250 | 500 Kilometers |

PANAMA
COLOMBIA
VENEZUELA
GUYANA

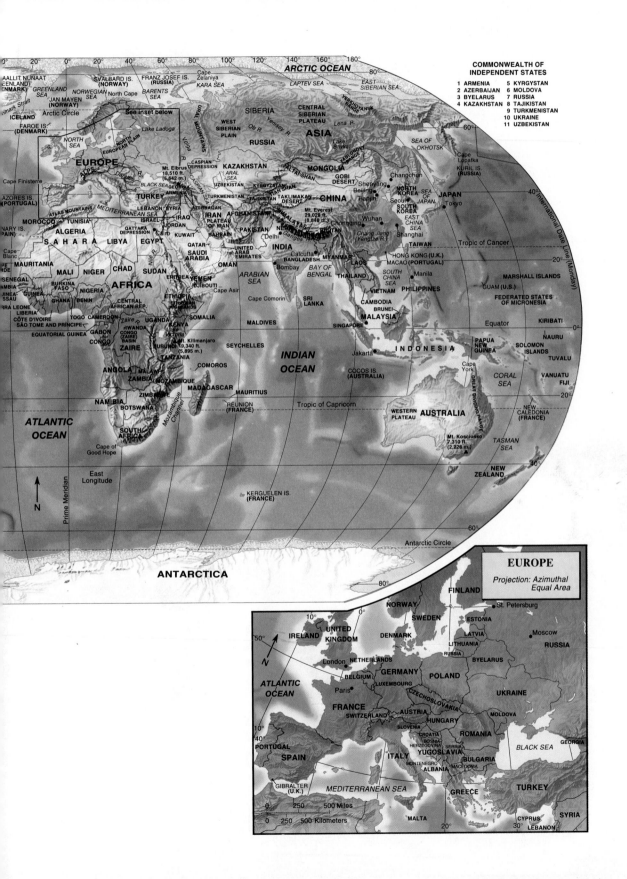

ARCTIC OCEAN

COMMONWEALTH OF INDEPENDENT STATES

1 ARMENIA 5 KYRGYSTAN
2 AZERBAIJAN 6 MOLDOVA
3 BYELARUS 7 RUSSIA
4 KAZAKHSTAN 8 TAJIKISTAN
9 TURKMENISTAN
10 UKRAINE
11 UZBEKISTAN

AALLIT NUNAAT (GREENLAND) (DENMARK)
GREENLAND SEA
NORWEGIAN SEA
SVALBARD IS. (NORWAY)
FRANZ JOSEF IS. (RUSSIA)
Cape Zelaniya
KARA SEA
LAPTEV SEA
EAST SIBERIAN SEA
BARENTS SEA
North Cape
JAN MAYEN (NORWAY)
Denmark Strait
ICELAND
Arctic Circle
FAROE IS. (DENMARK)
NORTH SEA
EUROPE
Lake Ladoga
URAL MOUNTAINS
WEST SIBERIAN PLAIN
SIBERIA
CENTRAL SIBERIAN PLATEAU
Ob R.
Yenisey R.
VERKHOYANSK RANGE
Lena R.
SEA OF OKHOTSK
ASIA
EUROPEAN PLAIN
RUSSIA
Lake Baikal
Cape Lopatka
Cape Finisterre
ALPS
Danube
Volga
CASPIAN DEPRESSION
Mt. Elbrus 18,510 ft. (5,642 m.)
CASPIAN SEA
KAZAKHSTAN
MONGOLIA
GOBI DESERT
KURIL IS. (RUSSIA)
AZORES IS. (PORTUGAL)
BLACK SEA
GEORGIA
ARMENIA
ARAL SEA
UZBEKISTAN
TIEN SHAN
ALTAI SHAN
Changchun
Shenyang
NORTH KOREA
SEA OF JAPAN
JAPAN
40°
MOROCCO
TUNISIA
MEDITERRANEAN SEA
TURKEY
LEBANON SYRIA
AZERBAIJAN
TURKMENISTAN
TAJIKISTAN
KYRGYZSTAN
TAKLIMAKAN DESERT
CHINA
Beijing
Tianjin
Seoul
SOUTH KOREA
Tokyo
EAST CHINA SEA
International Date Line (Monday)
NARY IS. (SPAIN)
ALGERIA
SAHARA
LIBYA
EGYPT
ISRAEL
JORDAN
IRAQ
KUWAIT
IRAN
PLATEAU OF IRAN
AFGHANISTAN
HIMALAYAS
Mt. Everest 29,028 ft. (8,848 m.)
NEPAL
Chongqing
Wuhan
Chang Jiang (Yangtze R.)
Shanghai
TAIWAN
Tropic of Cancer
Cape Blanc
MAURITANIA
MALI
NIGER
CHAD
SUDAN
Nile R.
Cairo
QATTARA DEPRESSION
SAUDI ARABIA
QATAR
UNITED ARAB EMIRATES
BAHRAIN
PAKISTAN
Delhi
Ganges R.
INDIA
Calcutta
BANGLADESH
MYANMAR
HONG KONG (U.K.)
MACAO (PORTUGAL)
SOUTH CHINA SEA
Manila
20°
SENEGAL
BURKINA FASO
NIGERIA
AFRICA
CENTRAL AFRICAN REP.
ERITREA
ETHIOPIA
DJIBOUTI
YEMEN
OMAN
Cape Asir
ARABIAN SEA
Bombay
BAY OF BENGAL
THAILAND
LAOS
VIETNAM
CAMBODIA
PHILIPPINES
GUAM (U.S.)
MARSHALL ISLANDS
GUINEA
GHANA
BENIN
CAMEROON
SOMALIA
Cape Comorin
SRI LANKA
BRUNEI
MALAYSIA
FEDERATED STATES OF MICRONESIA
RA LEONE
LIBERIA
CÔTE D'IVOIRE
TOGO
SÃO TOME AND PRINCIPE
EQUATORIAL GUINEA
GABON
CONGO
RWANDA
UGANDA
KENYA
Lake Victoria
MALDIVES
SINGAPORE
INDONESIA
Jakarta
Equator
KIRIBATI
NAURU
0°
ZAIRE
CONGO (ZAIRE) BASIN
BURUNDI
TANZANIA
Mt. Kilimanjaro 19,340 ft. (5,895 m.)
SEYCHELLES
INDIAN OCEAN
PAPUA NEW GUINEA
SOLOMON ISLANDS
TUVALU
ANGOLA
ZAMBIA
MALAWI
MOZAMBIQUE
ZIMBABWE
MADAGASCAR
COMOROS
MAURITIUS
Cape York
CORAL SEA
VANUATU
FIJI
NEW CALEDONIA (FRANCE)
20°
ATLANTIC OCEAN
NAMIBIA
BOTSWANA
Mozambique Channel
RÉUNION (FRANCE)
Tropic of Capricorn
WESTERN PLATEAU
AUSTRALIA
GREAT DIVIDING RANGE
SOUTH AFRICA
Cape of Good Hope
East Longitude
Mt. Kosciusko 7,310 ft. (2,228 m.)
TASMAN SEA
NEW ZEALAND
30°
Prime Meridian
N
KERGUELEN IS. (FRANCE)
60°
Antarctic Circle
80°
ANTARCTICA

EUROPE

Projection: Azimuthal Equal Area

St. Petersburg
FINLAND
NORWAY
SWEDEN
ESTONIA
LATVIA
Moscow
RUSSIA
IRELAND
UNITED KINGDOM
DENMARK
LITHUANIA
RUSSIA
BYELARUS
50°
N
London
NETHERLANDS
BELGIUM
GERMANY
POLAND
ATLANTIC OCEAN
Paris
LUXEMBOURG
CZECHOSLOVAKIA
UKRAINE
FRANCE
SWITZERLAND
AUSTRIA
HUNGARY
MOLDOVA
SLOVENIA
ROMANIA
GEORGIA
40°
PORTUGAL
SPAIN
CROATIA
BOSNIA HERZEGOVINA
SERBIA
YUGOSLAVIA
BULGARIA
BLACK SEA
MONTENEGRO
ALBANIA
MACEDONIA
GIBRALTER (U.K.)
MEDITERRANEAN SEA
ITALY
GREECE
TURKEY
MALTA
CYPRUS
LEBANON
SYRIA
0
250
500 Miles
0
250
500 Kilometers
20°
30°

Cape Flattery

125°   120°   115°   110°   105°   100°

Bellingham
Juan de Fuca Strait
Puget Sound
Seattle
Olympia ★ Tacoma
Mt. Rainier 14,410 ft. (4,392 m.) ▲

COLUMBIA PLATEAU

F.D. Roosevelt Lake
Spokane
Pend Oreille Lake

WASHINGTON

Portland   Columbia   River

Salem
Corvallis
Eugene

Mt. Hood 11,235 ft. (3,424 m.) ▲

OREGON

Medford

Mt. Shasta 14,162 ft. (4,316 m.) ▲

Goose Lake

River

Lewiston

BITTERROOT RANGE

ROCKY

Flathead Lake

Helena ★

Butte

IDAHO

Borah Peak 12,662 ft. (3,859 m.) ★ Boise

Idaho Falls

Twin Falls   Snake   River   Pocatello

Grand Teton Peak 13,770 ft. (4,197 m.) ▲

Missouri

Great Falls

Fort Peck Lake

MONTANA

Yellowstone   R.

Billings

Continental Divide

BIGHORN MTNS

WYOMING

Casper

Minot

Lake Sakakawea

Grand Forks

Farg

NORTH DAKOTA

★ Bismarck

Lake Oahe

Aberdeen

SOUTH DAKOTA

BLACK HILLS

Rapid City

Powder   River

★ Pierre

Sioux Fa

Missouri

45°

40°

Eureka
Cape Mendocino

COAST RANGES

CASCADE RANGE

SIERRA

Sacramento   River

Pyramid Lake
Reno
Lake Tahoe
Carson City ★
Sacramento
Stockton

San Francisco
Oakland
San Jose

San   Joaquin

Mono Lake

GREAT

BASIN

NEVADA

Fresno

Mt. Whitney 14,494 ft. (4,418 m.) ▲

Bakersfield

GREAT SALT LAKE DESERT

Great Salt Lake

Salt Lake City ★
Ogden

WASATCH RANGE

Orem
Provo
Utah Lake

UTAH

Rock Springs

Green   River

MOUNTAINS

Lake Powell

Ogden

Cheyenne ★

Fort Collins
Greeley
Boulder

Laramie

Mt. Elbert 14,433 ft. (4,399 m.) ▲

Denver ★

COLORADO

Pikes Peak 14,110 ft. (4,301 m.) ▲ Colorado Springs

Pueblo

Arkansas   River

North Platte   River

South   Platte   River

North Platte
Grand Island
Platte

Republican   River

NEBRASKA

Linco

GREAT

PLAINS

KANSAS

Salina

Hutchins

Wichita

35°

Point Conception

CALIFORNIA

SIERRA   NEVADA

MOJAVE DESERT

Death Valley -282 ft. (-89 m.)

Las Vegas

Lake Mead

Colorado   River

Los Angeles
San Bernardino
Riverside
Long Beach
Salton Sea
San Diego

PAINTED DESERT

Grand Canyon

Flagstaff

COLORADO PLATEAU

ARIZONA

Glendale   ★ Phoenix
Mesa
Gila   River

Yuma

Tucson

SANGRE DE CRISTO MTS

Continental   Divide

Rio   Grande

★ Santa Fe

Albuquerque

NEW MEXICO

Las Cruces

El Paso

Canadian   River

Amarillo

LLANO

ESTACADO

Roswell

Lubbock

OKLAHOM

Enid

Oklahoma City ★

Norman
Lawton

Red   River

Lak Texom

Brazos   River

Dall

Fort Worth

TEXAS

San Anton

30°

PACIFIC

OCEAN

GULF OF CALIFORNIA

120°   115°   110°

Pecos   River

EDWARDS PLATEAU

Austin ★

San Anton

Rio   Grande

Corpus Christi

MEXICO

Br

160°   155°

Kauai Channel
Kailua ★
Honolulu

HAWAII

PACIFIC OCEAN

20°

Alenuihaha Channel

Mauna Kea 13,796 ft. (4,205 m.) ▲
Hilo

20°

0   100 Miles
0   100 Kilometers

160°   155°

170°

0   250   500 Miles
0   250   500 Kilometers

50°

180°   170°

BERING SEA

ALEUTIAN ISLANDS

180°

180°   170°   160°   150°   140°

RUSSIA
Arctic Circle
Bering Strait
SEWARD PEN.

Pt. Barrow

BROOKS RANGE

ALASKA

Yukon   River

Bethel

Iliamna Lake

BRISTOL BAY

ALASKA PENINSULA

Denall (Mt. McKinley) 20,320 ft. (6,193m) ▲

Tanana   River

Fairbanks

ALASKA RANGE

Anchorage

Kodiak

Shelikof St.

GULF OF ALASKA

70°

60°

CANADA

Juneau ★

Sitka

130°

60°

140°   130°

APPENDIX G

CANADA

Lake of the Woods
Red Lake
Lake Superior
Duluth
MICHIGAN

St. Lawrence River
MAINE
Moosehead Lake
Bangor
Mt. Washington 6,288 ft. (1,903 m.)
Augusta
Lewiston
Lake Champlain
Burlington
Montpelier
N.H.
VT.
Concord
Manchester
Portland
MASS.
Cape Cod

MINESOTA
inneapolis
St. Paul
Minneapolis
Rochester

WISCONSIN
Green Bay
Appleton
Madison
Milwaukee
Racine

Grand Rapids
Flint
Lansing
Detroit
Ann Arbor

ADIRONDACK MTNS.
Lake Ontario
Rochester
Syracuse
Utica
Albany
Worcester
Springfield
Boston
Providence
Hartford
New Haven
R.I.
CONN.

Niagara Falls
Buffalo
Binghamton
NEW YORK

Mississippi River

City
IOWA
Dubuque
Cedar Rapids
Davenport
Des Moines
uncil Bluffs

Rockford
Chicago
Aurora
Joliet
South Bend
Gary
Hammond

Toledo
Fort Wayne
Cleveland
Youngstown
Akron
Canton
Erie
Lake Erie
Pittsburgh
Wheeling

PENNSYLVANIA
Susquehanna River
Harrisburg
Allentown
Newark
Yonkers
New York
N.J.
Trenton
Philadelphia
Camden
Wilmington
Dover

CENTRAL
LOWLAND
ILLINOIS
Peoria
Springfield
Decatur
Muncie
INDIANA
Indianapolis
Dayton
Columbus
OHIO
Parkersburg
WEST
VIRGINIA
Charleston
MD.
Baltimore
Arlington
Washington
D.C.
Annapolis
DEL.
DELAWARE BAY

Kansas City
Independence
Jefferson City
nce City
Harry S. Truman Res.
MISSOURI
Springfield

East St. Louis
St. Louis
Evansville
Louisville
Frankfort
Lexington
KENTUCKY
Owensboro
Cincinnati
River
Huntington
Charleston
Roanoke
VIRGINIA
Richmond
Newport News
Norfolk
CHESAPEAKE BAY

ATLANTIC
OCEAN

Wabash R.
Ohio River

Cumberland
Nashville
Knoxville
PLATEAU
TENNESSEE
Chattanooga
Tennessee River
Huntsville
APPALACHIAN
MOUNTAINS
Mt. Mitchell 6,684 ft. (2,037 m.)
Winston-Salem
Greensboro
Durham
Raleigh
Charlotte
Spartanburg
Greenville
NORTH
CAROLINA
Roanoke River
Cape Hatteras

OZARK
PLATEAU
ARKANSAS
R.S. Kerr Res.
Fort Smith
North Little Rock
Little Rock
Hot Springs
Pine Bluff
ake ufaula

Memphis
Birmingham
Tuscaloosa
ALABAMA
Montgomery
Meridian
Jackson
MISSISSIPPI
Hattiesburg
CUMBERLAND
Atlanta
Columbus
Macon
Albany
GEORGIA
Augusta
Columbia
SOUTH
CAROLINA
Charleston
Savannah
Chattahoochee River
COASTAL
PLAIN
Jacksonville

Shreveport
LOUISIANA
Toledo Bend Res.
Rayburn ervoir
Houston
Lake Charles
Lafayette
Baton Rouge
Lake Pontchartrain
New Orleans
Biloxi
Mobile
Pensacola
Alabama R.
Tallahassee
FLORIDA
Orlando
Cape Canaveral
Tampa
St. Petersburg
Lake Okeechobee
Palm Beach
Miami Beach
Miami
Cape Sable
Key West
Strait of Florida

GULF OF MEXICO

N

THE BAHAMAS

UNITED STATES

⊛ National capital
★ State capital
● Major city
○ Other city
— International boundary
— State boundary

0   100   200 Miles
0   100   200 Kilometers

Projection: Albers Equal Area

95°   90°   85°   80°   75° **671**

Topographic Map Symbols

Symbol Name		Symbol Name	
Primary highway, hard surface		Index contour	
Secondary highway, hard surface		Supplementary contour	
Light-duty road, hard or improved surface		Intermediate contour	
Unimproved road		Depression contours	
Railroad: single track and multiple track			
Railroads in juxtaposition		Boundaries: National	
		State	
		County, parish, minicipio	
Buildings		Civil township, precinct, town, barrio	
School, church, and cemetery	cem	Incorporated city, village, town, hamlet	
Buildings (barn, warehouse, etc.)		Reservation, National or State	
Wells other than water (labeled as to type)	o oil o gas	Small park, cemetary, airport, etc.	
	water	Land grant	
Tanks: oil, water, etc. (labeled only if water)	●●●		
Located or landmark object; windmill	⊙	Township or range line, United States land survey	
Open pit, mine, or quarry; prospect		Township or range line, approximate location	
Marsh (swamp)			
Wooded marsh		Perennial streams	
Woods or brushwood		Elevated aqueduct	
Vineyard		Water well and spring	
Land subject to controlled inundation		Small rapids	
Submerged marsh		Large rapids	
Mangrove		Intermittent lake	
Orchard		Intermittent streams	
Scrub		Aqueduct tunnel	
Urban area		Glacier	
		Small falls	
Spot elevation	×7369	Large falls	
Water elevation	670	Dry lake bed	

Solar System Information

Planet	Mercury	Venus	Earth	Mars	Jupiter	Saturn	Uranus	Neptune	Pluto
Diameter (km)	4878	12104	12756	6794	142796	120660	51118	49528	2290
Diameter (E = 1.0)*	0.38	0.95	1.00	0.53	11.19	9.46	4.01	3.88	0.18
Mass (E = 1.0)*	0.06	0.82	1.00	0.11	317.83	95.15	14.54	17.23	0.002
Density (g/cm³)	5.42	5.24	5.50	3.94	1.31	0.70	1.30	1.66	2.03
Period of Rotation days hours minutes **R = retrograde**	58 15 28	243 00 14$_R$	00 23 56	00 24 37	00 09 55	00 10 39	00 17 14$_R$	00 16 03	06 09 17
Surface gravity (E = 1.0)*	0.38	0.90	1.00	0.38	2.53	1.07	0.92	1.12	0.06
Average distance to sun (AU)	0.387	0.723	1.000	1.524	5.203	9.529	19.191	30.061	39.529
Period of revolution	87.97d	224.70d	365.26d	686.98d	11.86y	29.46y	84.04y	164.79y	248.53y
Eccentricity of orbit	0.206	0.007	0.017	0.093	0.048	0.056	0.046	0.010	0.248
Average orbital speed (km/s)	47.89	35.03	29.79	24.13	13.06	9.64	6.81	5.43	4.74
Number of known satellites	0	0	1	2	16	18	15	8	1
Known rings	0	0	0	0	1	thou-sands	11	4	0

*Earth = 1.0

Star Charts

Shown here are star charts for viewing stars in the Northern Hemisphere during the four different seasons. These charts are drawn from the night sky at about 35° North Latitude, but they can be used for most locations in the Northern Hemisphere. The lines on the charts outline major constellations. The dense band of stars is the Milky Way. To use, hold the chart vertically, with the direction you are facing at the bottom of the map.

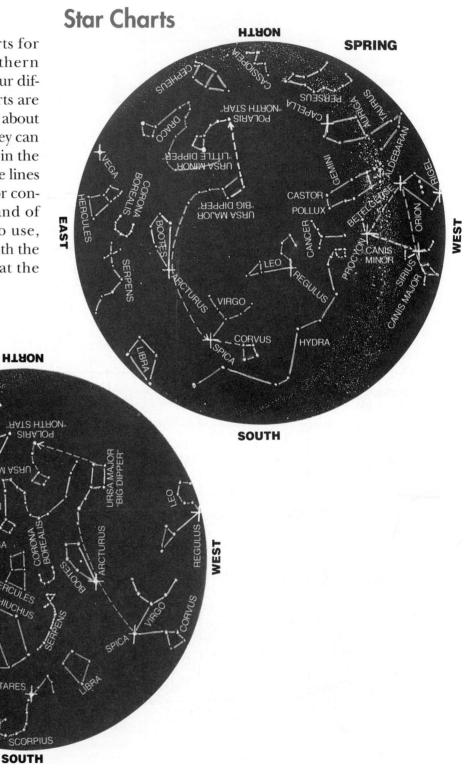

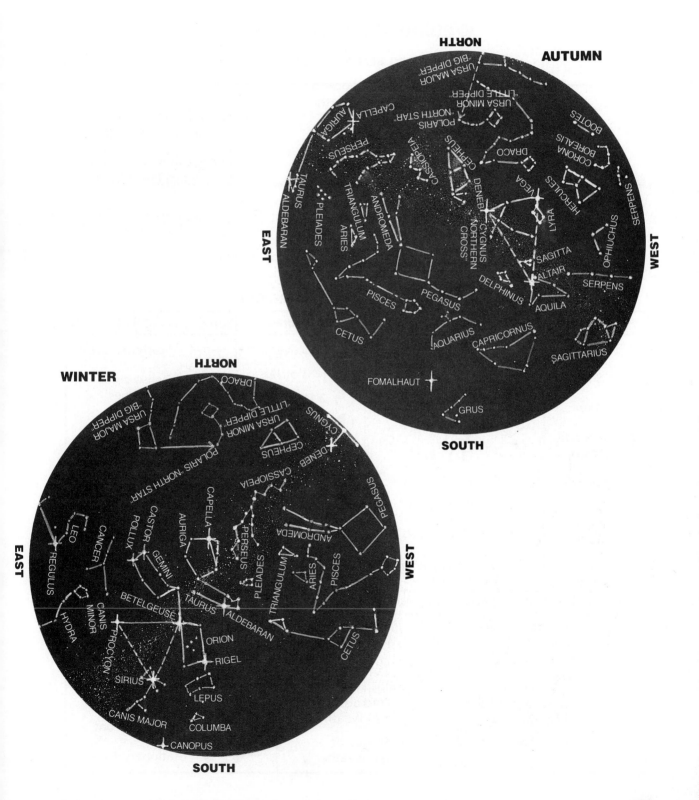

Weather Map Symbols

SAMPLE PLOTTED REPORT AT EACH STATION

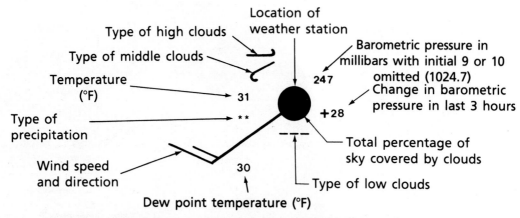

SYMBOLS USED IN PLOTTING REPORT

Precipitation	Wind speed and direction	Sky coverage	Some types of high clouds
Fog	0 calm	No cover	Scattered cirrus
Snow	1–2 knots	1/10 or less	Dense cirrus in patches
Rain	3–7 knots	2/10 to 3/10	Veil of cirrus covering entire sky
Thunder-storm	8–12 knots	4/10	Cirrus not covering entire sky
Drizzle	13–17 knots	½	
Showers	18–22 knots	6/10	
	23-27 knots	7/10	
	48-52 knots	Overcast with openings	
	1 knot = 1.852 km/h	Complete overcast	

Some types of middle clouds	Some types of low clouds	Fronts and pressure systems	
Thin altostratus layer	Cumulus of fair weather	(H) or High (L) or Low	Center of high or low pressure system
Thick altostratus layer	Stratocumulus	▲▲▲▲	Cold front
Thin altostratus in patches	Fractocumulus of bad weather		Warm front
Thin altostratus in bands	Stratus of fair weather		Occluded front
			Stationary front

APPENDIX L

Minerals with Metallic Luster

Mineral (formula)	Color	Streak	Hardness	Specific gravity	Crystal system	Breakage pattern	Uses and other properties
graphite (C)	black to gray	black to gray	1-2	2.3	hexagonal	basal cleavage (scales)	pencil lead, lubricants for locks, rods to control some small nuclear reactions, battery poles
silver (Ag)	silvery white, tarnishes to black	light gray to silver	2.5	10-12	cubic	hackly	coins, fillings for teeth, jewelry, silverplate, wires; malleable and ductile
galena (Pbs)	gray	gray to black	2.5	7.5	cubic	cubic cleavage perfect	source of lead, used in pipes, shields for X rays, fishing equipment sinkers
gold (Au)	pale to golden yellow	yellow	2.5-3	19.3	cubic	hackly	jewelry, money, gold leaf, fillings for teeth, medicines; does not tarnish
bornite (Cu_5FeS_4)	bronze, tarnishes to dark blue, purple	gray-black	3	4.9-5.4	tetragonal	uneven fracture	source of copper; called "peacock ore" because of the purple shine when it tarnishes
copper (Cu)	copper red	copper red	3	8.5-9	cubic	hackly	coins, pipes, gutters, wire, cooking utensils, jewelry, decorative plaques; malleable and ductile
chalcopyrite ($CuFeS_2$)	brassy to golden yellow	greenish black	3.5-4	4.2	tetragonal	uneven fracture	main ore of copper
chromite ($FeCr_2O_4$)	black or brown	brown to black	5.5	4.6	cubic	irregular fracture	ore of chromium, stainless steel, metallurgical bricks
pyrrhotite (FeS)	bronze	gray-black	4	4.6	hexagonal	uneven fracture	often found with pentlandite, an ore of nickel; may be magnetic
hematite (specular) (Fe_2O_3)	black or reddish brown	red or reddish brown	6	5.3	hexagonal	irregular fracture	source of iron; roasted in a blast furnace, converted to "pig" iron, made into steel
magnetite (Fe_3O_4)	black	black	6	5.2	cubic	conchoidal fracture	source of iron, naturally magnetic, called lodestone
pyrite (FeS_2)	light, brassy, yellow	greenish black	6.5	5.0	cubic	uneven fracture	source of iron, "fool's gold," alters to limonite

APPENDIX M

Minerals with Nonmetallic Luster

Mineral (formula)	Color	Streak	Hardness	Specific gravity	Crystal system	Breakage pattern	Uses and other properties
talc ($Mg_3(OH)_2Si_4O_{10}$)	white, greenish	white	1	2.8	monoclinic	cleavage in one direction	easily cut with fingernail; used for talcum powder; soapstone; is used in paper and for table tops
bauxite (hydrous aluminum compound)	gray, red, white, brown	gray	1-3	2.0-2.5	—	—	source of aluminum; used in paints, aluminum foil, and airplane parts
kaolinite ($Al_2Si_2O_5(OH)_4$)	white, red, reddish brown, black	white	2	2.6	triclinic	basal cleavage	clays; used in ceramics and in china dishes; common in most soils; often microscopic-sized particles
gypsum ($CaSO_4 \cdot 2H_2O$)	colorless, gray, white, brown	white	2	2.3	monoclinic	basal cleavage	used extensively in the preparation of plaster of paris, alabaster, and dry wall for building construction
sphalerite (ZnS)	brown	pale yellow	3.5-4	4	cubic	cleavage in six directions	main ore of zinc; used in paints, dyes, and medicine
sulfur (S)	yellow	yellow to white	2	2.0	ortho-rhombic	conchoidal fracture	used in medicine, fungicides for plants, vulcanization of rubber, production of sulfuric acid
muscovite ($KAl_3Si_3O_{10}(OH)_2$)	white, light gray, yellow, rose, green	colorless	2.5	2.8	monoclinic	basal cleavage	occurs in large flexible plates; used as an insulator in electrical equipment, lubricant
biotite ($K(Mg, Fe)_3AlSi_3O_{10}(OH)_2$)	black to dark brown	colorless	2.5	2.8-3.4	monoclinic	basal cleavage	occurs in large fexible plates
halite (NaCl)	colorless, red, white, blue	colorless	2.5	2.1	cubic	cubic cleavage	salt; very soluble in water; a preservative
calcite ($CaCO_3$)	colorless, white, pale, blue	colorless, white	3	2.7	hexagonal	cleavage in three directions	fizzes when HCl is added; used in cements and other building materials
dolomite ($CaMg(CO_3)_2$)	colorless, white, pink, green, gray, black	white	3.5-4	2.8	hexagonal	cleavage in three directions	concrete and cement, used as an ornamental building stone

Mineral (formula)	Color	Streak	Hardness	Specific gravity	Crystal system	Breakage pattern	Uses and other properties
fluorite (CaF_2)	colorless, white, blue, green, red, yellow, purple	colorless	4	3-3.2	cubic	cleavage	used in the manufacture of optical equipment; glows under ultraviolet light
limonite (hydrous iron oxides)	yellow, brown, black	yellow, brown	5.5	2.7-4.3	—	conchoidal fracture	source of iron; weathers easily, coloring matter of soils
hornblende ($CaNa(Mg, Al, Fe)_5(Al,Si)_2 Si_6O_{22}(OH)_2$)	green to black	gray to white	5-6	3.4	monoclinic	cleavage in two directions	will transmit light on thin edges; 6-sided cross section
feldspar (orthoclase) ($KAlSi_3O_8$)	colorless, white to gray, green and yellow	colorless	6	2.5	monoclinic	two cleavage planes meet at 90° angle	insoluble in acids; used in the manufacture of porcelain
feldspar (plagioclase) ($NaAlSi_3O_8$) ($CaAl_2Si_2O_8$)	gray, green, white	colorless	6	2.5	triclinic	two cleavage planes meet at 86° angle	used in ceramics; striations present on some faces
augite ((Ca, Na) (Mg, Fe, Al) (Al, Si)$_2 O_6$)	black	colorless	6	3.3	monoclinic	2-directional cleavage	square or 8-sided cross section
olivine ((Mg, Fe)$_2SiO_4$)	olive green	colorless	6.5	3.5	ortho-rhombic	conchoidal fracture	gemstones, refractory sand
quartz (SiO_2)	colorless, various colors	colorless	7	2.6	hexagonal	conchoidal fracture	used in glass manufacture, electronic equipment, radios, computers, watches, gemstones
garnet (Mg, Fe, Ca)$_3$ ($Al_2Si_3O_{12}$)	deep yellow-red green, black	colorless	7.5	3.5	cubic	conchoidal fracture	used in jewelry, also used as an abrasive
topaz (Al_2SiO_4 (F, OH)$_2$)	white, pink yellow, pale blue, colorless	colorless	8	3.5	ortho-rhombic	basal cleavage	valuable gemstone
corundum (Al_2O_3)	colorless, blue, brown, green, white, pink, red	colorless	9	4.0	hexagonal	fracture	gemstones: ruby is red, sapphire is blue; industrial abrasive

Organizing Information

Classifying

You may not realize it, but you make things orderly in the world around you. If your shirts hang in the closet together, your socks take up a particular corner of a dresser drawer, or your favorite cassette tapes are stacked together, you have used the skill of classifying.

Classifying is sorting objects or events into groups based on common features. When classifying, you first make observations of the objects or events to be classified. Then, you select one feature that is shared by some members in the group but not by others. Those members that share the feature are placed in a subgroup. You can classify members into smaller and smaller subgroups based on characteristics.

How would you classify a collection of cassette tapes?

You might classify cassettes you like to dance to in one subgroup and cassettes you like to listen to in another. The cassettes you like to dance to could be subdivided into a rap subgroup and a rock subgroup. Note that for each feature selected, each cassette only fits into one subgroup. Keep selecting features until all the cassettes are classified. The chart shows one possible classification.

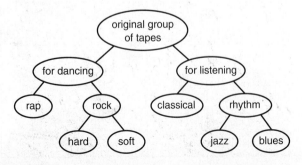

Remember when you classify, you are grouping objects or events for a purpose. Select common features to form groups and subgroups with your purpose in mind.

Sequencing

A common sequence with which you are familiar is students sitting in alphabetical order. Another use of a sequence would be the steps in a cookie recipe. Think about baking chocolate chip cookies. The steps in the recipe have to be followed in order for the cookies to taste good. A sequence is an arrangement of things or events in a particular order.

When you are asked to sequence objects or events, first identify what comes first, then what should come second. Continue to choose objects or events until they are all in order. Then, go back over the sequence to make sure each thing or event logically leads to the next.

Suppose you wanted to watch a movie that just came out on videotape. What sequence of events would you have to follow to watch the movie? You would first turn the television set to Channel 3 or 4. You would then turn the videotape player on and insert the tape. Once the tape has started playing, you would adjust the sound and picture. Then, when the movie is over, you would rewind the tape and return it to the store.

Outlining

Have you ever wondered why teachers ask students to outline what they read? The purpose of outlining is to show the relationships among main ideas and information about the main ideas. By doing this, outlining can help you organize, remember, and review written material.

When you are asked to outline, you must first find a group of words that summarizes the main idea. This group of words corresponds to the Roman numerals in an outline. Next, determine what is said about the main idea. Ideas of equal importance are grouped together and are given capital letters. These ideas are further broken down and given numbers and letters.

To familiarize yourself with outlines, compare the following outline with Chapter 10 of your textbook.

Notice that the outline shows the pattern of organization of the written material. The boldfaced title is the main idea and corresponds with I. The letters A and B and the numbers and letters that follow divide the rest of the text into supporting ideas.

Weather and Climate
I. What Is Weather?
  A. Factors of Weather
    1. What weather is
      a. present state of atmosphere
      b. current conditions
    2. Important factors are
      a. air pressure
      b. wind
      c. temperature
      d. amount of moisture in air
    3. Humidity is amount of water vapor in air
      a. amount of water vapor held depends on temperature
      b. warm air holds more water vapor

  B. Clouds and Precipitation
    1. Clouds are made when cooled air condenses
    2. When air condenses into large water droplets, the droplets may fall as precipitation

Thinking Critically

Observing and Inferring

Imagine that you and your friends have just finished a volleyball game. You hurry home to get a cold drink. Opening the refrigerator, you see a jug of orange juice on the back of the top shelf. The jug feels cold as you grasp it. "Ah, just what I need," you think. When you quickly drink the juice, you smell the oranges and enjoy the tart taste in your mouth.

As you imagined yourself in the story, you used your senses to make observations. You used your sense of touch to feel the cold jug, your hearing to listen as the liquid filled the glass, your sense of smell and taste to enjoy the odor and tartness, and you used your sight to find the jug in the refrigerator. The basis of all scientific investigation is observation. Scientists are careful to make accurate observations. When possible, they use instruments, like microscopes, to extend their senses.

Often they use instruments to make measurements. Because measurements are easy to communicate and provide a concrete means of comparing collected data, scientists use them whenever possible.

When you make observations in science, you may find it helpful to first examine the entire object or situation. Then, look carefully for details. Write down everything you observe before using other senses to make additional observations.

Scientists often make inferences based on their observations. An inference is an attempt to explain or interpret observations or to determine what caused what you observed. For example, if you observed a CLOSED sign in a store window around noon, you might infer the owner is taking a lunch break. But, it's possible that the owner has a doctor's appointment or has taken the day off to go fishing. The only way to be sure your inference is correct is to investigate further.

When making an inference, be certain to make accurate observations and to record them carefully. Analyze all of the data that you've collected. Then, based on everything you know, try to explain or interpret what you've observed. If possible, investigate further to determine if your inference is correct.

Comparing and Contrasting

Observations can be analyzed and then organized by noting the similarities and differences between two or more objects or events. When you examine objects or events to determine similarities, you are comparing. Contrasting is looking for differences in similar objects or events.

Properties	Earth	Venus
Diameter (km)	12 756	12 104
Average density (g/cm³)	5.5	5.3
Percentage of sunlight reflected	39	76
Daytime surface temperature (K)	300	750
Number of satellites	1	0

Suppose you were asked to compare and contrast the planets Venus and Earth. You would start by examining observations made of these planets. You would then divide a piece of paper into two columns. List ways the planets are similar in one column and ways they are different in the other. Then report your findings in a table or in a paragraph.

Similarities you might point out are that both are similar in size, shape, and mass. Differences include Venus having hotter surface temperatures, a dense cloudy atmosphere, and an intense greenhouse effect.

Recognizing Cause and Effect

Have you ever observed something happen and then tried to figure out why or how it might have happened? If so, you have observed an event and inferred a reason for its occurrence. The event is an effect, and the reason for the event is the cause.

Suppose that every time your teacher fed fish in a classroom aquarium, she tapped the food container on the edge. Then, one day she tapped the edge of the aquarium to make a point about an ecology lesson. You observe the fish swim to the surface of the aquarium to feed.

What is the effect and what would you infer would be the cause? The effect is the fish swimming to the surface of the aquarium. You might infer the cause to be the teacher tapping on the edge of the aquarium. In determining cause and effect, you have made a logical inference based on careful observations.

Perhaps, the fish swam to the surface because they reacted to the teacher's waving hand or for some other reason. When scientists are unsure of the cause for a certain event, they often design controlled experiments to determine what caused their observations. Although you have made a sound judgment, you would have to perform an experiment to be certain that it was the tapping that caused the effect you observed.

Experimentation Skills

Measuring in SI

The metric system is a uniform system of measurement developed by a group of scientists in 1795. The development of the metric system helped scientists avoid problems with different units of measurement by providing an international standard of comparison for measurements. A modern form of the metric system called the International System, or SI, was adopted for worldwide use in 1960.

Your text uses metric units in most of its measurements. In the activities and experiments you will be doing, you will use the metric system of measurement.

The metric system is easy to use because it has a systematic naming of units and a decimal base. For example, meter is the base unit for measuring length, gram for measuring mass, and liter for measuring volume. Unit sizes vary by powers of ten. When changing from smaller units to larger, you divide by ten or a power of ten. When changing from larger units to smaller, you multiply by ten or a power of ten. Prefixes are used to name larger and smaller units. Look at the following table for some common metric prefixes and their meanings.

METRIC PREFIXES			
Prefix	Symbol		Meaning
kilo-	k	1000	thousand
hecto-	h	100	hundred
deka	da	10	ten
deci-	d	0.1	tenth
centi	c	0.01	hundredth
milli-	m	0.001	thousandth

Do you see how the prefix *kilo-* attached to the unit *gram* is *kilogram* or 1000 grams? The prefix *deci-* attached to the unit *meter* is *decimeter* or one tenth (0.1) of a meter.

You have probably measured distance many times. The meter is the SI unit used to measure distance. To visualize the length of a meter, think of a baseball bat. A baseball bat is about one meter long. When measuring smaller distances, the meter is divided into smaller units called centimeters and millimeters. A centimeter is one hundredth (0.01) of a meter which is about the size of the width of the fingernail on your ring finger. A millimeter is one thousandth of a meter (0.001), about the thickness of a dime.

Most metersticks and metric rulers have lines indicating centimeters and millimeters. Look at the illustration. The centimeter lines are the longer numbered lines and the shorter lines between the centimeter lines are millimeter lines.

When using a metric ruler, you must first decide on a unit of measurement. You then line up the zero centimeter mark with the end of the object being measured, and read the number where the object ends.

Units of length are also used to measure surface area. The standard unit of area is the square meter (m^2). A square that's one meter long on each side has a surface area of one square meter. Similarly, a square centimeter (cm^2) is a square one centimeter long on each side. The surface area of an object is determined by multiplying the number of units in length times the number of units in width.

The volume of rectangular solids is also calculated using units of length. The cubic meter (m^3) is the standard SI unit of volume. A cubic meter is a cube one meter on a side. You can determine the volume of rectangular solids by multiplying length times width times height.

Liquid volume is measured using a unit called a liter. A liter has the volume of 1000 cubic centimeters. Since the prefix *milli-* means thousandth (0.001), a milliliter equals one cubic centimeter. One milliliter of liquid would completely fill a cube measuring one centimeter on each side.

During science activities you will measure liquids using beakers and graduated cylinders marked in milliliters. A graduated cylinder is a tall cylindrical container marked with lines from bottom to top.

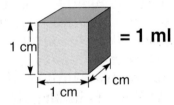

Scientists use a balance to find the mass of an object in grams. You will likely use a beam balance similar to the one illustrated. Notice that on one side of the beam balance is a pan and on the other side is a set of beams. Each beam has an object of a known mass called a rider that slides on the beam.

Before you find the mass of an object, you must set the balance to zero by sliding all the riders back

to the zero point. Check the pointer to make sure it swings an equal distance above and below the zero point on the scale. If the swing is unequal, find and turn the adjusting screw until you have an equal swing.

You are now ready to use the balance to find the mass of the object. Place the object on the pan. Slide the rider with the largest mass along the beams until the pointer drops below the zero point. Then move it back one notch. Repeat the process on each beam until the pointer swings an equal distance above and below the zero point. Read the masses indicated on the beams. The sum of the masses is the mass of the object.

Never place a hot object or pour chemicals directly on the pan. Determine the mass of a suitable container and place dry or liquid chemicals into the container. Then determine the mass of the container and the chemicals. Finally, calculate the mass of the chemicals by subtracting the mass of the empty container.

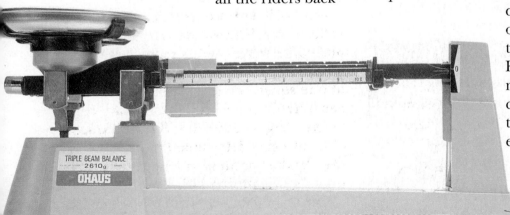

Hypothesizing

What would you do if the combination lock on your locker didn't work? Would you try the combination again? Would you check to make sure you had the right locker? You would likely try several possible solutions until you managed to open the locker.

Scientists generally use experiments to solve problems and answer questions. An experiment is a method of solving a problem in which scientists use an organized process to attempt to answer a question.

Experimentation involves defining a problem and formulating and testing hypotheses. A hypothesis is a testable prediction. Each hypothesis is tested during an experiment which includes making careful observations and collecting data. After analysis of the collected data, a conclusion is formed and compared to the hypothesis.

Imagine it's after school, and you are changing clothes. You notice a brownish-black spot on a favorite shirt. You problem is how to remove the stain from the shirt without damaging the shirt. You think that soap and water will remove the stain. You have made a hypothesis, or a prediction. But, making a prediction is not enough, the hypothesis must be tested. You try soap and water, but the stain doesn't budge.

You then observe the stain more carefully and decide that you will need to use a solvent. You have revised your hypothesis based on your observations. The new hypothesis is still only a proposed prediction until you test it and examine the results. If the solvent removes the stain, the hypothesis is supported. But, if the solvent doesn't remove the stain, you will have to revise and refine the hypothesis.

Using Variables, Constants, and Controls

When scientists do experiments, they are careful to manipulate or change only one condition and keep all other conditions in the experiment the same. The condition that is manipulated is called the independent variable. The conditions that are kept the same during an experiment are called constants. The dependent variable is any change that results from manipulating the independent variable.

Scientists can only know that the independent variable caused the change in the dependent variable if they keep all other factors constant in the experiment. Scientists use controls to be certain that the observed changes were a result of manipulating the independent variable. A control is a sample that is treated exactly like the experimental group except that the independent variable is not applied to the control. After the experiment, the change in the dependent variable of the control sample is compared to the change observed in the experimental group. Any observed differences may be the effect of application of the independent variable.

Suppose you were asked to bring your portable compact disc player on a weekend camping trip. You put in fresh dry cell batteries so that you and your friends can play CDs all weekend. But, the player loses volume about midday Sunday and soon won't play at all. You expected the dry cell batteries to last all weekend. Since you played the CDs louder than you do at home, you wonder if the volume of the player affects how long the batteries last and decide to design an experiment to find out. What would be your independent and dependent variables, constants, and control in your experiment?

This is how you might set up your experiment. You decide to compare the amount of time the player will operate at different volume settings. You purchase enough fresh dry cell batteries to operate the player at number 6, your normal listening volume, and for lower and higher volume settings. You first set the volume at number 6 and operate the player until you can no longer hear the music. You then repeat the experiment two more times using volume settings of 3 and 9. You record the amount of time the player operates for each volume setting in a data table. Your data table might look like this:

DURATION MUSIC IS HEARD	
Volume	Amount of Time
3	23 h, 46 min
6	18 h, 13 min
9	14 h, 53 min

What are the independent and dependent variables in the experiment? Because you are changing the volume setting of the compact disc player, the independent variable is the volume setting. Since the dependent variable is any change that results from the independent variable, the dependent variable is the number of hours and minutes music is heard on the player.

What factors are constants in the experiment? The constants are using identical dry cell batteries, playing the same compact disc, and keeping the compact disc player in the same environment for each test. What was the purpose of playing the compact disc player at your normal setting? The normal setting of the player is the control. The duration that music is heard for the normal volume setting will be used to compare the durations of lower and higher volume settings.

Interpreting Data

After doing a controlled experiment, you must analyze and interpret the collected data, form a conclusion, and compare the conclusion to your hypothesis. Analyze and interpret the data in the table. On which volume setting did the dry cell batteries last the longest? The batteries lasted the longest on number 3, the lowest setting. On which volume setting did the dry cell batteries last the shortest duration? The batteries lasted the shortest duration on volume setting number 9. What conclusion did you form? The data indicate that as the volume increases the dry cell batteries last for a shorter duration. How does the conclusion compare with your hypothesis for this experiment? Was your hypothesis supported by the experiment or not?

Graphic Organizers

Concept Mapping

If you were taking an automobile trip, you would likely take along a road map. The road map shows your location, your destination, and cities along the way. By examining the map, you can know where you are in relation to other locations on the map.

A concept map is similar to a road map. But, a concept map shows the relationship among ideas rather than cities. A concept map is a diagram that visually represents how science concepts are related. Because the concept map shows the relationships among science ideas, it can clarify the meaning of the ideas and terms and help you to understand what you are studying.

Look at the construction of a simple concept map called a network tree. Notice how some words are circled while others are written on the lines. The circled words are science ideas or terms called concepts. The lines in the map show related concepts, and the words written on them describe relationships between the concepts.

A concept map can also show more complex relationships between the concepts. For example, a line labeled "affected by" could be drawn from "weather" to "plants" or "animals," because plants and animals are affected by the weather. Another example of a relationship that crosses branches would be a line connecting "Earth changes" and "matter and energy" labeled "caused by interactions of." Earth changes are caused by interactions of matter and energy.

When you are asked to construct a concept map, state the topic and select the major concepts. Find related concepts and put them in order from general to specific. Branch the related concepts from the major concept and describe the relationships on the lines. Continue to write the more specific concepts. Write the relationships between the concepts on the lines until all concepts are mapped. Examine the concept map for relationships that cross branches, and add them to the concept map.

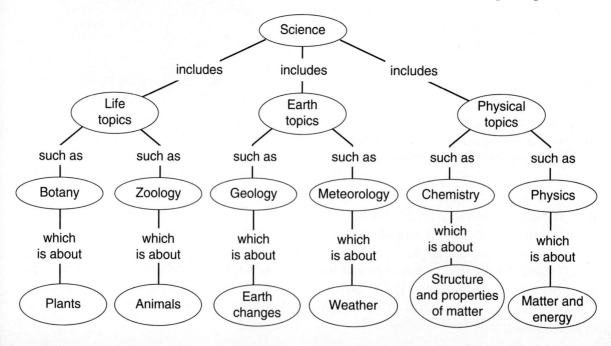

An **events chain** is another type of concept map. An events chain map is used to describe ideas in order. In science, an events chain can be used to describe a sequence of events, the steps in a procedure, or the stages of a process.

When making an events chain, you first must find the one event that starts the chain. This event is called the initiating event. You then find the next event in the chain and continue until you reach an outcome. Suppose your mother asked you to wash the dinner dishes. An events chain map might look like the one below. Notice that connecting words may not be necessary.

Initiating event:

| Mother asks you to wash dishes. |

↓

Event 2:

| You clear the table. |

↓

Event 3:

| You wash the dishes in soapy water. |

↓

Event 4:

| You rinse the dishes in hot water. |

↓

Event 5:

| You dry the dishes. |

↓

Final outcome:

| You put the dishes away. |

A **cycle concept map** is a special type of events chain map. In a cycle concept map, the series of events do not produce a final outcome. There is no beginning and no end to a cycle concept map.

To construct a cycle map, you first decide on a starting point and then list each important event in order. Since there is no outcome and the last event relates back to the first event, the cycle repeats itself. Look at the cycle map of physical changes of water:

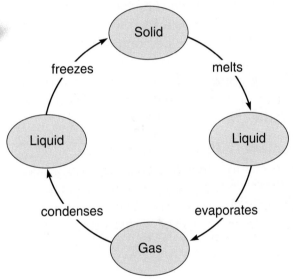

There is usually not one correct way to create a concept map. As you are constructing a map, you may discover other ways to construct the map that show the relationships among concepts better. If you do discover what you think is a better way to create a concept map, don't hesitate to change it.

Concept maps are useful in understanding the ideas you have read about. As you construct a map, you are constructing knowledge and learning. Once concept maps are constructed, you can use them again to review and study and to test your knowledge.

Making and Using Tables

Browse through your textbook, and you will notice many tables both in the text and in the activities. The tables in the text arrange information in such a way that it's easier for you to understand. Also, many activities in your text have tables to complete as you do the activity. Activity tables will help you organize the data you collect during the activity so that it can be interpreted easily.

Most tables have a title telling you what is being presented. The table itself is divided into columns and rows. The column titles list items to be compared. The rows headings list the specific characteristics being compared. Within the grid of the table, the collected data is recorded. Look at the following table:

EARTHQUAKE MAGNITUDE

Magnitude at focus	Distance from epicenters that tremors are felt	Average number expected per year
1.0 to 3.9	24 km	> 100 000
4.0 to 4.9	48 km	6 200
5.0 to 5.9	112 km	800
6.0 to 6.9	200 km	120
7.0 to 7.9	400 km	20
8.0 to 8.9	720 km	< 1

What is the title of this table? The title is "Earthquake Magnitude." What is being compared? The distance away from the epicenter that tremors are felt and the average number of earthquakes expected per year are being compared for different magnitudes on the Richter scale.

What is the average number of earthquakes expected per year for an earthquake with a magnitude of 5.5 at the focus? To find the answer you must locate the column labeled "Average number expected per year" and the row "5.0 to 5.9." The data contained in the box where the column and row intersect is the answer. Did you answer "800?" What is the distance away from the epicenter that tremors are felt for an earthquake with a magnitude of 8.1 on the Richter scale? If you answered "720 km," you have an understanding of how to use a table.

RECYCLED MATERIALS

Day of Week	Paper (kg)	Aluminum (kg)	Plastic (kg)
Mon.	4	2	0.5
Wed.	3.5	1.5	0.5
Fri.	3	1	1.5

To make a table, you simply list the items compared in columns and the characteristics compared in rows. Make a table and record the data comparing the mass of recycled materials collected by a class. On Monday, students turned in 4 kg of paper, 2 kg of aluminum, and 0.5 kg of plastic. Wednesday, they turned in 3.5 kg of paper, 1.5 kg of aluminum, and 0.5 kg of plastic. On Friday, the totals were 3 kg of paper, 1 kg of aluminum, and 1.5 kg of plastic. If your table looks like the one shown, you should be able to make tables to organize data.

Making and Using Graphs

After scientists organize data in tables, they often display the data in graphs. A graph is a diagram that shows a comparison between variables. Since graphs show a picture of collected data, they make interpretation and analysis of the data easier. The three basic types of graphs used in science are the line graph, bar graph, and pie graph.

A line graph is used to show the relationship between two variables. The variables being compared go on two axes of the graph. The independent variable always goes on the horizontal axis, called the x-axis. The dependent variable always goes on the vertical axis or y-axis.

Suppose a school started a peer study program with a class of students to see how it affected their science grades.

AVERAGE GRADES OF STUDENTS IN STUDY PROGRAM	
Grading Period	Average Science Grade
First	81
Second	85
Third	86
Fourth	89

You could make a graph of the grades of students in the program over a period of time. The grading period is the independent variable and should be placed on the x-axis of your graph. The average grade of the students in the program is the dependent variable and would go on the y-axis.

After drawing your axes, you would label each axis with a scale. The x-axis simply lists the grading periods. To make a scale of grades on the y-axis, you must look at the data values. Since the lowest grade was 81 and the highest was 89, you know that you will have to start numbering at least at 81 and go through 89. You decide to start numbering at 80 and number by twos through 90.

Average Grades of Students in Study Program

You next must plot the data points. The first pair of data you want to plot is the first grading period and 81. Locate "First" on the x-axis and "81" on the y-axis. Where an imaginary vertical line from the x-axis and an imaginary horizontal line from the y-axis would meet, place the first data point. Place the other data points the same way. After all the points are plotted, connect them with a smooth line.

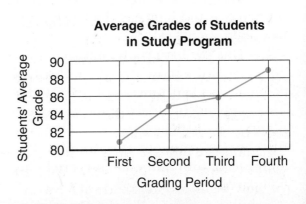

Average Grades of Students in Study Program

What if you wanted to compare the average grades of the class in the study group with the grades of another science class? The data of the other class can be plotted on the same graph to make the comparison. You must include a key with two different lines, each indicating a different set of data. Also change the title of the new graph to represent the data you are comparing.

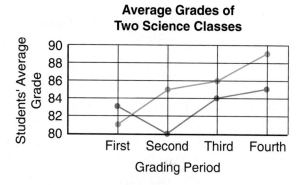

Average Grades of Two Science Classes

KEY   Class or study students ———

       Regular class ———

Bar graphs are similar to line graphs, except they are used to compare or display data that does not continuously change. In a bar graph, thick bars, rather than data points, show the relationships among data.

To make a bar graph, set up the x-axis and y-axis as you did for the line graph. The data is plotted by drawing thick bars from the x-axis up to an imaginary point where the y-axis would intersect the bar if it was extended.

Look at the bar graph comparing the amounts of the most abundant dissolved elements in a kilogram sample of seawater. The independent variable is the type of element, and the dependent variable is the number of grams in the sample. The amounts of different elements are being compared.

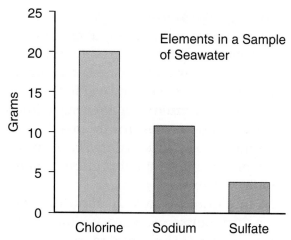

A pie graph uses a circle divided into sections to display data. Each section represents part of the whole. When all the sections are placed together, they equal 100 percent of the whole.

Suppose you had a rock collection and wanted to make a pie graph to show the percentage of rocks that are igneous, sedimentary, and metamorphic. You would have to determine the total number of rocks and the number of rocks of each type. You count the rocks and find that you have 25 rocks in the collection. Therefore, the whole pie will represent this amount.

You then place the igneous rocks in one group, the sedimentary in another, and the metamorphic in the last group. After counting the rocks in each group, you find you have 8 igneous rocks, 5 sedimentary rocks, and 12 metamorphic rocks.

To find out how much of the pie each section should take, you must divide the number of rocks in each group by the total number of rocks. You then multiply your answer by 360, the number of degrees in a circle. Round your answer to the nearest whole number. The percentage of igneous rocks would be determined as follows:

$$\frac{8}{25} \times 360° = 115.2° \text{ or } 115 \text{ degrees}$$

Use the formula to compute how much of the circle sedimentary and metamorphic rocks would take up. Sedimentary rocks would take up 72 degrees, and metamorphic rocks would take up 173 degrees.

To plot the groups on the pie graph, you need a compass and protractor. Use the compass to draw a circle. Then, draw a straight line from the center to the edge of the circle. Place your protractor on this line and use it to mark a point on the edge of the circle at 115 degrees. Connect this point with a straight line to the center of the circle. This is the part of the circle representing igneous rocks. Place your protractor on the line you just made and use it to mark a point on the edge of the circle at 72 degrees. Again draw a straight line from this point to the center of the circle. This part represents sedimentary rocks. The remaining part of the circle represents the percentage of metamorphic rocks. Complete the graph by labeling the sections of your graph and giving the graph a title. What title would you give the pie graph shown below?

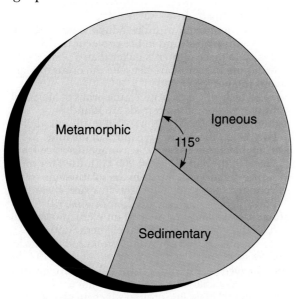

Interpreting Scientific Illustrations

Your science textbook contains many scientific illustrations to help you understand, interpret, and remember what you read. When you are reading the text and encounter an illustration, examine it carefully and relate it to the text you have just read. Also read the caption for the illustration. The caption is a brief comment that explains or identifies the illustration.

Some illustrations are designed to show you how the internal parts of a structure are arranged. Look at Figure 15-13 on page 406. The purpose of this illustration and the text it accompanies is to help you understand how calderas form. Notice that the caption of the illustrations identifies the location of this caldera and briefly describes the illustrations.

The illustrations of the caldera show what is called a cross section. A cross section is a section that is formed by cutting through an object. The illustration of the caldera is formed by cutting at right angles to the horizontal axis of the volcano.

You will notice many maps as you read the text. The map helps you understand your reading by showing you the locations of places described in the text.

Scientific illustrations similar to maps are two dimensional. A two-dimensional illustration has height and width. However, many of the illustrations in this text are three-dimensional. The illustration of the caldera is three dimensional. Notice that the illustration has not only height and width but also depth. Since an illustration in three dimensions is similar to the way you see the world, it is even more useful to help you understand the science ideas you are reading about.

GLOSSARY

This glossary defines each key term that appears in **bold type** in the text. It also shows the page number where you can find the word used. Some other terms that you may need to look up are included, too. We also show how to pronounce some of the words. A key to pronunciation is in the table below.

PRONUNCIATION KEY

a . . . b**a**ck (bak)	oh . . . g**o** (goh)	sh . . . **sh**elf (shelf)
ay . . . d**ay** (day)	aw . . . **so**ft (sawft)	ch . . . na**t**ure (nay chur)
ah . . . f**a**ther (fahth ur)	or . . . **or**bit (or but)	g . . . **g**ift (gihft)
ow . . . fl**ow**er (flow ur)	oy . . . c**oi**n (coyn)	j . . . **g**em (jem)
ar . . . c**ar** (car)	oo . . . f**oo**t (foot)	ing . . . s**ing** (sing)
e . . . l**e**ss (les)	ew . . . f**oo**d (fewd)	zh . . . vi**s**ion (vihzh un)
ee . . . l**ea**f (leef)	yoo . . . p**u**re (pyoor)	k . . . ca**k**e (kayk)
ih . . . tr**i**p (trihp)	yew . . . f**ew** (fyew)	s . . . **s**eed, **c**ent (seed, sent)
i (i + con + e) . . . **i**dea	uh . . . c**o**mma (cahm uh)	z . . . **z**one, rai**s**e (zohn, rayz)
(i dee uh), l**i**fe (life)	u (+ con) . . . flow**e**r (flow ur)	

A

abrasion: a type of erosion caused when windblown or waterborne sand grains strike other sand grains and rocks, breaking off small fragments. (163)

absolute dating: determining the age of rocks using the radioactive decay of atoms in them. (436)

absolute magnitude: a measure of the amount of light a star or other space object gives off. (630)

abyssal (a BIHS uhl) **plain:** the flat seafloor in the deep ocean. (313)

acid: any substance with a pH lower than seven; the lower the pH number, the stronger the acid. (526)

acid rain: precipitation that is very acidic because it contains sulfuric acid (from coal-burning power plants) and nitric acid (from car exhausts). (526)

air mass: a large body of air that has the properties of the surface over which it formed. (262)

alluvial fan: a deposit of sediment that occurs when water rushing down a slope abruptly slows at the bottom, depositing its sediment load. (150)

amphibians (am FIHB ee unz): vertebrate animals adapted to living both on land and in water; they return to water to reproduce. (459)

angular unconformity: a type of unconformity where tilted rock layers meet horizontal rock layers; this indicates that layers are missing and causes a gap in the time record.

anthracite: the hardest, cleanest burning coal, contains about 90 percent carbon. (482)

apparent magnitude: a measure of light received on Earth from an object in space. (630)

aquifer: a layer of permeable rock that has connecting pores and transmits water freely. (183)

arête (uh RAYT): a sharp-edged mountain ridge carved by glaciers.

artesian (ahr TEE zhun) **well:** a well in which water under natural pressure rises to the surface without being pumped. (184)

asbestos: a mineral with threadlike, flexible fibers used as insulation and in fire protection. (78)

asteroid: a piece of rock, smaller than a planet, that orbits the sun; most are between the orbits of Mars and Jupiter. (622)

asteroid belt: the area between the orbits of Mars and Jupiter where most asteroids are found.

asthenosphere (as THEN uh sfihr): the plasticlike layer below the lithosphere in Earth's mantle. (349)

astronomical unit (AU): the average distance from Earth to the sun (150 000 000 km), used for measuring distances to objects in the solar system. (608)

astronomy: the study of objects in space, including stars, planets, comets, and their origins. (9)

atom: the smallest particle of an element that still has all the properties of that element. (29)

atomic number: the number of protons in the nucleus of an atom.

Australopithecus: the earliest animals to have distinct humanlike characteristics; now extinct.

axis: an imaginary line around which an object spins; for example, Earth spins around its axis. (577)

B

barred spiral galaxy: a galaxy having two spiral arms extending from a large bar.

barrier island: a sand deposit that parallels the shore but is separated from the mainland. (310)

basaltic: dark-colored igneous rocks that form from magma rich in iron and magnesium. (93)

base: any substance with a pH above seven; the higher the pH number, the stronger the base. (526)

basin: a low area that contains an ocean. (283)

batholith: a large body of intrusive igneous rock that forms when magma cools underground and stops rising toward the surface. (404)

beach: a deposit of sediment that runs parallel to a seashore. (308)

benthos (BEN thohs)**:** animals that live on the ocean bottom, such as corals, snails, clams, sea urchins, and bottom-dwelling fish. (320)

big bang theory: the leading theory of the origin of the universe. (650)

binary system: a system of two stars orbiting one another. (645)

biomass fuel: organic matter used as fuel, such as firewood. (491)

bituminous coal: commonly used coal, contains 50 to 75 percent carbon; also called soft coal. (481)

black hole: the final stage in the life cycle of some stars; the remnant of a star that is so dense that not even light can escape its gravity field. (638)

brachiopods (BRAY kee uh pahdz)**:** fan-shaped marine invertebrate animals commonly found as fossils in Paleozoic Era rocks.

breaker: an ocean wave that tumbles forward and breaks up as it approaches the shore, because its top is moving faster than the bottom. (293)

buoyancy (BOY un see)**:** the lifting effect on an object immersed in water.

C

caldera (kal DARE uh)**:** the large opening formed at the top of a volcano when the crater collapses into the vent following an eruption. (406)

carbonic acid: a weak acid formed when water mixes with carbon dioxide from air.

carbonaceous film: a fossil impression in a rock, consisting only of a thin carbon deposit. (421)

cast: a type of fossil formed when an earlier fossil in rock is dissolved away, leaving behind the impression of that fossil (a mold), and new sediments or minerals enter the mold. (421)

cave: an large underground opening formed when groundwater gradually dissolves rock. (186)

cementation: a sedimentary rock-forming process in which sediments are glued together by minerals deposited between the sediments. (101)

Cenozoic (sen uh ZOH ihk) **Era:** the most recent era of Earth's geologic history; spans 65 million years ago to the present time. (466)

chemical properties: characteristics of an element or compound that determine how it will react with other elements or compounds. (35)

chemical weathering: the breaking up of rocks due to a change in chemical composition; occurs when water, air, and other substances react with the minerals in rocks. (124)

chemosynthesis (kee moh SIHN thuh sihs)**:** a process used by bacteria to produce food and oxygen by using dissolved sulfur compounds. (318)

chlorofluorocarbons (CFCs): a group of chemicals used as refrigerants and aerosol spray propellants. CFCs destroy the atmosphere's ozone layer. (237)

chromosphere: the intermediate layer of the three layers of the sun's atmosphere, lying between the photosphere and the corona. (643)

cinder cone: a type of volcano in which tephra (cinders) piles up into a steep-sided cone. (399)

circumpolar constellation: a constellation that appears to circle Polaris as Earth rotates.

cirque (SURK)**:** a bowl-shaped basin carved by a glacier at the glacier's place of origin.

clay: sediment particle less than 0.004 mm in size.

Clean Air Act: this 1990 U.S. law sets maximum levels for major air pollutants. (529)

Clean Water Act: this 1987 U.S. law gives money to the states for building sewage and wastewater treatment facilities. (537)

cleavage: the physical property of a mineral that causes it to break along smooth, flat surfaces. (71)

climate: the pattern of weather in an area.

coal: a sedimentary rock formed from compacted, decayed plants; burned as a fossil fuel.

coastal plain: a landform that is a broad, flat area along a coastline; also called a lowland.

cold front: the boundary that develops when a cold air mass invades a warm air mass.

comet: a mass of frozen gases and rock particles that orbits the sun, often developing a bright tail when it passes near the sun. (618)

compaction: a sedimentary rock-forming process that occurs when layers of sediment become compressed by the weight of layers above them. (101)

composite volcano: a type of volcano built of lava and ash layers that accumulate from repeated cycles of tephra eruptions and lava eruptions. (400)

composting: the piling up of grass clippings, dead leaves, and other organic matter, so they can gradually decompose. (514)

compound: a substance containing two or more chemically combined elements and having properties different from those elements. (34)

compression: squeezing forces that compress rocks together at convergent plate boundaries, causing them to rumple, fold, and sometimes break.

conduction: the transfer of energy that occurs when molecules collide. (241)

conic projection: a map projection made by projecting locations and lines from a globe onto a cone; it produces accurate maps of areas smaller than the whole Earth, such as a nation or state. (207)

conservation: the careful use of resources to avoid wasting them and damaging the environment; includes reusing and recycling resources. (513)

constellation: a grouping of stars that has a shape resembling an animal, mythological character, or other object and thus is named for it. (628)

container law: a law requiring you to pay a refundable deposit each time you buy a container of beverage. (518)

continental drift: a hypothesis that continents have moved around the globe thousands of kilometers over millions of years to reach their current locations. (340)

continental glacier: a type of glacier in Earth's polar regions that covers a vast area; existing now only in Greenland and Antarctica.

continental shelf: the part of every continent that extends out under the ocean. (312)

continental slope: a part of the continental shelf that dips steeply down to the seafloor. (312)

contour interval: the difference in elevation between two contour lines on a topographic map. (209)

contour line: a line on a topographic map that connects points of equal elevation. (209)

control: in an experiment, the standard for comparison. (17)

convection: the transfer of heat due to movement caused by density differences in fluids like water or air. (241)

convection current: a circular current in a fluid like air, water, or molten rock; caused when the fluid is unevenly heated, so that part of it rises, and then cools and sinks, causing a circular movement. (352)

convergent boundary: in plate tectonics, the boundary between two plates that are converging, or moving toward each other. (350)

Copernicus, Nicholas: Polish astronomer (1473-1543) who hypothesized a sun-centered solar system.

Coriolis (kohr ee OH lus) **effect:** the effect of Earth's rotation on the movement of air masses. (245)

corona: the outermost and largest of the three layers of the sun's atmosphere, extending from the chromosphere outward millions of kilometers into space. (643)

crater: the opening at the top of a volcano. (389)

creep: a type of mass movement in which sediments move down a hill very slowly, sometimes causing posts to lean. (144)

crest: the highest point of a wave. (292)

crinoids (KRI noyds): marine invertebrate animals that resemble plants, commonly found as fossils in Paleozoic Era rocks and still a living animal group.

crust: the outermost layer of Earth. (338)

crystal: a solid having a distinctive shape because its atoms are arranged in repeating patterns. (63)

crystal system: the pattern that atoms form in a crystal.

cyanobacteria: bacteria thought to be one of the earliest life-forms on Earth. (458)

D

data gloves: electronic gloves worn by a person controlling a robot; the gloves sense every movement the person makes and command the robot to perform identical moves. (611)

deflation: erosion caused by wind as it wears away sediments such as clay, silt, and sand. (162)

deforestation: the removal of forests, mostly by people who are clearing land for farming or construction. (275)

delta: a triangular deposit of sediment that occurs when a stream or river slows as it empties into an ocean, gulf, or lake. (150)

density: how tightly packed a substance's molecules are; expressed as the mass of an object divided by its volume, in g/cm^3. (41)

density current: an ocean current that occurs when denser seawater moves toward an area of less dense seawater. (289)

deposition (dep uh ZIHSH un): the dropping of sediments by running water, wind, gravity, or glaciers as their energy of motion decreases. (143)

desertification: the formation of a desert when livestock overgraze an area that receives little rain. (135)

dew point: the temperature at which air becomes saturated with water and condensation begins. (256)

dike: igneous rock that forms when magma is squeezed into a vertical crack and solidifies. (405)

disconformity: a type of unconformity in which the top rock layer is eroded before the next layer can be deposited, causing a gap in the time record.

divergent boundary: in plate tectonics, the boundary between two plates that are diverging, or spreading apart. (350)

doldrums: a zone at the equator where heated air rises vertically, so there appears to be no wind. (246)

Doppler shift: the change in wavelength that occurs in any kind of wave energy (light, radio, sound) as the source of the energy moves toward you (the wavelength shortens) or away from you (the wavelength lengthens).

drainage basin: the land area drained by a river system. (177)

dust bowl: the Great Plains area of the United States in the 1930s, when it was struck by devastating drought and dust storms.

E

Earth: in our solar system, the third planet from the sun; the only planet known to support life. (608)

earthquake: the movement of the ground, caused by waves from energy released as rocks move along faults. (360)

electromagnetic spectrum: the classification of electromagnetic waves, either by wavelength or frequency. (553)

electron: one of the three sub-atomic particles; orbits the atom's nucleus; has a negative electric charge. (31)

element: a substance that contains only one kind of atom; cannot be broken down into simpler substances. (29)

ellipse: an elongated, closed curve; the shape of planetary orbits. (579)

elliptical galaxy: the most common type of galaxy, shaped like a large, three-dimensional ellipse.

endangered: describes a species that has a small number living and thus is in danger of dying out. (454)

energy: the ability to do work. (480)

epicenter: the point on Earth's surface directly above an earthquake's focus. (367)

epochs: subdivisions of periods on the geologic time scale. (449)

equator: an imaginary line that circles Earth halfway between the North and South Poles. (202)

equinox: two times each year that the sun is directly over Earth's equator and the day and night are of equal length, the start of spring or fall. (581)

eras: the four largest subdivisions of the geologic time scale—Precambrian, Paleozoic, Mesozoic, Cenozoic. (449)

erosion (ih ROH zhun): the process that moves weathered rocks from one location to another. (142)

esker: a winding ridge of sand and gravel formed by streams flowing beneath a glacier.

extinct: describes an organism species that no longer lives anywhere on Earth. (426)

extraterrestrial life: life that may exist in the universe outside of Earth. (652)

extrusive igneous rocks: igneous rocks that form when magma extrudes onto Earth's surface and cools as lava. (92)

F

fault: a large fracture in rocks, from several meters to many kilometers long, where rocks not only crack but also move along either side of the break. (360)

fault-block mountains: mountains formed from huge, tilted blocks of rock. (200)

first quarter: the moon phase halfway between new moon and full moon, when half of the side facing Earth is lighted. (585)

fission: the splitting of the nuclei of atoms to release energy. (494)

floodplain: the broad, flat valley floor carved by a meandering stream and often covered with water when the stream floods. (179)

focus: in an earthquake, the point in Earth's interior where movement releases energy to cause the earthquake. (366)

fog: a stratus cloud that forms on or near the ground when air is cooled to its dew point. (257)

folded mountains: mountains created when forces cause rock layers to fold. (199)

foliated: a texture of metamorphic rock, created when mineral grains flatten and line up in parallel bands. (97)

fossil: the remains or traces of a once-living organism; usually preserved in rock. (419)

fossil fuel: a fuel made of the decayed remains of ancient plants and animals; includes coal, oil, and natural gas. (480)

fracture: the physical property of a mineral that causes it to break with rough or jagged edges. (71)

front: in weather systems, the moving boundary between two colliding air masses. (263)

full moon: the moon phase when the side facing Earth is completely lighted, because Earth is between the sun and the moon. (585)

fusion: the process that powers our sun and other stars; hydrogen fusion occurs when great temperatures and pressures fuse hydrogen atoms to form helium atoms and energy is released.

G

galaxy: a massive grouping of gas, dust, and stars in space, held together by gravity. (646)

Galileo: Italian astronomer (1564-1642) who supported a sun-centered solar system by discovering that Venus has phases similar to our moon.

gamma rays: electromagnetic waves having very short wavelengths and high energy.

Ganymede: one of Jupiter's four largest moons; the largest satellite in the solar system.

gasohol: a biomass fuel that is about 90 percent gasoline and 10 percent alcohol; used in cars and trucks.

gem: a mineral highly prized because it is rare and beautiful. (74)

geologic time scale: a chart of Earth's history showing events, time units, and ages. (447)

geology: the study of Earth and its matter, processes, and history. (8)

geothermal energy: thermal energy from the magma underneath volcanoes. (394)

geyser: a hot spring of groundwater that erupts periodically, shooting water and steam into the air. (186)

giant: a late stage in a star's life cycle where the core has contracted and grown hotter, causing its outer layers to expand. (637)

glacier: a moving mass of snow that has compacted into ice and is moving downhill. (154)

Glossopteris (glah SAHP tuhr ihs): a fossil fern providing evidence that continents once were joined.

granitic: light-colored igneous rocks, form from magma rich in silicon and oxygen. (93)

gravitational force: an attractive force that exists between all objects. (19)

Great Red Spot: a giant storm in Jupiter's atmosphere. (613)

greenhouse effect: the process by which heat radiated from Earth's surface is trapped and reflected back to Earth by gases in the atmosphere. (275)

groundwater: water that soaks into the ground and collects in the pore spaces between particles of rock and soil. (182)

Gulf Stream: an ocean current that flows out of the Gulf of Mexico, then northward along the East Coast of the United States, and then toward Europe.

gully erosion: a type of erosion in which water swiftly running down a slope creates large channels in the soil or rock. (149)

habitat: any place where organisms live, grow, and interact. (455)

hachures (ha SHOORZ): lines drawn at right angles to contour lines on a topographic map; they indicate depressions.

half-life: the time it takes for half of the atoms of an isotope in an object to decay. (437)

hardness: a measure of how easily a mineral can be scratched. (69)

hazardous waste: waste that is dangerous to organisms because it is poisonous, cancer causing, or radioactive. (510)

Hess, Harry: a Princeton University scientist who proposed the theory of sea-floor spreading in the 1960s.

high pressure system: an air mass with densely packed air molecules, where cold air descends and rotates clockwise (in the Northern Hemisphere).

Homo erectus: an ancestor of modern *Homo sapiens,* this extinct primate lived in Africa and Asia from 1.7 million to 250 000 years ago. (466)

Homo habilis: the earliest species to have fully human characteristics, this extinct primate evolved from *Australopithecus,* lived in Africa 1.5 to 2 million years ago, and regularly used tools. (466)

Homo sapiens: our modern human species, primates having large brains, use of language, and use of complex tools; evolved from *Homo erectus* about half a million years ago. (466)

horizon: a soil layer; most areas of Earth have three, called the A horizon (topsoil), B horizon, and C horizon. (129)

horn: a sharp mountain peak, pointed like an animal's horn, carved by glaciers.

hot spots: areas in Earth's mantle that are hotter than neighboring areas, forming magma that rises toward the crust. (392)

hot spring: a spring of warm groundwater, caused when the water is heated by rocks that contact magma under Earth's surface. (186)

humidity: the amount of water vapor in the air.

humus: dark-colored organic matter made of decaying plants and animals. (129)

hurricane: a large, swirling, low-pressure system with winds of at least 120 km/hour that forms over tropical oceans. (268)

hydroelectric energy: electricity produced by the energy of running water. (490)

hypothesis: a testable prediction for a problem. (16)

ice wedging: the breaking of rocks when water in cracks freezes and expands. (124)

igneous rock: rock formed from magma or lava when it cools. (90)

impermeable: rock or soil that has very small pores, preventing water from passing through. (183)

index fossil: a fossil of a species that existed briefly and was widespread geographically, used in determining the relative ages of rock layers. (424)

infrared waves: electromagnetic waves that are the heat waves that we feel.

inner core: the solid center of Earth. (336)

inner planets: the four solid, rocky planets closest to the sun—Mercury, Venus, Earth, and Mars. (602)

International Date Line: the 180° meridian, on the other side of Earth from the prime meridian; an imaginary line in the Pacific Ocean where we change calendar days. (205)

International System of Units (SI): the standard worldwide system of measurement; a modern version of the metric system. (18)

intrusive igneous rocks: igneous rocks that form below Earth's surface. (92)

invertebrates: animals without backbones.

ion: an atom with an electric charge. (36)

ionosphere: a high layer of Earth's atmosphere, made up of ions that reflect radio waves. (231)

irregular galaxies: galaxies having irregular shapes.

isobar: on a weather map, a line connecting points of equal atmospheric pressure. (271)

isotherm: on a weather map, a line connecting points of equal temperature. (271)

isotopes: atoms of the same element that have the same number of protons in their nuclei, but different numbers of neutrons. (32)

jet stream: narrow wind belts occurring near the top of the troposphere where trade winds and polar easterlies meet prevailing westerlies. (246)

Jupiter: in our solar system, the fifth planet from the sun; the largest planet, mostly gas and liquid. (612)

Kepler, Johannes: German mathematician (1571-1630) who discovered that the planets travel at different speeds and in orbits around the sun.

L

laccolith: a dome-shaped body of igneous rock created when the magma that forms a sill continues to push the rock layers upward. (405)

land breeze: wind blowing from land to sea at night because the land cools faster and cool air over the land flows over the sea. (248)

landfill: an area of land that is excavated and filled with waste. (510)

landforms: features that make up the shape of the land at Earth's surface, such as plains, plateaus, and mountains.

latitude: a distance north or south of the equator, expressed in degrees. (203)

lava: molten rock from a volcano flowing on Earth's surface. (91)

law: a "rule of nature" that describes the behavior of something in nature. (17)

law of superposition: a law stating that, in layers of undisturbed rock, the oldest are on the bottom, and rocks become younger toward the top. (430)

leaching: when minerals are dissolved in water and carried down through a soil profile. (131)

legend: a list of symbols used on a map that explains their meaning.

light pollution: the glow in the night sky caused by city lights. (558)

light-year: a unit used to measure distance in space; the distance that light travels in one year (about 10 trillion km). (631)

lignite: soft, brown coal that is about 30 percent carbon; smoky and polluting when burned. (481)

lithosphere (LITH uh sfihr): the rigid, outermost layer of Earth, about 100 km thick and including the crust and part of the mantle. (349)

Local Group: the cluster of about 25 galaxies that includes our galaxy (the Milky Way).

loess (LES): a thick deposit of very fine, wind-eroded sediments. (164)

longitude: a distance east or west of the prime meridian, expressed in degrees. (203)

longshore current: an ocean current that runs parallel to the shore, caused by waves hitting the shore at a slight angle. (307)

low pressure system: in weather systems, an area where warm air rises and rotates counterclockwise (in the Northern Hemisphere).

lunar eclipse: the passing of Earth between the sun and moon, so that Earth blocks sunlight from reaching all or part of the moon. (588)

luster: the physical property of a mineral that describes how light is reflected from its surface. (70)

magma: molten rock beneath Earth's surface. (64)

magnetometer: an instrument that measures the strength of Earth's magnetic field. (346)

magnitude: in earthquake studies, a measure of the energy released by an earthquake; the Richter scale is used to describe earthquake magnitude. (375)

main sequence: on a Hertzsprung-Russell diagram, the diagonal band that includes 90 percent of all stars. (634)

mammals: warm-blooded vertebrates.

mantle: the thickest layer inside Earth; it lies between the outer core and the crust and is solid. (337)

map scale: the relationship between the distances drawn on a map and actual distances on Earth. (210)

maria: dark, flat regions of ancient lava on the moon; viewed from Earth, they resemble oceans, the Latin word for which is *maria*. (589)

market: the people or businesses that want to purchase a product. (517)

Mars: in our solar system, the fourth planet from the sun. (608)

mass: the amount of matter in an object; SI unit is the gram. (18)

mass movement: the sliding of a volume of loose material down a slope, caused by gravity.

mass number: the sum of the protons and neutrons in the nucleus of each atom of an element.

matter: anything that takes up space and has mass. (28)

meander: a curve in a mature stream. (179)

mechanical weathering: the breaking up of rocks without changing their chemical composition. (123)

Mercator (mur KAYT ur) **projection:** a map projection method using parallel longitude lines; continent shapes are accurate, but areas are distorted. (207)

Mercury: in our solar system, the first planet from the sun; the second-smallest planet, it has a cratered surface like our moon. (606)

Mesosaurus (mes oh SAR uhs): a fossil reptile found in both South America and Africa, providing evidence that these continents once were joined.

Mesozoic (mez uh ZOH ihk) **Era:** the middle era of Earth's geologic history; spans 225-65 million years ago. (462)

metallic luster: the physical property of any mineral that has a shiny appearance resembling metal.

metamorphic rock: rock formed from existing rock when the temperature or pressure changes. (95)

meteor: a meteoroid that enters Earth's atmosphere and burns up as it falls. (620)

meteorite: a meteor that reaches Earth's surface. (621)

meteoroid: small pieces of rock that orbit the sun, resulting from the breakup of comets.

meteorologist: a scientist who studies weather conditions, draws weather maps, forecasts weather, and warns of severe weather. (270)

meteorology: the study of Earth's atmosphere, its processes, and weather. (8)

microwaves: electromagnetic waves that are shorter than radio waves, but longer than light waves; we use them for radar and transmitting voice, music, video, and data.

mid-ocean ridge: an underwater mountain range that extends through the middle of most oceans, formed when forces within Earth spread the seafloor apart, causing it to buckle. (313)

mineral: a naturally occurring, nonliving solid with a definite structure and chemical composition. (62)

mixture: a combination of different substances that keep their own physical and chemical properties despite being mixed. (36)

Moho discontinuity: the boundary between Earth's crust and the upper mantle; seismic waves travel slower above the Moho and faster below it. (370)

Mohs' Scale of Hardness: a list of common minerals and their hardnesses, developed by German mineralogist Friedrich Mohs.

mold: a cavity in a rock that has the shape of a fossil that was trapped there; water dissolved the fossil away, leaving its imprint. (421)

molecule: the smallest particle of a compound that still keeps all the properties of the compound; it is made of atoms. (34)

moon colony: a permanent structure on the moon in which people could live and work. (592)

moon phases: the changes in appearance of the moon as it orbits Earth every 29-1/2 days; for example, full moon and new moon. (585)

moraine: a ridge of rock and soil bulldozed ahead of a glacier and along its sides; left behind when the glacier melts.

N

natural gas: a mixture of gases formed as ancient plants and animals decayed; burned as a fossil fuel.

natural selection: the natural process by which some organisms survive and reproduce because they have traits favorable to survival in an environment, while others die out because they lack those traits. (450)

neap tide: a tide that is lower than normal because the sun, Earth, and moon form a right angle.

nebula: a large cloud of gas and dust in space that is the beginning of a star. (637)

nekton (NEK tuhn): sea-dwelling animals that swim, such as fish, turtles, whales, and seals. (319)

Neptune: in our solar system, the eighth planet from the sun; it is large and gaseous. (615)

neutron: one of the two particles that make up the nucleus of an atom; it has no electric charge. (31)

neutron star: the final stage in the life cycle of some stars, where the core collapses and becomes so dense that only neutrons can exist there. (638)

new moon: the moon phase when the side facing Earth is completely dark, because the moon is between Earth and the sun. (585)

nonfoliated: a texture of metamorphic rock, created when mineral grains change, grow, and rearrange but don't form bands. (97)

nonmetallic luster: a physical property of a mineral that does not resemble metal.

nonrenewable energy resources: energy resources (coal, oil, and natural gas) that we are using up faster than natural processes can replace them. (483)

normal fault: a pull-apart (tension) fracture in rocks, where rocks that are above the fault surface drop downward in relation to rocks that are below the fault surface, like this: $\leftarrow_{normal}/^{fault}\rightarrow$. (361)

nuclear energy: energy produced by the fission (splitting) of the nuclei of uranium atoms. (494)

nuclear reactor: a device in which uranium atoms fission to release energy, used to generate electricity.

O

observatory: a building that contains a telescope for observing objects in space. (554)

occluded front: in weather systems, the boundary that results when two cool air masses merge and force warmer air to rise between them.

oceanography: the study of Earth's oceans, their processes, and life within them. (9)

ocean trench: a deep trench in the ocean, caused when one piece of seafloor is pushed beneath another piece. (314)

oil: a liquid formed as ancient plants and animals decay; burned as a fossil fuel and used to make lubricants and plastics.

old stream: a stream that flows very slowly down a gradual slope, through a broad floodplain that it has made, often meandering.

Olympus Mons: the largest volcano in the solar system—on Mars.

Oort Cloud: a cloud of comets surrounding the solar system outside Pluto's orbit; it may be the source of most comets. (619)

orbit: the curved path followed by a satellite as it travels around a star, planet, or other object. (561)

ore: minerals or rocks that contain a useful substance, such as a metal, that can be mined at a profit. (75)

organic evolution: the gradual change in life-forms through time. (449)

organic matter: any material that originated as plant or animal tissue; decaying animals or plants that become sediment and a part of soils.

outer core: a liquid layer of Earth's core that surrounds the solid inner core. (337)

outer planets: the five planets farthest from the sun—Jupiter, Saturn, Uranus, Neptune, and Pluto. (602)

outwash: a glacial deposit left by streams flowing from a melting glacier. (159)

overgrazing: occurs when too many livestock graze too small an area and eat all the grass off the land.

oxidation: chemical weathering that occurs when a substance is exposed to oxygen and water. (126)

ozone layer: a layer of the stratosphere that contains ozone; absorbs ultraviolet radiation from the sun. (236)

P

Pacific Ring of Fire: the area around the Pacific tectonic plate where volcanoes and earthquakes are common due to tectonic movement. (391)

Paleozoic (pay lee uh ZOH ihk) Era: the second-oldest era of Earth's geologic history; began when organisms developed hard parts; spans 570 to 225 million years ago. (458)

Pangaea (pan JEE uh): the name Alfred Wegener gave to the landmass that he believed existed before it split apart to form the present continents. (340)

parallax: the apparent shift in position of an object when viewed from two different points, such as your left eye and right eye. (631)

peat: a low-grade, smoky fossil fuel made of decaying plants; the first stage in the development of coal. (481)

pebble: a sediment particle measuring 2.0 mm to 64 mm in size.

penumbra: during an eclipse, the lighter outer portion of the shadow.

periods: subdivisions of eras on the geologic time scale. (449)

permeable: describes rock or soil that has connecting pores that allow water to pass through easily. (183)

petrified remains: plant or animal remains that have been petrified, or "turned to rock"; this happens when minerals carried in groundwater replace the original materials. (420)

photochemical smog: a brown-colored air pollution that forms when sunlight chemically changes the pollutants released by burning fossil fuels. (524)

photosphere: the innermost of the three layers of the sun's atmosphere; radiates the light we see. (643)

photosynthesis (foh toh SIHN thuh sihs): the process that plants use to make food, using light energy and oxygen. (318)

pH scale: a number scale used to describe how acidic or how basic a solution is; an abbreviation of *p*otential of *H*ydrogen. (526)

physical properties: characteristics of an element or compound that affect weight, color, density, and such, but don't affect how it will react with other elements or compounds. (40)

plain: a landform that is a large, relatively flat area. (196)

plankton (PLANK tuhn): plants and animals that drift in seawater; most are microscopic. (319)

plateau: a landform created when forces within Earth raise a flat area of nearly horizontal rocks. (198)

plates: in plate tectonics, sections of Earth's lithosphere (crust and upper mantle). (348)

plate tectonics: the theory that Earth's crust and upper mantle (lithosphere) exist in sections called plates and that these plates slowly move around on the mantle. (348)

plucking: a type of glacial erosion in which rock fragments from sand size to boulders are broken off and carried by the glacier. (156)

Pluto: in our solar system, the ninth and last planet from the sun. (616)

polar easterlies: winds caused by cold polar air. (246)

pollutants: substances that cause harmful changes in the environment; they are produced by both human activities and natural processes.

pollution: the addition of harmful substances to an environment. (322)

population: the number of individuals of a particular species that exists in a specific area. (502)

population explosion: a large increase in the population of a species, due to a rapid reproduction, or a sharply reduced death rate, or both. (503)

Precambrian (pree KAM bree un) Era: the oldest and longest era of geologic time, including about 90 percent of Earth's history; spans 4.6 billion to 570 million years ago. (457)

precipitation: water or ice that condenses in the air and falls to the ground as rain, snow, sleet, or hail. (259)

prevailing westerlies: winds between 30° and 60° north and south of the equator that blow opposite to the trade winds and cause much of our weather. (246)

primary waves: waves of energy, released during an earthquake, that travel through Earth by compressing particles in rocks in the same direction the wave is traveling. (367)

prime meridian: an imaginary line running from the North Pole to the South Pole, passing through Greenwich, England; the 0° reference line for longitude. (203)

Project Apollo: a project of the U.S. space program in which astronauts first traveled to the moon in the spacecraft *Apollo 11*. (564)

Project Gemini: an early project of the U.S. space program in which two crewed *Gemini* spacecraft successfully linked in orbit. (563)

Project Mercury: an early project of the U.S. space program in which a crewed spacecraft orbited Earth and returned safely. (563)

prominence: a huge, arching column of gas extending above the sun's surface; associated with sunspots.

proton: one of the two particles that make up the nucleus of an atom; it has a positive electric charge. (31)

psychrometer (si KRAH muh tur): a device used by meteorologists to measure relative humidity.

R

radiation: the transfer of energy by electromagnetic waves that can travel through space and some materials. (239)

radioactive decay: the decay of an atom of one element to form another element, occurring when an alpha particle or beta particle is expelled from the original atom. (437)

radiometric dating: an absolute dating method that uses the rate of decay of radioactive isotopes in rocks. (438)

radio telescope: an instrument that uses a large antenna to gather radio waves from space, for use in studying space objects and communicating with artificial satellites and probes. (554)

radio waves: electromagnetic waves having long wavelengths; we use them to transmit voice, music, video, and data over distances.

recyclable: describes a product that can be reprocessed into the same product or a similar one; for example, an aluminum can might be recycled to make other aluminum cans or foil. (516)

red shift: a kind of Doppler shift in which light from a star that is moving away from us has its wavelength shifted toward the red end of the spectrum.

reef: in the ocean, a large underwater colony of coral animals that have become cemented together. (321)

reflecting telescope: an optical instrument that uses a concave mirror, a flat mirror, and a convex lens to magnify distant objects. (554)

refracting telescope: an optical instrument that uses two convex lenses to magnify distant objects. (554)

relative dating: determining the order of events and the relative age of rocks (older or younger) by examining the positions of rocks in layers. (431)

relative humidity: the amount of water vapor actually in the air, compared to the maximum it can hold; it varies with temperature and is between 0 percent and 100 percent. (256)

renewable energy resources: energy resources (sun, wind, and water power) that are constantly being replenished. (486)

reptiles: vertebrate animals having dry, scaly skin that prevents loss of body fluids so they can survive out of the water on dry land. (460)

respiration (res pur AY shun): the process used by all organisms to combine oxygen with food so that the energy in food can be used. (318)

reverse fault: a compression fracture in rocks, where rocks that are above the fault surface are forced up over rocks that are below the fault surface, like this: $\rightarrow^{reverse}/_{fault}\leftarrow$. (362)

revolution: the orbiting of one object around another, like Earth revolving around the sun. (579)

Richter (RIHK tur) **scale:** describes how much energy is released by an earthquake.

rift zone: an area in the middle of some oceans that contains a system of cracks where the seafloor is rifting, or spreading apart. (313)

rill erosion: a type of erosion in which water swiftly running down a slope creates small channels in the soil; these channels can enlarge into gullies. (149)

Robinson projection: a map projection method using curved longitude lines; continent shapes and land areas are accurate, with little distortion. (207)

rock: Earth material made of one or more minerals. (87)

rock cycle: the processes by which, over many years, Earth materials change back and forth among magma, igneous rocks, sedimentary rocks, and metamorphic rocks. (87)

rock-forming minerals: a group of minerals that make up most of the rocks in Earth's crust.

rotation: the spinning of an object around its axis. (577)

runoff: water that neither soaks into the ground nor evaporates, but instead flows across Earth's surface and eventually into streams, lakes, or oceans. (174)

S

Safe Drinking Water Act: this 1986 law sets safety standards for drinking water in the U.S. (536)

salinity: a measure of the amount of solids (mostly salts) dissolved in seawater. (284)

salt marsh: a saltwater marsh by the ocean that is a breeding ground for many ocean organisms. (300)

sand: a sediment particle measuring 0.06 mm to 2.0 mm in size.

sanitary landfill: a waste-disposal area that is excavated, lined with leakproof material, and filled with layers of waste and dirt. (510)

satellite: any object that revolves around another object; planets and human-made satellites are examples. (560)

saturated (SACH uh rayt id): condition when all the spaces in a solid, liquid, or gas are filled with another substance: air is saturated with water when the relative humidity is 100 percent; a saltwater solution is saturated when it can dissolve no more salt; a rock or soil is saturated with water when it can hold no more. (256)

Saturn: in our solar system, the sixth planet from the sun; it is the second-largest planet, is mostly gas and liquid, and has prominent rings. (613)

science: the process of observing, explaining, and understanding our world; means "having knowledge." (7)

scientific methods: the problem-solving procedures used by scientists that may or may not include the following basic steps: define the problem, make a hypothesis, test the hypothesis, analyze the results, and draw conclusions. (16)

scrubber: a device that "scrubs" the exhaust from coal-burning power plants to reduce the amount of sulfur gases released into the air. (531)

Sea Beam: a system of 16 sonar (sound echo) devices on a ship to measure the depth of the seafloor. (215)

sea breeze: wind blowing from sea to land during the day when the sun warms the land faster and cool air from above the water forces the warm air above the land to rise. (247)

sea-floor spreading: the theory that magma from Earth's mantle rises to the surface at the mid-ocean ridge and cools to form new seafloor, which new magma slowly pushes away from the ridge. (344)

seamount: an underwater volcano.

secondary waves: waves of energy, released during an earthquake, that travel through Earth by moving particles in rocks at right angles to the direction the wave is traveling. (367)

sediment: loose materials such as rock fragments and mineral grains that have been transported by wind, water, or glaciers. (100)

sedimentary rock: rock formed when sediments become pressed or cemented together. (100)

seismic-safe: describes structures that are resistant to movements from an earthquake. (380)

seismic waves: the energy waves that make the ground quake during an earthquake. (366)

seismograph: an instrument that records earthquake waves. (375)

seismologist: a scientist who studies earthquakes and seismic waves. (375)

shadow zone: the area where seismic waves cannot reach because Earth's liquid outer core bends primary waves and stops secondary waves.

shearing forces: along strike-slip faults, forces that push on rocks from various directions, causing them to twist and break.

sheet erosion: a type of erosion in which water flowing over a gentle slope slowly removes sediment from the entire surface. (149)

shield volcano: a broad volcano with gently sloping sides, built by quiet eruptions of runny basaltic lava, which spreads out in flat layers; example: the Hawaiian Islands. (399)

shore zone: the land area at the ocean's edge between high tide and low tide. (306)

silicate: a mineral containing silicon and oxygen (often with other elements); the largest group of minerals. (66)

sill: a small body of igneous rock that forms when magma is squeezed into a horizontal crack and then solidifies. (405)

silt: a sediment particle measuring 0.004 mm to 0.06 mm in size.

sinkhole: a depression in the ground caused when groundwater dissolves limestone beneath the hole, causing the ground to collapse.

slump: a type of mass movement in which loose material slowly moves downhill a short distance, leaving a curved scar. (144)

smog: air pollution seen around cities, resulting from burning fossil fuels.

soil: a mixture of weathered rock and decaying organic matter (plants and animals). (128)

soil profile: a vertical section of soil layers (horizons). (129)

solar cell: a device that collects solar energy and converts it into electricity. (488)

solar eclipse: the passing of the moon directly between Earth and the sun, so that the moon blocks sunlight from reaching Earth. (587)

solar energy: energy from the sun. (488)

solar flare: an intense bright spot in the sun's chromosphere, associated with sunspots and radio interference on Earth.

solar system: a system of nine planets and many other objects that orbit our sun. (601)

solstice: the two times each year that Earth's tilt makes the sun reach its greatest angle north or south of the equator, marking the start of summer or winter. (582)

solution: a mixture of different substances, occurring without chemical reaction. Usually one substance is dissolved in another.

sonar: the use of sound wave echoes to detect the size and shape of structures found under water. (215)

space probe: an instrument that travels through space to probe for information and transmit it back to Earth. (561)

space shuttle: a reusable spacecraft that transports astronauts, satellites, and other material between Earth and space. (568)

space station: a facility in space with living quarters, workspace, and its own environmental control and power generation equipment. (569)

species: a group of organisms that are similar to each other and that typically reproduce only with each other. (449)

sphere: a round, three-dimensional object whose surface at all points is the same distance from its center. (576)

spiral galaxy: a galaxy having spiral arms.

spring: the point at which the water table meets Earth's surface, causing water to flow from the ground. (184)

spring tide: a tide level greater than normal because the moon, Earth, and sun are aligned.

stalactite: an icicle-like deposit of calcite hanging from the ceiling of a cave.

stationary front: in weather systems, a warm front or cold front that has stopped moving.

station model: in weather forecasting, a group of meteorological symbols that depict weather information for a location on a weather map. (271)

streak: the color of a mineral when it is powdered, usually observed by rubbing the mineral on a ceramic streak plate. (70)

striations (stri AY shunz): long, parallel scars in rocks, caused by rock fragments being dragged across them, often by a glacier.

strike-slip fault: a break in rocks where rocks on either side of the fault move past each other (instead of above or below each other). (363)

strip mine: mine in which resources such as coal or iron ore are removed by digging at Earth's surface, instead of through underground tunnels. (108)

subduction zone: in plate tectonics, a boundary where an ocean plate collides with a continental plate, and the denser ocean plate slides beneath the less-dense continental plate. (350)

sulfurous smog: a gray-colored air pollution created when power plants and home furnaces burn fossil fuels, releasing sulfur compounds and smoke particles. (525)

sunspot: a dark spot on the sun's surface that shows up because it is cooler than surrounding areas. (643)

superconductor: a material that allows electricity to pass through it without resistance. (48)

supergiant: a late stage in the life cycle of a very large star, when the core reaches high temperatures, heavy elements form by fusion, and the star's outer layers expand. (638)

supernova: a late stage in the life cycle of some stars where the core collapses, causing the outer portion to explode.

surface current: an ocean current found in the upper few hundred meters of seawater. (288)

surface waves: waves of energy, released during an earthquake, that reach Earth's surface and travel outward from the epicenter in all directions. (367)

synfuel: a human-made energy source, usually involving conversion of a fossil fuel into a different form (*synthetic + fuel*). (491)

T

technology: the useful application of scientific knowledge. (10)

temperate zones: the two areas of moderate, seasonal weather that exist between the tropics and the polar regions. (272)

tension: stretching forces that can be strong enough to pull rocks apart at divergent plate boundaries.

tephra: lava that is blasted into the air by violent volcanic eruptions and solidifies as it falls to the ground as ash, cinders, and volcanic bombs. (399)

terraces: broad, steplike cuts in the side of a slope. (152)

theory: an explanation backed by results from repeated tests, experiments, or observations. (17)

thermal pollution: the addition of heat to a lake, stream, or ocean by power plants and other industries, which kills organisms that cannot quickly adapt to the warmer water. (324)

third quarter: the moon phase halfway between full moon and new moon, when half of the side facing Earth is lighted. (586)

tidal energy: electricity generated by the ocean tides.

tidal range: the vertical distance between high tide and low tide. (294)

tide: the periodic change in the surface level of the oceans due to the gravitational force of the sun and moon on Earth. (294)

till: a mixture of boulders, sand, silt, and clay left by a melting glacier. (159)

Titan: Saturn's largest moon.

topographic map: a map that uses contour lines to show the varying elevations of Earth's surface. (208)

topsoil: the top layer of soil, also called the A horizon; usually contains humus and is dark in color.

tornado: a small, violent, whirling, funnel-shaped, low pressure windstorm that moves in a narrow path over land. (266)

trace fossils: footprints, worm holes, burrows, and other traces of animal activity preserved in rock.

trade winds: steady winds, about 15° north and south of the equator, caused by cool descending air. (246)

transform fault: in plate tectonics, a boundary between two plates that are sliding past one another. (352)

trilobites (TRI luh bites): shield-shaped marine invertebrate animals commonly found as fossils in Paleozoic Era rocks but are now extinct.

Triton: Neptune's largest moon.

troposphere: the lowest layer of Earth's atmosphere, in which we live, and where clouds and weather occur. (231)

trough: the lowest part of a wave. (292)

tsunami (soo NAHM ee): an ocean wave caused by an earthquake. (377)

turbine: a machine with fan blades that spin when water or air pushes on them; it turns a generator to produce electricity. (299)

U

ultraviolet radiation: a type of energy that comes to Earth from the sun and is mostly absorbed in the ozone layer. (236)

ultraviolet waves: electromagnetic waves that are a little shorter than light waves; they cause sunburn and skin cancer.

umbra: during an eclipse, the darker central portion of the shadow

unconformity: one or more missing layers in a sequence of rocks; this causes a gap in the time record. (432)

uniformitarianism: a basic principle of geology stating that Earth processes occurring today are similar to those that occurred in the past. (439)

upwarped mountains: landforms created when forces within Earth push up the crust. (200)

upwelling: the rising of cold, nutrient-rich water from deep in the ocean to the surface. (291)

Uranus: in our solar system, the seventh planet from the sun; it is large, gaseous, and is the only planet that "lays on its side" in orbit. (614)

Valles Marineris: a huge rift on Mars that is more than 4000 km long.

valley glacier: the commonest type of glacier, occurring locally in mountain valleys where the average temperature allows snow to accumulate faster than it can melt.

variable: in an experiment, the factor that you change to see what will happen. (17)

vent: in volcanic regions, an opening in Earth's surface through which flow lava, ash, and steam. (389)

Venus: in our solar system, the second planet from the sun; it is very similar in size to Earth, is blanketed with dense clouds, and is very hot. (607)

vertebrates: animals with backbones; evolved during the Ordovician Period.

visible light: electromagnetic waves having short wavelengths; the only part of the electromagnetic spectrum that we can see.

volcanic mountains: mountains created when magma within Earth escapes to the surface, building cones of lava and ash. (201)

volcanic neck: the core of a volcano's vent that remains after the outer layers of lava and tephra have been eroded away from an extinct volcano. (405)

volcano: a mountain built of lava and volcanic ash, which erupt from a vent over rising magma. (388)

volume: the amount of space occupied by an object; SI unit is the cubic meter (m³).

waning: describes the moon as its visible lighted area grows smaller during the lunar cycle. (586)

waning crescent: the shrinking slice of lighted moon when the visible lighted area is decreasing from third quarter to new moon.

waning gibbous: the shrinking area of moon as the visible lighted area is decreasing from full moon to third quarter.

warm front: the moving boundary that develops when a warm air mass meets a cold air mass.

water cycle: the continual worldwide movement of water evaporating from the ocean into the atmosphere as water vapor, then to the ground as precipitation, and then back into the ocean through runoff. (173)

water diversion: changing the natural flow of water to another location by using dams, canals, or pipelines. (189)

water table: the top of the zone of saturation (the area where all of the pores in a rock are completely filled with water). (183)

wave height: the vertical distance between the crest and trough of a wave. (292)

wavelength: the distance between a point on one wave and the identical point on the next wave; for example, the distance between two crests. (292)

waxing: describes the moon as its visible lighted area grows larger during the lunar cycle. (585)

waxing crescent: the growing slice of moon when the visible lighted area is increasing from new moon to first quarter.

waxing gibbous: the growing area of visible lighted moon as the lighted area is increasing from first quarter to full moon.

weather: the behavior of the atmosphere—wind, temperature, pressure, precipitation—at a particular place and time. (254)

weathering: the breaking of rocks into smaller pieces, either mechanically or chemically. (123)

Wegener, Alfred: a German scientist who proposed the idea of continental drift in 1915.

weight: a measure of the force of gravity on an object. (19)

white dwarf: a late stage in a star's life cycle where its core runs out of fuel and its unstable outer layers escape into space, leaving the white-hot core. (638)

wind farm: a place having steady winds where windmills are installed to generate electricity. (490)

X rays: electromagnetic waves having very short wavelengths; they can penetrate many materials; we use them to see inside our bodies and some materials.

young stream: a stream that flows swiftly down a steep slope or a valley with steep sides, causing rapid erosion.

zone of saturation: an area where all the pores in a rock are completely filled with water, usually near the ground surface. (183)

The Index for *Merrill Earth Science* will help you locate major topics in the book quickly and easily. Each entry in the index is followed by the numbers of the pages on which the entry is discussed. A page number given in **boldface type** indicates the page on which that entry is defined. A page number given in *italic type* indicates a page on which the entry is used in an illustration or photograph. The abbreviation *act.* indicates a page on which the entry is used in an Activity.

PHOTO CREDITS

Cover, Galen Rowell/Mountain Light; **iv**, Tim Courlas; **v**, (l) Smithsonian Institution, (r) Jack S. Grove/Tom Stack & Associates; **vi**, (t) courtesy GeoGraphix, Inc., (b) Floyd Holdman/The Stock Solution; **vii**, (t) Studiohio, (b) Science Source/Photo Researchers; **viii**, (t) Studiohio, (b) courtesy Dr. Adam Dziewonski, Harvard University; **ix**, © Chip Clark; **x**, (t) Tim Courlas, (b) Studiohio; **xi**, (l) NASA, (r) Studiohio; **xii**, NASA; **xiii**, Doug Martin; **xv**, Tim Courlas; **xvi**, (t) Elaine Comer Shay, (b) Doug Martin; **xviii**, Studiohio; **xx**, Doug Martin; **2-3**, Steve Lissau; **4**, Tom Sanders/Adventure Photo; **5**, Kenji Kerins; **6**, Tim Courlas; **7**, (t) Hickson-Bender Photography, (bl) A. B. Dowsett/Science Photo Library/Photo Researchers, (br) Tim Courlas; **8**, (t) Krafft/Explorer/Photo Researchers, (b) Dan McCoy from Rainbow; **10**, (l) Hickson & Associates, (r) Milepost Corporation; **11**, (t) Merrill photo, (b) Tim Courlas; **12**, Bob Daemmrich Photography; **13**, Todd Powell/ProFiles West; **14, 16, 18**, Milepost Corporation; **19**, Hickson & Associates; **20**, (l) Milepost Corporation, (r) Doug Martin; **21**, Tim Courlas; **22**, Doug Martin; **25**, First Image; **26**, Milepost Corporation; **27**, Studiohio; **28**, Steve Lissau; **29**, Studiohio; **30**, (brc) Kenji Kerins, (others) Doug Martin; **31**, Animals Animals/Donald Specker; **32**, Studiohio; **33, 34**, Tim Courlas; **35**, courtesy IBM Corporation; **36**, First Image; **37**, Doug Martin; **38**, First Image; **40**, (l) Studiohio, (r) Tim Courlas; **41**, Gary Braasch/Woodfin Camp & Associates; **42, 43**, Studiohio; **44**, (t) Doug Martin, (b) Gary Ladd; **45**, Cameramann Internat'l. Ltd./The Image Works; **46**, Larry Ulrich/DRK Photo; **47**, NASA; **48**, Rich Brommer; **49**, Runk/Schoenberger from Grant Heilman; **52**, Hickson-Bender Photography; **54**, (t) Center for Astrophysics/Harvard-Smithsonian Astrophysical Laboratory, (b) courtesy Dr. Julian G. Rosenmann, Department of Radiation Oncology, University of North Carolina at Chapel Hill; **55**, (l) David Parker/Science Photo Library/Photo Researchers, (c) courtesy Bridgestone Corporation, Japan, (b) Allen Russell/ProFiles West; **56**, (tl, br) Doug Martin, (tr) Kenji Kerins, (bl) courtesy Corning Glass; **57**, "Nora, 1979," © David Em/Represented by Spieckerman Associates, San Francisco; **58-59**, Karen Kasmauski/Woodfin Camp & Associates, (inset) NASA; **60**, courtesy Akzo Salt, Inc.; **61**, Studiohio; **62**, (t) file photo, (others) Studiohio; **63, 64, 65, 67**, Doug Martin; **68**, (tl) Roger K. Burnard, (trc) Smithsonian Institution, (others) Craig Kramer; **69, 70**, Doug Martin; **71**, (t) First Image, (b) Doug Martin; **72**, Craig Kramer; **73**, Doug Martin; **74**, (l, r) Ward's Natural Science, (rc) Field Museum of Natural History, (lc) D.C.H. Plowes; **75**, (t) E. Alan McGee/FPG, (bl) Doug Martin, (br) Studiohio; **76**, courtesy Dr. Andrzej Badzian, Pennsylvania State University; **77**, Paolo Koch/Photo Researchers; **78**, (t) Craig Kramer, (b) Bob Daemmrich/The Image Works; **79**, Gold Information Center; **80**, John Chiasson/Gamma-Liaison; **82**, Elaine Comer Shay; **84**, P. & G. Bowater/The Image Bank; **85**, Studiohio; **86**, (b) Linda Young, (others) Doug Martin; **87, 88, 90, 91**, Doug Martin; **92**, (t) Doug Martin, (b) Soames Summerhays/Photo Researchers; **94**, (l) Doug Martin, (r) Earth Scenes/Breck P. Kent; **95**, Doug Martin; **96**, Michael Kreisler Photography, Fairfield, IA/courtesy Granitech Corp.; **97**, (l) Phil Degginger/Color-Pic, Inc., (r) Earth Scenes/E. R. Degginger; **98**, Alpha/FPG; **99, 100**, Doug Martin; **102**, G. R. Roberts; **103**, (t) Craig Kramer, (b) Tim Cairns; **104**, (t) Elaine Comer Shay, (b) Tom Bean; **105**, Aaron Haupt; **106**, (l) Studiohio, (r) Kevin Schafer/Tom Stack & Associates; **108**, Chris Niedenthal/Black Star; **110**, ODNR, Division of Reclamation; **113**, Ward's Natural Science; **114**, (t) Merrill photo, (b) Kennecott Explorations; **115**, (t) Tracy I. Borland, (b) Giraudon/Art Resource; **116**, (tl) Kenji Kerins, (tr) Hickson & Associates, (b) Doug Martin; **117**, SuperStock; **118-119**, Tom Bean, (inset) G. R. Roberts; **120**, Jack S. Grove/Tom Stack & Associates; **121**, Studiohio; **122**, (l) Bill Ross/Woodfin Camp & Associates, (r) Dale Jorgenson/Tom Stack & Associates; **123**, Studiohio; **124**, Bud Fowle; **125**, Doug Martin; **126**, Tom Bean; **127**, Weldon King/FPG; **129**, Studiohio; **130**, Doug Martin; **131**, William E. Ferguson; **132**, (t) Tim Courlas, (b) Doug Martin; **133**, (l) file photo, (r) Larry Koons; **134**, (tl) Studiohio, (tc) Tim Cairns, (tr) Tom Hollyman/Photo Researchers, (b) Studiohio; **135**, Library of Congress; **136**, Kenneth W. Fink/Photo Researchers; **138**, Studiohio; **140**, Ron Thomas/FPG; **141**, Studiohio; **142**, Grant Heilman from Grant Heilman Photography; **143**, Studiohio; **144**, Thomas G. Rampton from Grant Heilman; **146**, Lawrence S. Burr/Sygma; **147**, Curt Schieber; **149**, Tom Till/DRK Photo; **151**, NASA; **153**, SuperStock; **155**, (l) Wolfgang Kaehler, (r) Roger K. Burnard; **156**, Thomas Kitchin/Tom Stack & Associates; **157**, James Westwater; **158**, William D. Popejoy; **160**, John Barger; **161**, Doug Martin; **162**, (l) Debbie Dean, (r) Earth Scenes/M. J. Coe; **163**, Floyd Holdman/The Stock Solution; **164**, Michael Collier; **165**, Steve Lissau; **166**, Doug Martin; **168**, Studiohio; **170**, Doug Lee/Tom Stack & Associates; **171**, Studiohio; **172**, NASA; **174**, (l) Doug Martin, (r) Lindsay Gerard/Merrill; **175**, Grant Heilman Photography; **176**, Larry Hamill; **178**, (t) Pictures Unlimited, (b) First Image; **179**, Larry Hamill; **180**, Doug Martin; **181**, Wendy Shattil & Bob Rozinski/Tom Stack & Associates; **182**, Studiohio; **185**, Doug Martin; **187**, (l) M. Timothy O'Keefe/Tom Stack & Associates, (r) Steve Lissau; **188**, Tim Cairns; **189**, (t) Byron Augustin/Tom Stack & Associates, (b) Len Rue Jr./DRK Photo; **190**, (l) Gary Milburn/Tom Stack & Associates, (r) Joe Sohn/The Image Works; **194**, NASA; **195**, Studiohio; **196**, Wayne Lynch/DRK Photo; **198**, Peter French/DRK Photo; **199**, Earth Scenes/Jim Tuten; **200**, (t) Tom Till/DRK Photo, (b) Robert Frerck/Woodfin Camp & Associates; **201**, Michael Giannechini/Photo Researchers; **208**, USGS; **209**, courtesy of GeoGraphix, Inc.; **211, 212**, USGS; **213**, Doug Martin; **214**, NOAA; **216**, Doug Martin; **220**, (t) Allen Russell/ProFiles West, (b) David M. Dennis; **221**, (t) Ed Nagele/FPG, (b) NASA; **222**, (tl) Bob Daemmrich Photography, (tr) David R. Frazier/The Stock Solution, (bl) Studiohio, (br) Doug Martin; **223**, Mark E. Gibson; **224-225**, NASA/Science Source/Photo Researchers, (inset) Walter Stricklin/Stock South; **226**, SuperStock; **227**, Mary Lou Uttermohlen; **228**, Morgan Photos; **229**, Tony Freeman/PhotoEdit; **233**, Doug Martin; **240**, Earth Scenes/Doug Wechsler; **243**, Doug Martin; **251**, Studiohio; **252**, A. & J. Verkaik/The Stock Market; **253**, Mary Lou Uttermohlen; **254**, Robert Brenner/PhotoEdit; **256**, (t) Mary Lou Uttermohlen, (b) Doug Martin; **257**, SuperStock; **258**, (l to r, t to b) file photo, William D. Popejoy, Betty Crowell, David M. Dennis, Betty Crowell, William Tucker/Uniphoto, Betty Crowell, James Fullmer, David R. Frazier, David M. Dennis; **259, 261**, Doug Martin; **265**, Keith Kent/Science Photo Library/Photo Researchers; **266**, Larry Miller/Photo Researchers; **267**, NOAA; **269**, SuperStock; **271**, Bill Bachman/Photo Researchers; **275**, Jacques Jangoux/Peter Arnold, Inc.; **278, 279**, Science Source/Photo Researchers; **280**, Brian Parker/Tom Stack & Associates; **281**, Doug Martin; **282**, (l) Steve Ogden/Tom Stack & Associates, (r) SuperStock; **285**, Dan McCoy from Rainbow; **286**, Doug Martin; **287**, NOAA; **289**, O. Brown, R. Evans, and J. Brown/University of Miami/RSMAS; **290**, Studiohio;